NOT BY
SCRIPTURE ALONE

MW00659251

NOT BY SCRIPTURE ALONE

A Catholic Critique of the Protestant Doctrine of *Sola Scriptura*

Robert A. Sungenis

Foreword by Peter Kreeft

Queenship
PUBLISHING COMPANY
P.O Box 42028 Santa Barbara, CA 93140-2028
(800) 647-9882 • (805) 957-4893 • Fax: (805) 957-1631

NIHIL OBSTAT
Monsignor Carroll E. Satterfield
Censor Librorum

IMPRIMATUR
Monsignor W. Francis Malooly
Vicar General of the Archdiocese of Baltimore

Cover Picture: "The Sermon on the Mount" by Carl Bloch (d. 1890)

© 1997 Queenship Publishing

Library of Congress #: 97-76397

Published by:
Queenship Publishing
P.O. Box 42028
Santa Barbara, CA 93140-2028
(800) 647-9882 • (805) 957-4893 • Fax: (805) 957-1631

Printed in the United States of America

ISBN: 1-57918-055-8

Dedication:

This book is dedicated to **Pope John Paul II** who inspires us with his love of Scripture and his dedication to making Scripture reading and study a daily and abiding part of Catholic life.

Special Thanks to:

Mr. Steven Engle and **Mr. John Collorafi** for their editing of the manuscript. **Mr. Scott Butler**, **Mr. William Bora, Ms. Maureen Reed, Ms. Christina Lange** and **Mr. & Mrs. Ron Friddle** for their continual uplifting and encouragement throughout the course of this project. **Mr. Martin Schäffer** for his dedication to this work and his generous financial underwriting. The **Catholic University of America** in Washington for their personal help and use of the university library. All the contributors to this book: **Philip Blosser, Robert Fastiggi, Joseph Gallegos, Peter Kreeft, Patrick Madrid, Rev. Mitchell Pacwa, Mark Shea,** and the **Very Rev. Peter Stravinskas.**

Contributors:

Philip Blosser, Ph.D., is professor of Philosophy at Lenoir-Rhyne College in Hickory, North Carolina. He is a graduate of Sophia University in Tokyo and Westminster Theological Seminary in Philadelphia. He obtained his M.A. in Philosophy from Villanova University in Philadelphia and his Ph.D. from Duquesne University in Pittsburgh. He is the author of *Scheler's Critique of Kant's Ethics* (Ohio University Press, 1995), editor of *Friendship: Philosophic Reflections on a Perennial Concern* (Lanham, MD: University Press of America, 1997), and editor of *Japanese and Western Phenomenology* (Dordrecht, Holland: Kluwer Academic Publications, 1993).

Robert Fastiggi, Ph.D. is an associate professor of Religious Studies at St. Edward's University in Austin, Texas where he has worked since 1985. He holds his doctoral degree from Fordham University. He is the author of *The Natural Theology of Yves de Paris* (Atlanta: Scholar Press, 1991). He is a frequent speaker, debater and writer for Catholic apologetics. His articles appear in *The Thomist, Homiletic and Pastoral Review*, and *Crisis*.

Joseph A. Gallegos, is a graduate of the University of California, Irvine, and West Coast University, Los Angeles. He is very active in Catholic apologetics, having created Corunum Apolgetics BBS in 1992, and an international Web site (http://www.cin.org/users/jgallegos) for his expertise on patristic thought regarding the Papacy and Tradition.

Patrick Madrid, is the editor-in-chief of *Envoy* Magazine, a journal of Catholic apologetics and evangelization (www.envoymagazine.com).

His articles appear in magazines such as Catholic Dossier, Lay Witness, Regeneration Quarterly, New Oxford Review, and New Covenant. He is the editor of the best-selling book *Surprised By Truth* (Basilica Press, 1994), and author of *Any Friend of God's Is A Friend Of Mine* (Basilica Press, 1996). He did his undergraduate work at the University of Phoenix and is completing his Master's Degree in Theology at the University of Dallas. He is an internationally featured speaker on Catholic apologetics.

Rev. Mitchell Pacwa, S. J., Ph.D., was ordained a priest in 1976. He received his doctorate in Old Testament from Vanderbilt University. He is presently teaching at the Institute of Religious and Pastoral Studies at the University of Dallas. He is the author of two books: *Catholics and the New Age* (Servant Press, 1996) and *Father Forgive Me For I Am Frustrated* (Servant Press). Father Pacwa appears regularly on the Eternal Word Television Network (EWTN), teaching many theological and biblical topics. He also has engaged in many debates with prominent evangelicals, including the late Walter Martin of the Christian Research Institute.

Mark P. Shea, is a graduate of the University of Washington. He is a convert from Evangelicalism and is an internationally-known writer, speaker and lay Catholic apologist. In addition to his numerous articles, he is the author of the books: *By What Authority? An Evangelical Discovers Catholic Tradition* (Our Sunday Visitor, 1996); and *This Is My Body: An Evangelical Discovers The Real Presence* (Christendom College Press, 1993). He also writes the popular column *Heaven and Earth* for *New Covenant* magazine.

Very Rev. Peter M. J. Stravinskas, Ph.D., S.T.L., was ordained a priest in 1977 and is presently provost of the Newman House Oratory of St. Philip Neri in Mount Pocono, PA. He serves as adjunct professor of Education at Seton Hall University in South Orange, NJ, and as adjunct professor of Latin and Greek at Holy Apostles Seminary in Cromwell, CT. He holds a Ph.D. from Fordham University in New York and an S.T.D. from the Marian Institute at the University of Dayton; and a Licentiate of Sacred Theology from the Pontifical Faculty of the Immaculate Conception in Washington, D. C. He is the author of nineteen books and more than five hundred articles; the contributing editor of the *National Catholic Register*, and founding editor of *The Catholic Answer* magazine.

Robert A. Sungenis, M.A. is president of Catholic Apologetics International. He is a graduate of Westminster Theological Seminary and is pursuing doctoral studies at the Maryvale Institute in Birmingham, England. Robert is the author of *Shockwave 2000* (New Leaf Press, 1994) and *Not By Faith Alone: The Biblical Evidence for the Catholic Doctrine of Justification* (Queenship Publishing, 1997), contributor to *Surprised by Truth* (Basilica Press, 1994); contributor to *Jesus, Peter and the Keys* (Queenship, 1995) and has written various articles for Catholic periodicals. He has appeared in various debates with prominent evangelicals, and has been a frequent guest on the Eternal Word Television Network.

Abbreviations

AAOH	Teske, Roland, trans., John E. Rotelle, ed., *Arianism and Other Heresies.*
ACW	Quasten, J. and J. C. Plumpe, eds., *Ancient Christian Writers.*
ANF	Roberts, Alexander, et al, eds., *The Ante-Nicene Fathers.*
CCC	J. Stevenson, ed., *Creeds, Councils and Controversies: Documents Illustrating the History of the Church AD 337-461.*
CON	Congar, Yves, M. J. *Tradition and Traditions:An Historical Essay and A Theological Essay.*
ECC	Kelly, J. N. D. *Early Christian Creeds.*
ENO	Eno, Robert, B., *Teaching Authority in the Early Church.*
FOC	Berington, Jos., Rev. et al., *The Faith of Catholics.*
GILES	Giles, E. *Documents Illustrating Papal Authority.*
JUR	Jurgens, Williams, A., trans., *The Faith of the Early Fathers.*
NE	Stevenson, James, ed., *A New Eusebius: Documents Illustrating the History of the Church to AD 337.*
NPNF I	Schaff, Philip et al, eds., *A Select Library of Nicene and Post-Nicene Fathers of the Church*, 14 volumes, Series 1.
NPNF 2	Schaff, Philip, et al., eds., *A Select Library of Nicene and Post-Nicene Fathers of the Church*, 14 volumes, Series 2.
PAN	Amidon, Philip, R., S.J., ed. and trans, *The Panarion of St. Epiphanius, Bishop of Salamis: Selected Passages.*
PG	Migne, J. P., ed., *Patrologia Graeca Cursus Completus*, 161 vols.
PL	Migne, J. P., ed., *Patrologia Latina Cursus Completus*, 221 vols.
SS	*Sola Scriptura! The Protestant Position on the Bible*
WCF	Westminster Confession of Faith

Foreword

by Peter Kreeft

The divisions that make the Church visibly many rather than one are scandalous and intolerable. If you do not agree with that statement, then either you don't believe that the Bible is the revelation of God's own mind and therefore totally true, or else you can't read. The most serious division today, and the most serious one in history, is the division between Catholics and Protestants.

There are many disagreements between Catholics and Protestants — about the nature and number of sacraments, about the nature and authority of the Church, about the Pope, about saints, about Mary, about Purgatory, about Justification, about the Mass, about transubstantiation — a long list. Yet all of these disagreements are derived from a single one. On each of these divisive issues, Protestants say that Catholics believe too much, and Catholics say that Protestants believe too little. Protestants see Catholics as semi-idolaters, and Catholics see Protestants as semi-skeptics.

Why do Catholics believe too much, by Protestant standards, and why do Protestants believe too little, by Catholic standards? For one reason only: Protestants accept, and Catholics deny, the principle of *sola scriptura* — the idea that only Scripture is infallible divine revelation. All the Catholic doctrines and practices that Protestants reject are rejected because Protestants do not find them clearly in Scripture. And the reason Catholics accept them is not that they have reasoned each one out by independent, rational theological criteria. Rather, Catholics accept them on the authority of the Church. Catholics do not accept the principle of *sola scriptura*.

They believe what the Church teaches about herself: that her dogmatic teachings are also infallible and divine revelation. They argue that Jesus did not write a Bible, but He did establish a Church — which, in turn, wrote the New Testament. If the cause (the Church) is not infallible, how can its effect be infallible? By what authority do we know what books constitute the New Testament? The answer is not in doubt; it is as historically certain as the answer to the question who was the first American president. We know the canon of the New Testament by the *magisterium* (teaching authority) of the Catholic Church.

Since this single issue of *sola scriptura* is logically the root of all issues between Protestants and Catholics, if it could be resolved, then the greatest split in the Church would be healed. If Catholics accepted *sola scriptura*, they would become Protestants, and if Protestants rejected it, they would become Catholics.

There are two other "sola" issues, or "sola" formulas of the Protestant Reformation, especially Luther: *sola gratia* and *sola fide*. But these are not as fundamental as *sola scriptura*, for two reasons. First, it is not the case that all the disagreements derive from them, as they do from *sola scriptura*. Second, they are not clearly either/or issues, for the Catholic Church too accepts them in a sense. She explicitly accepts *sola gratia* — that we are saved by God's grace. This is clearly and forcefully taught by the Church Fathers, Augustine, Aquinas, the Council of Trent, and the new Catechism. But the Catholic understanding of this formula does not exclude free will, as Luther's understanding of it does. But, then, most Protestants agree with the Catholic Church rather than with Luther on this issue!

Hence, the logically most important issue of the Reformation is *sola scriptura*. This book is the single most important systematic, logical, sustained, direct, multifaceted treatment of this central issue that I know of. Therefore it should be a mighty means to the exalted end of finding the truth. And truth is the only possible basis for the Church reunion, because that is the business the Church is in: the truth business.

Reunion is possible because truth is one. "Pluralism" — the contemporary version of the medieval heresy of "double truth" — is false, indeed self-contradictory. If a doctrine is true for you but they are not ultimately subject to the Church and her Traditions.

It is the Catholic contention that Scripture, though esteemed as God's holy and inerrant Word, cannot be properly understood apart from the Church and her Tradition. I like to compare this to the beautiful goldfish I bought my children. They watch with keen interest as the fish swims from side to side, its golden scales glittering in the sunlight and its body floating like a kite. The children claim a great relationship with the goldfish and know him personally as "Goldy." But one day, my three year old took Goldy out of the fish bowl and threw him on the floor. He watched as the fish flailed about and gasped for air, all the while wondering why Goldy wasn't acting like the majestic creature he saw in the aquarium. I simply explained to him that God made fish to live only in water, and if you take them out, they will die. While I don't want to trivialize the controversy concerning *sola scriptura*, the Catholic contention is not much unlike the experience I had with my son and Goldy. As beautiful and majestic as Scripture is, once you take it out of its living environment, like Goldy, it will not look or act the same. It will be left gasping for air and perhaps be crushed on the floor by some unsuspecting toddler, and end up not resembling at all its original stately form. When Catholics see thousands of Protestant denominations being created as a result of taking Scripture out of its ecclesial and historical environment, all in the name of Scripture, we can't help but see evidence of the ironic axiom of life that 'we hurt most the one we love.'

All this talk of "Protestant this" and "Protestant that," however, is not to excuse the sometimes legitimate criticisms levied by our brethren against people of Catholic persuasion. Although the Catholic Church, we believe, has the unadulterated truth of God, it by no means contains perfect people who consistently and unhesitatingly skip to the tune of her historic teachings. Protestants can provide a whole litany of abuses that have occurred in the history of the Church, and still do occur. The axiom of 'hurting the one you love' is just as true with Catholics and their Church as it is with Protestants and their Scripture. Human beings are, well, *human*, and they will always be so, at least on this side of the grave. To this effect, Vatican II states in its *Decree on Ecumenism*:

> In this one and only Church of God from its very beginning there arose certain rifts, which the Apostle strongly censures as damnable. But in subsequent centuries much more serious dissensions appeared and large communities became separated from full communion with the Catholic Church — for which, often enough, men on both sides were to blame.[1]

In stating that "men of both sides were to blame," Vatican II admits that among human beings, including those in the Church, no one is perfect. All of us share the blame for the division that is upon us. With these words, and many others like them, the Council sought to open the doors to ecumenism that had been shut for virtually 450 years. Vatican II not only assigned to Catholic people of the 16th century their share of the blame for the divisions occurring at that time, it also recognizes the faults of the Church's current members:

> But their primary duty is to make a careful and honest appraisal of whatever needs to be renewed and done in the Catholic household itself... For although the Catholic Church has been endowed with all divinely revealed truth and with all means of grace, yet its members fail to live by them with all the fervor that they should. As a result the radiance of the Church's face shines less brightly in the eyes of our separated brethren and of the world at large, and the growth of God's kingdom is retarded.[2]

None of this, however, should stop us from striving for reconciliation between our two faiths. Life is hard enough as it is, but it is much harder when Christians are fighting one another instead of fighting their true enemy. We can love Scripture, but we must love Truth even more. We are not suggesting that the two are in any way mutually exclusive, but only that men, whether intentional or not, sometimes make them that way. In this regard, Vatican II states:

---

1 Vatican Council II: The Conciliar and Post Conciliar Documents, *Unitatis redintegratio 3*, ed. Austin Flannery, O.P., p. 455; CC, Section 817.

2 Vatican Council II, *Unitatis redintegratio 4.*

> It is, of course, essential that the doctrine be clearly presented in its entirety. Nothing is so foreign to the spirit of ecumenism as a false irenicism which harms the purity of Catholic doctrine and obscures its genuine and certain meaning. Furthermore, in ecumenical dialogue, Catholic theologians, standing fast by the teaching of the Church yet searching together with separated brethren into the divine mysteries, should do so with love for the truth, with clarity, and with humility.[3]

Regarding our present division, Vatican II states:

> Certainly, such division openly contradicts the will of Christ, scandalizes the world, and damages that most holy cause, the preaching of the Gospel to every creature... Everywhere large numbers have felt the impulse of this grace, and among our separated brethren also there increases from day to day a movement, fostered by the grace of the Holy Spirit, for the restoration of unity among all Christians.[4]

Leading us into the third millennium the Council continues:

> The sacred Council now pleads with all to forget the past, and urges that a sincere effort be made to achieve mutual understanding; for the benefit of all men, let them together preserve and promote peace, liberty, social justice and moral values.[5]

So, we have come full circle. There is a needy world awaiting us. Let us come to the table and voice our differences, but also a desire to obey Christ's commands for his Church — the Church we want to present to him in unity. To do so, this book will thoroughly investigate the Protestant doctrine of *sola scriptura*, and allow you to determine if it can indeed stand under its own weight. Our conclusion is that it cannot, and we demonstrate this by turning over every rock and looking into every crevice of the issue. We hope you come to the same conclusion. May you enjoy your reading.

Robert Sungenis

---

3 Vatican Council II, *Unitatis redintegratio* 11.

4 Vatican Council II, *Unitatis redintegratio 1.*

5 Vatican Council II, *Nostra aetate 3.*

Chapter 1

Sola Scriptura: A Blueprint for Anarchy

By Patrick Madrid

It's funny. For five centuries, Protestants have intimidated, cowed, browbeaten, flustered, put to flight, trodden down, bullied, vexed, and knocked the wind out of countless unwary Catholics by using the "Bible only" approach to religious arguments.

Actually, it's not *funny*, but it is ironic, because it shouldn't be this way. Catholics need not be disturbed (and our hope is that after reading this book they won't be) when a Protestant attacks the Catholic Church using Scripture as his cudgel. That's because the standard Protestant objections to Catholicism are all based on a fallacy — *sola scriptura* (Latin: by Scripture alone) — a fallacy that can be easily refuted by informed Catholics.

As Catholic apologists mount a concerted attack on *sola scriptura*, Protestant apologists have been scrambling to find new ways to bolster their case for *sola scriptura*. A spate of new books defending this most vulnerable of Reformation slogans have been printed in recent years.[1] This is due, I believe, to the recent dramatic rise in apologetics works by Catholics, e.g., articles, books, conversion testimonies, seminars, and debates specifically aimed at rebutting the Protestant claim of *sola scriptura*. This book you're now holding is

---

1 Cf. Don Kistler, general editor of *Sola Scriptura! The Protestant Position on the Bible* (Morgan, PA: Soli Deo Gloria, 1995); James White, *The Roman Catholic Controversy* (Minneapolis: Bethany House, 1996). Norman Geisler and Ralph E. MacKenzie, *Roman Catholics and Evangelicals: Agreements and Differences* (Grand Rapids: Baker, 1995).

the latest in that series of critiques, a joint effort by several Catholic apologists aimed at providing in a single volume the major outlines of the patristic, theological, exegetical, and epistemological evidence that demonstrates that *sola scriptura* is indefensible.

Sola scriptura is a grave theological error that has led countless souls to doctrinal ruin, a purely human construct that all Christians who love and obey God's Word should reject as a tradition of men that nullifies and distorts that Word.

Protestant writer Don Kistler, remarking on the state of the debate between Catholics and Protestants on *sola scriptura*, said, "The slugfest goes on."[2] Indeed it does, and the Protestant side is not getting the better of the exchange. The fire Catholics have been directing on *sola scriptura* is having visible, positive effects. Many converts to the Catholic Faith from evangelicalism report that their seeing *sola scriptura* disintegrate in the face of rigorous biblical, historical, and logical scrutiny, was the key to their conversion to the Catholic Church. They were shocked at the discovery that Christ did not teach *sola scriptura*, the apostles and Church Fathers did not teach it and, most ironically, the Bible does not teach it.

Catholics need to realize just how untenable *sola scriptura* is. The first step is to see the tremendous advantage gained by asking Protestants to prove *sola scriptura* from the Bible. Instead of being put on the defensive when purgatory or the Real Presence or some other doctrine is challenged by Protestants demanding that they be proven from Scripture,[3] the Catholic should begin by asking, "where does the Bible teach *sola scriptura*?"

This book focuses on the most devastating flaws of *sola scriptura*: (a) It is unhistorical, (b) It is unbiblical, and (c) It is utterly unworkable. This first chapter is designed to give you a "macro" look at the issues at stake. Later chapters will delve deeply into specific aspects, but to get ourselves properly oriented, let's stand back and look at the big picture.

---

2 Ibid., p. 277.

3 Scriptural evidence, whether explicit or implicit, can indeed be adduced for any given Catholic teaching, but those apologetics discussions are not our focus here.

What Is *Sola Scriptura*?

Reformed theologian Robert Godfrey issued, perhaps, the simplest rendition of the doctrine in a public debate: "The Protestant position, and my position, is that all things necessary for salvation and concerning faith and life *are taught in the Bible clearly enough* for the ordinary believer to find it there and understand it."[4]

This book is devoted to showing the many reasons why Godfrey's claim is false. We will prove that Scripture alone, apart from the Church and Tradition, is not sufficient (in the sense that Godfrey and other Protestant apologists argue) for "all things necessary for salvation and concerning the faith and life." Scripture is not always clear in all places so that any "ordinary believer can find it there and understand it." Millions of ordinary Christian believers over the centuries have found the Real Presence of Christ in the Eucharist there, they found baptismal regeneration there, they found the authority of the Church and the primacy of Peter there. The Church Fathers certainly found the Mass, the sacraments, and the necessity of Sacred Tradition there.

You can already see the problem. Godfrey's definition of (and, *a fortiori*, his arguments for) *sola scriptura* self-destructs, because his claim insists that all those "ordinary believers" who found the Mass, the sacraments, etc., were completely wrong in their interpretation of Scripture. These Catholic teachings, Godfrey and his fellow Protestant apologists contend, are actually not there in Scripture. But then he must also admit that Scripture was not clear on those doctrines, at least not clear enough to prevent 2000 years-worth of Christian believers from seeing them in Scripture. In his very definition of *sola scriptura*, Godfrey has exposed its fatal flaw: There is no way, under the *sola scriptura* rubric, to know with certainty who's interpretation of Scripture is correct and whose is "unbiblical." *Sola scriptura* is epistemologically unviable.

Let's begin the critique of *sola scriptura* by means of a simple analogy. Let's say a person, who lived 100 years ago, wrote the

---

4 This definition was reproduced verbatim in Godfrey's chapter in *Sola Scriptura! The Protestant Position on the Bible*, titled "What Do We Mean By *Sola scriptura*," pp. 1-26, (emphasis mine).

following sentence on a piece of paper: "I never said you stole money." Do you understand the meaning of that sentence? "Of course," you respond. "There is nothing complicated about that six-word sentence. It's simple. Sure I understand what it means." But do you really? For example, what if the man who wrote, "I never said you stole money," meant the statement to mean, "*I* never said you stole money," implying that *someone else said it.* Or what if he meant, "I never *said* you stole money," implying that he may have *thought* you stole money, be he never actually said so. Or maybe he meant, "I never said *you* stole money," implying that he said *someone else* stole money, not you. Maybe he meant, "I never said you *stole* money," implying he felt you mismanaged the money, or maybe you lost it, or you did something else with it he didn't approve of. But he wasn't saying you *stole* it. Or yet again, perhaps he meant to convey the sense that, "I never said you stole *money*," implying that it wasn't money you stole — you stole his *pig*. We can see from this simple exercise that there is a wide range of meanings that can legitimately be inferred from these six, simple words. Placing the emphasis on different words creates different meanings.

Now ask yourself: Which is more complicated, that six word sentence, or the Bible? If even a simple sentence can be interpreted in a variety of ways, is it not much more likely that Scripture will yield a huge number of possible meanings? Due to its size and complexity, Scripture can be and is understood in a vast multiplicity of ways. This leads us to a second question: How can we know for certain which of the many conflicting interpretations is right? How can we know, when we read a passage of Scripture, that we are understanding it properly? The answer is we cannot be certain, unless we ask the person who wrote it, or someone who knows the person who wrote it, e.g., the Church and her Tradition. Christ established the Church for the purpose of teaching and sanctifying all people. He promised his own authority to the Church: "He who listens to you listens to me, and he who rejects you, rejects me" (Luke 10:16). That is another reason why *sola scriptura* fails. It does not work — really, it cannot work — simply because the written Word cannot cry out to you, "Wait! You have misinterpreted me!" But the Church can.

The ironies of *sola scriptura* are endless. Chief among them, though, is that the Bible nowhere teaches it. When the Reformers pioneered the idea of *sola scriptura*, they were unwittingly propping up their theological system on the flimsiest of supports. When we examine the various classical Protestant creeds,[5] we find that *sola scriptura* becomes a self-refuting proposition. Perhaps the clearest example is found in the seventeenth century document titled *The Westminster Confession of Faith*:

> The whole counsel of God, concerning all things necessary for his own glory, man's salvation, faith, and life, is either expressly set down in Scripture, or by good and necessary consequence may be deduced from Scripture: unto which nothing at any time is to be added, whether by new revelations of the Spirit, or traditions of men...(1:6); All things in Scripture are not alike plain in themselves, nor alike clear unto all; yet those things which are necessary to be known, believed, and observed, for salvation, are so clearly propounded and opened in some place of Scripture or other, that not only the learned, but the unlearned, in a due use of the ordinary means, may attain unto a sufficient understanding of them... (1:7).

I call your attention to the statement, "All things necessary for...man's salvation, faith, and life, is either expressly set down in Scripture, or by good and necessary consequence may be deduced from Scripture." This means that the doctrine of *sola scriptura* itself must be found in the Bible — but it isn't, as this book you hold will amply prove.

How Protestants Distort and Misreport the Church Fathers

A ploy being adopted by a growing number of evangelical apologists is what I call the "hijacking" of the Church Fathers,

5 The other major creedal statements that arose during the heyday of the Reformation take essentially the same approach in asserting the formal sufficiency of Scripture, e.g., the Anglican *39 Articles of Religion*, the Baptist *London Confession of 1688*, and the Lutheran *Augsburg Confession*.

attempting to press them into service for *sola scriptura*. This ploy mimics the Jehovah's Witnesses and Mormons, who also attempt to defend their unorthodox teachings from behind a carefully-constructed facade of patristic quotes — quotes invariably taken out of their immediate context and without regard to the complete writings of the Fathers.

The practice of selective quoting from the Fathers — great Fathers such as Athanasius, John Chrysostom, Cyril of Jerusalem, Augustine, and Basil of Caesarea — is spreading. In fact, often the very Protestant apologists who misuse and twist the testimony of the Fathers to fit their hermeneutic of anachronism (i.e., reading their own views such as *sola scriptura* and *sola fide* back into Scripture and the Fathers) are themselves accusing Catholics of "misusing" or "prooftexting" the Fathers.[6]

But we insist that the quotes Protestants lift from the Patristic writers' works are invariably (mis)used and isolated from the rest of what the Father in question wrote about Church authority, Tradition, and Scripture. Selective quoting gives the appearance that these Fathers were hard-core Evangelical Protestants who promoted an unvarnished doctrine of *sola scriptura* that would have made John Calvin proud. But this appearance is a chimera, for in order to make selective "pro- *sola scriptura*" quotes from the Fathers of any value, the Protestant apologist's audience must have little or no firsthand knowledge of what these Fathers wrote. By looking at the totality of the Fathers writings on the subject of Scriptural authority, we see a very different picture emerge. A few patristic examples will suffice to demonstrate what I mean.

Basil of Caesarea has provided Evangelical polemicists with what they think is the "smoking gun" to deny Catholic claims and

---

6 See *Sola Scriptura! The Protestant Position on the Bible*, pp. 31f, where James White makes this charge. Some Catholic scholars and apologists who are familiar with White's allegation that the Catholic Church engages in "prooftexting the Fathers" may be tempted to dismiss his claim as absurd — the pedantic boast of one whose own knowledge of the complete Patristic testimony appears dubious — but they shouldn't. Though White's charge is absurd, of course, it nonetheless dupes many, and needs to be rigorously exposed as false. See chapters 5 and 8 of this book for a thorough refutation of White's and other Protestants' use of the Fathers.

uphold *sola scriptura*: "Therefore, let God-inspired Scripture decide between us; and on whichever side be found doctrines in harmony with the Word of God, in favor of that side will be cast the vote of truth (*Epistle ad Eustathius*). This, they think, means that Basil would have been comfortable with John Calvin's theology that, "All things in Scripture are not alike plain in themselves, nor alike clear unto all; yet those things which are necessary to be known, believed, and observed, for salvation, are so clearly propounded and opened in some place of Scripture or other, that not only the learned, but the unlearned, in a due use of the ordinary means, may attain unto a sufficient understanding of them" (*The Westminster Confession of Faith,* 7). But if Basil's quote is to be of any use to the Protestant apologist, the rest of Basil's writings should be consistent and compatible with the theology expressed in this quote from the Westminster Confession. But watch what happens to Basil's alleged *sola scriptura* mindset when we look at other statements of his:

> Of the beliefs and practices whether generally accepted or enjoined which are preserved in the Church, some we possess derived from written teaching; others we have delivered to us in a mystery by the apostles by the tradition of the apostles; and both of these in relation to true religion have the same force (*On the Holy Spirit*,27)... In answer to the objection that the doxology in the form 'with the Spirit' has no written authority, we maintain that if there is not another instance of that which is unwritten, then this must not be received [as authoritative]. But if the great number if our mysteries are admitted into our constitution without [the] written authority [of Scripture], then, in company with many others, let us receive this one. For I hold it apostolic to abide by the unwritten traditions. 'I praise you,' it is said [by Paul in 1 Cor. 11:1] 'that you remember me in all things and keep the traditions just as I handed them on to you,' and 'Hold fast to the traditions that you were taught whether by an oral statement or by a letter of ours' [2 Thess. 2:15]. One of these traditions is the practice which is now before us [under consideration], which they who ordained from the beginning, rooted firmly in the churches, delivering it to their succes-

> sors, and its use through long custom advances pace by pace with time *(On the Holy Spirit*, 71).

Such talk hardly fits with the notion that Scripture is formally sufficient for all matters of Christian doctrine. Basil's appeal to an authoritative body of unwritten apostolic Tradition within the Church is frequent in his writings.

Protestant apologists are also fond of quoting two particular passages from Athanasius:

> The holy and inspired Scriptures are sufficient of themselves for the preaching of the truth (*Contra Gentiles* 1:1); These books [of canonical Scripture] are the fountains of salvation, so that he who thirsts may be satisfied with the oracles contained in them. In these alone the school of piety preaches the Gospel. Let no man add to these or take away from them (*Thirty Ninth Festal Letter*).

We can show that in neither place is Athanasius teaching *sola scriptura*. First, in the case of the *Festal Letter*, as bishop, Athanasius was instructing his churches what they could and could not read as "Scripture." The context of his letter shows he was laying down a liturgical directive for his flock.

> Second, as in the case of Basil and the other Fathers whom Protestants attempt to press into service, their writings show no signs of *sola scriptura*; rather, they show a staunchly orthodox Catholicism. Athanasius, for example, wrote the following:
>
> The confession arrived at Nicea was, we say more, sufficient and enough by itself for the subversion of all irreligious heresy and for the security and furtherance of the doctrine of the Church (*Ad Afros* 1); [T]he very tradition, teaching, and faith of the Catholic Church from the beginning was preached by the apostles and preserved by the Fathers. On this the Church was founded; and if anyone departs from this, he neither is nor any longer ought to be called a Christian (*Ad Serapion* 1:28).
>
> And consider this quote from Cyril of Jerusalem's *Catechetical Lectures:*

> In regard to the divine and holy mysteries of the faith, not the least part may be handed on without the Holy Scriptures. Do not be led astray by winning words and clever arguments. Even to me, who tell you these things, do not give ready belief, unless you receive from the Holy Scriptures the proof of the things which I announce. The salvation which we believe is not proved from clever reasoning, but from the Holy Scriptures (4:17).

How should we understand Cyril? Well, Catholic patristic scholars would point out that his language here is consistent with his and the other Fathers' high view of Scripture's authority and its material sufficiency. This language, while perhaps more rigorous than modern Catholics are used to, nonetheless conveys an accurate sense of Catholic teaching on the necessity and material sufficiency of Scripture. Taken at face value, Cyril's admonition poses no problem for the Catholic. But it does, ironically, for the Protestant. Let's see how this happens.

The proponent of *sola scriptura* is faced with a dilemma when he uses the above quote from Cyril. Here are his options: First, Cyril was, in fact, teaching *sola scriptura.* If this is so, however, Protestants have a big problem. Cyril's *Catechetical Lectures* are filled with forceful teachings on the Mass as a sacrifice, the efficacy of expiatory prayers for the dead, the Real presence of Christ in the Eucharist, the theology of sacraments, the intercession of the saints, holy orders, baptismal regeneration, and a whole array of specifically "Catholic doctrines." These are the same Catholic doctrines that Protestants claim Scripture does not contain. So, if Cyril really held to the notion of *sola scriptura*, then it must be true that he believed he had found those Catholic doctrines in Scripture. Consequently, the Protestant would have to posit that Cyril was badly mistaken in his exegesis of Scripture. Of course, this tack leads nowhere for Protestants, for it would of necessity impugn Cyril's exegetical credibility, not to mention his claim to find *sola scriptura* in Scripture. The second option is that Cyril was not teaching *sola scriptura.* If so, that means any attempt to hijack his quote to support *sola scriptura* is futile (if not dishonest), since it would lead to a hopelessly incorrect understanding of Cyril's method of systematic theology, the doctrinal schema he sets forth in *Catechetical Lectures*, and his view of the authority of Scripture. Obviously, neither of these options is palatable to the Protestant apologist.

If the notion of the absolute[7] sufficiency of Scripture were indeed part of "the faith that was once for all handed on to the saints" (Jude 3), we would expect to find it everywhere taught and practiced in the early Church. We would expect to see the ancient Christian liturgical life dominated and shaped by the rule of *sola scriptura*. We would expect the Church Fathers preaching sermons and writing treatises on this issue (as they did on subjects such as the Real Presence of Christ in the Eucharist, purgatory, the authority of the Church, infant baptism and baptismal regeneration, the sacraments, and the Mass as a propitiatory sacrifice). But we don't see anything of the sort. The fact is, the writings of the Fathers and the councils, both regional and ecumenical, reveal that *sola scriptura* was completely alien to the thought and life of the early Church. Mind you, the early Church placed an exceedingly high emphasis on the importance and authority of Scripture to guide and govern the life of the Church, and the Fathers constantly employed Scripture in their doctrinal treatises and pastoral directives, but they never regarded (or used) Scripture as something that stood alone, self-sufficient and unreliant on Sacred Tradition and the magisterium.

In later chapters, which set forth the patristic case against *sola scriptura*, Robert Sungenis and Joe Gallegos will provide detailed evidence that the Fathers did not teach *sola scriptura*. They examine each of the patristic quotes Protestant apologists use to argue for *sola scriptura*, and demonstrate in each case that they quote the Fathers out of context and without regard to the rest of their statements on the authority of Scripture, Tradition, and the Magisterium. It will suffice for now, though, to remind you the reader that the early Church Fathers did not teach *sola scriptura*. You will see that no amount of clever "cut-and-paste" work by defenders of *sola scriptura* can demonstrate otherwise.

---

[7] That is, the distinct, formal sense that Protestants advocate, over against the Catholic position of Scripture's *material sufficiency*, which will be discussed later in this and other chapters.

Fallacies Protestants Commit In Arguing For *Sola Scriptura*

The following is a summary of the other fallacies inherent in the pro-*sola scriptura* arguments employed by Protestant apologists.

#1: The "Word of God" Fallacy

It never fails. In conversations with Evangelicals and Fundamentalists about biblical authority, this argument always comes up. The Protestant mistakenly assumes that every time the phrase "Word of God" appears in Scripture, it refers to the Bible. In reality, most of the time, when we pay attention to the context of the passage, we see that "the Word of God" does not refer to Scripture but to Christ, the Law, God's creative utterances, and apostolic and prophetic preaching. Here are some verses that prove this:

Luke 3:2-3 "[T]he word of God came to John the son of Zechariah in the wilderness; and he went into all the region about the Jordan, preaching a baptism of repentance..." This refers to the inspiration that St. John the Baptist received, as he was sent forth to preach the gospel of repentance and preparation for Christ.

Luke 4:44; 5:1 "[Jesus] was preaching in the synagogues of Judea. While the people pressed upon him to hear the word of God."

Luke 8:11-15 "Now the parable is this: The seed is the word of God. The ones along the path are those who have heard;...the ones on the rock are those who, when they hear the word, receive it with joy; but these have no root, they believe for a while and in time of temptation fall away... And as for that in the good soil, they are those who, hearing the word, hold it fast in an honest and good heart, and bring forth fruit with patience." Notice that the emphasis here is on hearing the word of God. This is an obvious reference both to Christ's own preaching as well as to apostolic preaching (cf., 1 Thess. 2:13), and the continual preaching of the Gospel by the Church to all creatures in all ages (c.f. Matt. 28:19-20; Rom. 10:14-15).

John 1:1, 14 "In the beginning was the Word, and the Word was with God, and the Word was God... And the Word became flesh and dwelt among us." This passage, of course, refers to the Incarnate Christ.

Acts 4:31 "And when they had prayed, the place in which they were gathered together was shaken; and they were all filled with the Holy Spirit and spoke the word of God with boldness."

1 Thessalonians 2:13 "[W]hen you received the word of God which you heard from us, you accepted it not as the word of men but as what it really is, the word of God, which is at work in you believers." Here Paul is specifically pointing to oral Tradition, not to Scripture. This was his first epistle to the Thessalonians. Notice that he doesn't enjoin them to go solely by what is found in Scripture, but he reminds them to adhere to the oral teachings he had handed on to them.

Hebrews 11:3 "By faith we understand that the world was created by the word of God, so that what is seen was made out of things which do not appear." Clearly, no Protestant will posit that "the world was created" by the Bible. (If he does, head for the door, quickly).

#2: The "Bible vs. the Church" Fallacy

Sola scriptura also demonstrates the "either-or" fallacy, known to logicians as the fallacy of the "false dichotomy." This fallacy pits the Church against Scripture. But the "either-or" approach simply is not what we see outlined in the New Testament. Rather, it's the Catholic "both-and" approach we discover. Furthermore, there exists among Protestants a pervasive suspicion of and hostility to the Catholic belief that "The Church" is far more than a mere "collection of like-minded believers from each denomination," but is, in fact, a unified supernatural organism — a unity directed by Christ, created and sustained by Christ, and operating with Christ's own authority. This "Bible vs. the Church" fallacy is partly to blame for the rise of *sola scriptura*. It entails a fundamental misunderstanding of the nature of the Church as much as a misunderstanding of the nature of Scripture. John H. Armstrong writes, "But Scripture has no equal precisely because Scripture alone has its source in God, who, by the Holy Spirit, is its author."[8]

Armstrong is wrong. True, Scripture indeed is what he describes, but so is the Church. She also has her source in Christ.

---

[8] *Sola Scriptura!: The Protestant Position on the Bible*, p. 121.

Catholics do not speak or think of the Church and Scripture in terms of "equals," rather, Christ constitutes each, and the two function in such a way that both are necessary and complimentary, which avoids the Protestant error of subjugating one to the other.[9]

Here are a few representative passages that speak of the nature and authority and necessity of the Church and its magisterium:

Matthew 16:18 "[O]n this rock I will build my Church, and the powers of death shall not prevail against it. I will give you the keys of the kingdom of heaven, and whatever you bind on earth shall be bound in heaven, and whatever you loose on earth shall be loosed in heaven".

Matthew 18:15-18 "[I]f he refuses to listen even to the Church, let him be to you as a Gentile and a tax collector. Truly, I say to you, whatever you bind on earth shall be bound in heaven, and whatever you loose on earth shall be loosed in heaven."

Luke 10:16 "He who hears you hears me, and he who rejects you rejects me, and he who rejects me rejects him who sent me."

1 Corinthians 10:8 "If I boast a little too much of our authority, which the Lord gave for building you up and not for destroying you, I shall not be put to shame."

1 Timothy 3:14-15 "[I]f I am delayed, you may know how one ought to behave in the household of God, which is the church of the living God, the pillar and bulwark of the truth."

#3: The "All Tradition Is Bad" Fallacy

Here's another Protestant bugaboo: the "T" word. When faced with a Catholic doctrine they dislike, and for which they deny there is any Scriptural warrant (i.e., most Catholic teachings), Protestants will invariably point to Matthew 15:1-9 and Mark 7:1-13, where Jesus excoriates "traditions of men" which "nullify the Word of God." What they fail to recognize in these passages is that our Lord was condemning *false* traditions; he wasn't condemning *tradition* itself. This is proven by the way the Apostles passed on the gospel to the infant Church:

---

9 Cf., Ibid., 129.

1 Corinthians 11:2 "I praise you because you remember me in everything and hold fast to the traditions, just as I handed them on to you."

1 Thessalonians 2:13 "[W]hen you received the word of God which you heard from us, you accepted it not as the word of men but as what it really is, the word of God, which is at work in you believers."[10]

2 Thessalonians 2:15 "So then, brethren, stand firm and hold to the traditions which you were taught by us, either by word of mouth or by letter" (cf., Titus 1:7-11).

2 Timothy 2:2 "And what you have heard from me through many witnesses [i.e., what Timothy personally heard Paul preach as well as the oral tradition that had been handed on to Timothy from other Christian leaders] entrust to faithful people who will have the ability to teach others as well" (cf., 2 Timothy 1:13).

This last passage not only points to the transmission of the deposit of faith through oral Tradition, it also gives us a glimpse of the beginnings of apostolic succession — a succession that was already the norm for the transfer of ecclesiastical authority (cf., Acts 1:15-26; 1 Tim. 4:14).

#4: The "*Sola Scriptura* Is Found In The Old Testament" Fallacy

In the Old Testament God gave authority to the priests to interpret his laws and issue binding doctrine based on those interpretations, even with regard to criminal and civil issues — both through divine revelation (cf. Lev. 20:1-27, 25:1-55). In the New Testament, he endowed the Church with a charism to teach infallibly. Deuteronomy 17:8-12 states:

> If any case arises requiring decision between one kind of homicide and another, one kind of legal right and another, or one kind of assault and another, any case within your towns which

[10] While the word "tradition" (Greek: *paradosis*) does not appear in this passage, nonetheless, Paul is explaining that the oral transmission of the deposit of faith (i.e., Sacred Tradition) carries the same weight as do the Scriptures, which convey the word of God in written form.

is too difficult for you, then you shall arise and go up to the place which the Lord your God will choose, and coming to the Levitical priests, and to the judge who is in office in those days, you shall consult them, and they shall declare to you the decision. Then you shall do according to what they declare to you from that place which the Lord will choose; and you shall be careful to do according to all that they direct you; according to the instructions which they give you, and according to the decision which they pronounce to you, you shall do; you shall not turn aside from the verdict which they declare to you, either to the right hand or to the left. The man who acts presumptuously, by not obeying the priest who stands to minister there before the Lord your God, or the judge, that man shall die.

Not only are there clear references to an authoritative body of teachers (constituted by God or by his appointed prophets and Kings), but there are also a number of examples in which authoritative oral Tradition is at work alongside Scripture in the Old Testament. Here are two examples:

2 Chronicles 29:25 [King Hezekiah] then stationed the Levites in the house of the Lord with cymbals, with harps, and with lyres, according to the command of David and of Gad the king's seer, and of Nathan the prophet; for the command was from the Lord through his prophets."

2 Chronicles 35:4 "Prepare yourselves by your fathers' households in your divisions [by tribe], according to the writings of David the king of Israel and according to the writing of his son Solomon."

What makes these two passages so striking as evidence against the "*sola scriptura* in the Old Testament" fallacy is that God commanded these reforms based on the oral tradition preserved many centuries before 2 Chronicles had been written. We don't find these commands anywhere else in the Old Testament, yet Hezekiah clearly regarded then as authoritative and binding. A Protestant writing on this very issue admitted that,

The fact that these words from God were never included in the [Old Testament] canon had absolutely nothing to do with

> the matter. These words from God, not preserved in Scripture, were consulted and applied authoritatively by the reformers [spoken of in 2 Chronicles]. The passages in 2 Chronicles are very clear and straightforward refutations of *sola scriptura*...[11]

Also, the Old Testament shows us repeatedly that the Lord had established a hierarchy of sorts (prophets, priests, and kings), wherein he charged each group with the task of promulgating, explicating, and enforcing the Divine precepts that were being set down occasionally in Scripture. Besides the fact that no individual Jew had a personal copy of the Bible (copies of Scripture were rare, being reserved only for the Temple priests, the king, and the synagogues), priests and prophets appointed by the Lord to give its interpretation. In fact, there are no Old Testament examples of Scripture functioning alone, apart from, or interpreted at variance with the authoritative tradition of the Old Testament hierarchy of priests and prophets.

#5: The "*Sola Scriptura* Is Found In The New Testament" Fallacy

Ditto for the New Testament. After all, it's here we would expect to find the strong proof texts supporting *sola scriptura* if, in fact, Christ and the apostles had taught and practiced it. But we don't because they didn't. There are no verses that either express or imply that Scripture is to be the sole rule of faith for the Church, especially in independence of the magisterium and sacred Tradition. Read the book of Acts and you will see how the early Church operated in this area. Acts describes how the Church constantly invoked apostolic authority, whether by an Apostle himself or one of his protégés (ie. the nascent Catholic magisterium) in the interpretation of Old Testament Scripture, as well as the transmission, often with detailed clarifications, of Christ's teachings.[12] In Acts 15, in the face of the serious issue of the status of Gentile converts, the apostles did not invoke *sola scriptura*. Rather, they called a plenary

---

[11] Gregory Krehbiel points out the 2 Chronicles argument in a privately distributed manuscript titled "A Critical Look at *Sola Scriptura*" 1993.

[12] These magisterial interpretations were rendered as binging on the Church; cf. Acts 15:1-35; Gal. 3:7-14; 1 Thess. 2:3-7, 13.

council to settle this doctrinal dispute. Furthermore, when the council sent Paul, Barnabas, Barsabbas and Silas to promulgate its teachings, they were not told to convince their hearers by using a "Thus sayeth Scripture" motif. Instead we find a "Thus sayeth the Holy Spirit through this council" motif (cf. Acts 15:27-29).

There are numerous Scriptural examples, explicit and implicit, of the apostles pointing to sacred Tradition as being an indispensable part of the Gospel. But nowhere will you see an apostle or an early Christian believing in, teaching, or operating under the principle of *sola scriptura*. Besides the many direct references to the authority of the Church that we looked at earlier, we also see a few curious episodes in which the apostles prefer not to use Scripture when teaching:

1 Corinthians 11:34 "And the rest I will set in order when I come."

2 John 12 "Although I have much to write to you, I do not intend to use paper and ink. Instead, I hope to visit you and to speak face to face so that our joy may be complete."

3 John 13 "I have much to write to you, but I do not wish to write with pen and ink. Instead, I hope to see you soon, when we can talk face to face."

#6: The "Scripture Interprets Itself" Fallacy

This fallacy is a fundamental element of *sola scriptura*.[13] Once again, the Westminster Confession of Faith lays a sure path into the confusion:

> All things in Scripture... which are necessary to be known, believed, and observed, for salvation, are so clearly propounded

[13] Robert Godfrey makes this mistake, albeit in a rather muddled way, in *Sola Scriptura! The Protestant Position on the Bible* (p. 24), where he says, "Roman apologists usually object to an appeal to Psalm 119 on the grounds that it speaks of the Word of God, not of the Bible, and therefore could include in its praise tradition as well as Scripture. But their argument is irrelevant to our use of Psalm 119, because *we are using it to prove the clarity, not the sufficiency of Scripture!*" (sic), (emphasis mine).

> and opened in some place of Scripture or other, that not only the learned, but the unlearned, in a due use of the ordinary means, may attain unto a sufficient understanding of them (1:7).

Such assertions might seem plausible at first, but in reality it's a scheme that simply does not — no, cannot — work. Protestantism has long asserted that the Bible is clear on essential issues. But how do they then explain the vast divisions that have fractured Protestantism from the start? Lutheran theology is markedly different from, and often directly contradictory with, central doctrines held by the Reformed Protestantism of John Calvin.[14] Baptists will tell you that both of those groups are wrong about a whole raft of key doctrines. Not surprisingly, the succession of Protestant doctrinal disputes continues unabated, each camp wrapping itself in the mantle of "Religious Truth" and claiming that it has the correct interpretation of Scripture. It's not hard to spot the problem here: By using Scripture alone, no one can know for sure which of all the many competing, squabbling Protestant sects is the right one.[15] And the best proof of this is Protestantism itself. Since the onset of the Reformation, Protestantism has been one roiling mass of protest. Its fragmented history aside, perhaps the most devastating evidence is that Christ and the apostles repeatedly remind us of the necessity of a teaching Church and its lived Sacred Tradition, and Scripture also warns us against *sola scriptura*:

2 Peter 1:20-21 "First of all you must understand this, that no prophecy of scripture is a matter of one's own interpretation, because no prophecy ever came by the impulse of man, but men moved by the Holy Spirit spoke from God. But false prophets also arose among the people, just as there will be false teachers among you, who will secretly bring in destructive heresies, even denying the Master who bought them, bringing upon themselves swift destruction." This passage hardly needs commentary. You might think this warning contains sufficient evidence that "destructive heresies" are

---

[14] E.g., infant baptism, baptismal regeneration, the Real Presence of Christ in the Eucharist, sacraments, the absolute assurance of salvation, etc.

[15] Cf., my written debates with Protestant apologist Douglas Jones in **Appendix 3** of this book.

the natural outgrowth of the "every man for himself" approach to the Bible — an approach that is the foundation of *sola scriptura*. But almost as if St. Peter had foreseen the rise of Protestantism, he added another prescient warning about private interpretation:

2 Peter 3:15-17 "There are some things in [Paul's letters] hard to understand, which the ignorant and unstable twist to their own destruction, as they do the other scriptures. You therefore, beloved, knowing this beforehand, beware lest you be carried away with the error of lawless men and lose your own stability."

Sola Scriptura Is Not Biblical

The fatal flaw of *sola scriptura* is that it is not taught in Scripture. This fact has been made clear to me in the several debates on *sola scriptura* in which I have participated against Protestant apologists, and in other debates between Catholic and Protestant spokesmen. In later chapters, Phil Blosser and Robert Sungenis take an Exacto knife to the various Scripture verses Protestants use to prop up *sola scriptura*, dissecting them from every conceivable angle.

But the over-arching biblical case against *sola scriptura* can be divided here into two primary divisions: *negatively*, that is, the Bible contains no evidence to support it; and *positively*, that is, the Bible contains overwhelming evidence that demonstrates that the Catholic tripartite model of authority i.e., Scripture, Tradition, and the magisterium[16] — is in fact the model Christ intended for the Church.

---

16 "The task of authentically interpreting the word of God, whether written or handed on, has been entrusted exclusively to the living teaching office of the Church, whose authority is exercised in the name of Jesus Christ. This teaching office is not above the word of God, but serves it, teaching only what has been handed on, listening to it devotedly, guarding it scrupulously and explaining it faithfully in accord with a divine commission and with the help of the Holy Spirit, it draws from this one deposit of faith everything which it presents for belief as divinely revealed. *It is clear, therefore, that Sacred Tradition, Sacred Scripture and the teaching authority of the Church, in accord with God's most wise design, are so linked and joined together that one cannot stand without the others*, and that all together and each in its own way under the action of the one Holy Spirit contribute effectively to the salvation of souls" (Vatican Council II, *Dei Verbum* 10, emphasis mine; cf., 23-25; *Catholic Catechism* 74-95).

In discussions with Bible-believing Protestants, the Bible-believing Catholic should always point out that the Catholic Church emphasizes the unique and indispensable role of Scripture in the life of the Church, its plenary inspiration, and its binding authority. But, and this is a very big but, Scripture was never intended to stand alone (*sola*) without recourse to Sacred Tradition (i.e., the Church's lived interpretation of Scripture and the unwritten mode of transmitting the single apostolic deposit of faith) and the Magisterium, which Christ charged with the task of safeguarding and authentically interpreting and promulgating the deposit of faith throughout the ages.

The terms *Scriptura*, *Traditio*, and *Magisterium* may be summarized this way: *Scriptura* is the object of the Church's interpretation; *Traditio* is the Church's lived interpretation of Scripture; and *Magisterium* is the authority of the Church that does the interpreting. Historically, the Catholic model, not *sola scriptura*, is the one we see the Church using, even from its earliest years. Protestant apologists will have you believe otherwise. For example, the *Westminster Catechism of Faith* says:

> The whole counsel of God, concerning all things necessary for his own glory, man's salvation, faith, and life, is either expressly set down in Scripture, or by good and necessary consequence may be deduced from Scripture: unto which nothing at any time is to be added, whether by new revelations of the Spirit, or traditions of men" (6). If this statement is true, then the doctrine of *sola scriptura* must itself be "expressly set down in Scripture, or ... deduced from Scripture.

But that's the rub. By asserting *sola scriptura*, Protestants are making the concomitant assertion that all the divine revelation necessary for the Church to possess comes down to us in Scripture alone. The Anglican Reformers put it this way:

> The Holy Scripture containeth all things necessary to salvation: so that whatsoever is not read therein, nor may be proved thereby, is not to be required of any man that it should be believed as an article of the Faith, or be thought requisite or necessary to salvation" (39 Articles of Religion, 6).

More specifically, as the *Westminster Confession of Faith* explains that "what is necessary" must be expressed or implied. That leads us to the question of *formal* versus *material* sufficiency. Many eminent Catholic theologians and doctors down through the centuries, most notably the Church Fathers, have taught that Scripture is materially sufficient[17] (i.e., it contains all the material or "stuff" of divine revelation, either in explicit or implicit form),[18] In fact, to gain an authentic understanding of the Fathers, it's crucial that one recognize their virtual unanimity on the issue of material sufficiency. The problem is that Evangelical Protestants who venture into patristic literature invariably come away with a faulty understanding of what the Fathers meant. Cardinal John Henry Newman observed this problem in a letter to an Anglican friend: "You have made a collection of passages from the Fathers, as witnesses in behalf of your doctrines that the whole Christian Faith is contained in Scripture, as if, in your sense of my words, Catholics contradicted you here."[19]

We must make a critical distinction here in order to understand the difference between the Father's teaching of the *material sufficiency* of Scripture and the Reformer's much narrower notion of *formal sufficiency*. At certain levels, the Catholic teaching intersects with the Protestant teaching of *sola scriptura*. But the fundamental difference is this: The Catholic Church holds that in order to properly understand the meaning of Sacred Scripture, the Church must have recourse to and rely on its living Tradition.[20] The Protestant understanding of "sufficiency" pushes well beyond the realm of material sufficiency into the province of formal sufficiency. Formal sufficiency means that all revelation necessary for the Church

[17] For a discussion of the history of the material sufficiency position among Catholic theologians, see George H. Tavard, *Holy Writ or Holy Church: The Crisis of the Protestant Reformation* (London: Barnes and Oates, 1959) and Yves M. J. Congar, O. P., *Tradition and Traditions* (San Diego: Basilica Press, 1997 edition).

[18] St. Thomas Aquinas: "*Sacra Scriptura ad hoc divinitus est ordinata ut per eam nobis veritas manifestetur necessaria ad salutem*" (*Quodl.* 7, 14).

[19] John Henry Newman, *Certain Difficulties Felt by Anglicans in Catholic Teaching, Considered in a Letter Addressed to the Rev. E. B. Pusey, D. D., on the Occasion of His Eirenicon of 1864*, Vol. 2, section 2, 2.

[20] Cf., Vatican Council II, *Dei Verbum* 7-10, 24.

to possess is presented formally in the pages of Scripture. This nuance, and make no mistake that it is a very important nuance, is precisely where the failure of *sola scriptura* occurs.

Sola Scriptura As "Canon Fodder"

Another problem for *sola scriptura* is the canon of the New Testament. There is no "inspired table of contents" in Scripture that tells us which books belong and which ones do not. That information comes to us from outside Scripture. Moreover, the knowledge of which books comprise the canon of the New Testament must be infallible; if not, there is no way to know for certain if the books we regard as inspired really are inspired. Further, this knowledge must be binding; otherwise men would be free to create their own customized canon containing those books they value and lacking the ones they devalue. This knowledge must also be part of divine revelation; if not, it is merely a *tradition of men*, and if that were so, Protestants would be forced into the intolerable position of championing a canon of purely human origin.

The above requirements do not square with the classic Protestant creeds, for example the Westminster Confession of Faith, which asserted that,

> The authority of the Holy Scripture, for which it ought to be believed and obeyed, dependeth not upon the testimony of any man or church, but wholly upon God (who is truth itself), the author thereof; and therefore it is to be received, because it is the Word of God. We may be moved and induced by the testimony of the Church to an high and reverent esteem for the Holy Scripture... yet, notwithstanding, our full persuasion and assurance of the infallible truth and divine authority thereof, is from the inward work of the Holy Spirit, bearing witness by and with the Word in our hearts.

This is pure Mormonism — the old "I know it's inspired because I feel in my heart that it's inspired" line that Mormon missionaries use. As a proof for the inspiration of Scripture, this bromide is useless. *Sola scriptura* becomes "canon fodder" as soon as the Catholic requires the Protestant to explain how the books of the

Bible got into the Bible. Under the principles implicit in *sola scriptura*, Scripture is placed in an epistemological vacuum, since it and the veracity of its contents "dependeth not upon the testimony of any man or church," If that's true, how then can anyone know with certitude what belongs in Scripture in the first place? The answer, of course, is that you can't.[21]

Without recognizing the trustworthiness of the Magisterium, which is endowed with Christ's own teaching authority (cf., Matt. 16:18-19, 18:18; Luke 10:16) guided by the Holy Spirit (cf., John 14:25-26; 16:13), and the living apostolic Tradition of the Church (cf., Luke 1:3-4; 1 Cor. 11:1; 2 Thess. 2:15; 2 Timothy 2:2), there is no way to know for certain which books belong in Scripture and which do not. As soon as Protestants begin to appeal to the canons drawn up by this or that Father, or this or that council, they inadvertently concede defeat, since they are forced to appeal to the very "testimony of man and Church" that they claim not to need.[22]

Specific Verses Protestants Use

Here is an overview of the more common Protestant arguments raised in defense of *sola scriptura*. The verse most often used is 2 Timothy 3:16-17. Since it speaks of God directly inspiring Scripture, Protestants assume that Scripture alone has the divine stamp of approval. Ironically, this passage is a minefield of difficulties for *sola scriptura*. The context of the passage shows Paul giving a lengthy series of directives and advice to his young episcopal protégé, Timothy. He concludes his practical advice on how to be a good bishop with this reminder and exhortation: "All Scripture is inspired by God (Greek: *theopneustos* = God breathed) and is useful for teaching, for refutation, for correction, and for training in righteousness, so that the man of God may be competent, equipped

[21] R. C. Sproul admits this when he says, "...the Protestant view is that the church's decision regarding what books make up the Canon was a fallible decision. Being fallible means that it is possible that the church erred in its compilation of the books found in the present Canon of Scripture" *(Sola Scriptura! The Protestant Position on the Bible*, p. 66).

[22] This is just an overview of the canon issue. In chapter 5 Robert Sungenis gives a detailed refutation of the Protestant arguments on the canon.

for every good work." The conclusion Protestants often draw from this passage is that 2 Timothy 3:16-17 teaches that the Bible is sufficient in all matters of Christian doctrine and practice because it will make the man of God equipped for these tasks.[23]

In one of my public debates on *sola scriptura*,[24] Protestant apologist James White attempted to make his case for the formal sufficiency of Scripture by using an analogy of a bike shop. He argued that just as the bike shop contains all the necessary accouterments for bike riding and can fully equip a bike rider, so too Scripture is sufficient to "fully equip" the man of God. Unfortunately for his case, this analogy, although superficially plausible, is faulty. The bike shop may provide all the necessary equipment, but the customer must first know how to ride a bike to make use of that equipment. This is analogous to the Christian knowing how to correctly use Scripture. Bike shops can certainly equip their customer with all the necessary paraphernalia, but they do not teach him how to ride.

White tried to get around my rebuttal by countering that 2 Timothy 3:17 says that the man of God is made fully equipped by Scripture, so there is no question that he'll know how to use Scripture correctly. But the problem with this argument is that there is no way to determine who is a "man of God," and who isn't. When challenged on this issue during the debate, White had no adequate answer. The debate was held in an Orthodox Presbyterian Church, moderated by the pastor, and there were a number of Protestant ministers of different denominations present that night in the audience. I reminded White that the pastor of that Presbyterian church believed in baptizing infants, because of the biblical evidence he saw. White, a Baptist, is hostile to the doctrine of infant baptism, also on biblical grounds.

---

23 Cf., John MacArthur in *Sola Scriptura! The Protestant Position on the Bible*, pp. 168-170; James White in *The Roman Catholic Controversy*, pp. 63-67; William Webster in *The Church of Rome at the Bar of History*, pp. 1-4; and Kim Riddlebarger in *Roman Catholicism: Evangelical Protestants Analyze What Divides and Unites Us*, pp. 235-237.

24 Cf., "Does the Bible Teach *Sola Scriptura*?" Patrick Madrid versus James White, available in a two-tape set from Catholic Answers, P.O. Box 17490, San Diego, CA, 92177.

"So which of you is the 'man of God'"? I asked White. He could not resolve the dilemma without taking the position that either he or the pastor was not a "man of God." That is a brief example of why his "Man of God" argument is vacuous as a defense for *sola scriptura*. If White had been consistent with his argument, he would have had to say that the pastor was not a man of God, because the pastor was "misusing" Scripture (at least on the issue of infant baptism). Remaining consistent, however, was not something White could do, for obvious reasons. To summarize, White's "bike shop" and secondary "man of God" arguments fall apart when subjected to even modest logical testing.

Protestantism is so divided over doctrinal issues (e.g. infant baptism, baptismal regeneration, the nature of justification, salvation, divorce and remarriage, etc.), that this "man of God" argument only begs the question. Each Protestant believes that he has embraced the "correct" interpretation of Scripture, but believing so includes the implicit assertion that all the other denominations do not have the correct interpretation on all things. If they did, why the need for denominations?

The answer to the Protestant claims of sufficiency for this passage is that Paul is not trying to establish Scripture as the sole, sufficient item that renders the man of God fit for these tasks. Rather, he is reminding Timothy of several things that, combined with God's grace and Timothy's faithful diligence, will make him so equipped.

In the year 434, Vincent of Lerins reflected on this problem:

> If one should as one of the heretics who gives you this advice, 'How do you prove [your assertion]? What ground have you for saying that I ought to cast away the universal and ancient faith of the Catholic Church? He has the answer ready: 'For it is written.' And forthwith he produces a thousand examples, a thousand authorities from the Law, from the Psalms, from the apostles, from the prophets, by means of which, interpreted on a new and wrong principle, the unhappy soul may be precipitated from the height of Catholic truth to the lowest abyss of heresy... Do heretics appeal to Scripture? They do indeed, and with a vengeance. For you may see them scamper through every single book of Holy Scripture... Whether among their own people or among strangers, in private or in

> public, in speaking or in writing, at convivial meetings or in the streets, hardly ever do they bring forward anything of their own which they do not endeavor to shelter under the words of Scripture... You will see an infinite heap of instances, hardly a single page, which does not bristle with plausible quotations from the New Testament or the Old" (*Commonitoria* 25, 26, 25).

Sola Scriptura Is Unworkable

We have reached that point at which the "rubber" of *sola scriptura* meets the "road" of everyday life. The final question we should ask the Protestant is this: "Can you show where in history *sola scriptura* has worked?"[25] In other words, where, throughout Protestantism's relatively brief life-span, can we find examples (just one will do) of *sola scriptura* actually working, functioning in such a way that it brings about doctrinal certitude and unity of doctrine among Christians? The answer: *nowhere*.

As a rule of faith that, without recourse to Sacred Tradition and an infallible Magisterium, promises doctrinal certitude and a unity of faith, *sola scriptura* fails miserably. The best evidence of this is Protestantism itself. There are today, thousands of distinct Protestant denominations in the world, each claiming to go by the "Bible alone," yet no two of them agree on what exactly the Bible teaches. In later chapters, you'll hear much of the "chaos" and "anarchy" that is the byproduct of *sola scriptura*. The blueprint for that doctrinal anarchy is laid out in the *Westminster Confession of Faith*:

> The whole counsel of God, concerning all things necessary for his own glory, man's salvation, faith, and life, is either expressly set down in Scripture, or by good and necessary consequence may be deduced from Scripture: unto which nothing at any time is to be added, whether by new revelations of the Spirit, or traditions of men...All things in Scripture are not alike plain in themselves, nor alike clear unto all; yet those things which are necessary to be known, believed,

---

[25] Refer to my asking Douglas Jones this question repeatedly — and getting no answer — in our written debates on *sola scriptura* in **Appendix 3** of this book.

> and observed, for salvation, are so clearly propounded and opened in some place of Scripture or other, that not only the learned, but the unlearned, in a due use of the ordinary means, may attain unto a sufficient understanding of them...The infallible rule of interpretation of Scripture, is the Scripture itself; and therefore, when there is a question about the true and full sense of any scripture (which is not manifold, but one), it may be searched and known by other places that speak more clearly. The Supreme Judge, by which all controversies of religion are to be determined, and all decrees of councils, opinions of ancient writers, doctrines of men, and private spirits, are to be examined, and in whose sentence we are to rest, can be no other but the Holy Spirit speaking in the Scripture" *(Westminster Confession of Faith* 6, 7, 9).

All of that sounds fine at first hearing, but upon close inspection, this framework falls apart rather easily. First, if "the whole counsel of God... is either expressly set down in Scripture, or by good and necessary consequence may be deduced from Scripture," then *sola scriptura* must itself appear somewhere in Scripture, but it does not. Thus, under the terms set forth in all the classical Protestant creeds (the *Westminster Confession of Faith* being one of the best examples of which) it is a self-refuting proposition.

Second, if "those things which are necessary to be known, believed, and observed, for salvation, are so clearly propounded and opened in some place of Scripture or other, that not only the learned, but the unlearned, in a due use of the ordinary means, may attain unto a sufficient understanding of them," then we have another problem. What are we to do with such things "necessary to be known, believed, and observed for salvation" as the doctrine that the Persons of the Trinity are *homoousios*, that in Christ there are two wills, the Hypostatic Union, the cessation of divine revelation upon the death of the last Apostle, the canon of Scripture, whether or not infants should be baptized, and a whole host of key issues that bear directly upon the core of the Christian faith?

Scripture alone — Scripture forced to stand apart from the infallible teaching Magisterium that Christ gave by his own authority to accurately interpret Scripture, and Sacred Tradition, which is the Church's living interpretation of those written words is insufficient to provide a stable model of authority. It leads to the myriad of conflicting, erroneous, and sometimes spiritually fatal "human traditions" (c.f. Matt. 15:3-9; Mark 7:6-7) that lead people away from Christ.

Scripture alone, as the tragic history of Protestantism has shown, becomes the private play toy of any self-styled "exegete" who wishes to interpret God's Word to suit his own views. The history of Protestantism, laboring under *sola scriptura*, is an unending kaleidoscope of fragmentation and splintering. It cannot provide any sort of doctrinal certitude for the Christian, because it is built on the shifting sand of mere human opinion what the individual pastor *thinks* Scripture means.

Martin Luther's protest against the admitted liturgical and other abuses that characterized much of 16th-century Catholic Europe, quickly blossomed into a full-blown case of rebellion against most of the tenets of the Catholic Faith. Within a short period of time, the cry of *sola scriptura*! was heard in pulpits across the land. Fieldhands, blacksmiths, milkmaids, and clerks in every burg and hamlet were encouraged by the Reformers and their disciples to grasp Sacred Scripture firmly in hand and, turning a scornful back on the "oppressive and corrupt" Roman system, interpret it for themselves. *Sola scriptura*! rang in their ears as they were cajoled and hectored and tsk-tsked into "thinking for themselves," prodded to decide for themselves just what Scripture means. That is what they did, and that is when the religious scene in Europe got really weird.

In the name of *sola scriptura*, every imaginable theological goulash, however exotic, was enabled to flourish and spread. Scripture had been wrested out of its rightful place in the Church, and had become the personal "Rubik's Cube" of anyone who picked it up and endeavored to figure out what it meant for himself. Naturally, some pretty striking differences of interpretation emerged among Protestants.

Martin Luther was hardly in the grave when the Calvinists were busy "reforming" Luther's reformation. Calvin's *Institutes of the Christian Religion* were aimed at codifying the doctrines of "true Christianity," and in so doing, correct the doctrinal aberrations in the Lutheran, Anglican, Anabaptist and other seminal Protestant denominations. But even as this "reformation of the Reformation" was chugging along in Geneva, the Anabaptists in England, France, and elsewhere were hard at work pointing out where both Luther and Calvin had misstepped in their interpretations of Scripture. By the end of the Sixteenth Century, scores, if not hundreds of new, theologically distinct Protestant sects were alive and well each claiming to possess "The Truth," each claiming to go by the Bible alone, yet no two of them agreeing on exactly what the Bible means. All of that brought to you, compliments of *sola scriptura*.

Tragically, the theological bickerfest known as Protestantism continues unabated into our own day. If anything, it has picked up steam. Each new denomination that splinters off claims to have the "correct" interpretation. But wait a bit, and sooner or later some folks in that new fellowship will dislike an interpretation the pastor plucks out of Scripture, and they will hive off and start a new "church" that contains the "correct" interpretation. Think I'm exaggerating? Just open the Yellow Pages and check for yourself how many different Protestant denominations exist in your city.

Catholics should not flinch when confronted with the alleged "biblical" and "historical" evidences in favor of *sola scriptura*. They fall apart. Scripture and history are the two best apologetic tools for effective evangelization in discussions with Protestants about *sola scriptura*. I know firsthand the importance of discussing *sola scriptura* with Protestants. Having engaged in a number of live public debates with Protestant ministers on this subject, I've seen Protestants flumoxed (some even converted to Catholicism) when they see that *sola scriptura* is indefensible.

Sure, *sola scriptura* is bogus and a failure, but we can at least admit that it has been an ambitious failure. As theological bellyflops go, it has sloshed more souls out of the Church than any other half-baked scheme that has come down the pike of Church history. Sadly, it is still at work, confusing and dividing sincere men and women who seek to follow Christ and yanking many Catholics out of the One True Church. That is why we who know better need to understand it and know how to refute it.

Chapter 2

What are the Philosophical and Practical Problems with *Sola Scriptura*?

by Philip Blosser

In this chapter, we will set the stage for our discussion with some remarks on the 16th-century and contemporary historical context of our debate (Part I), then address a number of immediate misapprehensions stemming from *sola scriptura* that have continued to cloud Catholic-Protestant dialogue concerning Scripture. In particular, we will address the practical effect of *sola scriptura* in substantially severing large portions of Protestantism from the living traditions of the Church (Part II). In the main body of the chapter, we will offer a detailed analysis of several philosophical and practical problems with the Protestant theological tradition of *sola scriptura*. This analysis falls broadly into two parts: (Part III) philosophical problems related to coherence and historicity, and (Part IV) practical problems of hermeneutical subjectivism, factionalism, and the undermining of pastoral authority and discipline.

Part I: Historical Background of the Debate

One of the most urgent needs among the various Christian traditions in our time is for an honest accounting of the issues stemming from the "Great Divorce" of the 16th century. After nearly five centuries it has become possible to see that the issues over which Catholics and Protestants divided were not black and white. There was truth in the claims and accusations made by both sides, and there were disastrous errors of judgment on both sides, which all converged to produce what Lutheran historian Jaroslav Pelikan has called the "tragic necessity" of the Reformation. What is needed today more than ever is a mutual sorting out of what was really "necessary" from what was "tragic" in the Protestant Reformation, as well as the good from the bad in the life of the Catholic Church in and since the 16th century. The urgency of this need is now beginning to be felt within those traditions that have been most vocal in past centuries about the "necessity" of the Reformation but silent about its "tragedy" — most happily, by a number of solidly conservative, evangelical and Reformed Protestants. This is attested not only by such fraternal efforts as Charles Colson's and Richard Neuhaus's book, *Evangelicals and Catholics Together: Toward a Common Mission,*[1] but by honest evaluations of agreements and differences by fair- minded evangelicals who seem sincerely willing to try to understand the position of their Catholic "separated brethren," such as Norman Geisler's and Ralph MacKenzie's *Roman Catholics and Evangelicals: Agreements and Differences.*[2]

But even many of the more polemical defenses of classic Protestant positions by such men as James White, R.C. Sproul, John

---

1 Charles Colson and Richard J. Neuhaus, *Evangelicals and Catholics Together: Toward a Common Mission* (Dallas: Word, 1996). One thinks also of cooperative efforts in such popular areas as music, as in the recent album, *Brother to Brother*, jointly produced by the evangelical, Michael Card, and the Catholic, John Michael Talbot (Word, 1996), and also of the collaboration in the pro-life movement between Catholics and (especially Baptist) evangelicals.

2 Norman Geisler and Ralph MacKenzie, *Roman Catholics and Evangelicals: Agreements and Differences* (Grand Rapids: Baker Books, 1995). While Catholics will find their discussion of areas of doctrinal differences (in Part Two) flawed, the tone is consistently civilized and the objections sincere; and the discussion of areas of doctrinal agreement and practical cooperation (in Parts One and Three) go far beyond any recent evangelical publication in clearing up areas of misunderstanding and uncovering our common unity from the evangelical side.

Armstrong, and others,[3] have demonstrated an increased willingness to wade out into the "strange divine sea" of Catholicism and to attempt, as far as differences of perspective permit, to engage in critical discussion. More specifically, some have shown a new appreciation of the importance of traditions of the ancient Church and have conceded that at least some of the common Protestant fears have been groundless or misguided. James White, for example, warns his readers against the common anti-Catholic paranoia about making the sign of the cross, crucifixes, candles, liturgy, and Catholic "conspiracies"; and, following Geisler and MacKenzie, who dedicated their book to J. von Staupiz — Luther's father confessor, who, like others in the Catholic tradition, "kept alive the Pauline and Augustinian doctrine of salvation by grace" — White concedes that Luther and earlier believers like Wycliff and Hus "found the truth of the Gospel" even while they were Catholics.[4] Other conservative Protestants, faced with the widespread indifference to history, ignorance of tradition, individualism, and focus on immediate experience that characterizes much of modern-day evangelicalism, demonstrate a renewed appreciation for the importance of (at least lower-case) "catholic" tradition, such as R. C. Sproul, who readily acknowledges that the NT Canon, for example, rests upon a "tradition," even though the concept of tradition "is often viewed by a jaundiced eye among Evangelicals" because of "guilt by association"; or John Armstrong, who chides the attitude

---

3 James White, *Fatal Flaw* (Southbridge, MA: Crowne, 1990), *Answers to Catholic Claims* (Southbridge, MA: Crowne, 1990), and *The Roman Catholic Controversy* (Minneapolis: Bethany House, 1996); R. C. Sproul, *Faith Alone* (Grand Rapids: Baker, 1995); John Armstrong, ed., *Roman Catholicism: Evangelical Protestants Analyze What Divides and Unites Us* (Chicago: Moody Press, 1987); Don Kistler, ed., *Justification by Faith ALONE* (Morgan, PA: Soli Deo Gloria, 1995), and *Sola Scriptura! The Protestant Position on the Bible* (hereafter cited as "*SS*") (Morgan, PA: Soli Deo Gloria, 1995); and James McCarthy, *The Gospel According to Rome* (Eugene, OR: Harvest House, 1995).

4 James White, *Roman*, 33-38, 27; Geisler and MacKenzie, 5 (Dedication). White would certainly insist that these Christians found truth *despite* the Catholic Church, not because of it; nevertheless it remains a significant concession, given his hostility to Catholicism, that he would admit that "the truth of the Gospel" could be found by anyone within the Church at all — almost as significant as Geisler's and MacKenzie's concession that the "Pauline and Augustinian doctrine of salvation by grace" could be kept alive by one, like J. von Staupiz, who remained a faithful Catholic all his life.

of those who choose to ignore the contributions of extrabiblical traditions as the "height of contemporary arrogance."[5]

The oft-rehearsed practical abuses that provoked the Protestant Reformation have been readily acknowledged on all sides — certainly by the Catholic Church (though this comes as news to many Protestants). As Sheldon Vanauken observes in a sequel to his celebrated *A Severe Mercy,* "In the very year that Henry VIII's obedient Parliament named him head of the English church, Pope Paul III went through the streets of Rome in sackcloth and ashes for the sins of his predecessors..."[6] Luther was *right* about Tetzel and his abuses. Someone clearly was not minding the store in the offices of the Church. Discipline was slack. Reform was necessary. Rome acknowledges this. Yet, as Louis Bouyer argues in his sympathetic study, *The Spirit and Forms of Protestantism,* the well-intended assumption that the only way of securing the needed reforms was by recourse to *sola scriptura* spelled tragedy by effectively cutting off Protestantism from that living and normative community of memory in which alone her positive reforms could be sustained.[7] The positive intent was plain enough: if the Church and her human traditions were corrupt, she could be reformed only by

---

5 R. C. Sproul and John Armstrong, in Don Kistler, ed., *SS,* 70f. and 145f., respectively. R. C. Sproul, in his article, "Unity and Purity and the Holy Catholic Church," *Eternity* (June 1988), begins by asking, "Whatever happened to the catholic church?"; then rehearses the core catholic doctrines of the historic Ecumenical Councils, laments the anti-catholic heresies of four widely known televangelists, and concludes by affirming the need for a healthy evangelicalism that "is as catholic as it is evangelical" (60).

6 "...but not for their errors in doctrine," adds Sheldon Vanauken, *Under the Mercy* (Nashville: Thomas Nelson, 1985; rpt. San Francisco: Ignatius, 1988), 226; rpt., "The English Channel: Between Canterbury and Rome," in *The New Catholics: Contemporary Converts Tell Their Stories,* ed. Dan O'Neill (New York: Crossroad, 1989), 129.

7 Louis Bouyer, *Du protestantisme à l'eglise* (Paris: Les Editions du Cerf, 1954; tr. by A.V. Littledale as *The Spirit and Forms of Protestantism* [London: Harvill Press, and Westminster, 1956; Maryland: Newman Press, 1956; rpt. London: Collins, Fontanta Library, 1963; rpt. Cleveland: World, Meridian Books, 1964]. The author, formerly a Lutheran minister and now a Catholic priest and eminent theologian, undertakes to retrace the steps by which he arrived at the conviction that the Catholic Church was "the only church in which the fullness of the positive elements of the Reformation could be exercised."

being subjected to an external authority, and what else could this possibly be but Scripture, unmediated and alone? The tragic consequences implicit in this reasoning, however, were not immediately apparent, and today they are so covered over by centuries of distorted, unhistorical discourse about "churches," "denominations," "ministers," "the Word," "human traditions," and the like, as to be virtually lost from view. This itself is part of the tragedy. Protestantism is no longer in a position to see how Christ meant the Church to be an essential part of his Gospel. Instead, the Gospel is experienced as communicated to individuals by the Spirit through Scripture, and only circumstantially as connected to "the church of one's choice," whatever choice that may be — as long as it is a Protestant and relatively conservative one!

The tragedy of *sola scriptura* is that it cuts off Protestants from sacred history *after* New Testament times — from the living, sacred memory of the Church. Suspicion is inevitably roused in the Protestant mind against those who claim that an earthly, human institution with flawed and fallible human leaders is not only "sacred" and "divine," but infallibly guided by the Holy Spirit. It is usually of little help to note that the New Testament refers to the Church as the "Body of Christ" (Eph 1:23; 1 Cor 12:27); or to point out — as the *Catechism of the Catholic Church* does (citing Gal 3:27-28) — that Christ is "the head of the body, the Church" (792) and "lives with her and in her" (807), and that the Holy Spirit may be described as her "soul" (813).[8] None of this language generally impresses the Protestant as applying to any specific, earthly, historical, or humanly administered body, but rather to a generic, transcendent, ultimate and spiritual reality embracing "all true Christians"; and the suspicion that Catholics want to identify that reality exclusively with their own "denomination" only raises the hackles of most Protestants. This reaction signifies the depth of the problem at issue: it is almost as difficult for the Protestant to fathom the Catholic notion that the all-too-human Church of history could have anything like God's actual divine nature or real divine authority, as it is for an agnostic to fathom that the all-too-human Jesus

---

8 The *Catechism of the Catholic Church*, USCC tr. (Rome: Libreria Editrice Vaticana, 1994); parenthetical numerals are section numbers.

could also be God Incarnate, or for the secular critic to fathom that the all-too-human Bible could also be the revealed Word of a living God. One of the reasons for this is that Protestantism has cut itself off from its historical sources of authority and of self-understanding available through the divine life of the Church.

Part II: *Sola Scriptura* Severs One from Living Traditions of the Church

One consequence of being thus cut off from the sacred memory of the divine life of the Church — by this "*sola scriptura* schism" — is the immediate difficulty residing in the Protestant's general lack of acquaintance with the orthodox Catholic's actual experience and understanding of Scripture. Peter Kreeft, in an appendix to *Fundamentals of the Faith*, compares how Protestants experience and understand the Bible with how they think Catholics experience and understand it, as a matter of principle.[9] (1) Protestants *experience* the Bible as sacred, certain, and true: it is God's Word, a rock, a sure anchor, spiritual food, a place where we meet Christ. (2) They *believe* it is inspired and infallible. So far, as Kreeft notes, this is all quite Catholic.[10] Only the "Protestant additions" of belief in the Bible's formal "sufficiency" (*sola scriptura*) and its authority independent of the Church, as well as their misplaced suspi-

9 Peter Kreeft, *Fundamentals of the Faith* (San Francisco: Ignatius, 1988), ch. 43, "Authority of the Bible," 272ff. The words "as a matter of principle" are important to forestall any misunderstanding or mischief that might arise from the futility of comparing the experiences and beliefs of less-than-faithful Protestants and Catholics.

10 One of the ironies of chapters like Joel Beeke's and Ray Lanning's "The Transforming Power of Scripture" in *SS*, 221-76, is that a faithful Catholic could wholeheartedly affirm virtually everything in it, even while its purpose is linked to the overall purpose of the volume, which is the defense of Protestantism against the perceived threat of Catholicism. In this light, the authors' comments on the Belgic Confession's affirmation of the canonical Scriptures as received because of the testimony of the Holy spirit, not Church approval, ring ironically hollow: "Note the sweeping claim made for the faith of the Reformers: *They believed without doubt all things contained in Scripture*." (emphasis theirs, 268). But *so do Catholics!* The difference is that Catholics see the Church's and Scripture's authority as identically Christ's.

cions about what Catholics really experience and what the Catholic Church officially teaches concerning the Bible, separate them from Catholicism.[11] (3) How do Protestants suppose we *experience* the Bible? They suspect that Catholics have always feared it and kept it from the laity, lest it expose Catholic doctrines as unscriptural. (4) What do they think we *believe* about the Bible? Commonly, that the Bible is less important than the Church, which teaches dogmas quite independently of it; that, like the Pharisees, we confuse human tradition with divine revelation, "teaching as doctrines the precepts of men,... making the word of God void through tradition" (Mk 7:7, 13).[12]

Such grievous misunderstandings stem from the tragic effects of the "*sola scriptura* schism," by which Protestants have effectively cut themselves off from the ancient and abiding truth about the Catholic experience and understanding of Scripture. Even granting the growing encouragement of a biblically literate Catholic laity and shift to a vernacular liturgy following the Second Vatican Council (1963-65), most Protestant statements about the modern Catholic "rediscovery of the Bible" come off sounding, to the historically informed, like patronizing nonsense.[13] Suffice it here to observe that if ever there was a safe truth, it is this: no higher view of Scripture and its authority exists in all of Protestantism than that which is to be found in the Catholic Church. It was never the lack of a sufficiently high view of Scripture that produced the "necessity" of the

---

[11] This is not to belittle the significance of these differences. Specifically, the removal of the *primary* locus of Scripture in the life of the believer *from* the context of liturgical proclamation within the authoritatively-summoned gathering of the Church, *to* the context of the individual's autonomous Bible study or quiet time, is a major shift.

[12] This biblical passage, of course, refers to a specific human tradition (small t) of positive law, not to what Catholics call sacred Tradition (big T) of divine authority.

[13] For example, Sinclair Ferguson suggests that "a major development" has occurred since Vatican II in terms of a new, positive Roman Catholic regard for Scripture, and adds: "For this we may be grateful. We should not grudgingly minimize the rediscovery of the Bible" (in *SS*, 217). In the same vein is Armstrong's remark that the Council of Trent "fundamentally rejected the Reformers' efforts to call the church back to the authority of the Word of God" (in *SS*, 123).

Reformation. This can be amply shown from the Catholic Church's (1) official teaching, (2) history of Bible translation, (3) practice of Bible-reading at Mass, (4) uncompromising Biblical interpretation, and (5) strict adherence to the Bible's moral teachings.

First, official statements and teaching of the Catholic Church have always affirmed and continue to affirm that Scripture is written wholly and entirely in all its parts through the inspiration of the Holy Spirit and that it is absolutely inerrant.[14] For example, Pope Leo XIII insisted in his encyclical, *Providentissimus Deus* (1892), that "it is absolutely wrong and forbidden either to narrow inspiration to certain parts only of Holy Scripture or to admit that the sacred writer has erred."[15] Pope Pius XII, in *Divino Afflante Spiritu* (1943), declared: "For as the substantial Word of God became like to men in all things, 'except sin' [Heb. 4:15], so the words of God, expressed in human language, are made like to human speech in every respect, except error"; in the same document Pius quoted St. Jerome's words: "To ignore the Scripture is to ignore Christ."[16] The Second Vatican Council reiterated these positions — against the aberrations, not only of Protestant Liberalism, but of Catholic dissidents flirting with it — in *Dei verbum* (1965), which declared that the sacred writers "consigned to writing whatever [God] wanted written, and no more," and that the "books of Scripture, firmly, faithfully and without error, teach that truth which God, for the sake of our salvation, wished to see confided to the sacred Scriptures."[17] Thankfully, this high Catholic view of Scripture is coming to be acknowledged to some degree, gradually, by some evangelical scholars, such as Geisler, MacKenzie, Sproul, Roger Nicole, and the late John Gerstner.[18]

---

[14] For a recent defense of the Catholic teaching on inerrancy, see William G. Most, *Free from All Error* (Libertyville: Prow Books, 1985).

[15] Leo XIII, *Providentissimus Deus* (1892), NCWC tr. (Boston: St. Paul Editions, N.d.), Part II, D, 3, "Inerrancy of Holy Scripture" (25f.).

[16] Pius XII, *Divino Afflante Spiritu* (1943), NCWC tr. (Boston: St. Paul Editions, N.d.), secs. 37 & 57 (21, 27); cf. also secs. 1-4 (pp. 5-8).

[17] Vatican II, *Dei verbum* (1965), in Austin Flannery, O.P., *Vatican Council II: The Conciliar and Post Conciliar Documents* (Northport, NY: Costello, 1987), ch. 3, sec. 11 (p. 757).

[18] See Geisler and MacKenzie, 19-33, 467-69; and Sproul, including his references to John Gerstner, in *SS*, 66-68.

Second, although this is seldom known or recognized among Protestants, this high view of Scripture is attested by the impressive historical record of Catholic translations of Scripture. While it is true that the illiterate peasant populations of the middle ages learned the Gospel primarily through the spoken word, illustrated in stained glass, and enacted in ritual, the Catholic Latin Bible was itself a translation into what was once the common "vulgar" tongue (hence: *Vulgate*) of the Church in the West. Furthermore, as Henry Graham points out in *Where We Got the Bible: Our Debt to the Catholic Church*, an abundance of vernacular Catholic translations of Scriptures existed (in Spanish, Italian, Danish, French, Norwegian, Polish, Bohemian, Hungarian, and English) *well before* the time of Wycliff.[19] *The New Catholic Encyclopedia*, in its discussion of pre-Reformation German versions alone, says that there was "no want of early German translations of Scripture," and that "some 18 German editions of the whole Bible were printed prior to Luther," the first "at Strassburg in 1466."[20] In its article on Pre-Reformation English Versions, it has sections on Anglo-Saxon and Middle English translations of the Bible (463f.), and its entire discussion of translations runs the gambit of European languages from Spanish to Russian. In fact, little about Luther's celebrated translation may have been original. The Swiss Reformer, Ulrich Zwingli, is quoted as having declared to Luther:

> You are unjust in putting forth the boastful claim of dragging the Bible from beneath the dusty benches of the schools. You forget that we have gained a knowledge of the Scriptures through the translations of others. You are very well aware, with all your blustering, that previously to your time there existed a host of scholars who, in biblical knowledge and philological attainments, were incomparably your superiors.[21]

---

19 Henry G. Graham *Where We Got the Bible: Our Debt to the Catholic Church* (St. Louis: B. Herder, 1911: Rockford, IL: TAN [Thomas A. Nelson], 1987), ch. 11: "Abundance of Vernacular Scriptures Before Wycliff," 98- 109.

20 *The New Catholic Encyclopedia*, ed. by William J. McDonald, et al. at Catholic University of America (New York: McGraw-Hill Book Co., 1967), II, 476; but see the entire article, "Bible IV (Texts and Versions)," 414ff.

21 *Alzog*. III, 49, quoted in Patrick F. O'Hare, *The Facts about Luther* (Rockford, IL: TAN [Thomas A. Nelson] Publishers, Inc., 1987), 191.

Third, the high Catholic regard for Scripture is attested in the role played by Bible reading during Mass. A cycle of prescribed lectionary readings — always including a reading from (1) a book of the Old Testament, (2) a Psalm, (3) an Epistle, and (4) one of the Gospels, whose pages are symbolically kissed after the reading — takes the practicing Catholic through major portions of Scripture on a regular basis, assuring a steady diet of Bible-reading uninfluenced by the pastor's whim, pet theological hobby horse, or disinclination to preach on certain topics. David Currie, in his book *Born Fundamentalist, Born Again Catholic*, describes an experiment he conducted in measuring the average clock time spent in actual Bible reading in different churches.[22] He chose two Protestant churches — one evangelical, the other fundamentalist — both with an average Sunday attendance well into the thousands. He found that the evangelical church, in the northwestern suburbs of Chicago, spent less than 6 percent of its Sunday service in Scripture, while the fundamentalist church in northwest Indiana spent 2 percent of its mornings in Scripture. By contrast, he found that Catholics spend an average of more than 26 percent of their time at Mass in Scripture. This should tell us something.

Fourth, the Catholic Church's high view of Scripture is attested, ironically, at those points where her straightforward and uncompromising interpretation is disputed by Protestantism. Despite what conservative Protestants may think about "Catholic additions" to the "simple Gospel" of Scripture, most of the Catholic distinctives that they criticize are rooted in taking Scripture at face value. As James Akin points out in his contribution to *Surprised by Truth: Eleven Converts Give the Biblical and Historical Reasons for Becoming Catholic*, it is not the Catholic Church, but the various factions of Protestantism that clamor over alternative interpretations and spiritualizing metaphors for the straightforward meanings of the text, and it is the Catholics who take Scripture at face value.[23]

---

[22] David Currie, *Born Fundamentalist, Born Again Catholic* (San Francisco: Ignatius, 1996), 99f.

[23] James Akin, "A Triumph and a Tragedy" in Patrick Madrid, ed., *Surprised by Truth: Eleven Converts Give the Biblical and Historical Reasons for Becoming Catholic* (San Diego: Basilica Press, 1994), 59-60; rpt. in *This Rock* VI, 4 (April 1995), 16.

In nearly every case where Protestant interpretations of scripture have diverged from *official* Catholic interpretation, the latter has taken the more conservative, even literal, view — whether it is the matter of eating the flesh and drinking the blood of Jesus (Jn 6:53), his Eucharistic declaration, "This is my body" (Lk 22:19), our being regenerated or even "saved" in some sense by baptism (Jn 3:5, Rm 6:3, 1 Pt 3:21), the indissolubility of marriage and prohibition of remarriage (Mk 10:11; Lk 16:18; Mt 5:32; 19:9; 1 Cor 7:10, 33), Christ's delegation of a real power of binding and loosing (Mt 16:18, 18:18), his transmission of real authority to forgive or retain sins (Jn 20:23), his building of his Church upon Peter the "rock" (Aramaic: *kepha*) and giving to Peter (whom Jesus specifically named "Cephas," *from* the Aramaic *kepha*) the keys of the kingdom (Mt 16:18-19; cf. Is 20:20).

Fifth, the Catholic Church's high view of Scripture is attested by her steadfast adherence to the moral teachings of our Lord in Scripture. No matter how far afield her most vocal and dissident theologians have strayed (like disobedient children from their mother), she has stood by her magisterial definitions of what is to be believed "of faith" (*de fide*). After all, whose voice is it that, as the spiritual leader of nearly one fifth of the earth's recalcitrant inhabitants, still dares to condemn as sin the commonplace practices of contraception, masturbation, abortion, divorce, remarriage, homosexuality, and to retain an uncompromising view of Scripture and insist on an exclusively male and celibate clergy? The voice of the Pope. Where else do you hear such a voice? From Canterbury? Lutheranism? Presbyterianism? Methodism? Evangelicalism? All of Rome's official teaching and reasoning is based, directly or indirectly, on the Bible — even her position on celibacy (1 Cor 7:32, 35; Mt 19:11-12). Further, with the exception of celibacy, Protestantism traditionally shared Rome's view of all these practices, including contraception.[24] Yet contemporary Protestant

[24] The Evangelical author, Charles D. Provan, *The Bible and Birth Control* (Monongahela, PA: Zimmer, 1989), explores not only biblical arguments against birth control, but the arguments of prominent Protestant theologians — from the Protestant Reformers to the 19th century — for opposing birth control. In fact, no Protestant denomination sanctioned contraception prior to the 1930's when the Episcopal Church became the first to officially go on record permitting birth control.

teaching has, to one degree or another, relinquished its traditional positions and sought rationalizations for more permissive views — even in evangelical circles.[25] It is a remarkable phenomenon that in a world where nearly one out of five persons (or nearly a billion people) is Roman Catholic — where, thus, the Church's uncompromising stance is bound to meet with constant resistance among even her own members — Rome continues to be unyielding in her adherence to her strict, biblically-based traditions on these issues. This clearly says: we don't *vote* on what we're going to let God's Word tell us.

Thus, as we have said earlier, the tragedy of *sola scriptura* — illustrated by widespread and continuing Protestant misunderstanding of facts such as these — is that it cuts off Protestants from sacred history, from the living memory of the Church. To the philosophical and practical problems resulting from that schism and separation, we now turn.

Part III: The Philosophical Problems of *Sola Scriptura*

The *sola scriptura* thesis suffers from two sets of broadly philosophical problems. These derive from the fact that it is (A) incoherent, and (B) unhistorical (treated in the next section).

---

25 Several notable recent cases of conservative Protestants abandoning their position of historical solidarity with the Catholic tradition come to mind. (1) The well-known Evangelical magazine, *Christianity Today*, turned the corner on the ordination of women in a "CT Institute supplement on women in the church" in its October 3, 1986 issue, under the editorial leadership of Kenneth S. Kantzer. (2) Respected Evangelical champion of "Focus on the Family," James Dobson, sidestepped the position of most conservatives in *Preparing for Adolescence* (Wheaton: Tyndale House, 1971) when he expressed his opinion that "masturbation is not much of an issue with God" (83). (3) The November 1993 issue of *Christianity Today* carried an article in its "Education" section stating that "the Wheaton College Gay and Lesbian Alumni Association has gained a membership of 100 alumni from classes spanning four decades," many of whom "call themselves evangelicals, including missions workers, church leaders, and Christian college teachers" (38).

A. Problems of Coherence

It is incoherent in two ways: it is (1) unbiblical, and (2) logically inconsistent.

1. It is unbiblical.

Why is it unbiblical? It is unbiblical because the Bible (a) nowhere teaches or assumes it; rather, the Bible assumes (b) a larger context of delegated ecclesiastical authority and normative tradition; (c) the continued normativity of extrabiblical traditions of divine instruction; and (d) the liturgical context of the worshipping community.

(a) *The Bible nowhere teaches or assumes it.*

For a Catholic to say that the Bible nowhere teaches or assumes *sola scriptura* is not to be disrespectful of the Bible's authority, but to defer respectfully to its authority in precisely *what it says...* and does *not* say, as in this case. Jesus, Paul, and others, do claim that Scripture has divine authority. It is "God breathed" in the profoundest sense, as B.B. Warfield so compellingly argues in his magisterial work on *The Inspiration and Authority of the Bible*.[26] Jesus is seen appealing constantly to its authority. But nowhere do the inspired authors of Scripture, or Jesus, assume that *what is written* is the *only* source of continuing divine authority and guidance. In order to prove *sola scriptura*, it is not enough to show that Scripture has divine authority, or even that it is the ultimate material deposit of divine revelation. One must show *from Scripture* that God's will throughout history has been to *commit wholly to writing all* revelation and instruction that He intended as an ongoing authority for the His people and their salvation.[27] But even the best texts typically adduced to support *sola scriptura* — 2 Tim 3:16f.; Acts 17:10-

[26] Benjamin B. Warfield, *The Inspiration and Authority of the Bible* (Philadelphia: Presbyterian and Reformed, 1948).

[27] This is essentially the position assumed in the opening paragraph of the Westminster Confession of Faith (WCF) on the subject of Scripture (I, 1).

12; 1 Cor 4:6; Dt 4:2; Rev 22:18f., etc. — simply do not *say* this; nor can they be made to *imply* this, without assuming in advance what is proper to one's exegetical conclusions. Evangelicals typically will say something like, "While 2 Tim 3:16-17 does not use the word 'sufficient' it does use the equivalent in the phrase 'competent, equipped for every good work.'"[28] But this merely begs the question, for the terms of the comparison are *not* clearly equivalent. One could arguably say that all of Billy Graham's books "are profitable for teaching, reproof, correction, and for training in righteousness, that the man of God may be complete, equipped for every good work"; but this would hardly warrant the claim that his books alone are a sufficient authority for the ongoing life and instruction of the Church. What the Bible says is that Scripture is inspired by God, infallible, useful for instruction, and shouldn't be tampered with. It does not say that it is the *only* standard by which God intends to administer the ongoing life of His Church.[29]

(b) *The Bible assumes a larger context of delegated authority.*

The Bible assumes a larger context of delegated ecclesiastical authority and normative tradition. God is never seen conferring his authority on Scripture in an historical and social vacuum. Scripture is always found, rather, within a community in which God has conferred authority also upon lawfully ordained human leaders. These leaders are always either (1) appointed by God Himself, and publicly confirmed in their appointment by a miraculous ministry, or (2) appointed in legitimate and lawful succession by authorities having their ultimate origin in the first category.[30] Even Moses'

---

[28] Geisler and MacKenzie, 185, n. 26.

[29] See chapter 3 on 2 Timothy 3:16-17 by Robert Sungenis in this volume for a more detailed treatment.

[30] In fact, the requirements for holding divine office were taken so seriously in the OT that, even among the sons of Aaron, who were ordained to the Levitical priesthood by law, those who could not *verify* their family line were excluded from becoming priests (see Ezra 2:62). I owe a debt of gratitude in this section to Gregory A. Krehbiel's *A Defense of Roman Catholic Doctrine Against Reformed Protestantism* (Laurel, MD: privately circulated unpublished manuscript, 1992), pp. v, 19.

first efforts in behalf of his oppressed people in Egypt came to nothing before God had called and confirmed him (Ex 2:11-15); but afterwards, God confirmed his call with miraculous signs. Nowhere in Scripture is any member of the laity — or those who lacked the lawful authority of Jesus, the apostles, prophets, or priests — ever praised for rebelling against lawfully-ordained authority on the basis of his private reading of Scripture.[31] In fact, in Moses' later ministry, when some rose up against him claiming that God was not only with Moses but with all the people, God opened fissures in the earth to swallow them up, sent fire to consume those offering incense illicitly, and a plague upon their supporters (Num 16; cf. 12:1-10). Jesus and the apostles are seen demanding obedience not only to the written Word of God, but to the living decisions of the Church (Mt 18:12-20; cf. Acts 15, 16:4). Paul demands that his readers "stand firm and hold to the traditions" they have received "either by word of mouth or letter" (2 Th 2:15), and calls the Church the "pillar and foundation of truth" (1 Tim 3:15). These verses can be tailored to a Protestant pattern, but the resulting fit is never quite natural. As Kreeft says, "We are not taught by a teacher without a book or by a book without a teacher, but by one teacher, the Church, with one book, Scripture."[32]

(c) *The Bible assumes extrabiblical traditions.*

The Bible assumes continued normativity of extrabiblical traditions of divine instruction. It does not assume the framework presupposed by *sola scriptura.* In fact, the position of *sola scriptura* is self- defeating, because it rests on a presupposition that cannot be proved from Scripture (let alone from history) — namely, that the *whole content* of God's revealed will for the ongoing instruction of His Church was committed "wholly to writing," so that *no unwritten residue* of divinely inspired instruction survived from the oral teachings of Jesus and His apostles that remained binding on God's

[31] Krehbiel notes that neither Jesus' nor the apostles' opposition to the "authorities" of their time serves as a precedent, since they themselves were the new authority in Israel, as God's Son and His commissioned apostles (19). Formally, God established this position of Jesus at His baptism.

[32] Kreeft, *Fundamentals,* 275.

people after the New Testament (NT) was written. This assumption, stated more or less audaciously, is ubiquitous among Protestants.[33] But *where* does Scripture say this? How could one claim to *know* this? The data of history and the Church Fathers weigh heavily against it. It does not even make good sense. First, if all bindingly authoritative oral instruction ceased with the death of the last apostle, and if the early churches did not have copies of all the New Testament books until well after that time, who spoke for the Lord Jesus and the apostles in the interim? Second, how can one plausibly *imagine* the transition from the *partially oral* framework of authoritative instruction (OT + teachings of Jesus and apostles) to a *wholly written* framework (OT + NT) required by this hypothesis? Gregory Krehbiel offers a wry scenario: "One imagines all the churches dutifully obeying Paul's oral instructions on the Eucharist [1 Cor 11:34] and anxiously awaiting the publication in the *Antiochian Post* of the last apostle's obituary, at which point they are to rewrite their book of church order and eliminate everything based on oral instructions."[34] The whole idea, of course, is ridiculous.

But then, what is the partisan of *sola scriptura* to say about those who remembered the oral instructions of the apostles — con-

---

[33] The Westminster Confession claims that the "whole counsel of God, concerning all things necessary for his own glory, man's salvation, faith, and life" has been committed "wholly to writing," and is either "expressly set down in Scripture, or by good and necessary consequence may be deduced from Scripture" (WCF, I:1 & 6).

John Armstrong says: "God revealed His Word orally and temporarily through prophets and apostles and then subsequently through the inscripturated text" (in *SS*, 110); and John MacArthur, Jr. says: "Protestants do not deny that the oral teaching of the apostles was authoritative, inerrant truth, binding as a rule of faith *on those who heard it*"; "Nor does *sola Scriptura* claim that everything Jesus or the apostles ever taught is preserved in Scripture. It only means that everything necessary, everything binding on our consciences, and everything God requires of us is given to us in Scripture" (*SS*, 166, 171, cf. 182).

Geisler and MacKenzie confidently assert: "All the traditions (teachings) that were revelations were written down and are inspired and infallible." As for the rest, "it is not necessary to claim that all these oral teachings were inspired or infallible, only that they were authoritative" in some fallible, nonbinding sense (188).

[34] Krehbiel, 4 (see above, n. 30).

cerning, say, the Eucharistic liturgy — who perhaps even wrote down and preserved these, even though they never made it into the NT canon? The writings of the early Church are filled with extrabiblical sayings of Jesus, practices of the Christian community, liturgical and Eucharistic formulas, and so forth, which presuppose the divine origin and authority of these things.[35] On the Catholic view, there is no problem here, since the writings of the NT are viewed as fragments of a larger normative tradition — not as a complete set of catechetical instructions for new believers, but as occasional writings with an "eye to the situation in the churches," often intended to correct abuses.[36] But what is the Protestant partisan to do with instructions and practices that claim to be apostolic

[35] On the early liturgies of St. James, St. Mark, etc., see Roberts and Donaldson, *Ante-Nicene Fathers*, VII (1886; rpt. Peabody, MA: Hendrickson, 1994). The Reformed-Protestant editors admit in their introductory remarks to the liturgical section of this volume that documented testimony to the authentic antiquity of some of these liturgies go back as early as Justin Martyr (c. A.D. 100-165), if not to the Apostles themselves. For example, of the Roman Liturgy, they state: "If Justin Martyr describes the liturgy used in Rome, when he lived there under the Antonines, then it was nearly identical with the 'Clementine,' and had reached them from the East" (533, n. 4). Of the Gallican Liturgy, they concede that an Oxford study by William Palmer "strives to show with great ingenuity that it is not improbable that [it] may have been originally derived from St. John," even while rejecting his arguments; and of the Liturgy of St. James (used in Jerusalem), they cite numerous scholars who "think that the main structure of this liturgy is the work of St. James," even if they are divided over whether it contains some interpolations or "the whole is the genuine production of the apostle" (533f.). And of the Liturgy of St. Mark (used in Alexandria), they cite the authoritative English scholar, J. Mason Neale, who says that it is "to all intents and purposes the same as that of St. Mark; and it seems highly probable that the Liturgy of St. Mark came, as we have it now, from the hands of St. Cyril, or, to use the expression of Abu'lberkat, that Cyril 'perfected' it" (534).

[36] *Dei Verbum*, ch. 5, sec. 19 (p. 761): "... The sacred authors, in writing the four Gospels, selected certain of the many elements which had been handed on, either orally or already in written form, others they synthesized or explained with an eye to the situation of the churches, the while sustaining the form of preaching, but always in such a fashion that they have told us the honest truth about Jesus." The Gospels are not catechetical in form at all, but presuppose catechesis. The Epistles are at best indirectly catechetical, as correctives, but nowhere present themselves as a complete catechesis.

but were never put in writing in the NT? Again, Krehbiel offers an imaginative scenario:

> Imagine, if you will, John Calvin, Bible in hand, visiting the church of Corinth in the year 125. Calvin notices some practices in the church of which he has never read specific mention in Scripture, and he rebukes the church for "adding to God's word."
>
> One of the presbyters approaches Calvin and says, "Have you not read in Paul's first epistle to this church, in the passage about the Lord's Supper, 'And the rest I will set in order when I come'? (1 Cor 11:34) Dear brother, I was a young man when the apostle visited this church. These church practices you condemn came from the apostle's very lips. Are you greater than Paul? We also have in our possession Paul's letter to the church of the Thessalonians. He commands them to continue in the traditions, whether delivered by word of mouth or by epistle. (2 Thess 2:15) Are we to obey you or the apostle?" (Krehbiel, 6).

By means of this simple historical fiction, Krehbiel illustrates the unbiblical and unhistorical nature of the assumptions required by *sola scriptura*. There is no reason to suppose that early Church practices are contrary to apostolic teaching or were intended to be only temporary, simply because we can find no explicit description of them in Scripture today. In fact, Krehbiel offers an interesting *biblical* refutation of this supposition from 2 Chronicles 29:25 and 35:4, where both Hezekiah and Josiah used extrabiblical teachings in their reforms, from prophets who had been dead for hundreds of years, in violation of the assumption that only those teachings preserved in canonical Scriptures are authoritative.[37] What is interesting about the first verse (29:25) is that the instructions of David, Gad and Nathan followed by Hezekiah are described as being the command of the Lord through His prophets, even though (1) they were long dead by the time of Hezekiah, and (2) there is no record in canonical Scripture that serves as a basis for Hezekiah's actions. The same is true of the writings of Solomon whose instructions Josiah is cited as following in the second verse (35:4).

What is also remarkable is the altogether unexceptional manner in which these actions are described. As Krehbiel observes, "In no case did the believing community rebuke Hezekiah or Josiah for violating *sola scriptura*. On the contrary, they accepted the fact that divine instruction, through the mouths of God's prophets, had been preserved for the church's use for hundreds of years *apart from Scripture*."[38]

(d) *The Bible assumes the liturgical context of the worshiping community.*

People in biblical times were not walking around with their own copies of the Bible. The primary locus of Scripture was the liturgy, not daily quiet time. The Word of God was heard when it was proclaimed in the authoritatively-summoned assembly of God's people. The Bible is *by design* a text intended to be publicly read and heard. We *lose* something when all we do is read it on our own. This privatized and bookish view is anachronistic and contrary to both the primary intended use of the Biblical texts and to the historical milieu of Scripture itself.[39]

2. It is logically inconsistent.

Sola scriptura is illogical in at least two ways: it is (a) self-referentially inconsistent, and (b) involves a tacit violation of the principle of sufficient reason.

---

[37] 2 Chron 29:25 — "[Hezekiah] then stationed the Levites in the house of the Lord with cymbals, with harps, and with lyres, according to the command of David and of Gad the king's seer, and of Nathan the prophet; for the command was from the Lord through His prophets."
2 Chron 35:4 — "prepare yourselves by your fathers' households in your divisions, according to the writing of David king of Israel and according to the writing of his son Solomon."

[38] Krehbiel, 7. Thus, Scripture can be seen to directly contradict views such as those of MacArthur, who says that "tradition had no legitimate place of authority in the worship of Jehovah" (in *SS*, 156).

[39] I am indebted in this paragraph to Kirk Kanzelberger (Fordham University) for his helpful remarks, based in part on ch. 3 of Louis Bouyer's *Liturgical Piety*.

(a) *It is self-referentially inconsistent.*

How? In several respects. First, as Kreeft notes, "it is self-contradictory, for it says we should believe only Scripture, but Scripture never says this! If we believe only what Scripture teaches, we will not believe *sola scriptura*, for Scripture does not teach *sola scriptura.*[40] This is analogous to other self-refuting hypotheses that fail to conform to their own criteria, such as the famous "verification principle" of the logical empiricist, A.J. Ayer.[41]

Second, it assumes that the "essential" teachings of Scripture are sufficiently clear to be understood by anyone, but is not itself sufficiently clear even to be considered a scriptural teaching by all.[42] In fact, *sola scriptura* represents a minority position among Bible-believing Christians; and historically it is a relative novelty, entertained by nobody explicitly prior to Wycliff in the 14th century.

Third, it claims that the Bible is the ultimate authority, but in fact subordinates the Bible to the extrabiblical (traditions of) interpretation of this or that individual, or group, about what the Bible says. This means, practically speaking, that *sola scriptura* leads to

---

40 Kreeft, 275.

41 According to Ayer, only empirically testable, synthetic *a posteriori* statements (such as "It's raining") or analytic *a priori* statements (such as "No bachelors are married") should be accepted as verifiable and therefore meaningful. The problem is that his own "verification principle" itself is not verifiable in either way. Cf. Currie, 56ff., for several other examples.

42 For example, Robert Godfrey says "that all things *necessary* for salvation and concerning faith and life are taught in the Bible clearly enough for the ordinary believer to find it there and understand" (in *SS*, 3). Geisler and MacKenzie write: "The perspicuity of Scripture does not mean that everything in the Bible is perfectly clear, but rather the essential teachings are. Popularly put, in the Bible the main things are the plain things and the plain things are the main things" (178). Neither the cavil that "Scripture interprets Scripture" (Geisler and MacKenzie, 179) nor the cavil that *sola scriptura* can be "logically deduced" from what is clearly taught in Scripture (*Ibid.*, 184), are of any help here, since it is not the most obscure but the clearest statements of Scripture (and what may be deduced from them) that are at issue. In short, if "*Sola scriptura* simply means that *all truth necessary for our salvation and spiritual life is taught either explicitly or implicitly in Scripture*" (MacArthur, in *SS*, 165), then *sola scriptura* must not belong to those truths "necessary for our salvation and spiritual life."

hermeneutical subjectivism. The claim that Scripture is "self-interpreting" is self-serving and sophistical at this point, because conflicting and even contradictory interpretations of Scripture are held by those asserting this claim. Recourse to what the Church (or "historic Christianity") has traditionally taught would be a Catholic option, but not consistent with *sola scriptura*. The proposition that the advocates of *sola scriptura* respect tradition insofar as it agrees with Scripture is empty, since their criterion for what is "biblical" remains their extrabiblical (tradition of) private *interpretation*. The retort that Catholicism also engages in circular reasoning is beside the point and misses the mark. (For a detailed discussion of this issue, see below, *Excursus on Circularity,* following this section).

Fourth, *sola scriptura* is self-referentially inconsistent because the Bible contains no inspired index of its own contents and cannot even be identified as a divine revelation except on extrabiblical grounds of tradition — but in violation of the *sola scriptura* principle. As evangelical James White concedes: "The single best argument presented by Roman Catholicism against the concept of *sola scriptura* is based on the assertion that without some kind of extrabiblical revelation it is not possible for us to know the canon of Scripture."[43]Ambitious attempts to answer this objection have hoped to preserve the integrity of *sola scriptura*, but with less than stellar results.

Some have suggested that Scripture is "self-attesting," either in the sense that it is self-evidently inspired or that some books of the Bible cite other books as "Scripture."[44] But the argument of self-

43 *The Roman Catholic Controversy*, 92.

44 As to the first sense, see John Calvin, *Institutes of the Christian Religion*, I, tr. Ford Lewis Battles (Philadelphia: Westminster, 1960), who states that Scripture is "self-authenticated" (*autopiston*), "exhibits fully as clear evidence of its own truth as white and black things do of their color, or sweet and bitter things do of their taste," and that, therefore, "it is not right to subject it to proof and reasoning" (76, 80). Cf. Godfrey's remarks about the Bible's "self- authenticating" character, in *SS*, 18ff. Geisler and MacKenzie rightly reject analogous appeals to subjectivity from the Catholic side, and so they should be rejected here (197). As to the second, see Sproul's statement (in *SS*, 73) that the Church had a "functional canon" from its beginning, in the sense that Peter can be seen referring to Paul's writings as included among "other Scriptures" (2 Pt 3:16), and Paul can be seen quoting Luke's Gospel (1 Tim 5:18).

evidence begs the question by overlooking the distinction between evidence as an objective property (brightness is an evident property of the sun) and as a subjective perception (its brightness is not evident on a cloudy day). The divine inspiration of Scripture is "self-evidencing" in the first sense, but not necessarily in the second. The argument that some biblical texts cite others as "Scripture" is credible as far as it goes; but it does not go far (we don't even know that the book which cites another is itself inspired), and it certainly does not provide the means by which to identify the entire canon.

James White himself argues that the "difficulty of the question is that it views the canon as a separate entity from Scripture," as a distinct "object of revelation"; whereas it is actually "a *function* of Scripture itself," as *defined* by God's inspiration, so that the "Roman error lies in creating a dichotomy between two things that cannot be separated, and then using that false dichotomy to deny *sola scriptura*" (*Roman*, 93). As compelling as this may seem at first, it distorts the issue: what is at issue is not (1) the *property* of being canonical (inspired), which Catholics would agree is "a *function* of Scripture," but rather (2) the *identification* of the canon. White's argument begs the question, since the ontological property of being canonical (inspired) does not even begin to answer the essential epistemological question at issue (how we identify the canon).[45]

---

[45] Ironically, having just condemned Rome for a "false dichotomy" that Rome does not make (separating the quality of canonicity from Scripture), White immediately proceeds to restore precisely the distinction Rome would insist upon as a condition for answering the question at issue, that is, between "(1) the canon's nature, and (2) how people came to know the *contents* of the canon" (94).

White believes the Catholic argument "falls apart" when applied to the OT, because he assumes that (1) an infallible authority for identifying the canon, equivalent to the Church as understood by Catholics, cannot be found, and (2) even if such a source existed, it could no longer be regarded as infallible by Catholics because of (a) Christ's abrogation or condemnation of certain OT practices, and (b) the Jewish rejection of the canon of Scripture accepted by Rome.

The answer to #1 is the "prophetical tradition," which John Henry Newman correctly saw as continued within the Church (*Lectures on the Prophetical Office*, 1837). The answer to #2a is that (1) certain practices condemned by Christ (e.g. the *corban* rule of Mt 15) were never taught by the infallible prophetical tradition, and (2) other demands (ceremonial laws) that were infallibly

Other Protestant approaches to identifying the canon, while rejecting the Catholic answer of an infallibly guided Church, have propounded various extrabiblical criteria but continued to maintain the adequacy of *sola scriptura.* Some have introduced criteria that cannot be measured objectively, such as the "testimony of the Holy Spirit," and confuse the question of the *motive* of faith with the question of the objective *evidence* for it. Others, like Luther, have proposed tests such as "what preaches Christ" (*was Christus triebet*), but then faced the dilemma of books in the canon that, in their opinion, seemed to fail the test. Still others have suggested criteria that are incapable of being applied to all the books in the present canon, or epistemically unverifiable in most cases, or otherwise debatable, e.g., "apostolic authorship," "imposition by the apostles as law," "propheticity" (*sic*), or "unanimity of testimony."[46]

---

45 cont. imposed in the OT were abrogated by the infallible prophetic office of Christ. Further, if this prophetic prerogative was not passed on to the apostles and their lawful successors, why do Protestants not abstain from the meat of strangled animals as required by the council of Jerusalem — a demand explicitly identified with the will of the Holy Spirit (Acts 15:28)? The answer to #2b is that Jews who rejected the canon accepted by Rome were non-Christian Jews whose "council of Jamnia" (AD 90) had no authority for Christians. It is ironic that Protestants appeal to a council of non-Christian Jews but reject the decisions of early Christian councils. Even F. F. Bruce writes, in *The Canon of Scripture* (Downers Grove: InterVarsity Press, 1988): "It is probably unwise to talk as if there was a Council or Synod of Jamnia which laid down the limits of the Old Testament canon" (34).

46 Criteria proposed by Protestants include: (1) testimony of the Holy Spirit: e.g., Calvin, *Inst.* I, 78-80, says that this testimony is "more excellent than all reason"; cf. WCF, I:4-5; James Montgomery Boice, *Foundations of the Christian Faith* (Downers Grove, IL: InterVarsity, 1986), 57; (2) "*was Christum treibet*": Luther, *Epistle to the Romans*, 3.21, cited in J.K.S. Reid, *The Authority of Scripture: A Study of the Reformation and Post-Reformation Understanding of the Bible* (New York: Harper, N.D.), 67; (3) apostolic authorship or approval: e.g., Armstrong, in *SS*, 114ff.; (4) imposition by the apostles as law: e.g., B.B. Warfield, *Revelation and Inspiration* (Grand Rapids: Baker, 1927), 45; (5) "propheticity" (*sic*): Geisler and MacKenzie, 166, 174.; and (6) unanimity of testimony: e.g., Godfrey, in *SS*, 18.

Criterion #1 confuses the motive of faith with the question of objectively assessable evidence for it; #2 sidesteps the fact that some canonical books in the OT, such as Esther, do not even refer to *God*, let alone Christ; ##3- 6 ignore the

The difficulty is worth dwelling on momentarily, because it illumines one of the chief difficulties of *sola scriptura.* How do you establish the canon? Do you leave it to each individual to weigh the merits of the contested books for himself, such as the Epistle of Barnabas, or Shepherd of Hermas? Do you trust the Holy Spirit to witness in the heart of each individual to the inspiration of each book — say, Jude, Philemon, or 2 John?[47] Or do you avoid the anarchy of individualism and subjectivism by recourse to tradition? But how do you do that without accepting ecclesiastical authority?[48] Do you let each individual sort out Church history for himself? The Protestant quandary at this point is nowhere more compellingly illustrated than in Luther's refusal to number Hebrews, James, Jude, or Revelation among the canonical NT books in his translation of the Bible, because in his opinion they failed to "preach Christ" in the manner of the Pauline epistles, and contradicted his understanding of the relationship between "justification by faith" and "works of the law."[49] Where did Luther get his criteria? Clearly not from the

---

46 cont. fact that early Christian opinion was anything but unanimous prior to the councils of the late 4th and early 5th centuries, as demonstrated by John Henry Newman, *An Essay on the Development of Christian Doctrine* (Notre Dame: University of Notre Dame, 1989), 123-25; so that, without a magisterium, there is no shelter in the Vincentian Canon ("*Quod semper, quod ubique, quod ab omnibus* ...") or any such principle of unrestricted consensus among Christians.

47 Krehbiel, 24, asks: "Does the Spirit witness to John 7:53-8:11 (a passage of disputed textual attestation)? It seems silly to ask... Of course no one claims that the testimony of the Spirit is so precise. But if it is not this precise, how can it be useful in establishing the canon?"

Further, the Protestant's appeal to the Holy Spirit's guidance in the heart of each individual looks disingenuous alongside his tacit denial that the whole undivided Church of the first millennium has been successfully guided in this way.

48 This is in fact how most individual Protestants seem to receive the biblical canon — by simply accepting tradition, without recourse to ecclesiastical authority. The inherent inconsistencies of such a position go unnoticed because it is accepted unreflectively.

49 Accordingly, in *Luther's Works* (hereafter *LW*) (St. Louis: Concordia, and Philadelphia: Fortress, 1955-1986), we see him declare: "... the Epistle of James is no truly apostolic epistle..."; "... it has nothing of the nature of the gospel about it"; "... it does not once mention the Passion, the resurrection, or the Spirit of Christ"; "In the first place it is flatly against St. Paul and all the rest of Scripture in ascribing justification to works [2:24]. It says that Abraham was

principle of *sola scriptura*, for his criteria resulted in "taking away" from Scripture (Dt 4:2, Rev 22:19). Luther's arbitrary "canon reduction" constitutes a *prima facie* case against the distinctive Reformation doctrines it was designed to support, and dramatically illustrates the perilous implications, inherent flaws, and inadequacy of *sola scriptura* in defining the canon of Scripture.[50]

Excursus on Circularity

When the inherent circularity of the *sola scriptura* thesis is pointed out to them, Protestants often retort by asserting that Ca-

---

[49 cont.] justified by his works when he offered his son Isaac [2:21]; though in Romans 4[:2-22] St. Paul teaches to the contrary that Abraham was justified apart from works, by his faith alone, before he had offered his son, and proves it by Moses in Genesis 15[:6]"; "James concludes falsely that now at last [Abraham] was justified after that obedience... But it does not follow, as James raves..." (*LW*, Vol. 30, p. 12; Vol. 35, pp. 362, 396; Vol. 4, pp. 133- 34). Luther translated the disputed books and included them in his Bible, but excluded them from the list of canonical Scriptures. In a footnote to Luther's Preface to the Epistle to the Hebrews, the editor writes: "In terms of order, Hebrews, James, Jude, and Revelation come last in Luther's New Testament because of his negative estimate of their apostolicity. In a catalogue of 'The Books of the New Testament' which followed immediately upon his Preface to the New Testament... Luther regularly *listed these four — without numbers — at the bottom of a list in which he named the other twenty-three books*, in the order in which they still appear in English Bibles, and numbered them consecutively from 1-23 (*WA*, DB 6, 12-13), *a procedure identical to that with which he also listed the books of the Apocrypha*" [emphasis added] (*LW*, Vol. 35, p. 394, n. 43; cf. 337, n. 1). This listing may be confirmed by examining D. Martin Luther, *Die gantze Heilige Schrift*, ed. Hans Volz (Münschen: Deutscher Taschenbuch Verlag GmbH & Co. KG, October, 1974).

[50] The case of Luther is oddly absent from Sproul's discussion of the problem of "canon reduction" (in *SS*, 82-89), although he offers a limping defense of Luther in another context by stating: "His question about James was not a question of the inspiration of Scripture but a question of whether James was in fact Scripture" (65). But this goes without saying: the question concerns Luther's arbitrary criteria for excluding four books from the NT canon. A striking reassessment of traditional Protestant assumptions about the relation of justification to "faith" and "works" is offered by James D. G. Dunn, *The Justice of God: A Fresh Look at the Old Doctrine of Justification by Faith* (Grand Rapids, Michigan: Eerdmans, 1994).

tholicism also resorts to circularity. Sometimes the claim is made that the Catholic Church uses circular reasoning in appealing to Scripture to support her authority while also claiming the *final say* in how to interpret Scripture.[51] But there is no circularity here, first, because she does not claim *sola scriptura*; and, second, because if she has the authority she claims, the case is no different logically from that of the NT writers appealing to the Old Testament (OT) for support while claiming divine warrant for their NT interpretations.

Others mistakenly claim the Church's position is circular because it boils down to saying: "we must believe Rome because Rome says so."[52] The concern here for avoiding self-serving abuses by those in authority is legitimate, but misplaced. The Catholic is not asked to submit to the Church because the Church says so, arbitrarily, but because God demands this in His public revelation and because Christ has appointed the Church and her lawfully ordained leaders, with many checks and balances, as administrators

---

51 See, for example, Ferguson's remarks in *SS*, 209; and James White's accusations about "circular reasoning" in *The Roman Catholic Controversy*, where he writes: "Roman Catholicism claims the final say in interpreting the Bible, yet it also points to Bible passages as the basis of its authority"; the issue is never "*what the actual text of Scripture says*, but what the Roman Catholic Church, claiming Christ's special empowerment, *says* it says" (47). First, Protestants do not avoid a similar appeal to what *they* think Scripture means, as noted above. Second, if the Catholic Church does possess "Christ's special empowerment," then "*what the actual text of Scripture says*," is precisely what she "*says* it says." The Church does not *get* its authority from the Bible; rather, the Bible supports the fact of the Church's authority. (See Shea, chapter 4, in this volume for a thorough discussion of this issue).

52 Godfrey raises a legitimate concern when he says: "The church must have a standard of truth by which to reform and purify itself when divisions arise. The church cannot claim that it is that standard and defend that claim by appealing to itself. Such circular reasoning is not only unconvincing; it is self-defeating. Rome's argument boils down to this: we must believe Rome because Rome says so" (in *SS*, 23). However, the Catholic claim is not that the Church *is* the standard in some *voluntarist* sense, but rather that God will always *keep* the Church to *His* standard. Nor is the Catholic claim the fideistic one of believing Rome "because Rome says so," any more than most Protestants would say they believe the Bible simply "because the Bible says so." See the following discussion.

of His commission.[53] The Church is *subject* to the Word of God (including the *message* of the Bible), even while she is guardian and master (as *Magisterium*) of the Bible's text and interpretation.[54] Her authority is not an "enabling" one but a "restraining" one, which prevents any reigning Pope from arbitrarily inventing heretical new doctrines, by binding him to an infallible tradition (including Scripture) traceable to the "apostolic deposit of faith."[55]

Still others mistakenly claim that Catholicism is circular because it bases our conviction of the Bible's inspiration on the

---

[53] God cannot be faulted for "circular reasoning." When God says, "Thou shalt not steal," and we ask why, and He responds by declaring, "I, the Lord, have spoken," there can be no quibbling about insufficient grounds or authority. The problem of "circularity" vanishes where there is authority or credentials of delegated authority. The issue is illustrated by Jesus' use of reasoning that would have to be dismissed as "circular" were it not for His own divine authority (cf. John 7:16-17; 8:14, 19). (I am indebted to R. Sungenis for drawing my attention to these verses).

[54] *Dei verbum* declares that the "Magisterium is not superior to the Word of God, but is its servant" (ch. 2, sec. 10, p. 756). St. Francis de Sales, a priest who reconverted 72,000 Calvinists near Geneva back to Catholicism, was expressing a Catholic belief when he wrote, in *The Catholic Controversy*, tr. Henry B. Mackey (1886; rpt. Rockford, IL: TAN, 1989): "The Christian faith is grounded on the Word of God.... Faith which rests on anything else is not Christian. Therefore, the Word of God is the true rule of right-believing" (83). The question at issue is whether all of God's instructions for His Church are contained in Scripture alone or whether His Word is preserved in a larger sacred tradition (of which Scripture is a part) in which the Church has an authoritative role as custodian and administrator of these instructions.

[55] The wording of Pope John Paul II's Apostolic Letter reserving priestly ordination to men alone, *Ordinatio Sacerdotalis*, is instructive: he says, quoting Pope Paul VI, that the Church "*does not consider herself authorized* to admit women to priestly ordination" (emphasis added). As Peter Kreeft remarks, in "Gender and the Will of God," *Crisis* (Sept. 1993): "The Catholic Church claims less authority than any other Christian church in the world; that is why she is so conservative. Protestant churches feel free to change 'the deposit of faith'... or of morals (e.g. by allowing divorce, though Christ forbade it), or of worship" (20).

Harold Berman, *Law and Revolution: The Formation of the Western Legal Tradition* (Cambridge: Harvard, 1983), notes that the theory of papal infallibility developed as "a *limitation* on papal authority: it meant that the infallible utterances of prior popes could not be reformed by the pope in power at any given moment" (emphasis added; 605, n. 21).

Church's infallibility, and the Church's infallibility on the word of an inspired Bible. But it does not. While it may appeal to the Church's infallible teaching in support of the conviction that Scripture is inspired, it does not have to argue for the Church's infallibility from the Bible alone. It can argue this from other sources of early Church tradition as well. Hence there is no logical circularity.[56] Furthermore, as Kreeft says, Church and Scripture "are not two rival horses in the authority race, but one rider (the Church) and one horse (Scripture). The Church as writer, canonizer, and interpreter of Scripture is not another source of revelation but the author and guardian and teacher of the one source, sacred tradition, which includes Scripture as its preeminent treasure and legacy. We are not taught by a teacher without a book or by a book without a teacher, but by one teacher, the Church, with one book, Scripture."[57] Hence, "authority" is not a univocal term. The deposit of revelation possesses the highest authority of its kind; and the teaching Church possesses the highest authority of its kind. One is the horse, the other is the rider; but they are one horse and one rider on the same team.

There is a larger sense, Protestant John Frame argues, in which some sort of circularity cannot be avoided in arguing for the *ultimate* criterion of a system.[58] A rationalist can prove the primacy of reason only by using a rational argument. An empiricist can prove the primacy of sense-experience only by some kind of appeal to sense-experience. A Christian can prove the primacy of divine revelation only by some kind of appeal to divine revelation. Why should one believe God's Word? Because it is the Word of God, of course! Any other reason we could offer in proof of this claim would al-

---

[56] White's charge of circularity (in *Roman*, 233, n. 4) against Karl Keating's argument in *Catholicism and Fundamentalism: The Attack on "Romanism" by "Bible Christians"* (San Francisco: Ignatius, 1988), 126, is thus fallacious, since Keating explicitly denies basing the Church's infallibility exclusively on Scripture.

[57] Kreeft, p. 274f.

[58] John M. Frame, *The Doctrine of the Knowledge of God* (Phillipsburg, NJ: Presbyterian and Reformed, 1987), 130- 33. See my review of this work by this philosophically astute disciple of Cornelius Van Til, in *Eternity* (May 1988), 36-37.

ways at some level already presuppose its truth. Every system is based, says Frame, on presuppositions that control its epistemology, argument, and use of evidence; and therefore *ultimate* circularity is philosophically inescapable.[59] While neither Aristotle nor St. Thomas Aquinas would have accepted the notion of ultimate circularity, they *would* have admitted that it belongs to no science to demonstrate its first principles, but to depend for their demonstration and defense on some higher science, and that the highest science (metaphysics) possesses principles which are strictly not demonstrable, though they are *evident* because they are principles of being. Yet even Frame, while accepting ultimate circularity, insists this does not mean that circularity is permissible in other (penultimate) sorts of arguments. Thus, on Frame's own principles we could say that "The Bible is inspired because the Bible says its inspired" is a circular argument whose circularity is not justified.[60] It lacks cogency. A document's self-attestation is insufficient warrant for accepting its claims. The argument that the Bible is di-

---

[59] James White is correct, accordingly, in objecting to an argument for biblical authority that begins with the neutralist assumption that the Bible can be taken "simply as history." The Bible "never claims to be simply history," he writes, and "people will not be convinced that Jesus is truly God merely on this basis," because such a conviction is "spiritually borne" (*Roman*, 233, n. 4). It is not clear, however, that Keating's argument (which White is opposing) is ever more than hypothetically neutralist; and it is certainly false, contrary to widespread Calvinist assumption, that Catholicism is essentially neutralist or nonpresuppositionalist in its approach to theory, as Arvin Vos demonstrates in *Aquinas, Calvin and Contemporary Protestant Thought: A Critique of Protestant Views on the Thought of Thomas Aquinas* (Grand Rapids: Eerdmans, 1985). If, as White assumes, "spiritually borne" presuppositions of faith are necessary for discerning the divine nature of Christ from the data of Scripture, the same are no less necessary, the Catholic would claim, for discerning the divine authority of the Church from the data of history.

[60] Frame would disagree, of course, since he holds to the Protestant principle of *sola scriptura*; and he ambitiously claims not only that Scripture "justifies itself," but that it is "the ultimate justification for all human knowledge" (129). As we have shown, however, Scripture does not view itself as the sole repository of God's Word for the continuing instruction of His Church, and *sola scriptura* cannot serve as a coherent first principle. Hence, the "self-justification" of Scripture is not admissible as an instance of *ultimate* circularity that unavoidably belongs to the first principles of a system.

vinely inspired can gain cogency only by enlarging its circle to include also the attestation of the Church and data of sacred and secular history. By contrast, "The Bible means what the Church says it means" is not circular in this way, since the Church's interpretation is not closed off from history, but empirically testable for fidelity and coherence both against Scripture and the other traditions of the Church.[61]

(b) *Sola Scriptura violates the principle of sufficient reason.*

As Kreeft notes, "it violates the principle of causality: that an effect cannot be greater than its cause. The Church (the apostles) wrote Scripture; and the successors of the apostles, i.e., the bishops of the Church, decided on the canon, the list of books to be declared scriptural and infallible. If Scripture is infallible, then its cause, the Church, must also be infallible."[62]

The retort that "God *determined*" the canon while the Church "merely *discovered*" the canon does not make its case.[63] No Catholic would deny this. Pope Leo XIII says in *Providentissimus Deus* that "the Church holds [the books of the Bible] as sacred and canonical not because, having been composed by human industry, they were

---

61 These extrabiblical historical data, of course, are preambles to *faith*, which is a gift by which we can attain certitude regarding the Bible and the Church. While it is true that the Church's interpretations are themselves open to a degree of interpretation, this openness is limited by the progressive refinement and definition of dogma by the Church in the history of the development of Christian doctrines. Even Protestants admit the progressive clarification of revelation through history (e.g., White, *Rome*, 82). Hence, it misses the point to ask "how is an infallible interpretation any better than the infallible revelation?" (Geisler and MacKenzie, 214). What use is God's "objective disclosure" (revelation) without an accurate "subjective discovery" (understanding) of it on the part of the Church?

Nor is it warranted to distinguish the "historical evidence used by Protestants" from the "religious tradition used by Roman Catholics" by saying: "The former is objective and verifiable; the latter is not" (Geisler and MacKenzie, 197). This is a distinction without a difference, for the former is a *part* of the latter. Nothing is more open to empirical testing than the historical credentials of the Catholic Church.

62 Kreeft, 275.

63 Geisler and MacKenzie, 192f.

afterwards approved by her authority; not only because they contain revelation without errors, but because, having been written under the inspiration of the Holy Spirit, they have God for their Author."[64] No Bible-believing Christian would deny that God determined the canon any more than that God is the primary author and cause of Scripture. But God obviously used secondary causes (human authors) to write Scripture. No Bible-believing Protestant has difficulty accepting the idea of God guiding fallible human authors to write infallible Scripture. But when it comes to the idea of God extending His infallible guidance to the decisions of post-apostolic bishops in deciding the final canon of Scripture, they suddenly smell Catholicism and balk. They adopt the fall-back position of admitting that the Bible is only a "fallible collection of infallible books," thereby hoping to avoid the consequence of granting the Church's bishops the divine authority implicit in the Catholic doctrine of the apostolic succession.[65] But the move is disingenuous, for it is immediately followed by various caveats implying that, for all practical purposes, they do believe in an infallible canon after all; and what they denied to the Church under the heading of "infallibility," they quickly restore under the heading of "providence."[66]

Protestants already accept implicitly the principle that God can infallibly guide fallible humans to teach infallibly, both in the oral teachings of the prophets and apostles, and in the writing of Scripture.[67] But there is no more reason why one should deny that God

---

64 Pope Leo XIII, *Providentissimus Deus* (1892) (Boston: St. Paul Editions, N.d.), Part II, D, 3.

65 Sproul, in *SS*, 66f., following the teachings of his mentor, John Gerstner.

66 For example, Sproul writes, "It is one thing to say that the church *could* have erred; it is another thing to say the church *did* err"; and, again, "It was also by [God's] providence that the original books of the Bible were preserved and accorded the status of Canon... That the Canon was originally established by a historical selection process, undertaken by fallible human beings and fallible institutions, is no reason to exclude from our consideration the role of the providence of God in these affairs" (in *SS*, 67, 93f.). See R. Sungenis in *Point/ Counterpoint* in chapter 5 of this volume for a refutation of Sproul's thesis.

67 As John MacArthur, Jr. says, "Protestants do not deny that the oral teaching of the apostles was authoritative, inerrant truth, binding as a rule of faith *on those who heard it*" (in *SS*, 166).

infallibly guided the process by which the Church "discovered" the canon any more than the process by which the Church "wrote" the books contained in it. The reluctance to accept the same principle in the formation of the canon is not only an arbitrary and largely an anti-Catholic reflex: it is a violation of the principle of causality. For Bible-believing Protestants don't hold to a doctrine of inspiration and infallibility in the abstract, but in relation to *this* book, the Bible. And to accept the stamp of divine authority in the effect (the Bible) and reject it in the causes that led to its formation (not only the primary cause, God, but the secondary causes — including not only the human writers but the human bishops who finally agreed, long after the death of the last apostle, on which books belonged in the canon), is to hold the fallacious view that an effect can be greater than its cause.[68] At the very least it logically requires admission that God temporarily allowed his human instruments (including early bishops and popes) to participate in the infallible process by which he guaranteed the creation and canonization of Scripture. If Scripture itself participates in divine infallibility, so did they.[69]

It should be noted that in Catholic teaching, "infallibility" in the absolute sense is predicable of God alone. In the sense in which it refers to the Church, the Pope and the bishops, it is the result of

[68] Statements like: "the Bible is a *direct* revelation *from God*. As such, it has *divine* authority, for what the Bible says, *God says*," (Geisler and MacKenzie, 178, emphasis added), while true, tend to overlook the secondary (human) causes by which God unerringly mediates his divine revelation to man.

[69] The assertion that God ceased revelatory intrusion after the death of the last apostle or NT writer, accordingly, is not in itself a sufficient basis for rejecting an infallible post-apostolic Church. There is no logical reason why the Holy Spirit could not have infallibly guided the bishops and popes of the Church, either in their decisions about which books to include in the Canon of Scripture in the fourth and fifth centuries, or in their magisterial definitions of Christian doctrine (both papal and conciliar) in the centuries up to the present. The empirical, historical and theological arguments supporting the continued infallibility of the Church beyond her definition of the Canon, however, deserve expanded treatment in an independent study. Suffice it here to note that the proponents of *sola scriptura* lack any adequate logical, historical, biblical, or theological grounds for restricting the charism of infallibility to the writers of Scripture alone. Such a position is both arbitrary and intellectually untenable.

divine assistance. The Church and her human leaders are not infallible of themselves, as individual men, but participate by virtue of their office (rooted in a sacrament) in the only infallibility there is, namely Divine Infallibility.

Since, as John Henry Newman notes, "It is very common to confuse infallibility with certitude,"[70] it may be helpful to say something here about Protestant arguments that trade on this confusion. James White, for example, offers three arguments of this kind against the Catholic claim of an infallible Church.[71] He sets the stage with a number of *ad hominem* remarks about how this claim offers people a false sense of security and lulls them with feelings of "infallible fuzzies" into seeking "certainty outside of personal responsibility before God," in the answers provided by the Church. First, *ad hominem* remarks are never more than personal attacks and always cut both ways: if Protestants can accuse Catholics of "infallible fuzzies," I suppose theological liberals could accuse evangelicals of something like "inerrancy fuzzies." Second, as for "personal responsibility before God," nobody who has read Newman on the subject of "conscience" could possibly think that Catholicism fosters personal irresponsibility.[72] The *real* issue here is White's tacit confusion of infallibility with certainty, which is already clear from the fact that his opposition to Rome's claim of infallibility (an objective property) begins with *ad hominem* remarks on certainty (a subjective feeling or judgment). But let the arguments speak for themselves.

First, says White, the Roman claim of infallibility is illusory because "you have to make a fallible decision to buy into the plan,

70 Newman, *Essay*, 81, n. 1. Cf. Kreeft's remarks on "certitude" in his notes to Q. I, 5 of St. Thomas Aquinas' *Summa Theologica*, in Peter Kreeft, *A Summa of the SUMMA* (San Francisco: Ignatius, 1990), 40f.

71 White, *Roman*, 49f., 91, 107.

72 John Henry Newman, Section V from the "Letter to His Grace the Duke of Norfolk" (1875), in *Newman and the Thoughtful Believer*, ed. Mary Katherine Tillman (Florence, KY: Brenzel, 1993), quotes Cardinal Gousset's words, "He who acts against his conscience loses his soul"; and the Jesuit, Busenbaum, who wrote, "A heretic, as long as he judges his sect to be more or equally deserving of belief, has no obligation to believe [in the Church]"; and concludes by stating: "I shall drink, — to the Pope, if you please, — still, to Conscience first, and to the Pope afterwards" (10f.).

and any certainty offered thereafter rests solely on the first — fallible — choice that was made."[73] This links the Church's infallibility to our fallible choices, trading on the lack of subjective certainty that often attaches to the latter. But one could reply that a person's decision to follow Christ is also a decision of a fallible human being. Does this mean one should feel uncertain about following Christ? Certitude is a relative thing, as Newman observes: "I may be certain that two and two makes four, even though I often make mistakes in long addition sums... I may be certain that the Church is infallible, while I am myself a fallible mortal; otherwise I cannot be certain that the Supreme Being is infallible, unless I am infallible myself."[74] The fact that I am fallible does not mean that the object of my belief (God, the Bible, or the Church) cannot be infallible; or even that I cannot have a well-grounded certitude in the object of my belief.

Second, White argues, "Once Rome speaks, the fallible person must still interpret the supposed infallible interpretation," so "the element of error remains."[75] This move is a variation of the first, but deals specifically with interpretation. Here one could reply by noting that the fallibility of the evangelical's interpretation of Scripture does not undermine his confidence in the Bible's infallibility. Demonstrating the infallibility of the Church may be no easier than demonstrating that of the Bible, but neither the difficulty of demonstrating one nor the other necessarily undermines the certitude of infallibility.[76] Just as having an infallible Bible is clearly an advantage over having none, despite the fallibility of our interpretations,

---

73 White, *Roman,* 50.

74 Newman, *Essay*, 81f., n. 1. There is, of course, the theoretical possibility of absolute skepticism, which holds that no subjective certitude is possible; but that would doubtfully contribute little to our discussion here.

75 White, *Roman,* 91.

76 Newman admitted that by strict philosophical standards, the Catholic position could only speak of the "probable infallibility" of the Church (*Essay*, 80), a position comparable to the "fallible collection of infallible books" position of some Protestants (Sproul, in *SS*, 66). I am reminded of Pascal's remark in the *Pensées* that there is apparent evidence on both sides of the argument concerning God's existence, enough light to give hope to the seeker, enough darkness to blind the arrogant unbeliever and keep the believer humble. The same could be said for the evidence supporting the infallibility of the Bible and the Church.

so having an infallible Church to interpret the Bible is an advantage over having an infallible Bible alone. The infallibility of the Church's interpretations does not depend on a comparable infallibility in her members, or even on their certitude of her infallibility.[77]

Third, White argues, "defenders of the Roman Catholic Papacy cannot merely demonstrate that the Roman position is *probably* true, or that it is *likely* to be true, but must demonstrate that it is true *beyond question*"[78] — clearly an impossible demand. But what leads him to draw this conclusion? Presumably the premise that "Rome claims absolute authority" or "infallible teaching authority." But this is not only fallacious but conspicuously misleading. It simply does not follow that defenders of Rome must provide indubitable, apodictic proof of their position just because Rome claims infallible authority. One could reply by pointing out that there is nobody whose claims are more absolute than God's. Does this mean that Christian evangelists and missionaries must be able to offer philosophical demonstrations that prove the existence of God "beyond question" before they should be taken seriously? Of course not. The logic simply does not follow.

B. Problems of Historicity

The second set of broadly philosophical problems are historical. They could be called "historical" problems, simply, except that we treat them from the point of view of intellectual history, with particular attention to their philosophical implications. These problems derive from the fact that *sola scriptura* is *unhistorical*: it both stems from and reinforces ignorance of Church history. This results in at least seven problems: it is (1) improbable, (2) inconsistent with the practice of the NT Church, (3) overlooks the

---

77 Moreover, although there is a potential for the distortion of even infallibly true Church teaching, especially in the process of dissemination of this teaching among various levels of the Catholic population, Catholics nevertheless know where to go to obtain infallible teaching — a fact which, in turn, serves to limit factionalism and divisiveness, especially when compared to the multitudes of sects among Protestantism. (I am indebted to R. Sungenis for this observation.)

78 White, *Roman,* 107.

extrabiblical influences on its adherents, (4) overlooks the extrabiblical historical influences on itself, (5) assumes Scripture can be understood apart from tradition, (6) leads to misinterpretation of the Church Fathers, and (7) leads to unhistorical understandings and distortions of fact.

1. *It is improbable*

The doctrine that Scripture *alone* is sufficient to function as the *regula fidei* — the infallible rule for the ongoing faith and life of the Church — is of highly improbable orthodoxy since (among other reasons dealt with under #5 below) it had no defender for the first thirteen centuries of the Church.[79] It does not belong to historic Christianity. Only in the 14th century did Wycliff first broach the notion, and then merely as a defense mechanism to justify a specific disagreement he had with the Pope. Meanwhile his own university colleagues at Oxford condemned him. It wasn't until the theologians of the Protestant Reformation elevated the notion into a principle in the 16th century that it became widespread. As Newman put it, "the Christianity of history is not Protestantism. If ever there were a safe truth, it is this. And Protestantism has ever felt it so... in the determination... of dispensing with historical Christianity altogether, and of forming a Christianity from the Bible alone... To be deep in history is to cease to be a Protestant."[80]

This raises an interesting question about the burden of proof in connection with *sola scriptura*. On whom does the onus lie in proving or disproving it, and what is the nature of this onus? As a defender of *sola scriptura*, Godfrey writes: "Our opponents need to show not that Paul referred to his preaching as well as his writing as

[79] This is not the same as the conviction, which *can* be found from earliest times, that Scripture is inspired, authoritative, and the ultimate material deposit of God's Word to man. At most this would be *prima scriptura*, not *sola scriptura*. But nowhere do you find a defense of the notion that the Bible is the *exclusive and sufficient* rule for the ongoing instruction of the Church. White's use of "*regula fidei*" to stand for *sola scriptura* (*Roman*, 54, 59) is entirely unhistorical. (See chapter 8 by Joseph Gallegos in this volume for a detailed discussion of this issue).

[80] Newman, *Essay*, 7f.

the Word of God — I grant that; they need to show that Paul taught that the oral teaching of the apostles would be needed to supplement the Scriptures for the Church through the ages. They cannot show that because Paul did not *teach* that, and the Scriptures *as a whole* do not teach that!"[81] But not only is this untrue — and Godfrey has no way of proving that it is true — it also begs the question. The onus does not lie on the Catholic to prove the necessity of continuing extrabiblical traditions *from Scripture*, simply because he rejects *sola scriptura*. All he must be able to show *from Scripture*, at least logically, is that it does not contradict such traditions — though in fact, as we have seen, he can show considerably more. Further, *from history* he must be able to show that a preponderance of the data support such traditions but do not support *sola scriptura* — a task facilitated by the overwhelming testimony in his favor.

On the other hand, the proponent of *sola scriptura* must be able to show *from Scripture* that the whole content of God's revelation for the ongoing instruction of His Church was committed wholly to writing without residue, and also that verses referring to the necessity of holding fast to oral as well as written apostolic traditions (such as 2 Th 2:15) are limited in their reference to the first century.[82] Moreover, he must be able to show *from history*, that a preponderance of the data support *sola scriptura* but do not support the extrabiblical traditions of the Church — a considerably more difficult task. The onus is clearly on the proponent of *sola scriptura*, not on the opponent.

2. *It is inconsistent with the practice of the New Testament Church*

It certainly was not the belief of the early Church, for it is contradicted by the historical practice of the first generations of Christians, who did not have the NT, but only the Church — the apostles and their successors — to teach them how the New Covenant fulfilled and surpassed the Old Covenant inscripturated in the OT. It does not suffice to reply (1) that they had, at least, the OT Scrip-

[81] *SS*, 9f.

[82] I am indebted to R. Sungenis for pointing out the connection with 2 Th 2:15.

tures, and that was enough; (2) that they still had the apostles to teach them and didn't yet need the NT; or (3) that the only infallible authority to succeed the apostles was the NT.[83] First, the OT does not contain God's further revelation concerning the New Covenant. Thus, it required the supplemental oral teaching of Christ and the apostles. Second, the apostles died centuries before the NT was fully canonized, and well before each church had copies of all the books that would later make up the NT. Yet someone had to be "in charge" during these years — someone who had the authority to declare, "This is orthodox," and "That is heterodox." The authorized successors to the apostles were the ones in charge.[84] Third, to recognize the authority of the apostles' oral teaching but to assume that this teaching was transmitted without residue into the NT requires jiggery-pokery. One must assume either that everything they ever taught was included in the NT, or cobble together some sort of arbitrary criterion for explaining why those teachings and instructions that were not included the NT either (a) lacked authority, (b) ceased to have authority after the apostles died, or (c) may have had some sort of authority but lacked infallibility, divine inspiration, or the like.[85] But then, what sort of criterion could be offered that would

[83] Geisler and MacKenzie, 194

[84] Geisler and MacKenzie, 209-11, seem to confuse (1) the succession of authority delegated by the apostles to their successors, and (2) the office of apostle, which cannot be transmitted. For example, they argue from the fact that the apostles had to be eyewitnesses of the resurrection and were confirmed in their ministry by certain "signs" and "powers," to the conclusion that, "there could be no true apostolic succession in the pope or anyone else," and that "no one since the first century has possessed apostolic authority." But it does not follow from the premise that no successors of the apostles can *be* apostles, to the conclusion that no successors can have authority delegated by the apostles in a line of succession from them.

[85] For example, Geisler and MacKenzie (188) say: "it is not necessary to claim that all these oral teachings were inspired or infallible, only that they were authoritative. The believers were asked to 'maintain' them (1 Cor 11:2) and 'stand fast in them' (2 Thess 2:15). But oral teachings *about* Christ (not the words *of* Christ) and the apostles' affirmations were not called inspired or unbreakable or the equivalent unless they were inscripturated in the Bible (2 Tim. 3:16)." But this is obfuscation. Do these passages teach that fallible "traditions of men" are "authoritative"? Is Paul asking his readers to "maintain" and "stand fast in" what could be erroneous?

avoid the circularity of arguing that only what is inscripturated is inspired because what is not inscripturated is not inspired?

3. *It overlooks extrabiblical influences on its adherents*

As a philosopher recently noted, there is no "point of view from nowhere." Everybody has a perspective; and perspectives are historically influenced. It might be a perspective that is "individualistic" or "communitarian," American or Continental, contemporary or traditional, "evidentualist" or "presuppositionalist," "free-will" or "predestinarian," Arminian or Calvinist, "high church" or "low church," congregationalist or episcopalian, Baptist or Lutheran. Everyone is situated in some tradition, which consciously or unconsciously forms his presuppositions. The important question is whether or not the tradition in question is the one that Christ instituted and committed to his apostles to be passed down as a living, developing reality under the guidance of the Holy Spirit through His Church.[86]

[86] Some traditions originate in explicit teachings of the prophets, Christ, or the apostles — such as Paul's teaching which links our fallen condition and hope of salvation, respectively, to Adam's sin and Christ's redemption (1 Cor 15:22). Other traditions originate later — either in normative "developments" or illicit "corruptions." In one or the other category would have to go the Ecumenical Councils' formulation of the "Trinity," Luther's doctrine of "justification by faith alone," the Zwinglian interpretation of the Eucharist as a strictly symbolic "memorial," and the Anabaptist insistence on an exclusively adult, "believer's baptism."

One of the more egregious examples of how a Protestant bias can skew an interpretation is Sinclair Ferguson's representation (*SS,* 192-216) of remarks by Joseph Fitzmyer, a Jesuit, about the difference between Pauline and Tridentine formulations concerning faith and justification as a tacit *concession* that Catholic teaching is unfaithful to Scripture! Nothing could be farther from the truth, or from Fitzmyer's meaning! One may as well interpret the admission by a Protestant that "nowhere does the Bible formally and explicitly state the doctrine of the Trinity" (Geisler and MacKenzie, 184) as a concession that Protestant acceptance of the doctrine of the Trinity is a faithless departure from Scripture. Fitzmyer is simply observing what any good Scripture scholar and good Catholic recognizes — that Paul's writing sometimes looks about as different from the Council of Trent's as an acorn looks from an oak tree, even though the latter is wholly consistent with the former. Fitzmyer

A certain disdain for history and lack of historical consciousness fostered by *sola scriptura* can make its adherents particularly vulnerable to extrabiblical historical influences on their own thinking. Especially noteworthy among American evangelicals is the influence of the intuitivist "common sense" philosophy of the Scottish Enlightenment (Hutcheson, Reid, Smith, Stewart), which, combined with American individualism, led to an outlook of antihistorical immediatism[87] that produced what Mark Noll calls, in his book by that title, *The Scandal of the Evangelical Mind.*[88] Noll shows how evangelicals successfully aligned themselves with national ideals through the individualism and populism of their Great Awakenings, and through their embrace of the intuitivist outlook of the Scottish Enlightenment — but at the cost of producing an ethos which led them to abandon the universities in the secular post-Civil War climate, to withdraw into fundamentalist ghettos, and to embrace disastrous and anti-intellectual obsessions with dispensational millenarianism, speculations about the Antichrist, and the like. The ironies of evangelicalism are well illustrated by what Noll calls the "conundrum" of Jonathan Edwards, one of the profoundest evangelical intellects of American history. Despite all his erudition and Christian commitment, the revivalist movement of which he was a part fostered a populist, charismatic style of leadership that undercut the traditional authority of churches and planted the seeds of

---

[86 cont.] recognizes that Paul "does not say all that the Tridentine decree says," but he says that Paul's teaching is "open to later dogmatic development." He clearly believes that the Tridentine formula is a perfectly legitimate development of NT teaching — perhaps even "an exact theological transposition" — even though it exhibits a precision not to be found in the Pauline writings. (Joseph A. Fitzmyer, *Romans* [New York: Doubleday, 1993], 347f., cf. 342f.)

[87] This is essentially the view that, much as one can become personally "contemporaneous" with Christ through a direct, spiritual relationship with him in a way that could lead one to regard the data about the historical Jesus to be "secondary," so one can become "contemporaneous" with the eternal truths of God through a direct, intuitive apprehension of them in a way that could lead one to regard the data of biblical scholarship or ecclesiastical history to be "secondary."

[88] Mark A. Noll, *The Scandal of the Evangelical Mind* (Grand Rapids: Eerdmans, 1994). See my review of this work in *New Oxford Review* (April, 1995), 27-28. On the influence of the Scottish Enlightenment, see also Alasdair MacIntyre, *Whose Justice? Which Rationality?* (Notre Dame: University of Notre Dame, 1988), 209-325.

anti-historical individualism and immediatism that would help undermine the evangelical mind. The legacy of this influence can be seen in the antihistorical immediatism with which evangelicals often approach the Bible as a self-contained repository of timeless, revealed facts.[89] This accounts, in part, for their susceptibility to the philosophical currents of evidentialism, positivism, and empiricism, which, in turn, leave them vulnerable to post-modern philosophical currents of anti-foundationalism and deconstructionism.[90]

---

[89] A classic example of this outlook can be found in Charles Hodge's *Systematic Theology* (1872; rpt. Grand Rapids: Eerdmans, 1952), I, 10f.: "The Bible is to the theologian what nature is to the man of science. It is his store-house of facts; and his method of ascertaining what the Bible teaches is the same as that which the natural philosopher adopts to ascertain what nature teaches... The duty of the Christian theologian is to ascertain, collect, and combine all the facts which God has revealed concerning himself and our relation to him. These facts are in the Bible." Contemporary examples abound in appeals to the "plain meaning" of Scripture (e.g., Armstrong, in *SS*, 143), and rhetorical questions such as: "Are we to believe that the Bible is so unclear... that we cannot arrive at the truth through an *honest, wholehearted effort* at examining the *evidence?*" (White, *Roman*, 92, emphasis added). The assumption is that if the interpreter can simply lay aside his personal perspective and examine the "facts" of Scripture in an objective, rational manner, that they will "speak for themselves" — a classic positivistic or logical-empiricist view of "fact."

[90] Richard Rorty's *Philosophy and the Mirror of Nature* (Princeton: Princeton University, 1979) represents a milestone marking the recognition, within the Anglo-American "analytic" tradition of philosophy, of what had been long recognized in the Continental tradition by philosophers such as Martin Heidegger and Jacques Derrida: the bankruptcy of the older logical-empiricist and positivist epistemologies, which had attempted to lay a foundation in indubitable rational intuitions or empirical facts.

The challenge posed by the postmodernist movement of "deconstructionism," spearheaded by the French philosopher Jacques Derrida, in which textual meanings are semiotically dismantled by means of the decentering logic of textual surplus of meaning with no recourse to a "transcendental" index of signification, should alone suffice to illustrate the inadequacy of *sola scriptura* as an ultimate standard. A text does not stand alone, but requires an interpreter. Ultimately, not even that is enough to secure a realist response to deconstructionism. The Catholic argument that Scripture is analogous to a constitution and would be inadequate without the supreme court to interpret it, itself does not go far enough. A court filled with deconstructionist jurors would be inadequate too. One would need a court capable of defining "original intent," which, in the case of infallible biblical interpretation, would require a divine charism (which the Church claims to have).

4. *It overlooks the extrabiblical historical influences on itself*

What were the historical influences that contributed to the rise of *sola scriptura*? Doubtless there were many factors, some of them political and economic (like the desire for independence from Rome's hegemony and the need to theologically justify defying her authority), and some of them social and cultural (like the invention of printing, which not only made Bibles widely available, but reinforced the individualism of the act of reading, as opposed to hearing, Scripture). Still other factors were intellectual and spiritual. It was certainly no accident that the Protestant Reformation began in the academy (the perfect environment for the consummate individualist: me, my books, and the Holy Spirit — with the accent on the autonomous academic intellect); or that the academic setting was that of the slightly skeptical *via moderna* schools of the nominalist tradition. My own hunch is that the most significant influences on *sola scriptura* stemmed from a profound shift in intellectual and spiritual climate during the late middle ages, associated with the rising influence of nominalism.

In scholastic philosophy, nominalism involved a skeptical dismissal of "universals" as mere "fictions" — as mere "words" or "names" (Latin *nomina*), from which we get "nominalism." It attracted theological attention only after it was used to interpret the Eucharist. Berengar of Tours (c. 1000-1088) was the first scholastic to insist on the ultimacy of the evidence of the senses in interpreting the Sacrament, and was the first recorded case in Church history of a theologian denying the real bodily Presence of Christ in the Eucharist.[91] His position both reflected and contributed to a shift away from a world of timeless universals as the basis for understanding reality, and toward the physical world of changing individual, empirical facts. It was a shift that produced, in many quarters, an atmosphere of skepticism about the rational intelligibility of God's nature and purposes, as defined by the Church; a skepticism resulting not merely in the rejection of the divine realities

---

[91] Cf. "Nominalism," in Dagobert D. Runes, *Dictionary of Philosophy* (Totowa, NJ: Littlefield, Adams & Co., 1962), p. 211.

communicated in the sacraments as such, but in a rejection of the whole outlook of sacramental realism that pervaded the very identity and self-understanding of the Church and her claim to speak, on earth, for God in heaven. This meant a new skepticism, not merely about the connection between an "outward sign" (like baptism) and a real "inward grace" (like regeneration), but about any real, naturally mediated, intelligible connection between the temporal and eternal, the earthly and heavenly.[92]

The resulting atmosphere was one naturally conducive to proto-Protestant sentiments — a "symbolic" view of the sacraments, a "forensic" view of justification, and a "spiritual" view of the Church. As Christ could be present in the Eucharist only "nominally"; as sinners could be made just only "nominally" — so the One Holy Catholic and Apostolic Church could exist in the world only "nominally." The finite could not contain the infinite. Nature could not serve as a channel for grace. The authority of God's Word (in the order of eternity) could be preserved from the contamination of earthly mediations (in the order of time) only by sequestering it within a sanctuary of pure propositions by means of *sola scriptura*. So, at least, it was widely thought. But the effect was quite different. The seat of real authority was removed from the Church, as the

---

[92] This is not to say that theological nominalists were necessarily always individually heretical or anti-Catholic. While it is true that Luther was schooled in the nominalist tradition of Gabriel Biel and William of Ockham's *via moderna*, some of his staunchest Catholic opponents, such as Johannes Eck, as well as some of the most influential participants at the Council of Trent, such as Jacob Lainez, were indebted to that tradition as well. See Heiko Oberman, *The Harvest of Medieval Theology: Gabriel Biel and Late Medieval Nominalism* (Grand Rapids, Michigan: Eerdmans, 1967), 427, and A.G. Dickens, *The Counter Reformation* (London: Harcourt, Brace & World, 1969), 132, cf. 36.
But nominalism did produce a decisive shift in outlook. Louis Dupré, in his magisterial *Passage to Modernity: An Essay in the Hermeneutics of Nature and Culture* (New Haven: Yale University Press, 1993), says that the effect of nominalist theology was to remove God from creation so that nature came to be seen as linked only externally to God. The burden of interpreting nature and constituting meaning then fell to the human self, as the world's signs of intrinsic intelligibility seemed attenuated in proportion to God's distance from it. See also Vos's critique of the "Protestant textbook tradition" of misreading Aquinas on "nature and grace," which stems, in his view, from these late medieval and early Renaissance developments (Vos, *Aquinas*, 152-60).

teacher of Scripture, and placed in the individual interpreter of Scripture alone; where it was never meant to be.[93] Thus the extrabiblical influence of late medieval nominalism, together with various practical exigencies involved in trying to justify revolt against the Church and the whole ecclesiastical tradition, combined to facilitate the development of *sola scriptura* and to make each Protestant, in principle, his own pope.

5. *It assumes that the Bible can be understood apart from tradition*

Sola scriptura assumes no ultimate need for the larger context of the Church's tradition and teaching. However, not only is the canon of Scripture incapable of being identified apart from tradition, as we have seen, but the meaning of Scripture cannot be fully grasped. Protestants argue that Scripture is *clear*, but they disagree even among themselves as to what it means. If they admit that parts of Scripture are unclear, they argue that the *essentials* are clear and that the unclear parts can be interpreted in light of the clear. But their disagreements are not merely over unclear passages, but over the "clear" ones — about the very meaning of precisely those things that Jesus commanded us to do in His name: "Take, eat; this is my body... do this in remembrance of me... Go... baptize... teach them to observe all that I have commanded you." If they admit that Scripture is not expressly clear on an essential subject, they argue that it can "by good and necessary consequence" be *deduced* from Scripture. But they disagree over *what* can be

---

93 This nominalistic view of the Church as a purely human institution eviscerated of all of her proper divine attributes, such as her infallibility, is evident in Calvin's remarks throughout his *Institutes*: "As if the eternal and inviolable truth of God depended upon the decision of men!" he writes, referring to the Church's role in canonizing Scripture. Again, he asks, "what will happen to miserable consciences seeking firm assurance of eternal life if all promises of it consist in and depend solely upon the judgment of men?" (75). It is evident that the Church has no more than a nominal authority in his view. The finite cannot contain the infinite (never mind the Incarnation, the Blessed Sacrament, the Bible, the Arc of the Covenant, the Holy of Holies in the Tabernacle, the Pillar of Fire, or the Burning Bush, for starters).

deduced from Scripture.[94] If they admit that Church tradition can help, they annul this help by the circular argument that it can be trusted only where it agrees with (their interpretation of) Scripture.

The fact is that Scripture is only a part of what has been handed down to us in sacred tradition. By itself it was never intended to communicate the whole of God's instruction for the ongoing life of the Church and is quite ill-suited to that purpose. In addition, it contains many things that were not at first understood, but took time to become clear through decades and centuries of reflection and definition, often in contradistinction from emergent heresies.[95] It contains many references which cannot be understood apart from the larger context of sacred tradition.[96] Not only is it many-faceted

---

[94] For example, the great champion of Lutheranism against Rome, Martin Chemnitz, in his *Examination of the Council of Trent*, tr. Fred Kramer (St. Louis: Concordia, 1971), I, 249, maintains that the practice of infant baptism can be deduced "from clear testimonies of Scripture by way of good, certain, firm, and clear reasoning" — a conclusion that any well-trained Baptist would dispute with joyful vociferousness.

[95] Thus Newman writes, "It is indeed sometimes said that the stream is clearest near the spring. Whatever use may fairly be made of this image, it does not apply to the history of a philosophy or belief, which on the contrary is more equable, and purer, the stronger, when its bed has become deep, and broad, and full... Its beginnings are no measure of its capabilities, nor of its scope" (*Essay*, 40).

[96] Numerous Bible texts could be adduced which cannot be understood in terms of *sola scriptura* and require recourse to Church tradition. David Currie discusses a few, including the reference to future sacrifice in Zech 14:20f. (45); Jesus' command to "practice and observe whatever they tell you" who "sit on Moses' seat," in Mt 23:2f. (53); the Jerusalem Council's identification of the Holy Spirit's will with its *own* authority in Acts 15:28 (64f.); the apostles' authority to pass on the office vacated by Judas to Matthias, in Acts 1 (66); the power to forgive or retain sins in Jn 20:22f. (66f.); the reference to the deuterocanonical "Daniel" in Ez 14:14, 20 (104f.); the reference to Jesus' "brothers," whose father was either Alphaeus or Cleophas, in Mt 10:3, Jn 19:25, cf. Mt 27:56 (157-59; cf. Keating, 282-89). The cavil that such texts do not touch the "essentials" of the Gospel begs the question, since the question as to what is "essential" is part of the issue. To the retort that the Catholic also begs the question by insisting that such texts can be properly understood only within Church tradition, I would respond by saying: either there is a divinely authorized *magisterium* with a normative tradition of interpretation, or there is not; and if there is, then there's no material cause for objection.

and complex; it does not often clearly specify what is didactic or historical, fact or vision, allegorical or literal, idiomatic or grammatical, enunciated formally or occurring *obiter*, temporary or of lasting obligation, as Newman notes.[97] In this sense, it is *not* "self-interpreting." As Newman writes: "We are told that God has spoken. Where? In a book? We have tried it and it disappoints; it disappoints us, that most holy and blessed gift, not from fault of its own, but because it is used for a purpose for which it was not given. The Ethiopian's reply, when St. Philip asked him if he understood what he was reading, is the voice of nature: 'How can I, unless some man shall guide me?' The Church undertakes that office."[98] The question has nothing to do with whether the Ethiopian was a Christian or Jew, as Blomberg suggests,[99] any more than it has to do with whether the text was from the OT or NT. What he needed was a teacher (*magister*) who could instruct him in what God intended him to understand; that is what the eunuch received in Philip, and that is what we have in the *magisterium* of the Church.

Furthermore, even while claiming that Scripture is their only standard, Protestants typically *presuppose* Church tradition in ways

---

[97] John Henry Newman, *On the Inspiration of Scripture*, ed. J. Derek Holmes and Robert Murray (Washington: Corpus Books, 1967) writes: "It is antecedently unreasonable to suppose that a book so complex, so unsystematic, in parts so obscure, the outcome of so many minds, times, and places, should be given us from above without the safeguard of some authority; as if it could possibly, from the nature of the case, interpret itself. Its inspiration does but guarantee its truth, not its interpretation. How are private readers satisfactorily to distinguish what is didactic and what is historical, what is fact and what is vision, what is allegorical and what is literal, what is idiomatic and what is grammatical, what is enunciated formally and what occurs *obiter*, what is only of temporary and what is of lasting obligation? Such is our natural anticipation, and it is only too exactly justified in the events of the last three centuries, in the many countries where private judgment on the text of Scripture has prevailed. The gift of inspiration requires as its complement the gift of infallibility" (111).

[98] Newman, *Essay*, 88.

[99] Craig Blomberg, in a letter to the editor of the *New Oxford Review* (Sept. 1991), responding to an article by Richard Becker ("On the Authoritativeness of Scripture — A Contribution to Catholic-Evangelical Dialogue"), declared that the quote from Newman on the Ethiopian eunuch is irrelevant, because the latter was not "a Christian who lacked the insights of the Magisterium," but "a Jew (or God-fearer) who had not yet heard of Jesus — the one who was to become the key to a Christian understanding of the Old Testament" (5). But this is a distinction without a difference (see below).

they are often unaware. Mark Shea, for instance, offers a detailed analysis of certain fundamental commitments of evangelicals and argues compellingly that some of them — such as their commitment to the sanctity of human life in the pro-life movement, their rejection of polygamy, and their adherence to the doctrine of the Trinity — are actually based more on tradition than on explicit Scripture. In fact, in some cases, such non-negotiable commitments are only weakly attested in the Bible, he notes, yet treated as revealed doctrines in much the same manner as Catholics accept sacred tradition as a channel of revelation.[100] Other examples, cited at random, would include the traditional commitment of Presbyterians to infant baptism, Methodists to the episcopacy, Lutherans to baptismal regeneration and the Real Presence in the Eucharist, and so forth — none of which would go uncontested by other Protestant interpretations of Scripture despite their mutual agreement upon it as their only standard; whereas, to the Catholic at least, it is obvious that they are all in fact banking on Church tradition.[101]

---

[100] Mark Shea, *By What Authority?: An Evangelical Discovers Catholic Tradition* (Huntington, IN: Our Sunday Visitor, 1996); cf. Mark Shea, "When Evangelicals Treat Catholic Tradition Like Revelation," *New Oxford Review* (Sept. 1996), 6-15.

The claim that "the Trinity was always in Scripture; the *terms* used to describe it and creedal *formulation* of the doctrine were progressively unfolded" (Geisler and MacKenzie, 198, n. 50) is only a half-truth, belied by the *prima facie* credibility of the "adoptionist" interpretation of the NT in the early Christological controversies. Not many dogmas could be called syllogistic deductions from Scripture; many more are inductive inferences from the larger context of tradition.

[101] As illustrations of the same principle, Currie cites the acceptance of Sunday as the Lord's Day (54). Further, the same principle holds for the OT and Judaism, as Currie argues: "As I read the Old Testament, I was struck by several major issues. The most revolutionary for me was that I saw that no one could have established or maintained Judaism in the way God desired from the data found only in the Bible. There were too many holes and gaps: so much was assumed. I saw that a tremendous amount of what was involved in being a God-rearing, God-pleasing Israelite must have been passed down from generation to generation in an oral instruction (tradition). You want just one example? Try to reconstruct the process of offering a sin offering from the Old Testament alone. You can't get to first base! Reconstructing worship that would be pleasing to God from the Old Testament alone is impossible" (52).

6. *It leads to misinterpretation of the Church Fathers*

Protestant interpretations are sometimes so far-fetched that they would be amusing, were they not so misleading. If there is any truth to James White's accusation that Catholic apologists are sometimes guilty of "anachronistic interpretation" and "out-of-context citations,"[102] this charge applies to defenders of *sola scriptura* in spades. This should come as no surprise, since their chief principle is one that ties them to a disembodied text, and not to the embodying, living and ongoing tradition which gave rise to it, and of which it continues to be a part. It is no great task to find (1) a Church Father who affirms that Scripture is uniquely and divinely inspired, and uniquely authoritative as the supreme written record of the material deposit of faith. The Church grants that. The real task is to find (2) a Church Father who affirms that the whole content of God's revelation for the ongoing instruction of His Church was committed wholly to Scripture without residue, so that it serves in that capacity as a text, *apart* from the larger sacred tradition and ongoing community of memory of which it is a part. But for *sola scriptura* apologists to produce examples only of the former (Church Fathers who affirm biblical inspiration and authority), and none of the latter (Fathers who confine divine authority to Scripture), and then to boldly suggest that the Church Fathers entertained views even resembling *sola scriptura*, is simply ridiculous; for there is no case. Against such a suggestion, the weight of the patristic evidence stands like an incontrovertible colossus of steel and bronze.

A good example of this Protestant misuse of the Church Fathers is furnished by James White. He typically begins his foray into the Fathers in search of evidence for *sola scriptura* with a quote from Cyril of Jerusalem's *Catechetical Lectures*, in which he says: "not the least part [of the mysteries of the faith] may be handed on without the Holy Scriptures... Even to me, who tell you these things, do not give ready belief, unless you receive from the

---

[102] *SS*, 52f.

Holy Scriptures the proof of the things which I announce."[103] Taken in isolation, the passage may seem mildly promising to the Protestant, but the key issue here is the meaning of Scriptural "proof." The term is open to wide and narrow meanings. We cannot, in a narrow sense, "prove" many doctrines from Scripture (e.g. the Trinity, or infant baptism). But in a wider sense, the Church that teaches these doctrines can look for "proofs" from Scriptures. What does *Cyril* mean by "proof"? As Patrick Madrid points out:

> If Cyril was in fact teaching *sola scriptura* [in this passage], Protestants have a big problem. Cyril's *Catechetical Lectures* are filled with his forceful teachings on the infallible teaching office of the Catholic Church (18:23), the Mass as a sacrifice (23:6-8), the concept of purgatory and the efficacy of expiatory prayers for the dead (23:10), the Real Presence of Christ in the Eucharist (19:7; 21:3; 22:1-9), the theology of sacraments (1:3), the importance of frequent Communion (23:23), baptismal regeneration (1:1-3; 3:10-12; 21:3-4), indeed a staggering array of specifically 'Catholic' doctrines.[104]

It is clear, therefore, that Cyril didn't mean Scriptural "proof" in the narrow sense, and he certainly wasn't teaching *sola scriptura.*

In case after case — whether the Church Father is Irenaeus, Athanasius, Augustine, Basil of Caesarea, or any of the like — the same scenario is repeated time after time: a quotation is found that *looks* like a "smoking gun" in favor of *sola scriptura*, but a review of the textual setting confirms that this is *not* the case. Moreover, the larger context of the Father's corpus of writings invariably reveals a pattern of assumptions that is anything but Protestant, and cannot possibly have been derived from *sola scriptura*. The whole

---

[103] Cyril's *Catechetical Lectures* 4:17, cited by White, in *SS*, 27. White's chapter in this volume offers many choice examples of quotations from Fathers such as Irenaeus, Augustine, Athanasius, and Basil of Caesarea, all enlisted in service of *sola scriptura*, but only by ignoring the larger context of their work. Another good example is the similar use of quotations from Augustine in Geisler and MacKenzie, 199f.

[104] Patrick Madrid, "Sola Scriptura: A Blueprint for Anarchy," *Catholic Dossier* (March/April 1996), 25. See chapter 1 of this book for further explication.

world of the Church Fathers *breathes* Catholicism — whether we look at *Irenaeus'* deference to Roman primacy, his transformational view of the Eucharist, or his Mariology; or at *Athanasius'* confidence that God speaks through Ecumenical Councils, his belief in the perpetual virginity of Mary, his view that bread and wine become Christ's body and blood when consecrated by priests, his familiar references to the "sign of the cross," to the "archbishop," to the martyrdom of Peter in Rome, to "Apostolical tradition" and "Canons" (rules) received from the Apostles; or at *Augustine's* belief in Mary's perpetual virginity and sinlessness, his belief in purgatory, his acceptance of the episcopate, or his practice of praying to Mary; or at *Basil of Caesarea's* acceptance of the unwritten sacred traditions for consecrating the bread and wine in the Eucharist.[105] After witnessing case after case in which Protestant treatments of the Church Fathers ignore the overwhelming evidence of their explicitly Roman Catholic commitments, one cannot help being driven to the inexorable conclusion that *sola scriptura* cannot be supported by an appeal to tradition. It is not the opponents of *sola scriptura* who ignore the *context* of the Church Fathers' remarks, but the proponents.

---

[105] For Irenaeus see *Against Heresies* in Roberts and Donaldson, *Ante-Nicene Fathers* (Peabody, MA: Hendrickson, 1994), I, 415f., 526, 454f., 547; for Athanasius, William A. Jurgens, *The Faith of the Early Fathers* (Collegeville, MN: Liturgical Press, 1970), I, 330, 343, 345, and Schaff and Wace, *Nicene and Post-Nicene Fathers* (hereafter *NPNF*), Series II (Peabody, MA: Hendrickson, 1994), IV, 115f., 199, 283, 564; for Augustine, see William A. Jurgens, *The Faith of the Early Fathers* (Collegeville, MN: Liturgical Press, 1979), III, 111, 116, the brief resumé by Alan Schreck, *Catholic and Christian: An Explanation of Commonly Misunderstood Catholic Beliefs* (Ann Arbor: Servant, 1984), 98, 177, and 198, cf. 157f., and for a specific prayer to Mary by Augustine, see "To Mary, mother of the Church," in *Praying with the Saints*, ed. William Lane (Doublin: Veritas, 1987), 19; for Basil of Caesarea, see *NPNF*, Series II, I, 40-42. See also Madrid's previously-cited article for point-by-point refutations of common Protestant misreadings of Basil of Caesarea, Athanasius, and Cyril of Jerusalem.

7. *It leads to unhistorical understandings and distortions of fact*

Distortions can cover a great variety of issues, such as the erroneous belief that the early Church had no episcopal hierarchy; that the demand of priestly celibacy shows that Catholic doctrine has departed from Scripture; that liturgy is a medieval invention and nothing but empty ritual; that Papal infallibility means the Pope supposedly cannot err in *anything*; that the "extra" books in the Catholic Bible were not part of the Scriptures used by the NT writers; that Catholic devotions such as the Rosary and Stations of the Cross have no basis in Scripture; that doctrinal "development" in Catholicism means doctrinal "creation"; that certain Catholic doctrines — such as purgatory, baptismal regeneration, prayers for the dead, the sinlessness of Mary, and the transformation of bread and wine into Christ's body and blood — are medieval inventions. While these cannot all be treated here, they can all be easily refuted with a little time and study.[106]

(a) *Failure to distinguish matters of dogma from matters of discipline*

Some misunderstandings, such as the general belief that Catholic doctrine has departed from Scripture, stem in part from a failure to appreciate the historical distinction drawn by the Church between matters of dogma (which are unchangeable) and matters of discipline (which may be changed to meet the pastoral demands of particular times and places).[107] Thus, priestly celibacy — like "Fish on Fridays" (the requirement to abstain from meat) and Communion

---

[106] Some of these misapprehensions are dealt with in this essay; as to the others, the truth about them can be tracked down easily enough by beginning with some of the sources I have cited, such as Keating's *Catholicism and Fundamentalism* (a popular treatment), and Newman's *Essay* (a 19th century classic).

[107] See Keating, 66, *passim*, whose work amply illuminates from fundamentalist sources the foibles that result from failing to make this distinction. Currie's division of ecclesiastical data into "deposit, dogma, doctrine, discipline, and devotion" is also helpful, as well as his discussion of these categories (84-87), even if they are unofficial.

in one kind (the withholding of the Cup from the laity) prior to Vatican II — was never a matter of unchangeable dogma, but a prudential discipline imposed (in the case of celibacy) for the sake of fostering single-minded devotion to God and service in the ministry.[108] Furthermore, despite the existence of married apostles, Scripture often encourages celibacy for those who can accept the gift (1 Cor 7:32, 35; Mt 19:11-12). The fact that the Church has changed some of her practices in the interests of discipline does not mean that her teaching is inconsistent or that her dogma has changed.

(b) *Failure to understand the principle of doctrinal development*

Misunderstandings can also stem from a failure to understand the nature of doctrinal development. John Henry Newman offered the classic study of this idea in his *Essay on the Development of Christian Doctrine* (1845). He compared the process to that of an acorn growing into an oak. The oak looks very different from the acorn; yet this is to be expected, for the ordinary process of growth is healthy, natural and organic; and the fact that the oak *looks* different is no necessary indication of a "corruption" or transmutation of the organism into something altogether different. Analogously, everything necessary for the proper development of Christian doctrine was contained in the original deposit of faith (the teaching of Christ and the apostles). But all the doctrines that would later unfold in their fuller development were not immediately apparent in the original deposit. Thus, nowhere does the Bible formally and explicitly state the doctrine of the Trinity, as even Prot-

[108] The purpose of the Friday abstinence, in the words of the *Catholic Encyclopedia*, ed. Peter Stravinskas (Huntington, IN: Our Sunday Visitor, 1991), was to "unite the believer through a discipline of self-sacrifice to the sacrificial love of Christ and to free the person from self-centeredness, in order to facilitate deeper prayer and more generous charity" (31); and even now, Catholics are encouraged by the Church to abstain from meat on Friday, or to do some corporeal work of mercy on that day. The practice of withholding the Cup from the laity was a prudential decision for the avoidance of "certain dangers and scandals" involving the desecration of the Blessed Sacrament under the species of wine (Newman, *Essay*, 129f.).

estants admit.[109] But the doctrine is clearly a development based on the teachings of Christ and the apostles — a natural outgrowth of later reflections on their traditions (including Scripture) and the process of defining Christian doctrine over against various challenges to the faith. And the same is true, the Catholic would argue, of other doctrines that do not at first strike the Protestant as likely to have grown from the "acorn," or as clearly "implicit" in Scripture as the Trinity — such as the Church's teachings on purgatory, transubstantiation, papal supremacy, and the like. Not only are these doctrines well-attested in the early Church (for example, Newman shows that there is stronger evidence for belief in purgatory in the early Church than for belief in original sin); they are also implicitly grounded in Scripture (e.g., purgatory in 1 Cor 3:12-15; transubstantiation in Jn 6:54-59; papal supremacy in Mt 16:18) — which, for a Cyril of Jerusalem, might be considered "proof."[110]

At this point the practical difference from the Protestant *modus operandi* is not so great as may first be imagined. The Protestant insists that the deposit of faith is exhausted without residue in Scripture and, therefore, that only those doctrines that are "implicit" in Scripture can be "deduced" from Scripture as valid "developments." Accordingly, most would agree that the Trinity is a legitimate development. However there is a problem here, first, because the obviousness of the Trinitarian "deduction" is belied by the *prima facie* credibility of some interpretations of the NT in the early Christological controversies that would later be judged heretical, as Mark Shea has shown. It took more than Scripture to decide between competing inferences from Scripture to judge what was orthodox and heterodox. Second, Baptists will not agree with Lutherans that infant baptism or baptismal regeneration are legiti-

---

[109] Geisler and MacKenzie, 184; cf. 198, n. 50.

[110] See the discussion of Cyril of Jerusalem in Section 6 above. For Newman on purgatory, see his *Essay*, 21; and see 92-98 for a brief analytical resumé of the logical relations connecting the developments of various Catholic doctrines. See R. Sungenis' detailed exegesis of 1 Cor 3:15 in *Not By Faith Alone: The Biblical Evidence for the Catholic Doctrine of Justification* (Queenship Publishing, 1997), as a case in point. See also *Jesus, Peter and the Keys* by S. Butler, N. Dahlgren and D. Hess (Queenship Publishing, 1996) for a superlative treatment of Scriptural evidence for papal supremacy.

mate "deductions" from Scripture. Therefore *sola scriptura* is neither a compelling criterion for determining what is a normative "development," *nor the effective criterion ultimately employed by Protestants.* In this sense, the Protestant position resembles the position of those Catholics who accept the "material sufficiency" of Scripture, according to which, in Newman's words, "all the definitions or received judgments of the early and medieval Church rest upon definite, even though sometimes obscure sentences of Scripture."[111] Whether one's "deductions" and "developments" from Scripture are those of a Catholic, a Lutheran, or a Baptist, it is obvious that there is a principle of interpretation at work that is not itself derived from Scripture alone but from an extrabiblical tradition. Thus, the difference does not ultimately lie in the fact that some doctrines are "deduced" from "sometimes obscure sentences of Scripture" under the influence of extrabiblical traditions of interpretation. Such "deductions" are part of every tradition. The difference lies in the question of the relative authority of the respective traditions that influence or govern the "deductions."

(c) *Failure to distinguish official teaching from private opinion*

Other misunderstandings stem from a failure to distinguish official teaching from private opinion. Thus, it is just as erroneous to assume that every Catholic theologian or Church Father necessarily speaks always and everywhere for Rome as it is to assume that theological conflict among Catholic theologians and Fathers means that the Church is divided in her own teaching. Some contemporary Catholic theologians (such as Hans Küng) are dissenters against Church teaching at points, while some theologians of the early

---

[111] Newman, *Essay*, 72. The Catholic theory of "material sufficiency" says that the whole content of Revelation is present in Scripture if only implicitly, and denies that extrabiblical tradition offers any separate revelational material. It asserts *totum in Scriptura, totum in traditione*, as opposed to *partim in Scriptura, partim in traditione*. However, this does not necessarily mean that what is in Scripture cannot be illumined or amplified by what is in extrabiblical tradition, any more than it means the opposite could not occur. What is implicit in either one may be comparatively explicit in the other. (See chapter 7 by Rev. Peter Stravinskas in this volume for a more detailed discussion of this matter.)

Church (such as Tertullian and Origen) have been judged heretical in certain aspects of their writings. A related misunderstanding is illustrated by the Church's condemnation of Galileo, which Protestants sometimes mistake for a case of a fallible magisterium, confronting the Church with the dilemma "of how an infallible pronouncement of the Catholic church could be in error."[112] But Galileo's conflict with the Roman curia over cosmology was a conflict that involved Rome in practical judgments about the implications of private speculative opinions, not the dogmatic definition of doctrine. The Vatican's motivation was a practical, pastoral concern for protecting the spiritual well-being of the faithful, and in the conflict of private opinions over the matter, some of her spokesmen erred. But their errors were errors of practical judgment expressing private opinion, for they were not involved in the business of defining doctrine. The Church has never claimed that the private opinions of any human being are infallible. The earth-centered Ptolemaic cosmology contested by Galileo was supported by widespread opinion at that time, including the Protestant Reformers, but formed no part of official Catholic dogma.[113] Catholics readily accept that Popes can make errors of private judgment, even in public pronouncements. As Newman writes: "What have excommunication and interdict to do with Infallibility? Was St. Peter infallible on that occasion at Antioch when St. Paul withstood him? was St. Victor infallible when he separated from his communion the Asiatic Churches? or Liberius when in like manner he excommunicated Athanasius? And, to come to later times, was Gregory XIII, when he had a medal struck in honour of the Bartholomew massacre? or Paul IV in his conduct towards Elizabeth? or Sextus V when he blessed the Armada? or Urban VIII when he persecuted Galileo? No Catholic ever pretends that these Popes were infallible in these acts."[114] Official Church teaching and tradition is one thing; private

[112] Geisler and MacKenzie, 219.

[113] What got Galileo into trouble was his insistence that his heliocentrism not only "saved the appearances," but was a "physical fact." The conflict, therefore, was really more over the nature of physical theory itself than over a particular theory. This is why Galileo was censured, but not Copernicus.

[114] Newman, "Letter to His Grace the Duke of Norfolk," 9. Similar qualifications apply to Pope John Paul II's remarks before the Pontifical Academy of Science on the subject of the Theory of Evolution on Oct. 22, 1996.

opinion is another. The dogma of the Holy Trinity is one thing; speculative opinion about how the world was created is another.

(d) *Failure to reckon with history*

Still other misunderstandings seem to stem simply from historical ignorance. Some of these are perhaps less significant than they are egregious, such as the confused suggestion that Catholic devotions such as the Stations of the Cross have "no biblical basis whatsoever."[115] Others touch on matters of consequence for Church government, such as the common evangelical insistence that the early Church had only two ecclesiastical offices — "elder" (or "presbyter") and "deacon" — which is hard to maintain in the face of the historical evidence that the distinction of three offices — "bishop," "presbyter" and "deacon" — is one of the earliest and most clearly attested matters one can find.[116] Instead of asking whether their commitment to *sola scriptura* has so cut them off from history and tradition that they may no longer be reading the Bible as it was intended to be read, evangelicals seem intent on maintaining *sola scriptura* even if they think it requires interpretations that fly in the face of the obvious facts of Church history. For example, Godfrey

---

115 MacArthur, in *SS*, 157f. The stations of the cross, of course, are almost entirely based *explicitly* on the events of Christ's passion in the Gospel accounts.

116 While the distinctive functions identified with these three offices in the full-blown diocesan system clearly took time to develop, it is also clear that *some* kind of implicit distinction between them was recognized from the beginning. For example, St. Ignatius of Antioch, who personally knew the Apostle John and was martyred during the reign of the Emperor Trajan (A.D. 98-117), wrote: "Take care to do all things in harmony with God, with the *bishop* presiding in the place of God and with the *presbyters* in the place of the Apostles, and with the *deacons*, who are most dear to me..." (*Letter to the Magnesians*, 6,1); "In like manner let everyone respect the *deacons* as they would respect Jesus Christ, and just as they respect the *bishop* as a type of the Father, and the *presbyters* as the council of God and college of Apostles" (*Letter to the Trallians*, 3,1); and "Give heed to the *bishop* and the *presbytery* and the *deacons*" (*Letter to the Philadelphians*, 7, 1; all quoted from Jurgens, 19, 20, 23; emphasis mine). It is also noteworthy that the English word "priest" is etymologically a contraction of the Greek "presbyter," even if its commonly received connotations are not the same, and even if this association is not the *basis* for their connection in Catholic theology.

writes, "The Bible teaches that the office of bishop and presbyter are the same office (Titus 1:5-7), but tradition says they are different offices," and concludes that tradition must be wrong.[117] But from the perspective of Catholic tradition, the answer to this is simple: a "bishop" is *also* a "presbyter" — one whose office came, in time, to be distinctively identified with overseeing a number of presbyters and their parishes. So they have the same office in one respect, and different offices in another. Evangelicals are not helped by their commitment to a principle that leads them to ignore or reject the principle of development, which applies to institutions as well as doctrine, or to fear Catholic teaching and tradition as though they were the enemy of biblical exegesis.[118]

---

[117] Godfrey, in *SS*, 13.

[118] The foregoing quote from Godfrey represents the first of seven points, he says, in which Luther and others in the 16th century discovered through Bible study how Church traditions "contradicted the Bible." It may be instructive to see how these apparent contradictions may be resolved — adequately if not exhaustively — within a perspective informed by Catholic tradition, beginning with his second point:

(2) "The Bible teaches that all have sinned except Jesus (Romans 3:10-12, Hebrews 4:15), but tradition says that Mary was sinless." Reply: we know from history that early Church Fathers like St. Augustine clearly believed in Mary's sinlessness (Jurgens, III, 111). So what could Paul have meant? Since neither infants nor the insane are capable of actual sin, he could not have meant that every individual has actually sinned. From the context of his remarks in Romans, as he compares Jews and gentiles, as well as from the OT context he cites (Ps 14, which contrasts "my people" with "evildoers" in v. 4), it is clear that Paul is saying that no group of people — Jew or gentile — is sinless; which does not mean that individuals within the groups cannot avoid sinning. As for original sin, which is another question, Mary clearly had to have God's grace to be saved from it just as everyone does, only in her case the grace was preventative, not remedial.

(3) "The Bible teaches that Christ offered His sacrifice once for all (Hebrews 7:27; 9:28, 10:10), but tradition says that the priest sacrifices Christ on the altar at mass." Reply: tradition affirms that Christ's original sacrifice was indeed made once-for-all and that the Mass is nothing other than the means God gave us of participating in that once-for-all sacrifice. Since there is but one victim, offered by Christ and by us, there is but one sacrifice. As Karl Adam writes, in *The Spirit of Catholicism*, rev. ed., tr. Dom Justin McCann (Garden City, NY: Image, 1954): "In the Sacrifice of the Mass we are not merely reminded of the Sacrifice of the Cross in a symbolical form. On the

(e) *Failure to translate Scripture accurately*

One of the most serious abuses to which unhistorical understandings and distortions can lead is the mistranslation of Scripture itself. This happened already with Luther, who added the "*sola*" of his fateful "*sola fide*" in his translation of Romans (3:28) — "For we hold that a man is justified by faith [***alone***] apart from

---

118 cont. contrary the Sacrifice of Calvary, as a great supra-temporal reality, enters into the immediate present. Space and time are abolished. The same Jesus is here present who died on the Cross" (197).

(4) "The Bible says that we are not to bow down to statues (Exodus 20:4-5) — but tradition says that we should bow down to statues." Reply: what is forbidden is idolatry, not the making of images, for God commanded Moses to make gold images of cherubim for the ark (Ex 25:18) and a bronze image of a serpent (Num 21:8-9) — or veneration of those we love and respect through photographs or statues of them like Michelangelo's "Pieta."

(5) "The Bible says that all Christians are saints and priests (Ephesians 1:1, 1 Peter 2:9), but tradition says that saints and priests are special castes within the Christian community." Reply: Catholic tradition does not deny that all Christians are "saints" and "priests" in this sense, yet also affirms the distinctive priestly ministry of the ordained clergy and the distinctive "saintly" quality of those who, unlike us, are perfectly sanctified and glorified in heaven.

(6) "The Bible says that Jesus is the only Mediator between God and man (1 Timothy 2:5), but tradition says Mary is co-mediator with Christ." Reply: tradition affirms that Jesus is the only Mediator in the unique sense of 1 Tim 2:5, yet also affirms that others throughout history — pastors, evangelists, missionaries, parents, Sunday School teachers, intercessory "prayer warriors" — have served as "mediators" of God's grace in a secondary sense. By virtue of their cooperation with the purposes of Christ, they could be said to be "co-mediators" with Him. Mary is simply an elevated example of a "co-mediator" in this secondary sense, in that she accepted the task of mediating the Incarnation of Jesus, Son of God and Son of Mary!

(7) "The Bible says that all Christians should know that they have eternal life" (1 John 5:13), but tradition says that all Christians cannot and should not know that they have eternal life. Reply: if "know" is taken to mean a "firm hope," there is no problem — we have the "assurance" of Christ's promises; but if "know" is taken to mean "syllogistic certitude" that one will personally persevere to the end of one's life and be saved, there is a problem; for as St. Thomas Aquinas says (*Summa Theologiae*, 12ae, Q. 112, Art. 5), such certitude would require either knowing everything God knows about one's future (which is impossible), or a private revelation from God, and, short of that, would involve the sin of presumption.

works of law" (RSV).[119] He thought he was offering the "dynamic equivalent," but little did he see how he was reading back into Paul's opposition to Pharisaical legalism the 16th-century bias of his own quarrel with Rome over "works righteousness" — which was not the same thing[120] — and would lead him to exclude the Epistle of James from the NT canon; and little did he foresee the implications that this seemingly minor alteration would have centuries later in the recrudescences of antinomian tendencies among evangelicals, as in the recent writings of Zane Hodges.[121]

But no less disturbing than Luther's case, is that of current evangelical versions of Scripture that systematically expunge the "Catholic" overtones of certain passages by means of translations that significantly alter the meanings of these texts. Some examples of this are furnished by the Reformed scholar, James R. Payton, Jr., who criticizes the deliberate "de-catholicizing" of Scripture in the New International Version (NIV), a widely-respected and otherwise excellent evangelical translation.[122] He illustrates this "de-catholicizing" in the NIV's handling of a number of passages dealing with two key elements of the Church's "catholic" heritage: the Lord's Supper and tradition. He points out, for example, that there are thirteen instances of the term *paradosis* (usually in its plural form, *paradosis*) in the NT, of which ten are critical of human traditions that have departed from God's Word. In the other three cases, Paul *commends* traditions to the churches to whom he writes (1 Cor 11:2; 2 Thes 2:15; 3:6). Significantly all ten of the negative references are translated by the NIV as "traditions," while all three

---

[119] Luther's original German translation reads: "So halten Wir es nu/ das der Mensch Gerecht werde/ on des Gesetzes Werck/ *alleine* durch den Glauben" (Luther's, *Heilige Schrift*, 2274; emphasis added).

[120] For a thorough treatment of these issues, see Robert Sungenis, *Not By Faith Alone: The Biblical Evidence for the Catholic Doctrine of Justification* (Queenship Publishing, 1997) pp. 1-46 and 517-554.

[121] Zane Hodges, *Absolutely Free! A Biblical Reply to Lordship Salvation* (Dallas: Redencion Viva, 1989), *Gospel Under Siege: Faith and Works in Tension*, 2nd ed. (Dallas: Redencion Viva, 1992).

[122] James R. Payton, Jr., "The New International Version and the De-Catholicizing of Scripture," *Perspectives* (Nov. 1993), 10-13. (*Perspectives* absorbed the former *Reformed Journal* several years ago).

of the positive references are deliberately mistranslated as "teachings" — the translation for *didaskalia* or *didachê*, not *paradosis*. Payton concludes: "The NIV is not just invitingly easy to read; it is regrettably tendentious and parochial. From the perspective of the catholicity of the church that Christians confess, the NIV is not a good translation of the Word of God; it is a partisan version in which the translation is slanted in such ways that North American evangelicalism's tastes are not offended and its predilections are confirmed. In the NIV, catholicity is sacrificed on the altar of evangelical sensibilities; in matters where evangelicalism has fallen short of embracing the catholic heritage of the church, the biblical testimony for that heritage is muted. The ironic consequence is that those who profess to follow the Word of God alone are kept from hearing it."[123]

This comment is the governing thesis of the seventh and last point of this section of the essay: namely, that "*sola scriptura* leads to unhistorical understandings and distortions of fact." The misunderstandings include failure to appreciate the distinction between matters of dogma and matters of discipline; failure to understand the principle of doctrinal development; failure to distinguish official teaching from private opinion; and historical ignorance. *Sola scriptura* leads to these misunderstandings because it abstracts the text of Scripture from the context of its living tradition in which these distinctions and principles have living authority. It effectively cuts off its adherents from that context and that tradition, preventing them from hearing Scripture as it was intended to be heard, within the authoritative community of living memory in which these distinctions and principles can be properly discerned and have abiding meaning.

Part IV: Practical Problems

The *sola scriptura* thesis also suffers from at least three practical problems that result from the effective subjectivism and individualism of its hermeneutic, especially for those who allow no explicit role for tradition. It results in: (A) hermeneutical anarchy,

[123] Payton, 13.

(B) denominational factionalism, and (C) the undermining of pastoral authority and discipline.

A. Hermeneutical Anarchy

The fact that hundreds of denominations, each professing to derive its teaching by means of the Holy Spirit's guidance from "Scripture alone," cannot agree even on the fundamentals of the faith, such as the meaning of baptism or the Lord's Supper or even the means of salvation, constitutes a powerful *prima facie* case against it. The principle itself becomes impracticable and self-undermining — a recipe for anarchy. As some Catholic apologists have suggested, it would be like being given the U.S. Constitution but no administrative branches of government to apply it; or like vesting each citizen with the right to interpret the Constitution however he wished.

The quandary can be seen from the very inception of the Protestant movement. The seeds of it are embedded in the subjectivism and individualism of Luther's stand against the Church, which is exemplified in his dramatic declaration before the Diet of Worms: "Unless I am convinced by Scripture and plain reason — I do not accept the authority of popes and councils, for they have contradicted each other — my conscience is captive to the Word of God. I cannot and I will not recant anything, for to go against conscience is neither right nor safe."[124] Luther is correct about conscience, of course. The problem is with how one's theological conscience is formed. But note the emphasis: unless *I* am convinced. It is as if there were suddenly no Church, no tradition, no corporate guidance by the Holy Spirit, no father confessor Staupiz pointing him to the Epistle of Romans or to St. Augustine, but only the individual Luther thrown back upon his own resources — himself, his conscience, and his private interpretation of Scripture. The tragic irony, then, as Krehbiel points out, is to see how the outlines of a familiar pattern begin to emerge in the similar response to *Luther's* doctrine offered by Caspar Schwenckfeld, an Anabaptist reformer: "[If Dr. Luther] would convince me by Holy Scripture and persua-

[124] Roland H. Bainton, *Here I Stand* (New York: New American Library, 1978), 144.

sive reasons that I am straying or mistaken in any point of Christian doctrine or faith, also with respect to life... I would not only be willing to cease and desist from everything that is not right, but also praise and thank him for his love."[125] The rest is history.

The problem is not with the emphasis on personal experience as such. As Krehbiel says: "Martin Luther's special insight was that the individual must come to God entirely unaided or thwarted by human interference. He must have a personal encounter with Jesus Christ. This, itself, is a very Catholic doctrine. Yet when that personal experience becomes a matter of doctrine — essentially a claim to inspiration — apart from the teaching office of the church, this entirely biblical and Catholic idea becomes heretical."[126] Luther confused these; and the resulting fragmentation of teaching authority in Protestantism has produced a proliferation of Protestant positions disagreeing over baptism, Communion, worship, divorce, remarriage, women's ordination, altars, pictures, statues, kneelers, alcohol, cigarettes, cards, Zionism, contraception, premillennialism, the use of musical instruments in worship, and the like. By its very nature, this cacophony of conflicting claims must lead the honest Bible student to stand back and wonder where the system has gone wrong. After all, did not the Apostle Paul say (in 1 Cor 14:33) that "God is not a God of confusion"?

The honest Protestant Bible student has little ground for easily presuming that his private interpretation of the issues that divide the Protestant denominations is necessarily the right one, or that the 2000 year-old consensus of millions of Catholics on every inhabited continent is necessarily wrong. It would be untoward ignorance to assume that he is the first person in history to have carefully examined Scripture; and presumptuous arrogance to assume that he is the first to have understood it. Where was the Holy Spirit for these two thousand years? What about the centuries upon centuries through which the Christian faith was preserved, passed down

---

125 George H. Williams, ed., *Spiritual and Anabaptist Writers* (Philadelphia: Westminster, 1957), 165. I am indebted to Krehbiel (15) for the connection between Luther and Schwenckfeld.

126 Krehbiel, 15.

from generation to generation, and carried by missionary monks to our barbarian ancestors in Europe? What about the millenia of godly champions of the faith, such as St. Augustine, St. Jerome, Pope Leo, Pope Gregory, St. Benedict, St. Anselm, St. Bonaventure, St. Bernard, St. Francis of Assisi, St. Thomas Aquinas, St. Francis Xavier (the first missionary to Japan), and John Henry Newman, for starters? What about the early bishops who personally knew the apostles, like Ignatius of Antioch (the third successive bishop of that city), and who claimed to have had passed on to them the delegated authority of the apostles to stand in their place as divinely commissioned guardians and interpreters of the apostolic faith, and passed on this conviction (together with this claim of authority) from generation to generation through the laying on of hands? What about the popes and bishops who settled the Trinitarian and Christological controversies of the early Ecumenical Councils, who declared "This is orthodox" and "That is heterodox," "This is canonical" and "That is not," and preserved and passed down the Bible and the meaning of its message to us? Were they all mistaken in their "Romish" beliefs? Were these all partially confused, partially misinformed, partially benighted unfortunates who lost their way under the bondage of Rome, until, at last, with the advent of the modern Protestant Bible student, with his NIV Study Bible and Zondervan Concordance and CD-ROM Bible Dictionary, the light of truth has finally dawned?

B. Denominational Factionalism

As a result of its hermeneutical anarchy, *sola scriptura* has splintered into denominational factionalism. It has spawned thousands of denominations, and sects and cults and conventicles. According to the *Oxford Encyclopedia of World Christianity*, published in 1982, there are more than 28,000 recognizable denominations of Christianity.[127] "Spirit-led" Protestant leaders have split congregations and founded new denominations over disagreements

[127] *Oxford World Christian Encyclopedia* , ed. David B. Barrett, (Oxford: University Press, 1982), pp. 15-18.

sometimes serious and sometimes trifling. Not infrequently, their pretensions have been anything but irenic or temperate. For example, when the Rev. Alexander Craighead led his congregation to secede from the New Side Presbytery in 1743, they gathered at Middle Octorara, Pennsylvania, in a solemn ceremony with four swords pointed to the four winds, and established the Covenanter or Reformed Presbyterian Church in America by ceremonially reading "The Declaration, Protestation, and Testimony of a Suffering Remnant of the Anti-Popish, Anti-Lutheran, Anti-Prelatick, Anti-Erastian, Anti-Latitudinarian, Anti-Sectarian, True Presbyterian Church of Christ, in America."[128] It is one thing to wish to avoid sacrificing truth for the sake of unity; it is another to have a profusion of separate Christian communities of faith, each insisting on points of doctrine that conflict with the others, and many of them claiming to be the one true Church of Christ.

One must ask what has gone wrong here. Something about this picture is not quite commensurable with our Lord's call for unity (Jn 17:21) and the repeated warnings throughout the NT about dissent against divinely ordained authority, factionalism, division, and the literal "denominationalism" of those who claimed, "I belong to Paul," "I belong to Apollos," or "I belong to Cephas."[129] No great leap in logic is required to see how these warnings extend to those who claim to belong to Luther, Calvin, Knox, Cranmer, Wesley, Menno, and so forth. Christ's promise of the "Spirit of truth" to guide His Church "into all the truth" (Jn 16:13) was not made to disparate individual followers (or disparate individual readers of John's Gospel), each preparing to figure out what this would

---

[128] Maurice Armstrong, et al., eds., *The Presbyterian Enterprise: Sources of American Presbyterian History* (Philadelphia: Westminster, 1956), 57f. The schism was over the Rev. Craighead's demand that the New Side Presbytery should renew the historic Scottish National Covenant (1581) and the Solemn League and Covenant (1643), thus committing themselves to the extreme Covenanter position of opposition to the existing British Government — a demand that the Presbytery declared to be full of "treason, sedition and distraction."

[129] 1 Cor 1:10-13; cf. 11:18-19, 12:25; Rm 16:17; Heb 13:17; and compare the discussion of Num 16 and 12:1-10 in connection with the unbiblical character of *sola scriptura* towards the beginning of this chapter.

mean on his own, but to the *apostles* — those whom He had authorized and specially commissioned to be His representatives on earth. The Apostle Paul says that the "pillar and foundation of truth" is the *Church* (1 Tim 3:15), not "Spirit-led" individuals hiving off to start their own independent thing.

Disagreement among Protestants extends beyond the circle of conservatives, of course, to include also liberal Protestants. This is important to note because, despite their difference in orthodoxy, the personalizing and subjectivizing logic animating liberal Protestantism is no different *in principle* from that of the first Reformers. The Reformers rejected what they considered to be Roman "additions" to the religion of the Bible, and embraced *sola scriptura* as their authority. But having rejected the teaching office of the Church as their guide in interpreting Scripture, and having made the subjectivizing move to private interpretation, the next logical step was for the Reformers' liberal stepchildren to ally themselves with the congenial subjectivizing epistemologies of the Enlightenment and to begin chipping away at the authority of Scripture itself. The relation between the modern philosophical turn to subjectivism (Descartes) and the anti-Catholic turn to private interpretation (Luther) is itself an interesting question.[130] But, in any case, once these moves were made, questions about traditional interpretations of isolated passages in the Bible led, by a natural and seemingly inexorable logic, to questions about the inerrancy and inspiration of those passages, and, eventually, to the full-blown demythologizing hermeneutics of "higher criticism." In turn, the postmodernist critique of the modern Enlightenment epistemologies to which liberal Protestantism allied itself, has left it vulnerable to the cultural relativism and nihilism of our own day in a way

[130] J. Bottom writes, in "Roman Roads: The Catholic Alternative to Nihilism," *Regeneration Quarterly* (Summer 1996): "The personalizing and subjectivizing of modern thought were certainly signaled, if not caused, by the anti- Catholic movements of the Reformation" (21). The connection between them lies in their common rejection of the objective authority represented by the Catholic Church, and their common turn to the individual rational subject as the ultimate authority by which the world (in the philosophies of Descartes and Kant) or Scripture (in Protestantism) is to be interpreted and understood.

that Rome is not.[131] It is hardly necessary to repeat the litany of apostasies in mainstream Protestant denominations, many of which are now on record endorsing not merely the serialized polygamy of divorce and remarriage, but also endorsing abortion and euthanasia as acts of Christian stewardship, and flirting with the ordination of gays and lesbians (having already ordained women), and with the acceptance of "same sex marriages." All of this places an additional burden on *conservative* Protestants to show the philosophical coherence of *sola scriptura* without appeal to ecclesiastical authority (see the discussion above under Part III, Section A: "Problems of Coherence").

It will not do to object that the charge of Protestant disunity can be turned back on the Catholic Church. It is true, as Protestant apologists enjoy pointing out, that the "scandal of liberalism" and disunity can be found among Catholics just as it is among Protestants. But there is an ineluctable difference. The problem of disunity on the Protestant side is the disunity between the *official* teachings of different denominations, not, as on the Catholic side, the disunity between official Church teaching and the *views* of various dissidents who happen to also be (at least nominally) church members. Hence it is beside the point that we find liberal theologians and even professing atheists who call themselves "Catholics," perhaps in some cultural sense, even as there are secular Jews.[132] This does not mean that Catholic teaching is divided against itself. The

[131] J. Bottom comments: "We have more or less seen it coming: For some time it has been possible to discern in some unclear way that the Reformation churches that allied themselves with the liberal, modern Enlightenment were doomed. 'Rome and the atheists have gained,' the American novelist Herman Melville wrote in 1876; 'These two shall fight it out — these two; Protestantism being retained for base of operations solely by Atheism.' But it is now unavoidably obvious. To recognize the need for a publicly held Christian ethics to temper unbridled capitalism, to understand that the principles that demand a secular society end by denying the existence of any moral claim, to assert the objective intelligibility of a universe existing beyond personal 'readings' — to do anything like these things is to be compelled to think about the church. And to think about the church is to come, slowly but inevitably, home to Rome" (Ibid., 21).

[132] Geisler and MacKenzie, 193, cites the "scandal of liberalism" among Catholics and the case of an author who had "a Catholic teacher at a Catholic university who claimed to be an atheist."

conflict is between the Church's *unified* teaching and the dissenting opinions of various dissident individuals and groups. By contrast, Protestant disunity is between the conflicting *official* teachings of various denominations.[133]

Hence, it will not do to protest that charges of Protestant hermeneutical anarchy and denominational chaos involve an unfair comparison of "Roman theory with Protestant practice," for they do not.[134] The question here is: which *theory* is right? Catholic or Protestant? And if not the Catholic, then which Protestant one? the Baptist? Presbyterian? Episcopalian? Methodist? Lutheran? Nazarene? Pentecostal? Conservative? Liberal? The *practical* problem resulting from *sola scriptura* is a problem of *theoretical* chaos.

Nor will it do to fall back on the assertion that Protestant conservatives, at least, are united on "essentials"; for the question as to what is "essential" and what is not, is itself part of what is at issue.[135] Lutherans consider baptism essential, while Quakers do not. Baptists consider an "adult" profession of faith to be an essential prerequisite for baptism, while Presbyterians do not. Presbyterians

---

133 Geisler and MacKenzie get the matter half-right: "When Catholic apologists claim there is significantly more doctrinal agreement among Catholics than Protestants they must mean between *orthodox Catholics* and *all* Protestants (orthodox and unorthodox), which clearly is not a comparison" (193). The half-wrong part is the reference to "orthodox and unorthodox" Protestants, since the question as to what constitutes "orthodoxy" is precisely what is at issue in their disunity.

134 Godfrey, in *SS*, writes: "Our Roman opponents will want to compare Roman theory with Protestant practices. That is not fair. We must compare theory with theory or practice with practice" (21f.). But what Catholics are interested in comparing is not Roman theory with Protestant practice, but the consequences of the Catholic theory with the consequences of Protestant theory (the theory of private interpretation of Scripture).

135 Examples of this assertion of Protestant unity on "essentials" can be found in Geisler and MacKenzie, 193; Godfrey, in *SS*, 21; and Armstrong, in *SS*, 132-34.

A related group of arguments (in Geisler and MacKenzie, 194) include J.I. Packer's claim (1) that "the real deep divisions have been caused not by those who maintained *sola Scriptura*, but by those, Roman Catholic and Protestant alike, who reject it"; (2) that "when adherents of *sola Scriptura* have split from each other the cause has been sin rather than Protestant biblicism"; and Geisler's and MacKenzie's claim (3) that a "bad hermeneutic is more crucial

consider the predestination of the elect to be an essential doctrine, but Free Methodists do not. Nazarenes consider personal holiness an essential prerequisite for salvation, while Lutherans do not. Calvinists consider the "irresistibility of grace" an essential belief, while Lutherans do not. Episcopalians consider sacraments essential, but the Salvation Army does not. Presbyterians regard the belief in the "total depravity" of man essential, but Methodists do not. The Dutch Reformed consider creeds and confessions essential, but Baptists do not. Mennonites view nonparticipation in military service as essential, but Baptists do not. Baptists consider "altar calls" essential, but Presbyterians do not. Q.E.D. — we rest our case.

It will not suffice to fall back on the excuse that external unity does not matter as long as there exists a "true spiritual unity" of genuine believers, who can be identified (on the basis of John 13:35) by their love for one another (e.g., Geisler and MacKenzie, 193). While it is true that genuine believers share a spiritual unity which is authenticated by their love, this cannot serve as a sufficient criterion for deciding between true and false doctrine; and doctrine is what is at issue. This argument begs the question, both as to what constitutes being a "genuine believer" and as to what constitutes the "true unity" of Christians. And while it is true that genuine Christians will manifest love for one another, recognizably genuine human love is not limited to conservative Protestants or even to Christians.

---

135 cont. to deviation from orthodoxy than is the rejection of infallible tradition from the Roman Catholic Church."

#1 confuses (a) the authority of Scripture, which both Catholic and conservative Protestants accept, and which is important to orthodoxy, with (b) *sola scriptura*, which, as we have seen, can arguably be judged to have contributed to the development of Protestant liberalism and sectarianism. #2 implicitly links a practical cause (sin) to a theoretical effect (doctrinal disunity), with the aim of acquitting "Protestant biblicism" (shorthand for *sola scriptura*). This is an example of what logicians call the genetic fallacy. The fact that sin may be the cause of doctrinal disunity implies nothing about the guilt or innocence of the principle of "Protestant biblicism." Invariably, the possibility is all-too-easily dismissed that belief in *sola scriptura* is itself a sin. #3 begs the question at issue by assuming that "orthodoxy" can be defined independently of Rome's infallible tradition, without showing how — i.e., without showing why a bad hermeneutic (like that of Arius or Nestorius) is "bad."

Nor will it help to assert that even if Rome's teaching is unified, this has not insured a well-catechized, biblically-literate, informed unity among her members *in practice*. Such unity is a practical goal, and a very important one, as the pontificate of Pope John Paul II has stressed by its production of a magisterial new *Catechism* and steady output of doctrinally intensive encyclicals, such as the magnificent *Veritatis Splendor*. However, the relative success of securing unanimous informed assent to official Church teaching among 1,000,000,000 Catholics, besides being an exhilarating challenge, is a practical ideal, not a theoretical criterion by which to adjudicate doctrinal differences. Hence, it is those who try to turn the charge of doctrinal chaos back on Rome, at this point, who conflate "theory" with "practice," not their opponents.[136] For in the case of Rome, the disunity is a matter of practice (the disobedience or ignorance of some Catholics), while in the case of Protestantism, it is a matter of theory (the conflict of denominationally distinctive doctrines). Even apart from this fact, the charge of Catholic disunity does nothing to rebut the charge of doctrinal disunity and factionalism among Protestants.[137]

Nor does it help to argue that "orthodox Protestant 'denominations,' though there be many, do not differ much more significantly than do the various 'orders' (such as Dominicans, Franciscans, and Jesuits) and factions of the Roman Catholic Church" (Geisler and MacKenzie, 193). First, the delimiting reference to "orthodox" Prot-

---

[136] Accordingly, James White is mistaken when he suggests that the Roman apologist's charge of Protestant chaos is "inconsistent" and self-refuting because Rome "has not brought about the desired unity even among Roman Catholics" (*Rome*, 89f.), as well as Godfrey, when he draws the same fallacious inference (in *SS*, 21f.).

[137] A related objection is that even if Rome has an infallible magisterium, its teaching is still subject to fallible interpretation (White, *Roman*, 91). This is true, but the magisterium's teaching is also subject to possible future *infallible* interpretation. Each infallible magisterial definition progressively clarifies the body of Church teaching through history so that there is a clear advantage to having authoritative interpretation, even if, by its very nature, all interpretation leaves a measure of indeterminate meaning. Cf. my earlier discussion of this argument in connection with *sola scriptura's* violation of the principle of sufficient reason.

estant denominations begs the question, since the definition of "orthodoxy" is what is at issue. Second, Catholic religious orders differ from Protestant denominations precisely in their collective submission to the singular teaching authority of Rome, whereas each Protestant denomination represents an autonomous teaching authority subject only to (its own interpretation of) Scripture. Precisely because of this, the Catholic has a point of reference for distinguishing between more or less "orthodox" Protestant denominations, as well as more or less orthodox Catholics; but what common point of reference do the Protestant denominations have for making such a judgment? It cannot be the Bible, because that falls back again upon their respective interpretations. Accordingly, they lack any mutual standard by which to evaluate one another's "orthodoxy" at those points in which they differ, so that either these points must be dismissed as "unessential" matters, or else it must be admitted that on significant points of difference Protestants lack a common definition of what is "orthodox." Third, the reference to Catholic "factions" confuses the matter by introducing individuals or groups that dissent from *official* Catholic teaching, as we have seen.

Nor will it help, finally, to concede that denominational differences are a result of the fact that people are "sinful" and "fallible."[138] First, this is certainly no justification for the doctrinal disunity and conflict that exist between Protestant denominations, or for the Protestants who broke from Rome. If anything, it should serve as a spur to overcome disunity by working out areas of difference. Second, sometimes it is assumed that by locating the cause of Protestant doctrinal disunity in sin, fallibility, or human finitude, that it will be possible to acquit the principle of *sola scriptura* itself of any culpability in the matter.[139] However, this involves what logicians call a genetic fallacy. The identification of the cause of doctrinal disunity here (sin, fallibility or finitude) implies nothing about the truth or falsehood of *sola scriptura*; unless it is that, as one of those beliefs that divide us, *it* may be the result of sin, fallibility or finitude. Indeed, Catholicism is on record as condemning private

[138] White, *Roman*, 51, 91.

[139] See the discussion of J. I. Packer's argument above, n. 134.

interpretation of Scripture as sin. Third, the claim that "people are fallible" is itself one of the questions at issue. For it is the Catholic claim that there are certain conditions under which not all people are fallible. Jesus was a man who was infallible in his teaching because he was divine. The Apostles Paul, Peter, Matthew, Mark, John, and the other NT writers were not fallible while writing Scripture. And it is a Catholic claim that those serving in the ongoing teaching office of the Church are likewise protected by the infallible guidance of the Holy Spirit from error in their continuing task of clarifying and defining the apostolic deposit of faith.

C. The Undermining of Pastoral Authority and Discipline

Finally, *sola scriptura* effectively undermines pastoral authority and discipline. Scripture plainly teaches that Christians are to submit to their spiritual leaders (Heb 13:17). Protestants recognize this and concur. They also recognize the need to beware of false prophets (Mt 7:15) and, therefore, the need to test everything (1 Th 5:21) to make sure it is of God. Hence, spiritual leaders must be obeyed only insofar as their instruction agrees with God's will. There is nothing wrong with this reasoning. Catholics would agree. No serious Catholic would believe a priest who claimed it was permissible to have an extramarital affair. Thus, it is not only appropriate, but it is one's duty, to test the teaching he receives against things otherwise known to be true.[140] The question is: How does one know whether his religious leaders agree with God? The Protestant's answer of *sola scriptura* is insufficient at this point, because the interpretive autonomy and individualism it permits, as well as the profusion of conflicting interpretations it has fostered historically, run into unavoidable conflict with one of the funda-

[140] Protestants often point to the Bereans, who "searched the Scriptures daily to see if these things were so" (Acts 17:11), as supporting *sola scriptura*. However, they were checking Paul's new revelation against previous revelation, not *deriving* his teaching from the OT, which would have been impossible. The passage supports the common practice of checking new data against what is already known, not *sola scriptura*. (See chapter 3 by R. Sungenis in this volume for a more detailed discussion of Acts 17.)

mental functions of Church authority, which is to settle matters of doctrinal dispute (e.g., Acts 15).[141]

Here the Protestant finds himself on the horns of a dilemma. What does he do if his beliefs conflict with those of his denomination? Does he go looking for one that agrees with *him*? Does he start his own? Such options would indeed open a Pandora's box full of abuses. But "abuses" by *whose* standards? His? His denomination's? What does it mean for *him* to "submit" to his spiritual leaders? Clearly the Bible enjoins him to do so. But to which leaders? And what does it mean for him to *submit*, if his spiritual leaders are to gain his submission only in so far as their leadership and teaching agree with (his own interpretation of) Scripture? What would we think of someone who said: "I will accept and respect the words of Jesus and follow them whenever I agree with them"? The question, of course, is: How do we know whether *these spiritual* leaders are instructing us as Jesus intended? But the effect of this question is logically the same as the previous one. It likewise redounds back upon the private judgment of the individual Protestant. In principle, the problem is one of logical circularity. In practice, if Protestant beliefs do not seem so utterly arbitrary as might be thought possible, this is due to a variety of historical and traditional restraints that ameliorate the viciousness of their circular reasoning, usually in inverse proportion to their denomination's historical drift and distance from its sources in Catholic tradition.

---

[141] This is especially true in contemporary moral doctrine. Scripture *alone* does not give definitive answers to every question concerning contraception, self-induced orgasm, in-vitro fertilization, surrogate motherhood, genetic engineering, cloning, and a host of other modern questions that have arisen in the fields of medical ethics, legal ethics, business ethics, social theory, economic theory, political theory, etc. How, then, do Protestant Christians truly know if they are truly glorifying God in what they do? Either they must proceed on the basis of their best individual insights, hunches, and speculative "deductions" from Scripture, or they must trust their pastors or denominational leaders to do the same for them, realizing in either case that their own prayerfully-reached conclusions are contradicted by other, equally-prayerful Protestants, equally trusting God to guide them. See "Point/Counterpoint: Protestant Objections and Catholic Answers" by R. Sungenis in chapter 5 of this volume for more discussion on this issue.

But in principle the circle is vicious, and this poses a tremendous theoretical problem for the Protestant.

For example, what if one's denomination decides to accept the ordination of women and actually installs a woman as a pastor, in the face of protests from individual members (based on 1 Tim 2:12 and 1 Cor 14:34) that the Bible does not allow women to be pastors? He might be told that a denominational study commission has determined that these texts apply only to the temporary situation in the first century and are no longer binding today; that the commission's interpretation makes sense historically, is not ruled out by any clear teachings of Scripture, and is supported by other passages, such as Paul's statement that in Christ "there is neither male nor female" (Gal 3:28); and that, since the commission's findings have been approved by the denomination's authorities, he ought to defer to his spiritual leaders (on the basis of Heb 13:17) in the interest of unity. His pastor might tell him: "You have to trust that God leads through the elders. We'd like you to understand and agree with our reasons — and I encourage you to continue to study — but we're not always going to see eye to eye. That's why God put leaders in the church. Otherwise we'd just have a mess with everybody doing their own thing."[142] Indeed. Need we say more?

What should the Protestant do? If his denomination represents a valid ecclesiastical authority, he should submit. If it does not, he should not. But how does he know? The answer to the question "Which religious authorities are valid?" cannot be "Those whose doctrines are biblical," because that is exactly what is under dispute. It would be as redundant as saying: "The only biblical leaders are those who are biblical." While this is true, it is tautologous and unhelpful; since it offers no guidance in identifying what is "biblical." The Lutherans say that their doctrines are biblical, as do the Methodists, Presbyterians, Pentecostals, Baptists, Nazarenes, Mennonites, Moravians, Plymouth Brethren, Seventh Day Adventists, and Disciples of Christ — and Catholics. "Lord, to whom should we go?"

---

[142] I am indebted to Krehbiel (pp. iv, 17f.) for the foregoing quotation, as well as for the construction of the example of the female pastor, and a number of insights in the following paragraph.

In the final analysis, there would seem to be no more than two alternatives: either we are left with nothing but personal opinion, illumined as it may or may not be by private interpretations of others — which means it comes down to this: every man for himself, interpreting Scripture as best he can and joining whatever group or denomination agrees most closely with his personal understandings; ***or*** God has established some kind of identifiable authority, with a promise of protection against error, to guide the Church — so that we may trust that the religious authority to whom we defer is delegated by Christ in the same manner as those to whom He said "He who hears you hears me" (Lk 10:16), permitting us to reply to this authority with Peter's words: "You have the words of eternal life" (Jn 6:68).

The problem stems from ecclesiology. In brief, it is this. Traditionally there have always been two meanings subsumed under the single term "Church." On the one hand, the Church is the *submissive recipient* (Latin: *ecclesia discens*)of God's grace and His Revelation; the Bride of Christ, willingly subordinating herself to His authority and will, obedient to His law, and subject to the message of Scripture. On the other hand, it is the *authoritative administrator* (Latin: *ecclesia docens*)of God's will and His law, the divinely-commissioned mediator of His grace through Word and Sacrament, dispensing justice through church discipline; the authorized teacher and interpreter of His revealed will and guardian of the meaning of Scripture.

Protestants have little trouble seeing themselves (and even "born-again" Catholics) as belonging to the "Church" in the first sense. However, they run into problems with their theory (*sola scriptura*) and their practice (*denominationalism*) when considering the second option. They typically balk at the thought of identifying *any* historical institution with the "Church" in the second sense; unless, with due modesty, it is their *own* denomination — but then usually only in a provisional and etiolated sense. While they clearly recognize themselves as recipients of God's grace and as desiring to submit to His authority, their theory and practice nudge them towards two, conflicting — equally unattractive — conclusions about how that authority is mediated. Their *theory* (*sola scriptura*) inclines them to deny the existence of any particular earthly institution that is uniquely-authorized to interpret God's Word and administer His sacramental grace and moral discipline; while their *practice* (denominationalism) inclines them to presume, against all modesty and with abiding fear of embarrassment, that this awesome office is borne, in some manner, by their own particular denomination.[143] Needless to say, the position is an awkward one for a denominationalist. The first conclusion leans towards the abyss of relativistic subjectivism, while the second leans toward specious presumption, with the fear that one may be caught in the compromising position of merely play-acting at submitting to real authority.

This has led to a pattern of ambivalence and equivocation in Protestant statements about ecclesiastical authority. The following are a couple of typical examples: (1) "Calvin does not dismiss the role of the authority of the church. That authority, however, must be subservient to the Scriptures"; and (2) "For we also say that the church is the interpreter of Scripture, and that the gift of interpretation resides only in the church: but we deny that it pertains to particular persons, or is tied to any particular see or succession of men."[144] Each statement concedes that the Church has authority. The second even concedes that the gift of interpreting Scripture resides *only* in the Church. But then this power or authority of the Church is immediately qualified in such a manner as to annul it as an effective reality, and ultimately puts it in direct opposition to the autonomy of the individual interpreter of Scripture. The *appeal* is to the primacy of Scripture, but in reality the Church is made subservient to the biblical interpretations of particular individuals or denominations. The statements look like classic cases of trying to eat one's cake and have it too. Newman noted this equivocation among his contemporary English evangelicals, when he described them as "safe" men who could guide Protes-

---

[143] I am reminded of a meeting of the American Catholic Association in Philadelphia about fifteen years ago, at which Alvin Plantinga, a good-humored member of the small (Dutch) Christian Reformed denomination, began his lecture by inviting any disgruntled Catholics to meet with him afterwards who might be interested in returning to the "Mother Church"!

[144] #1 is from Geisler and MacKenzie, 179; #2 is from William Whitaker's *A Disputation on Holy Scripture* (1849), quoted by Godfrey, in *SS*, 3.

tants "through the channel of no-meaning, between the Scylla and Charybdis of Aye and No."[145]

Why is it important for the advocate of *sola scriptura* to also affirm ecclesiastical authority? Because if the Church has no authority, there is no discipline. There is ecclesiastical anarchy. In his heart, the Protestant knows this. He knows, implicitly, that if the Church has no real authority, then she has no privileged interpretation of Scripture; and if she lacks that, she has no special privilege by which to settle doctrinal disputes; and if she lacks that, she has no effective discipline. Implicitly knowing this, the Protestant has no choice but to continually equivocate, now asserting his right of private judgment, now asserting his duty of deference to those in religious authority, ever trying to keep his balance between preserving his autonomy of opinion and his toehold on some fragment of ecclesiastical authority — for ballast — even if it is only a provisional pretense.

Given their commitment to *sola scriptura*, it is interesting to see how far Protestants will bend over backwards, at times, to affirm their commitment to ecclesiastical authority. At times, their statements, if taken in isolation, can sound almost Catholic. For example, James White declares:

> Sola scriptura is not a denial of the authority of the Church to teach God's truth... the individual priesthood of the believer does not mean there is no Church. It does not mean there are no pastors and teachers. It does not... do away with the biblically based authority of elders to teach and train and rebuke, nor does it give license to anybody and everybody to go out and start some new movement based on their own 'take' on things. While this may happen, it is an *abuse* of the doctrine, not an *application* of it.[146]

While he is discussing the priesthood of all believers in the quote, the point White is making applies no less to *sola scriptura*. The relevant question at this point would be: How does a legiti-

---

[145] John Henry Cardinal Newman, *Apologia Pro Vita Sua*, ed. David J. DeLaura (1864; rpt. New York: Norton, 1968), 88.

[146] White, *Roman*, 57, 52f.

mate "application" of *sola scriptura*, as opposed to an "abuse" of it, allow the Church to exercise her real authority over Protestants, to teach, train, rebuke, and prevent them from going out to start some new movement based on their own "take" on things? How can the Church have any real authority if the final authority is Scripture alone? Over against the perceived threat of interpretive anarchy implicit in *sola scriptura,* Protestants quite rightly sense the need for Church authority and the ballast of tradition. But they undermine this authority and this ballast by insisting that the Church and tradition are infallible only when they are truly "biblical"; or, as Armstrong puts it, "only when the church speaks biblically is its authority absolute."[147] The problem is that Scripture and tradition require authoritative interpretation. Protestants are often quick to humbly deny that they have any special authority in themselves, since Scripture *alone* (they insist) is their ultimate authority. But they just as often end up *tacitly* claiming and exercising — either individually or denominationally — the prerogatives of the very kind of infallible authority they condemn the Catholic Church for *explicitly* claiming, despite the fact that they lack the apostolic credentials that the Church possesses.

The Venerable Cardinal Newman's summary of "Evangelical Religion" is, if anything, as apt a description of our muddled world of contemporary American Protestantism as it was of English evangelicalism a century ago. He writes:

> It has no straightforward view on any one point, on which it professes to teach, and to hide its poverty, it has dressed itself out in a maze of words... It does not stand on intrenched ground, or make any pretense to a position; it does but occupy a space between contending powers... Then indeed will be the stern encounter, when two real and living principles, simple, entire, and consistent, one in the Church, the other out of it, at length rush upon each other, contending not for names and words, or half-views, but for elementary notions and distinctive moral characters.

[147] Armstrong, in *SS*, 116; cf. 146.

> In the present day... mistiness is the mother of wisdom. A man who can set down a half-a-dozen general propositions, which escape from destroying one another only by being diluted into truisms, who can hold the balance between opposites so skillfully as to do without fulcrum or beam, who never enunciates a truth without guarding himself against being supposed to exclude the contradictory, — *who holds that Scripture is the only authority, yet that the Church is to be deferred to,* that faith only justifies, yet that it does not justify without works... — this is your safe man...; this is what the Church is said to want, not party men, but sensible, temperate, sober, well-judging persons, to guide it through the channel of no-meaning, between the Scylla and Charybdis of Aye and No.[148]

Conclusion

Sola scriptura is a philosophically incoherent and practically disastrous tradition of men. It is intellectually untenable, unbiblical, unhistorical, and the mother of ecclesiastical chaos. It has cut Protestantism off from its moorings in historic Christianity, and left it reeling in the capricious and devastating winds of doctrine that have swept across the last five centuries. It is one of the tragedies of the Reformation, not one of its necessities. By contrast, all the good and true and necessary things of the Protestant experience — above all, the clarion call to personal conversion to Jesus Christ — can be preserved and exercised to full effect only by being reestablished firmly upon the foundation that Christ laid for the ongoing instruction and life of His people, and that is the authority He delegated and continues to entrust to our Homeland's Embassy on earth: the Rock of St. Peter and the apostles united with him, and their delegated successors, the Pope and bishops united with him in the Catholic Church.

---

[148] Newman, *Apologia*, 88; emphasis mine.

Chapter 3

Does Scripture Teach *Sola Scriptura*?

By Robert Sungenis

All Scripture is Inspired and Profitable — 2 Timothy 3:16-17

"All Scripture is inspired and profitable for teaching, for reproof, for correction, for instruction in righteousness, in order that the man of God may be fit, fully equipped for every good work." [1]

2 Timothy 3:16-17 is used by both Protestant scholar and layman to support the notion of *sola scriptura*. When asked where Scripture teaches that it is the sole or final authority, Protestants commonly begin by quoting the first portion of 2 Timothy 3:16, "All Scripture is given by inspiration of God..." By focusing on the word *inspiration*, they imply that the Bible is the Christian's sole or final authority. Their underlying premise is that Scripture is the only truth that is divinely inspired, therefore it can and must be our only divine authority.

---

1 Commenting on 2 Timothy 3:16-17, Vatican II declared in Dei Verbum 11: "...we must acknowledge that the books of Scripture, firmly, faithfully and without error, teach that truth which God, for the sake of our salvation, wished to see confided to the sacred Scriptures." (Cf., St. Augustine, Gen. ad Litt., 2, 9, 20: PL 34, 270-271; Epist. 82, 3: PL 33, 277; CSEL 34, 2, p. 354. — St. Thomas. De Ver. Q. 12, a. 2, C. — Council of Trent, Session IV, de canonicis Scripturis: Denz. 783 (1501) — Leo XIII, Encycl. Providentissimus: EB 121, 124, 126-127. — Pius XII, Encycl. Divino Afflante: EB 539.

Some theologians may have an even more detailed argument. They will appeal to the words "fully equipped"[2] in 2 Timothy 3:17, claiming that since the word of God completely equips the Christian, therefore, Scripture is *sufficient,* in and of itself, to be the final rule for the Christian life and is not dependent on tradition or ecclesial authority.

In order to answer these arguments, a few preliminary remarks will be helpful. First, when we closely examine the few verses that Protestants have collected which they claim support the concept of *sola scriptura*, we find that such texts merely extol the unique *quality* of Scripture but are passed off as dogmatic proof for *sola scriptura*, 2 Timothy 3:16-17 being no exception. We can understand why this is so. Since Scripture contains no explicit statement that teaches that Scripture is the sole or final authority, Protestants have no choice but to appeal to texts that were never intended to support such a notion. We will show by examining both the context of 2 Timothy 2-3 and the specific words Paul uses in 2 Timothy 3:16-17, that drawing out a doctrine of *sola scriptura* from this passage is at best unprovable, and at worst, a gross distortion both of Scripture and of biblical hermeneutics in general.

An Analysis of Paul's Terminology in 2 Timothy 3:16-17

In appealing to 2 Timothy 3:16-17 to support *sola scriptura*, Protestant theologians draw our attention to Paul's use of the Greek noun *artios* ("fit") and the participle *exartismenos* ("fully equipped") in verse 17.[3] Since some lexicons include *sufficient* as

[2] 2 Timothy 3:17 reads: ἵνα ἄρτιος ᾖ ὁ τοῦ θεοῦ ἄνθρωπος πρὸς πᾶν ἔργον ἀγαθὸν ἐξηρτισμένος. A more literal reading would be "in order that the man of God may be fit, having been fully equipped for every good work." The word "fit" stands for the Greek noun ἄρτιος while "fully equipped" for the appositional perfect passive participle, ἐξηρτισμένος. These words appear in a Greek *purpose clause*, introduced by the word ἵνα, denoting that the purpose of God-inspired Scripture is to make one "fit" and "fully equipped" for every good work.

[3] One of the more detailed attempts at exegeting 2 Timothy 3:16-17 appears in *Roman Catholics and Evangelicals: Agreements and Differences* by N. Geisler and R. MacKenzie (Grand Rapids: Baker Books, 1995) pp. 184-185; *The Roman Catholic Controversy* by James R. White (Bethany House, 1996), pp. 63-67, and *Sola Scriptura: The Protestant Position on the Bible* (Soli Deo Gloria Publications, 1995) ed. Don Kistler, in "What Do We Mean By Sola Scriptura" by W. Robert Godfrey, pp. 1-26.

one of the meanings of the two words, many conclude that 2 Timothy 3:17 teaches Scripture is *sufficient*, in and of itself, to stand as the Christian's only or final rule of faith, in need of no other source of divine revelation to supplement it, nor an infallible authority to interpret it. To begin our critique, we will first do a grammatical study on the words used in 2 Timothy 3:16-17.

The Lexical Derivatives of *Artios* and *Exartismenos*

Greek lexicons are somewhat varied in their definition of both *artios* and *exartismenos*. Standard lexical works authored by such prestigious names as Walter Bauer, Liddell and Scott, Ardt and Gingrich, and Louw and Nida contain a range of meanings from "fit" and "capable" to "complete" or "perfect"[4] The definitions of "fit," "capable," or "ready" show a preparedness to accomplish a given task but do not guarantee the outcome. The definitions of "complete" and "perfect" speak more to the expected result. Suffice it to say that, coupled with the very infrequent usage of these words in both classical and Koine Greek, the variations in meaning suggests that the understanding and application of the words will depend heavily upon the context in which they are placed. We will investigate this dimension of our study momentarily.

Observing Paul's play on words further helps us to understand the use of *artios* and *exartismenos* in 2 Timothy 3:17. The adjective *artios* and the perfect passive participle *exartismenos* derive from the same verb *artidzo*. The prefix *ex* (from the Greek εξ) puts a perfective force on *exartismenos*, which denotes the meaning of "altogether" or "fully." In a somewhat repetitive way Paul describes the kind of man he envisions (a fit or capable man), and then explains the result of that capability (he is now fully equipped for every good work).

4 Liddell and Scott define ἄρτιος as: (1) "complete, perfect of its kind, exactly fitted" (2) "active, quick, ready." It defines ἐξαρτίζω as "to complete, finish, to be completely furnished" (Abridged version, Oxford, Clarendon Press, 1977) pp. 105, 233. Walter Bauer defines ἄρτιος (as "complete, capable, proficient=able to meet all demands." He defines ἐξαρτίζω as: (1) "finish, complete" and (2) "equip, furnish." (2nd edition, revised by Gingrich and Danker, University of Chicago Press, Chicago and London, 1957, 1979), pp. 110, 273.

The New Testament uses *artios* only here in 2 Timothy 3:17, while it uses *exartidzo* (from which *exartismenos* is derived) twice, the other occurrence appearing in Acts 21:5 in the infinitive form, normally translated as "accomplished" or "ended" ("But when those days were ended, we departed and went our way..."). In the Septuagint *exartidzo* appears only in Exodus 28:7 where it is translated as "fastened," and *artios* appears only once, as a temporal adverb in 2 Samuel 15:34, translated as "until now." *Artios* and its derivatives come from the root *ar*, which means "appropriateness, suitability, usefulness, aptitude."[5] The cognate *katartidzo*, its oldest derivative in classical Greek, means "to put in order, restore, furnish, prepare, equip." These various meanings have a common origin in the basic concept "to make suitable, fitting." The Septuagint uses *katartidzo* 19 times, standing for no less than 9 different Hebrew words, e.g., in the sense of "complete" (Ezra 4:12), "to set up, establish" (Psalm 74:16), "to hold fast" (Psalm 17:5), "God's equipping" (Psalm 40:6), "to restore" (Psalm 68:9). *Katartidzo* is also used in the New Testament as "repair" (Matthew 4:21), "prepare" (Hebrews 10:5), "to establish," "to form" (Hebrews 11:3), "to equip" (1 Peter 5:10). From these various meanings and contexts, we understand Paul to teach that Scripture prepares the man of God to function properly — his function being to do "every good work."[6]

Artios and *Exartismenos* as Used in Context

One of the most important points about 2 Timothy 3:16-17 for the present discussion on *sola scriptura* is that neither the adjec-

---

5 *Dictionary of New Testament Theology*, editor, Colin Brown, Vol. III, 4th printing, Zondervan, 1979), p. 349.

6 Commenting on these varied meanings, the *Dictionary of New Testament Theology* states: "*artios* here does not imply perfection, as was originally thought, doubtless because of the variant reading *teleios*, perfect, in Codex D. Rather it refers to the state of being equipped for a delegated task. So too, in Eph. 4:12 *katartismos* refers to the preparation of the church for becoming perfect, but not to this perfection itself, as can be seen from the use of *teleios* (complete, mature; → Goal), *helikia* (stature; → Age, Stature), and *pleroma* (→ fulness) in v. 13 (cf. Also 1 Cor. 1:10). The terms *artios* and *katartismos* thus have not so much a qualitative meaning as a functional one" (Ibid., p. 350).

tive *artios* nor the participle *exartismenos* is describing "Scripture"; rather, they are both describing the "man of God." However strong the definition one assigns to *artios* or *exartismenos*, support for a doctrine of *sola scriptura* is limited by the fact that Paul does not say *Scripture* is "perfect" or "complete" to accomplish the task at hand. In their interpretation of 2 Timothy 3:16-17, some Protestant theologians make an unwarranted exegetical leap by assigning the concept of sufficiency to Scripture, although Paul never said this. Yet others who realize such a leap is unjustified will nevertheless argue that if opponents insist that only the "man of God" is perfectly equipped, does not this imply Scripture is the perfect equipper? Let us focus on this specific question.

First, as noted earlier, one cannot prove that the only or even primary meaning of *artios* or *artidzo* is "perfect" or "sufficient." There are many other words Paul could have used to denote the concept of perfection or absolute sufficiency which he obviously did not use in the context of 2 Timothy 3. Moreover, the specific meanings of these words are conditioned, or are relative to, the context in which they are contained. We will speak on both of these points shortly. Second, while in verse 17 Paul uses the adjective *artios* and the participle *exartismenos* to describe the "man of God," he uses a much weaker word, *ophelimos* ("profitable"), in verse 16 to describe Scripture. *Ophelimos* means "helpful, beneficial, useful, advantageous."[7] It is not a word that connotes solitary sufficiency and certainly nothing close to the absolute or formal sufficiency that Protestants must assign to Scripture to support the doctrine of *sola scriptura*. In fact, there is an implied insufficiency or

---

7 Greek: ὠφέλιμος. Bauer's lexicon defines it as: "useful, beneficial, advantageous, what is particularly helpful" (op. cit., p. 900). The adjectival form ὠφέλιμος (appears in two other places in the New Testament, e.g., "for physical training is of *some value*" (1 Tim. 4:8) and "these things are excellent and *profitable* for everyone" (Titus 3:8). The verbal form ὠφελέω appears 16 times, denoting the concept of "profitability" or "value," e.g., Rom. 2:25; 1 Cor. 13:3; Gal. 5:2; Heb. 4:2. The noun form ὠφέλεια appears twice, once translated as "advantage" in Jude 16. If Paul wanted to teach the sufficiency of Scripture, he could have used a word such as αὐταρκεία, which is lexically defined as "the state of one who supports himself without aid from others; contentment, self-sufficiency" (Bauer, op. cit., p. 122).

limitation in *ophelimos*. If Scripture is merely "profitable" in order to make the "man of God" perfect or complete, this implies that there are other things that have brought him to a near perfect or complete state while or before Scripture is being administered to him. Scripture may be considered a crucial or final ingredient that the man of God needs in order to complete his training or make him perfect, but not the only ingredient. Other sources have prodded him along the way and now that he is about to face a more difficult task (as is implied in Paul's closing words to Timothy in 2 Timothy 4:1-5), he must learn how to apply Scripture more fervently to his task of doing every good work. By using all the ingredients, including Scripture, he will be a perfect man, able to accomplish any spiritual task set before him.

Ophelimos is certainly not the kind of word one would choose if he desired to teach that Scripture is the ***only*** means to perform the task at hand. If Paul had used a play on words on this order: "All Scripture is inspired of God and sufficient to make a sufficiently equipped man of God" then perhaps a case could be initiated for the ultimate sufficiency of Scripture. Instead, Paul's deliberate use of the fractional word "profitable" indicates he may have had more than Scripture in mind to accomplish the task of making Timothy a fit man of God equipped to do every good work. And we must add, that since 2 Timothy 3:16-17 is one of the only places Paul specifically describes the nature, purpose, and effect of Scripture in his epistles, this context was the perfect opportunity to make the exclusive use of Scripture, either then or in the future, very clear to Timothy, if indeed that concept was in his thoughts.

To show the intent of Paul's description of Scripture as profitable, a simple analogy from Scripture will help illustrate the point. In Ephesians 6:10 Paul instructs Christians to "Put on the full armor of God so that you can stand against the devil's schemes." Included in the full armor is "the belt of truth," the "breastplate of righteousness," the "feet fitted with readiness," the "shield of faith," the "helmet of salvation," and the "sword of the Spirit which is the word of God" (Ephesians 6:11-18). We notice here that Paul includes many aspects of the Christian walk in making one prepared to fight evil (the same evil Paul instructs Timothy to fight in 2 Timothy 2-4), e.g., truth, righteousness, readiness, faith, salvation and the word of God. We also notice that Paul considers the "word of God" but one of many components of the "full armor" of God. The "full armor" of Ephesians 6:11 is analogous to being "fully equipped" in 2 Timothy 3:17. Finally, Paul adds prayer to the list of items to ward off the devil as he says, "Pray also for me, that whenever I open my mouth, words may be given me so that I will fearlessly make known the mystery of the gospel" (Eph. 6:19).

We see from this analogy that Paul intends his message to reveal ***all*** the things necessary to teach and defend the gospel and lead a good and wholesome Christian life, not to give a lesson on using only Scripture. Even if we were to allow the definition of "sufficiency" for the sake of argument, one cannot presume that a sufficiently equipped man has been made that way only by Scripture. Certainly Scripture plays a large part in his equipping, but Paul does not tout it as the *only* source to help in this process, nor a source that will automatically do so.

The General Context of 2 Timothy 3:16-17

In 2 Timothy 3:16, Paul states that Scripture is profitable for "teaching, for reproof, for correction, and training in righteousness." It goes without saying that the reason Scripture can be so beneficial in producing such virtuous results and tools for teaching is that it contains God's inspired truth. In the context that Paul gives us, however, we notice that he is not at all interested in setting up a contest between Scripture and oral tradition, or Scripture and church authority, or addressing whether Scripture is the only authority. We insist that since Paul develops no such contests between competing authorities in the context, using 2 Timothy 3:16-17 as a proof text for *sola scriptura* is simply begging the question. Paul is interested in demonstrating only that inspired Scripture is a profitable means of equipping the man of God for good works; he is not trying to present a treatise on epistemology and revelation.

Scripture certainly provides the raw data that helps in making a "fit" or "fully equipped" man of God to do every good work. Even then, as the history of Protestant biblical interpretation has shown, "men of God" in each denomination have their own view of how Scripture can be interpreted to teach, reprove, correct and train for righteousness, so that, in being exposed to the multitudinous interpretations of Scripture, one can never be sure he has correctly understood the teaching of Scripture at all. Hence, at least the *result* of Scripture study can hardly be considered "sufficient" as the rule of the Christian life. To avoid this confusion, God works in many other ways that will be profitable in making a "fit man, equipped for every good work." As we shall see shortly, Paul mentions these instruments in the context of 2 Timothy 2-3, e.g., a virtuous Christian life, knowledgeable and trustworthy teachers to explain Christian truths on faith and morals, oral tradition, infallible guidance of the Holy Spirit, saintly models, prayer and meditation.

In 2 Timothy 2:21 we see that there are means other than the inspired written word to accomplish the goal of making a "fit and fully equipped man of God." Paul says, "...If a man cleanses himself from the latter, he will be an instrument for noble purposes, made holy, *useful* to the Master and *prepared to do every good work.*" Here Paul specifies one of the primary ingredients needed to make a "useful" man of God, namely, the cleansing away of bad influences and behavior. What is most interesting in this passage (and thus helpful in understanding his meaning in 2 Timothy 3:16-17), is the phrase "every good work" in 2 Timothy 2:21. It is the identical Greek phrase used in 2 Timothy 3:17.[8] Hence, we notice that the end result in 2 Timothy 2:21 is the same as in 2 Timothy 3:17, that is, to make a "*fit*" or "*useful*" man so that he is "*prepared*[9] *to do every good work.*" Both verses are looking to the same

---

[8] The Greek phrase is πᾶν ἔργον ἀγαθὸν, used, without variation, in both 2 Timothy 2:21 and 2 Timothy 3:17.

[9] "Prepared" is the Greek perfect passive participle ἡτοιμασμένον, from ἑτοιμάζω, appearing over 40 times in the New Testament and understood as "ready" or "prepared." It has the same semantic range as the root *artidzo* (αρτίζω) in 2 Timothy 3:17. It can refer to an ordinary preparation or a superlative divine preparation (cf., Matt. 20:23; 22:4; 1 Cor. 2:9). On this issue we beg to differ with Protestant James R. White who claims that there is no relation between the two. He states: "The term "prepared" is not *artios* or *exartizo* (as in 2 Timothy 3:16). It is a term that differs markedly in its semantic domain and meaning: ἑτοιμάζω (hetoimazo), which specifically speaks of making preparation, of becoming prepared and ready" (*The Roman Catholic Controversy*, p. 240). We reply that obviously *hetoimazo* refers to preparedness. The issue,

goal yet have different sources from which to draw. If we were to use the concept of "sufficiency" that Protestants force into 2 Timothy 3:17, we could claim, in light of the similar language in 2 Timothy 2:21, that refraining from bad influences and behavior is ***all*** that is needed to make a man useful for every good work. However, knowing Paul's goal from the general context and his liberal use of language, we are confident that he does not mean that only avoiding bad influences will make one "useful for every good work." Good conduct is a profitable means but not the only means. A Christian man depends on many things, both from within and without himself, to make him a vessel of honor suitable to his Master.[10]

Paul uses the phrase, "every good work" six other times in his epistles.[11] As in the context of 2 Timothy 2-3, these verses shed much light on how we are to understand Paul's meaning in 2 Timothy 3:16-17. For example, in 2 Corinthians 9:8 Paul says, "God is able to make all grace abound toward you in order that always

---

[9 cont.] however, is the *degree* of preparedness, whether perfect or imperfect, and thus the word contains the same range of applicability as *artios*, which can refer on the lesser side to being "fit" but on the stronger side to being "perfect." White also attempts to dismiss using 2 Timothy 2:21 because it is not speaking about the "source of the man of God's ability to engage in the work" but "of sanctification in the person's life." By forcing this dichotomy into the discussion, White makes it appear as if "sanctification" cannot be considered a "source" from which the man of God can draw in order to do "every good work." White conveniently confines "source" to revelatory dimensions and thereby misses the whole point of Paul's contextual argument — an argument designed not to single out or make exclusive revelatory sources but to direct Timothy to *whatever* will help him become the man of God he desires to be and to teach others to do the same.

10 The epistle of James also uses similar language. James says in 1:4, "*Perseverance must finish its work so that you may be mature and complete, not lacking in anything.*" One could not conclude from this verse that "perseverance" is all that is needed to make one mature and complete. "Perseverance" is the final or crucial virtue that "completes" each one of the "testings" (1:2-3) that come upon the Christian, but perseverance, in itself, is not what makes one mature and complete.

11 πᾶν ἔργον ἀγαθὸν (2 Cor. 9:8; Col. 1:10; 2 Thess. 2:17; 1 Tim. 5:10; Tit. 1:16; 3:1; cf., Heb. 13:21). The phrase itself is ambiguous as to what it specifically refers, but it would appear from the general context that it includes both practice and doctrine (cf., 2 Tim. 2:22f; 4:2-5; 1 Tim. 4:16).

having all sufficiency in everything, you may abound in *every good work*." Here the same goal of preparing the individual for "every good work" is evident. Although the passage does not refer to Scripture, it contains language that *sola scriptura* advocates would be most happy to see associated with Scripture (i.e., "always having all sufficiency[12] in everything"). It is the "grace" of God, not Scripture, however, that makes the person all sufficient in everything.[13] But God's grace is manifold, coming through his Spirit in an array of dimensions, e.g., love, faith, knowledge, encouragement, energy, zeal, wisdom, etc., that equips one for every good work. Scripture is but one of these graces, and, as is obvious from our own reading of 2 Corinthians 9:8 above, Scripture informs us that God makes us sufficient through his graces, but Scripture itself is not the sufficient source for every good work.

In 2 Thess. 2:16-17, Paul similarly connects God's grace with the ability to do "every good work." He writes, "God, our Father, has loved us and given us eternal comfort and good hope by grace; may he comfort your hearts and strengthen you in every good work and word." Here again it is God's grace that comforts and strengthens the individual for every good work. This comfort and strength comes not only from reading Scripture, but through the inner working of God's grace in the soul of the individual. It is the peace of God, evoked by his response to our prayer, that guards the hearts and thoughts of those who seek him, or the terror of God that afflicts with madness and confusion of mind.[14]

As Paul moves on in his letter to Timothy, we notice that his chief concern is that Timothy not be weakened in his faith through the influence of corrupt men who pass themselves off as spiritual.

---

12 "Sufficiency," from the Greek αὐταρκεία, used only one other time in the New Testament (1 Tim. 6:6), is lexically defined as "the state of one who supports himself without aid from others; contentment, self-sufficiency" (Bauer, op. cit., p. 122). A similar word is ἱκανός which can sometimes be translated as "sufficient" (2 Cor. 2:6, 16; 3:5) or "qualified" or "able" (2 Tim. 2:2); and ἀρκέω which means "sufficient" or "content" (cf., John 14:8; 2 Cor. 12:9; 1 Tim. 6:8), but none of them are used to describe Scripture.

13 The Greek of the passage exhibits a paronomasia on the word πᾶν, using it four times in the verse, showing the superlative ability of God's grace.

14 Cf., Philippians 4:6f; Deut. 28:28.

These men have "a form of godliness but deny the power thereof" (2 Timothy 3:5). Paul also warns Timothy, by citing examples in Paul's own ministry, that he will be persecuted for standing up for the truth. Paul says, "You, however, know all about my teaching, my way of life, my purpose, faith, patience, love, endurance, persecutions, sufferings" (2 Timothy 3:10). Hence, one of the main sources from which Timothy can draw in order to help him remain faithful to God is by recalling Paul's "teaching," and also by modeling himself after Paul's "way of life." Paul continues and says, "But as for you, continue in what you have learned and become convinced of, because you know those from whom you learned it..." (2 Timothy 3:14). He commands Timothy to "continue in what he has learned," which again refers to Paul's teaching and his model way of life in the midst of persecution. Hence, Paul's teaching and experience are two other sources upon which Timothy can draw to become a "fit man of God" or a "useful vessel to his Master."

Paul also refers to what Timothy has "become convinced of," which shows that Timothy has been thinking and meditating on the teachings, reasoning them out in his mind so that they will help in his efforts to be the fit man of God he desires to be. Thus we have another source for Timothy's quest to be a "fit" or "useful" man, that is, his own reasoning abilities.

Paul assures Timothy of these teachings by saying, "because you know *those* from whom you learned it..." By the use of the plural "those" Paul is referring not only to himself but to other teachers Timothy has had. In fact, Paul makes the effectiveness and veracity of the instruction Timothy received dependent on the fact that Timothy "knows" (i.e., personally trusts) his teachers.

Finally, Paul continues into another source of truth that Timothy has had at his disposal: "...and how from childhood you have known the holy Scriptures, which are able to make you wise for salvation..." In addition to cleansing himself from bad influences, his modeling of Paul, his other teachers and his own reasoning ability, Timothy has the Scriptures which he can study. Even if the conjunctive "and" (Greek: καὶ) were indicating that the oral teaching Timothy received included the Scripture, (which it most likely did), still, the proper study of Scripture includes verbal explanation and elaboration from trusted teachers. Timothy, being in childhood[15] when first introduced to the Scriptures, certainly could not grasp its deep truths by himself, especially since the Old Testament, to which this verse could only apply,[16] contained only the obscure or veiled references to "faith in Jesus Christ" that Paul ascribes to the Old Testament Scriptures in 2 Timothy 3:15. Only a very astute and informed individual could explain the mysteries of "faith in Jesus Christ" from the Old Testament alone, thus proving that knowledgeable teachers are very important in making a fit man of God (cf. Colossians 1:26-27; Luke 24:27; Acts 8:30-35; 1 Peter 1:10-12). Timothy was dependent on his teachers (his grandmother Lois and his mother Eunice in his childhood (2 Timothy 1:5); Paul and other leaders in his adulthood), who could rightly divide the word of truth, to make him a fit man for every good work. In fact, Timothy's use and interpretation of Scripture is dependent on the hermeneutical principles he learned from Paul and other his other teachers.

---

[15] From the Greek word βρέφος, normally understood as (1) unborn child, embryo, or (2) baby, infant (Walter Bauer, *A Greek-English Lexicon of the New Testament and Other Early Christian Literature* (University of Chicago, 1979, 2nd edition) p. 147). Used in Luke 1:41, 44 for a child in the womb, or Luke 2:12,16 as a newborn infant. As opposed to τέκνον, a general Greek word for children, βρέφος would describe a very young child, most likely one not yet able to read and comprehend on his own.

[16] Some Catholic apologists, e.g., John Henry Cardinal Newman, have used the argument that the reference to the "scriptures" in 2 Timothy 3:14-16 refers only to the Old Testament. Based on the context of 2 Timothy 3, we agree with that conclusion. Since the New Testament Scriptures were not in existence when Timothy was an infant, it would be futile for Protestants to argue against this point. However, as Paul is writing the very verse (2 Timothy 3:16), at that instant it becomes Scripture in the fullest sense of the word and therefore falls under the rubric Paul is using. Hence, one could project the reference to "all scripture is inspired" to refer to the creation of New Testament Scriptures as well. Further, Paul seems to distinguish between "holy Scriptures" in verse 15 and "all Scripture" in verse 16, the latter, used in the singular, seeming to be a more general reference to both the Old and New Testaments. In support of this thesis, one could argue that Paul had already quoted from Luke 10:7 in his first letter to Timothy (1 Timothy 5:18), showing that at least some New Testament Scripture already existed and was recognized as Scripture.

Another aspect of the relationship between Scripture and the other elements which make Timothy a "fit" man of God is Paul's wording in 2 Tim. 3:15: "you *know* the holy Scriptures which are *able* to make you *wise* to salvation." The word "know" denotes a present intellectual apprehension of Scripture, and as such, it, itself, is not saving wisdom but only a means to saving wisdom. Timothy must turn his intellectual knowledge of salvation into a spiritual embracing of salvation. The *process* of attaining salvation is implied in Paul's use of the present tense verbs "know" and "are able."[17] As noted earlier, Timothy must combine his faith and obedience to what he knows of Scripture in order to secure his salvation. Not surprisingly, Paul says to Timothy in 1 Tim. 4:15-16, "Be diligent in these matters: give yourself wholly to them, so that everyone may see your progress. Watch your life and doctrine closely. Persevere in them, because if you do, you *will save* both yourself and your hearers"; in 1 Tim. 6:11-12, "But you, man of God, flee from all this, and pursue righteousness, godliness, faith, love, endurance and gentleness. Fight the good fight of the faith. *Take hold of the eternal life* to which you were called..."; and in 2 Tim. 2:12, "if we endure, we will also reign with him. If we disown him, he will disown us." We see that Timothy's salvation is not an absolute certainty. Scripture is trustworthy (i.e., inspired revelation) and thus it is "profitable" for what leads to salvation, but it itself does not produce or guarantee salvation.

A parallel concept is found in Romans 15:4 where Paul says, "For everything that was written in the past was written to teach us, so that through endurance and the encouragement of the Scriptures we might have hope." Similar to the context of 2 Timothy 2-3 in which Paul seeks to accomplish the goal of making Timothy a

---

[17] The phrase "you know" is from the Greek οἶδας which is the perfect form (lit. "you have seen") of the present εἴδω ("to see"), thus "you have seen" is understood in the present as "you know." The verb "are able" translates the present tense participle of the Greek δύναμαι ("to have power"). The present tense participle could very well be translated, "the holy Scriptures are enabling you to be wise for salvation." The present tense shows that the assimilation of the knowledge of salvation provided in Scripture is an ongoing process, with its hopeful end in the salvation of the individual.

fit man of God for every good work, so Paul has a similar goal in mind for the Romans. His desire is to generate brotherhood and unity in the church. One way of accomplishing this goal is by giving "encouragement" to the brethren. This is also seen in verse 5 as Paul says, "May the God who gives endurance and encouragement give you a spirit of unity..." The Scripture is certainly one source of the encouragement on which the Romans could rely, but surely it could not be concluded from this context that Scripture is their only source of encouragement. People can be encouraged in many ways, one of the best ways is brotherly love as Paul says, "We who are strong ought to bear with the failings of the weak and not to please ourselves..." Paul is not trying to show the superiority of the Scripture, rather, he is pointing out the various sources to which one can turn to help reach perfection in his Christian life.

Paul's prescription in Romans 15:4-5 also includes "endurance." This is not "endurance of the Scripture," as some might read it, but the endurance that Paul expects to be coming from the virtuous life of the Roman Christians. They can hope by, 1) enduring through their trials, and 2) by reading the Scriptures for encouragement. There are two sources for the hope that Paul wishes to generate in them— their own Christian virtues and the Scriptures. This is followed by a third source, God himself, as Paul says in verse 5, "May the God who gives endurance and encouragement give you a spirit of unity..." God's working is also seen in verse 13 as Paul says, "May the God of hope fill you with all joy and peace as you trust in him, so that you may overflow with hope by the power of the Holy Spirit." Similar to the "grace" we have seen Paul deem as sufficient in 2 Cor. 9:8 and 2 Thess. 2:16-17, these are spiritual powers that God instills in the Christian, independent of any other source. One could merely pray for hope and joy and God would fill that person with the Holy Spirit so that they could feel those emotions and be closer to God and their brothers. Scripture, to be sure, points one in the direction of hope in God but it is not the only or *formally sufficient* source to accomplish this task. As noted previously in the exegesis of 2 Timothy 2-3, Paul calls on the virtues and prayer of the person himself, the help and teaching of others, God, and the Scriptures, in order to make a fit man of God for every good work, or in the terminology of Romans 15, a Christian filled with hope, joy and peace. Paul is not giving a treatise on *sola scriptura* in Romans 15:4. He is merely showing some of the sources one has at his disposal for the hope that he wishes to generate within himself.

Hearing The Word Of God

Although the Scriptures were certainly at Timothy's disposal, Paul's consistent theme in these epistles is that the word of God comes to a man upon hearing it, not necessarily upon reading it in print. Apparently, the Scriptures Timothy possessed were useful to give him insights into the nature of "faith in Jesus Christ" as well as for "teaching, rebuking, correcting, and training in righteousness," but Paul, never teaching that the Old Testament was sufficient, only "profitable," did not tell Timothy to pay more and more attention to the Old Testament and less and less to other beneficial sources. The Scriptures, though useful in providing rudimentary truth about "faith in Christ," were simply not enough for what Timothy needed to know about the mysteries of the New Testament gospel and about administering the New Testament Church. Timothy was a Jewish convert who, knowing the Scriptures very well, may have wondered, now that he was a New Testament Christian, just how the Old Testament fit in with this new faith. Since Paul often talked about the rejection of the law for grace, Timothy may have wondered to what degree the Old Testament Scriptures were relevant. Paul settles this question by telling him that those Scriptures could even bring one to "faith in Christ," and that they are very profitable in Timothy's effort to convert other Jews like himself to Christianity. What better way to convert a Jew than to show him from his own Hebrew Scriptures how one could have "faith in Christ" even in Old Testament times. Paul himself did this many times (cf. Rom. 1:17; 3:10-17; 4:1-26; 9:25-30; 10:5-21; 1 Cor. 10:1-12; Luke 24:27; Heb. 11:26, et al).

But as useful as the Scriptures are, Paul insists to Timothy in 2 Timothy 1:13, "What you have **heard** from me keep as the pattern of sound teaching...guard the good deposit that was entrusted to you." It is what Timothy "heard" from Paul that is called the "good deposit," showing that the mere hearing of the word from Paul's lips made an indelible mark on the conscience of Timothy and provided the basis for his understanding of the gospel and his quest to be a fit man of God. Similarly, in 2 Timothy 2:2, Paul says, "And the things you have **heard** me say in the presence of many witnesses entrust to reliable men..." Again, even though the Scriptures are at his disposal, Timothy is to rely just as much or more on what he "**heard**" from Paul.[18]

In 2 Timothy 2:15 Paul tells Timothy, "Do your best to present yourself to God as one approved, a workman who does not need to be ashamed and who correctly handles the word of truth." This is very similar to the language of 2 Timothy 3:16-17 in which the man of God is striving to be a "fit" (i.e., "approved") man of God. Protestants often ignore this matchup by claiming that "the word of truth" in 2 Timothy 2:15 is identical to the "inspired Scripture" of 2 Timothy 3:16, concluding that it is the written word of God *alone* that makes the workman of God "approved." But we must hasten to add that the "word of truth" in 2 Timothy 2:15 does not necessarily refer to the written word, but more likely refers to the spoken word, or refers to both without one taking precedence over the other. As noted above, Paul has not mentioned the Scriptures once in his opening remarks to Timothy, and only does so in the

[18] Protestant James White attempts to dismiss the emphasis on "hearing" the teaching of Paul by claiming that "The deposit of teaching that has been given to Timothy is not different from what we have in Acts, Romans, or Galatians" (*The Roman Catholic Controversy*, p. 98). This kind of analysis is very misleading. White fails to clarify what "is not different" means, and thus makes it appear that oral teaching cannot be distinguished in any way from written teaching. Certainly, with respect to the general knowledge of the *gospel* (i.e., "faith in Jesus Christ" from 2 Timothy 3:15), oral teaching is "not different" from written teaching. But with respect to specific knowledge regarding the gospel, oral teaching may very well be different in that it could contain additional information that written revelation merely touches upon. For example, in 1 Corinthians 11:34 Paul is teaching how to observe the Lord's Supper but terminates his remarks by saying, "And when I come I will give further instructions." We assume that because Paul would eventually speak to them face to face that the additional instructions were given orally and were just as authoritative as his previous written instruction in the remainder of 1 Corinthians 11. Certainly one could not conclude that this oral teaching was any "different" with respect to the nature of the gospel at large, but certainly it was different in regard to additional details of Eucharistic celebration.

passage in question, 2 Timothy 3:14-17. Instead, he has consistently referred to what he had taught Timothy by word of mouth.[19]

In other epistles, Paul uses the phrase "word of truth" to refer to more than Scripture. For example, in Ephesians 1:13, Paul says, "And you also were included in Christ when you heard the **word of truth**, the gospel of your salvation. Having believed, you were marked in him with a seal, the promised Holy Spirit." Here it is evident that the "word of truth" is not necessarily associated with written revelation but with the gospel that the Ephesians had "heard"[20] (cf. Romans 10:17). This oral message was, in itself, powerful enough to effect their *belief* and *seal* them with the Holy Spirit. The same is true in Paul's letter to the Colossians. In Colossians 1:5, Paul says, "...and that you have already heard about in the **word of truth**, the gospel that has come to you." The "word of truth" is that which the Colossians had "heard," not necessarily read. We might also add that in 2 Timothy 2:15 Timothy is first told to "correctly divide the word of truth" and immediately after, "but avoid profane and empty speech."[21] The contrast is between

19 Paul mentions Scripture in the first epistle to Timothy but only in a minor way (1 Timothy 4:13; 5:18). They are not demonstrating the superiority of Scripture over inspired oral teaching or church authority. Rather, as is usually the case, Paul is appealing to Scripture as a witness in order to support what he has taught Timothy by word of mouth.

20 It is interesting to note that in Acts 20:20, 27, 31 Paul says to the Ephesians, "You know that I have not hesitated to preach anything that would be helpful to you but have taught you publicly from house to house. I have declared to both Jews and Greeks that they must turn to God in repentance and have faith in our Lord Jesus...for I have not hesitated to proclaim to you the whole will of God...Remember that for three years I never stopped warning each of you night and day with tears." Here Paul preaches orally the "faith in Christ" (the same "faith in Christ" of which he spoke in 2 Timothy 3:15) which he calls the "whole will [or counsel] of God" and which was disseminated over a "three year" period. We would assume that Paul gave them an abundance of information about "faith in Christ" over this three-year period. Yet Paul says in Ephesians 3:3 that he had only "written briefly" of the mystery of revelation given to him. We must assume that Paul gave the Ephesians much more by oral teaching than what was contained in the Ephesian epistle.

21 The Greek begins verse 16 with τὰς δὲ which should be translated "but," not "and." The word "but" shows that what follows it is a contrasting, not an additional, statement.

right speech and wrong speech, not between the good written word and the bad spoken word. In other words, when he dialogues with men, Timothy should be careful to know what things are important to be said and what things only lead to dissension and unrest (cf., 2 Timothy 2:23-26; 1 Timothy 6:4-5). He must ***speak*** the word of truth correctly. This analysis shows that the command of Paul in 2 Timothy 4:2 to "preach the word"[22] does not refer only to Scripture but includes Paul's inspired oral teachings and the understanding Timothy has of them. To promote a doctrine of *sola scriptura* Paul could simply have said "preach the Scriptures" or "preach the Scriptures only" but he was careful not to do so.

Is Scripture the Only Infallible Source of Divine Truth?

Protestants will argue that Scripture is the only "infallible" source among other sources and therefore stands alone as the sufficient source of divine truth. We have previously dealt with this argument; let us now present specific conterarguments. First, we showed that the context of 2 Timothy 1-3 referred several times to Paul's *oral* teaching. Did Paul consider his oral teaching merely his own ideas? No; according to 1 Thessalonians 2:13 he considered them the very words of God:

> "And we also thank God continually because, when you received the word of God, which you heard from us, you accepted it not as the word of men, but as it actually is, the word of God, which is at work in you who believe."

Here we see that Paul's oral teaching was inspired by God just as were his written words.[23] If these words were inspired by

---

[22] "word" is from the Greek λόγον, a general term referring to any form of revelation.

[23] Of course, not all of Paul's oral speaking was inspired. Not everything Paul wrote was inspired either. We might also consider that Paul dictated some of his canonical letters (Romans 16:22) which would make the actual letter a product of an inspired oral revelation — a process known as *amanuensis*. Thus, some of Paul's orally inspired messages were enscripturated while others (e.g., those in 1 Thessalonians 2:13) were not.

God, they were infallible. If the inspired oral preaching was infallible, Timothy had another infallible source from which to draw to help make him a fit man of God prepared for every good work. Therefore, by the principle of infallibility, Paul cannot be teaching the concept of *sola scriptura* in 2 Timothy 3:16-17.

Second, we must point out that the use of the word *inspiration* in 2 Timothy 3:16 does not imply or prove that Scripture is our only source of inspired revelation. Certainly God inspired men to write the Scripture, but he also inspired them to speak his words, some of which were written down (Romans 16:22), and some not (Matthew 2:23; 10:19; 1 Thessalonians 2:13; 1 Corinthians 15:2; Ephesians 1:13). Paul commands that the word of God given by "word of mouth" was to be obeyed and preserved just as much as the written (2 Thessalonians 2:15). Though much of what was orally inspired probably overlapped in content with what was inspired into writing, evidently some details of truth contained in orally inspired teachings Paul chose not to put in written revelation, otherwise there would be little reason for Paul to command that both forms, oral and written, be obeyed and preserved. If at that time the written word contained the complete and only necessary revelation of God to preserve, it would have been superfluous for the first Christians to preserve any oral revelation. But since Paul did command the first Christians to preserve and obey oral revelation, the Catholic Church has always taught that oral revelation serves as an additional source of revelation alongside the written word. Therefore, Scripture is not our sole authority.

Third, attempts to use 2 Timothy 3:16-17 to prove the notion of *sola scriptura* lead to an untenable anachronism. If Protestants believe 2 Timothy 3:16-17 teaches *sola scriptura*, then they must also believe that Timothy was meant to understand 2 Timothy 3:16-17 as teaching *sola scriptura*. Obviously, Scripture cannot be interpreted one way for us and another way for Timothy. But if Timothy is to see *sola scriptura* in this passage, neither entertaining nor seeking any other interpretation, then what was Timothy to do with Paul's orally inspired teaching given at the same time as the writing of 2 Timothy, and which Paul told him to "keep" and "guard"?[24] It will do no good for Protestants to argue that oral revelation was eventually confined to Scripture, for even if this were true, they are still left with the fact that in Timothy's day oral revelation was an abiding concern. If Timothy was to see the same interpretation as Protestants do in 2 Timothy 3:16-17, this imposes on Timothy the requirement to make a strong mental effort to stop referring to Paul's orally inspired teaching and cease from passing it on and entrusting it to reliable men as he once was commanded. But Paul never told Timothy anything of the sort. Paul commanded that his oral teachings were to be preserved and propagated throughout the church. He gave no indication that one day orally inspired teaching should be ignored, demoted, or looked upon with suspicion after Paul died, when the Scripture was completed, or when the Bible was canonized. It is only reasonable to conclude that if on his death bed Paul wanted to leave Timothy with a doctrine of *sola scriptura* — a doctrine which would have made such a monumental difference in how Timothy arrived at truth — he would have said so explicitly and clearly. As it stands, he did not.

As the above analysis should make clear, one cannot overstate the principle that, in relation to written teaching, oral teaching was just as much, or even more so, the basis upon which Timo-

---

[24] Evangelical James White admits: "Protestants do not assert that *sola scriptura* is a valid concept during times of revelation. How could it be, since the rule of faith to which it points was at the very time coming into being" ("A Review and Rebuttal of Steve Ray's Article *Why The Bereans Rejected Sola Scriptura*," 1997, on web site of Alpha and Omega Ministries). By this admission, White has unwittingly proven that Scripture does not teach *sola scriptura*, for if it cannot be a "valid concept during times of revelation," how can Scripture teach such a doctrine since Scripture was written precisely when divine oral revelation was still being produced? Scripture cannot contradict itself. Since both the 1st century Christian and the 21st century Christian cannot extract differing interpretations from the same verse, thus, whatever was true about Scripture then must also be true today. If the first Christians did not, and could not, extract *sola scriptura* from Scripture because oral revelation was still existent, then obviously those verses could not, in principle, be teaching *sola scriptura*, and thus *we* cannot interpret them as teaching it either.

thy learned the gospel and the means to become a fit man of God, fully equipped for every good work. Once we understand that Paul's inspired oral teaching was just as inerrant as his inspired written teaching, then we can also understand that Paul, in 2 Timothy 3:14-17, was not saying that the Scripture was Timothy's only authority or final source of revelation. Since Paul mentions the "hearing" of the gospel three times within the immediate context of 2 Timothy 1-3, it is hard to avoid this vehicle as the major source of Paul's teaching and of Timothy's learning to make him a fit man of God. As we pointed out previously, however, Paul in 2 Timothy 1-3 is not trying to formulate an argument positing Scripture against another source of teaching or revelation, or even address the strengths and limitations of revelation in general; he is interested only in gathering all the ingredients needed to make a "fit man of God" or "useful vessel to his Master." Elsewhere in Scripture, when Paul wants to oppose one authoritative source against another, he makes his intentions clear (e.g., 1 Corinthians 1:18-2:16; Galatians 1:6-9; 3:2; Colossians 2:8-23), but he is not doing so in 2 Timothy 2-3. Since the goal of being *fit* and *useful* is his only purpose, Paul takes great pains to mention all the sources upon which a man can draw to accomplish this noble task. Paul's concern in 2 Timothy 2-3 is not to give a treatise on the superiority or exclusiveness of Scripture, but rather to encourage Timothy to tap into every available resource at his disposal, especially Scripture, in order to reach his goal. In this regard, Scripture is "profitable" to make him fully equipped, but it is not his only tool. In fact, even taking Paul's words in 2 Timothy 3:17 in their most superlative meaning, Timothy can become the perfect man of God not merely because he has Scripture at his disposal but because when he adds Scripture to all the other sources of help, it is all these together that make him the fit and perfect man of God he desires to be. Attempts to use this passage to prove the notion of *sola scriptura* are injecting something into the text that Paul never even considered. Paul does not refer to Scripture as the 'final court of appeal' but as a 'profitable source to equip the man of God.'

The Case of the "Noble" Bereans

Acts 17:11

"Now the Bereans were of more noble character than the Thessalonians, for they received the message with great eagerness and examined the Scriptures every day to see if what Paul said was true."

For those predisposed to believe in the concept of *sola scriptura*, Acts 17:11 is touted as a definitive proof text. It is reasoned that because of the Berean's appeal to Scripture and the Thessalonian's apparent lack thereof, Luke, the writer of the Acts of the Apostles, judges that the former "were of more noble character" than the latter and should serve as the model for each Christian to emulate. Obviously, the Berean's appeal to Scripture suggests a people very familiar with the word of God who did not bend with every new wind of doctrine that came breezing their way, even from an apostle like Paul. Their "every day" examination of Scripture evokes a picture of studious and intelligent people who did not give God lip-service on the Sabbath but from sun-up to sun-down had, as the Psalmist of old, the word of God on their heart. They did this *daily* because Paul, as Acts 17:17 specifies, "reasoned in the synagogue with the Jews...*day by day* with those who happened to be there."[25] Luke tells us that not only did the Bereans examine the Scriptures, but they did this purposely "to see if what Paul said was true." Hence the actions of the Bereans, if we are to take them as our model, seem to set Scripture up as the *sole judge* of what a teacher is proclaiming. For *sola scriptura* advocates, Scripture is portrayed as the *given*, but Paul was the *new-comer* who had to be authenticated. The passage seems to assert, or at least strongly suggest, that in judging anything claiming to be from God, Scripture must be the sole and final authority.[26]

---

25 Cf., Acts 19:9; 18:4; 19:8.

26 Typical comments about the Bereans of Acts 17 in defense of *sola scriptura* are as follows: "They are called noble because they evaluated everything on the basis of the written Word of God... If we would be faithful children of God, if we would be noble, we must proceed as the Bereans did" (W. Robert Godfrey

But is Scripture as the sole or final authority the message Luke is trying to impart here? Let's examine the context of this passage to find out. Acts 17:2 records:

> As his custom was, Paul went into the synagogue, and on three Sabbath days he reasoned with them from the Scriptures, explaining and proving that the Christ had to suffer and rise from the dead."

Here we see that it was not only the Bereans who were steeped in Scripture, but rather Paul himself, who in this regard had led the way in all the synagogues in which he taught. At this early time in Christian history, the synagogue was still the main meeting place, for Jews as well as Greeks. It was Paul's "custom" to visit the synagogues in each city of his missionary journey. For example, on his trip to Antioch recorded in Acts 13:14, Luke tells us that "on the Sabbath," Paul and his companions "entered the synagogue and sat down...reading from the Law and the Prophets..." As he would later do in Thessalonica and Berea in Acts 17, Paul made it a continual practice to read and teach from the Scriptures — in this case, the Old Testament. Hence we see that Paul's teaching sessions in the synagogue were to a people who knew their Scripture, used it often, and were willing to exchange ideas about it. If Paul appealed to Scripture, then it was to Scripture the people would go to check "if what Paul said was true."

[26 cont.] in *Sola Scriptura! The Protestant Position on the Bible*, pp. 24-25); "Further, the Bereans are commended as the most noble of all early Christians because 'they searched the Scriptures daily' to see if the oral teachings of even an apostle were faithful to the text (cf. Acts 17:11). Again, the assumption is that in truly searching the Scriptures truth can be clearly discovered" (John Armstrong, Ibid., p. 136); "It is highly significant that the Bereans are explicitly commended for examining Scripture. They had the priority right: Scripture is the supreme rule of faith, by which everything else is to be tested. Unsure of whether they could trust the apostolic message — which, by the way, was as inspired and infallible and true as Scripture itself — the Bereans erased all their doubt by double-checking the message against Scripture. Yet Roman Catholics are forbidden by their Church to take such an approach!" (John MacArthur, Ibid., p. 178).

But there was a special reason that Paul may have stimulated (or agitated), his hearers. In Thessalonica, Acts 17:2 records that Paul not only read from the Scripture but that he "*reasoned*[27] with them from the Scriptures, *explaining*[28] and *proving*[29] that the Christ had to suffer..." Apparently, Paul was deducing from already known Scripture new understandings about what that Scripture meant in light of the events that had just taken place a decade or so earlier.

In Luke's wording we notice a slight difference between what Scripture said and what Paul taught. In the beginning of verse 3 he says that Paul was "proving that the *Christ* had to suffer and rise from the dead," but in the latter part he records Paul saying, "This *Jesus* I am proclaiming to you is the Christ..." The difference between the two is that Paul is *interpreting* "the Christ" of the Old Testament to be the "Jesus" of the New Testament. Since the Old Testament did not use the name of "Jesus" to identify the Messiah (i.e., the Christ) Paul's message was a new application of Scripture. Further, the Jews did not believe that their coming Messiah had to "suffer," let alone "rise from the dead." Most of the Jews expected their Messiah to be a powerful king who would relieve them of Gentile rule. In their view, he would not have to rise from the dead because he would establish himself as an eternal king who would rule forever over the Jews' enemies. They simply did not understand the many Old Testament passages which spoke of the Messiah as a suffering servant who had to die — a suffering he underwent precisely for their sin of disbelief in him.[30]

---

27 From διαλέγομαι which is understood either as "to dispute" (e.g., Mark 9:34, Jude 9); or as "to argue" or "to reason" (Acts 17:2, 17; 18:4, 19:8-9; 20:7, 9; 24:12, 25).

28 From διανοίγω, which is used exclusively for "opening" or "opening up" (e.g., Mark 7:34, 35; Luke 2:23; 24:31, 32, 45; Acts 16:14).

29 From παρατίθημι, meaning "to set before" (Acts 16:34) or "commit" (Acts 20:32). The word does not mean "proof," per se, but "to show" or "to exhibit." A synonym is used of Apollos in Acts 18:28 which says that he was "*proving* from the Scripture that Jesus was the Christ." The word "proving" is from the Greek ἐπιδείνυμι which also means "to show" (cf., Matt. 16:1; 22:19; 24:1; Acts 9:39: Heb. 6:17). The normal word for "proof" is δοκιμαζω (cf., 1 Cor. 3:13; 2 Cor. 8:8; 13:5; 1 Thess. 5:21; 1 Tim. 3:10), but this word is not used in Acts, nor is it used elsewhere to equate the Christ with Jesus.

30 Cf. Isaiah 53:10-12; Luke 24:46.

In Thessalonica, it was Paul's statement that "the Christ" of the Old Testament was the "Jesus" of the New which caused such contention and jealousy among the Jews. In Acts 17:5-9 Luke records their response:

> But the Jews were jealous; so they rounded up some bad characters from the marketplace, formed a mob and started a riot in the city. They rushed to Jason's house in search of Paul and Silas in order to bring them out to the crowd. But when they did not find them, they dragged Jason and some other brothers before the city officials, shouting: "These men who have caused trouble all over the world have now come here, and Jason has welcomed them into his house. They are all defying Caesar's decrees, saying that there is another king, one called Jesus."

It is apparent by their last words, "one called Jesus," that the Jews were simply not ready to accept the Christ of the Old Testament as the Jesus of the New. Hence Paul and the Jews of Thessalonica were not contending about the veracity or usefulness of Scripture; rather, it was Paul's *interpretation* of Scripture that they could not accept. Everyone believed Scripture's prophecy about the coming Messiah. But the information that the Christ was "Jesus" who had recently suffered and died at the hands of the Jews was something Paul was getting from another source outside Scripture. This new information would, of course, correlate with Scripture but it would nonetheless be in addition to Scripture. Such was the case, in fact, in Paul's own conversion. He had to be convinced through additional divine revelation that the people who followed "Jesus," and whom he was persecuting, were in actuality followers of "the Christ." In Acts 9:5, after being knocked off his horse by a flash of light, the Lord said to Paul, "I am *Jesus*, whom you are persecuting..." At that instant Paul recognized that his long-awaited Messiah was the "Jesus" who had suffered and died a decade or so earlier.[31] It was not Scripture that brought him to this point but a

---

[31] Notice the attention Acts gives to identifying Jesus as Messiah, cf., Acts 1:1, 11; 2:22, 32, 36; 3:13, 26; 4:27-33; 5:30; 7:55; 8:35; 10:38; 13:23; 18:5, 28; 25:19; 28:23.

revelation from Jesus himself showing Paul how the Old Testament Scriptures were to be interpreted.

When Paul arrived in Berea, he acted just as he did in Thessalonica — he went to the synagogue to teach. We may assume that he engaged in similar "reasoning," "explaining and proving" from Scripture with the Bereans that he had done with the Thessalonians. We may also assume that Paul, as in Thessalonica, made it a point to teach the Bereans that the Christ of the Old Testament was the Jesus of the New. The Bereans received Paul's interpretation of Scripture without hesitation. Luke records in Acts 17:11

> Now the Bereans were of more noble character than the Thessalonians, for they received the message with great eagerness and examined the Scriptures every day to see if what Paul said was true. Many of the Jews believed, as did also a number of prominent Greek women and many Greek men.

Here we see that these Berean Jews "received the message with great eagerness." We can surmise from his previous encounter with the Thessalonians that the main message the Bereans were receiving with eagerness was Paul's news that Jesus of Nazareth was the Christ. Because they believed Paul's message about the identity of the Messiah, Luke concludes that they were "of more noble character[32] than the Thessalonians." Moreover, their "nobility" was also demonstrated when they "examined the Scriptures every day to see if what Paul said was true." It showed that they cared greatly for God's revelation, in whatever form it came. We can imagine that their counterparts in Thessalonica perhaps did not investigate the testimony of Scripture after Paul told them that Jesus was the Messiah. They had a blinded or one-sided view of Scripture and did not care for Paul's interpretation. They were not willing to "rea-

---

[32] "Noble character" is from the Greek noun εὐγενής, appearing 3 times in the New Testament (Luke 19:12; Acts 17:11; 1 Cor. 1:26). It is clear from Luke's wording that he considered the Jews of Berea "noble" because of their positive reaction and open-mindedness to Paul's message, not necessarily because they were previously known to be of more virtuous character than the Thessalonians. The church at Thessalonica actually became one of Paul's model churches (cf. 1 Thess. 1-3).

son" from Scripture's circumstantial evidence that the Messiah was indeed Jesus, thus, they were not noble, open-minded people.

But why, we ask, did Luke consider the Jews of Berea more "noble" than the Jews in Thessalonica, when, according to Luke's description of the Thessalonians in Acts 17:4, "some of the Jews [in Thessalonica] were persuaded and joined Paul and Silas, as did a large number of God-fearing Greeks and not a few prominent women." It is obvious that *not all* the Jews in Thessalonica had rejected Paul's interpretation of Scripture. Wouldn't Luke consider these Jews "noble" for accepting Paul's message? The answer is yes, but these noble Jews were so badly outnumbered by the jealous and riotous Jews who rejected Paul's message that Luke was forced to sum up the situation in Thessalonica as one of general unbelief. We see this also in the way he describes how many people were positively influenced by Paul's message. Regarding the Thessalonians in Acts 17:4 he points out that only "*some* of the Jews were persuaded," while in regard to the Bereans in Acts 17:12 he says "*many* of the Jews believed..."[33] Apparently, the number of believing Jews in Berea were of a sufficient quantity that Luke could designate them, at large, as "noble" in contrast to the overall negative disposition of the people in Thessalonica. Moreover, the unbelieving Jews of Thessalonica further justified Luke's negative assessment since they caused riots among the people both in Thessalonica and later in Berea (cf., 17:5-9 and 17:13-15).

In view of the above facts, is it reasonable to conclude that the Bereans, because they "examined the Scriptures every day to see if what Paul said was true," are models of the modern theory of *sola scriptura*? Is Luke trying to teach us that "nobility" consists in using Scripture as the final authority in determining the veracity of oral teaching? When we look at the evidence fairly and accurately, the answer is a resounding, no. Any attempt to extract from this short pericope a teaching of *sola scriptura* is simply reading into the text one's doctrinal bias. First, the text is simply a narrative of events that occurred in two respective cities, not a treatise on the nature and extent of Scripture and its authority. Granted, the passages suggest how Paul and his hearers used and understood Scrip-

33 "Some" is from the Greek τινές "many" is from πολλοὶ.

ture, but neither Paul or his commentator Luke say anything definitive about the doctrine of Scripture. Second, we have seen from our comparison of the Jews in Berea with the Jews in Thessalonica that Luke considered the former noble not because they merely examined Scripture, but mainly because they believed Paul's *oral revelation* that the Christ of the Old Testament was the Jesus of the New. Luke attributes nobility to them because they "received the [oral] message with great eagerness." The Bereans believed that the apostle's oral message had just as much divine authority as the Scripture. In Acts 17:13 Luke specifies Paul's oral proclamation as: "Paul was preaching the word of God[34] at Berea," making it clear that the Bereans considered Paul's oral message to be the very word of God. Paul was not merely speaking *about* the word of God, he was speaking the *actual* word of God. Elsewhere, Paul's own assessment of his oral teaching to the Thessalonians confirms its superlative distinction, for in 1 Thessalonians 2:13 he states:

> We also thank God continually because, when you received the word of God, which you heard from us, you accepted it not as the word of men, but as it actually is, the word of God, which is at work in you who believe.

This is a pivotal passage because it shows that Paul considered his oral message to the Thessalonians in Acts 17:1-4, (which revealed that Jesus was the Christ), and by necessary extension his oral message to the Bereans in Acts 17:11-13, as divine revelations on a par with Scripture. In fact, no one could know the real meaning of Scripture, as obscure as it was at times, unless accompanied by an equally authoritative divine interpretation. This is the essential teaching of the Berean encounter.

Since the Old Testament did not explicitly identify "the Christ" as "Jesus," it was impossible for the Jews of Berea, using the Old Testament alone, to have proven from Scripture that Jesus was the Messiah. One could certainly "reason," "explain" and "prove" that the Christ had to suffer and rise from the dead, but there was no explicit evidence, other than Paul's authoritative testimony, that

[34] Greek: ὁ λόγος τοῦ θεοῦ.

the one who was prophesied in the Old Testament to suffer and rise was the Jesus who walked the earth just a decade or so earlier. The Bereans were noble because they accepted Paul's apostolic authority on the identity of the Messiah, not because they could extract for themselves from the Old Testament that Jesus was indeed the Messiah. Thus, their "examination" of Scripture was limited to re-evaluating those passages which spoke of the Messiah as the one who had to suffer, die, and rise again; not to prove or disprove that Jesus was the Messiah. Before Paul's teaching, the Bereans, like most Jews, thought that the Messiah would be recognized by a majestic appearance and a subsequent conquering of the Gentiles. It was not until Paul pointed out that the Old Testament passages which spoke of God's servant as one who had to suffer must be interpreted to apply to the Messiah and, more importantly, that his name was *Jesus*. The typical Jew, although he knew his Scripture, invariably skipped over the numerous passages in the Old Testament that suggested his Messiah had to first come as one to suffer and die. As Paul says in 2 Corinthians 3:14-16:

> But their minds were made dull, for to this day the same veil remains when the old covenant is read. It has not been removed, because only in Christ is it taken away. Even to this day when Moses is read, a veil covers their hearts. But whenever anyone turns to the Lord, the veil is taken away.

After Paul was done teaching, the now enlightened Jew could read a passage like Isaiah 53 and see it in a whole different light (cf. Luke 24:26; Acts 8:26-35). It was in connecting Paul's divine revelation of the person of Jesus with the suffering passages of the Old Testament that the Berean "examined Scripture to see if what Paul said was true." The Berean did not first believe that Jesus was the Messiah and then examine Scripture to see if Paul's identifying of Jesus as the Messiah was true. No, he examined the Scriptures that spoke of the suffering servant and then accepted by *faith* that the "Jesus" about whom Paul spoke was indeed the Messiah. His faith was based on accepting Paul's authority to interpret Scripture, while Scripture served mainly as a *witness* to what Paul preached. Scripture could not serve as the sole determinant of what

Paul taught for the simple reason that Scripture never identified "the Christ" specifically as "Jesus." He was designated with names like "the prophet" (Deut. 18:15) or "Immanuel" (Isaiah 7:14) but never "Jesus" (Matt. 1:21). The Bereans, as their Old Testament prescribed, needed at least two or three witnesses to prove the veracity of a certain person or event (cf. Deut. 19:15; 2 Cor. 13:1). Paul was one witness and Scripture was another, and both were necessary for the truth to be known and understood. Hence, Acts 17:11 cannot support the concept of *sola scriptura*. If anything, it implicitly denies such a teaching.[35]

"Not Beyond What Has Been Written"

1 Corinthians 4:6

> ***"Now these things, brothers, I have applied to myself and Apollos because of you, that in us you may learn not to go beyond what has been written, that you not be puffed up one for one against the other."***

Searching for biblical support for the theory of *sola scriptura*, many Protestant apologists have begun to appeal to the cryptic phrase in 1 Corinthians 4:6, "...not beyond what has been written..." These apologists claim that in this simple six-word statement Paul is declaring that no one can go beyond the written corpus of Scripture for authoritative revelation. Ironically, the quest to use 1 Corinthians 4:6 is in the face of a history of Protestant interpretation which concludes almost unanimously that not only does this verse not support *sola scriptura*, in reality it is one of the most

---

35 As Catholic apologist Steven Ray has stated: "If one of the two groups of Jews could possibly be tagged as believers in *sola scriptura*, who would it be, the Thessalonians or the Bereans? The Thessalonians, of course. They also, like the Bereans, examined the Scriptures with Paul in the synagogue yet they rejected his teaching. They did not accept the new teaching, deciding after three weeks of deliberation that Paul's word contradicted Torah...They reasoned from Scripture alone and concluded Paul's new teaching was "unbiblical" (*This Rock*, 1997).

difficult and ambiguous statements in the entire New Testament. But finding no other explicit verses in Scripture to support their position, modern Protestant apologists are almost irresistibly drawn to use 1 Corinthians 4:6 to advance the theory of *sola scriptura*.[36] We will show, however, that doing so only wraps the Protestant's theological noose that much tighter. When the strongest verses put forward can be dismissed so easily, there is little left to discuss. Let us observe how this happens.

Possibilities For the Meaning Of "Has Been Written"

One of the main questions concerning 1 Corinthians 4:6 is the referent for the perfect passive verb "has been written."[37] Biblical commentators have offered numerous suggestions, some similar, some unconventional. In fact, some believe that the phrase does

[36] Typical comments from Protestants regarding 1 Cor. 4:6 in support of *sola scriptura* are as follows: "Do not rest your confidence on the wisdom of men who claim infallibility. Stand rather with the Apostle Paul who wrote in 1 Corinthians 4:6, 'Do not go beyond what is written'" (W. Robert Godfrey in *Sola Scriptura! The Protestant Position on the Bible*, p. 25); "What is certain is that all that is necessary is in Scripture — and we are forbidden 'to exceed what is written' (1 Corinthians 4:6)" (John MacArthur, Ibid., p. 167); "...the Bible constantly warns us 'not to go beyond what is written' (1 Cor. 4:6)" N. Geisler and R. MacKenzie, *Roman Catholics and Evangelicals: Agreements and Differences*, p. 186). Invariably, the appeals to 1 Corinthians 4:6 are made without offering any exegesis of the passage to support their claims. In another instance, I wrote to the head of the New Testament department at Westminster Theological Seminary (Philadelphia, PA) in October 1993 inquiring where the Bible taught *sola scriptura*. Noting in the return letter that he was "pressed for time," this professor offered just one verse, 1 Corinthians 4:6, without any explanation why he felt it supported *sola scriptura*. In another letter I received, the associate New Testament professor offered Romans 15:14 as his main support (letters on file).

[37] Greek: γέγραπται. Difficulty arises in interpretation since some Greek texts precede γέγραπται with τὸ μὴ ὑπὲρ ἃ ("not above what things"), while others precede it with τὸ μὴ ὑπὲρ ὃ (Byzantine minuscules, Codices Bezae Cantabrigiensis (D) and (G), and the Syriac Peshito), and follow with γέγραπται φρονεῖν ("not to think above what has been written") (Codex Ephraemi Rescriptus (C), minuscule 33, Byzantine minuscules, most Syriac versions).

not even belong in the Greek text, suggesting instead that it was originally the marginal note of a scribe whose subsequent copyist mistakenly put it into the biblical text. In sorting out the various interpretations offered, the phrase in question has proven to be one of the most difficult passages in the whole Bible to interpret. One translator of the New Testament, Protestant scholar J. B. Moffatt, simply refused to translate the phrase in question. In his New Testament translation he put a dotted line in its place with a marginal note explaining his utter frustration at making sense out of it.[38]

Because of the inherent difficulty of the passage, at least eight plausible suggestions have been offered as to its interpretation. Let us now examine these:

(1) Some commentators believe that "not beyond what has been written" refers to a Rabbinic maxim or proverbial saying that Paul thought appropriate to include in his admonitions to the Corinthians. According to this argument, the Greek article (τὸ) sets off the phrase in question and treats it as a quotation, the quotation in this case being from an extra-biblical source. Various renditions of this line of thinking are seen in some modern translations, "remember the maxim: Keep to what is written" (*Jerusalem Bible*), or "so that you may learn through us the meaning of the saying 'Nothing beyond what is written'" (*New Revised Standard Version*), or "so that you may learn from us the meaning of the saying, "Do not go beyond what is written" (*New International Version*).

Those who use such translations in support of *sola scriptura* argue that Paul's citing of a Rabbinic maxim shows that the principle of *sola scriptura* was ancient and well-known. As the argument goes, if the Rabbis felt very strongly about only using Scripture as authoritative revelation, surely Paul would want the same rules for the New Testament church. Though this seems to be a logical deduction, appealing to such extra-biblical sources would in actuality weaken Paul's argument for *sola scriptura.* If *sola scriptura* were indeed a biblical doctrine, why would Paul cite an

---

[38] Moffatt, James B. *The New Testament, A New Translation* (Harper and Brothers Publishers, New York, London, 1935 ed.) p. 415.

extrabiblical source to prove his point? Would he not be compelled to cite Scripture for support? Citing an extra-biblical source without any biblical proof texts would defeat the whole principle of *sola scriptura*, since the theory presupposes that Scripture is sufficient to be its own authority. In fact, Paul quotes the Old Testament six times in the first four chapters of 1 Corinthians thus demonstrating his working knowledge of its precepts when writing to the Corinthians, but not once does he cite anything in support of or in reference to *sola scriptura*.

Regarding the intent of the Rabbis, no commentator who has suggested that Paul is referring to some sort of maxim has ever shown us where such a maxim can be found in Rabbinic or proverbial sayings. Finding such documentation would be difficult, if, as the above translations suggest, the phrase was only a "saying" rather than a written prescription. If it is merely a "saying," the question would surface as to why Paul would appeal to an *unwritten* source to support a principle that one should only accept as authoritative that which was *written*. It would be totally illogical and contradictory for Paul to appeal to non-written tradition to support the concept of *sola scriptura*. The mere citing of such a tradition would automatically eliminate *sola scriptura* as a candidate to be the referent for "has been written." In light of such tradition, we should also be note that the Rabbis were not known for adhering only to those things documented by Scripture. In addition to Scripture they consulted many of their own writings and also appealed to a handy circle of tradition within the Rabbinic community. In short, appealing to the Rabbis to support sola scriptura is self-defeating.

Further, it would be out of character for Paul to cite Rabbinic maxims as proofs for biblical/theological concepts since he does not do so elsewhere in this epistle, nor is there any indication that he is doing so in the immediate context of 1 Corinthians 4:6. Paul cites only Old Testament quotations in this and other epistles. Moreover, it would be rather strange for Paul to issue Rabbinic maxims to a young Gentile church. In the Greek culture of Corinth, Judaistic sayings would not be well known or hold much influence. In other passages addressed to Gentile churches, Paul makes a point of ignoring Judaistic traditions, branding them as short-sighted and vain (cf., Col. 2:8; Phil. 3:5; Matt. 15:1ff).

As for the suggestion that Paul is citing a well-known proverb, this would also be out-of-character for him. Paul never cites extra-biblical proverbs in his writings. The only passage in all his writings where Paul refers a biblical proverb is in Romans 12:20, in reference to Proverbs 25:21-22. It is introduced by the normal means, *viz.*, "it is written," phrasing that does not appear in 1 Corinthians 4:6. When other New Testament writers reference biblical proverbs there is a clear indication they are citing biblical wisdom literature (cf., Heb. 12:5-6; James 4:6/1 Peter 5:5; 2 Peter 2:22). In addition, nothing in biblical proverbs resembles the phrasing in 1 Corinthians 4:6.

Finally, although one may argue that the Greek neuter article (τὸ) can sometimes set off a particular part of a sentence to form a parenthetical saying, this is not always the case, and when it does set something off, it is difficult to tell exactly why. For example, the Greek article introduces a separate clause in Galatians 5:4 and Luke 22:37, but these passages clearly cite Scripture, which is not the case in 1 Corinthians 4:6. Although the Greek article could introduce a parenthetical saying, on the other hand it may simply attach itself to the nearest referent.[39] Moreover, various commentators have shown that the addition of the article may simply be an idiosyncrasy of Paul's.[40] It is commonly known that Luke and Paul had a particular penchant for inserting a superfluous article in their sentence structure.[41]

(2) Other commentators interpret "what has been written" as an idiomatic expression to describe a consensus or agreement. Various translations bring out this idea in the phrasing "and learn to keep within the rules, as they say" *(New English Bible)*, or "so that you may learn what the saying means, Observe the proper rules" (*Today's English Version*). Here the saying is not necessarily concerned with writing, per se, but rather, means that everyone should adhere to the previously agreed-upon rules. On the one hand, these

---

[39] An example is Galatians 6:9 where, if the article attaches to καλὸν the translation can be either the saying: "let us not grow tired" or the question: "what is good."

[40] C. F. D. Moule, *An Idiom Book of New Testament Greek*, 2nd edition. (London: Cambridge University Press, 1959).

[41] *International Critical Commentary,* Romans 8:26.

translations, like the ones above, treat the phrase as a *saying* but, on the other hand, seem to take unwarranted liberties in paraphrasing the verb "has been written." Supporting this translation commentator John Parry suggests that 1 Corinthians 4:6 does not use "has been written" in the normal sense. From Milligan and Moultan's *Vocabulary* he shows that "graphein" ("to write") had current use in referring to law or contracts, and that "kath a gegraptai" commonly referred to the terms of a contract. He concludes that Paul could very well mean that one is "not to go beyond the terms of the agreement," i.e., of the commission as teacher.[42]

(3) Another interpretation of "what has been written" in 1 Corinthians 4:6 is that it is a direct quote from the Old Testament. Since Paul has already quoted from the Old Testament six times up to this point in the epistle, it would be natural to think he is doing so again in 1 Corinthians 4:6. The major problem with this solution is that no passage in the Old Testament makes a specific reference to "not beyond what has been written." As an outside possibility this phrase could be in the category of citations from Scripture in which the exact verse being quoted is uncertain, but even in such instances the New Testament writer at least specifies that his citation is from "Scripture" (e.g., James 4:5; John 7:38). In other cases, the New Testament writer refers to what was "said" by the prophets but was apparently not written in Scripture (e.g., Matthew 2:23). There is one instance in the context of 1 Corinthians 1-4, however, where Paul does not introduce an Old Testament reference by the normal phrase "it is written." This is "For who has known the mind of the Lord that he may instruct him" in 1 Cor. 2:16 (cf. Isaiah 40:13). Yet even in this passage one can readily find the quotation in the Old Testament, which is not true of the phrasing in 1 Corinthians 4:6.

(4) Another possibility is that since "what has been written" is not a direct quote from the Old Testament, it could refer to the general principles contained therein. The Old Testament touches upon many of the themes Paul assembles in the Corinthian epistle,

---

[42] *Expositor's Times*, W.F. Howard, xxxiii (July 1922).

the major concern being the unnecessary emulation of men and the penetration of worldly wisdom into the Church. Paul uses this method of "written" proof in other parts of the epistle, most notably 1 Cor. 10:11, in which he says, "these things happened to them as an example, and *have been written down* as a warning to us..." In this case, Paul reveals that the Old Testament writings were created precisely to serve as documented examples in the New Testament of God's dealing with men.

(5) Another possibility is that, rather than having the whole Old Testament in mind, Paul could be referring only to the Old Testament passages he cites in the opening chapters of 1 Corinthians. In the first three chapters, Paul quotes from the Old Testament a total of six times. Interestingly, all these references address the same theme: the wisdom of God versus the pseudo-wisdom of man. It is apparent from the context that the Corinthians had assumed a wisdom from the world that was contrary to God's wisdom displayed in Christ. This created major divisions in the Corinthian church as each person sided with the teacher he thought was wiser, stronger, or more eloquent. The Old Testament passages that Paul chooses strike right at the heart of this problem in the Corinthian church concerning the pride of man in thinking that he is wiser than God. Here are the precise citations:

a) 1 Cor. 1:19: "I will destroy the wisdom of the wise, and the cleverness of the clever I will set aside." Paul takes this quote from Isaiah 29:14, in a context of God's judgment in which Isaiah states that the Lord has taken away the understanding of the prophets and seers (v. 10). He quotes the Lord as saying that the people of Israel honor him with their lips but their hearts are far from him. For reverence to God they obey the tradition of men (v. 13). He sternly warns those who hide their wicked ways from the Lord and say, "who sees us?" Isaiah states that in their pride and false wisdom they were making themselves equal to their maker and were claiming that God did not have any knowledge about them (v. 16).

b) 1 Cor. 1:31: "Whoever boasts should boast in the Lord." Paul introduces this passage by referring to how God chooses the foolish, weak, and base things of the world to confound the wise so that no one can boast before God (vv. 28-29). He takes the quote from Jeremiah 9:23, in a context forecasting God's judgment upon Israel. The people were boasting of their wisdom, might, and riches, but had forgotten God and the practice of the virtues of loving kindness, justice, and righteousness (v. 24). Paul says similar things of the Corinthians in the context in question (cf., 1 Cor. 4:8-10).

c) 1 Cor. 2:9: "The eye has not seen nor the ear heard, neither has it entered into the heart of man, what things God has prepared for them that love him." The preface to this quotation is the contrast between the wisdom of men and the power and wisdom of God. God's wisdom is mysterious, hidden, and predetermined (vv. 4-7). As in the crucifixion of Christ, in which no one had even an inkling of God's secret plan or ultimate purpose (v. 8), Paul quotes from Isaiah 64:3, which focuses on those who wait patiently for the hidden wisdom of God to answer their call in an unexpected and miraculous way. Paul also states that God hides his face from evildoers (v. 7).

d) 1 Cor. 2:16: "For who has known the mind of the Lord that he should instruct him." Paul does not introduce this statement with the normal phrasing, "it is written," as he does the other quotations, but this statement is an allusion to Isaiah 40:13. The chapter contains beautiful imagery describing the greatness of God as expressed in the creation. God regards the nations as "less than nothing" (v. 17) and considers the inhabitants of earth as "grasshoppers" (v. 22).

e) 1 Cor. 3:19: "I will catch the wise in their own craftiness." Paul takes this quote from Job 5:13. It is similar to 1 Cor. 1:19 cited above which demonstrates the greatness of God and the foolishness of men. Although men think they are wise, God is wiser and uses their own pseudo-wisdom to trap them.

f) 1 Cor. 3:20: "The Lord knows the thoughts of the wise that they are vain." Paul takes this quote from Psalm 94:11 in a context in which the people are complaining that God does not pay attention to them when their enemies attack them. God tells them not to worry, since the wisdom and plans of their attackers are nothing compared to God's plans. God will come to the rescue and at the same time teach the righteous his wise and mysterious ways.

g) We could also add 1 Cor. 4:5: "The Lord...who will bring to light the hidden things of darkness and disclose the motives of the heart..." This passage alludes to a saying of Jesus in Luke 12:1-3 which warns of Pharisaical hypocrisy, and states that there is nothing covered up that will not be revealed at judgment day. This correlates with Paul's warning in 1 Cor. 3:13 of the fire that will test the quality of each man's work, and with the theme of the above citations that God is wiser than men, upsetting their plans and exposing their vain thoughts.

(6) Another possibility for the meaning of "what has been written" is that it is referring to Paul's own writings to the Corinthians. Supporting this possibility are Paul's frequent references in the Corinthian epistle to his own writings. For example, in 1 Cor. 4:14, which is in the same context as the phrase in question, Paul sums up all the admonitions he has given them by saying, "I *write* not these things to confound you, but I admonish you as my dearest children." This is a general statement referring to all that Paul has written to the Corinthians thus far in the epistle, which at this point encompasses only four chapters. The reference in verse 14 to "writing" in order to "admonish" is very similar to the reference in verse 6 to "what has been written" in order to admonish them not to be "puffed up." In addition, "what has been written" could even hearken back to similar admonitions Paul had given the Corinthians in previous letters. Paul cites these letters, e.g., 1 Cor. 5:9 ("I wrote to you in my letter") and 2 Cor. 10:10 ("...his letters [plural] are severe and forceful...") even though they did not end up in the canonical corpus.[43] If Paul is citing his

---

[43] 1 Corinthians 5:9 appears to refer to an epistle written before 1 Corinthians. 1 Corinthians 5:9 specifies "not associating with fornicators" but nowhere does the epistle of 1 Corinthians mention this command. Hence, a previous epistle may have contained this command. Paul's use of the plural "epistles" in 2 Corinthians 10:9-10 seems to necessitate more than one previous epistle. See also Phil. 3:1: "...to write the same things to you again..."

own writings in 1 Corinthians 4:6, a more idiomatic rendering of the verse could be "so that you learn from our example, not going beyond the warnings [I have] written to you [about false wisdom], so that you do not puff yourselves up one against the other."

(7) Yet another possibility for the meaning of "what has been written" is that it refers to the names and deeds "written" in the book of life — an allusion to the final judgment mentioned in Revelation 20:12 (cf., Exodus 32:33). Since Paul refers to the final judgment in the verse immediately prior to the phrase in question, the connection between the two has some plausibility. In essence, Paul would be telling the Corinthians not to think of themselves as chosen to salvation since no one knows whose names are "written" in the book of life. By judging themselves as already on their way to heaven they were in effect "going beyond what has been written" in the book of life. Although this interpretation is certainly interesting and in line with Paul's theme, it draws from specifics that are not explicit in the context. It limits the meaning of "what has been written" to concepts extraneous to the text at hand. Moreover, in none of Paul's writings does he equate that which is "written" with the "book of life" or with election.

(8) Finally, as mentioned previously, various commentators either hold that the Greek phrasing of "has been written" is so obscure as to be untranslatable, or that the phrase is not an original part of the inspired text. Such arguments are very plausible. Peake was one of the first commentators to suggest that the text of 1 Corinthians 4:6 was corrupt. Although he felt that Paul was telling the Corinthians not to transgress the injunction of Scripture, he admits that the Greek eliptical form and the overall obscurity of the language makes the verse very difficult to interpret. Other commentators have suggested that "what has been written" is a marginal gloss. Plummer critiques this notion, saying that a gloss would have taken some other form. W.F. Howard counters that Plummer's analysis may be true for an interpretive gloss but not for a textual gloss. In support of his theory, Howard cites Johannes Weiss's commentary which also argued that the Greek text is corrupt and unintelligible.[44] The French scholar Bousset and the Dutch scholar Baljon provide further arguments in this regard.[45] Both treat the phrase as a scribe's marginal comment. The remaining text would simply read "that in us you learn that one be not puffed up against the other," coinciding with the third discrepancy of Weiss noted above.[46]

Finally, as noted previously, the Protestant scholar and New Testament translator James B. Moffatt was so thoroughly frustrated

---

44 Weiss points out four areas of discrepancy that lead to his conclusion: (1) there is a suspicious repitition in "τὸ μὴ ὑπὲρ" and "ἵνα μὴ εἷς ὑπὲρ," suggesting that the scribe may have copied "μὴ ... ὑπὲρ" twice but only one was present in the text. (2) the Latin texts do not translate the "ἵνα μὴ," which suggests that it was not in the original from which they copied. (3) the object of "μάθητε" ("to learn") seems to be juxtaposed, suggesting that the phrase "not above what has been written" would fit better *after* the clause "that one be not puffed up against the other." It would make more sense if the Corinthians were to learn that they shouldn't be puffed up rather than learn not to go above what has been written. The latter has no precedent in this epistle whereas the former continues very well the general theme of 1 Corinthians 1-4. The Douay-Rheims version takes note of this juxtaposition and translates accordingly by placing "what has been written" at the end of the sentence (i.e., "...that in us you may learn, that one be not puffed up against the other for another, above that which is written."). (4) the striking absence of "μὴ" ("not") in uncials D (Codex Bazae) and E (Codex Laudianus), which suggests that it was not part of the inspired text.

45 *Die Schriften des New Testament*, 3rd edition, 1917.

46 For Bousset, "τὸ μὴ ὑπὲρ ἃ γέγραπται" is understood as a marginal note instructing the copyist that, "the μὴ is written above the alpha" (i.e., the final letter of "ἵνα"). According to Baljon, the phrase in question is the comment of a scribe who found the "μὴ" added over the "εἷς" (written in the form of a numerical symbol "a"). Weiss starts the gloss from "ἃ" in ("ἃ γέγραπται ἵνα μὴ εἷς") which would read: "the ἃ has been written, [read it as] 'ἵνα' not 'εἷς'" This would necessitate the verb to be an infinitive (Greek: φυσιοῦθαι) rather than the present indicative (φυσιοῦσθε) or subjunctive. Curiously, a corrected version of Codex Sinaiticus (א) contains the infinitive form of the verb. We might also add at this point that though the Greek "ὑπὲρ" with the accusative normally means "above" or "beyond" as noted in the various translations recorded, it can also have the meaning of "over" in the local sense. This again may suggest that the phrase in question was a marginal note to subsequent copiers. It could have crept into the Greek text and become "not beyond what has been written" when it originally was the marginal directive "the μὴ is written *over* the alpha" alerting the scribe that the Greek word "μὴ" had been written "over" the alpha of the word "ἵνα."

with the phrase in question that he made this marginal note in his 1935 edition: "the text and the meaning of the phrase between "μάθητε" [learn] and "ἵνα μὴ" [the second "that"] is beyond recovery."[47] Moffatt does not even attempt to translate the phrase, instead, he makes an unprecedented move in New Testament translation by inserting a dotted line in the place where "what has been written" would normally be. He does not make dotted line emendation for any other verse in his New Testament translation. The closest would be a minor comment about the obscurity of Acts 24:17, but there he still ends up attempting a translation.

Other Grammatical and Textual Considerations in The Exegesis of 1 Corinthians 4:6

For further insights into the direction of Paul's thinking in 1 Corinthians 4:6, an analysis of his Greek grammatical construction yields some interesting clarifications but raises questions as well. The two statements (1) "that in us you may learn" and (2) "that no one of you be puffed up one against the other" both begin with the Greek word "ἵνα" (translated as "that" or "in order that"), but with the second ἵνα clause in grammatical apposition to the first. Some translators see such an intimate connection between the two that they make the clauses consecutive: i.e., "I have in a figure transferred these things to myself and Apollos for your sakes *that* in us you may learn *that* one be not puffed up against the other, not beyond what is written" (Douay-Rheims).[48]

---

47 op. cit., p. 415.

48 As noted previously, the seeming juxtaposition of the object of "μάθητε" ("learn") was one of the issues raised by the Protestant commentator Weiss in an argument which if followed leads to the Douay-Rheims rendition. (This is in spite of the fact that some versions of the Latin Vulgate contain the word order: "ut in nobis discatis illud ne supra quae scripta sunt ne unus pro alio inflemini adversus alterum" (Novum Testamentum Latine, Eberhard Nestle, ed. (Wurttembergische Bibelanstalt, Stuttgart, 1906, 1952) p. 431). By putting the second ἵνα clause directly after the first, this translation teaches that the primary lesson Paul wanted the Corinthians to learn was "not to become puffed up." We see support for such a grammatical structure in the way Paul uses two consecutive ἵνα clauses in other places (e.g., Gal. 4:5).

To complicate matters even further, another possible rendering of 1 Corinthians 4:6 is "...that you might learn in us not *to think* above that which is written..." Sufficient manuscript evidence al-

---

48 cont. Another facet to the Greek grammar that produces the same results as above is that the first ἵνα clause is in the normal subjunctive mood whereas the second is in the indicative, the latter mood being one of the very few instances in the New Testament, independent of textual variants, of a ἵνα clause in the present indicative. The passages which include the subjunctive mood in the manuscript variants are John 5:20; 17:3; Gal. 6:12; Titus 2:4; 1 John 5:20; Rev. 12:6, while Gal. 4:17 and 1 Cor. 4:6 are the only cases of a pure, non-variant, indicative mood with "ἵνα." Even then, some commentators say that these two instances may just be irregularly contracted subjunctives, e.g., "φυσιοῦσθε" in 1 Cor. 4:6 could be "φυσιωσθε" in which the omicron plus eta makes an omega. Similarly, "ζηλοῦσιν" of Gal. 4:17 may be standing in for "ζηλωσιν." Though plausible, these replacements cannot be proved. The indicative form is what appears in the text. The use of ἵνα with the indicative would suggest a dependency on or clarification of the previous statement, that is, the second ἵνα clause would be specifying what has actually been "written," *viz.*, that they do not become puffed up. Keeping the same word order, the sentence could conclude "that in us you may learn not beyond what has been written [concerning] that no one of you be puffed up one against the other" (I insert the word "concerning" to denote the intention of the ἵνα clause in the indicative mood). This reading shows that the primary lesson the Corinthians are to learn is not to be puffed up with pride against one another, while "what has been written" specifies the resource of information on how one avoids becoming puffed up, namely, all that has been written about the pride of man.

A feature of the second ἵνα clause which suggests yet another direction to Paul's thoughts is the use of the negative "ἵνα μὴ" (literally: "that not") which would read: "that not one for one you be puffed up against the other. (This analysis is in spite of the evidence that "μὴ" is missing from Uncials D and E, as noted prior). In Greek, "ἵνα μὴ" can also be translated as "lest" (cf., 1 Cor. 1:15,17; 8:13; 9:12; 2 Cor. 3:3). The sense is: "learn from us... *lest* you puff yourselves up against one another." In other words, if the Corinthians don't live up to the stipulations in the first ἵνα clause ("learn from us"), the consequences will be the results of the second ἵνα clause ("puffing up"). Conversely, introducing the second ἵνα clause only with "that," as many translations do, would more readily connote that what the Corinthians are to learn is *primarily* "not to be puffed up," rather than saying the *result* of not learning is that they will be puffed up. Hence, to say that they were "puffed up above what has been written" is one possible solution but it is also valid to say that they are to learn "not above what has been written *lest* they become puffed up."

lows for the reading of "to think" (Greek: φρονεῖν) to the text.[49] The one translation relying on the Textus Receptus and adding "to think" to 1 Corinthians 4:6 is the King James Version. These translators also added "of men" in italics to show that the text implies a personal reference. The complete translation is: "that ye might learn in us not to think of men above that which is written, that no one of you be puffed up for one against another." Grammatically, it makes the object of "that in us you might learn" to be "that which is written" and, as suggested above by the use of the word "lest," treats the second ἵνα clause as a resultative statement. The addition of "of men," although not absolutely necessary, helps the reader to eliminate extraneous thoughts as to the meaning of "has been written." It limits the phrase in question to all that has been written about men's pride and false wisdom. Since, as the context specifies, the Corinthians were emulating men beyond that which was proper and acceptable, hence Paul warns them that they should not view men beyond these parameters "lest" they become "puffed up for one against another." The parameters within which they must remain were delineated by "that which is written" in the beginning chapters of the epistle.

---

49 The Textus Receptus, a corrected version of Codices Sinaiticus and Bazae, a possible reading of Codex Ephraemi and Rescriptus, one Vulgate manuscript, and all Syriac witnesses, all contain this verb. The manuscripts that omit "φρονεῖν" from the text include Papyrus 46, the original Codices Sinaiticus and Bazae, Codices Vaticanus and Alexandrinus, the three Uncials F, G, U from the ninth century, the fragmentary Uncial 81, and three minuscules. Since many reliable studies have warned against viewing the Textus Receptus as less accurate than other manuscripts, the reader should be wary of dismissing its impact on the discussion (For example, see *The Byzantine Text Type and New Testament Textual Criticism*, doctoral dissertation, by Harry A. Sturz, 1979, et al). Another textual variant uses the relative pronoun "what" in the clause "has been written" (Novum Testamentum Graece, Nestle-Aland, 26th ed., Deutsche Bibelstiftung, Stuttgart, 1979, p. 446). Those manuscripts adding "φρονεῖν," seen from the Textus Receptus above, usually include the nominative or accusative neuter singular "ὃ," whereas the non-Textus Receptus manuscripts contain the nominative or accusative neuter plural "ἃ." The plural form would be translated as "what things" to distinguish it from the singular "what." This textual discrepancy seems to have no bearing on the exegesis of the text, however.

Even if the King James translators took too much liberty by adding "of men," the same idea is nevertheless implied when "to think" is used by itself. Wrong "thinking" was the main problem with the Corinthians. They went beyond what was written by "thinking" themselves to be better than they were. As noted previously, they *thought* they were "rich," and had become "kings," were "wise," "strong" and "held in honor" (cf., 1 Cor. 4:8-19; 3:18); they *thought* they were "eloquent" (cf., 1 Cor. 1:17; 2:4); they "boasted" (cf., 1 Cor. 1:31; 3:21) and *thought* they were the elect of God (1 Cor. 4:1-5). Paul wants to straighten out this self-inflated *thinking* by referring them back to his previous writings condemning such lofty attitudes.[50]

Preliminary Conclusion

As one can surmise from all the possible translations, possible glosses, grammatical irregularities, textual inconsistencies, and contextual problems, the phrase "has been written" in 1 Corinthians 4:6 has not proven to be an easy statement to authenticate, let alone been proven capable of supporting a major doctrine of biblical theology such as *sola scriptura.* Despite this evidence, *sola scriptura* advocates seem to be so oblivious to these difficulties. They unwittingly attempt to classify "not beyond what has been written" as an *a-priori, prima facie* concept of Paul's buried deep within his theological sub-

[50] Other translations rejecting the wording of the Textus Receptus render the clause as: "that you may learn by us not to go beyond what is written" (RSV); "that in us ye might learn not to go beyond the things which are written" (ASV); "that in us you might learn not to exceed what is written" (NASB); "so that you may learn from us not to go beyond what is written (NAB). These translations claim the existence of an ellipsis and thus allow the insertion of "to go" or "to exceed" into the text. Note here that in rejecting "φρονεῖν" ("to think") of the Textus Receptus, these translators are forced to add their own infinitive to make sense out of the verse. Although helpful in one sense, the addition of "to go" or "to exceed" may mislead by implying that the Corinthians were familiar with interpreting written documents and hence were being warned not "to go" beyond these documents. But nowhere does the context suggest that the Corinthians were so in the habit of claiming inspired revelation beyond what was written in Scripture as to require such an abrupt admonition to adhere to Scripture alone.

conscious that somehow bubbles to the surface for the first and only time at this inconspicuous point in his writings. These advocates lead us to believe that Paul, as he suddenly squeezes in a six-word statement in a context that has nothing to do with such high-order theological concepts as *sola scriptura,* is establishing a fundamental rule of biblical hermeneutics. They inflate this small and modest six word statement into a doctrinal proposition on the order of the Incarnation and Justification, doctrines that are replete with scriptural material for discussion whereas *sola scriptura* has virtually no explicit scriptural proofs as to its existence. Like many other verses used to support their position, 1 Corinthians 4:6 becomes the victim of the overly zealous searching for that one succinct verse, the magic bullet, as it were, that will quell their opponents and prove their case. How ironic, then, that the very concept of *sola scriptura*, one that by its very nature can only depend on the perspicuity or clarity of Scripture to sustain its life, should have as its major prop a verse (1 Corinthians 4:6) that is one of the most unverifiable, ambiguous and exegetically difficult passages in the whole Bible.

1 Corinthians 4:6 In Light Of Its General Context

One of the best helps in understanding the meaning of a particular passage of Scripture is to examine the context within which it is contained. Let us bring the context of Paul's letter to bear on this puzzling statement, "not beyond what has been written."

First, since Paul's reference in 1 Corinthians 4:6 to himself and Apollos in the statement "I have transferred these things to myself and Apollos for your sakes" comprehends in "these things" the entire epistle up to this point, it seems evident that our interpretation of 1 Corinthians 4:6 must relate directly to all of the previous chapters. Accordingly, we see the first reference to "Paul" and "Apollos" in 1 Cor. 1:12 where Paul alludes to the popular sayings, "I am of Paul, I am of Apollos..." Paul refers to the same grouping again in 1 Cor. 3:4 using the phrasing, "I am of Paul...and I am of Apollos..." and again in 1 Cor. 3:22, "whether it be of Paul or Apollos..." These references to "Paul and Apollos" show that the context surrounding the references must have a direct bearing on 1 Corinthians 4:6, especially since Paul uses the same names

("I have transferred these things to myself [Paul] and Apollos") to introduce the very phrase in question.

Paul's words in 1 Corinthians 4:14, "I am writing you this...to admonish you...even if you should have countless *guides...*" suggest that the context of the verse in question extends all the way back to Paul's first mention of the various "guides" to Christ. Accordingly, the "guides" to Christ is the first issue Paul addresses in the epistle (1 Cor. 1:10-17). Here Paul speaks of disagreements, divisions, and rivalries among the Corinthians. Paul identifies the various factions by echoing their respective pledges, "I am of Paul, I am of Apollos, I am of Cephas..." From the text we understand that the Corinthians were probably aligning themselves with the person who baptized them.

After introducing the divisions at Corinth, Paul begins a series of statements (1 Cor. 1:18-2:16) concerning the preaching of the "cross of Christ" as opposed to the rhetoric and wisdom of the world. We gather from this additional information that the Corinthians' affection was for certain leaders who ignored the simple message of the cross and subsequently attracted a following by their eloquence of speech, worldly beliefs regarding wisdom, and the power of persuasion, all of which Paul judges to be against the pure gospel. To the Corinthians, the cross of Christ meant weakness and was therefore unattractive. To Paul, the cross was the real power of God—a predetermined, hidden mystery whose power and timing no one suspected (1 Cor. 2:8). As each new worldly idea surfaced, the Corinthians formed another party line in their church. From Paul's comments we understand that the Corinthians had either disdained or watered down the gospel in favor of worldly wisdom.

In chapter three, Paul begins to emphasize the immaturity of the Corinthian's faith, saying that they are "carnally minded" and think like the men of the world. These immature practices center on their false allegiances to Paul, Apollos, and others. In contrast, Paul explains that he and Apollos are mere servants of Christ, planting and watering to be sure, but not to be overly emulated since only God gives the increase. Paul begins a lengthy section (1 Cor. 3:10-23) that indicates the responsibility of every Christian to build the temple of God correctly. Paul warns against forming allegiances to their favorite teacher and mixing the gospel with the wisdom of the world, since each man's work will be judged. Ultimately, those who destroy God's temple, God will destroy (1 Cor. 3:17). Paul warns them that the wisdom of this world is foolishness and that they should not be building the church by such means. Emulating men based on eloquence of speech, worldly knowledge, and contempt for others, etc., will destroy the church, not make it grow (1 Cor. 3:21). The Corinthians had the same problem the apostles had had in the early years of Jesus' ministry. They were vying for position, trying to determine who was the greatest among them. Jesus instructed them that the kingdom of God is not like that at all. It is a kingdom built on the premise that we are to be servants of one another (Matt. 20:20-28).

An even more likely possibility for the identity of the leaders in the competing factions in Corinth is the various teachers within the church itself. Rather than being concerned over whether they are unnecessarily emulating Paul and Apollos, Paul may have been only pointing out that the Corinthians were emulating various Corinthian teachers over other Corinthian teachers. In this case, Paul used his and Apollos's names only to represent these factious Corinthian teachers. This may be the reason why Paul uses the Greek word "μετεσχημάτισα" in 1 Cor. 4:6 ("I have *transferred* these things to myself and Apollos for your sakes"). It is a common teaching tool in which one speaks in the first person to represent the second person. Paul used the same principle in 1 Cor. 4:1-5 when he explained that if he doesn't judge himself as worthy before God, surely the Corinthians should not judge themselves as superior to him. Although Paul doesn't name them, he strongly implies that these divisive and error-filled teachers permeate the Corinthian church.

The direction of Paul's thinking in chapter four is further supported by the verse immediately preceding 1 Cor. 4:6. As the previous chapters (1-3) had expressed Paul's wish that the Corinthians not use their personal wisdom to evaluate men and understand the gospel — a pseudo wisdom which only leads to divisions and false allegiances — Paul reinforces this theme in 1 Corinthians 4:1-5 by telling the Corinthians not to make rash or false judgments about men in general, especially of Paul. In order to drive this point home to the Corinthians, Paul tells them that even he, one of the "ministers of Christ and stewards of the mysteries of God" (1 Cor. 4:1), one who has great authority and knowledge, cannot even judge himself accurately (4:3: "for neither do I judge myself"). Paul goes on to say in verses 4-5 that though his conscience does not condemn him, that alone does not clear him of wrongdoing because the Lord, who knows the secrets of men's hearts, is the ultimate judge of them ("For I am not conscious of anything, yet thereby I am not justified; but he that judges me is the Lord...who will bring to light the hidden things of darkness, and will make plain the counsels of the heart"). God, who is omniscient, may discover sins which Paul, partial to himself, may have dismissed. Hence, if Paul, being the privileged spiritual man that he was, dare not say that he was justified before God, how can the Corinthians, who are so spiritually immature (1 Cor. 3:1-3), judge the hearts of men and rate themselves or another superior to someone else. As Paul says later in the text, many of them were "puffed up" with pride, thinking themselves wiser than and superior to Paul (cf., 1 Cor. 4:6, 18, 19; 5:2).

When Paul speaks of the Lord's coming in which he will "bring to light the hidden things of darkness and will manifest the counsels of the heart" (1 Cor. 4:5), he is referring to judgment day when the Lord will determine who shall receive "praise" from God and who shall be condemned (cf., 1 Cor. 3:13; Luke 12:2-10). Paul had warned earlier that "those who destroy the temple of God, him shall God destroy" (1 Cor. 3:17). Similarly, in 1 Cor. 6:8-10, Paul warns the Corinthians that in defrauding their brother they shall be judged and not receive the kingdom of God (cf., 2 Cor. 12:21). In 1 Cor. 15:1-2, Paul tells them that they are saved only if they hold fast to what Paul had preached to them (cf., 2 Cor. 13:5). In all these instances we see that Paul does not allow them to take their salvation for granted. Paul does not even presume his own faithfulness as is evident in 1 Cor. 9:27, "but I buffet my body and make it my slave lest, perhaps, when I have preached to others, I myself should become reprobate."[51] Similarly, in Phil. 3:10-12 Paul says

---

[51] The Greek word for "reprobate," ἀδόκιμος, is used eight times in the New Testament, preponderantly in contexts of falling from the faith (e.g., 2 Cor. 13:5; 2 Tim. 3:8; Tit. 1:16; Heb. 6:8).

of himself, "...the resurrection from the dead. Not that I have already obtained it, or have already become perfect, but I press on in order that I may lay hold of that for which also I was laid hold of by Jesus Christ." Despite his impeccable Christian life, Paul does not presume that he is destined for the resurrection of life.

Paul's allusion to the Lord's final judgment upon men in 1 Corinthians 4:5 implies that he was admonishing the Corinthians because they had already judged themselves as being among the elect of God — those who did not have to worry about the future judgment. Certainly, if Paul did not judge his own motives and ultimate salvation, how much less were the Corinthians qualified to be their own judges, especially when their judgments were resulting in superior and "puffed up" attitudes toward Paul and their brethren. How different is Paul who, in his humility dares not even call himself 'just,' in comparison to these imposters who teach that a man is justified merely because he believes it to be so.

We gain further insight into Paul's humble attitude in contrast to the Corinthians' superior attitude in the remainder of chapter four. Continuing the theme of "learn in us" in 1 Cor. 4:6,[52] Paul again beseeches the Corinthians to follow his example in 4:16: "Therefore, I urge you, be imitators of me." Paul contrasts his way of life with the Corinthians, bringing their "puffed up" attitudes to the fore by a series of satirical statements. He says he was a "fool for Christ" but they were "wise in Christ." They were "strong" and "held in honor" while he and other apostles were "weak" and "held in disrepute" (1 Cor. 4:8-10). This language is similar to Paul's description of himself in 1 Cor. 2:3: "I came to you in weakness and fear and much trembling." Basically, the Corinthians are a proud lot — they think themselves wiser and stronger than Paul and ultimately wiser than God himself. Paul wants them to learn to be humble like himself. In this way they will not cause divisions nor pervert the pure gospel of Christ-crucified.

---

[52] "In us" is the Greek instrumental or exemplary form meaning: "that, by considering our example, you might learn" (C. F. D. Moule, op. cit., p. 77).

Bringing The Context To Bear on The Exegesis Of 1 Corinthians 4:6

The exegesis of 1 Corinthians 4:6 should address one of the main questions regarding the passage: when Paul says, "that in us you may learn," what specifically does he want the Corinthians to learn? If the phrase in question ("not beyond what has been written") is an actual part of the inspired text, then whatever this phrase means remains a possibility as the primary lesson Paul wants them to learn. The other and more likely choice, however, is that Paul wants them to learn not to become "puffed up, one against another." These two possibilities relate to the apparent juxtapostion of the object of "to learn" that led commentators Howard and Weiss, cited earlier, to suspect that the phrase in question was a marginal gloss. If the phrase in question is not part of the text, then clearly the object of "to learn" can only be "not being puffed up..." Perhaps we need not go as far as to reject the phrase as part of the inspired text; nevertheless, if "not beyond what has been written" were the object of "to learn," nothing in our analysis so far suggests that Paul wants to impose on them the rigors of accepting only divine revelation that comes in the form of writing, i.e., *sola scriptura*. Moreover, nothing in Paul's statements or examples in all of the preceding or subsequent chapters suggests that the phrase, "not beyond what has been written," or its textual counterparts, should be absolutized to mean that the Corinthians must be cautious from this point on to use only the Scripture for authoritative revelation. Paul often requires the Corinthians to follow his way of life, yet he *never* requires them to "follow my example by not using anything but the Scripture for authoritative revelation." When Paul says in 1 Cor. 4:6 "learn in us" and in 1 Cor. 4:16, "Therefore I urge you to imitate me," he is asking the Corinthians to follow the example of his humble lifestyle, not to assume a narrow view of divine revelation. After all, Paul makes quite a big deal over the private revelations he received from God outside the Scriptures, which he in all likelihood forwarded directly to the Corinthians but apparently did not reduce to writing (e.g., 2 Cor. 12:1-9; Gal. 1:15-20). In addition, the Corinthians also had their own oral revelations directly from God in the form of prophecies and tongues (cf.,

1 Cor. 12-14), revelations which obviously did not confine the Corinthians to relying only on the written word.

The main message is that the Corinthians were "arrogant" and "puffed up." Introducing a theological tenet like *sola scriptura* was not going to cure that problem. In fact, confining their resources to Scripture would only have made the problem worse. First, the Corinthians would have had only the Old Testament, as dark and obscure as it was, to shed light on the new gospel. Reading the Old Testament alone without divine revelation to guide its interpretation is not the best method to understanding the complete gospel (cf., Acts 8:32-35; Luke 24:25-27). New Gentile Christians were not even familiar with the Old Testament, let alone capable of understanding it without qualified guidance. If by this time some parts of the New Testament were available to them, this would not have solved the problem either. A partially created New Testament, missing some of the greater and more complete truths of the faith, would only have left them confused and groping for clarification. The New Testament is hard enough to understand in its complete form, let alone in a partial form. Second, confining them to Scripture would have resulted in each teacher proclaiming his own verses with his own interpretation of those verses, further exacerbating the divisions among them. With their ever-present "puffed up" attitudes and dependence on worldly wisdom, unleashing them to try their fortunes in unbridled Scriptural exegesis would only have compounded the problem already present. Looking in hindsight, have not the differing interpretations of Scripture been the very cause of the proliferation of countless denominations and sects in our day? Third, introducing the doctrine of *sola scriptura* would have increased the tension already existing between Paul and the Corinthians. We can venture a guess, if 1 Corinthians 4:6 was teaching *sola scriptura,* as to the Corinthian reaction the next time Paul gave them oral instruction. Paul would issue an oral teaching but the proud and arrogant Corinthians would retort, "Well, Paul, didn't you tell us yourself, 'not to go beyond Scripture' for our instruction? Aren't you contradicting yourself to tell us to stick to Scripture and then expect us to listen to your or another teacher's oral teaching?"

The third reason cited above is not at all far-fetched. Paul was engaged in a constant tug-of-war with the Corinthians concerning his authority over them. Hints of this problem appear repeatedly throughout the two Corinthian epistles. We see the first indication in the false allegiances they proclaimed. When they said, "I am of Apollos, I am of Cephas, and I am of Christ" they were not only forming parties for their own theological preferences; they were also attempting to challenge Paul's authority over them. What better way to get out from under Paul's thumb then to claim an authority higher or better than Paul.[53] Paul, unimpressive in appearance and lacking personal charisma, had to struggle constantly to make a favorable impression with the Corinthians. At times he found himself having to "boast" about his personal revelations from God so that they would respect his authority over them (2 Cor. 12:1ff). Paul had enough problems convincing the Corinthians of his personal revelations from God, without making his teaching of these revelations even more difficult by telling the Corinthians to heed Scripture alone. It is much more likely that Paul was appealing to the written word for help in confirming his own teaching, authority, and his own inspired revelations (cf., 1 Cor. 2:12-13). After all, Paul appealed to Old Testament Scripture six times in those four chapters to back up the admonitions he was giving the Corinthians about pride and false wisdom. It would only be natural for him to allude to these writings in 1 Corinthians 4:6. Perhaps he thought he could persuade the Corinthians more effectively by putting things in writing, especially since they did not think too highly of Paul personally. Paul is the Corinthians's spiritual father who is pleading with them to become his faithful sons. He is trying to bring them under his loving care and gentle authority. One of the hardest tasks in all human relations is to convince those who see your frailties that you have authority over them. Everyone agrees that God is the highest authority and that he has spoken in the Scriptures, but many struggle with the idea that God has spoken to men individually and delegated his authority to them. Paul was not exempt from this problem nor was the church that succeeded him. It should be clear from this context that Paul was not citing written revelation to supplant

[53] Other instances of this tension between Paul and the Corinthians appear in the following passages: cf., 1 Cor. 5:2-3; 9:1-3; 14:36-38; 2 Cor. 3:1; 5:12; 6:11-13; 7:2; 10:8-12; 11:5, 13, 15, 21-12:13, 19.

his or other teacher's oral teaching; he was only using it as a confirming witness to bolster oral teaching (cf., 1 Cor. 15:3-4).

Given Paul's focus on the Corinthians' attitude of smug superiority towards himself and to the gospel of Christ in general, his reference to "what has been written" must in some way draw on sources which would curtail such self-indulgent thinking. If the phrase in question is indeed part of the inspired text, and given that the context does not absolutize the phrase into a teaching of *sola scriptura*, its most likely referent is either the written material in the Old Testament or the writing of Paul himself. A hybrid possibility is that Paul's writings include the statements he quotes from the Old Testament that support the lessons from his own inspired pen.

Our analysis has shown that Paul cites six Scriptures in the first four chapters of 1 Corinthians. We found that all these Old Testament passages address the same theme: the wisdom of God versus the pseudo-wisdom of man. False wisdom, and the pride that either initiated it or stemmed from it, was the main problem of the Corinthian church. They had assumed a wisdom of the world, and with it the arrogance that was contrary to God's wisdom displayed in Christ. Without this criterion to judge truth, divisions developed in the church as each person began to side with the teacher he thought was wiser, stronger, or more eloquent. Since Paul in their eyes had none of these qualities, they spurned his authority and teaching. The Old Testament passages Paul quotes to defend himself against their taunts strike right at the heart of their problem.[54]

Conclusion

Significantly, the admonition of 1 Corinthians 4:6 concerning "not beyond what has been written" does not appear again in the

---

[54] Ironically, John Calvin's interpretation of 1 Corinthians 4:6 is similar to ours. A staunch supporter of *sola scriptura* on theological grounds, Calvin did not see 1 Corinthians 4:6 as supporting his argument. He said of the verse: "The phrase, 'beyond that which is written,' can be explained in two ways, as referring either to what Paul has written, or to the scriptural proofs he has adduced. But because this is not very important, readers are free to choose whichever they prefer." (*Calvin's New Testament Commentaries, First Corinthians*, translated by T. A. Smail (Grand Rapids: MI, Eerdmans Publishing) p. 90).

New Testament. Neither does the remainder of the Corinthian epistles clarify or elucidate this statement. Such a glaring absence from the rest of Scripture confirms that it is relevant only to the situation at Corinth — a situation in which the Corinthians, steeped in worldly wisdom, were inappropriately emulating various men, and thereby causing destructive divisions in the church. When we examine the controversies in the churches of Galatia, Colosse, Rome, or the issues brought up in the pastoral epistles of Timothy and Titus, we do not see Paul defending precepts of truth by an appeal to a doctrine of Scripture alone. If *sola scriptura* was in Paul's mind, he certainly did not make it clear to his readers. The volumes he wrote defending other church doctrines leave us aghast at his total neglect of what we would assume to be an equally important doctrine, if not the most important doctrine of all. Moreover, the multitude of translations, grammatical difficulties, and textual variants surrounding 1 Corinthians 4:6 all testify to the obscurity of the passage. It is certainly ironic that Protestant apologists, who are trying to defend the perspicuity of and exclusive recourse to Scripture to obtain clear and unambiguous truth, would deem such a non-perspicuous verse to be one of the primary proof-texts for *sola scriptura*.

Jesus Condemns the Tradition of the Pharisees

Mark 7: 5-13

So the Pharisees and teachers of the law asked Jesus, "Why don't your disciples live according to the tradition of the elders instead of eating their food with 'unclean' hands?" He replied, "Isaiah was right when he prophesied about you hypocrites; as it is written:

"'These people honor me with their lips, but their hearts are far from me. They worship me in vain; their teachings are but rules taught by men.' You have let go of the commands of God and are holding on to the traditions of men." And he said to them: "you have a fine way of setting aside the commands of God in order to observe your own traditions! For Moses said, 'Honor your father and your mother,'

and, 'Anyone who curses his father or mother must be put to death.' But you say that if a man says to his father or mother: 'Whatever help you might otherwise have received from me is Corban' (that is, a gift devoted to God), then you no longer let him do anything for his father or mother. Thus you nullify the word of God by your tradition that you have handed down. And you do many things like that."

This incident, along with its companion passage in Matthew 15, has become one of the favorite verses of Protestant apologists in their efforts to neutralize Catholic tradition and support *sola scriptura*. Because Jesus puts the tradition of the elders and Pharisees in a bad light, Protestants make the conclusion that Jesus casts a suspicious eye on all tradition. Despite the fact that many Protestants adhere to various traditions and confessions in their own denominations, nevertheless, when it comes to Catholic traditions very little, if any, allowance is made. Whether the tradition is considered apostolic or a practice created in the life of the church over the centuries, "tradition" is a hot-bed of controversy in Protestant / Catholic relations.

To quiet this controversy, a realistic and sensible understanding of this passage is required. We can accomplish this first by focusing on the main themes that Jesus points out in his discussion on tradition. First, three times in the passage Jesus shows his standard of judgment against the tradition of the elders and Pharisees. In verse 8 he says, "You have let go of the commands of God..." In verse 9 he says, "You have a fine way of setting aside the commands of God..." and in verse 13, "Thus you nullify the word of God..." Obviously, Jesus is not condemning tradition, in itself, but specifically tradition that *sets aside God's clear commands*. But, of course, this would be true of any teaching, past or present, which sets aside God's law. It is not the idea of tradition, per se, that Jesus is condemning, but anything that is taught by men which is contrary to God's mandates. Any false doctrine, whether antiquated or modern, can serve as the object of Jesus' condemnation in this passage.[55]

[55] In this passage Jesus uses both the Greek word παράδοσιν ("tradition" in verses 5, 8, 13) and διδασκαλίας ("teachings" in verse 7) in his condemnation.

In order to get the full impact of what Jesus is teaching, we must observe the two phases of his answer to the Pharisees. In the first phase, verses 1-8 focus on a tradition of the Pharisees which prohibited them from eating food with unclean hands. The Pharisees inquire of Jesus why his disciples don't do the same. We must understand that there is nothing particularly wrong with observing a tradition that requires one to wash his hands before eating. In fact, it is the most hygienic way to prepare to eat. Those who don't wash before they eat are considered barbaric in many societies. The Pharisees, however, are washing their hands more for religious reasons than for hygienic reasons. Thus, when Jesus answers the Pharisees, he does not condemn the tradition itself. Instead, he attacks the heart and motivations of the Pharisees. In a word, Jesus points out their religious hypocrisy. They are the kind who clean the outside of the cup, but within themselves they are utterly corrupt (cf., Luke 11:37-41). They give the appearance of being religious but they are full of contempt and hatred for God and man. Perhaps there is nothing wrong, per se, in a tradition that requires one to wash his hands before eating, but it is totally wrong to judge others by such external standards and make oneself superior to those one judges. Their tradition has become superior to God's basic laws of love and kindness and in effect, they have supplanted God's laws with their own laws. Similarly, in Luke 11:42, in a context where the Pharisees had accused Jesus of not washing before he ate, Jesus then says of them, "Woe to you Pharisees, because you give God a tenth of your mint, rue and all other kinds of garden herbs, but you neglect justice and the love of God. You should have practiced the latter without leaving the former undone." We see that Jesus is not condemning the tradition of tithing, in itself. He tells them that they should keep tithing, but not to the extent of ignoring God's more important laws of justice and love. Hence, Jesus ends the first phase of his teaching in Mark 7:8 by saying, "You have let go of the commands of God and are holding on to the traditions of men." What we have learned here is that it was not a crime to have a tradition of washing hands before meals, but it was a crime to ignore God's laws that required love for God and man.

In the second phase of his answer, verses 9-13 penetrate deeper into the traditions of the Pharisees and show that some traditions can be evil practices themselves. To set this up, Jesus brings to the fore two specific commands given by Moses (honoring one's parents and putting to death those who curse parents) and shows how these commands have been set aside and replaced by one all-pervasive teaching called the law of Corban — a law which said that one was not required to requite his parents, rather, whatever was done for them was voluntary, and was actually not done for them personally but was done for God. In effect, the Pharisees were trying to turn the neglect of man into an honor for God. This is a much more serious charge, for now the Pharisees have been accused of teachings that are morally evil. It was the worst kind—presenting something evil to God as if it were good.

In analyzing this passage, we can point out four comparisons and contrasts with tradition as we know it. First, whether Catholic or Protestant, any teaching that purposely sets aside God's laws is condemnable. Whether from antiquity or from more modern times, men create traditions, some of which are good, others which are not to the glory of God. Jesus' condemnation applies to any individual or group that attempts to usurp God's authority and replace it with their own. In this light, we must turn the tables on our Protestant brethren, for if the teachings they hold distinct from Catholicism are indeed incorrect, then they have created man-made traditions, many which stem from the Reformation period, which replace God's truth with man's inventions. For example, if baptismal regeneration is a true doctrine but most Protestants reject it in favor of symbolic baptism, then their doctrine of baptism is a tradition of men, and it is no less a condemnable tradition than the tradition Jesus condemned in Mark 7.

Second, despite Protestant aversion to Catholic tradition, it remains an incontrovertible fact that the New Testament values oral tradition and commands the Church to preserve it (2 Thess. 2:15). No amount of exegetical contortions can dismiss this fact. No Protestant has ever shown where Paul's command to preserve oral tradition was ever rescinded in the New Testament. Hence, we must insist that when one studies Scripture's teaching on tradition, he must be willing to accept that there are two ways in which Scripture judges tradition — on the one hand, it highly praises tradition that is divinely authentic, and on the other hand it castigates tradition that obscures or neutralizes divine teaching.

Third, the problem with the Pharisees was not tradition, per se, but their refusal to form a synthesis of Scripture and divine Tradition that preserved the teaching of Scripture but allowed tradition to serve its main purpose, that is, to expound and enhance Scripture. They made their tradition contradict Scripture instead of using tradition to support Scriptural teaching. This principle is seen more clearly in the passage Jesus quotes from Isaiah. In Isaiah 29:11 the prophet speaks of the neglect of Scripture among the Jews:

> For you this whole vision is nothing but words sealed in a scroll. And if you give the scroll to someone who can read, and say to him, "Read this, please," he will answer, "I can't, it is sealed." Or if you give the scroll to someone who cannot read, and say, "Read this, please," he will answer, "I don't know how to read."

Here we see Isaiah complaining that the people have rejected the words of God written in scrolls by giving child-like excuses, i.e., "it is sealed" and "I don't know how to read." This language reveals that the people had reached such a point in their apostasy that they refused even to read God's words. We also find that their blindness to God's revelation is a product of God's wish to blind them to his truth because of their unrepentance. Isaiah 29:10 records:

> The Lord has brought over you a deep sleep: He has sealed your eyes (the prophets); he has covered your heads (the seers).

Here we see that God is not neutral when men reject him. He will increase and prolong their blindness to his truth. The result of the blindness is that they make excuses that scrolls are sealed and they are unable to read. In effect, their inability to consult and discern God's word is from the condition of blindness that God has given them. Not being able to consult God's word, they resort to a man-made religion of trivial, useless, and often immoral traditions.

What must be made clear, however, is that Israel, as represented by Isaiah and the rest of the prophets and godly people, were true worshipers of God, had read Scripture and obeyed it, and preserved the true tradition that had been passed down since the time of Abraham. These traditions did not set aside God's laws but enhanced and explained them. The same is true in the New Testament. Jesus set up the Church to perpetuate the Scripture and Tradition originating from the Old Testament saints. If man-made traditions seep into the thinking of the people, it is the Church's mandate to separate the good from the bad. Just as she separated true Scripture from that which only purported to be God's word, so she separated divine tradition from that merely produced by men. Just as Jesus was able to separate God's teaching from man's teaching, so the Church he established was given the mandate to do the same, for the Church is Christ's body.

The New Testament prescribes that Scripture and Tradition serve as witnesses to the same truth — in which one witness does not contradict the other. When there is no contradiction between Scripture and Tradition on any given topic, there is truth. Is this not the way that Jesus recognized the means of coming to truth when he told the Jews: "In your own Law it is written that the testimony of two men is valid. I am one who testifies for myself; my other witness is the Father, who sent me" (John 8:17-18). Tradition and Scripture stand as two witnesses verifying one truth. Just as Jesus, being only one witness, calls on the witness of the Father, so Scripture is dependent on the witness of Tradition. All in all, Mark 7 is teaching that it is damnable to deliberately set aside Scripture with man-made traditions, not that Scripture and Tradition cannot exist side by side.[56]

---

[56] See **Appendix 2** by Rev. Mitchell Pacwa for more detailed information on Mark 7 and Matthew 15. See Chapter 5, "Point/Counterpoint: Protestant Objections and Catholic Answers" for analysis of other Scriptures that are purported to support the doctrine of *sola scriptura*.

Chapter 4

What is the Relationship Between Scripture and Tradition?

By Mark P. Shea

Sacred Scripture is the written portion, but not the totality, of Revelation which is given to us by the apostles with the authority of Christ Jesus himself. This is the basic Catholic teaching. But what follows from this is not always clear to our Protestant brethren. The reasons for this unclarity are numerous. Giving up *sola scriptura* and embracing the Catholic understanding of a revelation which comes to us as both written and unwritten is a true paradigm shift and, as such, takes time and patience. For one thing, there is the simple fact that many people imagine they have never put their weight on Sacred Tradition before, so there is a lingering hesitance that the ice, which seems solid, will crack and we will drown wondering, "Why did I ever stop relying on Scripture alone?" In other words, there is the nagging fear in the devout Protestant soul that to give up *sola scriptura* and really embrace Sacred Tradition as revelatory is to overthrow the inspiration and authority of Scripture itself. And this is not a difficult thing to understand, given what seems to many a "Bible-only" believer to be the loud and clear verdict of Scripture which appears to be riddled with condemnation, and nothing but condemnation, for Tradition. For example, "Why do you break the command of God for the sake of your tradition?" says our Lord (Matthew 15:3). "You nullify the word of God for the sake of your tradition," he complains (Matthew 15:6). To the Pharisees he says, "You have let go the commands of God and are holding on to the traditions of men." (Mark 7:8). He specifically warns of teachings that "are but rules taught by men" (Mark 7:7).

The same is true for the apostles. Paul, for instance, cautions the Colossians against "hollow and deceptive philosophy which depends on human tradition and the basic principles of this world rather than on Christ" (Colossians 2:8), and prophesies that the day will come when "some will abandon the faith and follow deceiving spirits and things taught by demons" (1 Timothy 4:1). Peter also warns of the empty way of life "received by tradition from your fathers" (1 Pet 1:18). Further, Luke records Paul's warning to the Ephesian elders that "After I leave, savage wolves will come in among you and will not spare the flock. Even from your own number men will arise and distort the truth in order to draw away disciples after them" (Acts 20:29-30).

This is sinister stuff. And all of it appearing to finger Sacred Tradition as the villain of the piece. However, the operative word here is "appearing." For as we shall see, this is not all the Scriptures have to say about Tradition. But before we find out what Scripture says, it is important to understand what Catholics mean by the term Sacred Tradition.

To answer that, we must first ask, what is tradition? Essentially, tradition is a thing *handed down* from one generation to the next. This is precisely the meaning of the biblical word for tradition: *paradosis*.[1] Tradition greets us in many forms and we may make distinctions between "large T" and "small t" traditions even in secular and folk culture. "Small t" traditions are things which "dress" life and which express some bit of a heritage yet which, in a pinch, could probably be done without and not irreparably damage that heritage (though the deprivation would sting). Some "small t" traditions (like toasting the bride and groom) are very ancient and can cross many cultures. Some (like fireworks on the Fourth of July) are fairly new and may be confined to only one culture. Some

---

[1] *Paradosis* is a transliteration of the Greek word παράδοσις which appears thirteen times in the New Testament (cf., Matt. 15:2-6; Mark 7:3-13; 1 Cor. 11:2; Gal. 1:14; Col. 2:8; 2 Thess. 2:15; 3:6). The word is made up of two components: "para" meaning "alongside of" and "dosis" meaning "to give."

have religious significance (like blessed wedding rings), some are just ingrained customs (like a birthday cake and candles). Human culture is awash in a veritable sea of such "small t" traditions ranging from throwing wedding rice, to setting out menorahs, to celebrating bachelor parties, to Homecoming Dances, to having annual vacations in Fort Lauderdale. And, as such, nobody fears tradition. It is a profoundly human thing.

However, tradition is more than the mere cultural window dressing of "small t" traditions. It is not *just* charming customs. It is also a way of being, thinking and perceiving the world which powerfully (and often *unconsciously*) colors and influences how we order our lives and even our relationship with God. Americans, for example, have a long-standing heritage of self-governance and a certain distrust of the powerful which influences our outlook on life far more deeply than the mere tradition of fireworks on the Fourth of July. Compared to the "small t" tradition of sparklers on July 4th, the deep-rooted distrust of kings and princes is Tradition with a capital T in the American psyche. It is the secret fuel of everything from the American Revolution, to the Civil War, to the Vietnam protests. Its powerful grip on the way we live can hardly be overestimated, precisely *because* such a grip is often largely unconscious. In short, Americans, if they had to, could celebrate July 4th without fireworks; but they could only mourn and hate a July 4th without representative government and freedom of speech.

Now this distinction between "small t" and "large T" tradition holds true in the realm of the sacred as well, according to Catholic teaching. That is, there are aspects of Christian life which, the Church teaches, are principally handed on to us, not so much through Scripture as through the Tradition of the Church. Some of this tradition, says the Church, is "small t" stuff: candles, styles of prayer, favorite carols and songs, popular forms of devotion, beloved books, treasured old rituals like blessing the children at bedtime, foods associated with particular holidays, legends like the Little Drummer Boy, nursery rhymes and jingles, and a billion other such adornments to the life of faith. All such things are part of the warp and woof of an ordinary human life immersed in ordinary human culture. We first learn the faith, not from trained theologians or from our Bibles, but from our mommies and daddies. And we do so, not by elaborate discourses on the Christology of St. Paul, but by hearing and absorbing the *Tale of Martin the Cobbler* or by prayers like "Now I lay me down to sleep."

Yet, when push comes to shove, we also know that none of these "small t" traditions, though they are vital and living, are *essential* to the Faith. Rather than the *Tale of Martin the Cobbler*, our parents could just as easily have told us the story of the *Stubborn Donkey Who Carried Jesus* and they would not have been maiming the Faith thereby. For it is the nature of "small t" tradition to be somewhat mutable. But if they neglected to tell us that Jesus Christ is "God from God, Light from Light, True God from True God, Begotten, Not Made", they would have truly been failing to hand down not a tradition, but Tradition. For as the Church makes very clear, there are some aspects of the Tradition that are emphatically *not* mutable and can be neglected only at the cost of radically injuring the Christian Faith.

It is really here that the worries of Bible-only Christians get stirred into the mix. For while Catholics are worrying about what will happen if you *subtract* from Tradition handed down in both written and unwritten form, our Bible-only brothers and sisters are worrying about what will happen if you *add* to it. The big question for them is "What if essentially human things get muddled with essentially divine things? As the Pharisees with their rules and regulations (and their cancerous religious pride) make clear, when such muddling happens it is quite possible for human beings to become so obsessed with observing their own traditions that they set aside the commands of God."

Yet the Catholic can, I think, allay these fears — and call the Bible as an ally and a witness to both their faith and to the primary concerns of their brother and sister Evangelical Christians. For at bottom, both the Bible-only Christian and the Catholic Christian have the same concern: the corruption of revelation. And that is precisely the core of the biblical denunciation of certain traditions: they are "traditions of *men*" (Mark 7:8), "rules taught by *men*" (Mark 7:7), not the commands of God but "*your* tradition" (Matthew 15:3). In a word, "*human* traditions" (Colossians 2:8) masquerading as revelation from God. It is this, and only this, which the Bible, like Catholic teaching, condemns.

But the Catholic faith, in its wariness of human tradition usurping divine revelation, sees a bit further. For it knows the ironic truth that fear of human tradition can *itself* become a human tradition and set aside the commands of God. How? By ignoring the *rest* of what Scripture has to say about Tradition and assuming that *all* Tradition, simply because it is Tradition, must therefore be merely human — a claim the Bible never makes. Thus, some people feel justified in adopting the Bible-only mentality that revelation can *only* be in the form of written Scripture.

But is this what Scripture itself says? Does Scripture condemn *all* Tradition as necessarily human tradition? To answer this, let us begin by looking at two passages from 2 Thessalonians. First, Paul tells the Thessalonians:

> So then, brethren, stand firm and hold to the traditions which you were taught by us, either by word of mouth or by letter.(2 Thess. 2:15—RSV)

> Now we command you, brethren, in the name of our Lord Jesus Christ, that you keep away from any brother who is living in idleness and not in accord with the tradition that you received from us. (2 Thess. 3:6 —RSV)

If all tradition without exception is the nemesis of Scripture, Paul does not seem to be aware of it here, despite what he has said elsewhere. For he specifically commands the Thessalonians to "hold to the *traditions*" (Greek: *paradosis*) they were given "by word of mouth". Indeed, he specifically warns them to steer clear of those who *don't* hold to the Traditions they have received from him. If the formula is Scripture=Revelation/Tradition=Human Corruption, what are we to make of this command and this warning?

Many believers propose the following solution to the problem: "The New Testament," they say, "had not yet been written when Paul said this (the letters to the Thessalonians being two of the earliest Christian documents). Therefore, it was necessary for the Church to rely on the oral teaching of the apostles until the Bible was complete. Once the Bible *was* complete, however, it said *everything* that had constituted the *paradosis* Paul mentions. So apostolic 'tradition' means, for us, Scripture and only Scripture." The Evangelical *New Bible Dictionary* puts it this way:

> Apostolic tradition was at one time oral, but for us it is crystallized in the apostolic writing containing the Spirit-guided witness to the Christ of God. Other teaching, while it may be instructive and useful and worthy of serious consideration, cannot claim to be placed alongside the Old Testament and New Testament as authoritative without manifesting the same defect as condemned Jewish tradition in the eyes of our Lord.[2]

So, the argument goes, when perfection comes, the imperfect will disappear (1 Corinthians 13:10). When Scripture came, it swallowed up the *paradosis* of which Paul spoke so that there is no revelation passed on to us anywhere but in Scripture.

This seems, at first glance, to be a reasonable theory for reconciling Scripture's endorsement of Tradition with current denial of it in Bible-only Christianity. But upon closer examination the theory reveals some very significant flaws.

First, where in the biblical text is the basis for the Bible-only belief that Scripture swallows Tradition? Certainly it is not in 2 Thessalonians or 1 Corinthians 13. Nor is it made clear anywhere else that the *paradosis* of which Paul spoke would someday be "crystallized" in Scripture alone. On the contrary, Paul's command in 2 Thessalonians 2:15 gives no sign whatsoever that he regards the Tradition he had given them as being in any special need of "crystallization." Granted, Paul clearly regards his writings as invested with apostolic authority and therefore as the word of God (1 Thessalonians 2:13), but he nonetheless speaks, not of some future complete New Testament, but of "the teaching you received from us" as the one and only source of revelation—a teaching which was almost entirely oral and which 1 and 2 Thessalonians are written to underscore, not replace. Thus, in contrast to the *New Bible Dictionary*, Paul refers the Thessalonians to the oral *paradosis* of the *past*, not to the completed canon of the future; to what they

---

2 *New Bible Dictionary*, 2nd Edition, J.D. Douglas, Organizing Editor, (Wheaton: Tyndale House, 1984) p. 1212.

have already *heard*, not merely to what he is writing or will someday be written by him and others. He does not think of the Tradition as "imperfect" and of the written as "perfect". Rather he thinks of the whole thing, both spoken and written, as apostolic and therefore as authoritative.

And Paul is not alone. Luke also writes to underscore, not replace, the apostolic Tradition Theophilus has *already received.* Thus, he begins by saying, "It seemed good to me to write an orderly account for you, most excellent Theophilus, so that you may know the certainty of *the things you have been taught*[3] [that is, the *paradosis* 'by word of mouth']" (Luke 1:3-4). In other words, Luke also offers his writing in union with, not in replacement of, the *paradosis.* He too thinks Theophilus should hold fast to the Traditions that he was taught, either by word of mouth or by letter.

Likewise, John twice acknowledges that his written record of Jesus does not deny other extrabiblical traditions (John 20:30; 21:25), so long as these traditions do not *oppose* his teaching and that of the other apostles (cf. 1 John 2:18-19; 4:1-3; 2 John 7-9). For John, as well as Luke, the test for authentic Christian teaching is not "Is this written?" but "Is this apostolic?"

In short, there is no New Testament evidence that the apostolic *paradosis* was an "imperfection" designed to be "crystallized" in writing. Neither Jesus (who never wrote any Scripture) nor the Twelve (who were never commanded to commit *anything*—much less *everything*—to writing, except for the book of Revelation (Revelation 1:19)), nor any other New Testament author, provide an ounce of support for the idea that the biblical writings swallowed apostolic Tradition and completely "crystallized" or "perfected" the entirety of the *paradosis* once handed on by word of mouth.

That is the first problem with the Bible-only theory. The second is this: Exactly how, on the basis of the Bible alone, do we *know* that the content of the *paradosis* handed on by letter and the *paradosis* handed on by word of mouth are absolutely identical? Paul does not tell us what he said to the Thessalonians "by word of

---

3 The word "taught" is from the Greek κατηχήθης, from which we get the English word "catachesis" or "catechism."

mouth." Therefore, any claim to know that the content of his oral *paradosis* is identical to the content of his written *paradosis* is just whistling in the dark. The fact is, we can't know, based on the text of Scripture alone. The theory is simply a bold guess, and thus a very weak support for Bible-only revelation.

The third and most glaring problem with the Bible-only theory lies hidden in the five little words "once the Bible was complete." For, of course, the question which eternally dogs *sola scriptura* is the question of how, based on Scripture alone, we know *what* books constitute a complete Bible. Apart from Sacred Tradition and the authority of the Church as the basis for knowing what a complete Bible looks like (the validity of which are denied in Bible-only circles), we find ourselves simply arguing in a circle, saying, "We know Scripture is the totality of revelation because we know the totality of revelation is Scripture."

Thus, rather than explaining away this problem of Paul's endorsement of Tradition, we have simply lost sight of it momentarily in a bit of fog. But when the fog clears, the question remains, if Scripture condemns *all* Tradition as merely human, why does Paul commend and even command our faith in it? To find out, the best thing to do is begin by placing Paul's comments about Tradition (both the positive and the negative) in the context of the rest of Scripture. Let's begin with the Old Testament.

Extrabiblical Tradition in the Old Testament

When we begin to examine the Old Testament with a view to its treatment of Tradition, we discover a curious thing. The Old Testament seems to have the same odd view of Tradition that the New Testament does. Sometimes the Old Testament fiercely condemns tradition (for example, from false prophets, e.g., Jeremiah 28). It is not for nothing that Jesus' condemnation of tradition is borrowed from the words of Isaiah (Isaiah 29:13). The prophets, like our Lord, are quite ferocious in their opposition to those who "call evil good and good evil" (Isaiah 5:20) and who replace the word of God with the words of men (cf. Isaiah 13:10; Jeremiah 14:14; Micah 2:6-11). In this, they are also like Moses, who opposed Korah and his merely human assertions of authority (cf.

Numbers 16; Jude). For the Old Testament writers, like the New, vehemently oppose substituting the word of God with the traditions of men.

Like Paul, however, they do not therefore conclude that all Tradition is, *ipso facto*, *human* tradition. How do we know? Because the Old Testament writers received enormous amounts of extrabiblical (or more precisely *pre*biblical) Tradition as revelation. How, after all, does the author of Genesis know about the Adamic, Noahic and Abrahamic Covenants if not from Sacred Tradition? All these events occur centuries before the birth of Moses and none of them are written down till the book of Genesis is composed. Similarly when God reveals himself in the Burning Bush, Moses knows who God is talking about when the Voice declares, "I am the God of your father, the God of Abraham, the God of Isaac, and the God of Jacob" (Exodus 3:6). How do Moses and all the rest of the children of Israel know about these figures from Israel's remote past? Because the stories preserved in Genesis were quite obviously passed down in Tradition, and neither Moses nor the children of Israel saw anything inherently unsatisfactory or evil about this. In short, they recognized that tradition can be a vehicle not only of human opinion, but of divine revelation as well.

The same applies to much of the Old Testament. The writer of Joshua makes it clear that the events he relates are stories separated from his own day by a long period of time (Joshua 4:9; 6:25). Likewise, whole books such as Judges, 1 and 2 Kings and 1 and 2 Chronicles are clearly composed many years (sometimes centuries) after the events they describe. How then do the authors know of the things they are recording? The same way Moses knows of events hundreds of years before his birth: Sacred Tradition. And again, we have no hint that the Tradition recorded by the authors of Scripture is somehow dubious.

"No," replies our Bible-only friend, "but then neither are they still traditions. For as we have just noted, the traditions were preserved in Scripture *alone*, not in Scripture and Sacred Tradition. That is why Christ and the apostles never say 'it is said' or 'it is in our tradition...' Rather, they always say 'it is written.' For whatever may be the case with the Old Testament, the fact remains that the New Covenant is superior to it. And under that New Covenant, there is no revelation handed down in Sacred Tradition along with the books of the Old Testament. Christ and the apostles refer their hearers exclusively to Scripture as the authoritative source of revelation." That is the claim. Now let us see what the New Testament writers say.

Extrabiblical Tradition in the New Testament

It is, of course, quite true that the New Covenant is superior to the Old. Paul makes this clear in, among other places, the epistle to the Galatians when he describes the provisional and temporary nature of the Old Covenant, saying, "What, then, was the purpose of the law? It was added because of transgressions until the Seed to whom the promise referred had come." (Galatians 3:18). The Seed, of course, is the Messiah, the Seed of Abraham, the Incarnate Word. And one of the signs his covenant is superior is because it is a covenant made through the Son of God himself and not merely through a creature as the law of Moses was. For as Paul points out, the law was put into effect, not by God directly, but "through angels" (Galatians 3:19). The author of Hebrews concurs with Paul and warns, "For if the message spoken by angels was binding, and every violation and disobedience received its just punishment, how shall we escape if we ignore such a great salvation?" (Heb 2:2). Likewise Stephen, the first martyr, makes precisely the same claim just minutes before he is martyred. Speaking to the Jews of Jerusalem, he cries out "and now you have betrayed and murdered him—you who have received the law put into effect through angels but have not obeyed it" (Acts 7:53).

So it is quite clear: the New Testament does indeed teach the New Covenant to be greater than the Old. And one of the principal signs of this superiority is that the Old Covenant was put into effect through angels while the New Covenant was put into effect by the Incarnate God himself. However, this faces the advocate of Bible-only revelation with a serious problem. *For there is no place in the entire Old Testament which teaches the Mosaic Covenant was given through angels.*

Where then do these New Testament figures get this teaching? From extrabiblical Tradition known, not only to these writers, but to other Jews as well.[4]

Nor is this New Testament citation of Tradition an isolated incident. Paul, for instance, also writes to Timothy this warning concerning deceivers in the Church:

> Just as Jannes and Jambres opposed Moses, so also these men oppose the truth — men of depraved minds, who, as far as the faith is concerned, are rejected. But they will not get very far because, as in the case of those men, their folly will be clear to everyone. (2 Timothy 3:8-9)

Who are Jannes and Jambres? Well, the Old Testament doesn't mention them, but if you consult a handy Bible reference work, you find they are the Egyptian magicians who opposed Moses. So... if these gentlemen are not in the Old Testament, how do Paul (and Timothy) know their names? The same way thousands of their contemporaries knew. For, in fact, Paul is again drawing on (and assuming Timothy will draw on) a widely known extrabiblical *Tradition,* and treating it as authoritative revelation.[5]

Jude does the same thing — twice! First, he speaks of the time the Archangel Michael disputed with Satan over the body of Moses (v. 8-9). His Old Testament reference? There is none. For it is a Tradition found only in the non-canonical book, the *Assumption of Moses*. Evidently both Jude and the author of the *Assumption of Moses* regard this extrabiblical Tradition as important. Then, a few verses later, Jude again draws on extrabiblical Tradition and refers (vrs. 14-15) to a prophecy of Enoch recorded, not in the Old Testament, but in the book of Enoch, another non-canonical book. The book of Enoch was composed about a century or two before Christ. However, according to Genesis 5:18-24, Enoch himself lived long

---

4 *The Jerome Biblical Commentary*, Vol. 2, Raymond E. Brown, S.S., Joseph A. Fitzmyer, S.J., Roland E. Murphy, O. Carm., eds., (Englewood Cliffs: Prentice-Hall, 1968) p. 243. (According to this commentary this tradition is attested, not only by these New Testament writers, but by such sources as Josephus' *Antiquities of the Jews* and the *Book of Jubilees*).

5 *New Bible Dictionary*, p. 551

before *Noah*. Thus for Jude to quote a prophecy of Enoch's as inspired revelation is Jude's acknowledgment that Tradition—in this case the Tradition of Enoch's prophecy—is revelation.

Then there is the epistle to the Hebrews. The author writes of the suffering Old Testament prophets:

> Some faced jeers and flogging, while still others were chained and put in prison. They were stoned; *they were sawed in two*; they were put to death by the sword. (Heb 11:36)

Again the champion of Bible-only revelation is faced with a problem. For nowhere in the Old Testament is any hero or prophet martyred by being *sawed in two*. What, then, is the author of Hebrews talking about? He is talking about a Tradition preserved, not in the Old Testament, but in the *Ascension of Isaiah* 5:1-14, another piece of late Old Testament-era literature which was never canonized.[6] For it was a well-known Tradition that Isaiah met his end this way—a Tradition preserved both by the author of Hebrews and by the author of the *Ascension of Isaiah*.

But most striking of all (for the Bible-only advocate) is our Lord himself. For like the apostles, he, too, turns out to be perfectly willing to accept Tradition as a vehicle of revelation. For he tells his disciples:

> The teachers of the law and the Pharisees sit in Moses' seat. So you must obey them and do everything they tell you. But do not do what they do, for they do not practice what they preach. (Matthew 23:2-3)

As with all the other aspects of Tradition cited above, nowhere in the Old Testament do we find reference to "Moses' seat" as the title for the teaching authority in Israel. Like all the other facets of New Testament teaching we have seen above, it too is found only in Tradition![7] Yet Jesus honors and even exalts such a position of authority and its traditional name, and even binds his followers to honor it. In short, our Lord, too, acts just the way Paul

---

6 *The Jerome Biblical Commentary*, Vol. 2, p. 402.

7 Ibid., p. 102.

says we should: he condemns *only* human tradition, but honors authentic divine *paradosis* whether it comes by word of mouth or by Scripture. It is not the Tradition of God, but the tradition of men, that is condemned.

Very well then, the Tradition of God is handed down "both by word of mouth and by letter" all through the Christian revelation. And there is no indication that the reliance on that Tradition which characterizes huge stretches of the Old Testament, is abrogated in the New. On the contrary, in book after New Testament book, and author after New Testament author (not to mention our Lord himself), there remains a very clear awareness that revelation is sometimes handed down in writing, but is also sometimes handed down by the Tradition of God preserved in the life of the Old Israel and then in the life of the New Israel.

But, comes the objection, Paul implies Scripture is sufficient to equip the man of God (2 Timothy 3:16). What need is there, then, of Tradition?

Formal vs. Material Sufficiency of Scripture

The Catholic Faith can agree that Scripture *is* sufficient. But (Theological Technobabble Alert!) it also warns that there is a distinction between *material* and *formal* sufficiency. What's the difference between material and formal sufficiency? Simply put, it is the difference between having a big enough pile of bricks to build a house and having a house made of bricks. Material sufficiency means that all the bricks necessary to build doctrine is there in Scripture. However, it also teaches that since the meaning of Scripture is not always clear and that sometimes a doctrine is implied rather than explicit, other things besides Scripture have been handed to us from the apostles: things like Sacred Tradition (which is the mortar that holds the bricks together in the right order and position) and the Magisterium or teaching authority of the Church (which is the trowel in the hand of the Master Builder). Taken together, these three things—Sacred Scripture, Sacred Tradition, and the Magisterium — are *formally* sufficient for knowing the revealed truth of God.

In contrast, those who hold to Bible-only revelation hold the notion that Scripture *alone* is formally sufficient and therefore does not need Sacred Tradition or the Magisterium to elucidate its true meaning. The idea of the formal sufficiency of Scripture has been asserted in various ways, but all the attempts to do so depend on a confusion. Typically, there is the persistent idea (despite all the biblical evidence we have already seen to the contrary) that the "word of God" refers simply and solely to Scripture. Thus, in argument after argument, those who hold to the formal sufficiency of Scripture warn darkly that setting Scripture in the context of Sacred Tradition will inevitably put Scripture *under* the Church. The fear, in fact, is that to admit the revelatory nature of Sacred Tradition will necessarily subjugate Scripture to merely human agendas. For despite the biblical evidence that Tradition can sometimes be authoritative revelation, there remains the lingering notion that, when all is said and done, Scripture alone is the basis of the Church in the same way, for example, the Constitution is the basis of the United States of America. In short, the foundation of the Church is the word and the word is the Bible. Any appeal to Tradition is therefore seen as an attempt to move the House of God off its foundations.

But is this the way Scripture is treated in the New Testament? Is the word of God always regarded as synonymous with a written word? Is the Church seen as founded on a formally sufficient Bible? On the contrary, history and common sense clearly place the Church *before* the completed Bible — decades before it was all written and centuries before it was fully collated and canonized. That is why there was a Thessalonian *Church* to whom Paul could write the earliest parts of the New Testament.

So the question is: If the early Church was not founded on the formally sufficient Scriptures, in what sense *was* it "founded on the word of God"? To find out, let us begin by looking at the way in which the Apostle Paul encountered the gospel.

The conversion of Saul of Tarsus truly begins with the martyrdom of Stephen. Saul heard Stephen preach, a goad that stuck in Saul's conscience (Acts 26:14). Yet we must emphasize that what distinguishes Stephen when he preaches to the Sanhedrin in Acts 7 is not so much his faith in the written word of God as his faith in the *unwritten* word of the apostles. After all, everybody in Stephen's audience knows their Scripture as well as Stephen. Both Stephen and his hearers have been reading it for years and know by heart its stories, lessons and prophecies. But only Stephen sees in the pile of bricks that is the Hebrew Bible a clear message concerning the life and person of Jesus of Nazareth. What, then, is the word of God Stephen is really offering Saul and the Sanhedrin? Not the Bible, but the apostolic *paradosis*. It is this *paradosis* which is the mortar that builds the bricks of the materially (but not formally) sufficient Hebrew Bible into the revelation of Christ. It is also this *paradosis* which provokes the elders (and also Saul) to notice something of a difference between the way they read *their* Bibles and the way Stephen reads *his* — and to stone him to death.

But, of course, as we know from Acts, Saul later changes his mind, rather radically, about the gospel of Stephen. What causes this change? More diligent Bible study? No, change is effected when Saul comes to accept that the bricks of Scripture must be assembled with the same materials and according to the same plan which Stephen used—the revelation of Christ *and* the *paradosis* of the apostles. For as Paul repeatedly says, Christ not only revealed himself in a moment of mystical ecstasy on the Damascus Road, he revealed himself just as reliably through the word of God which was handed down to him through the unwritten apostolic *paradosis*.

"What?" say some, "I thought Paul told the Galatians he did not receive his gospel "from any man, nor was I taught it, rather, I received it by revelation from Jesus Christ" (Galatians 1:12). So he did. But that does not mean he thereby disavowed any dependence on the Tradition handed down by the Twelve. Rather, by those words he aimed to deny the claims of certain critics that he did not really have apostolic authority from Christ (cf. 2 Corinthians 3-4). In the same way, the Pauline teaching that Christ is the Son of God does not thereby disavow the equally true claim that Christ is the Son of Man. Neither doctrine conflicts with the other in Paul's mind.

To prove this, note that Paul, a few lines later, specifically notes that he went to Jerusalem to present his preaching to the apostles and make sure that they *approved* of his doctrine, "for fear I was running or had run my race in vain" (Galatians 2:2). Further, a quick reading of his letters shows that Paul often relies on all sorts of unwritten apostolic Tradition in the form of doxologies (cf., Gal.1:5; Phil. 4:20; Rom. 11:36; Eph. 3:21), hymns (cf., Phil. 2:6-11; Col. 1:15-20; Eph. 5:14), stories (1 Cor. 11:23-25), and prayers (1 Cor.

16:22), which he hands down to his churches as authoritative revelation with no qualms at all. This reliance on apostolic *paradosis* is precisely why, even though he did not know Christ during his time on earth, Paul nonetheless has extensive knowledge of his life, trial, death, resurrection and ascension. For example, Paul knows Jesus is a Jew of the House of David (Romans 1:3); that John the Baptist was his prophet and had rejected any claim to be Messiah (Acts 13:24-25); that his Big Three disciples were Peter, James and John (Galatians 2:9); that he had predicted his return "like a thief" (1 Thessalonians 5:4); that he had instituted the Eucharist on the night he was betrayed (1 Corinthians 11:23-25); that he had been rejected by the Jewish leaders (1 Thessalonians 2:15), tried under Pontius Pilate (1 Timothy 5:13) and crucified for us (Galatians 3:1); that he was laid in a tomb (Acts 13:29); that he had been raised from the dead and seen by many witnesses (an already standardized list of five hundred people whom Paul recites in 1 Corinthians 15:3-8); and that he had ascended (Ephesians 4:9-10). All these data are clearly treated by Paul as part of a common deposit of apostolic Tradition to which all Christians are privy, not as things mystically revealed to him on the Damascus Road.

And it is no wonder. For Paul was taught, like every other new Christian, that Christ had told the Twelve, "He who listens to you listens to me" (Luke 10:16) and thus to make no distinction whatever between the Tradition of the apostles and the authoritative revelation of Christ. Therefore it makes perfect sense that Paul "went up to Jerusalem to get acquainted with Peter and stayed with him fifteen days" (Galatians 1:18). It makes perfect sense that during his long years in Tarsus and Antioch before his first missionary journey he would have done what Scripture said all new Christians did: learn the "elementary teachings about Christ" and "instruction about baptisms, the laying on of hands, the resurrection of the dead, and eternal judgment" (Heb 6:1-2). And it would make perfect sense that he would thereafter spend the rest of his life appealing to Tradition handed down from the Twelve in a way which plainly shows such Tradition is, for him, "from the Lord."

Thus, Paul repeatedly tells the Corinthians "what I received I passed on to you" (1 Corinthians 11:23; 15:3). What did Paul receive and pass on? In these passages, it is the stories concerning the

Lord's Supper and the Resurrection. From whom did Paul receive these stories? "From the Lord," says Paul (1 Corinthians 7:10; 14:34). Is Paul therefore saying Jesus Christ gave a direct account of these (and all the other events of his life) on the Damascus Road? No. Paul is saying he received the apostolic *paradosis*; the same one Stephen knew and the same one Peter, James, John and the other apostles preached. For in using the terms "receiving and handing on," Paul is, in fact, using common rabbinical jargon which means literally, "I am transmitting, without addition or subtraction, a *Tradition* I have been taught."[8] And since, for Paul, as for every other early Christian, "he who listens to the apostles listens to Christ" (Luke 10:16), Paul simply refers to the Traditions as "from the Lord" since they are, in fact, the heart and soul of what Christ has commissioned the apostles to preach.

This accounts for why the two gospel stories related in 1 Corinthians (the institution of the Eucharist and of the Resurrection) bear an almost word-for-word resemblance to other accounts of these events (in the written gospels) which are separated from this epistle by decades, mountain ranges and seas. Matthew, Mark, Luke and Paul all drew on a common *paradosis*, known to all the churches, which set the most important parts of the story (such as the story of the Passion—including the institution of the Eucharist and the narrative of the Resurrection) in a kind of liturgical concrete that admitted very little variation. It is precisely adherence to this common *paradosis* which the apostle applauds when he tells the Corinthians:

> I commend you because you remember me in everything and maintain the traditions even as I have delivered them to you. (1 Corinthians 11:2 — RSV)

Here, once again, the apostle is commending adherence to the apostolic *paradosis* and here, once again, he is thinking not merely of written Scripture but of extrabiblical apostolic Tradition as well. As with the Thessalonians, the very thing Paul does *not* do is give

---

8 *The Jerome Biblical Commentary*, Vol. 2, p.449, n. 29; James H. Moulton and George Milligan, *The Vocabulary of the Greek New Testament Illustrated From the Papyri and Other Non-literary Sources*, (London: Hodder and Stoughton, 1930) p. 483.

the Corinthians the slightest hint that writing alone is the word of God or that Scripture will someday contain everything he has delivered extrabiblically. Quite the opposite, he praises them for holding to the *paradosis* which has *already been handed on to them before his letters were written* and urges them to stick to both his letters *and* this extrabiblical Tradition. Thus, in Corinth as well as in Thessalonica, the total *paradosis* — the complete word of God— is the formally sufficient brick house of Scripture, Tradition and Apostolic authority — not merely the materially sufficient pile of Scripture bricks alone. It is upon this that the churches are founded.

This also is the case in the Acts of the Apostles. For the book of Acts in no way portrays Scripture alone as the foundation of the nascent churches (though a few things occasionally get written). This is not, of course, to say the apostles reject Scripture as the word of God any more than Catholics do. But it is to say that the plain record of Acts is that nobody spends much time writing Scripture. Why? They are too busy preaching. And it is this *preached* Tradition in union with Scripture which virtually always constitutes what the New Testament calls "the word of God" (Ephesians 1:13; 2 Timothy 2:15).

Thus, just like the Catholic Church, Paul calls the writings of the Old Testament the "words of God" (Romans 3:2). Moreover, when the apostles do occasionally write something, they teach their churches to regard this, too, as authoritative; "not as the word of men, but as it actually is, the word of God" (1 Thessalonians 2:13). But these words are authoritative *not* because they are written but because they are *apostolic*. That is why, again and again, the apostles also refer to their preached message — the message "by word of mouth" as "the word of God" (cf. Acts 2:41; 4:4; to name just a couple of references). Indeed, in the book of Acts, "the word" *always* means a preached apostolic message. It *never* refers to Scripture.[9] Again, it is this total apostolic Tradition — a Tradition handed

[9] An interesting (and eye-opening) exercise for one interested in discovering Sacred Tradition in Scripture is to read through the rest of the New Testament and discover the overwhelming number of instances where 'the word of God' refers, not to Scripture, but to a preached tradition of Christ on the lips of the apostle.

down in both written and unwritten form—which is the word of God in the New Testament.

At this point it is common for someone to invoke what I call the Berean Fallacy. The argument proceeds this way: "You keep speaking of unwritten Tradition. But Acts *tells* us what Paul taught them 'by word of mouth.' He 'reasoned with them *from the Scriptures*, explaining and proving that the Christ had to suffer and rise from the dead' (Acts 17:2-3). And this principle holds throughout the New Testament. From Peter's quotation of the prophets and psalms on Pentecost to Paul's preaching in Rome you have a message that is steeped in Scripture. Moreover, Scripture commends the churches for doing likewise. Take the Bereans. Acts says clearly:

> Now the Bereans were of more noble character than the Thessalonians, for they received the message with great eagerness and examined the Scriptures every day to see if what Paul said was true (Acts 17:11).

"So" the Bible-only believer concludes, "it is untrue that the apostles founded their churches on Tradition. The Church was founded on the Scripture alone." Now this argument certainly has a piece of truth to it. For nobody (least of all the Catholic Church) denies the apostles quoted Scripture, regarded it as the inspired word of God, and encouraged their disciples to know it. But the fact remains that the notion the apostles founded their Churches on the Bible alone is an optical illusion. For in reality, the apostles founded the Church on their *paradosis* of Jesus Christ. Then, as it was appropriate, they called on the Old Testament Scripture to act as a *witness* to that Tradition.

What, after all, did the Bereans *receive* from the apostles? Was it the Old Testament? Obviously not. For like the Jews who stoned Stephen, *the Bereans already had that*. Rather, they received from Paul a Tradition — mostly oral and occasionally written — about a *new* and *final* revelation that was, says Paul, "*not* made known to men in other generations as it has now been revealed by the Spirit to God's holy apostles and prophets" (Ephesians 3:5). Indeed, one of the constant themes of the New Testament is the need for the completion of Scripture by the apostolic *paradosis*. That is why

Paul insists we cannot grasp the meaning of the Jewish Scriptures apart from the revelation of Christ. They remain, says Paul, "veiled" until the gospel he *preaches* (that is, the apostolic *paradosis*) comes to take the veil away by the power of the Spirit (2 Corinthians 3:14). According to Paul, the new revelation was *hidden in* the Old Testament writings, not revealed there. The new revelation was Jesus, who gave us first and foremost, not a collection of New Testament documents, but an apostolic Body of Christ. It was this Body whose proclamation is the Tradition — both written and unwritten — of which Paul spoke.

This is clearly the teaching of Acts. For nobody in Acts *derives* the gospel from their supposedly formally sufficient Bibles as we derive a sum from a set of numbers in a math problem. Nobody picks up a Torah and figures out from it that Messiah will be handed over for crucifixion, rise from the dead, bestow his Spirit on the Church at Pentecost, call the Gentiles into covenant with him and promise to come again in glory to judge the living and the dead. Quite the contrary: nobody sees this coming, *particularly* the apostles. Rather, as St. John notes, until Jesus opened their eyes — by his death and resurrection, not a Bible study — "they still did not understand from Scripture that Jesus had to rise from the dead," even when they stood staring at his graveclothes (John 20:9).

That is why the New Testament talks as though Scripture is materially, not formally sufficient, just as the Catholic Church does. This is why it speaks of understanding Scripture as the Ethiopian eunuch did: "How can I, unless someone explains it to me?" (Acts 8:31). For the Eunuch, as for the Bereans, Paul and for all the other characters in Acts, the materially sufficient bricks of Scripture must be assembled and mortared together by the apostolic *paradosis* using the trowel of apostolic authority in the hand of the Holy Spirit. Again, according to Scripture, it is the Tradition (both written and unwritten) and the apostolic authority of the Church which constitute the fullness of the revelation of Christ.

That is why Paul *never* says that the gospel is derived from Scripture. Rather, he says the Law and the Prophets "testify" to the righteousness revealed in Christ "apart from the Law" (Romans 3:21). The Law and the Prophets are road signs. They *bear witness* to Christ. But he is also truly *hidden* in them until God, through the written and unwritten *paradosis* of his holy apostles, reveals Christ.

This also clarifies 1 Peter 1:23-25 which speaks of the "living and enduring word of God" and which most people mistakenly take to be a comment on the inspiration of the Old Testament. Admittedly the confusion is understandable. After all, St. Peter quotes Isaiah 40:6-8 saying:

> The grass withers and the flowers fall, but the word of the Lord stands forever.

Yet the fact is, Peter (though he does, of course, regard Isaiah as inspired) is *not* targeting Isaiah as the living and enduring word of God here. Rather, he is, like Paul, *calling Isaiah as a witness to his own preached apostolic message of Christ*. For Peter, the living and enduring word of God is not only the written word of Scripture; it is "the word that was preached to you" — that is, the apostolic Tradition of God. He too is taking the materially sufficient bricks of Scripture and joining them with Apostolic Tradition and Authority to build the formally sufficient brick house of revelation.

And small wonder. For this is precisely what his Master did on the day of his resurrection. For Christ too reveals himself as the new revelation *hidden* in the Old Testament, inaugurating an entirely new way of seeing the Scripture by inaugurating in his risen person the source of the apostolic *paradosis*.

> "How foolish you are, and how slow of heart to believe all that the prophets have spoken! Did not the Christ have to suffer these things and then enter his glory?" And beginning with Moses and all the Prophets, he explained to them what was said in all the Scripture concerning himself. (Luke 24:25-27).

What we are seeing here again is that Scripture alone was only *materially* sufficient, not *formally* sufficient, to reveal Christ. All the bricks of the Christian revelation were there in Moses and the Prophets. But, like the Ethiopian eunuch, the disciples on the Emmaus Road could not understand it unless someone (and someone with authority delegated by God himself) explained it to them, showing them how the bricks fit together and how to mortar them so they would not fall. Indeed, so opaque were the Scriptures to the disciples on the Emmaus Road that the Risen Christ had to *appear* to them and rub their noses in these books they had been reading all their lives before they finally began to see his gospel and himself concealed there.

The Continuity of the Biblical Pattern

This then is the pattern of discernment of doctrine and governance set up in the teaching and actions of our Lord and his apostles: Scripture, Tradition and Apostolic Authority. What is more, it is, not surprisingly, the exact same pattern adopted by their successors, the bishops, who had to do the same work of discernment and governance afterwards. Why did they adopt this pattern? Because the apostles taught them no other way. For the fact is, at the end of the apostolic age, a buzzer did not sound nor did a booming voice ring out in the heavens, saying, "Okay Church, the Scripture isn't just materially sufficient anymore. Now it's formally sufficient. All of apostolic Tradition has now been completely crystallized in writing and you no longer need to do what Christ and his apostles did. From now on, just read Scripture."

On the contrary, at the end of the apostolic age, the Church had two things bequeathed to it by the apostles: Tradition (both written and unwritten) and a whole bunch of apostolic successors (technically known as *presbyters* or, in English, *bishops*) in all the places the apostles planted churches. Who were these bishops and what were they supposed to do anyway?

To begin finding out, we need look no further than Scripture itself. For unlike the doctrine of Bible-only revelation (which, as we have seen, is nowhere in Scripture), apostolic succession is very clearly in evidence in germinal form at several points in Scripture.

According to Catholic teaching, the Church's authority is a line that leads straight back through the bishops to the apostles and finally, to Jesus Christ. Beginning with the gospels we have a picture of authority delegated first by the Father to the Son, and then by the Son to the Twelve ("He who receives you receives me, and he who receives me receives him who sent me" (Matthew 10:40)). But what then? Does this Christ-delegated authority die with the Apostle John?

On the contrary, a look at the book of Acts shows clearly that this line of authority is plainly being set up by the apostles to cruise right out of the apostolic period and into history. For wherever the apostles founded churches, they delegated successors to govern in their place. Thus, for example, Acts 14:23 tells us that "Paul and Barnabas appointed elders for them in each church and, with prayer and fasting, committed them to the Lord in whom they had put their trust." Likewise, Peter speaks to the elders of the churches, not as though they have no authority, but as though they share his authority as "fellow elders" (1 Pt 5:1).

These successors are, then, no mere figureheads. They have authority, not merely to preach or to be examples of niceness, but to *command* — to render authoritative judgment on whether a doctrine agrees with apostolic teaching (1 Timothy 1:3), and even to discipline unruly members of the Body (1 Timothy 5:20). Thus, when the hubbub over circumcision develops, it is not just the apostles but the *elders* (that is, the appointees of the apostles) who meet at the Council of Jerusalem to discern the mind of Christ (Acts 15:6). What is their big beef with the circumcision party? Not that they acted without authority from Scripture, but that they "went out from *us* without *our authorization*" (Acts 15:24). Likewise, it is not merely the apostles but the *elders* who promulgate the decision of the council and bind the Church to it.

In short, these apostolic delegates are delegated apostolic *authority*. In turn, they have one overriding obligation: "*Guard* yourselves and all the flock of which the Holy Spirit has made you overseers" (Acts 20:28). "So be on your *guard*!" (Acts 20:31). "*Guard* what has been entrusted to your care" (1 Timothy 6:20). "*Guard* the good deposit that was entrusted to you — *guard* it with the help of the Holy Spirit who lives in us" (2 Timothy 1:14).

What is this "good deposit" they are to guard? Certainly, the revelation of Scripture. But Paul means much more than that. For he explicitly and repeatedly commands Timothy to guard, not only the Scripture, but "what you *heard* from me" (2 Timothy 1:13). Likewise, he commands Timothy to adhere closely, not only to his letters but to "the things you have *heard me say* in the presence of many witnesses" (2 Timothy 2:2). In other words, the Bible does not say the *paradosis* is being entirely crystallized in writing now that the gospel is passing to the next generation. It says the apostolic successor is under solemn obligation to preserve the total *paradosis*, whether he received it by word of mouth or by letter. It says, in short, that the Church is to go on functioning in the post-apostolic age just as it did in the apostolic age, relying on Tradition (both written and unwritten) and on the apostolic authority of the apostolic successors. The one and only development implied by Paul (and confirmed by the Tradition of the Church) is that the bishops have no authority to promulgate *new* revelation. On the contrary, public revelation is closed with the death of the apostles. All bishops may do is guard old revelation.

Moreover, this setup is intended to be perpetual. How do we know? Because Paul goes on in the same verse to say that Timothy must himself pass on this written and unwritten Tradition to "reliable men who will be qualified to teach others" (2 Timothy 2:2). Similarly, Paul commands Titus to appoint successors whose job, once again, is to "teach what is in accord with sound doctrine" (Ti 2:1) with "the Holy Spirit's help" (2 Timothy 1:14).

This is precisely what Timothy, Titus, and the many other apostolic successors in the various churches did. For in the years immediately following the apostles, we find each of the many post-apostolic communities governed by a string of successors who see their task in just the way Paul told them to: guarding the good deposit entrusted to them and, as the Church grew, appointing successors to themselves with the help of the Holy Spirit, just as Timothy and Titus did. And so the biblical record sails right into the historical record.

Apostolic Succession: The Witness of the Fathers

Clement of Rome, who had heard the apostles with his own ears, writes (around 80 AD, well within the lifetime of the Apostle John and the generation that knew the apostles):

> The Apostles received the gospel for us from the Lord Jesus Christ; and Jesus Christ was sent from God. Christ, therefore, is from God, and the Apostles are from Christ. Both of these orderly arrangements, then, are by God's will. Receiv-

> ing their instructions and being full of confidence on account of the resurrection of our Lord Jesus Christ, and confirmed in faith by the word of God, they went forth in the complete assurance of the Holy Spirit, preaching the good news that the Kingdom of God is coming. *Through countryside and city they preached; and they appointed their earliest converts, testing them by the Spirit, to be the bishops and deacons of future believers.*[10]

Further, Clement confirms that the apostles desired their authority be handed down forever:

> Our Apostles knew through our Lord Jesus Christ that there would be strife for the office of bishop. For this reason, therefore, having received perfect foreknowledge, they appointed those who have already been mentioned, *and afterwards added the further provision that, if they should die, other approved men should succeed to their ministry.*[11]

There is also Irenaeus. Historical records show that he was a disciple of a man named Polycarp, who was a disciple of the Apostle John. Irenaeus writes in France (about 180):

> It is possible, then, for everyone in every Church, who may wish to know the truth, to contemplate the tradition of the Apostles which has been made known throughout the whole world. And we are in a position to enumerate those who were instituted bishops by the Apostles, and their successors to our own times...[12]

To prove this, Irenaeus picks out the Roman church as an example.

> The blessed Apostles [Peter and Paul], having founded and built up the Church [of Rome], they handed over the office of the episcopate to Linus. Paul makes mention of this Linus in

---

10 Clement, *Letter to the Corinthians*, 42, 1-4 (JUR Vol. 1, #20).

11 Ibid., 44, 1-3 (JUR Vol. 1, #21).

12 Irenaeus, *Against Heresies*, 3, 3, 1 (JUR Vol. 1, #209).

> the Epistle to Timothy. To him succeeded Anencletus; and after him, in the third place from the Apostles, Clement was chosen for the episcopate... To this Clement, Evaristus succeeded; and Alexander succeeded Evaristus. Then, sixth after the Apostles, Sixtus was appointed; after him, Telesphorus, who as was gloriously martyred. Then Hyginus; after him, Pius; and after him, Anicetus. Soter succeeded Anicetus, and now, in the twelfth place after the Apostles, the lot of the episcopate has fallen to Eleutherus. In this order, and by the teaching of the Apostles handed down in the Church, the preaching of the truth has come down to us.[13]

Because of this direct delegation of apostolic authority, yet another early Christian (Ignatius) writes (about 110): "You must all follow the bishop as Jesus Christ follows the Father, and the presbytery as you would the Apostles."[14]

And so it goes. All the early churches function as though apostolic succession is a given, just as they function as though Sacred Tradition is a given. Nobody talks as if the apostles told them revelation would be "crystallized" in writing alone, and everybody conceives of revelation in just the way Scripture does, as a union of Tradition (both written and unwritten) and of the apostolic teaching authority of the Church in union with the bishops and with Peter — as at the Council of Jerusalem in Acts 15. The typical arch-conservative attitude of the Church after the apostles is voiced by Basil the Great (c. 374):

> Of the dogmas and kerygmas preserved in the Church, some we possess from written teaching and others we receive from the tradition of the Apostles, handed on to us in mystery. In respect to piety both are of the same force. No one will contradict any of these, no one, at any rate, who is even moderately versed in matters ecclesiastical. Indeed, were we to try to reject unwritten customs as having no great authority, we would unwittingly injure the Gospel in its vitals."[15]

---

[13] Ibid., 3, 3, 3 (JUR Vol. 1, #211).

[14] Ignatius, *Letter to the Smyrnaeans*, 8, 1 (JUR Vol. 1, #65)

[15] Basil the Great, *The Holy Spirit*, 27:66 (JUR Vol. 2, #954).

In short, so far from being given to zany new innovations every few months or so, the documents of the early Church reveal a community that looks very, very conservative, very, very suspicious of innovation and very, very Catholic. And it looks like it got that way because the apostles made it so.

Development of Tradition: The Biblical Witness

Now at this point we meet a difficulty with our Bible-only friends that needs to be addressed. For despite all the biblical evidence for Sacred Tradition and apostolic succession, there remains some doubt and confusion, particularly when we begin to confront what we know as Catholic "doctrinal developments". For on the one hand, we have this portrait of a conservative Church insisting her Tradition comes from the apostles and must not be altered by addition or subtraction while, on the other hand, She appears to add novel doctrines to the Faith in broad daylight under the claim they had been there all along (e.g., the 19th and 20th Century definitions of the Immaculate Conception, Papal Infallibility and the Assumption of Mary).

In response, the exasperated Protestant cries, "If these doctrines have been there all along, then where the blazes is the Immaculate Conception of Mary in Scripture and why did it not become a teaching of the Church until 1854!?" This is, of course, a very good question. When the Church (at the Council of Trent, for example) replies that "this truth and teaching are contained in written books *and* in the unwritten traditions that the apostles received from Christ himself or that were handed on, as it were from hand to hand, from the apostles under the inspiration of the Holy Spirit, and so have come down to us"[16] this is seen as an attempt to say in effect, "Okay, so the Immaculate Conception *isn't* in Scripture. It's in, uh... Tradition! Yeah! That's the ticket! Tradition! And it always has been (as every *bishop* knows because it was passed on at the Secret Tradition-Passing-On Ceremony that bishops all have to go through in the dungeons beneath the Vatican)."

[16] Council of Trent, *Decree on Sacred Scripture and Tradition*: Denziger 783 (1501).

Thus, one can often hear not only believers in *sola scriptura* but even those who are coming to disbelieve it still speaking of Sacred Tradition as though it were a *separate*, *secret* and *parallel* revelation transmitted from bishop to bishop ("Psst! Mary is Immaculate, Ever-Virgin and Assumed into Heaven, pass it on!") and leaked into official documents of the Church by dribs and drabs over the centuries when Rome felt the time was right to tell the ordinary believer. And such an absurd picture of Tradition is one reason why, not to put too fine a point on it, the Catholic appeal to Tradition, for all the compelling evidence in its favor, smells like a rat to a Bible-only nose. In fact, so sinister does it seem to some of our more fundamentalist brothers and sisters that, confronted with the baffling discovery of an early Church that looks pretty Catholic, yet also confronted with a modern Catholic Church riddled with what appears to be dogmas having no discernible connection to Scripture, they solve the problem of the obvious connection between the early Church and the modern Catholic Church by positing the theory of the "hidden, true Church of Bible Christians" that was driven underground by a mass apostasy at the end of the apostolic era. It was, they say, this "hidden Church" that preserved the gospel through the long night of pre-Reformation error in which the Church appeared Catholic but really wasn't. It is, so the theory goes, the documents of this fallen away "catholic" church that we are reading when we read the works of writers like Clement of Rome, Irenaeus, Polycarp, Basil and all the other Fathers who make the Church look so Catholic.[17]

The difficulty with the "hidden Church" theory is that it is a picture perfect example of the absurd separate, secret and parallel revelation it claims Catholic Sacred Tradition is. For, despite all their faults and failings, we at least *know* what the supposedly apostate Catholic Church was up to for 15 centuries. In addition to the inevitable sins of its human members, it was busy defending Scripture from people who wanted to destroy it, preserving the doctrine of the Trinity against the assaults of Arianism; holding the Great

---

[17] For a fairly typical exposition of the "hidden church" theory, see J. M. Carroll's *The Trail of Blood* (Lexington, Kentucky: Ashland Avenue Baptist Church, 1974) 55 pp.

Ecumenical Councils which settled the most bedeviling questions concerning the person and work of Jesus Christ; withstanding the onslaught of Islam and Viking invasions; laying the foundations for the rule of law in Dark Ages Europe; converting nation after nation to Christ; ordering the reading of Scripture in all of its worship and prayer; renewing art and science and philosophy; inspiring saints like Thomas Aquinas and Francis of Assisi; building hospitals and universities; evangelizing the New World and working energetically to do all the sorts of things commanded by the gospel. Meanwhile, if any Church lived a separate, secret, and parallel existence, it is the supposed "hidden church of true Christians" which, for 15 centuries, did nothing, said nothing, accomplished nothing, and was so invisible that we do not even find record of *opposition* to it by the supposedly apostate Catholic Church which usurped its place the moment St. John was dead. Thus, if we want to argue that the memory of the "hidden Church" was obliterated by sinister Catholics who won the battle and wrote the history books, we have to account for the mysterious fact that it is *only* this "hidden Church" that seems to have been written out of the historical records. All the other groups the Church opposed (e.g., Gnosticism, Arianism, Sabellianism, Manichaeism, Modalism, Paulicianism, the Bogomils, the Albigensians and a host of other movements) show up again and again in the polemical writings of the Church as movements to beware of. Only the "hidden Church" is completely absent from sight. This was the Church whose light so shone that men praised their Father in heaven? This is the City on the Hill that cannot be hid? This is the light of Christ burning for all the nations to see?

It seems pretty obvious then that the "hidden Church" theory is neither biblical nor very good history or common sense. Are there other ways to account for the apparent contradiction of an extremely Catholic-looking Church whose Tradition "never changes" and yet always seems to be changing? To answer that, we need to first ask, "Is Sacred Tradition really a separate, secret and parallel revelation?" And to that we find the answer of the Catholic Church is "No. Indeed, it is precisely this view of Tradition which the Church has always condemned." For, despite appearances, the belief that salvation lies in some secret knowledge given only to the elite is the essence, not of Christianity, but of Gnosticism. And the Catholic Church has always been its mortal foe. That is why Irenaeus writes the following in the 2nd Century:

> For if the Apostles had known hidden mysteries which they taught to the elite secretly and apart from the rest, they would have handed them down especially to those very ones to whom they were committing the self-same Churches. For surely they wished all those and their successors to be perfect and without reproach, to whom they handed on their authority.[18]

If, then, the Church does not see Sacred Tradition as a separate, secret, and parallel form of revelation whence the Church can suddenly produce brand new dogmas like rabbits from a hat, then how *do* they see it? Answer: They see Tradition as the living and growing truth of Christ contained, not only in Scripture but in the *common teaching, common life*, and *common worship* of the Church. It is this common teaching, common life and common worship which is implied by the behavior of the disciples in Acts 4:42 when they devote themselves, not simply to Bible study but to the fullness of "the apostles' teaching and to the fellowship, to the breaking of bread and to prayer." The 'apostles teaching' is teaching given, as Paul says, both by word of mouth and by letter. In its unwritten form it is not separate, secret, and parallel to Scripture, but common and widely known, as Irenaeus points out. It is, for example, how the Church knows that Holy Communion is a rite to be performed by the Church on a continuous basis, but the washing of feet is not, even though both rituals were performed by Jesus at the Last Supper and even though Jesus commanded his disciples in both cases to imitate him. On the basis of the text alone, we are powerless to make such a distinction. But since the Church of Acts had the common apostolic *paradosis* concerning *how* to read these accounts of the Last Supper, it was able to make this distinction. For it received the 'apostles teaching' both by word of mouth and by letter.

Likewise, the "fellowship" and "the breaking of bread and prayer" means more than just chummy glad-handing and church

[18] Irenaeus, *Against Heresies*, 3, 3, 1 (JUR Vol. 1, #209)

socials. The early Christians "devoted themselves" to the common life ("fellowship") and the common eucharistic, liturgical worship of the Church ("the breaking of bread and prayer") — a life and worship that is essentially public and communal, not private and esoteric. And for the Church in the New Testament as for the Catholic Church today, this common teaching, common life and common worship is a *living thing*—a truth which was planted as a mustard seed in first century Jerusalem and which has not ceased growing — as our Lord prophesied in Mark 4:30-32. The mustard plant may not look like the seed anymore, but it is, if anything, more mustardy than ever. Just as every branch and flower shooting out of the plant is hidden in the seed, so every dogmatic development which shoots out of the Church was hidden in the Seed of Tradition (and borne witness to by the materially sufficient Scriptures, even though the connection with Scripture may not be plain at first). This is an entirely biblical pattern.

To see this, let us return once again to the circumcision controversy in Acts 15 and study the way in which the very first doctrinal development of the Church took place. What was the genesis of the circumcision controversy? In a nutshell, the controversy flared up in the apostolic church as the result of the increasing number of Gentile converts flooding into the Church in its first two decades. The Church, of course, began as an almost totally Jewish sect. Its members were all Jews, its Lord was a Jew and the only Scriptures it possessed when the circumcision question arose were Jewish Scriptures. Not surprisingly then, the Jewish Christians, confronted with the problem of all these eager Gentile converts were thrown into a tailspin by the question of how they ought to proceed in admitting them to fellowship. Let us, for a moment, join the Council of Jerusalem in Acts 15 and imagine ourselves to be delegates from the supposed Bible-only "hidden Church" of the first century, trying to resolve the question of whether to circumcise Gentiles who want to join the Covenant People. What is written in our Bible? Well, we read that God gave Abraham the covenant of circumcision "as an everlasting covenant" (Genesis 17:7). It is the sign that is enjoined, not only on descendants of Abraham, but upon "those who are not your offspring" (Genesis 17:12) that is, those who wish to join the Covenant People by conversion (Exodus 12:48). Thus, the Patriarchs are all circumcised. Moses is circumcised and the covenant of circumcision is renewed and reinforced in the Mosaic Law (Lev 12:3). All the prophets are circumcised. The apostles are all circumcised. Even the Lord Jesus himself is circumcised (Luke 2:21). And he himself says that not one jot or tittle of the law would by any means pass away (Matthew 5:18). Meanwhile he is remarkably silent in issuing any command that Gentiles be exempted from the immemorial requirement of circumcision for all who wish to join the Covenant People. Thus, on the basis of Scripture alone, it is apparent that the case for circumcision is really very strong. And so, the Church meets in Council and, in light of all this obvious scriptural teaching, declares....that circumcision for Gentiles is *against* the will of the God who does not change.

How do we Bible-only folks respond? One way to do so is to hold the Council of Jerusalem to the same standard of Bible-only principles as we hold the dogma of the Immaculate Conception or Papal Infallibility, and cry out in exasperation, "If this doctrine is the teaching of the God who does not change, then where the blazes is the Circumcision Exemption for Gentiles in Scripture and why did it not become a teaching of the Church until 48 AD!?"

However, there *is* another way to proceed. For we can just as easily hold these supposedly preposterous Catholic doctrinal developments to the standards of the biblical Council of Jerusalem. We can then propose that what happened at Jerusalem is the model for every single development of doctrine throughout Catholic history right down to the Assumption of Mary. That is, we can recognize that, despite appearances, dogmatic definitions of the Church do *not* just pop up with absolutely no relation to Scripture. In these later developments we can come to recognize what we already recognize of the Circumcision Exemption: that such developments are always rooted in the Tradition of the Church, both written and unwritten. And that Tradition is not a separate, secret and parallel body of revelation, but the common teaching, common life, and common worship of the Church, known to all the faithful.

How does the interplay between the written and unwritten aspects of Tradition work to give such surprising results at the Council of Jerusalem? First of all, there were several elements of apostolic *paradosis* through which the light of Scripture was focused like a lens. For example, there was the apostolic *paradosis* of Christ's command to preach the gospel to the whole world (Matthew 28:19); there was the apostolic *paradosis* of Peter's mystical revelation by the Holy Spirit ("Do not call anything impure that God has made clean" [Acts 10:15]); there was the experience of Paul and Barnabas in preaching to the Gentiles (Acts 15:12); there was the work of Philip among the Samaritans (Acts 8:4). At Jerusalem, all these facets of the *paradosis* crystallize as the apostles and elders gather, and it is *through* these facets that Scripture is read. That is why, when the Council meets, they do *not* do a topical Bible study on circumcision and derive their opinion on the matter from Scripture as the sole formally sufficient rule of faith. On the contrary, they begin by arguing clamorously in accord with the old Jewish proverb "Two Jews, three opinions." When the arguing winds down Peter stands up and appeals, not to Scripture, but to the apostolic Tradition of the Church and to his own Christ-delegated apostolic authority. He says, "Brothers, you know that some time ago God made a choice among you that the Gentiles might hear from my lips the message of the gospel and believe. God, who knows the heart, showed that he accepted them by giving the Holy Spirit to them, just as he did us. He made no distinction between us and them, for he purified their hearts by faith " (Act 15:7-9). Notice that there is no mention of 2,000 years of Scripture here, just an appeal to apostolic authority and the Spirit's revelation to the Church.

Then Paul and Barnabas stand up and describe the events which have marked their missions: miracles, signs and wonders. Like Peter, they also appeal, not to Scripture, but to the apostolic *paradosis* and to their Christ-delegated magisterial apostolic authority. It is only *after* this that we finally get around to the scriptural references, wherein James quotes from the prophet Amos. Yet note this: James does not *derive* from Amos the idea that the Gentiles don't have to be circumcised. Rather, in light of the fullness of Christ's revelation through the lens of apostolic *paradosis*, James is able to see in the prophet Amos a *witness* to this ingathering of Gentiles and to the Council's decision. In short, James *derives the revelation from the apostolic Tradition and magisterial authority of the apostles in union with Scripture*. James, like everyone else at the Council, places the Church on the judge's seat and the Scripture in the witness box, saying of the Church's authoritative judgment that, "The words of the prophets agree with this" (Acts 15:15).

Thus, through the lens of apostolic Tradition, Scripture that seemed to say one thing about circumcision is suddenly seen to be saying something vastly different, just as the black and white cubes in an optical puzzle miraculously face the opposite direction, depending on how we see them. The materially sufficient bricks of Old Testament revelation, which at first seemed to build a synagogue of circumcision, are stacked and mortared with apostolic Tradition by the trowel of the Church's magisterial authority, and turn out to make a cathedral instead. The Council of Jerusalem, just like the Catholic Church, behaves as though Scripture is materially, not formally, sufficient to reveal Christ. The Council of Jerusalem, just like the Catholic Church, places Scripture in the context of the Church's Tradition and magisterial, apostolic authority. The Council of Jerusalem, just like the Catholic Church, speaks with apostolic authority and declares, "It seemed good to the Holy Spirit and to *us*..." (Acts 15:29). And so, the Council of Jerusalem, just like the Catholic Church, makes a step which, to Bible-only eyes, appears to flatly nullify Scripture yet which, upon closer inspection, turns out to uphold it (Romans 3:31).

Very well then, what is sauce for the New Testament goose is sauce for the Catholic gander. For every one of the Catholic Church's doctrinal developments — all the way down to the Assumption of Mary — proceeds in exactly the same fashion as the development of doctrine about circumcision in Acts 15. Each development has a basis in the text of Scripture either implicitly or explicitly, but the connection of the text to the doctrine cannot always be seen clearly apart from the Tradition as it is discerned by the Body of Christ.

Take, for instance, the Perpetual Virginity of Mary (formulated as dogma at the Second Council of Constantinople in 553). Here is a dogma which, to Bible-only Christians, seems to be either a bizarre extrapolation from a couple of texts (as though some medieval theologian sat down with a Bible and said, "Let's see. What is the most tortured and extreme reading I can get out of Matthew 1:25 today? I know! How about we say Mary remained a virgin perpetually!") or else an attempt by the Church to perversely defy the plain meaning of Scripture (which speaks repeatedly of Jesus' "brothers"). Thus, no matter how you slice Scripture (from a Bible-only perspective), you have a dogma which is at best weakly attested by Scripture or at worst flatly contradicted by it.

How then does it come to be declared a dogma? Answer: the same way the Circumcision Exemption did—not by sitting down and *deriving* the dogma from the tortured reading of a few isolated texts of Scripture, but by placing the Scripture in the context of the Tradition handed down by the apostles and the interpretive office of the successors they appointed.

It is quite true that Mary is not explicitly described as a perpetual virgin anywhere in Scripture, just as it is quite true that Jesus is not explicitly described as "God from God, light from light, true God from true God." However, just as all orthodox Christians agree that the Nicene Creed accurately expresses apostolic belief, so the Catholic Church says the doctrine of the Perpetual Virginity of Mary also summarizes apostolic belief. Similarly, just as we can say that verses which appear to deny the doctrine of the Trinity (such as Jesus' question, "Why do you call me good?" (Luke 18:19), or his statement that "The Father is greater than I" (John 14:28)), have always been understood in a way compatible with Trinitarianism, so the Church says those verses which appear to speak of Jesus' siblings or Mary's relations with Joseph after the birth of Christ have always been understood in a way compatible with her perpetual virginity. The verses which appear to attribute siblings to Jesus need not mean anything more than cousins in the Jewish milieu in which the Scriptures were written. The passage in Matthew which says Joseph "had no union with her until she gave birth to a son" (Matthew 1:25) does not necessarily imply anything about Mary's subsequent relationship with Joseph since the word "until" is ambiguous. This is seen, for instance, in Deuteronomy 1:31, where Moses tells Israel that, "the LORD your God carried you, as a father carries his son, all the way you went *until* you reached this place." Moses does not mean that God stopped carrying Israel once they reached Canaan, for he has just finished saying God will continue to fight for them just as he always has. Likewise, in Deuteronomy 9:7 Moses tells Israel, "From the day you left Egypt *until* you arrived here, you have been rebellious against the LORD." Moses is not saying that Israel, once they arrived at the border of Canaan, ceased being rebellious. Similarly, when Luke tells us that John the Baptist "lived in the desert *until* he appeared publicly to Israel" (Luke 1:80), he does not mean to imply that John stopped living in the desert after he began his public ministry. For as the Baptist himself says (and Luke records) John's ministry was precisely "A voice of one calling in the desert" (Luke 3:4). In the same way then, Matthew is not implying that Mary, once she brought forth Jesus, ceased being a virgin. He simply is saying that she conceived him in virginity and making no implications whatever about any post-partum sexual relations between Mary and Joseph. Therefore, Scripture does not forbid the Catholic understanding of Mary's virginity.

By the same token, neither does Scripture *command* us to believe in Mary's perpetual virginity. Why then does the Church read the Scripture in this way? Because of the Tradition handed down to it by the apostles, *through* which the Scripture is read, just as it was at the Council of Jerusalem. And again, this Tradition is *not* a separate, secret and parallel revelation but the common teaching, common life and common worship of the faithful—a common Tradition which is at work in many ways and at many levels in the life of the Church.

It is, for instance, why the Church of the first century knows, without it being written down, that beer or milk is not the appropriate thing to use for baptism. Nothing in Scripture forbids it, it is just not the *way* we read Scripture. It is why the Church of the second century knows, without it being written down, that marriages are not validly contracted simply by a man and a woman saying, "I love you. Let's go to bed together tonight." Nothing in Scripture forbids it, it is just not the *way* we read Scripture. It is why the Church of the third century knows that abortion and polygamy are forbidden, even though Scripture says nothing about the former and appears to endorse the latter. Nothing in Scripture clearly forbids these things, but we know they are forbidden because it is the *way* the apostles taught us to read Scripture. It is why the Church of the fourth century knows that, whatever the Scripture appears to say about the superiority of the Father to the

Son, it does not mean that the Son is a mere godlet or vague "divinity", but very God and one in being with the Father. Nothing in Scripture unequivocally demands this, it is just the *way* the apostles taught us to read Scripture. It is why the Church of the fifth century knows, even though it is not written down, that public revelation was closed with the death of the apostles. Nothing in Scripture demands this, it is just the *way* the apostles taught us to understand revelation. And it is why the Church of the sixth century knows, even though it is not written explicitly in the New Testament, that Mary is Ever-Virgin. Nothing in Scripture explicitly demands this, it is just the *way* the apostles taught the Church to understand Scripture. For the Church of the post-apostolic era has received from the apostles, not only their written Tradition, but their unwritten Tradition as well. And the Tradition is not a separate, secret, parallel revelation, but the common teaching, common life and common worship of the Church.

But, says the Bible-only believer, why should we think this perpetual virginity Tradition was handed down by the apostles and not invented later on by a Church given to adding legends to the apostolic teaching? After all, it doesn't show up in the written records of the Church for nearly three centuries after the apostles.

The Church's reply: This is true, but then neither does the term "Trinity" show up in the Church's records until about 150 years after the apostles. This does not mean the deity of Christ was *invented* at that time. It just means that is the earliest *documentation* we have of a Tradition that was already very old. That the Tradition has been around for a lot longer is attested, not by the surviving piece of paper which documents it, but by the character of the people who wrote on the paper. For the Fathers of the early Church who attest the Perpetual Virginity of Mary are emphatically *not* avant garde flakes hankering to add legends to the gospel, but staunch, hardcore, arch-conservative traditionalists like St. Athanasius.[19] Recall for a moment that the people who are charged with adding legends to the apostolic teaching are the same people who fought bitter struggles to keep just this kind of stuff out of the Church. That is why they wrangled about the Trinity and fought

19 Athanasius, *Discourses Against the Arians*, 2, 70 (JUR Vol. 1, #767a).

with Arius when he proposed a view of Christ the Church had never heard before. That is why they fought to keep legends like the *Protoevangelium of James* and the *Gospel of Thomas* out of Scripture. That is why they wrote incessantly about the purity of the Faith and went to their persecutions, sufferings, exiles, and tortured deaths rather than compromise one little bit with those who wanted to add newfangled material to the deposit of Faith. To maintain the charge that people like Athanasius were willing to face exile, death threats, and years of their life spent in fights over picayune details of Trinitarian language yet were simultaneously willing to say, "What the heck! Let's make up a novel doctrine of Mary's Perpetual Virginity just for the fun of it!" is to strain credibility well past the snapping point.

So the fact is, the evidence for the dogma of the Perpetual Virginity of Mary is attested by the very same strong witnesses we trust when we accept the dogma of the Trinity. And both aspects of Tradition point, not to an inventive fourth century church, but to an apostolic first century church handing down these aspects of Tradition along with its Scripture. Therefore, the Church at the Second Council of Constantinople, knowing what the Church at the Council of Jerusalem knew, acts like the Church at the Council of Jerusalem did: it reads its Scripture in light of that apostolic Tradition, just as it did concerning circumcision. Operating, as Athanasius and many other Church Fathers[20] did, in light of the apostolic Tradition that Mary was Ever-Virgin, the Church reads Scripture in light of this fact and sees things emerging from it that we Bible-only Christians did not see before (just as the Church began to see interesting things in the "everlasting covenant of circumcision" texts at the Council of Jerusalem).

We find, for instance, that Mary reacts with astonishment at the news that she, a woman betrothed, will bear a son. Notice that the angel does not say "You *are* bearing a son." He says "You *will*

[20] Among them Gregory of Nyssa (JUR Vol. 2, #1020a), Didymus the Blind (Ibid., #1073), Epiphanius of Salamis (Ibid., #1111), Jerome (Ibid., #1361), Augustine (Ibid., Vol 3, #1518), Leporius (Ibid., #2048), Cyril of Alexandria (Ibid., #2133), Peter Chrysologus (Ibid., #2177), Pope Leo I (Ibid., #2194), Gregory of Tours (Ibid., #2288b), Sophronius of Jerusalem (Ibid., #2289), and John Damascene (Ibid., #2383, 2390).

bear a son." This is a promise that has been made to other women in Jewish history (among them, Sarah, Hannah, and the Shunammite woman). All of them understand the promise to mean, "Your husband will be able to get you pregnant." Why then should this astonish Mary, a young woman who also plans to marry... unless, of course, she had already decided to remain a virgin even after marriage?

Then again, there is the curious fact that, in light of the Tradition of Perpetual Virginity we begin to see the New Testament subtly but very clearly identifying Mary with the Ark of the Covenant, wherein dwelt the Presence of God. Luke 1:35, for instance, quotes the angel as saying, "The Holy Spirit will come upon you, and the power of the Most High will overshadow you." This is very clearly an allusion to the Shekinah glory which overshadowed the Tabernacle and the Ark in the Old Testament (Numbers 9:15). John also makes this connection in his Revelation, where we see first the Ark of the Covenant (Revelation 11:19) and then immediately afterward we see an image of a woman clothed with the sun who gives birth to a "male child, who will rule all the nations with an iron scepter" (Revelation 12:5). The connection between Mary and the Ark, once it is made, is hard not to see. Knowing the identity of Mary's "male child," it would be an easy mental connection for any pious Jew to immediately think of her as a kind of Second Ark.

Well, Joseph of Nazareth *was* a pious Jew. And, after his dream (Matthew 1:23) he *did* know the identity of Mary's "male child". He also knew, as a Jew steeped in the Old Testament, what happens to people who touch the Ark without authorization (2 Sm 6:6-8). So it becomes very psychologically probable that Joseph, knowing what he knew, also would have chosen celibacy in this rather unusual situation.

Please note what is happening here. We are *not* reading isolated proof texts from Scripture and saying, "Let's see... How can we put a bizarre and extremist construction on this chance phrase in order to wring some ridiculous new doctrine out of it that nobody ever heard of before?" Rather, the Church is seeing Scripture in light of the Tradition handed on by the apostles just as the Council of Jerusalem and, later on, Athanasius and the Fathers did. Once we have this clearly in mind, we begin to see what is actually going on: namely, that the Church, just like the Council of Jerusalem, is again putting Scripture not on the judge's bench, but in the witness stand. The texts, seen in light of the Tradition handed down from the apostles, bear witness (often in an unexpected and satisfying way) to the Tradition. In the words of James of Jerusalem, they "agree with" it. The Tradition is not *derived* from the Scripture any more than the decision of the Jerusalem Council was derived from words of Amos. And this is the case for every single doctrinal development in the history of the Catholic Church. This pattern, so far from being foreign to Scripture, is at the very heart of Scripture. And it is the pattern the Church follows in every single development of doctrine right down to the doctrines of the Immaculate Conception, Papal Infallibility and the Assumption of Mary.

Conclusion

In summary then, Scripture says a great deal about Sacred Tradition—all of it agreeing perfectly with the picture of the Catholic Church drawn by the Second Vatican Council. In Scripture, as today, it is human tradition, not Sacred Tradition, that is condemned by Christ and his Church. In Scripture, as today, revelation is handed down "both by word of mouth and by letter." In Scripture, as today, "Sacred Tradition and Sacred Scripture form one sacred deposit of the word of God"[21] so that the Bible is part, not the whole, of the apostolic *paradosis*. In Scripture, as today, the Bible is materially, not formally, sufficient to reveal the fullness of the gospel of Christ. In Scripture, as today, both written and unwritten Tradition are from Christ and made by him to stand inseparably united like hydrogen and oxygen that fuse to form living water or like the words and tune of a single song.

Similarly, the picture of apostolic succession drawn by Catholic teaching bears an uncanny resemblance to the picture drawn by Scripture. In Scripture, as today, successors to the apostles are appointed by predecessors who received their authority from predecessors who received their authority ultimately from the hands of Christ himself. In Scripture, as today, these apostolic successors

[21] Vatican II, *Dogmatic Constitution on Divine Revelation*, II, 10.

have apostolic authority to bind and loose, just as they did at the Council of Jerusalem. In Scripture, as today, these successors are responsible to preserve, not just Scripture, but the whole Tradition of the apostles.

Finally, the picture of the development of Tradition shown by Scripture looks just like the picture drawn by the Catholic Church in its subsequent developments of doctrine. In Scripture, as today, the Church reads the Bible in light of apostolic Tradition. In Scripture, as today, this Tradition is not some separate, secret and parallel revelation, but the common teaching, common life, and common worship of the whole Church. In Scripture, as today, this Tradition grows like the mustard seed and, as a result, gets more mustardy, not less. In Scripture, as today, the Church in council sits on the judge's bench and listens to the testimony of Scripture in light of its Tradition in order to discern how best to define that Tradition more precisely.

And all this is because, in Scripture, as today, the Tradition, both written and unwritten, comes to us through the Body of Him Who is Truth: the one, holy, catholic and apostolic Church Paul calls "the fullness of him who fills everything in every way" and the "pillar and foundation of the truth" (Ephesians 1:22; 1 Timothy 3:15). Therefore, it never occurs to Paul to pit the Church against the Scripture or the Scripture against the Tradition. Rather, he refers the authority of the Spirit-breathed book to the authority of the Spirit-filled Body and reminds Timothy that the God-breathed Scripture can be trusted, not because it is the formally sufficient source of all revelation, but "because you know those from whom you learned it" (2 Timothy 3:15)—the Body on whom Christ himself breathed and said, "Receive the Holy Spirit" (John 20:22; Acts 2:4). That is why, three centuries later, an apostolic successor named Augustine of Hippo echoed Paul and said, "I would not believe in the Gospel myself if the authority of the Catholic Church did not influence me to do so."[22] It is also why, twenty centuries later, the Catholic Church remains the Church of Jesus Christ in continuity with the apostles and with their Sacred Tradition. For in Scripture, as today, Sacred Tradition—the

[22] Augustine, *Against the Letter of Mani*, 5, 6 (JUR Vol. 3, #1581).

common apostolic teaching, life and worship handed down to us in written and unwritten form — and the magisterial authority of the one, holy, catholic and apostolic Church are as inseparably united as the Father, Son and Holy Spirit.

That, and nothing less, is what Scripture says about Sacred Tradition.

Chapter 5

Point/Counterpoint: Protestant Objections and Catholic Answers

by Robert Sungenis

In this chapter we focus on specific Protestant Objections to Catholic doctrine in a point-by-point fashion. We cite Protestant objections verbatim from their present published works. This is not an exhaustive catalog of objections but only a representative sample of the prevailing Protestant views on *sola scriptura.*

Scripture

Objection #1: "*Sola Scriptura* simply means that all truth necessary for our salvation and spiritual life is taught either explicitly or implicitly in Scripture."[1]

Answer: First, any proposed definition of *sola scriptura* is by its very nature meaningless, except, perhaps, as a starting point to debate its existence or non existence. The definition is strictly a product of its adherent, who, wishing to promote the teaching, formulates his definition to encompass what he desires *sola scriptura*

---

1 John MacArthur, *Sola Scriptura! The Protestant Position on the Bible,* ed., Don Kistler. Contributors: W. Robert Godfrey, James White, R. C. Sproul, John Armstrong, John MacArthur, Sinclair Ferguson, Joel Beeke, and Ray Lanning (Morgan, PA: Soli Deo Gloria Publications, 1995) p. 165. Herein referred to as *Sola Scriptura!*

to be. Since no statement in Scripture defines *sola scriptura,* any proposed definition is in reality begging the question and is subject to the biases and misconceptions of its proponent. Not only must he extract the *principle* of *sola scriptura* from a Scripture which does not explicitly teach the doctrine, he must perform the more difficult task of formulating a *precise definition* of *sola scriptura* based on this same lack of information.

This problem becomes even more apparent when we witness how different are the definitions of *sola scriptura* offered by different Protestant theologians. Sometimes the proposed definition is so generic that it can apply to almost anything spiritual; thus, it does not adequately distinguish Scripture from other authorities. Such is the case with the above definition. The dictum "all truth necessary for our salvation and spiritual life" could describe the Church, or even a good spiritual book which explains the essence of Christianity. Even a four-page gospel tract or a verbal explanation of the gospel can provide adequate information for one's salvation. On the one hand, the more general the definition of *sola scriptura,* the easier it is for the Protestant to show that it describes the essence of Scripture. For example, adding the term "spiritual life" creates a definition that is so wide-open to interpretation that the meaning becomes almost irrelevant. What is the extent and limitation of the term "spiritual life"? Does it include everything a Christian must decide in his life, or only some things? Similarly, the use of "explicitly or implicitly" is sufficiently general and pervasive to provide *sola scriptura* with a very wide but undefined latitude in its imposition on the Christian life. We can guess that the Protestant will assign to this term as many variations as there are Protestant denominations — denominations which believe very different things amongst themselves concerning doctrine and morals.[2] On the other hand, the more specific the definition, the harder

---

2 Protestant disagreements in essential areas of doctrine are so common that its theologians often seem unaware that their differences virtually destroy the tenets of *sola scriptura.* For example, note the following statement by Geisler and MacKenzie: "Since Protestants believe that the Bible alone is sufficient for faith and practice, they take seriously any attempt by Catholics to support their doctrine from Scripture. And while the authors acknowledge that some Protestants (e.g., Anglicans and Lutherans) believe in baptismal regeneration, we

it is to prove how Scripture fits the description. We will cover this aspect of the problem momentarily.

Objection #2: "There is much we do not understand, but Scripture does teach all that we need to know to obtain eternal life and to live to the glory of God (2 Timothy 3:15)."[3]

Answer: This definition of *sola scriptura* limits its parameters to the areas of "eternal life" and "the glory of God." Let us examine the verse from which this definition if extracted, 2 Timothy 3:15. Although 2 Timothy 3:15 teaches that the Old Testament Scripture is able to lead one to salvation, it does not specifically mention "living to the glory of God." Discussions on the "sufficiency" of Scripture often confuse these two points. Granted, part of living to God's glory is attaining to salvation, but that is not all that is involved in glorifying God. This is particularly true in much of Protestant thinking, which understands "salvation" as a one-time event which occurs when one 'accepts Christ as Savior,' with many believing that this salvation cannot be lost once it is attained. Regardless of his view on Justification, the Protestant well knows that after 'being saved' he must lead a whole life of sanctification — and lead it to the glory of God. Moreover, he knows he will confront a whole host of difficult issues in his life, and that he must decide each to the glory of God. Generally speaking, he knows that he must love God and his neighbor, for this is the summation of all the commandments. But what if life confronts him with something that Scripture does not cover, and if he does not have the

[2 cont.] believe the Reformed/Baptist rejection of this doctrine is a more consistent Protestant approach" *(Roman Catholics and Evangelicals: Agreements and Differences*, p. 480). We wonder how the authors can say in one breath that "the Bible alone is sufficient for faith and practice," and in the next openly admit that other denominations disagree with them on one of the most important doctrines of the Christian faith that both claim to draw from the supposedly "sufficient" Scriptures. Trying to euphemize the difference on such a grave matter of salvation by saying that they have a "more consistent Protestant approach" leaves the impression that the difference is just a matter of perspective. In reality, however, one of these "perspectives" is teaching heresy.

[3] John Armstrong, *Sola Scriptura!* p. 133.

answer, how does he know if he is glorifying God? For example, note the following issues: contraception, abortion, artificial insemination, test-tube fertilization, genetic engineering, surrogate motherhood, sterilization, masturbation, sex education, eugenics, cloning, equal rights for women, capitalism and the use of wealth, the use of alcohol and mind-altering drugs, usury, cremation, psychology, resistance to tyranny, labor strikes, war, slavery, or church/state relations, and many others like these. Are these part of his "spiritual life"? One would be hard-pressed to deny that they are. If they are, would he not need correct answers to them in order to "glorify God"? Scripture does not address many of these topics, and even to those that it does address, its answer is often unclear. If, indeed, our belief about them is wrong, does such a belief glorify God? And what if God has given answers to these questions through the teaching office of the Church but we have refused, because of believing that the Bible is our "only authority," to obey these teachings? Are we glorifying God? Even if Scripture addresses some of these issues "implicitly" (as our Protestant apologist suggests), who has the authority to make *explicit* and specific doctrine of them? Are we to believe that God left us with the task of glorifying him through the agency of best guesses and sanctimonious opinions? Scripture teaches that when we sin we 'fall short of the glory of God,' but how do we know we have sinned unless we have correct answers to the questions above?

Objection #3: "Scripture is therefore the perfect and only standard of spiritual truth, revealing infallibly all that we must believe in order to be saved, and all that we must do in order to glorify God."[4]

Answer: This is the second definition for *sola scriptura* that this apologist offers, and it is more specific and precise. Adding the word "infallibly" changes the complexion of the argument, for what is now implied is that Scripture is the *only* infallible source of God's truth on earth. Indeed, definitions of *sola scriptura* that only appeal to Scripture as containing 'all that is necessary for salvation' are superfluous. It goes without saying that Scripture contains what

---

4 John MacArthur, *Sola Scriptura!*, p. 166.

is necessary to be saved, the same, as suggested above, that a four-page gospel tract may contain. What is different between Scripture and a four-page gospel tract is that the former is inerrant. But again, this presents a dilemma for the *sola scriptura* advocate. If the main difference between one spiritual source and another is infallibility, is it not required of the infallible source to claim that (1) it is the *only* infallible source, and (2) disclaim other sources that are logical candidates for infallibility? This is where the issue becomes most crucial. Catholic theologians, although they recognize that Scripture testifies to its own inerrancy, do not find in Scripture a claim that it is the *only* infallible authority, nor do they find Scripture disclaiming other worthy candidates to infallibility, such as the Church or Tradition. In fact, as we noted above, Scripture does more than merely imply that it recognizes these two other sources as infallible right along with itself (cf., Matthew 16:18-19; John 16:13; 2 Thess. 2:15; 1 Timothy 3:15). When we add to this the dilemma we face with the issues enumerated above that Scripture does not address, (e.g., contraception, abortion, in-vitro fertilization, etc.) it becomes obvious that if we truly want to "glorify God" we sorely need an infallible guide, for God is not glorified by ignorance or popular opinion. If he saves us it will only be because he has overlooked our ignorance. Is not God truly glorified when his people have answers to all the crucial questions of faith and morals so they can live lives that, without doubt, please him?

Objection #4: "The Thirty-nine Articles of the Anglican Church include this statement on sola Scriptura: 'Holy Scripture containeth all things necessary to salvation: so that whatsoever is not read therein, nor may be proved thereby, is not to be required of any man, that it should be believed as an article of the Faith, or be thought requisite or necessary to salvation."[5]

Answer: We assume that the apologist agrees with this particular definition of *sola scriptura*, even though it comes from a denomination other than his own. This would seem so in light of a previous statement he makes: "It [*sola scriptura*] only means that ev-

[5] Ibid., p. 167.

erything necessary, everything binding on our consciences, and everything God requires of us is given to us in Scripture."[6] One major problem with such a definition is that, like the difference between Newtonian physics and quantum mechanics, Scripture can perhaps be considered a sufficient guide only until you reach the level of life where Scripture does not penetrate. For example, the Anglican Articles were written in the 16th century, long before men could understand and define the precise biological processes occurring in the conception and gestation of the human baby inside the female uterus. They just assumed that the womb was sacred and should not be violated. But in modern times, men have seen the gestation process under a microscope, assigning terms to the primitive stages of development such as zygote, blastula, embryo, and fetus. Not surprisingly, some of these same men have claimed that a blastula is not really human but is a mere mass of 'undeveloped tissue.' Therefore, if the pregnancy becomes inconvenient, many people feel there is no moral requirement to inhibit them from terminating the existence of the 'undeveloped tissue.' Going to Scripture is little help, for while Scripture alludes to life in the womb (cf., Exodus 21:22-24; Psalm 139:13-16; Luke 1:39-45), it does not define when human life begins, nor does it give any information on the reasons life could be artificially aborted in-utero. One could claim, then, using the premise given by the Anglican *Thirty-nine Articles*, that since Scripture does not forbid aborting a blastula, it is perfectly alright to do so. But the Catholic Church insists that it is precisely in these particular areas of life, areas which Scripture either does not address clearly or does not address at all, that Christians need infallible and 'God-glorifying' answers. Thus, the Catholic Church has taught that life begins at conception. Thus, no abortion is morally legitimate, no matter what stage the preborn has reached, and no matter what the cause of the pregnancy (e.g., rape and incest).[7] In short, sufficiency and infallibility are of

---

6 Ibid., p. 166.

7 This is in contrast to various Protestant spokesmen who have claimed otherwise, e.g., Carl F. H. Henry claims that abortion is permissible for imbecility. When it is convenient to use *sola scriptura* as a weapon, however, Henry states: "...it is not surprising that liberation theology grew in Catholic soil, where the principle of *sola Scriptura* has never been accepted" ("Biblical Authority and

no use unless they can be applied to all areas of faith and morals, not merely on how to be saved and live a "spiritual life."

Objection #5: "...Do we need to know the daily menu of apostolic meals? Do we need descriptions of the clothing worn by Judas Iscariot? Certainly not! It is obvious that the Bible does not need to be *exhaustive* to be *sufficient* as our source of divine truth. Instead, the Bible must provide to us *what God intends for us to have* to function in the manner described by the doctrine of *sola scriptura*."[8]

Answer: Perhaps in referring to "meals" and "clothing" the apologist is using hyperbole to make his point. Nevertheless, he has not

---

7 cont. Social Crisis" in *Authority and Interpretation: A Baptist Perspective*, pp. 208- 209). Walter Martin, the late host of the famed *Bible Answer Man*, believed and taught that abortion was permissible in cases of rape and incest. All in all, there are six distinct positions on abortion in Evangelical Protestantism. We also find it puzzling that Geisler and MacKenzie can say: "For Catholics, as well as many Protestants, natural law is the moral basis from which social issues are addressed. Issues such as abortion, euthanasia, and homosexuality can and are dealt with from the perspective of natural law. One of the authors [Geisler] made a convincing argument against euthanasia to the medical staff of a large hospital, using the natural law concept *exclusively*" (*Roman Catholics and Evangelicals*, p. 25, emphasis mine). Being Catholics, we welcome Geisler's appeal to natural law in such areas. We must insist, however, that the appeal to natural law does not lend credence to the concept of *sola scriptura*. Of the three social issues Geisler mentions, only one (homosexuality) is addressed in Scripture. Further, unlike the Protestant appeal to natural law, Catholicism does not stop with natural law. Natural law is a means to an end, but it is not the end in itself. Natural law reaches its highest validity because its teachings are dogmatized in the Catholic Church, and therefore, her teachings against abortion, euthanasia, and homosexuality are infallible doctrine. As noted above, bare natural law has led Protestants to six views on abortion. In light of this, we find it revealing that in the section defending the need for "Special Revelation," Geisler and MacKenzie quote Aquinas' remarks on natural law: "human reason is very deficient in things concerning God. A sign of this is that philosophers, in their inquiry into human affairs by natural investigation, have fallen into many errors, and have disagreed among themselves" (Ibid., p. 27, taken from *Summa Theologica* 2a, 2ae. 2, 4). We insist that if one replaces the word "philosophers" with "Protestant denominations," and the words "natural investigation" with "sola scriptura," Aquinas' conclusion would still be as true.

8 James White, *The Roman Catholic Controversy*, p. 57.

escaped the problem implicit both in the concept of *sola scriptura* and in his proposed definition of *sola scriptura*. Granted, no source of information has to be exhaustive to be sufficient, that is, as long as everyone agrees as to what the source is sufficient ***for***. The apologist has proposed that the answer to the nature of Scripture's sufficiency is "what God intends for us to have." That answer, however, is sufficiently vague as to say nothing at all. First, we wonder why the apologist does not include the word "all" in his definition, to say "all what God intends for us to have," for this seems to be what he wants to denote. The reason we point out this distinction will be evident below. Second, just what are the extent of and limitations to "what God intends for us to have"? The answer "all God intends us to have is contained in Scripture" simply begs the question. Does Scripture claim that it contains all that God 'intends for us to have'? Granted, Scripture provides us with enough information that we can "believe that Jesus is the Christ, the Son of God, and that by believing you may have life in his name" (John 20:31), but Scripture does not claim that this is *all* that God intends for us to have. A person may come to salvation by reading merely one passage of Scripture that happens to touch his heart, but it would be absurd to conclude that this is all God wants him to have. In order to build on and maintain his salvation, avoiding sin and facing the harsh realities of life, he must know much more than just to believe in Jesus. Again, let's apply the litmus test developed in answer to Objection #4. What if the Christian wants to know if abortion in the case of rape or incest is permissible?[9] Scripture does not tell him the answer, but surely one cannot conclude from this that God does not want him to know the answer; after all, a human life (if his particular denomination has defined the fertilized egg as a human life) is at stake.

Even Scripture itself teaches us that such difficult issues will invariably arise, and obviously in such cases the Christian must have an authority to appeal to for correct answers. For example, in Romans 14 Paul is addressing a problem that arose in the Church concerning eating meat offered to idols. We can see the impor-

9 We choose this particular moral dilemma since (1) the issue is obviously a serious one, and (2) it is precisely on this issue that Protestant opinion diverges so radically.

tance of this issue in Paul's warning that arriving at the wrong answer may "cause someone to stumble" and "destroy your brother for whom Christ died" (Romans 14:15-20). This is not an area of simply "believing in Jesus," per se, but an area of *maintaining* one's belief in Jesus, as we noted above. Faced with this problem, Paul gives the Romans a general principle to live by: "Let us therefore make every effort to do what leads to peace and to mutual edification...All food is clean, but it is wrong for a man to eat anything that causes someone else to stumble..." Now, let's apply to this principle the litmus test we proposed in answer to Objection #4 concerning abortion for rape and incest. How are Christians going to know what the correct answer is unless someone steps in and tells them, as Paul did with the Romans? Granted, we can conclude from reading Romans 14 that Scripture has been *sufficient to give us the account* of Paul's deliberations and reasoning with the Romans, and sets an example for us to follow, but it is *not sufficient* to answer the specific question of whether abortion is permissible for rape and incest. For this question, Scripture needs a supplement — another witness who can explicitly determine dogma from implicitly revealed truth, providing an abiding answer for all Christians for all time.

Tradition, of course, is such a witness. Many of the Church Fathers spoke against abortion and the early Church made official statements condemning it. But even then we may have a problem. What if the Fathers have merely proclaimed that abortion, in general, is wrong, but did not address the specific area of rape and incest? Now what do we do? This is where the Magisterium of the Church must step in. It gathers all possible information — from the principles developed in Scripture, the witness of Traditional teaching, and any other pertinent information — in order to make a 'God-glorifying' decision for God's people to live by. It will do no good to claim that the Magisterium need not make an *infallible* decision, for a wrong answer is certainly not "what God intends for us to have" in a matter so vital to life, happiness, and even salvation. Unless the answer is absolutely correct, Christianity is no better than the best guesses and vacillating opinions of the world that surrounds it.

Objection #6: "By *sola Scriptura* orthodox Protestants mean that Scripture alone is the primary and absolute source of authority, the final court of appeal, for all doctrine and practice (faith and morals)... Second, Scripture is the sufficient and final written authority of God. As to sufficiency, the Bible — nothing more, nothing less, and nothing else — is all that is necessary for faith and practice...Further, the Scriptures not only have sufficiency but they also possess final authority."[10]

Answer: As noted above, the first problem with such a formulation is that it is an arbitrary, man-made, definition. Words like "primary," "absolute," "final court," and "all doctrine" help Protestants set the parameters and strictures around the concept of *sola scriptura*, but none of these words, nor their lexical equivalents, does Scripture ever apply to itself. This is especially true of the latter part, which claims that Scripture is sufficient for "all that is necessary." The immediate question surfaces as to what, exactly, is "necessary" for faith and practice. Second, if we look closely, we see that the above definition proposes two distinct components. It says Scripture is the "final court of appeal," referring to Scripture's *level* of authority; but it also claims that Scripture is "sufficient" for "all that is necessary for faith and practice," referring to Scripture's *extent* of authority. We make this distinction because Scripture could be the "final authority" in the areas of faith and morals without being "sufficient for all that is necessary for faith and practice." The apologists have not proven, only assumed, that Scripture addresses all the areas "necessary" for faith and morals. If Scripture does not address all that is necessary then it is not sufficient, yet it could remain the "final court of appeal" for areas it does address. By the same token, Scripture could be sufficient for many areas of faith and morals without being the final court of appeal simply because in order for one to know what the final court is really saying he must be able to interpret the court accurately. We make appeals to a court precisely because an opponent has sought and received a judgment from the court with which he may

---

10 Geisler and MacKenzie, *Roman Catholics and Evangelicals*, p. 178.

disagree. Since Scripture is not a 'thinking personality' that can evaluate and decide among the multitudinous problems, situations, and nuances of faith and morals, it acts more as *evidence of,* or as a *witness to,* truth than as a personal judge of truth. Appealing to Scripture's infallibility does not override these facts: clearly because Scripture speaks in human words — words which everyone realizes may mean different things to different people — Scripture's infallibility, though esteemed in its own right, is only as good practically as the interpretation placed upon it.

Objection #7: [Commenting on medieval theology the apologist says the following]: "...scripture and scripture alone, was regarded as the materially sufficient source and norm of Christian theology. No other theological source could be regarded as having this status. Is not this what is expressed by the Reformation principle of sola scriptura?"[11]

Answer: If the early Protestant theologians understood Scripture as the "materially sufficient source and norm," then perhaps we would not have much controversy left to sort out. Perhaps in phrasing his comment as a question, this apologist is not certain himself whether such was the prevailing view in 16th century Protestantism. In any case, his assertion is not sensitive to the major distinction, at least in modern Protestant circles, between "formal" and "material" sufficiency. "Formal" sufficiency requires that doctrine be formulated only from explicit statements in Scripture, whereas "material" sufficiency requires only that Scripture contain implicit statements. Catholic theologians, by and large, do not have much of a problem with material sufficiency, but they will always deny formal sufficiency, and, in fact, claim that Scripture is *formally insufficient*.[12] Moreover, as we have seen in the other chapters of this book, and will see in this one, the medieval theologians, as much as they esteemed Scripture, did not hesitate to appeal to *Tra-*

[11] Alister McGrath, *The Intellectual Origins of the European Reformation*, pp. 140-141.

[12] So, Congar, *Tradition and Traditions*, p. 410.

dition as a binding authority to make their case for truth.[13] To use an analogy, Scripture's contents are like the contents of the book we used in college for General Chemistry. Such books touch on a variety of Chemistry topics, and if the book is good enough, it will mention and briefly explicate all the other areas of Chemistry that are available for study (Organic, Inorganic, Physical, Nuclear, etc). But it does not cover every problem that will confront the chemist. It only strives to be truthful in what it *does* address. Scripture does not address every problem of life either. As the Apostle John intimated, if Scripture were to address every problem it would have to be more voluminous than "all the books in the whole world" (John 21:25). The only thing of which John assures us is that in Scripture "his testimony is true" (John 21:24).

Objection #8: "Third, the Bible is clear (perspicuous). The perspicuity of Scripture does not mean that everything in the Bible is perfectly clear, but rather the essential teachings are."[14]

---

[13] As Robert Preus has concluded: "In Thomas and Duns we see how difficult it is to maintain *sola Scriptura* against the encroachments of reason on the one hand and of church authority on the other" (as quoted in *Inerrancy*, by Norman Geisler, pp. 368-372). As Catholic apologist James Akin has reminded us: "Protestants call the idea that Scripture is clear the perspicuity of Scripture. Their doctrine of *sola scriptura* combines the perspicuity of Scripture with the claim that Scripture contains all the theological data we need. It is important to make these distinctions because, while a Catholic cannot assert the formal sufficiency (perspicuity) of Scripture, he can assert its material sufficiency, as had been done by such well-known Catholic theologians as John Henry Newman, Walter Kaspar, George Tarvard, Henri de Lubac, Matthias Scheeben, Michael Schmaus, and Joseph Ratzinger. French theologian Yves Congar states, '[W]e can admit *Scriptura sola* in the sense of a material sufficiency of canonical Scripture. This means that Scripture contains, in one way or another, all truths necessary for salvation. This position can claim the support of many Fathers and early theologians. It has been, and still is, held by many modern theologians. . . .[At Trent] it was widely ... admitted that all the truths necessary to salvation are at least outlined in Scripture.... [W]e find fully verified the formula of men like Newman and Kuhn: *Totum in Scriptura, totum in Traditione,* 'All is in Scripture, all is in Tradition.' ... 'Written' and 'unwritten' indicate not so much two material domains as two modes or states of knowledge" (*Tradition and Traditions* [New York: Macmillian, 1967], 410-414). "Material and Formal Sufficiency" *This Rock*. October, 1993. p. 15.

[14] Geisler and MacKenzie, p. 178.

Answer: As in the previous attempt in Objection #6 to define the authoritative *level* and *extent* of Scripture, the apologists now wish to set the parameters on Scripture's *complexity/non-complexity*. Again, however, they make such definitions arbitrarily, for Scripture does not describe itself as either perspicuous or non-perspicuous, let alone say that it is perspicuous on its "essential teachings," whatever they are. Moreover, perspicuity is a relative term that depends on the intrinsic nature of the object in view. For example, we can say that the formula $E=mc^2$ is perspicuous (i.e., to find the amount of energy, one has only to multiply the mass of an object by the square of the speed of light), but the theory of relativity behind it, when studied in depth, is very complex. Similarly, Paul's answer to the Philippian jailer in Acts 16 on how to be saved is "Believe on the Lord Jesus" — an answer that is certainly perspicuous on one level, but since it incorporates all knowledge about God and his dealings with man (e.g., the Trinity, the Incarnation, the Virgin birth, original sin, predestination and free will, the nature of justification, perseverance, and a host of other topics), on another level it is indeed very complex.

Objection #9: "Fourth, Scripture interprets Scripture...When we have difficulty in understanding an unclear text of Scripture, we turn to other biblical texts, since the Bible is the best interpreter of the Bible."[15]

Answer: This is a variation on the previous Objection. First the apologist, as in the philosopher Descarte's supposedly bedrock dictum "I think, therefore I am," wishes to find a verse or verses of Scripture that are so clear as to be indisputable, and then use this knowledge to answer what he feels are the more complex passages. But because he is left to his own fallible judgment, he can never be sure that he is indeed interpreting correctly even the bedrock Scriptures that he claims to know absolutely. Second, the Bible does not claim to be the "best interpreter of the Bible." In fact, the Bible

[15] Ibid., p. 179.

simply does not claim to be its own interpreter, good or bad. Protestants invariably confuse *interpretation* with *testimony*. Interpretation must be done by a thinking personality, whereas Scripture can only offer *testimony* to a certain fact of history or soteriology. For example, when the Sadducees denied the resurrection, Jesus referred them to the testimony of Exodus 3:6 which states, "I am the God of Abraham, the God of Isaac, and the God of Jacob." Left to themselves, the Sadducees would have walked away in consternation. But Jesus *interprets* the passage for them and reasons from his own thinking ability that God cannot be the God of the dead, but only of the living; therefore, Abraham, Isaac, and Jacob are still living but apparently in another realm of existence. What Jesus did is called *interpretation*. The Bible neither claims to do this nor has the ability to do so, for it cannot think as humans do.

We can add a very practical example of this problem. If "Scripture interprets Scripture," let's take a typical Protestant doctrinal controversy. The present apologists often refer to the "Calvinist" perspective on Scripture, and, in fact, do so on the same page as his "fourth" objection cited above regarding *sola scriptura*. John Calvin, as most know, was a predestinarian theologian who did not believe in free will.[16] Norman Geisler, one of our present Protestant apologists, has declared in his writings that he [Geisler] *does* believe in free will. To be fair to both Calvin and Geisler, a whole host of Scriptures support predestination, and an equal number support free will. Now which set of passages are the "clearer" set, the predestination passages or the free will passages? Which set of passages should serve as the foundation for interpreting the other set of passages? And if there is a synthesis between the two, who decides what the degree of balance is? Scripture cannot serve as the interpreter because Scripture, with all due respect to it's being God's Word, is what occasioned the problem in the first place. Anyone who has studied in depth the issue of predestination versus free

---

[16] See my work, *Not By Faith Alone: The Biblical Evidence for the Catholic Doctrine of Justification* (Queenship Publishing, 1997) for full documentation of Calvin's theology of predestination.

will knows that Scripture gives a lot of ambiguous and incomplete information on the subject. It takes quite an astute mind — a thinking personality — to interpret the issue correctly.[17]

To illustrate the intractable nature of this problem, we must mention that many "Calvinists" hold that the doctrine of predestination is an "essential" of the faith, so much so that they say those who believe in free will ("Arminians") do not understand or even possess the true gospel of salvation. Arminians, likewise, castigate Calvinists as cold-hearted, ivory-tower theologians who don't understand the gospel. This is what we can expect when theologians make arbitrary decisions as to what is "essential" and what is not.

Finally, let us add one more issue to the pile to emphasize this subject's importance. On the previous page of his work, the apologist claims that: "...classical Protestantism denies any salvific value of natural (general) revelation, believing one can only come to salvation through special revelation."[18] Observe closely what this theologian is saying. In effect, he, as a mere man, is setting the parameters as to how God can save or not save someone. Those who do not receive "special revelation" cannot, in his view, be saved. And, of course, we cannot fail to mention the apologist claims that Scripture alone constitutes "special revelation." First, where does Scripture say that 'Scripture alone' constitutes "special revelation," and second, where does Scripture teach that no one can be saved unless they receive "special revelation"? Not only has this apologist said something that is untrue, he has also neglected his own theory of *sola scriptura* by failing to cite chapter and verse where Scripture teaches such things. This is where the matter of *sola scriptura,* and Scripture being "its own interpreter," impinge on the very gospel

---

[17] Problems of this type are pervasive in Protestant Evangelicalism. A recent venue of popular books attempt to address the controversy by providing the reader with four or five opposing views on a particular subject. For example: *Predestination and Free Will: Four Views of Divine Sovereignty and Human Freedom* (1986); *Four Views on Salvation in a Pluralistic World* (1996); *Five Views on Law and Gospel* (1996); *Are Miraculous Gifts for Today: Four Views* (1996); *Women in Ministry: Four Views* (1989); *The Meaning of the Millennium: Four Views* (1977);

[18] Geisler and MacKenzie, p. 178.

itself, sticking its ugly head into affairs that are none of its business. Who but God can decide who will be saved and who will not be saved, especially in light of so many passages in Scripture that speak of this prerogative being only God's, whether or not the person is receiving "special revelation"?[19]

Objection #10: First, as Catholic scholars themselves recognize, it is not necessary that the Bible explicitly and formally teach *sola*

---

[19] cf. Psalm 62:12; Romans 2:4-15; 2 Peter 3:9; Matt. 16:27; Rev. 20:11-15. Vatican II, *Dei Verbum* 3; 6, states: "God, who creates and conserves all things by his Word (cf. Jn 1:3), provides men with constant evidence of himself in created realities (cf. Rom. 1:19-20)...The Sacred Synod professes that 'God, the first principle and last end of all things, can be known with certainty from the created world, by the natural light of human reason' (Rom. 1:20). It teaches that it is to his Revelation that we must attribute the fact 'that those things, which in themselves are not beyond the grasp of human reason, can, in the present condition of the human race, be known by all men with ease, with firm certainty, and without the contamination of error.' (Ibid., Denz. 1785 and 1786 (3004 and 3005)." In light of this, Geisler's and MacKenzie's statement that "Both traditional Roman Catholics and conservative Protestants agree that general revelation is insufficient to lead one to a saving knowledge of the gospel" (*Roman Catholics and Evangelicals*, p. 26) is essentially incorrect. Catholicism does not believe that salvation is limited to those who receive special revelation, rather, God will judge each person based on what he knows and does. Romans 2:5-15 is very clear about such matters, yet it is precisely in Geisler's and MacKenzie's failure to address this passage throughout their entire 538 page book which shows a glaring inconsistency and contradiction in their theology. Moreover, because of Geisler's and MacKenzie's view that salvation cannot be procured unless special revelation is made available, in effect, their prior appeal to natural law to combat the social ills of "abortion, euthanasia, and homosexuality" (Ibid., p. 25) has a very hollow ring to it. If one cannot strive for moral righteousness with the added dimension that through this God would be pleased to provide salvation to that same individual, then what good is moral righteousness or the striving for it? Wouldn't it be better for that individual to "eat, drink, and be merry" (cf. 1 Cor. 15:32; Acts 10:1-35) rather than risk his life for good causes? Or, do Geisler and MacKenzie really believe the same concept about natural law as their mentor John Calvin, whom they refer to with the words, "He [Calvin] explicitly called this moral awareness 'natural law' which is 'sufficient for their righteous condemnation' (Ibid., p. 128). Calvin sees no lasting blessing or salvific goodness in natural law, but only a means through which God can condemn men. See my book *Not By Faith Alone: The Biblical Evidence for the Catholic Doctrine of Justification* (Queenship Pub., 1997) for a more thorough analysis on this matter.

Scriptura in order for this doctrine to be true. Many Christian teachings are a necessary logical deduction of what is clearly taught in the Bible. For example, nowhere does the Bible formally and explicitly state the doctrine of the Trinity...the doctrine of the Trinity is validly based in Scripture alone. Likewise, it is possible that *sola Scriptura* could be a necessary logical deduction from what is taught in Scripture"[20]

Answer: No responsible Catholic apologists with which we are aware have ever published a statement saying that *sola Scriptura* need not be formally taught in the Bible to be believed.[21] In asserting this, the Protestant apologist is merely making an inference based on Catholic scholars having extracted the doctrine of the Trinity from implicit documentation in Scripture. Unfortunately, these kinds of discussions throw the doctrine of the Trinity around like the proverbial ragdoll, and the present case is no exception. The comparison is inappropriate for the following reasons. (1) However "implicit" the doctrine of the Trinity is in Scripture the fact remains that the Ecumenical Councils saw fit to extract the doctrine of the Trinity from Scripture, but did not see fit to extract a doctrine of *sola scriptura*. No council in Christian history ever declared Scripture as the 'sole and sufficient authority' or 'the final court of appeal.' Hence it is misleading to propose that "it is possible that *sola Scriptura* could be a necessary logical deduction" without pointing out to the reader that the very Councils to which the apologist appeals did not see it as "possible." We must also point out that the Church arrived at their specific doctrine of the Trinity not because it was the "only possible" solution but because it was the only *orthodox* solution. Theologians participating in the Council proposed many "possible" solutions (e.g., Modalism, Sabellianism, etc), but only one was correct. (2) The Councils based their doctrine of the

---

20 Geisler and MacKenzie, p. 184.

21 There are some Catholic theologians who use the term *sola scriptura*, but their remarks are always qualified to say that it is not the same as the Protestant conception of *sola scriptura*. It concerns the debate over whether there is constitutive tradition outside of Scripture, but does not deny the existence of inerrant Tradition and infallible Magisterium (See Gabriel Moran's *Scripture and Tradition*, pp. 20-26).

Trinity on more than Scripture alone. If one reads the accounts of the early Fathers on the matter of the Trinity and the Incarnation, one finds frequent references to the Tradition of the Church that was handed down to them, especially in opposition to groups like the Arians who denied the Trinity and the Incarnation claiming Scripture did not teach such doctrines. Further, no Father ever defended the *formal sufficiency* of Scripture or cited the Tradition of the Church as upholding such a doctrine. (3) One of the main reasons that Scripture is vague on the subject of the Trinity is that it is a very complex concept — one, in fact, that the mind of man cannot understand. It is impossible for Scripture to explain to us how 'three are in one yet one are in three' because it does not make any logical sense to our finite minds. Using trite formulas like "1 x 1 x 1 = 1" to explain the Trinity do us more harm than good.[22] *Sola scriptura*, on the other hand, is not complex at all. If Scripture meant to teach such a doctrine, it would have no difficulty at all in explaining the doctrine to us. All we would need is some clear statement that conveys: (a) Scripture is formally sufficient and the final court of appeal; (b) oral Tradition is not to be preserved and is not authoritative after the completion of Scripture; and (c) the Church is not the final authority on the interpretation of Scripture. If Scripture stipulated just one of these three principles, there would be cause to consider a doctrine of *sola scriptura*; but so far, no one has been able to show us where Scripture clearly teaches any of these stipulations. If the early Councils could not see it in Scripture, they who were closest to the apostles, why should *we* be expected to see it?

Objection #11: "Now, since both Catholics and Protestants agree that there is no new revelation beyond the first century, and since even what the apostles said apart from these revelations could not make them void, it would follow that these texts support the Protestant principle of *sola Scriptura*. For if there is no normative revelation after the time of the apostles and even the prophets themselves were not to add their teachings to the revelations God gave them in the Scriptures, then it follows that the Scriptures are the only infallible source of divine revelation."[23]

---

[22] Geisler and MacKenzie, p. 43.

[23] Ibid., 186.

Answer: The apologist has taken one component of agreement between Catholics and Protestants concerning inspired revelation and has concluded that Catholics should therefore logically accept Scripture as the only infallible source of divine revelation. Whether inspired revelation has ceased or not has nothing to do with whether God can give infallible guidance to the Church on an ongoing basis. The apologist is confusing the *vehicle* of infallibility with the *gift* of infallibility. The apologist is correct in stating that the Catholic Church believes that inspired revelation has ceased, but the Church does not say that "private" revelation, or the charism of infallibility, have ceased in the Church. The former allows for such things as the validity of approved Marian apparitions, the latter serves to prohibit the Church from dogmatizing errors in faith and morals. Infallibility is the very reason, for example, that the Catholic Church holds to an *infallible* 27-book New Testament — something our Protestant brethren do not have the privilege of asserting. Although God did not give inspired revelation to the Church of the fourth century, he protected them from error in formulating the canon by the charism of infallibility. We will say more on this topic later.

Objection #12: "The Bible teaches *sola Scriptura* by stressing that it is a revelation from God (Gal. 1:12; cf. 1 Cor. 2:11-13) as opposed to the words of men. Paul's contrast vividly illustrates the difference...(Gal. 2:1-2). It is important to note here that "human being" includes the other apostles, of whom Paul adds, "nor did I go up to Jerusalem to those who were apostles before me" (2:17). So even the preaching of an apostle is not on the same level as the "revelation" (disclosure) from God; neither are the words of an angel (Gal. 1:8). This is argument for sola Scriptura."[24]

Answer: First, one cannot conclude that because Scripture is a "revelation from God" that it is the *only* revelation from God. Paul is clear in 1 Thess. 2:13 that his oral words were understood as the "words of God" not the "words of men" (cf., 1 Cor. 2:13; 14:37; 2 Cor. 13:3; 2 Pet. 3:2; Acts 2:42-47). In addition, in Galatians 1:12, from which this apologist bases his argument, Paul is not necessar-

---

[24] Ibid., pp. 186-187.

ily contrasting *inspired* teachings to the revelation from Christ. Paul does not indicate in Gal. 1:12 whether the "human being" or what was "taught" were inspired. Moreover, in Gal. 2:17 he does not claim that the apostles in Jerusalem (those he did not go up to see) possessed inspired revelation at that particular time. In fact, when Paul does finally see the apostles three years later it is for the mere purpose of "getting acquainted" with them and thus he stays with Peter 15 days (Gal. 2:18). Hence, the apologist is attempting to draw out a contrast between the inspired oral revelations given to the apostles and the revelations given directly to Paul that is simply not explicit in the context of the passage. Thus, Paul is not attempting to establish a doctrine of *sola scriptura* but is merely trying to validate his own *apostleship* by showing everyone that he, as the other apostles did, received his revelations directly from God. (A man could only be considered an apostle if he received his revelations directly from God, cf. 1 Cor. 9:1; Acts 9, 22, 26).

Second, we must also point out that nowhere in the Galatian epistle does Paul say that all his revelations from God were going to be confined to Scripture. A parallel situation occurs in his dealings with the Ephesians. In Acts 20:25-31 Paul explains that he was with the Ephesians for three years. He says that during this time he preached "the whole counsel of God" to them. Yet in Ephesians 3:2-3 Paul says, "Surely you have heard about the administration of God's grace that was given to me for you, that is, the mystery made known to me by *revelation*, as I have already *written briefly*." Here Paul is speaking about the same kind of *revelations* he received in Gal. 1:12, yet he adds that he has only *written briefly* about these revelations to the Ephesians. We can only conclude that not all of Paul's divine revelations were confined to Scripture.

Objection #13: "Romans 15:14 indicates that Paul thinks of a sufficiency of the gospel...The point of Romans 15:14 is that the Roman Christians already had a situation of 'complete in knowledge' on the basis of the gospel that they knew."[25]

[25] Personal letters to me, on file, dated October 22, 1993 and December 28, 1993 from Dr. Vern S. Poythress of Westminster Theological Seminary, Phila., PA.

Answer: First, although we can agree that the "gospel" and Scripture are related, and can, in certain instances, be used interchangeably, it is not appropriate to make such an interchange when technical discussions concerning *sola scriptura* are at issue. "Gospel" is a more general word than "Scripture." The "gospel" was preached as much or more by word of mouth than by writing, apparently in nuances which Scripture does not record in detail (2 Thess. 2:15). Missionaries had taught the "gospel" orally and its hearers gradually memorized it.[26] They learned the gospel without the help of most of the New Testament since at that time it did not exist in anything close to its final form, let alone in an undisputed canon of 27 books. The "gospel" could be something that Christians carried in their hearts and minds as general knowledge without necessarily having to depend on chapter and verse of Scripture.

More importantly, the passage cited above in support of *sola scriptura* actually does quite a good job of *refuting* the doctrine, when one examines closely the context in which it is placed. As Paul says in Romans 15:14 that they are "complete in knowledge,"according to verse 15 this state of mind existed *before* he wrote the Roman epistle to them, for he says, "I have written you quite boldly on some points, as if to remind you of them again..."[27] Paul is writing the epistle only to remind them what he

[26] In fact, Paul makes this clear in the context when he says that he should only go to places that have not heard the gospel. For this reason he has been "hindered from coming" to them. Apparently, the Romans had already heard the gospel from other missionaries.

[27] From the Greek ἐπαναμιμνῄσκων, appearing only once in the New Testament, but also in classical literature to "call to mind, remember, remind." Peter uses the same concept in 2 Peter 1:12, "Wherefore, I intend always to remind you concerning these things, though you have known and been established in present truth." As with Paul's "complete knowledge," Peter says that the Christians to whom he writes "know" and are "established" in the truth that they presently have. What they already know could not be referring only to Peter's first epistle, since it does not contain all the truths necessary for the Christian life. Peter's "reminding" is reinforcing the knowledge of the Christian faith that they had received by word of mouth. His epistle, written to a wide audience (2 Peter 2:1), serves only to heighten and support the pervasive oral teaching all these Christians from different lands had received and preserved. Moreover, if what they "knew" was sufficient in and of itself, Peter would not need to remind them of these truths.

or other missionaries had taught them orally, and even then, he writes only on "some points"[28] of what they were previously taught, not on *all* they were taught. This fact is even more significant when we realize that the epistle to the Romans contains some of the most profound theological truths of the Christian faith. By only "reminding" them of such truths, Paul is attributing to oral revelation the ability to communicate the most technical and deepest truths of the gospel. Apparently the missionaries were well trained and the Romans were good students. We can surmise from this prevalence of oral teaching that a concept of *sola scriptura* does not seem to have been floating around in the first century. In effect, Scripture was serving as the *witness* to the gospel, not as a judge of the gospel. We should also add that since the letter to the Romans was one of Paul's earliest inspired epistles, we can safely conclude that the New Testament was not in wide enough circulation for these Roman Christians to glean *complete knowledge* from Scripture. Certainly, they had the Old Testament Scriptures (Romans 1:2f; 15:4), but these were not the complete revelation from God. Moreover, as Gentiles who did not know the ancient Scriptures as well as their Jewish counterparts, surely the Romans could not have obtained from the Old Testament the *formally sufficient* knowledge Protestant apologists may wish to apply to Romans 15:14.

As many Protestant commentators agree, the phrase "complete knowledge" is simply hyperbole to show that Paul is impressed with what they already know and have put into practice. It is not a technical/theological term Paul uses in an effort to teach such a profound concept as *sola scriptura*. Paul, being the astute theologian he was, certainly would have known what a crucial difference a belief in *sola scriptura* would have made upon the understanding of the Christian faith.

The phrase "complete knowledge" is literally translated "having been filled with all knowledge." Anyone familiar with the Bible's usage of the word "all" knows that it is not a technical or absolutistic term denoting that there is no other knowledge they could desire or even need. This is supported by the fact that before using the phrase in question Paul says, "you yourselves are **full** of good-

---

[28] From the Greek ἀπὸ μέρους which is literally "in part."

ness." He does not mean that the Roman Christians were perfectly good without the slightest stain of sin. They were "full" of goodness in a relative sense — to a degree that Paul could be proud of them and their progress as Christians. They were not, however, so *full* of knowledge that they did not need to learn anything else, nor did they possess a written source of information that answered all their questions about the faith. They were full of knowledge in the sense that they could conduct themselves as mature men in Christ.

Objection #14: "I warn everyone who hears the prophetic words in this book: if anyone adds to them, God will add to him the plagues described in this book, and if anyone takes away from the words in the prophetic book, God will take away his share in the tree of life" (Rev. 22:18-19). As Jesus declared (Matt. 15:3-6), tradition sometimes adds to the words of Scripture teachings that make void what Scripture affirms. Sola Scriptura could hardly be stated more emphatically."[29]

Answer: Attempts to use such passages as Revelation 22:18-19, Deuteronomy 4:2; 12:32 or Proverbs 30:6 to support *sola scriptura* are really quite naive. First, we won't bog ourselves down in this discussion by arguing that John's command in Rev. 22:18-19 only refers to the book of Revelation. We will assume by extension that any addition to God's word that God does not authorize is indeed a violation of the *principle* in Rev. 22:18-19. It is futile, however, to accuse those who believe in authoritative Tradition of disregarding these verses if, as is indeed true, Scripture itself commands its readers to obey and preserve oral tradition (2 Thess. 2:15; 2 Tim. 1:13-2:2). In verses such as Deut. 4:2 and Rev. 22:18, the sacred authors are merely condemning any attempt by man, whether from "tradition" or from a document which is claimed as inspired but is not, to add to God's inspired word. They cannot add their own words to God's and claim that they are divinely authorized, nor can they subtract from God's word claiming that some of it is not inspired. This atrocity happened in Old Testament times as well as New Testament times. Invariably, throughout Christian history, men have

---

[29] Geisler and MacKenzie, p. 186.

claimed to be "inspired" by God to give additional revelation in contradiction to the Church's clear statement that God's inspired revelation has ceased.[30] If the apologist wishes to limit the definition of *sola scriptura* to prohibiting additional inspired revelation to Scripture, we would certainly oblige.

We find it interesting that the apologist says, "...tradition *sometimes* adds to the words of Scripture..." showing either that he realizes that not all tradition is harmful or that the Scripture allows for tradition. But we must insist he claim that tradition either adds to God's word or it does not. Tradition cannot "sometimes" add to God's word. If apostolic oral tradition is inspired, as the Catholic Church claims, then it is not "adding" to God's word because it already *was* God's word before Rev. 22:18 was penned. If the apologist responds that Catholic tradition is formed after the cessation of general revelation, we reply that post-apostolic tradition that the Catholic Church has deemed divinely authoritative is based only on the apostolic tradition from whence it originates.

Objection #15: "We read, in words that came from the lips of our Lord: 'Search the Scriptures' (John 5:39). This counsel would be meaningless unless all readers can know the truth through the Scriptures."[31]

Answer: When we study this verse closely, we find that in actuality it may be saying exactly the *opposite* of what this apologist has attempted to portray, even to the point of being one of the strongest verses *denying* the concept of *sola scriptura*. The Greek of John 5:39 literally reads: "*You* search the scriptures because in them you think you have eternal life..." The word "search" is a second person verb, which for this particular word can either be an indicative or an imperative, since both are spelled the same in Greek. If it is in the indicative, Jesus is saying that the Jews regularly consult Scripture for dogmatic truth. If it is an imperative, Jesus is *telling* the Jews to consult Scripture. The imperative is the form that the

---

30 Vatican II, *Dei Verbum* 4: "...no new public revelation is to be expected before the glorious manifestation of our Lord, Jesus Christ..."

31 John Armstrong, *Sola Scriptura!* p. 136.

apologist hopes to see here. The more likely grammatical form, however, is the indicative, since the phrase in question is immediately followed by a relative clause which gives the very reason the Jews search Scripture, i.e., "because" in them they think they have found eternal life. The indicative is also the more likely, since Jesus' next statement, "...and they are they which testify of me," is an attempt to show the Jews that even though they searched Scripture, they failed to extract the essential truth and reasoning that Jesus is the Son of God.[32] Irrespective of this analysis, even if Jesus was using the imperative form, the same accusation would hold against the Jews, namely, that even though they think they have found by searching Scripture a key to eternal life, they have nonetheless failed to reason from Scripture that Jesus was the long-awaited Messiah, which was a far more important truth to discover. Thus, whether indicative or imperative, the message that radiates from this passage is that the Jews think, by their interpretation of Scripture, that they have already gained entrance into heaven. In reality, they have not gained it at all, because they have failed to extract from Scripture that Jesus was the Savior who could either grant or deny their claims to heaven.

Tradition

Objection #16: "Indeed, to assume that oral traditions of the apostles not recorded in the Bible are necessary to interpret what is

[32] The translation "search" or "you search" is derived from the Greek word ἐρευνᾶτε, which is either a second-person plural imperative, or a second-person plural indicative. Both the present indicative and the present imperative of the verbal root ἐρευνάω have the same form in Greek. Because, however, ὅτι clause follows immediately after the use of ἐρευνᾶτε, it is almost certain that John intended the indicative "you search." In other words, Jesus is not commanding them to now begin searching Scripture; he is saying, rather, that they had already searched Scripture and concluded that they possessed eternal life without seeing that Jesus was the Messiah. Other translations bring this grammatical nuance to the fore, e.g., "You diligently study the Scriptures because you think that by them you possess eternal life" (NIV); "You search the Scriptures because you think that in them you eternal life" (RSV); "You search the Scriptures because you think that in them you have eternal life" (NASB).

recorded under inspiration is to argue in effect that the uninspired is more clear than the inspired."[33]

Answer: The apologist draws an incorrect conclusion because the premise is false. It is precisely because the oral traditions of the apostles were *inspired*, not uninspired, that they are sufficient to interpret and add to Scripture on the issues which Scripture does not completely clarify or does not address. Granted, the apostles probably said many things in their everyday conversation that were not inspired by God, but the Catholic Church does not regard these conversations as apostolic Tradition.

Objection #17: It is utterly presumptuous to assert that what a fallible human being writes is clearer than what the infallible Word of God declares! Further, it insists that words of the apostles that were not written down are more clear than the ones they did write! We all know from experience that this is not so."[34]

Answer: The apologist is engaging in a mild form of *ad hominem* argumentation when he asserts it is "utterly presumptuous" to suggest that what fallible human beings write can be clearer than the infallible Word of God. First, we must point out that the clarity of a given writing does not depend on whether the writer is fallible or infallible. Infallibility only means that what is written is without error, not that it is the clearest presentation of what the writer intends to convey. A child, for example, can often say and write things more clearly than an adult, but that does not mean that the child is superior in intellect to the adult or makes fewer mistakes. Further, one can declare even things that are *not true* with the same clarity as things that are true. We must be careful not to confuse truth with clarity. Moreover, Scripture itself testifies that its propositions are not always clear or easily understood (2 Peter 3:16), and that it often gives revelation in veiled form; its "clarity" being dependent on whether God opens one up to its understanding (Matt. 13:1-23). We also "know from experience" that what people write is often

---

[33] Geisler and MacKenzie, p. 190.

[34] Ibid., p. 190.

vague and ambiguous, needing further clarification, since the person writing does not put down everything he wishes to say (e.g., John 20:30-31; 21:25), nor think of all the possible nuances, situations, and ambiguities his writing may encounter in various peoples and cultures. Often even in a simple letter to a friend the friend may ask "what did you mean by that statement?" It is simply naive to think that statements in written form have some magical power that can't be improved upon or explained by oral examination and elucidation.

Objection #18: "What the Catholic must prove (and cannot) is that the God who deemed it so important for the faith and morals of the faithful to inspire the inscripturation of twenty-seven books of the apostolic teaching would have left out some important revelation in this book. So, however authoritative the apostles were by their office, only their inscripturated words are inspired and infallible (2 Tim. 3:16-17; cf. John 10:35). There is no evidence that all the revelation God gave them to express was not inscripturated in the twenty-seven books of the New Testament."[35]

Answer: We find it interesting that the apologist asks Catholics to "prove" that God did not inscripturate all his revelation, but at the same time keeps referring to a "twenty-seven book New Testament" which he claims contains all this revelation, but which he can't "prove" is really the canon of Scripture, for he does not claim any infallible means of knowing that the New Testament should contain 27 books. We can all play the "proof" game, but that is not going to get us very far in these discussions. We also find it interesting that the apologist is trying to prove his case by an argument from silence, through the double-negative "There is *no* evidence that all revelation was...*not* inscripturated." By the same token, there is no evidence that Mars does not contain little green men, but that does not mean that green men exist on Mars. It is precisely at this point that we must turn the tables and insist that it is this apologist who must prove his assertion that all revelation was eventually confined to Scripture, especially in the face of numerous and ex-

[35] Ibid., p. 188.

plicit passages of Scripture that speak against his assertion (cf., John 20:30-31; 21:25; 1 Cor. 11:34; Eph. 3:3; 2 John 12; 3 John 13; 2 Thess. 2:15, et al). As for basing his argument on the supposition that God could not have "left out some important revelation in this book" we need only point out one example of a "missing piece" of revelation, among many that are available, to prove our point: why did God leave out of Scripture whether infants are to be baptized, if, as even some Protestant denominations believe (Lutherans, Anglicans, Churches of Christ, Methodists), that baptism is the very means of grace and salvation?

Objection #19: "To claim that all God's revelation was not written down is to claim that the prophets were not obedient to their commission not to subtract a word from what God revealed to them."[36]

Answer: No, the writers of Scripture can only write in Scripture what God inspires them to write. If God chooses not to inscripturate all of his revelation, it is not the fault of the writer, nor is he *subtracting* from God's word. He is writing what God wanted him to write. Further, in making such a claim, the apologist must prove that every single oral revelation alluded to in Scripture was indeed confined to Scripture. This is certainly an impossible task, not only because the apologist does not know what oral revelations were given, and not only because Scripture does not claim to confine oral revelation to Scripture, but mainly because Scripture gives much evidence that oral revelations were obviously not confined to Scripture. For example, Scripture specifies that Philip had four unmarried daughters who "prophesied," yet none of their revelations were recorded in Scripture (Acts 21:9). Acts 11:28 briefly describes one prophecy of Agabus but this is only in passing, and Scripture records none of the revelations of the other prophets that were with him. Surely they would not be called *prophets* if they had not received divine revelation. If one objects that these prophets were not apostles, we can point to the tongues and prophecies given to the church of Corinth in 1 Cor. 12-14 (cf., 1 Thess 5:20; Eph. 2:20; 3:5; 4:11), of which Paul himself says that he speaks

[36] Ibid., p. 189.

more than all the rest (1 Cor. 14:18). Where does Scripture record these tongues, along with their interpretations, and these prophecies? And even if they were recorded, where does Scripture distinguish between an inspired writing and an oral revelation that became inscripturated? To claim a distinction between the two without evidence that Scripture itself makes such a distinction is pure speculation.

Objection #20: "Tradition in effect becomes a lens through which the written word is interpreted. Tradition therefore stands as the highest of all authorities, because it renders the only authoritative interpretation of the sacred writings."[37]

Answer: First, it is incorrect and misleading to convey that Tradition is the "highest of all authorities" based on its claim to interpret Scripture. If we use the same logic for Protestant dogmas, we even could consider Protestant interpretations of Scripture a higher authority than Scripture, since Protestants also produce what they consider dogmatic and unchangeable interpretations of Scripture, e.g., justification by faith alone. Because such dogmas form a single, authoritative interpretation of Scripture, they become, in effect, an unalterable, and virtually infallible, Tradition.[38] The only way the Protestant could disclaim this principle is to concede that every one of his interpretations, including justification by faith alone, could be wrong, for if he feels that just one dogma is of unquestionable certainty, then, according to the same logic he has imposed on Catholicism, he has assumed authority over Scripture. Since further study of Scripture may reveal that his previous interpretation is incorrect, he can never claim, even in the most important doctrines, that he has error-free and unalterable truth.

Second, we must also say that it is fallacious to argue against Catholic Tradition on the ground that it provides single, authoritative interpretations of Scripture. Since a given passage can have

37 John MacArthur, *Sola Scriptura!* p. 152.

38 As Yves Congar has reasoned, "Protestants add that the normative value of such confessions is completely conditioned, conditional and revisable. But in fact these confessions have no more been revised than the conciliar dogmas, and their normative value is just as absolute" (*Tradition and Traditions*, p. 422).

only one true interpretation, Tradition cannot be faulted when it claims to hold that single interpretation. An authentic Tradition could only hold to one interpretation.

Objection #21: "Whenever tradition is elevated to such a high level of authority, it inevitably becomes detrimental to the authority of Scripture. Jesus made this very point when he confronted the Jewish leaders. He showed that in many cases their tradition actually nullified Scripture. He therefore rebuked them in the harshest terms: '...Neglecting the commandment of God, you hold to the tradition of men.'"[39]

Answer: Again, it is fallacious to assume that because Tradition interprets Scripture it is detrimental to Scripture. There is nothing more detrimental to Scripture than divorcing it from the interpretation given in ancient Tradition and Councils, and subsequently turning it over to the interpretive whims and biases of men in the distant future. More importantly, let us notice precisely what Jesus is saying to the Jews. He is not saying that Tradition is necessarily detrimental to Scripture. He is only saying that in the Jews' use of Tradition they *neglected* the commandments of God. In other words, the Jews were not forming interpretations based on a synthesis of Scripture and Tradition; rather, they purposely ignored Scripture's commands and replaced it with their own, man-made teaching. They made their tradition contradict Scripture instead of using Tradition to support Scriptural teaching. Unlike the Jews, the Catholic Church uses Tradition the correct way — with Scripture and Tradition as witnesses to the same truth — where one witness does not contradict the other. When there is no contradiction between Scripture and Tradition on any given topic, there is truth. Is this not the means of coming to truth that Jesus taught when he told the Jews: "In your own Law it is written that the testimony of two men is valid. I am one who testifies for myself; my other witness is the Father, who sent me" (John 8:17-18). Tradition and Scripture stand as two witnesses verifying one truth. Just as Jesus, being only one wit-

---

[39] John MacArthur, *Sola Scriptura!*, p. 153.

ness, calls on the witness of the Father, so Scripture depends on the witness of Tradition.[40]

Objection #22: "So the revealed word of God, and nothing else, was the supreme and sole authority in Judaism. This alone was the standard of truth delivered to them by God Himself. Moses was instructed to write down the very words God gave him (Exodus 34:27), and that written record of God's Word became the basis for God's covenant with the nation (Exodus 24:4,7)..."[41]

Answer: First, nothing in the passages this Protestant apologist cites says that Scripture was the "supreme and sole authority in Judaism." *God* was the supreme authority in Judaism, and the decrees of God came in various forms (e.g., written, oral, ephod, seer, vision, and miracle), each holding equal authority because they were all directly from God. Second, the written portion of God's word was read *to* the people, not read *by* the people (Exodus 24:7: "Then he took the Book of the Covenant and read it to the people. They responded, 'We will do everything the Lord has said; we will obey'"). The people in the assembly did not possess their own personal copy

---

40 Vatican II, *Dei Verbum* 10, "It is clear, therefore, that, in the supremely wise arrangement of God, sacred Tradition, sacred Scripture and the Magisterium of the Church are so connected and associated that one of them cannot stand without the others." Dei Verbum 9, "Sacred Tradition and sacred Scripture, then, are bound closely together, and communicate one with the other. For both of them, flowing out from the same divine well-spring, come together in some fashion to form one thing...And Tradition transmits in its entirety the Word of God which has been entrusted to the apostles by Christ the Lord and the Holy Spirit. It transmits it to the successors of the apostles so that, enlightened by the Spirit of truth, they may faithfully preserve, expound and spread it abroad by their preaching. Thus it comes about that the Church does not draw her certainty about all revealed truths from the holy Scriptures alone. Hence, both Scripture and Tradition must be accepted and honored with equal feelings of devotion and reverence...(10) Sacred Tradition and sacred Scripture make up a single deposit of the Word of God, which is entrusted to the Church...(21) She has always regarded, and continues to regard Scripture, taken together with sacred Tradition, as the supreme rule of her faith...It follows that all the preaching of the Church, as indeed the entire Christian religion, should be nourished and ruled by sacred Scripture."

41 John MacArthur, *Sola Scriptura!*, p. 154.

of the Covenant, nor did they question the interpretation or teaching of Moses. Third, what they heard from Moses' reading of the Covenant was mostly simple commands of moral behavior (e.g., 'do this, don't do that), not theological treatises on the finer points of theology that the first centuries of Christendom would debate. In fact, concerning God's commands in the covenant, Moses says in Deut. 30:12: "Now what I am commanding you today is *not too difficult for you or beyond your reach*...For I command you today to love the Lord your God, to walk in his ways, and to keep his commands, decrees and laws; then you will live and increase."

Objection #23: "*Sola Scriptura* was therefore established in principle with the giving of the law. No tradition passed down by word of mouth, no rabbinical opinion, and no priestly innovation was to be accorded authority equal to the revealed Word of God as recorded in Scripture."[42]

Answer: We grant that "rabbinical opinion" and "priestly innovation" are not equal in authority to the Word of God. That goes without saying. But to conclude that the Jews had no oral teaching authority accompanying and supplementing the written word is simply incorrect. Not only did God and his prophets speak God's word directly to the people and then perpetuate them among the people by word of mouth, but even the written word makes reference to authoritative, independent oral traditions, and oral traditions of inspired writings that were not canonical.[43] Moreover, in order to avoid "opinion" and "innovation," God set up leaders in Israel to administer his law and hold the populace accountable (Deut. 17:8-13; 2 Chr. 19:6-8). These leaders dealt very harshly with instances of "opinion" and "innovation" (cf. Num. 12:1-15; 16:1-50).

Objection #24: "The Scriptures therefore were to be the one standard by which everyone who claimed to speak for God was tested:

---

[42] Ibid., p. 155.

[43] (cf. 1 Sam. 9:9; 2 Chr. 29:25-30; 9:29; 12:15; 33:18-19; Is. 30:10; Jer. 26:18; Zech. 1:4-6; 7:7; 8:9; cf., Matt. 2:23; 1 Cor. 10:4; 2 Tim. 3:8; Jude 14; James 5:14).

'To the law and to the testimony: if they speak not according to this word, it is because there is no light in them' (Isaiah 8:20, KJV)."[44]

Answer: The problem with this conclusion is that the apologist is assuming that "law and testimony" refer only to the written portion of God's word. Actually, "Law and testimony" refer to any divine mandate given to the people. We see this first in the previous verses, Isaiah 8:16-19 where Isaiah says:

> Bind up the testimony, seal the law among my disciples. And I will wait upon the Lord, that hideth his face from the house of Jacob, and I will look for him...And when they shall say unto you, 'Seek unto them that have familiar spirits, and unto wizards that peep, and that mutter: should not a people seek unto their God? For the living to the dead? (KJV).

These verses, which establish the context of the passage quoted in the objection, show that the problem in Israel was not Scripture versus Tradition, but God's revelation versus the occult. Instead of seeking God's truth, Israel sought revelation from the dead. Thus, when Isaiah says, 'Bind up the testimony, seal the law among my disciples' in verse 16, or 'to the law and the testimony' in verse 20, he is commanding God's true followers to reject the necromancy of their apostate brethren and remain true to the revealed word of God, in whatever form that came.

We should hasten to add that the terms "law and testimony," although they certainly include God's written revelation, also have other meanings in the Old Testament. The word "testimony," for example, specifies "witness" more than it does written revelation. For example, in the only other usage of this Hebrew word, Ruth 4:7, it serves as a witness to an exchange of pledges between two people.[45]

---

[44] Ibid., p. 156.

[45] The Hebrew word is תְּעוּדָה (teudah), appearing only three times in the Old Testament. Ruth 4:7 records: "Now this was the manner in former time in Israel concerning redeeming and concerning changing, for to confirm things; a man plucked off his shoe, and gave it to his neighbor: and this was a *testimony* in Israel." Cognates, such as עדות (eduth) and עדה (edah) are also used in reference to all of God's revelation.

Objection #25: The Catholic Church in particular has its own body of tradition that functions exactly like the Jewish Talmud: it is the standard by which Scripture is to be interpreted. In effect, tradition supplants the voice of Scripture itself."[46]

Answer: As developed in answer to objections 19-24, Tradition, if understood and used correctly, does not supplant Scripture but enhances it as does no other medium on earth, simply because it provides the true interpretation of Scripture and does not allow Scripture to be distorted by the whims and biases of men. In addition, Catholic Tradition, although similar to the Jewish Talmud in that both are tradition, differs greatly from the Jewish Talmud because Catholic Tradition claims infallibility, not just authority. This is the very reason why Catholic Tradition can provide the correct interpretation of Scripture, something the Jewish Talmud did not claim or attain, especially since there are many and varied interpretations in the Talmud by the various rabbis who wrote it.

Objection #26: "Fierce debates raged in the early church over such crucial matters as the deity of Christ, His two natures, the Trinity, and the doctrine of original sin. Early church councils settled those questions by appealing to Scripture as the highest of all authorities. The councils themselves did not merely issue *ex cathedra* decrees, but they reasoned things out by Scripture and made their rulings accordingly. The authority was in the appeal to Scripture, not in the councils per se."[47]

Answer: No one will argue that the councils appealed to Scripture to settle doctrinal controversy. But it is simply incorrect to say that their authoritative appeal was *limited* to Scripture. Scripture contained the rudiments of doctrines, but often the councils did not define their final formulations in purely Scriptural terms, e.g., the relation of God to Christ was defined by the council of Nicea under the nonbiblical Greek term *homoousios* (Christ was of the *same substance* as God) in contrast to the Arian term *homoiousios* (Christ was merely *like* God). It was precisely because the Arians often

---

[46] John MacArthur, *Sola Scriptura!* p. 156.

[47] Ibid., p. 157.

appealed to Scripture, and because on the surface many of their arguments seemed quite cogent, that the Councils appealed to the authoritative Church Tradition passed down from early centuries. Such was the case, for example, in Augustine's debates with the Arian theologian Maximinus. In fact, it was Arians like Maximinus who insisted that anything not explicit in Scripture was to be rejected, and he even quoted 2 Timothy 3:16 in support of his position.[48] Conversely, when Scripture was vague, ambiguous, or did not sufficiently cover a particular topic, the Fathers and Councils did not hesitate to base their arguments on Tradition.

Objection #27: "Unfortunately, the question of Scriptural authority itself was not always clearly delineated in the early church, and as the church grew in power and influence, church leaders began to assert an authority that had no basis in Scripture."[49]

Answer: The presupposition behind this objection is that *sola scriptura* is the correct view of Scripture. If that is what the apologist means then we can agree that the early church did not have the same view of Scripture as did the Protestant theologians of the sixteenth century. The early Church certainly "clearly delineated" the authority of Scripture — they understood it as the inspired revelation of God — but the Church and its Tradition, in order to curtail the rampage of heresy, had to control Scriptural interpretation. As for the importance of Scripture in the early church, even before the Church canonized the Bible in the late fourth century, the Church Fathers had made voluminous citations of Scripture in their teaching and defense of the gospel. It was these same Fathers, moreover, who saw in Scripture itself the "basis" for their own authority to do so. They interpreted passages such as Matthew 16:18-19; 18:15-18; John 20:23; 2 Thessalonians 2:15; 1 Timothy 3:15; Hebrews 13:17 and many others, as vesting authority in the Church and its Tradition.[50]

---

[48] (See chapter 8 by Joe Gallegos on the Church Fathers in this volume for more detailed information).

[49] John MacArthur, *Sola Scriptura!* p. 157.

[50] For an excellent commentary on the biblical and historical basis for the papacy, see *Jesus, Peter and the Keys* by S. Butler, N. Dahlgren, D. Hess (Santa Barbara, CA: Queenship Publishing, 1996).

Objection #28: "In other words, the official Catholic position on Scripture is that Scripture does not and cannot speak for itself. It must be interpreted by the Church's teaching authority and in light of "living tradition." *De facto* this says that Scripture has no inherent authority, but like all spiritual truth, it derives its authority from the Church."[51]

Answer: This statement confuses two separate issues. Scripture can certainly "speak for itself," at least in certain senses. After all, it is God's perfect word. But the crucial issue is not Scripture speaking for itself as much as it is the mind of man who interprets Scripture. It is a travesty to make Scripture "speak" something it was not intended to speak. Fallible men will invariably produce fallible interpretations of Scripture. When they do so, Scripture is not speaking for itself; rather, someone who does not understand how Scripture wishes to speak is, as it were, 'forcing words into its mouth.' Moreover, to say that Scripture "has no inherent" authority because the Church and its Tradition interprets it is akin to saying that the US Constitution has no inherent authority because the authority of the US Supreme Court interprets it. In reality, the job of the Supreme Court is to protect the inherent authority of the Constitution, just as the job of the Church is to protect the inherent authority of Scripture. Ironically, private interpretation, because it produces an array of conflicting views, tends to undercut the practical authority of Scripture. Since no one can be sure what Scripture is saying, Scripture becomes just one more confusing source of information amidst all the other confusion in the world.

Objection #29: "...Moreover, in effect it [Tradition] renders Scripture superfluous, for if Catholic tradition inerrantly encompasses and explains all the truth of Scripture, then the Bible is simply redundant."[52]

Answer: This is simply an illogical argument. Claiming that Tradition makes Scripture "redundant" is like saying that having more

---

[51] John MacArthur, *Sola Scriptura!* p. 160.

[52] Ibid., p. 161.

than one witness to a murder is redundant — the court has one witness; why does it need any more? It needs more simply because truth, especially in this fallen world of ours, needs corroboration to confirm its validity. Scripture itself recognizes this principle when it stipulates the necessity for two or three witnesses to establish truth that is in contention or subject to misinterpretation (cf. Deut. 19:15; John 8:17-18; 2 Cor. 13:1).

Objection #30: "2 Timothy 2:2...Here the apostle Paul instructs Timothy, a young pastor, to train other faithful men for the task of leadership in the church. There is no hint of apostolic succession in this verse, nor is there any suggestion that in training these men Timothy would be passing on to them infallible tradition with authority equal to the Word of God."[53]

Answer: First, although this single passage may not conclusively prove apostolic succession, to say that "there is no hint" of it here is a bit extreme. Since apostolic succession would incorporate passing on acquired divine revelation to qualified men of the Church, 2 Timothy 2:2 could certainly be alluding to some type of succession. The doctrine of apostolic succession, however, has support from so many passages of Scripture that, in the aggregate, bring us to conclude that it is a divine teaching.[54] Moreover, the Fathers of the Church believed in apostolic succession (we will document momentarily). Hence, both Scripture and Tradition confirm this teaching. Attempts to deny it based on one verse of Scripture are irresponsible.

Second, we must challenge the statement that there is no "suggestion that in training these men Timothy would be passing on to them infallible tradition with authority equal to the Word of God." Since in 1 Thess. 2:13 Paul considers his oral teaching an authority equal to Scripture, and then in 2 Thess. 2:15 commands the Thessalonians to preserve this oral teaching, it is certainly reasonable to conclude that the oral teachings given to Timothy, and later

53 Ibid., p. 169.

54 *Jesus, Peter and the Keys* (Queenship Publishing, 1996) for a treatment of the biblical basis for apostolic succession.

entrusted to other reliable men, possessed an authority equal to that of Scripture. To deny such a conclusion there must be substantial proof that the Catholic interpretation has no possibility of being correct. Moreover, nothing suggests that the oral teaching to the Thessalonians possessed more authority than the oral teaching to Timothy and his men.

Third, Paul tells Timothy in 1 Timothy 1:13-14: "What you heard from me... Guard the good deposit through the Holy Spirit indwelling in us." We see that Timothy is to guard what he heard from Paul *through the Holy Spirit*. Timothy is not on his own. Since Paul is speaking in a context of church leaders, the Holy Spirit's assistance in preserving this truth is not merely the general filling of the Spirit in the masses, but the localized working of the Spirit as a charism in its chosen leaders. It is the Spirit which leads the apostles [and by extension their successors] into all truth (John 16:13); it is the Holy Spirit who worked with the apostles and presbyters to arrive at an error free consensus (Acts 15:28); and it is the Spirit's influence that distinguishes inspired, authoritative teaching from the mere teaching of men (1 Cor. 2:4-14). Hence, it should come as no surprise when Paul tells Timothy that it is the *Spirit* in the church's leaders that will allow him, and his reliable men, to preserve the orally inspired teaching delivered to him. Timothy received this charism by the laying on of hands (1 Tim. 4:14; 2 Tim. 1:6); something he also did for the reliable men following him (1 Tim. 5:22), and thus perpetuated the same gift.

Objection #31: "Word-of-mouth tradition is *never* said to be *theopneustos*, God breathed, or infallible."[55]

Answer: First, 1 Thessalonians 2:13 assures us that Paul's oral teaching is God's word as much as Scripture is God's word; hence, both must be infallible. Second, *theopneustos* is a term used to describe Scripture not as a technical term which seeks to distinguish the infallible nature of Scripture from the purported fallible

---

55 John MacArthur, *Sola Scriptura!* p. 172. *Theopneustos* is the transliteration of the Greek word which is translated in 2 Timothy 3:16 as either "inspired" or "God-breathed." *Theopneustos* appears only in 2 Timothy 3:16.

nature of Tradition. *Theopneustos* means that Scripture, though written by men, is in actuality a unique combination of the words of God and the words of men — Scripture is "God-breathed" in the analogous sense that God breathed life into man at the creation. To claim, however, that "word-of-mouth" tradition is not equal to Scripture simply because the word *theopneustos* is not used to describe inspired oral teaching and its subsequent tradition is short-sighted, unprovable, and begging the question. Scripture uses various terms to describe divinely originated revelation, e.g, "the word of God," (1 Thess. 2:13) "the Spirit of your Father speaking through you" (Matt. 10:20); "in spirit" (Matt. 22:43); "filled with the Holy Spirit" (Acts 4:8), and many others. None of these descriptions is of less divine origin and authority than *theopneustos*.[56]

Objection #32: "The Greek word translated "tradition" is paradosis...The Greek root contains the idea of transmission, and

---

[56] Note the following statements by prominent Protestant apologists: **Greg Bahnsen**: "Therefore, according to the Scripture's own witness, the verbal form and content of the apostolic publication of the gospel message should be deemed wholly true and without error." *Inerrancy of the Autographs*. **Carl F. H. Henry**: "Inerrancy pertains only to the oral or written proclamation of the original inspired prophets and apostles" (quoted in *Inerrancy of the Autographs*). **J. I. Packer**: "The concept of biblical inspiration is essentially identical with that of prophetic inspiration... It makes no difference whether its product is oral or written. When in the past evangelical theologians defined God's words of inspiration as the producing of God-breathed scriptures, they were not denying that God inspired words uttered orally as well. Indeed, in the case of prophets and apostles, the biblical way to put the point is to urge that the words in which these men wrote or dictated are no less God-given than the words they shared orally with the individuals and congregations, for the spoken word came first ... and the Spirit speaking in them directed both what was said and how is was said (Matthew 10:19-20)" (*The Adequacy of Human Language*). **Norman Geisler**: "Whereas it is true that the oral pronouncements of the living apostles were as authoritative as their written ones (1 Thess. 2:13)..." Also, in the section, "Direct Claims For The Inspiration Of The New Testament," Geisler states: "Earlier he had reminded them, 'It was the word of God which you heard from us' (1 Thess. 2:13)" (*From God To Us*, Geisler and Nix, pp. 43, 45). **Bruce Milne**: "This high view of their teaching and preaching applied as fully to their written as to their spoken statements" (*Knowing The Truth,* p. 32).

the idea is no doubt doctrine that was transmitted by oral means. In this case, however, it refers only to Paul's own preaching — not to someone else's report of what Paul taught."[57]

Answer: This is partially correct. Catholicism understands Paul's orally inspired words as *apostolic tradition*. It is this Tradition that is divinely inspired and infallibly authoritative. If the Church appeals to tradition after the apostolic age, it is only because the Church understands that the subsequent tradition has its origin in the apostolic tradition. It is the origin of the Tradition that is at issue.

We can also apply the same principle to the transmission of Scripture. Since the original autographs upon which Paul wrote are no longer extant, all we retain of his inspired writings are copies — copies which contain many differences among themselves. Would we dare to conclude that those people in the centuries following Paul did not really possess his inspired written teachings? Of course not. Even though the copied manuscripts had errors, the Church still claimed to possess the inspired word of God. The Church did not reject the copies based on their fallibility, since she understood that it is the origin of Scripture that is the real issue.[58] Even on a theoretical basis, oral teaching, even though some parts may have been forgotten or corrupted along the way, could certainly retain the preponderance of truth it had originally contained. For example, if it was the practice of the apostles to baptize infants — a fact that Scripture does not address and is thus in need of verification — it is certainly reasonable to conclude that the Church could preserve this simple tradition and passed it down to successive generations. In fact, it is much more likely that

---

57 John MacArthur, *Sola Scriptura!* p. 173.

58 An exhaustive investigation into a standard Protestant Greek text of the New Testament (Nestle-Aland *Novum Testamentum Graece* (Stuttgart: Deutsche Bibelstiftung, 1979) reveals that of the 7,948 total verses from Matthew to Revelation, 6,176 verses contain textual variants. In other words, 78% of the New Testament verses are to some extent corrupted. The variations range from simple letters which change a word or its tense, to whole sentences which are either missing or significantly different.

infant baptism, being so important to the faith, would be preserved rather than be lost.[59]

Objection #33: "Oral transmission is far more subject to change, deviation and corruption than written communication. With written manuscripts (e.g., as in the study of Scripture) we can compare texts and various manuscripts and families of manuscripts, all the time seeking to get back to the source itself. This simply could not be done for long with oral communication."[60]

Answer: If the Protestant apologist wants to make the *degree* of corruption the central issue in deciding the veracity of the written as opposed to the oral, he has not escaped his problem. First, *corruption* is a relative term. On the one hand, proportionally speaking, perhaps it is true that the oral is more prone to corruption than the written. On the other hand, quantitatively speaking, since the written is much more voluminous than the oral, the sum of corruption in the written could be much more than the oral. But that is all beside the point. Once one admits that the written, to whatever degree, is corrupted, then one really has no basis to reject the oral because he thinks it is a "little more" corrupted. When we add to this that it is mostly in the writings of the early Fathers, liturgies and Councils, that the Church preserved its oral tradition, the "oral" is much less prone to corruption than the proverbial *gossip chain* that Protestants often use to make a caricature of Catholic Tradi-

---

59 "Even long after the more occasional use of script, the oral transmission of 'spiritual' knowledge was considered normal. In the East learning by heart is unto this day the normal way of transmitting even the longest written texts...With the Jews both Mishna and Talmud were orally transmitted for centuries; in the synagogue it was long forbidden to say the Torah from a written scroll; also the Aramaic and Greek translations were originally given orally, but in a traditional fixed form...The remnant of Israel was obliged to have the old sacred tradition written down in order to keep the connection with its spiritual foundation. But even learning by heart continued to be the normal form of transmission..." (*The Interpreter's Dictionary of the Bible*, eds. George Buttrick, et al., (Nashville: Abingdon Press), Vol. 4, pp. 684-685.

60 John Armstrong, *Sola Scriptura!*, p. 108.

tion.[61] For example, a prominent tradition of the Church concerns the nature and recipients of baptism. Although Scripture is unclear on the former and literally silent on the latter, we do not have to rely on some primitive transmission of oral communication or ecclesial gossip chain to know that the Church believed in both baptismal regeneration and infant baptism. We can know from the writings of the Fathers and the decisions of the Councils that these two doctrines indeed are apostolic. They are not true because the Church Fathers said so, inasmuch as the Church Fathers did not make up their own doctrine. They preserved and transmitted only what was passed down to them from the apostles and the apostle's immediate successors. Perhaps not every "oral tradition" has the same degree of documentation (e.g, baptismal regeneration versus the Assumption of Mary) but the Church will not elevate something to dogmatic status that does not have at least some documentation and authenticity from antiquity. By the same token, the Protestant holds that the inspired Scripture has large portions of text that are of questionable authenticity because they have very little witness among the earliest manuscripts (e.g., Mark 16:9-20; John 8:1-12; 1 John 5:7-8). Does he then hold in suspicion *all* of the written Scripture because there is considerable doubt about the authenticity of a few passages? Certainly not. Likewise, he does not reject more obscure oral traditions just because they do not measure up to the authenticity of the more verifiable oral traditions. In the end, just as someone has to judge whether John 8:1-12 is indeed authentic Scripture, so someone has to judge whether the Assumption of Mary is indeed authentic oral tradition. What better judge of these things do we have than the Church that Jesus said he would guide and protect till the end of time?[62]

We must also emphasize that at this point in the discussion the Protestant is in a "want your cake and eat it too" situation. On the

---

61 "Gossip chain" is a term used to describe the phenomenon of telling one person a message and having each successive person tell the message to another person. The process often introduces serious distortions, sometimes to the point that the original message is lost.

62 The Council of Trent, and further ratifications by subsequent Popes, judged that the aforementioned passages are all inspired Scripture.

one hand, he willingly sides with tradition when he accepts the 27-book canon of the New Testament passed down by means of tradition in the first four centuries. On the other hand, he is unwilling to have the same process applied to the oral teachings of the apostles. He claims that it is "too easy" for the inspired oral teaching to be corrupted and therefore it is unreliable. But we must make two logical replies: (1) As shown above, Scripture itself has been corrupted by the tradition-preserving process. These copies were certainly not infallibly protected from error. Hence, there is room for corruption in the transmission of both written and oral revelation. (2) The real reason he rejects oral tradition is not, as he claims, because it is too easily forgotten, corrupted, or not infallibly protected. In fact, as a matter of principle, he will not accept *any* oral tradition. His position claims that the early church was under no obligation to preserve any of the New Testament author's oral teachings, and therefore, anything claiming to be tradition from the apostles is, *de facto*, false.

Objection #34: "By contrast, what is not written is more easily polluted, as the New Testament illustrates. John 21:22-23 records how an unwritten "apostolic tradition"...was based on a misunderstanding of what Jesus said. The disciples wrongly assumed that Jesus said that John would not die. John, however, debunked this false tradition in his authoritative written record."[63]

Answer: This analysis contains several problems and irrelevancies. First, the rumor saying that John would not die was not an inspired apostolic oral tradition but precisely the opposite — an uninspired interpretation of what Jesus said. If anything, this passage, rather than suggesting corruption in perpetuating apostolic oral tradition, shows how easy it is to misinterpret something without the proper guidance. Moreover, John is merely *recording* the difference between right tradition and wrong tradition, not suggesting that Scripture is more accurate or authoritative than apostolic oral tradition. In the same way, while Paul tells Timothy to hold on to his oral teaching, he also tells Timothy to avoid "myths

---

[63] Geisler and MacKenzie, p. 195.

and legends" (cf. 1 Tim. 1:3-4; 4:7; 2 Tim. 2:14-16; Tit. 3:9). The saying that John was not going to die was just such a "myth."

Objection #35: "It is acknowledged by all, even by Catholic scholars, that there are contradictory Christian traditions. In fact, Abelard noted hundreds of differences. For example, some church fathers (like Augustine) supported the Apocrypha, while others (like Jerome) opposed it... Some great teachers (like Aquina) opposed the immaculate conception of Mary, while others (like Scotus) favored it. This very fact makes it impossible to trust tradition, certainly in any ultimately authoritative sense, for the question always arises: *Which of the contradictory traditions should be accepted*?"[64]

Answer: First, we can spend all day cataloguing the instances where the early Fathers and medieval theologians disagreed with one another on various points. Once the Church Councils defined a doctrine, however, the orthodox Fathers and medieval theologians came to consensus both with each other and with the Church. Such was the case in all the examples which the Protestant apologist cites above. Such was the case with the 27-book canon of the New Testament that Protestants accept today. For four centuries there were disagreements among most of the Fathers as to which books belonged in the canon. But when the Council of Rome in 382 A.D., a council confirmed by Popes Damasus and Innocent I), through the Council of Carthage in 419 AD, finally formalized the canon, there was virtually no more discussion or disagreement as to what belonged in the canon.[65] Will

---

[64] Ibid., p. 196.

[65] The exceptions to this were: John Damascene (676-754 to 787) who, in his *An Exact Exposition of the Orthodox Faith*, had assigned 22 books to the Hebrew Old Testament as he found them in the work of Epiphanius (314-403) *De pondeibus et mensuris*, a work completed before the Councils which formulated the Christian canon (*Catholic Encyclopedia*, eds., Charles G. Herbermann, et al. (New York: Robert Appleton Co. 1910), Vol VIII, p. 461); and Hugh of St. Victor (b. 1096) in *De Sacramentis Christianæ Fidei* (c. 1134) which questions the canonicity of Tobit, Judith, Maccabees, Wisdom and Ecclesiasticus; and Nicholas of Lyra (d. 1270-1340) who deferred to the Hebrew canon in his commentaries. Thomas Aquinas was perplexed as to the exact standing of the Deuterocanonicals, as was Cardinal Cajetan during the Protestant Reformation. Other medieval theologians did not accept their canonicity without at least some doubts.

the apologist say that it is virtually impossible to trust the tradition of canon formation simply because early on there were disagreements among the Fathers? Certainly not. We should also understand that the Fathers and medieval theologians, despite their differences, agreed by and large, on the doctrines of the Church. Second, everything the apologist has said above about Tradition can also be said about the transmission of Scripture itself. There are major manuscripts that, although they agree in the majority of their respective texts, have significant differences in various places. As we noted previously, among all the Greek manuscripts a 78% corruption rate exists in the sum total of verses in the New Testament. Without going into the details here, would the apologist conclude that "this very fact makes it impossible to trust" Scripture transmission? We dare say not. He is willing to accept a significant degree of corruption in the written documents in order to retain the essential truth of Scripture. He should do the same with Tradition. After all, Tradition is the vehicle for Scripture transmission.

Objection #36: "Third, the apostolic tradition is nebulous. As has often been pointed out, 'Never has the Roman Catholic Church given a complete and exhaustive list of the contents of oral tradition. It has not dared to do so because this oral tradition is such a nebulous entity.' That is to say, even if all extra-biblical revelation definitely exists somewhere in some tradition (as Catholics claim), which ones these are has nowhere been declared."[66]

Answer: First, the Church does what is necessary, when it is necessary. For example, many of the doctrines that the Catholic Church has dogmatized (e.g., the doctrines of grace in 529, Transubstantiation at the Fourth Lateran Council in 1215, the Immaculate Conception in 1854, et al) became so not because they were not believed in prior centuries but only because certain theologians began to question the validity of these long-established beliefs. The same was true of the doctrines of the Trinity, the Incarnation, the inspiration of Scripture, and the canon of Scripture in the early years of the Church—they were not dogmatized until a contro-

[66] Geisler and MacKenzie, p. 198.

versy arose. Likewise, when it becomes necessary to divulge, catalog, and dogmatize these truths, the Church only then delves into Tradition and extracts what she needs. We find the same kind of approach to law and dogmatizing in the Old Testament. Many of the civil and ceremonial laws of Israel were introduced when an abuse of or challenge to the accepted system occurred. For example, the whole Levitical priesthood was created due to Israel's sins in worshiping a golden calf (cf. Ex. 32ff; Lev. 1-27).

Second, the charge of "nebulous" that the apologist has levied against Tradition can also be levied against Scripture itself. Protestants seem to have a pristine concept of Scripture as if it just dropped down pure and undefiled from heaven, but this is far from the case. With 78% of New Testament verses being in some form of corruption, this apologist must use his own words and admit that, "intra-biblical revelation definitely exists somewhere in some Scriptural documents," and "which ones these are nowhere has been declared" simply because Protestants have no infallible way of knowing what they are. The Catholic Church can declare, and has done so on occasion, what variants in Scripture are the true Scripture, and she could do so with all the variants of Scripture if this became necessary. But just as it is unnecessary to extract and catalog every fact of Tradition, so it has never become necessary to determine the true Scripture from every single variant that exists.

Objection #37: "Second, support from tradition for the dogma of the bodily assumption of Mary is late and weak. Yet in spite of the lack of any real evidence from Scripture or any substantial evidence from the teachings of the early church fathers, Rome chose to pronounce this an infallible truth of the Catholic faith. In short, Roman Catholic dogmas are not the product of rationally weighing the evidence of tradition but rather of arbitrarily choosing which of the many conflicting traditions they wish to pronounce infallible."[67]

Answer: First, we cannot help but see a smoke screen in this apologist's complaint. Let's say we agree, for the sake of argument, that documentation on the Assumption of Mary is "late and

---

[67] Ibid., p. 198.

weak." But now let us turn the tables: documentation on *Baptismal Regeneration* and the *Real Presence of Christ in the Eucharist* are two of the most thoroughly addressed and substantiated doctrines in the writings of the Church Fathers, yet this particular Protestant apologist believes in neither of them. So, is "documentation," whether early or late, the real issue for him? Obviously not. In effect, it is this apologist who is "arbitrarily choosing" which dogmas from the Church Fathers he wishes to believe, despite the overwhelming evidence of views contrary to his.

Second, we must insist that whether "late" or "weak" in this apologist's opinion, the fact remains that the Church Fathers wrote enough, and Scripture said enough, to warrant the Church to investigate and judge whether the doctrine of the Assumption was valid. The issue is not the amount of evidence but the Church's right to warrant a judgment on the available evidence, just as a judge in a court of law can call for a hearing and from this decide whether there is sufficient evidence for a trial and verdict. The issue is the authority of the Church, not the Assumption of Mary, per se.[68] Second, Protestants have no evidence from either Church Fathers or Scripture that the Assumption of Mary is not true. If, as they claim, Scripture is silent on the issue, well, Scripture is silent on a lot of issues, but that does not make the particular issue untrue or nonexistent. Third, the concept of being assumed into heaven is not foreign to Scripture (e.g., Enoch, Elijah, and possibly Moses). Fourth, the doctrine of the Assumption of Mary, since it is consistent with the *concept* of assumption in Scripture, is not in the least detrimental to the sensitivities and logic of the Christian faith.

---

[68] Pius XII wrote in *Munificentissimus Deus*: "Since, then, the universal Church, in which the Spirit of Truth flourishes, who infallibly directs it to achieve a knowledge of revealed truths, has through the course of the ages repeatedly manifested its own faith; and since the bishops of the whole world with almost unanimous consent request that the truth of the bodily Assumption of the Blessed Virgin Mary into heaven be defined as a dogma of the divine and Catholic faith — a truth which is founded on the Sacred Scriptures, has been fixed deeply in the minds of the faithful in Christ, has been approved by ecclesiastical worship even from the earliest times, is quite in harmony with the other revealed truths, and has been splendidly explained and declared by the zeal, knowledge, and wisdom of the theologians..."

Objection #38: "2 Thessalonians 2:15...Certainly nothing here suggests that the tradition Paul delivered to the Thessalonians is infallibly preserved for us anywhere except Scripture itself."[69]

Answer: This is argumentation from silence. In fact, it would be more true to assert that nothing in 2 Thess. 2:15 suggests that Paul's oral teaching was preserved in Scripture. Why recommend two sources if the latter embraces all of the former? Irrespective of this, we can certainly agree that some of Paul's oral teaching is similar or perhaps identical to his written teaching. But we cannot conclude from such information that *only* Scripture houses his oral teaching. There is simply no evidence of this, and Paul never teaches in Scripture that his oral teaching would eventually be confined to Scripture. Since *sola scriptura* advocates are limited in their conclusions by the information that Scripture gives them, we must insist that if Scripture does not say that oral tradition was preserved only in Scripture then it is unscriptural to draw such a conclusion.

First, let's take a case in point. As he gives instruction on the Lord's Supper, Paul tells the Corinthians in 1 Cor. 11:34: "If anyone is hungry, he should eat at home, so that when you meet together it may not result in judgment. *And when I come I will give further directions*." Paul is addressing a very serious problem in the Corinthian church. People were abusing the Lord's Supper and, according to verses 29-30, God was casting sickness and death upon those who did. Thus, in verses 17-34, Paul is giving them written instructions in his letter as to the nature of this sin and what they must do to halt it. Apparently, however, his written instructions are not complete, for Paul says, "And when I come I will give further directions." Paul plans to speak to them face to face instead of in writing. This is not uncommon for New Testament authors (cf. 2 John 12; 3 John 13-14). We must assume that these "further directions" were at least in part dealing with the same serious problem that Paul expounded upon in 1 Corinthians 11:1-33. Considering the importance of these oral instructions in

[69] Geisler and MacKenzie, p. 177.

the face of the sickness and death occurring in the church, would not we expect Paul to desire the Corinthians to preserve this oral teaching, since it would help prevent the death of other Christians? And would not his oral teaching be as authoritative as Paul's written instruction? If people were becoming sick and dying because they abused a sacrament, would we not expect the Corinthians to hold Paul's instructions in the highest regard, and subsequently spread them to all the churches as they did his other teachings (cf. 1 Cor. 14:33)? The New Testament records that other instances of abuse that received a death sentence spread abject fear upon the whole church (Acts 5:11). In such a serious matter, why would we expect the church to "forget" these instructions, or claim that because they are not written in Scripture they are no longer valid or necessary? How could this be when Paul tells the church specifically to hold on to these oral teachings, as well as to the written teachings (cf. 2 Thess. 2:15; 3:6)?

Second, some try to get around the clear teaching of 2 Thess. 2:15 by claiming that the oral tradition Paul wanted preserved refers only to the written material he left them in the first epistle to the Thessalonians, e.g., the exhortation to work and not be idle in 1 Thess. 4:11-12. Again, some oral instruction may have overlapped with the teachings of 1 Thessalonians, but this does not mean that all of Paul's oral teaching was confined to that first epistle. Moreover, Paul nowhere in 2 Thessalonians says that his oral instruction was confined to the letter of 1 Thessalonians. In fact, as Paul is reminding the Thessalonians about the future appearance of the "man of sin," he says in 2 Thess. 2:5, "Don't you remember that when I was with you I used to tell you these things." We must assume that "these things" refers to the future appearance of the man of sin. Specifically, Paul had told them that the day of the Lord could not come until the man of sin had been revealed. But we will search in vain to find this teaching in 1 Thessalonians. The closest Paul comes to such information is his speaking in 1 Thess. 4:13-18 about the rapture of the saints and the rising of dead Christians when the Lord returns, but there is no mention of the man of sin in this context. Thus, it is obvious that Paul's reference to "Don't you remember..." in 2 Thess. 2:5 refers only to his oral teaching that perhaps related to the material in 1 Thessalonians but was not identical with it.[70] This understanding is reinforced as we contemplate Paul's command to the Corinthians in 1 Cor. 11:2 and 15:1-2 to hold on to the teachings he *preached* to them. In this case, they were to hold on to something that was spoken, not written.[71]

Third, probably the most devastating Catholic argument in connection with 2 Thess. 2:15 and similar verses is that neither Paul nor any other writes, gives any statement which commands that the Church retire oral revelation, either during the writing of Scripture or once Scripture was completed. Since the Protestant is required to form his doctrine only from mandates found in Scripture, the burden of proof rests on his shoulders to show that Scripture teaches that the propagation of apostolic oral revelation must cease with the completion of Scripture. Since Catholicism finds no such command in Scripture, and, in fact, finds Scripture mandating a continuing propagation and preservation of the original apostolic oral teachings, in reality, the debate should stop here until the Protestant can furnish the Scriptural proof for his position. If he believes in *sola scriptura*, then he is required to give answers from *sola scriptura*, not answers based on what he *thinks* is correct and logical.

Objection #39: "Paul does not say 'by word of mouth *and* by letter" (which would be expected if each one was a different tradition and both were necessary); instead, Paul says 'by word of mouth *or* by letter' (Greek, *eite* [εἴτε]), implying that one or the other is equally sufficient to convey Paul's message, and that both are essentially the same."[72]

---

[70] Vatican II, *Dei Verbum* 8, "Hence the apostles, in handing on what they themselves had received, warn the faithful to maintain the traditions which they had learned either by word of mouth or by letter (cf. 2 Th. 2:15); and they warn them to fight hard for the faith that had been handed on to them once and for all (cf. Jude 3). Council of Nicea II: Denz. 303 (602). Council of Constantinople IV, Session X, can. 1: Denz. 336 (650-652).

[71] Paul uses the word παραδόσεις ("traditions") in 1 Cor. 11:2, but εὐαγγέλιον ("gospel") in 1 Cor. 15:2, showing the intimate connection between the two forms.

[72] Eric Svendsen, *Protestant Answers*, p. 55.

Answer: First, attempting to make a major distinction in Paul's thought by hairsplitting the meaning of conjunctions, or what Paul "could" have said, is not going to prove anything. Often, the conjunction "and" is ambiguous because we cannot tell whether it is requiring the second proposition to be included in the first before either of the propositions can be fulfilled, or whether either of the propositions taken separately will satisfy what is intended to be fulfilled. We sense that even the apologist himself is unsure of the distinction he is trying to make, since he concludes with words such as "implying" and "are essentially the same." Does "implying" mean that Paul is making this a doctrinal teaching or not? Does "essentially the same" mean that they *are* the same or not? No Catholic would disagree that Scripture and Tradition are "essentially the same," for they both are pointing to the same redemptive truths, but we must insist that if there is even just *one* Tradition that says something that Scripture does not specifically say, then one must conclude that Paul is saying that Tradition is both necessary and in addition to the information provided in Scripture.

Objection #40: "Paul is not encouraging the Thessalonians to receive some tradition that had been delivered to them via second or third hand reports. On the contrary, he was ordering them to receive as infallible truth only what they had heard directly from his own lips."[73]

Answer: This is another instance of "reading into" the passage more than is there. In one sense we can agree that Paul is not encouraging second or third hand reports, but only because second or third hand reports are *not under discussion* in 2 Thessalonians 2:15, not because Paul has an aversion to men perpetuating and preserving his oral teaching by second and third hand parties. Of course, Paul expects the receivers of this truth to be "reliable men who are qualified" (2 Tim. 2:2) and that the preservation is to be done "through the Holy Spirit" (2 Tim.

[73] John MacArthur, *Sola Scriptura!* p. 177.

1:14),[74] but he never intimates that his readers should *not* obtain and preserve his truth from second and third hand parties. Moreover, 1 Thess. 2:13 and 2 Thess. 2:15 and 3:6 do not use the pronoun "I" but "we." In each case where Paul is instructing them about the nature and preservation of oral truth, he says that it is not from *his* lips only that they are to gather this information, but from *all* the teachers affiliated with Paul. Were all these other teachers divinely inspired as Paul was? Perhaps, but perhaps not. We are not even sure who the "we" of the above passages comprises. If they were not inspired, then we must conclude that at least some of the teachers included in the "we" were giving the people Paul's inspired messages second and third hand.

Objection #41: "At the beginning of his public ministry, Jesus faced the focused temptation of the devil in the wilderness...And how did he face that temptation? He did not appeal to the oral tradition of Israel...He did not even appeal to His own divinity or the inspiration of the Holy Spirit. Our Savior, in the face of temptation, turned again and again and again to the Scriptures. 'It is written,' He said."[75]

Answer: There are many arguments against this apologist's conclusion. First, the way he formulates his answer proves too much for his case. If he is asserting that Jesus "did not appeal to His own divinity or the inspiration of the Holy Spirit" but only to Scripture, does his kind of logic require us to exclude not only the oral

---

[74] Vatican II, Dei Verbum 10; 8, "It [the Magisterium] teaches only what has been handed on to it. At the divine command and with the help of the Holy Spirit, it listens to this devotedly, guards it with dedication and expounds it faithfully...The Tradition that comes from the apostles makes progress in the Church, with the help of the Holy Spirit. There is a growth in insight into the realities and words that are being passed on...Thus, as the centuries go by, the Church is always advancing towards the plentitude of divine truth, until eventually the words of God are fulfilled in her...(23) The spouse of the incarnate Word, which is the Church, is taught by the Holy Spirit. She strives to reach day by day a more profound understanding of the sacred Scriptures, in order to provide her children with food from the divine words."

[75] W. Robert Godfrey, *Sola Scriptura!* pp. 8-9.

tradition of Israel from being a reliable source to fight the devil but also Jesus' divinity and the inspiration of the Holy Spirit? The problem with his formulation is that Matthew is not attempting to specify the *only* source from which we are to make our appeal against the devil. Granted, on many occasions Jesus uses Scripture against the forces of evil, and rightly so, but not on every occasion. Many times he *does* appeal to his divinity, his miracles, and the Holy Spirit to fight the opposition against him (cf. John 5:32-47; 6:32-65; 7:16-19; 8:12-58; 10:1-34; 12:44-50; 14:9-31; 16:1-33). Hence, just because Jesus calls Scripture as a witness against the devil in Matthew 4:1-11 one cannot therefore conclude that Jesus believed in *sola scriptura*. Would we say that the devil believed in *sola scriptura* because he quoted verbatim to Jesus from Psalm 91:11? Of course not.

One reason Jesus may not be appealing to his divinity in his discourse with the devil is that it is precisely the identity of Jesus that the devil wishes to discover. Knowing this, it is Jesus' wish, at least in the early part of his ministry, to keep this information from the devil in order for God's plan to be accomplished (cf. 1 Cor. 2:8; Eph. 6:12; Matt. 8:4). Hence, in Jesus' three appeals to Scripture in Matthew 4:1-11 he does not affirm that he *is* the Son of God, but only that (1) *man* lives not by bread alone but by the word of God, (2) *man* should not test God, and (3) *man* should worship and serve God only. These three stipulations could apply to any man, not just Jesus, and from this the devil may have thought Jesus to be just a man at that time. Thus, Jesus thwarted the devil by withholding the very information the devil was trying to extract from him — his divinity.

We should also add that even in Jesus' specific appeal to Scripture, there is good evidence that he did not intend to teach or even suggest *sola scriptura*. For example, his first reference is to Deuteronomy 8:3: 'Man does not live on bread alone, but on *every word* that comes from the mouth of God.' Notice here the specific reference to "every word" that comes from God's mouth. Since God recorded his words not only in Scripture but also by speaking directly to the people, the term "every word" certainly cannot be limited to Scripture. Jesus is merely calling Scripture as a *witness* to the basic truth that *all* God's revelation is to be heeded, not saying that Scripture is the *only* source of God's word. The same applies in New Testament times: "every word" of God includes both his written and oral inspired truth (cf. Eph. 1:13; Col. 1:5-6; Acts 20:27; Gal. 1:12; 1 Thess. 2:13; 2 Thess. 2:15). More importantly, if Jesus was not teaching *sola scriptura* at that time, then how can these verses be interpreted as teaching *sola scriptura* today? The interpretation of Scripture does not change with the passing of time.

Lastly, we cannot leave this passage without pointing out its implicit warning against the misuse of Scripture. It is precisely the devil's misuse of Psalm 91:11 which shows us that interpretation, when the interpreter is not under the proper authority, only leads to error and apostasy.

Objection #42: "The position I am defending certainly is what is taught in the Bible itself. For example, Deuteronomy 31:9 states: 'Moses wrote down this law...'...The people do not need any additional institution to interpret the Word. The priests, prophets, and scribes of Israel certainly function to help the people ministerially. But the Word alone was sufficient for salvation."[76]

Answer: Again, the definition of *sola scriptura* with which this apologist is working is sufficiently general to apply to any single book or relevant passage of Scripture or other spiritually-centered teaching. Nothing here distinguishes *sola scriptura* as a dogma from forms of revelation that are not dogmatized. This is probably why the apologist does not feel any inadequacy in defending *sola scriptura* from the Old Testament. Normally, *sola scriptura* advocates limit their appeals to the New Testament, since quoting from the Old Testament would make *sola scriptura* an easy victim of anachronism, and therefore tend to disqualify itself. Defending *sola scriptura* from Scripture that is less than one-fifth complete is rather self- defeating. Moreover, since the interpretation the apologist is extracting from Deuteronomy 31 (i.e., an interpretation of *sola scriptura*) must also be the interpretation that a 15th century BC Jew would have to extract from the passage, he has opened up a

---

[76] Ibid., *Sola Scriptura!*, pp. 3-4.

series of issues that are difficult to apply to this historical figure. For example, the apologist's more expanded definition of *sola scriptura* would be difficult to apply, i.e., "The Protestant position, and my position, is that all things necessary for salvation and concerning faith and life are taught in the Bible clearly enough for the ordinary believer to find it there and understand."[77] In this definition the apologist has added things "concerning faith and life" to his other statement which said "the Word was sufficient for salvation." First, he does not tell us if "faith and life" are equal to or in addition to "salvation," but we assume by his use of the conjunction "and" that he wishes to extend the applicability of *sola scriptura* beyond "salvation," per se, to include other aspects of "life," whatever they are in his mind. Second, since the "Bible" that the 15th century BC Jew possesses is limited to the first five books of the Old Testament, a sum of less than one-fifth of the Scripture that would eventually be produced, does the Jew really have all that he needs for "faith and life"? Apparently, the apologist wishes to make the issues of "faith and life" which define the parameters of *sola scriptura* relative to the time and place in which a particular Scripture was written, for he must admit that the Old Testament Jew did not have to grapple with many of the doctrines and controversies ("faith and life") that the apostles and early Fathers of the Church did. Moreover, the fifteenth century BC Jew lived in a time when God was still speaking through oral revelation as well as through Scripture. The apologist offers no explanation as to how this fact squares with his imposition of *sola scriptura* onto Deuteronomy 31. Hence we see that this apologist's proposed definition and Scriptural support of *sola scriptura*, though general enough to escape detailed criticism, come back to haunt him; the definition really say nothing substantial, and, in effect, makes the concept of *sola scriptura* a free-floating, nebulous entity that can hardly be pinned down and scrutinized. No one would disagree that the Old Testament was sufficient to give the knowledge of salvation, but whether Moses was teaching that the Mosaic Law was the "final court of appeal" for the people of Israel is another issue altogether. It is

---

[77] Ibid., p. 3.

Moses' interpretation of the Law, and ultimately God's interpretation of that same Law, that is the final court of appeal (cf., Num. 15:32-36; 9:8; 5:20-22; Deut. 1:17; 17:8-13).

Numbers 15:32-36 is especially important in this regard because it illustrates very poignantly that problems will arise that are difficult to answer, indeed, cannot be answered, unless there is additional divine guidance. The passage in question describes a man who is caught picking up sticks on the Sabbath day. Although the leaders were aware of the original command that no work was to be done on the Sabbath (Exodus 31:14-15, et al), they did not know whether this general law applied to the specific situation at hand. Thus, "they kept him in custody, because it was not clear what should be done to him. Then the Lord said to Moses, 'The man must die. The whole assembly must stone him outside the camp.'" Apparently, the Sabbath law given previously was not sufficient to answer the question, or, at the least, the answer was not perspicuous. Thus God had to intrude and offer an infallible judgment on the situation. It will not suffice for Protestants to argue that because Numbers 15:32-36 is included in Scripture then Scripture has sufficiently answered the question. Such an admission necessarily implies that there were, or would be, many other areas of legislation that required the same *fine tuning* of the Law that was demonstrated in the case of illegal stick gathering. This is precisely what an authoritative source outside of Scripture does — it *fine tunes* the information contained in Scripture for the purpose of correctly answering a specific problem or area of concern not contained in Scripture. The passage in Number 15:32-36 is teaching us this principle as well as setting a precedent for New Testament times.

The availability of divine guidance which was over and above written law and oral tradition is evident also in the priest's use of the Urim and Thummim which assured correct decisions on matters of importance. Exodus 28:30 states: "Also put the Urim and the Thummim in the breast piece, so they may be over Aaron's heart whenever he enters the presence of the Lord. Thus Aaron will always bear the means of making decisions for the Israelites over his heart before the Lord." Also, Numbers 27:21 states: "He is to stand before Eleazer the priest, who will obtain decisions for him by inquiring of the Urim before the Lord." We see that although God had given Israel his sure and steadfast written word, it was intermittently supplemented by his personal instruction in order to provide infallible interpretation on issues of faith and morals. It is no coincidence that this charism comes through God's divinely appointed minister — the *priest* of Israel. This is not unlike the divine guidance God gives to his special ministers in the New Testament Church.

The Canon

Objection #43: "The church, it is argued, gave us the canon of Scripture, and the church, with its proper disciplinary function in every age, expounds and interprets the Word of God. These arguments, in themselves, are again, correct. What is wrong is to assume that they *prove* that the authority of the church is equal or greater than the authority of the Scripture itself."[78]

Answer: First, the Catholic Church does not consider itself an authority greater than Scripture, rather, she considers herself the servant of Scripture.[79] But just as a servant wants his master to be highly respected and not misrepresented to the people who are under him, so the Church desires that the people of God give the highest possible esteem and not misinterpret the Word of God. The Church wishes only to preserve Scripture's original meaning and intent. She can only do this if Scripture's divine author guides her on how best to present, but not misrepresent, his message.

Second, to base one's argument on "proof" is fallacious in itself. There is no more proof that the Bible is the Word of God than that the Church is infallibly guided to interpret that Word. "Proof," if we are using such a term in the legal sense rather than the colloquial sense, requires undeniable evidence. The only way one could claim to have "proof" that the Bible is the Word of God would be

[78] John Armstong, *Sola Scriptura*! pp. 110-111.

[79] Vatican II, *Dei Verbum* 10, "...Yet this Magisterium is not superior to the Word of God, but is its servant. It teaches only what has been handed on to it. At the divine command and with the help of the Holy Spirit, it listens to this devotedly, guards it with dedication and expounds it faithfully..."

for God to come down intermittently out of heaven and reveal to us that the Scripture is indeed his Word. If he hasn't done this, then we must believe by *faith* that the Scripture is God's Word. But if such is the case, it doesn't take that much more faith to believe that the Church is God's institution and that he has infallibly guided her, especially considering that we have overwhelming historical, not to mention biblical, evidence that she indeed fills this role. If one can accept the canon of Scripture by faith, certainly one can accept a dogmatically error-free church by faith.

Objection #44: "In the third place, we must see that the canon of Scripture is, in a real sense, established by the Scripture itself, because the canonical books are self-authenticating. As God's revelation, they are recognized by the people of God as God's own word. As Jesus said, 'I am the good shepherd; I know My sheep and My sheep know Me. They...will listen to my voice' (John 10:14-16). In the deepest sense we cannot judge the Word, but the Word judges us."[80]

Answer: This is the solution forced upon Protestants in their attempt to explain the final compilation of the books of the Bible — if one can't accept the Church as an authority to determine the canon, then the only possible answer is to say that the Scripture determines itself. Thus they tell us that Scripture is "self- authenticating," that is, it is of such a nature that the people of God, in their own judgment, will ultimately be able to recognize its authenticity as the word of God. We sense, however, some equivocation in this apologist's assertion, since he adds the phrases "in a real sense" and "in the deepest sense." What do these phrases really mean? Are there any "senses" in which the Scripture is not self-authenticating? Further exacerbating the problem is that this apologist has not given us any criteria for the mental process by which the people of God should finally judge the canon. He only makes a casual reference to John 10:14-16 in which the "sheep listen to the shepherd's voice" as proof of his claim. But let's

---

80 W. Robert Godfrey, *Sola Scriptura!* p. 18.

examine this more closely. Is the context of John 10:14-16 speaking about such esoteric topics as determining the canon of Scripture? Certainly not. It is speaking about simple obedience to Jesus' known commands. Moreover, since Jesus never says what constitutes the canon, how can we expect these people to "hear his voice" on that specific subject? Even if John 10 did apply to the canon, would this apologist also say that these sheep heard the words of the shepherd infallibly? If not, what kind of shepherd would lead them to fallible information? If he doesn't lead them to green pastures but to dry weeds he is no better than the hired hand he criticizes.

We should also add that if it is the precise *nature* of Scripture that leads people to determine the canon, what is this definitive mark of canonicity? And if someone does propose such a definitive mark, who has the authority to judge if it is accurate and complete? If one cannot specifically catalogue and limit, can those who take it upon themselves to determine the canon rely on a mere *feeling* that a certain book is the word of God? Just what is the final criterion for the determination of the canon? It seems from what this apologist is saying that the criterion is more the fallible sheep rather than the infallible Scripture.

Compounding the problem of the *sheep* judging the word of God, certain books of the canon hardly meet even the general criterion for canonicity suggested for other books. For example, the book of Philemon lacks many of the traits of canonicity that Protestants usually associate with other books of the Bible such as Romans or Galatians. Philemon contains no gospel/salvation message, per se. It is just a short letter expressing concern about the fortunes of a runaway slave. Nor can one claim Philemon is canonical merely because it claims Paul as its author, for not only is such an assertion unprovable but Paul wrote other letters that were not accepted as canonical (cf. 1 Cor. 5:9; 2 Cor. 10:10; Phil. 3:1; Col. 4:16). One can raise the same questions about intrinsic worth of such books as 2 John and 3 John, and other New Testament books. When we recall that some Protestant theologians of the sixteenth century either demoted or outright rejected even long-accepted books of the canon, such as James, Hebrews, and Revelation, which *do* speak heavily about gospel/salvation issues, we sense that determinating the canon is not simply a matter of the lowly sheep hearing the shepherd's voice.[81]

Objection #45: "The self-authenticating character of the canon is demonstrated by the remarkable unanimity reached by the people of God on the canon."[82]

Answer: Far more than the intrinsic nature of Scripture, or what this apologist elsewhere calls the "self- authenticating" quality of Scripture, underlies the unanimity of the canon of Scripture. A whole tradition passed down from the apostles and fathers, finalized in the dogmatic pronouncements of the Councils, formulated the canon. The Church Fathers refer to Tradition as one of their chief unifying criterion in determining the canon, and Fathers subsequent to the Councils refer back to the Councils for verification of the canon's constitution.[83] The councils did not determine canonicity based solely on the nature of Scripture, for no one was sure just what that "nature" was, as attested by books of the Bible that are quite diverse in their "nature," e.g., Philemon compared to Romans; 2 John compared to Revelation; Jude compared to Acts.

In addition, should we not insist that if this apologist sees unanimity as the criterion for canonicity, then he should make the same evaluation for all the other doctrines of the early Church that had the same unanimity of belief? For example, no Father, nor any Council, rejects baptismal regeneration. No Father or Council rejects the Real Presence of Christ in the Eucharist. No Father or Council rejects confession of sins to a priest. The Fathers held unanimously

---

[81] For example, Luther called James "an epistle of straw, compared to these others, for it has nothing of the nature of the gospel about it" (LW 35, 362). Martin Chemnitz was not too far behind: "No dogma ought therefore to be drawn out of these books which does not have reliable and clear foundations in other canonical books" *(An Examination of the Council of Trent*, Part 1, p. 189).

[82] W. Robert Godfrey, *Sola Scriptura!* p. 19.

[83] Vatican II, *Dei Verbum* 8, "By means of the same Tradition the full canon of the sacred books is known to the Church and the holy Scriptures themselves are more thoroughly understood and constantly actualized in the Church. Thus God, who spoke in the past, continues to converse with the spouse of his beloved Son."

to a whole host of "Catholic" doctrines. So on what basis does this apologist accept the unanimity of the Church on the canon but reject its unanimity on other doctrinal issues? Such a double-standard betrays the built-in biases Protestant apologists have when they examine history.

Objection #46: "In the fourth place, we must see that historically the canon was formed not by popes and councils; these actions simply recognized the emerging consensus of the people of God as they recognized the authentic Scriptures."[84] "God determined the canon by inspiring these books and no others. The church merely discovered which books God had determined (inspired) to be in the canon."[85]

Answer: The issue is not whether the Councils "recognized" Scripture. We agree that there had to be a "recognition" process of some kind.[86] The real question that this and other Protestant apologists have yet to answer is the precise *nature* of this "recognition." It is certainly true, as John Calvin stated, that 'God gave us the canon of Scripture,' — that goes without saying. But the real question is ***HOW*** did he give us the canon, and how were the people of God able to recognize it? The moment "recognition" is added to the issue, we then enter into the whole realm of how man perceives and distinguishes truth from error, real from unreal, objective from subjective. Knowing man and his dubious propensities, "recogni-

---

[84] W. Robert Godfrey, *Sola Scriptura!* p. 19.

[85] Geisler and MacKenzie, p. 192.

[86] As Yves Congar points out: "This intervention by authority, and the earlier rather more vague intervention of the *ecclesia*, does not imply that the Church could create the normative value of Scripture; it can only recognize it...There is, however, in the establishment of the canon, that is to say in the giving of a character of normativity to certain definite writings to the exclusion of others, *an act of the Church* which is posited in virtue of a charism quite distinct from the apostolic inspirational charism, although in continuity with it, with a view to completing its work for mankind's benefit." He continues: "The recognition of canonicity is thus a structural factor, analogous to *lectio divina*, the sacred reading of Scripture. In both cases, Scripture demands Tradition and the Church; the act which made Scripture requires a second divine act occurring both outside Scripture and in continuity with it..." (*Tradition and Traditions*, pp. 419-20).

tion" is an open mine-field of uncertainty. In fact, using human recognition as a criterion inadvertently makes our knowledge of the canon even more indecisive, because it is then subject to the unpredictable musings of human behavior. In reality, the only thing man should recognize when he finds himself claiming that he can recognize canonical Scripture is that his "recognition theory" is seriously flawed. In order for man to have any certainty that he has recognized the canon correctly, God must intrude, in some way, to make certain and confirm this knowledge.[87]

If, as the previous apologist claimed, the canon is revealed to "the sheep who hear his voice," are these sheep able to recognize his voice infallibly? If not, then he must fully admit to his audience that he does not have an infallible canon; that, in fact, he cannot be sure at all what books actually constitute Scripture. In all honesty, before he preaches his Sunday sermon or teaches a class about the Bible, should he not warn his parishioners and students that he cannot say infallibly that the books from which he quotes and teaches doctrine are indeed the word of God? Without such a disclaimer would he be completely honest?

Yes, the issue is "recognition," but it is a recognition that unless infallibly and directly guided by the Holy Spirit would turn out to be nothing more than the best guesses and conjectures of men. The Catholic Church holds that, in conjunction with the Tradition passed down from the apostles and the intrinsic nature of Scripture, an infallible charism of the Holy Spirit guided the Councils to "recognize," without error, the books of the canon. After all, it was Jesus who said he would give the Spirit to lead the Church into all truth, and bring to mind all the things that were taught, *till the end of the age* (John 14:16- 17, 26; Matt. 28:20).

---

[87] Protestant B. B. Warfield tries to answer this question, stating: "the principle of canonicity was not apostolic authorship, but *the imposition by the apostles as 'law'*" (cited in David Dunbar's, "The Biblical Canon" in *Hermeneutics, Authority and Canon*, p. 357. Dunbar goes on to say, "The seeming reluctance at an early period to designate the apostolic writings as 'Scripture,' the undifferentiating appeal to oral or written tradition, and the uncertainty over the status of certain books demand some adjustments in the traditional Evangelical approach" (Ibid).

Objection #47: "So the question of canonicity is not one ultimately decided by the church either. It is one principally decided by authorship: 'Was it written by an apostle or with apostolic approval and involvement (as examples of the latter category we include Mark and James)?' This is the important question."[88]

Answer: First, the above criterion "was it written by an apostle or with apostolic approval and involvement," though it contains some legitimacy, is still an arbitrary, man-made criterion. On what authority or from what source does this apologist set up such a specific criterion for canonicity? And what is apostolic "involvement"? What are its parameters and characteristics? In addition to failing to precisely define his terms, he has not gotten past the hurdle that the Bible makes no dogmatic assertion as to what qualifies a book as canonical. Every time the apologist tries to answer the question by taking the issue back another step, he ends up just exposing another layer of unprovable assumptions. Second, the evidence in the accepted canon does not support even his own criteria. For example, although Matthew's name is commonly ascribed to the writing of the first gospel, the text nowhere claims that Matthew is its author. The same is true of the other three gospels — they are all anonymous. Thus the Protestant does not even know if an "apostle, or one approved by an apostle," wrote these gospels. Similarly, the book of Hebrews claims no specific author, neither apostle nor one approved by an apostle. We can also add the book of Acts, and the epistle of Jude to the list for the simple reason that Luke, who claims to write Acts, and Jude, were neither apostles nor those claiming to be approved by an apostle.[89] Further, given that some of Paul's writings, though perhaps inspired, were not considered canonical, then even the criterion of apostleship is insufficient for canonicity. The apologist's addition of "or with apostolic approval" to his criterion for canonicity is an attempt to deal with the anomaly of non-

[88] John Armstrong, *Sola Scriptura!* p. 115.

[89] As even F. F. Bruce has admitted, "Traditionally they are ascribed to Luke, but if we wish to examine the validity of this tradition, we have to consider which Luke is meant, and what the probability is of their being the work of that Luke" (*The Canon of Scripture*, p. 256).

apostolic authors in the New Testament, but in doing so he inadvertently weakens "apostleship" as an absolute criterion. Catholicism has no problem with these issues since her tradition and councils provide the answer to the authorship of Matthew and Hebrews and the authenticity of Luke's writings. We end up in the same place every time. The Church, after it gathers all the evidence for canonicity, is the final judge of a book's canonicity, just as a judge in a courtroom, after all the evidence is presented before him, must make the final decision. The only difference is that if we want to claim an inerrant canon, then it can only come from an infallible judge. Best guesses will never settle the issue of what is God's word. God has settled that issue in heaven and has infallibly communicated the result, bot in its content and in its confines to his people through his Church.

Objection #48: "First, as discussed earlier in this chapter, the Council of Trent chose to follow the tradition that had less support in pronouncing the apocryphal books inspired. The earliest and best authorities, including the translator of the Roman Catholic Latin Vulgate Bible, Jerome, opposed the Apocrypha."[90]

Answer: As is often the case, Protestant summations of Catholic canon formation distort the truth considerably. First, the apologists represent the Council of Trent as the first council to include the Deutero-canonical books into the Scripture. On the contrary, before the Council of Trent in 1545, the Deutero-canonicals were understood as inspired Scripture at the Council of Rome in 382, at the Council of Hippo in 393, at the Councils of Carthage from 397-419, the Second Council of Nicea in 787, and the Council of Florence in 1442.[91] Thus, the tradition of including these books was

[90] Geisler and MacKenzie, p. 198.

[91] It is true, however, that the first formally infallible "canon" was issued at the Council of Trent. Although the same listing of inspired books at Trent were given at prior Councils, these Councils did not formally use the words "canon" or "canonical" (e.g., The Council of Florence in 1442). We also note, however, that even though the Council of Trent had some dissenters, the Council did not arrive at its infallible canon by lengthy examination or debate of the issue, rather, it forthrightly accepted the long-held tradition stemming from

long-standing and one which the whole Church accepted. In addition, although Jerome had some reservations about the Deutero-canonicals, various fathers had reservations about other books of the Old Testament. For example, Athanasius, another father who opposed the Deutero-canonicals, also opposed the book of Esther, which was an accepted part of the Palestinian Hebrew canon.[92] Examples of such anomalies can be multiplied.[93] What all this means is that there were disagreements about the canon right up until the Councils confirmed what books belonged in Scripture. This is to be expected, for such controversy occurred for almost every doctrine of the church up until the time such teachings were dogmatized by the Councils. In 382, Jerome capitulated to Pope Damasus and the Council of Rome and accepted the Deutero-canonicals as Scripture. After these Councils, there was little discussion among the medievals as to what constituted Scripture. This also demonstrates Jerome's explicit allegiance to the Church as his authority.

Objection #49: "Such books [the Deutero-canonicals] do not claim for themselves ultimate divine authority. Consider the boldness of

---

[91 cont.] earlier fourth-fifteenth century Councils and considered themselves bound by their decrees. Through this, the Council of Trent laid to rest the permissibility of doubt in regard to the Canon of Scripture (Session IV, April 8, 1546). Vatican Council I ratified the Canon from the Council of Trent (Session III, April 24, 1870). Similarly, the canon of the New Testament, which also contained its "deutero-canonical" books (those which were thought to have less authenticity and authority, e.g., Hebrews, James, 2 Peter, 2 and 3 John, Jude, and Revelation) were finally and formally canonized at the Council of Trent. Although these seven New Testament deutero-canonicals were heavily disputed among the early Fathers and some medieval theologians, Trent made its decision to include them based on the consensus of tradition laid before it, just as it had done with the seven Old Testament deutero-canonicals.

[92] *Easter Letter* XXXIX, NPNF, Vol. 4, p. 552.

[93] Protestant H. B. Swete states: "Thus, Clement of Rome places the story of Judith side by side with that of Esther; the Wisdom of Sirach is cited by Barnabas and the Didache, and Tobit by Polycarp; Clement of Alexandria and Origen appealed to Tobit and both the Wisdoms, to which Origen adds Judith. Our earliest manuscripts of the Greek Bible confirm the impression derived from the quotations of the earliest Christian writers" *(Introduction to the Old Testament in Greek*, p. 224).

Paul's writing ('if anyone thinks he is spiritual, let him acknowledge that what I write is the commandment of the Lord' — 1 Cor. 14:37-38; if anyone 'preaches any other gospel than what we preached to you, let him be accursed' — Gal. 1:8). Then contrast the insecure tone of the author of II Maccabees: 'if it is poorly done and mediocre, that was the best I could do' (15:38)."[94]

Answer: Arguing against a book's canonicity, as this apologist does, by citing statements which demonstrate the human weakness or incomplete knowledge of the writer, are invalid. God can inspire a statement demonstrating the weakness or doubt of an author as much as he can inspire a statement demonstrating his strength and certainty. For example, in 1 Cor. 7:40 Paul says to the widow: "In my judgment, she is happier if she stays as she is — and I think that I too have the Spirit of God." Paul seems somewhat equivocal on this issue. Essentially, he is giving his opinion on this matter. He recognizes that the Lord has not given a command in such matters and thus Paul can only "think" that he knows God's will. Despite the apparent weakness of his statement, Paul's words were still inspired by God. God wanted us to know it was only Paul's opinion. Likewise, God wanted us to know the "insecure tone" of the writer of 2 Maccabees.

Objection #50: "Hahn has insisted that the Pharisees, being in Moses' seat, held ecclesiastical authority; and that, because of this authority, they were to be regarded as accurate in what they taught. But if that is true, why doesn't Hahn accept the Canon that was used by the Pharisees? The Hebrew Scriptures in Jesus' day did not include the apocryphal books that are included in the Catholic Bible. Hahn is in a precarious position. He cannot concede that the Pharisees (being successors of Moses) may have been wrong in their understanding of the Hebrew Canon, for that would mean that the Catholic church (whose pope is the successor of Peter)

---

94 Greg Bahnsen, "The Concept and Importance of Canonicity" in *Antithesis*, Vol. I, No. 5, 1990, p. 44.

may be wrong in its understanding of the Canon. Yet if he agrees with the Canon accepted by the Pharisees, then he must acknowledge that the Catholic reckoning of the Old Testament Canon is wrong. Hahn can't have it both ways."[95]

Answer: First, there is simply no proof that "the Hebrew Scriptures in Jesus' day did not include the apocryphal books." Granted, *some* Hebrew compilations of the Old Testament did not include the "apocryphal" books, but some of the known compilations include them.[96] Since many New Testament quotes originate from the Greek Septuagint which contained the "apocryphal" books, we

---

[95] Eric Svendsen, *Protestant Answers*, p. 55. The Protestant apologist is here referring to Professor Scott Hahn, Ph.D. of Franciscan University.

[96] We maintain the existence of an Alexandrian canon in spite of the objections raised by David Dunbar that this would be unlikely since the Alexandrians capitulated to the canon preferred by the Council of Jamnia, or that the LXX was a 'Christian production' ("The Biblical Canon" in *Hermeneutics, Authority and Canon*, p. 308). First, Judaism at the time of the supposed council of Jamnia was in no condition after the onslaught of the Roman invasion of 70 AD, let alone had authority, to determine the Old Testament Canon. Jamnia may very well display the spell of Palestinian-Jewish tradition that originated in the controversies between the apostle Paul and the Judaizers of the early and mid- first century Church and had not died out until the second destruction of Jerusalem in 146 AD. Despite Jamnia, it is an incontestable fact that the sacredness of certain parts of the Hagiographa of the Palestinian Bible (Esther, Ecclesiastes, Song of Solomon) were disputed by some rabbis as late as the second century AD (Mishna, Yadaim, III, 5; Babylonian Talmud, Megilla, fol. 7); and none of them are cited in the New Testament. Further, some of the most reliable and prominent Greek manuscripts which date at the time the canon was declared by the Catholic Church, contain the Deutero-canonical books (e.g., Codex Vaticanus (B) contains all except 1 & 2 Maccabees; Codex Sinaiticus (א) contains Tobit, Judith, 1 & 2 Maccabees, Wisdom, and Ecclesiasticus; Codex Alexandrinus (A) contains all of the Deutero-canonicals, (not to mention the discovery of Hebrew originals of Ecclesiasticus and Tobit, but the absence of Esther, among the Qumran manuscripts, and the acceptance of the Wisdom of Solomon in the Muratorian Canon). There is absolutely no cause to suggest that the LXX is not representative of prior Greek manuscripts from the pre-Christian era, unless we want to accuse the early Christians of a gross effort at revisionist history.

have at least circumstantial evidence that the New Testament writers recognized them as canonical.[97] Second, Jesus is not speaking about the canon of Scripture in Matthew 23 but only of moral obedience to God's simple commands. Injecting the canon issue into Jesus's statement is simply reading into the text. Third, the Pharisees were not the only leaders of Israel who assumed authority or "sat in Moses' seat." There were also Sadducees, scribes, elders, and priests, not to mention the different schools of the Pharisees themselves (*viz*., the well-known schools of Hillel and Shammai). Fourth, the "seat of Moses" could not, and did not, define the canon anymore than Moses did in the fourteenth century BC, not only because they did not have the authority to do so but for the simple reason that *the canon was not complete*. No one in Israel knew whether or not God was going to add more revelation to the al-

---

[97] Out of 350 texts that the New Testament cites from the Old Testament, 300 are derived from the Greek version. Early Fathers such as Clement, Polycarp, the Shepherd of Hermas, et al., contain references to most all the Deutero-canonicals, and with the same force of authority that they refer to the Proto-canonicals. Justin Martyr, Irenaeus, Origen, Hippolytus, Tertullian and Cyprian confirm the canonicity of some or all of the Deutero-canonicals. In fact, all of the Deutero-canonicals, except Tobias, Judith and additions to Esther are cited by the Fathers. Jerome, though he doubted the canonicity of the Deutero-canonicals, wrote in the Vulgate preface of Judith that the Council of Nicea (325 AD) had accepted it as canonical. There are also allusions to Deutero-canonical books in many New Testament passages: cf., Heb. 1:3 and Wis. 7:25-27; Heb. 11:35-37 and 2 Macc. 6:18-7:42; James 1:19 and Ecclus. 5:13; 1 Pet. 1:6-7 and Wis. 3:5-6; Matt. 6:15 and Ecclus. 28:2; Matt. 11:28-30 and Ecclus. 51:23f; Matt. 9:16-17 and Ecclus. 9:10; Luke 12:16-20 and Ecclus. 11:18-19; John 10:22 and 1 Macc. 4:49/2 Macc. 10:8; Rom. 1:20f and Wis. 13-14; 1 Cor. 10:9-10 and Judith 8:24-25; 1 Cor. 6:13 and Ecclus. 36:20. All in all, there are over two dozen such allusions between the Deutero-canonicals and the New Testament. Though these are not prefaced by the common "it is written" phrase of many Proto-canonical books, even so, not all Proto-canonical books are not prefaced by any type of scribal introduction in the New Testament (e.g., 1 Corinthians 2:16; 15:32; Romans 11:33-36). "...Similarly, more careful studies of quotation formulas in the NT and early Christian literature have shown that formulas containing 'the scripture' or 'it has been written' have no canonical connotation since they are used indiscriminately of noncanonical, heretical, and non-Christian writings as well" (*The Interpreter's Dictionary of the Bible*, Vol. 3, p. 136)

ready known Scriptures. There cannot be a formally defined canon until there are no more books to add. Granted, the Jew of the fourteenth through the first centuries had a working knowledge of the then-accepted books of the Scripture (cf. 2 Kings 22:8; Rom. 3:2), but he did not have a final and formal canon as we know it today. Only when God stopped adding to Scripture could a definitive canon be formalized. The only time in history that a formal canon was, and could be, dogmatized occurred in the fourth century AD when the Church, after officially stating that inspired revelation had ceased, defined the composition and extent of the whole Bible.[98] But this act, of course, also demands that the Church have the authority to declare that the charism of inspiration had ceased — something Scripture itself does not specify, but that Protestants nevertheless affirm.

Objection #51: "...the Protestant view is that the church's decision regarding what books make up the Canon was a fallible decision. Being fallible means that it is possible that the church erred in its compilation of the books found in the present Canon of Scripture."[99]

---

[98] In light of this, Albert Sundberg cautions his Protestant brethren: "...It now appears that the bases upon which Luther and subsequent Protestants separated the books of the Apocrypha [Deutero-canonicals] from the Christian Old Testament are historically inaccurate or misleading. Not only was the so-called Palestinian or Hebrew canon not closed in Jesus' day, but a *de facto* Hebrew canon paralleling the later Jamnia canon did not exist either" ("The Protestant Old Testament Canon: Should It Be Reexamined?" in "A Symposium on the Canon of Scripture," CBQ 28 (1966). Likewise, Marvin Tate in "Old Testament Apocalyptic and the Old Testament Canon" in *Review and Expositor* 65 (1968): 353, says, "It seems clear that the Protestant position must be judged a failure on historical grounds, insofar as it sought to return to the canon of Jesus and the Apostles. The Apocrypha belongs to this historical heritage of the Church." See also Richard Lyon Morgan, "Let's Be Honest about the Canon: A Plea to Reconsider a Question the Reformers Failed to Answer," *Christian Century* 84 (1967): 717-19; and A. C. Sundberg, "'The Old Testament': A Christian Canon," CBQ 30 (1968): 143-45. Cited in David Dunbar's "The Biblical Canon" op. cit., p. 429. Dunbar's disagreement with such a leading historian as Sundberg, however, simply shows how indecisive the Protestant conception of canon really is.

[99] R. C. Sproul, *Sola Scriptura!*, p. 66.

Answer: Obviously, this Protestant apologist has quite a different view of the canonical process than the previous apologist, yet he insists on calling his view "the Protestant view." This is in the face of a subsequent statement he makes on the next page that "...the formula has often been met with both consternation and sharp criticism in evangelical circles." Thus we wonder if *his* view really is "the Protestant view." What we can say is that his view is the most logically consistent view Protestants can hold, for if Protestants cannot believe in a divine charism of infallibility vested in the Church after the apostolic age, then they have no recourse but to conclude that the canon of Scripture, as we have it today, may not be correct. Why has such a formula "met with consternation and sharp criticism in evangelical circles"? Because these evangelicals can also reach another logical conclusion: if the canon of Scripture is fallible, then how can a preacher honestly wave his Bible from the pulpit on Sunday morning and declare "Thus saith the Lord" when he does not know for certain that the Lord has said thus? Indeed, these evangelical's fears are not unreasonable. Sproul himself complains in pages following that certain Protestant theologians, *viz.*, Rudolph Bultmann, have engaged in "canon reduction," attempting to get to the "kernel" of the gospel by removing all the "myth" that the original writers have attached to it. Granted, Bultmann is wrong, but on what basis can this apologist make such a judgment if he himself believes the canon is fallible and perhaps might include things that are myth and legend? It is simply a case of "the pot calling the kettle black." Bultmann is merely following the Protestant theory to its logical conclusion.[100]

Objection #52: "It is one thing to say that the church *could* have erred; it is another thing to say that the church *did* err."[101]

Answer: Again, we can't help but see in this proposition a convenient way for the apologist to "have his cake and eat it too." On the

---

[100] Without infallible controls, Protestants, if they are honest with themselves, have no other recourse than to agree with Karl Barth that, "the canon, as a list made by the Church, can be revised, and writings could be added to or subtracted from it" (cited in *Tradition and Traditions* by Yves Congar, p. 420).

[101] Ibid., p. 67.

one hand, from a theoretical perspective, he maintains the possibility of error in the Church so as to allow himself to be free of Church rule on issues with which he disagrees. If he can reserve for himself the prerogative of saying *when* the Church has erred, then he can dismiss the Church's rule when *he* deems it necessary. On the other hand, since he is not comfortable with having his theoretical proposition of the canon become fact, he disclaims that the church has, in fact, erred in its decision on the canon. What is his basis for making this distinction? It is supported by another theory about the "providence" of God a few pages later. He writes, "It was also by His providence that the original books of the Bible were preserved and accorded the status of Canon" (p. 94). This is quite convenient for him. He can simply attribute all that has occurred to the "providence of God" and out of this convince himself that he possesses an error-free canon. This apologist has fallen into the trap of thinking that "as long as it agrees with what I believe, it is certainly the providence of God working in my life." The problem is, however, that the "providence of God" can apply to all that exists. Everything is in God's control and plan. But this also means that very bad things are in the "providence of God." The rebellion of Satan, the sin of Adam, the Bubonic plague, the Hitler regime, were all in the "providence of God," but that doesn't mean at all that they were good or error-free. In fact, in basing the argument on God's providence, there is equal justification from the Protestant perspective to say either that the Church received a fallible canon or that it received an infallible canon. Moreover, using the "providence" argument, Catholics can claim that God "providentially" gave the early Church the very doctrines with which this Reformed apologist disagrees — and there are many of them (e.g., Baptismal Regeneration, the Real Presence, etc.). We all want God's providence to be on "our side" and accomplish the things *we* desire, but that is not the way the real world operates. We cannot just invoke God's providence to judge whether a certain event in history is good or bad, true or false. Providence means only that, whatever happens, good or bad, all is in God's control and he will work it out the way he sees fit. Thus, the "providence" line of argumentation does not help this apologist escape his problem. In actuality, it shows how very weak his position is, since its foundation is so weak.

Objection #53: "Although it is highly important that this historical process be studied and analyzed as a part of our effort to comprehend the implications of the Church's doctrine of Scripture, we also insist that the comprehension of the whole development depends on a recognition of divine control of history and of the special guidance of the Spirit of God."[102]

Answer: In addition to the "providence of God" line of argumentation, another apologist adds "the special guidance of the Spirit of God." But, we ask, just what is the *nature* of the Spirit's guidance and what *vehicle* does He use to accomplish this guidance? Is "special" guidance different than "ordinary" guidance, and if it is, what are its distinguishing marks? It will do no good to dress up words in superlatives unless we provide precise meanings for them. If there is such a thing as "special" guidance, Catholicism insists that, according to Jesus' dictum that the Church retains 'the keys of the kingdom of heaven, so that what it binds God binds,' and Paul's dictum that 'the Church is the pillar and ground of the truth,' the vehicle for the Spirit's "special" guidance resides in the Church, and consequently her decisions on the canon. More importantly, if the apologist claims that the canon is known by the "special guidance of the Spirit" would this not necessitate that the Spirit give us *infallible* guidance, for who would want to accuse the Spirit of God of giving us erroneous or misdirected guidance? If He did, it wouldn't be so "special" after all. The real problem is that Protestants do not want to admit the existence of an infallible vehicle for the canon because, as Hermann Ridderbos has admitted, it would "eventuate in affirming the infallibility of the church, as in Roman Catholicism."[103] This, of course, would necessitate that, in addition to the canon, the Church is also infallible on other issues, which would, of course, necessitate that every God-fearing Protestant become Catholic — immediately.

Objection #54: [After quoting Luke 11:50-51, the apologist states the following]: Jesus is here referring to the generally accepted

[102] Ned B. Stonehouse, as concurred with, and cited by David Dunbar in *Hermeneutics, Authority and Canon*, p. 359.
[103] Ibid., p. 359-60.

Hebrew Canon which began with the book of Genesis and ended with the book of 2 Chronicles. He cites the first murder (Abel) and the last murder (Zechariah) recorded in the Hebrew Canon. This Canon, although arranged differently, is otherwise identical to the Protestant Old Testament Canon. Jesus is, in essence, defining the limits of the Old Testament Canon for us— a Canon with which Catholics differ."[104]

Answer: This is another case of "reading into" the passage what one wants to see. Since Jesus is making no formal statement on the canon, it is highly inappropriate to say that he is "defining the limits of the Old Testament Canon for us." Jesus is talking about the murders that occurred in Jewish history, not about the canon. One reason he may be limiting his historical markers to Abel and Zechariah is that this encompasses the time period up until the Babylonian captivity, when Israel ceased to be a nation. This was the most cataclysmic event in Israel's history and therefore serves as the most appropriate time-marker. During the Babylonian captivity, Jews did not murder their own Jewish prophets, nor does the Bible record that Jews murdered prominent Jews at the regathering of Israel under Ezra and Nehemiah. (Even if there were such murders in Ezra/Nehemiah, would this apologist conclude, based on his own theory, that Jesus is eliminating Ezra and Nehemiah from the canon because he did not include them in Luke 11:50-51? This is especially significant since scholars agree that there was no established order of books in the Hebrew canon at the time of the Babylonian captivity). In the time of the Maccabees, Romans were murdering the Jews but the Bible does not record that Jews murdered Jews, at least Jews of any redemptive significance. Hence, it is obvious that none of these more remote time periods would have fit into Jesus' statement in Luke 11:50-51.

Objection #55: "We can accept the general reliability of those who collected the Canon — and thank them for their contribution, acknowledging that the Holy Spirit gave infallible guidance to them!

[104] Svendsen, p. 56.

[footnote]: This is far different from ascribing infallibility to the ecclesial body itself!"[105]

Answer: Here is another case of "wanting your cake and eat it too." This apologist wants infallibility for what is dear to him (the canon of Scripture) but he reserves himself the right to deny it for anything else that "those who collected the Canon" deemed infallible truth. First, we must ask who he thinks "those who collected the Canon" were if he does not believe they were the very "ecclesial body" which he questions. The Fathers of the Church did not consider themselves outside the "ecclesial body," nor did the Councils that collected and defined the canon. The apologist is simply reading back into early Church history his own Protestant mindset — a mindset that believes there can be a legitimate separation between the Church at large and individual Christians. None of the Fathers ever entertained such a notion. Second, we can surmise that he does not want to say that the "ecclesial body" (i.e., the Church) has infallibility, probably because he does not want to accept many of the doctrines taught by the Catholic Church. If they were infallible, but he denied them, he would be signing his own death warrant. But how can he claim that "those who collected the Canon" had "infallible guidance" in only *one* area of the faith but not in other areas? Where does Scripture, the Church, Tradition, or any other source, ever even hint of such a single deposit of infallibility? It is only the musing of one who knows he cannot dogmatically claim that Scripture is Scripture without infallibility, yet one who does not want to accept the logical conclusion that if "those who collected the Canon" were granted infallibility in one important area they would also be granted infallibility in other important areas. Third, the apologist has not explained how such an extraordinary event as the intrusion of the Holy Spirit to provide infallibility took place, and what vehicle He used to accomplish this. Did the Holy Spirit implant this infallible certitude directly into the minds of "those" men? Unless he defines the nature of this divine intrusion he simply has no precedent or right to define its limitations and its recipients. It is similar to the undefined and ambigu-

[105] Ibid., p. 59.

ous claim presented by the previous apologist that we can know the canon because "the sheep hear the voice of the shepherd." Fourth, many of "those who collected the Canon" in the first four centuries of the Church included the Deutero-canonical books of the Old Testament, and it was some of these very Fathers who were presiding at the early Councils who decided that these books were indeed canonical. What the apologist ends up having to say is that of "those who collected the Canon" the Holy Spirit infallibly guided only the ones who agreed with the Protestant version of the canon. One can readily see that this kind of "cut and paste" recounting of ecclesiastical history is a total distortion of truth, not to mention being illogical.

Objection #56: "The institution of an infallible pope has not created theological unity in the Roman Church."[106]

Answer: First, Jesus himself, the infallible, incarnate word of God, did not create unanimous theological "unity" among his hearers. In fact, Jesus was disheartened that so many people argued with him and rejected his message of truth. At many points, his message divided more than it unified. Paul encountered the same opposition, among both Jews and Gentile converts. Hence it is very short-sighted to suggest that infallibility is the criterion of unity. Unity, at least demographic unity, occurs when the people obey what they hear. If one voice is teaching them, the possibility for practical unity is much greater than if there are thousands of voices all teaching something different.

Second, the unity that the Catholic Church claims to promote in her charism of infallibility is not that every bishop, every priest, and every lay person will automatically believe what she teaches. She claims that truth resides in the decrees and doctrines the Magisterium promulgates, regardless of how the remaining clerics and laity interpret the Magisterium's teachings. One has no more right to deny the charism of infallibility to the Magisterium because of disagreements among its hearers than to deny it to Jesus or the apostles because of disagreements among their hearers. To

[106] W. Robert Godfrey, *Sola Scriptura!* p. 22.

make the one dependent on the other is not only illogical, it has no Scriptural precedent.

Objection #57: "We should not be surprised that there are divisions in the church....The Apostle Paul told us that such divisions are useful. He wrote: 'No doubt there have to be differences among you to show which of you have God's approval'! (1 Corinthians 11:19). Differences should humble us and drive us back to the Scriptures to test all claims to truth. If we do not accept the Scriptures as our standard and judge, there is indeed no hope for unity."[107]

Answer: Here it seems that the apologist is attempting to find a rationale for the Protestant Reformation. He implies that God ordained the Protestant differences with the Catholic Church which "drove them back to Scripture," thus demonstrating that God "approved" of Protestantism. If this is his intent, we would strongly suggest an alternative scenario. We can agree that God can turn any evil into good. As Joseph said to his brothers in Genesis 50:20, "You intended it for evil but God intended it for good." But we must also insist that Paul is not even remotely referring to a wholesale rejection of the established Church such as occurred when Protestantism broke off from Catholicism. In the rest of the Corinthian epistle Paul tells us that he is appalled at even rudimentary division in the Church (cf. 1 Cor. 1-4). Although God can bring good out of evil, nevertheless it is precisely those who cause divisions in the Church whom Paul severely castigates. In Romans 16:17 Paul says, "I urge you, brothers, to watch out for those who cause divisions and put obstacles in your way that are contrary to the teaching you have learned." It is those who depart from the established "teaching you have learned" that are to be marked and avoided (cf. Gal. 5:20; 2 Pt. 2:1). Korah's rebellion against the established teaching and authority of Moses, though a "necessary" evil in terms of 1 Cor. 11:19, had one outstanding feature — it disapproved Korah and approved Moses (Num. 16:1-35; Jude 11). Likewise, 1 Cor. 11:19 indicates that those who rebelled against the established teaching were not the approved ones. In the same way, Protestants are

[107] Ibid., p. 23.

hard-pressed to prove that sixteen centuries of prior Church teaching was not the "teaching you have learned."

We must also say that holding "the Scriptures as our standard and judge" so that we can have "hope for unity" is the elusive mirage of Protestant thinking. Their history has proven that it is precisely the incessant referral to Scripture, without the guide of the Church and its Tradition, that has produced division upon division in the non-Catholic world. According to the Oxford World Encyclopedia of Religion, there are approximately 28,000 distinct Christian groups in the world, with five new ones arising every week.[108] There is enough dissension among Catholics who disagree with the established authority and dogma of the Church, let alone the division and anarchy that occurs in non-Catholic churches where thousands of dogmas and authorities exist. It is high time we learn that "going back to Scripture," while sounding very pious and noble, really means nothing without a controlling criterion for determining, among all the possible interpretations, what Scripture is actually saying.

Objection #58: "Furthermore, it seems singularly inconsistent for Catholic scholars to claim they need another mind to help them interpret Scripture correctly for them when the mind God gave them is sufficient to interpret everything else, including some things much more difficult than Scripture. Many Catholic scholars, for example, are experts in interpreting classical literature, involving both the moral and religious meanings of those texts. Yet these same edu-

---

[108] According to the *Oxford World Christian Encyclopedia*, in 1982 there existed 20,800 organized churches and denominations within Christendom, "...with a projected 22,190 by 1985." The authors attribute this to "...local disagreements in how to indigenize and inculturate the Christian faith. The inevitable result has been a vast increase in the number of distinct, discrete, separate and divergent Christian denominations in many countries of the world...The present net increase is 270 denominations each year (5 new ones a week). In many countries this produces serious overlapping, competition, rivalries, clashes, violence, and even lawsuits and protracted litigation" (ed. David B. Barrett, Oxford University Press, 1982, pp. 15-18). If this growth has continued at the 1985 rate, this would amount to over 28,000 churches and denominations at the present date.

cated minds are said to be inadequate to obtain a reliable religious and moral interpretation of the texts of their own Scriptures."[109]

Answer: First, the Catholic Church does not teach that an individual cannot glean reliable truth from reading Scripture. The Church encourages her members to read Scripture fervently.[110] The individual may discover great and wonderful truths that have not been noticed or explained previously. But whatever he claims to find, the Church's only requirement is that it be in accord with previously dogmatized truth. Previously dogmatized truth gives the individual interpreter a solid foundation and guide to interpret the rest of divine truth. If the Church is to maintain truth, it is only reasonable to expect that her members will abide by this logic. Second, it is misleading to compare the study of classical literature with formalized dogma of the Church. The finest expert in classical literature is still going to make mistakes in his interpretation of that literature. This doesn't mean he is "inadequate" for the task but only that he must recognize his individual fallibility in whatever he interprets. In addition, although truth and infallible dogma share the same nature, not all truth is infallible dogma. Infallible dogma is the Church's way of *formalizing* a certain truth — of bringing to the attention of all interested parties the absolute truth on very important matters. The Church is not saying that there is no truth outside of the arena of infallibility. It is only saying that in areas of the gravest importance (i.e., faith and morals) there is no room for error in God's Church since people's eternal souls are at stake. If this apologist would be honest with himself he should

[109] Geisler and MacKenzie, p. 215.

[110] In one of many statements he has made, Pope John Paul II stated on July 20, 1997: "Today I would like to emphasize in particular the importance of listening to the Word of God...Sacred Scripture is in fact 'a pure and lasting fount of spiritual life,' and 'the supreme rule of her faith.' It is like thirst-quenching water and food that nourishes the life of believers. I therefore invite everyone to cultivate a more intense and frequent contact with the Word of God, letting its healing and creative power work in us...Learning to read Sacred Scripture is fundamental for the believer: it is the first step of a ladder, which continues with meditation and, thus with real prayer. Prayer based on biblical reading is the principal way of Christian spirituality..." (*L'Osservatore Romano*, July 23, 1997).

now be able to recognize that 475 years of Protestantism, with its incessant division over the very interpretation of Scripture he is emulating, has not proven his case at all, but has only reinforced the adage about the emperor who failed to admit what kind of clothes he was actually wearing.

Objection #59: [Under the title "Philosophical Problems With Infallibility" the apologist proposes the following argument]: "The supposed need for an infallible magisterium is an epistemically... insufficient basis for rising above the level of probable knowledge. Catholic scholars admit, as they must, that they do not have infallible evidence that there is an infallible teaching magisterium. They have merely what even they believe to be only probable arguments."[111]

Answer: Reducing the argumentation to this level is clever but it is not going to help this apologist. We can all play the "proof" card in a *faith-based* religion such as Christianity and find cracks in each other's position. Engaging your opponent in "mutually self-destructive" apologetics is futile and irrelevant. From where this apologist has taken the argument, we can even go further. There is no "proof" that God exists because, as even John 1:18 says, no one has seen him at any time. We only have circumstantial evidence (cf. Rom. 1:20; Heb. 11:1-2). Hence, unless the apologist wants to become a Nihilist, it is pointless to argue his case as he has done. Man must use his reason and his faith to assent to God. Thus, we would suggest that this apologist introduce this section of his remarks with some other title than "Philosophical Problems with Infallibility," since it is not only Infallibility's philosophical problem but *Protestantism's* philosophical problem.

Objection #60: "In summation, since to be an apostle one had to be an eyewitness of the resurrected Christ, and since these select individuals known as apostles were given certain unmistakable 'signs of an apostle' to establish their authority — which ceased during their lifetime — it follows that no one since the first century

[111] Geisler and MacKenzie, p. 216.

has possessed apostolic authority...What remains today is the *teaching* of the apostles (in the New Testament), not the *office* of an apostle or its authority. The authority of the *living* apostles has been replaced by the authority of the *writings* of the apostles."[112]

Answer: This is a roundabout way of promoting *sola scriptura*, but all the supposed facts are either wrong or unprovable from Scripture. First, although the apologist tries to make a case on the previous page (p. 210) that miracles ceased after the apostolic age, there is simply no direct statement in the New Testament that this is so. Just because God gave miracles to the apostles to confirm their office does not mean that miracles could not be given at that time or a later time for *other* reasons. Miracles recorded in the Bible were neither confined to apostles nor to the confirmation of apostles (cf. Mark 9:39; 1 Cor. 12:10, 28; Gal. 3:5). Jesus and the apostles performed many miracles just to help people in their desperate situations. Further, because Paul did not miraculously heal certain individuals in certain instances (e.g, Phil 2:26; 2 Tim. 4:20) does not prove that miracles ceased. The apologist inadvertently admits this himself as he speaks of these events with the qualification that "Paul was *apparently* not able to heal them" and "apostle- confirming miracles *apparently* ceased even before some apostles had died"[113] (emphasis mine). Further, if miracles were only for the purpose of confirming the apostolic office, then it follows that a premature cessation of miracles in Paul's lifetime could even question the continuity of *his* office at that time.

Second, this apologist's desire to eliminate any direct communication between God and his Church after the first century is not only an attempt to dismiss the authority of the Catholic Church which sanctions such divine intrusion, but he seems to be promoting a semi-Deistic understanding of the universe — a universe in which God is said to create the world, like a watchmaker makes a watch, but then leaves it on its own to wind down. The only difference between seventeenth century Deism and this apologist's view is that the latter claims God "works in his heart" to know the truth.

---

[112] Ibid., p. 211.
[113] Ibid., p. 210.

But the proof of this is as subjective as the subjective nature of its manifestation, especially since his fellow Protestants also claim to be guided by the Spirit yet believe doctrines of major importance contrary to his.

Third, Scripture does not teach that the "teaching" of the apostles remains in the Church but not the "office" or "authority." Granted, statements from Scripture lead Catholics to agree that the apostles were numerically confined to twelve men, but Scripture also teaches that the authoritative "office" is transferred to the successive leaders of the Church. Among the many evidences, we will cite one. In Acts 1:20, Peter undertook the task of replacing Judas with another apostle. To validate his action, Peter quotes from Psalm 108 [109]:8 ("The office of him let another take"). Here we see that the precedent for succession of "office" was already established in the Old Testament since the directive for Peter to do so is contained in this specific Psalm. The Psalm says nothing about apostles, bishops, elders, or the like. The Psalmist is speaking about evil men in his day who were in "office" but were soon to be replaced by others more faithful. These, no doubt, were officials in David's court. Yet, without any mention of apostleship in the Psalm, Peter extracts this obscure Old Testament passage as a precedent and directive for the preservation of the apostolic office. This shows that the concept of "office" and its succession is larger than apostleship. These facts become all the more significant when we find that the word Peter uses for "office" in Acts 1:20 is the same word used only one other place in the New Testament regarding the office of bishop in 1 Timothy 3:1 (lit. "...if a man aspires to the office[114] he desires a good work"). We know that the office of bishop is in view since in the next verse Paul says, "It is necessary for a bishop[115] to be without reproach..." Hence it is obvious that the

[114] The word "office" is from the Greek ἐπισκοπή, appearing only four places in the New Testament. Twice the semantic range allows it to be used of "visitation" (Luke 19:44; 1 Pet. 2:12), but the other two references are confined to "office" (Acts 1:20; 1 Tim. 3:1).

[115] The word "bishop" is from the Greek ἐπίσκοπος, appearing five times in reference to the leading office of the Church (cf., Acts 20:28; Phil. 1:1; 1 Tim. 3:2; Tit. 1:7; 1 Pet. 2:25).

"office" in 1 Tim. 3:1 is intimately and directly connected to the office in Acts 1:20, and to the succession of that office mandated in Psalm 108 [109]:8. The mandate of Psalm 108 [109]:8 is that the "office" — a word by which the New Testament refers not only to an apostle but also to a "bishop"— is to be succeeded. It is a *mandate* because Peter interprets it to be such for us. His interpretation shows that the Psalm, and of course the whole Old Testament behind the Psalm, is a clear and biblically interpreted precedent for succession of office, which, according to the New Testament's use of the term, includes the elected bishops of the Church. Thus, Scripture does show that the authority of the office and its succession continue as long as bishops exist in the Church.

Objection #61: "The Bible tells us that the Word of God is the light that enables us to walk in the ways of God... Roman opponents usually object to an appeal to Psalm 119 on the grounds that it speaks of the Word of God, not of the Bible, and therefore could include in its praise tradition as well as Scripture. But their argument is irrelevant to our use of Psalm 119, because we are using it to prove clarity, not the sufficiency of Scripture."[116]

Answer: We do not wish to fault appeals to Psalm 119 to support the clarity or sufficiency of Scripture, that is, if we understand what Psalm 119 is clear and sufficient ***for***. As we said earlier, almost any book of the Bible is clear and sufficient to bring someone the knowledge of God and salvation, regardless of how rudimentary the information is. God has already built into man a knowledge of Himself and His laws (cf., Romans 1:18-20; 2:14-15; Jeremiah 31:33-34). Any true teaching of God, be it from Scripture or from some other qualified source, draws out and enhances what men already know intuitively. The issue at stake is this: is the Bible sufficient to answer all questions that face man in his quest to know and glorify God on earth? The answer is: no. As we pointed out earlier, often the Bible, both in theological doctrine and in morals, does not address a particular issue. When it does address an issue, sometimes it does so without giving a definitive judg-

---

[116] W. Robert Godfrey, *Sola Scriptura!* pp. 23-24.

ment (slavery; capital punishment; alcohol usage; Rahab's lie; Jephthah's oath); often we cannot tell whether its language is figurative or literal (the creation story; the book of Revelation; Joshua's stopping of the Sun; the Eucharist);[117] it leaves out information on

---

[117] As John Henry Cardinal Newman argued: "...It is antecedently unreasonable to suppose that a book so complex, so unsystematic, in parts so obscure, the outcome of so many minds, times, and places, should be given us from above without the safeguard of some authority; as if it could possibly, from the nature of the case, interpret itself. Its inspiration does but guarantee its truth, not its interpretation. How are private readers satisfactorily to distinguish what is didactic and what is historical, what is fact and what is vision, what is allegorical and what is literal, what is idiomatic and what is grammatical, what is enunciated formally and what occurs *obiter*, what is only of temporary and what is of lasting obligation? (*On the Inspiration of Scripture*, cited in Karl Keating's *Catholicism and Fundamentalism*, p. 128). Newman also argued against Evangelical Religion with the following insight: "It has no straightforward view on any one point, on which it professes to teach, and to hide its poverty, it has dressed itself in a maze of words...mistiness is the mother of wisdom. A man who can set down half-a-dozen general propositions, which escape from destroying one another only by being diluted into truisms...who never enunciates a truth without guarding himself against being supposed to exclude the contradictory,— who holds that Scripture is the only authority, yet that the Church is to be deferred to..." For an example of "holding to Scripture...yet deferring to the Church," note these statements from a prominent Protestant: "...he deposited this treasure [the gospel] in the church...he furnished them with authority...away from her bosom one cannot hope for any forgiveness or sins or any salvation...it is always disastrous to leave the church...God, who could in a moment perfect his own, nevertheless desires them to grow up into manhood solely under the education of the church...all those who spurn the spiritual food, divinely extended to them through the hand of the church, deserve to perish in famine and hunger...but [God] added priests as interpreters from whose lips the people might ask its true meaning...we hear his ministers speaking just as if he himself spoke...More detestable than this attitude is that of the apostates who have a passion for splitting churches, in effect driving the sheep from their fold and casting them into the jaws of wolves...the church is a multitude gathered from many nations; it is divided and dispersed in separate places, but agrees on the one truth of divine doctrine...[the church] where the preaching of the gospel is reverently heard and the sacraments are not neglected...no one is permitted to spurn its [the church's] authority, flout its warnings, resist its counsels, or make light of its chastisements — much less to desert it and break its unity...It is of no small

important practices (infant baptism; musical instruments for worship, frequency of the Lord's Supper, the number of sacraments); it seems contradictory or unclear on certain topics (divorce and remarriage; social economy; where unbaptized infants go upon death; predestination; baptism of the dead; blasphemy against the Holy Spirit; discrepancies in the Synoptic gospels; justification in Paul and James; the role of women; celibacy); it lacks precise terminology to combat heresy (consubstantial; homoousios); it does not tell us which Old Testament practices are to be modeled and which are to be ignored (the civil laws of Israel; Sabbath observance of the third commandment; tithing); it does not tell us whether some practices are sin (masturbation; polygamy); it fails to give us additional information taught to the Churches (1 Cor. 11:34; Eph. 3:3); it does not specify whether God would give additional revelation after Scripture was completed; it does not tell us which books are canonical or who wrote some of the books. The list can go on and on. But there is one thing that becomes clear to us. The Bible begs to be supplemented by an authority who can explain how to interpret correctly what Scripture does cover, and provide us with the truth about issues Scripture does not cover. It should come as no surprise that for many of the Scriptural ambiguities listed above, a distinct Protestant denomination has been created. Yes, Psalm 119 is clear and sufficient in its own right, but it is not clear and sufficient to answer virtually any of the questions and dilemmas raised above, and neither is any other part of Scripture capable of doing so. Rather, Psalm 119 is a plea for the man of God to meditate and adhere to God's general laws, but as we have just witnessed, often bare Scripture is not suffi-

---

[117 cont.] importance that it is called 'the pillar and ground of the truth'...by these words Paul means that the church is the faithful keeper of God's truth in order that it may not perish in the world...and provides everything that makes for our salvation...it follows that separation from the church is the denial of God and Christ...for in it alone is kept safe and uncorrupted that doctrine in which piety stands sound and the use of the sacraments ordained by the Lord is guarded" (John Calvin, *Institutes of the Christian Religion*, 2:4:1 to 2:4:17, ed. John T. McNeil (Phila., Westminster Press, 1960), pp. 1011-1032). It is amazing that a man can write these words, yet totally reject the Catholic Church.

cient to tell us all of what God's wishes comprise. Since it does not, then if we rely only on Scripture, we cannot be glorifying God in the best way possible

Some Protestants also appeal to verses like Psalm 19:7: "The law of the Lord is perfect, reviving the soul, the statutes of the Lord are trustworthy, making wise the simple." The argument is: if Scripture is perfect, why does one need Tradition? First, the Psalmist is speaking about the *quality* of Scripture only, not the *quantity* of God's revelation. We see this when he speaks of God's law as "trustworthy" in verse 7, as well as "right" and "radiant" in verse 8. In other words, wherever and whenever one contemplates God's law, he can be certain that it will not steer him wrong. God's laws are perfect, but this does not mean that God will not or cannot add other "perfect" revelation in whatever form he chooses. The mere fact that the remaining 131 Psalms add more information on the nature of God's laws shows that God continually adds "perfect" revelation. All of his laws are perfect, but this does not prove or suggest that God limits his revelation to these perfect laws.

The Church Fathers

Objection #62: [One Protestant apologist quotes Irenaeus as saying]:

> We have learned from none others the plan of our salvation, than from those through whom the gospel has come down to us, which they did at one time proclaim in public, and, at a later period, by the will of God, handed them down to us in the Scriptures, to be the ground and pillar of our faith" (NPNF, *Against Heresies*, III.1.1).

[The apologist then comments]:

> Irenaeus here clearly believes in the Protestant principle of a self-retiring apostolic oral tradition. As Irenaeus notes, whereas at one time the apostles orally proclaimed their message, later they committed their message to writing in the Scriptures. It is there that their continued legacy is to be found,

> and it is there that the church is to find the "ground and pillar" of its faith — not in oral tradition...[118]

Answer: This is a case of "reading into" a passage from the Fathers what one wants to see, rather than interpreting the words in context, and in relation to what else the father said that might contradict the proposed interpretation. The above quote is from Irenaeus's *Against Heresies*, Book III, Chapter 1, Article 1. To show how this quote can be easily misinterpreted, we will look on the very next page at Chapter 2, Article 2 of Irenaeus' work:

> But, again, when we refer them to that tradition which originates from the apostles, and which is preserved by means of the successions of presbyters in the Churches, they object to tradition, saying that they themselves are wiser not merely than the presbyters, but even than the apostles, because they have discovered the unadulterated truth.

This second quote is giving us something far different from what we would expect based on the Protestant apologist's assessment of Irenaeus. Obviously, Irenaeus believes not only in Scripture, but in the *tradition* that originates from the apostles. Moreover, Irenaeus also believes in the perpetuation of that tradition through the unbroken succession of presbyters (bishops or priests) in the Churches. How can Irenaeus be teaching that the oral tradition of the apostles was retired if he believes that the presbyters preserve it by means of successive generations? Protestant apologists who cite the first quotation of Irenaeus as evidence of *sola scriptura* do so without understanding that Irenaeus is merely saying that the miracle of inspiration (the divine influence the apostles were under when they publicly proclaimed the gospel in the first century), stopped at a specific point in time, namely, at the death of the last apostle. Catholics and Protestants accept as fact that after the first century God ceased the charism of divine inspiration. Hence Irenaeus is not saying that the preservation and perpetuation of the

---

118 Eric Svendsen in *Protestant Answers*, pp. 58-59, as quoted from the book *Roman Catholicism*: "Did I Really Leave the Holy Catholic Church?" by Protestant apologist William Webster, p. 273.

apostles' oral tradition was retired, but only that the charism of inspiration had ceased. If anything, Irenaeus is assuring us that responsible and qualified men had systematically preserved the apostles' orally inspired messages. Thus we have further proof of an unwritten Tradition that existed alongside the written Scripture in the life of the Church.

The same apologist quotes Cyril of Jerusalem as saying:

> Let us be content with this knowledge and not busy ourselves with questions about the divine nature of hypostasis. I would have spoken of that had it been contained in Scripture. Let us not venture where Scripture does not lead, for it suffices for our salvation to know that there is Father, and Son, and Holy Spirit...But the Holy Spirit himself has not spoken in the Scriptures about the Son's generation from the Father. Why then busy yourself over something that the Holy Spirit has not expressed in the Scriptures? You do not know all the Scriptures, and yet must get to know what is not in the Scriptures?![119]

The same apologist concludes from Cyril's comments:

> What is Cyril's view of Scripture's sole authority? Is it that of the Catholic church? Hardly. Cyril sounds much more like a Protestant in his view of Scripture than a Catholic.

Here again, we have another case of "reading into" the writing of a father without taking into account the context of the citation, nor what else the Father has stated. On the surface, Cyril's statement does seem to be more Protestant than Catholic, that is, until we understand with an open mind what he is really trying to say. Is Cyril teaching that Scripture is our only authority, and thereby denying any authority to Tradition? Let's see what else Cyril says on the same page in Article 11:

[119] Ibid., p. 58. Taken from Cyril of Jerusalem's *Catechetical Lectures*, XI, Article 12 in NPNF, p. 67.

> The Father then begat Him not in such wise as any man could understand, but as Himself only knoweth. For we profess not to tell in what manner He begat Him, but we insist that it was not in this manner. And not we only are ignorant of the generation of the Son from the Father, but so is every created nature.

So far, Cyril is telling us that man cannot know the precise nature of the Father begetting the Son. Only God himself knows how this took place. Next, Cyril gives a list of those who do not understand what "begetting" means:

> Why then art thou cast down, O man, at being ignorant of that which even the heavens know not? Nay, not only are the heavens ignorant of this generation, but also every angelic nature. For if any one should ascend, were it possible, into the first heaven, and perceiving the ranks of the Angels there should approach and ask them how God begat His own Son, they would say perhaps, "We have above us beings greater and higher; ask them."....and even if any one should reach them, which is impossible, they also would decline the explanation, for they know it not.

Notice precisely what Cyril is attempting to do here. He is telling his opponents not to speculate about things that only God can comprehend. Neither men, nor angels, nor thrones, nor principalities can comprehend it, thus, it is useless to speculate about such esoteric subjects. If only God himself can know what "begetting" really is, then certainly Tradition cannot contain its explanation, nor, as Cyril points out, does Scripture contain it. But we cannot conclude from this that Cyril is saying that Scripture is our only authority, nor that he is opposing Scripture against Tradition and the Church. Cyril is merely reacting against *unbridled theological speculation* that is out of the realm of divinely revealed truth, especially in such highly esoteric areas as how the Father 'begets' the Son. Simply put, no analogy on earth can even begin to explain how such an event as 'begetting' takes place. It is as enigmatic as the Trinity itself. Colloquially speaking, Cyril is saying, "Look, even Scripture, which you treasure as the very words of God, doesn't attempt an explanation to the nature of 'begetting,' so why do you take it upon yourself to answer such questions from your own limited human reasoning?"

The same explanation applies to Cyril's oft quoted statement on Scripture from Lecture IV, Article 17:

> For concerning the divine and holy mysteries of the Faith, not even a casual statement must be delivered without the Holy Scriptures; nor must we be drawn aside by mere plausibility and artifices of speech. Even to me, who tell thee these things, give not absolute credence, unless thou receive the proof of the things which I announce from the Divine Scriptures. For this salvation which we believe depends not on ingenious reasoning, but on demonstration of the Holy Scriptures.

The context of this passage concerns the nature of the Holy Spirit. According to Lecture XVI, Chapters 6-10, Cyril explains that there were many heresies floating around at this time about the nature of the Holy Spirit. In the preceding Lecture (IV, Chapter 16), Cyril voices his concern:

> Believe thou also in the Holy Ghost, and hold the same opinion concerning Him, which thou hast received to hold concerning the Father and the Son, and follow not those who teach blasphemous things of Him.

Notice first that Cyril tells them to hold on to the teaching of the Holy Spirit in the same way that "thou hast received to hold" the teaching of the Father and the Son. This implies that there was a general body of truth which had been passed on to them regarding the Trinity, and which they were to "hold" onto. Again, the Trinity was an esoteric and enigmatic article of the faith. It was prone to misrepresentation and error. It took the Church four centuries to draw parameters around the nature of the Trinity, and even then they told you primarily what you could *not* say about the Trinity, not what it *is in essence*. Cyril's concern is that unbridled speculation about the Trinity is the cause of much heresy. He describes these speculations not as authentic Church tradition, but as “casual statements,” “mere plausibility and artifices of speech” from high-minded yet presumptuous men. Again, Cyril sets Scripture against speculation, not Scripture against authentic Tradition. Further, when Cyril says, “Even to me, who tell you these things, give not absolute credence...” he is not setting Scripture over and above Tradition or the Church at large, but Scripture over and above a single, fallible man, Cyril or anyone else, who purports to know the truth without verification.

Finally, to show how dangerous it can be to quote from a Father without examining the context of his quote, or all that he says on a given subject, we will observe a case of selective quoting, which if not scrutinized, seems to support the *sola scriptura* position. The same Protestant apologist quotes Cyril as saying:

> For these articles of our faith were not composed of human opinion, but are the principle points collected out of the whole Scripture to complete a single doctrinal formulation of the faith.[120]

The implication the apologist is attempting to draw from this quote is that only Scripture, not human tradition, has been amassed in all its parts to form the doctrinal stipulations of our faith. This seems like a plausible interpretation, that is, until we read the remainder of Cyril’s paragraph and the beginning of the next paragraph:

> Take heed, then, brethren, and hold fast the traditions which ye now receive, and write them on the table of your heart. Guard them with reverence, lest per chance the enemy despoil any who have grown slack; or lest some heretic pervert any of the truths delivered to you.[121]

---

[120] Eric Svendsen, *Protestant Answers*, p. 57, citing Lecture V, Article 12 of Cyril’s *Catechetical Lectures*.

[121] NPNF, Vol. 7, p. 32. It is interesting to note that this quote, which is in the same paragraph as another sentence which Svendsen extracts to support the concept of *sola scriptura* is left out of Svendsen’s citation of Cyril.

Here Cyril is paraphrasing the famous passage in 2 Thessalonians 2:15 ("So then, brothers, stand firm and hold to the teachings we passed on to you, whether by word of mouth or by letter") which stipulates both oral ("word of mouth") and written ("by letter") as divine revelation and the Tradition Paul wanted the Thessalonians to preserve. Cyril's citation of 2 Thess. 2:15 comes only two sentences after the quote extracted by the Protestant apologist which he used to teach that Cyril believed in *sola scriptura*. We must assume that this apologist did not bother to read Cyril's entire paragraph, or, more likely was quoting a secondary source whose objectivity he did not question.

Objection #63: "The Reformers also discovered that tradition contradicted tradition. For example, the tradition of the Roman church teaches that the pope is the head of the church, a bishop over all bishops. But Gregory the Great, pope and saint at the end of the ancient church period, said that such a teaching came from the spirit of Antichrist ('I confidently affirm that whosoever calls himself *sacerdos universalis*, or desires to be so called by others is in his pride a forerunner of Antichrist')."[122]

Answer: Although this is a little off the topic of *sola scriptura*, this apologist has included it in his book defending *sola scriptura*. Because of this, and because it is such an egregious misrepresentation of Gregory the Great's intent, we must address it. As with many quotes taken from the Fathers, apologists often gather citations from secondary sources without consulting the origin of the citation (in this case, *Cambridge Medieval History*, (New York: MacMillian Co. 1967) Vol. II, p. 247).

First, the general context is Gregory's *Epistles,* made up mostly of letters he wrote in his papal office to all the archbishops, bishops and deacons, as well as to the Patriarchs/Bishops of the eastern churches. There are over 800 letters, divided between 14 books. The passage in question appears in Book VII, Epistle XXXIII. We see an example of Gregory's high position and authority over all these bishops in the way he begins the very first epistle: "Gregory,

[122] W. Robert Godfrey, *Sola Scriptura!* p. 14.

servant of the servants of God, to all the bishops constituted throughout Sicily."[123] In Epistle I:XXV, to John, Bishop of Constantinople, he writes: "...and with mind consoled give myself to the care of my pontifical office, I am deterred by consideration of the immensity of this very task." In Epistle I:XXVII, to Anastasius, Archbishop of Corinth, he writes: "...how the Lord had vouchsafed that I, however unworthy, should preside over the apostolic See." In Epistle II:XVIII, to Natalis, Bishop of Salona, he writes: "Wherefore let thy Fraternity, even after the admonition so often repeated, repent of the error of thy wrongdoing, and restore the aforesaid Honoratus to his post immediately on the receipt of my letter. Which if thou shouldest defer doing, know that the use of the pallium, granted thee by this See, is taken from thee."[124] Thus we see that, as Pope and 'servant of the servants of God,' Gregory commanded the submission of his bishops. His letters are filled with proclamation after proclamation, and instruction after instruction, for all the bishops, priests, deacons, and churches in the world.

In the specific context of the epistle in question (Epistle XXXIII to Mauricius Augustus), Gregory is concerned about a certain bishop in the province of Augustus who had given himself the title of Universal Priest. Gregory writes:

> "I have however taken care to admonish earnestly the same my brother and fellow-bishop that, if he desires to have peace and concord with all, he must refrain from the appellation of a foolish title...Now I confidently say that whosoever calls himself, or desires to be called, Universal Priest, is in his elation the precursor of Antichrist, because he proudly puts himself above all others."[125]

Hence we see that Gregory is not suggesting that he, as Pope, is not the head of the church or not a bishop over all bishops, but is saying only that someone who is merely the bishop of a certain

---

[123] The Latin reads: "Sanctus Gregorius primus omnium se in principio epistolarum suarum servum servorum Dei satis humiliter definivit."

[124] All quotes taken from NPNF, Vol. 12, pp. 73-104.

[125] Ibid., pp. 225-226.

region cannot call himself a universal bishop or priest. We can glean from just a cursory reading of his letters that Gregory considers himself the head of these bishops. Almost every page drips with evidence of his supreme rule over both the western and eastern churches. Critics of Gregory's rule should first read his epistles in their entirety before drawing conclusions!

Objection #64 (a): "Another statement of Augustine's often cited by Roman apologists, reads: 'I would not have believed had not the authority of the catholic church moved me.' That seems very strong and clear. But in another place Augustine wrote: 'I would never have understood Plotinus had not the authority of my neo-Platonic teachers moved me." This parallel shows that Augustine is not talking about some absolute, infallible authority in the church, but rather about the ministerial work of the church and about teachers who help students understand."[12]

Answer: Unfortunately, this Protestant apologist has drawn a conclusion about Augustine that is true neither of this particular citation nor of any of Augustine's other remarks on the Church. First, it is quite inappropriate to compare Augustine's quote on the Church with his quote on Plotinus. Augustine in any of his writings never encouraged allegiance to Plotinus, but he consistently encouraged and required allegiance to the Church. We can glean this fact directly from the citations given above, by the respective authorities Augustine associates with each, for he speaks of "believing" [in God] as opposed to merely "understanding" Plotinus. When we took philosophy in college we came to "understand" the meaning of Immanuel Kant because we had a college professor who was an authority on his philosophy, but we didn't necessarily "believe" in Mr. Kant. In fact, many of his theories are quite wrong.

Second, if the apologist had bothered to cite the rest of Augustine's quote (he provides neither the reference to Augustine's quote on the Church nor the quote on Plotinus in his citation), it would most assuredly show *what* Augustine meant when he said he "believed in the authority of the Catholic Church," a meaning

---

[126] W. Robert Godfrey, *Sola Scriptura!* p. 17.

which the reader misses because the apologist, instead of giving the quote in full, attempts to prove his point by appealing to an obscure reference to Plotinus. The quote of Augustine's allegiance to the Church is taken from Augustine's *Letter Against Manichaeus*. Manichaeus was a heretic who denied the authority of the Catholic Church and thought of himself as a true apostle. In context Augustine writes:

> I do not believe Manichaeus to be an apostle of Christ...For my part, I should not believe the gospel except as moved by the authority of the Catholic Church...for it was at the command of the Catholics that I believed the gospel...do you think me such a fool as to believe or not to believe as you like or dislike, without any reason? It is therefore fairer and safer by far for me, having in one instance put faith in the Catholics, not to go over to you...To convince me, then, you must put aside the gospel. If you keep the gospel, I will keep to those who commanded me to believe the gospel; and in obedience to them, I will not believe you at all...for it was through the Catholics that I got my faith in it...And who the successor of Christ's betrayer was we read in the Acts of the Apostles; which book I must needs believe if I believe the gospel, since both writings alike Catholic authority commends to me.[127]

In the chapter just prior to these quotes, Augustine says:

> ...the Catholic Church, there are many other things which most justly keep me in her bosom. The consent of peoples and nations keeps me in the Church; so does her authority, inaugurated by miracles, nourished by hope, enlarged by love, established by age. The succession of priests keeps me, beginning from the very seat of the Apostle Peter, to whom the Lord, after His resurrection, gave it in charge to feed His sheep, down to the present episcopate.[128]

---

[127] NPNF, *Against the Epistle of Manichaeus*, Vol. 4, Ch. 5, Art. 6, p. 131.
[128] Ibid., p. 130.

These do not at all sound like Augustine thought of the Church as a mere "teacher who helps students to understand." No, Augustine put his whole faith in what the Catholic Church believed and taught him.

Objection #65: "Even Augustine's famous statement that he 'should not believe the gospel except as moved by the authority of the Catholic Church' should be understood historically, not magisterially, for several reasons...In brief, Augustine argues that, were it not for the historic apostolic truths preserved by the Catholic Church, which contain the revelation given to the apostles and confirmed by miracles, he would not have known the gospel..."[129]

Answer: The apologist has given us a half-truth and has distorted what Augustine really believed. Granted, Augustine, like all the Fathers, held the apostolic tradition preserved by the Catholic Church as infallible. First, in light of this, we will not fail to remind the apologist that the Catholic Church held to many doctrines (e.g., Baptismal Regeneration and the Real Presence of Christ in the Eucharist) that she insisted came from apostolic tradition but from which this apologist dissents. Second, in the previous citation of Augustine's letter to Manichaeus Augustine said: "And who the successor of Christ's betrayer was we read in the Acts of the Apostles; which book I must needs believe if I believe the gospel, since both writings alike Catholic authority commends to me." Augustine wrote this piece to Manichaeus in the year 397 AD, the year the Council of Carthage had given the third conciliar statement on the canon of Scripture (the first was the Council of Rome in 382 and the second the Council of Hippo in 393). Thus we see that when Augustine tells Manichaeus that he accepts the canonicity of the book of Acts, he is accepting the *magisterial* authority of the Catholic Church to determine the canonicity of this book, not merely her historical authority. Augustine, as did all the Fathers, believed that the Church's magisterial decision on the canon was God-ordained and without error.

---

[129] Geisler and MacKenzie, p. 200.

Objection #66: "Augustine declared that 'it is to the canonical Scriptures alone that I am bound to yield such implicit subjection as to follow their teaching, without admitting the slightest suspicion that in them any mistake or any statement intended to mislead could find a place.' This is not an isolated statement, taken out of context, where Augustine gives supreme authority to Scripture alone."[130]

Answer: Although the apologist pleads that this quote from Augustine is not "taken out of context," this is exactly what he has done. First, it is obvious from the discourse with Manichaeus cited previously, Augustine deferred to the Church as his supreme authority, especially in the interpretation of Scripture. Second, in the citation quoted by the apologist, Augustine is writing a letter to Jerome in which he questions Jerome's use of the term *ladamus* (Latin for "let us amuse ourselves") in his description of the character of his discussion about Scripture with Augustine. Augustine explains that he has a very high respect for Jerome's ability to interpret Scripture. Yet as much as he respects Jerome as his superior and one more learned (a very humble approach), nevertheless he tells Jerome that it is not Jerome's ideas that convince him of truth, but the Scriptures alone. In other words, Augustine is telling Jerome, and rightly so, that Scripture is higher than Jerome or the status Jerome has achieved as a Church theologian. This is where the discussion stops. Contrary to what the Protestant apologist is attempting to extract from this discussion, Augustine does not pit Scripture against the Church's authority or its Tradition. He pits Scripture against Jerome, and Jerome only. Yes, it is very dangerous to have citations "taken out of context."

Objection #67: "In the *City of God* Augustine declared that 'He [God] also inspired the Scripture, which is regarded as canonical and of supreme authority and to which we give credence concerning all the truths we ought to know and yet, of ourselves, are unable to learn' (11:3)."[131]

---

130 Geisler and MacKenzie, p. 199, taken from Augustine's *Letters* 82:3 in NPNF, Vol. 1, p. 350.

131 Geisler and MacKenzie, p. 199.

Answer: What the apologist has failed to do is quote the first and last parts of the citation from Augustine. The citation begins as follows: "This Mediator, having spoken what He judged sufficient first by the prophets, then by His own lips, and afterwards by the apostles...and has besides produced the Scriptures which are called canonical..." This shows that Augustine has more in mind than just Scripture as the means by which God has spoken to us. He cites "the prophets," "his [Jesus'] own lips," and "the apostles." It is these *also* that the Church looks to for the voice of God. Further, the last part of the passage reveals Augustine's real intent in extolling Scripture: "For if we attain the knowledge of present objects by the testimony of our own senses, whether internal or external, then, regarding objects remote from our own senses, we need others to bring their testimony, since we cannot know them by our own..." Here Augustine is contrasting *human sense perception* with divine revelation, not pitting Scripture against apostolic Tradition or the authority of the Church. Yes, context is important. (NB: In the remaining citations the apologist gathers from Augustine, the same "out of context" analysis is made). Finally, we may state categorically that in all of Augustine's writings, he never once pits Scripture against the Church's authority or against the apostolic Tradition handed down to him from his predecessors. In every passage where Augustine extols Scripture it is against inferior forms of knowledge and authority.[132]

Objection #68: [After quoting two references to Irenaeus's support of tradition for dogmatic truth (*Against Heresies*, 3, 4:1; 1, 10:2), the Protestant apologist adds the following comments] "Citations such as these seem to carry great weight, until, that is, one looks more closely at the contexts. In both instances one discovers a very important fact. Our author did not fail to define for us exactly what his "tradition" was: 'These have all declared to us that there is one God, Creator of heaven and earth, announced by the

---

[132] This is also true of all the citations from Augustine given by James White in *Sola Scriptura! The Protestant Position on the Bible*, pp. 39-41. Augustine defers to Scripture on many occasions merely because it is the only document to which the heretics and debaters will give allegiance.

law and the prophets; and one Christ, the Son of God...' [*Against Heresies* 3, 1:1]...Here is Irenaeus's "tradition," and we note immediately how it doesn't look anything like Rome's version. The important thing to see, aside from the fact that such items as papal infallibility and the Bodily Assumption of Mary are missing from Irenaeus's definition (items that Rome has defined on the basis of tradition), is that these truths *are derived from the Scriptures themselves*. There is not a single item listed by Irenaeus that cannot be demonstrated directly from the pages of Holy Writ...Irenaeus' view is not a Roman Catholic one."[133]

Answer: What this apologist's juggling of quotes leads us to believe is that Irenaeus did not believe in any Catholic doctrine outside of Scripture; and that Irenaeus believed from Scripture all the doctrines that were "Protestant" and not necessarily Catholic. Protestant apologists commonly take this approach — either they will say that a certain Church Father deferred to Scripture when confronted with a choice between Scripture and Tradition, or they will say that the concept of Tradition in a certain Father is not the same as that of the Catholic Church. The present apologist has chosen the latter argument in this instance.

To answer this, we must first point out that Irenaeus is combating the Gnostic heresy of his day, a heresy which held that God emanated from matter and that Christ was a mere man. Most of his work *Against Heresies* deals with the problem of Gnosticism. Thus, there is no reason for Irenaeus to mention traditions concerning "papal infallibility" and the "Bodily Assumption of Mary" which the Protestant apologist says are "missing from Irenaeus's definition" of tradition. These are arguments from silence. Irenaeus concerns himself only with showing that God is the Creator of all things and that Jesus Christ was God in the flesh because the Gnostics were denying these specific truths. Hence the claim that Irenaeus has a different conception of tradition, merely because he does not mention the papacy and Mary in this particular section of his writings, has no basis whatsoever.

---

133 Ibid., pp. 33-34.

Second, we must point out that although God as Creator and Christ as his divine Son are certainly teachings "derived from the Scriptures themselves," this is just what we would expect. Nothing in Tradition will contradict Scripture. Further, that one can derive from Scripture these two doctrines (God as Creator and Christ as divine Son) does not prove that Irenaeus rejected other doctrines that were only in Tradition but not in Scripture. For example, Irenaeus believed Mary was the new Eve — a doctrine nowhere found in Scripture but readily apparent in Catholic tradition (PG 7, 3, 22, 4; JR 224). He believed that Peter established his ecclesial office in Rome (JR 208); that Matthew wrote his gospel in Hebrew (JR 208); that Mark's gospel is a rendition of Peter's preaching (JR 208). Hence, one cannot claim that all Irenaeus's beliefs from Tradition were "derived" from Scripture.

Third, Irenaeus also believed in doctrines that Tradition says are based on Scripture but that the Protestant apologist would say are not in Scripture. For example, Irenaeus believed in baptismal regeneration (JR 219, 220); infant baptism (JR 201); the real presence of Christ in the Eucharist (JR 234, 249); the Mass as a sacrifice (JR 232, 230); the apostolic succession of bishops (JR 209, 237); and he names the Popes that coincide with the succession (JR 211). Irenaeus bases his belief in these doctrines both on Tradition and Scripture. But if Irenaeus's beliefs are "derived from Scripture," the above list of beliefs certainly do not agree with the Protestant apologist's understanding of Scripture. Hence, not only is Irenaeus' *Tradition* not the same as this Protestant apologist's, but his *interpretation* of Scripture is different as well. Moreover, it is very misleading to claim an affinity with Irenaeus based only on the doctrine that God is Creator and Christ is his divine son. Many Christian, and some non-Christian, religions have similar overlaps with patristic beliefs, but that does not necessarily form an intimate bond between the two.

Fourth, we must take a closer look at Irenaeus's understanding and dependence on Tradition. In *Against Heresies* 1:10:2,3; 2:9:1, Irenaeus writes:

> ...the Church, having received this preaching and this faith, although scattered throughout the whole world, yet, as if oc-

> cupying but one house, *carefully preserves it.* She also believes these points [of doctrine] just as if she had but one soul, and one and the same heart, and she proclaims them, and teaches them, *and hands them down, with perfect harmony*, as it she possessed only one mouth...Nor will any one of the rulers in the Churches, however highly gifted he may be in point or eloquence, teach doctrines different from these...nor, on the other hand, will he who is deficient in power of expression *inflict injury on the tradition*...while the Catholic Church possesses one and the *same faith throughout the whole world*, as we have already said...The Universal Church, moreover, through the whole world, has *received this tradition from the apostles.*

It is very difficult for anyone to read these words and conclude, as the Protestant apologist has so boldly attempted to do, that Irenaeus did not fully ascribe to the Catholic Church and her apostolic Tradition — a Tradition, we have seen above, which included doctrines of Mary, sacramentalism, and clerical succession.

We also see Irenaeus's trust in unwritten Tradition in the very passage posed by the Protestant apologist. In the remainder of *Against Heresies* 2:4:2, he writes:

> Those who, in the *absence of written documents* have believed this faith, are barbarians, so far as regards our language; but as regards doctrine, manner, and tenor of life, they are, because of faith, very wise indeed; and they do please God, ordering their conversation in all righteousness, chastity, and wisdom. If any one were to preach to these men the inventions of the heretics...they would at once stop their ears, and flee as far as possible...Thus, by means of that *ancient tradition of the apostles*, they do not suffer their mind to conceive anything of the [doctrines suggested by the] portentous language of these teachers, among whom *neither Church nor doctrine has ever been established.*

Here Irenaeus explains that those without written documents can, by the established tradition of the apostles as propagated by the Church, be very wise and resist heresy. In view of these statements, does it seem that Irenaeus has a "Protestant" view of Tradition and Scripture? We think not. In truth, those who oppose the truth of the Church, in the words of Irenaeus, "consent neither to Scripture nor to tradition" (*Against Heresies*, 3:2:2).

Objection #69: [After quoting a passage from Basil's *On the Spirit* in NPNF 8:40-41 that supports the belief in tradition for dogma, the Protestant apologist makes the following comment], "Surely here we have the Roman position, do we not? An extrabiblical "tradition" is here posited that would fit quite nicely with Trent, would it not?...No matter how we might view Basil's beliefs, one thing is certain: the matters that he lists as being addressed by 'tradition' are not the very matters that Rome would have us to believe comprise their 'oral tradition.'...Does Rome say we must face to the East in prayer? Does Rome insist upon triune baptism after the Eastern mode? Yet these are practices that Basil defines as being derived from 'tradition.'[134]

Answer: The Protestant apologist is asserting that there were some traditions that Basil cites as originating in the Catholic Church but which the Church no longer practices. From this he implies that Basil's tradition is not the same as the Catholic Church's tradition. Of the eight traditions that Basil cites in his quote, the apologist picks the two that are no longer practiced in the Catholic Church. The other six (i.e., the sign of the cross, the words of invocation during the Eucharist, the blessing of the water of baptism, the blessing of the oil of chrism, the anointing with oil) the apologist leaves out, most likely because they continue to this day in the Catholic Church.[135] The impression that he leaves with the reader is that because there is a conflict between Basil and Rome on just two of these items, therefore, Basil's tradition is not Rome's tradition. Nothing could be further from the truth.

First, anyone familiar with Catholic doctrine knows that the Church reserves the right to change or eliminate *practices* (the very word also used by the Protestant apologist) but not *dogma*. For example, in the 1960's the Catholic Church dispensed with requir-

---

[134] James White, *Sola Scriptura!* pp. 35-37.

[135] They are still practiced, however, in Eastern rite Catholic Churches.

ing its members to abstain from meat on Friday. Theoretically, she could also dispense with the practice of celibacy for her priests, if she desired to do so. The Catholic Church, however, cannot and will not change dogmas such as the deity of Christ, the inspiration of Scripture, the existence of hell and eternal punishment. In light of this distinction, the beliefs of facing east at prayer and triune immersion are just such *practices* that the Church can alter, if indeed the Church had even officially accepted them in the time of Basil. This process of evaluating practices conforms with both Tradition and Scripture. For example, in 1 Cor. 11:5 Paul requires women to wear a head covering in worship. Most churches today, however, do not follow this practice, precisely because they deem it culturally irrelevant. Similarly, in Acts 15 the Church gave specific injunctions to new Gentile converts to abstain from eating blood, strangled animals, or meat offered to idols. Not only does the Church not prohibit these practices today, but just a few years into the New Testament Paul had already relaxed the prohibition against eating meat offered to idols (cf., 1 Cor. 8, 10; Rom. 14).

Lastly, we must turn the tables against the Protestant apologist by focusing on one item in Basil's list of traditions, that is, the tradition of the blessing of and anointing with oil. Though Basil does not mention the biblical reference to this practice, most Protestants will recognize that the most prominent place in New Testament Scripture that records the anointing with oil is James 5:14-15. We point this passage out because James appears to be giving a clear and dogmatic injunction that the Church bring its sick and dying before the elders to be anointed with oil for the purpose of physical and/or spiritual healing. Indeed, the Catholic Church has abided by this stipulation by making the anointing of the sick one of its seven sacraments. On the contrary, one can hardly find this clear biblical teaching anywhere in Protestant churches, including the one to which the present Protestant apologist belongs. Why is this? On what basis can anyone set aside this clear teaching of Scripture, especially since Scripture does not instruct us to dispense with the practice? We might ask the same question about the foot washing Jesus performed in John 13 — a practice that Jesus desired his followers to do ("...Now that I...have washed your feet, you also should wash one another's feet. I have set you an example that you should do as I have done for you"). Granted, the Catholic Church does not require foot-washing either, but she appeals to her authoritative tradition and magisterium for validation. Since Tradition does not serve as a dogmatic authority for Protestantism, on what basis can it eliminate biblical foot-washing? Scripture certainly does not give any validation for dispensing with it. Hence, we have anointing with oil and foot-washing: how do we answer the question as to which one to eliminate, or whether we should eliminate both or neither, if, as is apparent, Scripture gives no explicit information on which to base the decision? In light of this, we must insist that *Sola Scriptura* has not only painted the Protestant into a corner, it has become the very tool that, on the one hand, steals glory from God and graces from his people (especially the graces God offers through the seven sacraments), and on the other hand, leaves the Christian in a sea of doubt about important areas of Scripture that an appeal to Scripture alone simply cannot resolve.[136]

Objection #70: "What is more, other statements from this same Father fly in the face of the Roman claims. For example, when addressing truly important doctrinal truths, such as the very nature of God, Basil did not appeal to some nebulous tradition. How could he, especially when he encountered others who claimed that their traditional beliefs should be held as sacred? Note the words to Eustathius the physician:

> Their complaint is that their custom does not accept this, and that Scripture does not agree. What is my reply? I do not consider it fair that the custom which obtains among them should be regarded as a law and rule of orthodoxy. If custom is to be taken in proof of what is right, then it is certainly competent for me to put forward on my side the custom which

[136] Protestants have the same problem with the role of women in the church. Those who say that women can serve as bishops or elders do so by claiming that Paul's prohibitions against female involvement were intended only for the women of the first century. Their opponents, of course, disagree, but Scripture offers neither side has explicit support Only the Catholic Church can, and does, bar women from the clergy based on Tradition.

> obtains here. If they reject this, we are clearly not bound to follow them. Therefore let God-inspired Scripture decide between us; and on whichever side be found doctrines in harmony with the word of God, in favor of that side will be cast the vote of truth.

"A sentiment hardly in line with Trent!"[137]

Answer: First, we should point out that patristic scholars recognize the above quote as originating in the writings of Gregory of Nyssa, not Basil.[138] Nevertheless, we will deal with the citation as it appears in Basil in NPNF. Our assumption is that the apologist chose this citation from Basil to prove that Basil believed in the doctrine of *sola scriptura*, and indeed, a first reading of it might give such an impression to the uniformed reader. But let's look very closely at what Basil is saying. First, Basil states that his opponent's tradition is *not* to be regarded as the "rule of orthodoxy." Then he says, "If custom is to be taken in proof of what is right, then it is certainly competent for me to put forward on my side the custom which obtains here" showing that it is *his* tradition which is the correct tradition. Thus, on the basis of tradition versus tradition, Basil declares himself the winner. If anything, he is establishing and defending the tradition of the Church, not demoting it. He reinforces his reliance on tradition by saying, "If they reject this [the Church's tradition], we are clearly not bound to follow them.

Having said this, Basil now proceeds to Scripture and suggests that Scripture serve as the judge between them. Considering what Basil said above about his reliance on tradition, are we to assume

---

137 James White, *Sola Scriptura!* pp. 37-38.

138 Patristic scholar Johannes Quasten writes: "Epistle 189 to Eustathius on the Holy Trinity...is generally considered today to be a letter of Gregory of Nyssa written against the Pneumatomachi...The greater part of this treatise is found among the letters of St. Basil as Ep. 189, to whom it has been falsely attributed. This is perhaps the reason that in Migne's edition it does not appear among the works of Gregory" (*Patrology*, 4 vols. (Westminster, Maryland: Christian Classics, 1950-1986) 3:225, 260). The NPNF series includes the citation in both Basil and Gregory of Nyssa (cf. Vol. 8, p. 229 with Vol. 5, p. 327). Perhaps the confusion occurred because Basil and Gregory were brothers.

that Basil is suddenly rejecting his belief in Tradition in favor of Scripture? Not at all. Basil is doing the same thing many of the other Fathers were forced to do: if the opponent did not accept Church tradition or authority then the Father had no recourse but to argue the case from Scripture. Even then, disputes remained unsettled because their opponents would insist on their own interpretation of Scripture, as even Irenaeus complains in *Against Heresies*.[139] Hence Basil is doing the same thing any apologist would do: if the opponent does not accept one arm of his institution, he will use the arm the opponent does accept — in this case, Scripture. We do the same thing in this book. Not often do we argue for Catholic doctrine from Tradition (unless it is obvious that only Tradition has the answer, as in the case of foot-washing and anointing with oil noted above). For the most part we argue from Scripture, because that is all our opponents will accept as authoritative.

We must also add that in Basil's argument from Scripture with his opponents, he spends most of his time *reasoning* out conclusions from the rudimentary but incomplete information that Scripture contains. For example, in the letter to Eustathius that the Protestant apologist cites, Basil is trying to convince his opponents of the divinity and personality of the Holy Spirit. For anyone familiar with Scripture, this is no small task, since Scripture's references to these two characteristics of the Holy Spirit are sparse at best. Hence we find Basil drawing conclusions from Scripture which, from the particular passage he cites, neither speak directly about the Holy Spirit nor contain the conclusion he reaches. Consequently, we find Basil relying mostly on his *reasoning* from Scripture rather than explicit statements in Scripture about the nature of the Holy Spirit. He writes: "Wherefrom *I judge* it *right to hold* that the Spirit, thus conjoined with Father and Son in so many sublime and divine senses, is never separated" (Letters, 189:5); "...there is *no reasonable ground* for refusing to allow the same association in the case of that word alone..." (ibid); "...about things which are beyond our

[139] 3:1:1 - "When, however, they are confuted from the Scriptures, they turn round and accuse these same Scriptures, as if they were not correct, nor of authority, and assert that they are ambiguous, and that the truth cannot be extracted from them by those who are ignorant of tradition."

knowledge *we reason* on probable evidence...fire does not freeze; ice does not warm; differences of natures implies difference of the operations proceeding from them" (189:6); "...nevertheless any one, arguing from what is known to us, would find it *more reasonable* to conclude that the power of the Spirit operates even in those beings..." (189:7); "*It follows* that, even if the name of Godhead does signify nature, the community of essence proves that this title is *very properly* applied to the Holy Spirit" (ibid); "...since we find no variation in the nature, we *reasonably define* the Holy Trinity to be of one Godhead" (189:8).

In light of Basil'smethod, we note also that where the Fathers offered *reasonable* conclusions to be drawn from Scripture concerning the nature of the Holy Spirit, it was the Catholic Councils, affirmed by the respective Popes, that took from Tradition and the *reasoned* conclusions of the Fathers the information they needed to formulate dogmatic proclamations concerning the divinity and personality of the Holy Spirit.

Now, let's treat the passage as it originates in Gregory of Nyssa's writing. Gregory's context is very similar to Basil's. He is in a battle with the Pneumatomachi, who, based on their own tradition, accuse Gregory of "preaching three Gods" or "they allege that while we confess three Persons we say that there is one goodness..."[140] Gregory then states: "But the ground of their complaint is that their custom does not admit this, and Scripture does not support it." Gregory then gives the same reply that Basil gives. Since the Pneumatomachi will not listen to the Tradition or authority of the Church, Gregory goes to Scripture to defend his case. As for Gregory's dedication to the Church and her Tradition he writes:

> For it is enough for proof of our statement, that the tradition has come down to us from our Fathers, handed on, like some inheritance, by succession from the Apostles and the saints who came after them.[141]

---

[140] NPNF, Vol. 5, p. 326.
[141] *Against Eunomius* 4:6.

Objection #71: [Quoting Basil in JR 2:972, the Protestant apologist adds] "Plainly it is a falling away from the faith and an offense chargeable to pride, either to reject any of those things that are written or to introduce things that are not written."[142]

Answer: We would expect the apologist to add this quote, since he has already shown that he misunderstands Basil's view of Tradition and Scripture. As he leaves the quote without explanation, it seems that the apologist desires his reader to assume that the phrase "things that are not written" refers to Church tradition. Perhaps, without even thinking, the reader assumes that this quote proves Basil rejected any teaching that was not in Scripture. By now, however, the reader should readily be able to see the fallacy in this conclusion. Not only does this particular quote not specify what Basil means by "things that are not written," we have already noted, as given to us previously from the Protestant apologist himself, that Basil said, "On what written authority do we do this? Is not our authority silent and mystical tradition?"[143] Hence there are absolutely no grounds for implying that Basil is equating Catholic tradition with "things that are not written"; rather, he is referring to *any extraneous teaching* that was not included in either Tradition or Scripture. Paul tells Timothy the same thing in 1 Timothy 4:1: "Have nothing to do with godless myths and old wives' tales." Yet it was the same Paul who told Timothy "hold onto the traditions given to you, whether by word of mouth or by letter...what you have heard from me keep as the pattern of sound teaching" (2 Thess. 2:15; 2 Tim. 1:13).

Objection #72: [After quoting a section from *To Serapion* in JR 1:336 regarding Athanasius' support of Tradition, the Protestant apologist makes the following objection], "This section is quoted because it is surely liable to be read with modern eyes and understanding, is it not? 'Aha!' comes the cry, 'See! Athanasius speaks of tradition!' But, what does Athanasius *mean* by "tradition"? [Af-

---

[142] James White, *Sola Scriptura!* p. 38.
[143] Cited on page 36 of *Sola Scriptura!* from NPNF 2:8:40-41.

ter quoting the rest of the above citation he continues]: "This is very important, for it is beyond dispute that Athanasius develops, and defends, the Trinity on the basis of Scripture. He does not appeal for this truth to some unwritten revelation that exists *outside* of Scripture..."[144]

Answer: No one will argue that Scripture is part of Athanasius' understanding of Tradition, for that is the Catholic belief as well. But to imply or conclude from this that Athanasius did not hold to unwritten Catholic tradition, or to traditional teaching about Scripture that is in direct opposition to modern Protestant interpretations of Scripture, is simply to misrepresent him. In fact, nowhere in his writings does Athanasius say that Tradition is confined to Scripture. As we have seen with Irenaeus and Basil (the two other Fathers the apologist cited), Athanasius believed in all the doctrines of the Catholic Church (NPNF 4:116, 453, 567); the authority of the Ecumenical council (NPNF 4:104); Mary as 'Mother of God' (JR 788); Mary's perpetual virginity (JR 767a); the stainlessness of Mary (NPNF 4:40); the necessity of baptism (JR 752a); baptismal regeneration (NPNF 4:443); the real presence of Christ in the Eucharist (JR 802); apostolic succession (JR 753; NPNF 4:116); celibacy (NPNF 4:557); the jurisdiction of Rome (NPNF 4:178, 110-118, 282); and many other Catholic doctrines.

As we have seen with other Fathers battling against heretics, most of Athanasius' battle is against those who misinterpret and misuse Scripture. He writes:

> ...in her craft and cunning, affects to array herself in Scripture language, like her father the devil...the author of heresies, because of the ill savor which attaches to evil, borrows Scripture language, as a cloak wherewith to sow the ground with his own poison also, and to seduce the simple...they fall back upon passages of divine Scripture, and here too from want of understanding...they discern not their meaning; but laying down their own irreligion as a sort of canon of inter-

[144] Ibid., p. 43-44.

> pretation, they wrest the whole of the divine oracles into accordance with it.[145]

Objection #73: "How do modern Roman apologists handle statements made by heretics claiming Scriptural backing? Do they not quickly refer to the need of something more than Scripture? Do we not often see the cults and "isms" used as examples of why *sola scriptura* doesn't work? Yet we don't find any such song of praise to "oral tradition" here in Athanasius..."[146]

Answer: Let's just assume, for the sake of argument, that Athanasius did not believe in any teaching not addressed, either implicitly or explicitly, in Scripture. Let's assume that Athanasius desires only to prove his arguments from Scripture, just as the apologist proposed of Basil (or Gregory of Nyssa) when he said, "Therefore let God-inspired Scripture decide between us..." Would we then be forced to conclude that Athanasius did not believe in or rely on Tradition? Not according to Athanasius's following words:

> Afterward, because there were men who used his words, but chose to hear them as suited their lusts...he immediately proceeded to say, "And as I have delivered to you traditions, hold them fast."...But after him and with him are all inventors of unlawful heresies, who indeed refer to the Scriptures, but do not hold such opinions as the saints have handed down, and receiving them as the traditions of men, err, because they do not rightly know them nor their power.[147]

Notice that Athanasius first refers to the Scriptural reference about tradition in 1 Corinthians 11:2. Athanasius complains that these heretics have their own interpretation and "do not hold such opinions as the saints have handed down." Thus, although he often argues from Scripture with his opponents, he does not rest his case with *his* ability to interpret Scripture but with the saints of previous centuries who have handed down the correct interpretation of

---

[145] NPNF 4: *Discourse 1*, pp. 306, 310, 337.

[146] James White, *Sola Scriptura!* p. 46.

[147] NPNF, *Easter Letter II*, 4:511

Scripture. Moreover, he says that the heretics will not accept what the saints have handed down because they receive them as traditions of men rather than as genuine apostolic and ecclesiastical traditions. These heretics did the same thing that many do today — they claimed that *any* teaching outside of Scripture is a "tradition of men." Athanasius says that these heretics "do not know them [the traditional teachings] nor their power [their divine power]." This is precisely why Protestantism has a most difficult time in accepting Catholicism — they invariably fail to distinguish good tradition from bad tradition, preferring to dispense with all tradition under the illusion that Scripture will solve all their problems. Moreover, it will do no good to argue that Athanasius is merely referring to the doctrine of the resurrection — a fact already included in Scripture — when he speaks of tradition in this context. Athanasius insists that Christians accept Tradition's interpretation of the resurrection to rightly understand Scripture's teaching on that doctrine. As we have noted earlier, many teachings in Scripture are highly disputed for the simple reason that Scripture is often unclear about certain topics. For those Protestants who appeal to Athanasius as their mentor, we only need remind them that Athanasius sided with the Catholic interpretation handed down from Tradition on two of the most important, yet arguably two of Scripture's more difficult teachings, that is, Baptismal Regeneration and the Real Presence of Christ in the Eucharist. In fact, virtually no one in patristic Catholic tradition disputed these doctrines. Hence, while Athanasius was certainly a lover of Scripture, he was neither a despiser of Tradition nor a mentor of Protestantism.

Objection #74: "What then of the positive testimony from Athanasius? We note first and foremost the plain words from his work against the heathen: 'For indeed the holy and God-breathed Scriptures are self-sufficient for the preaching of the truth.'...he begins where Protestants and Roman Catholics part company: with the sufficiency of Scripture...The high view of Scripture is continued in this passage from Athanasius's work on the Incarnation of the Word of God: ... 'But you, taking occasion by this, if you light upon the text of the Scriptures, by genuinely applying your mind to them, will learn from them more completely and clearly the exact detail of what we have said. For they were spoken and written by God, through men who spoke for God.'"[148]

Answer: The first thing we must recognize in order to understand Athanasius's "high view of Scripture" is that in much of his writing he is referring to the doctrine of the Incarnation. Much of what Athanasius wrote concerns his controversy with the Arians, who did not believe in the deity of Christ. Athanasius puzzles at why the Arians distort such seemingly clear passages as Isaiah 7:14 and Matthew 1:23: "But what does that mean, if not that God has come in the Flesh?" (NPNF 4:577). In Athanasius's opinion, these Scriptures are clear and sufficient to provide the necessary truth about the nature of Christ. We have the same frustrations today when we battle with Jehovah Witnesses who deny the deity of Christ. What seems clear to us in John 1:1 is not clear to them. Be that as it may, even if Scripture is as clear as Athanasius believes it to be on the issue of Christ's deity, he concedes that Scripture does not precisely define the issue as perhaps other God-given authorities can define it, namely, the Council of Nicea which introduced the term *homoousios* into dogma to clarify Christ's nature more exactly (NPNF 4:172). This council's definition forever sealed the line of demarcation between orthodoxy and heterodoxy. It was the Magisterium that came to the rescue to clarify the "sufficient" Scripture.

In these arguments we must remember that "sufficiency" is a relative term, subject to the conceptions of those who use it. The main question is: what is Scripture sufficient ***for***? Is it sufficient for general knowledge of salvation, how we can best glorify God, specific doctrines and practices, history and science? And what degree of sufficiency can one expect from Scripture? Does Scripture exhaust a particular dogma, is its information implicit or explicit, does it ignore certain dogmas, and if it does ignore them what are we to believe and to whom do we go for answers? Hence to argue that Athanasius stood for the "sufficiency" of Scripture is an open mine-field, subject to a high degree of misrepresentation

[148] James White, *Sola Scriptura!* p. 49.

and distortion. This is especially true since "sufficiency," as much as Athanasius preferred to use Scriptural terminology, is not a term Scripture uses to describe itself.[149] What we have discovered so far, however, is that as much as Athanasius used Scripture, probably more than some Protestants do today, he still remained faithful to all the doctrines of the Catholic Church, claiming to find in Scripture the very doctrines that most Protestants deny today, including the present Protestant apologist. We have also discovered that Athanasius, though he was one of the most competent and

---

149 Quoting from Athanasius's statement, "...and God-breathed Scriptures are self-sufficient for the preaching of the truth," in footnote 41, p. 61, White focuses on Athanasius's use of the Greek word αὐτάρκεις, which Bauer and others define as "sufficiency, a competence" and "contentment, self-sufficiency." White then cites the use of αὐτάρκεις in 2 Corinthians 9:8 as biblical support for this definition of the word. In reply, we argue that αὐτάρκεις means "sufficiency," but αὐτάρκεις never appears in connection with Scripture. The word appears twice in the New Testament (2 Cor. 9:8 and 1 Tim. 6:6). In the first passage it is the *grace of God*, not Scripture, which Paul deems as sufficient. Since the grace of God is multifaceted, we can understand why Paul would assign "sufficiency" to it but not to Scripture, since Scripture is one-dimensional revelation.

We would also take issue with White's next footnote, #42, where he faults Catholic apologists for attempting "to weaken the term ὠφέλιμος" ("profitable") in 2 Tim. 3:16. White claims that Athanasius's statement "γραφὰς ἱκανὰς εἶναι πρὸς διδασκαλίαν" ("Scripture is good [or worthy, sufficient] for instruction") is parallel to and serves as a commentary on Paul's use of "ὠφέλιμος." He concludes with the statement, "Roman apologists must utterly reject Athanasius' obvious understanding of the term 'profitable' in 2 Timothy 3:16 as referring to sufficiency and adequacy" (p. 62). In reply we must first point out that if there ever was an opportunity for Paul to use either αὐτάρκεις or ἱκανὰς to describe Scripture, (if indeed he had the concept of sufficiency in his mind), that opportunity would have been in 2 Timothy 3:16 where he is describing Scripture's very nature and purpose. Moreover, White's strained connection between Athanasius and 2 Timothy 3:16 becomes apparent when we discover that: (1) the New Testament never refers to *Scripture* as ἱκανὰς, but rather refers to *men* in 2 Tim. 2:2 who are able to teach *sufficiently* after having received oral instruction, and (2) Athanasius never exegetes or even refers to 2 Timothy 3:16 in all of his writings. Thus, while this Protestant apologist has offered many suppositions, he has not presented any positive proof or even strong evidence that what he is claiming for Athanasius is indeed true. We would suggest that if one wants to define and describe the usage of biblical words then one must start by examining the way the *Bible* uses those words.

knowledgeable Scripture scholars of his day, consistently deferred the ultimate interpretation of Scripture to those who had gone before him, *never once* denying any traditional interpretation that had been handed down to him. If the Protestant apologist could demonstrate instances in which Athanasius had rejected the official dogmatic interpretation of the Church prior to him, he would have reason to question Athanasius's view of Tradition; but, in fact, there are no such instances.

As we close this section on Athanasius, let us go back to our present apologist's initial quote from Athanasius: "...the Scriptures, by genuinely applying your mind to them, will learn from them more completely and clearly the exact detail of what we have said. For they were spoken and written by God, through men who spoke for God."[150] What the apologist did not quote was the rest of the paragraph, which reads: "But we impart of what *we have learned from inspired teachers who have been conversant with them*, who have also become martyrs for the deity of Christ, to your zeal for learning, in turn." Again, Athanasius is not resting on his own laurels as a mighty exegete of Scripture, but on the *inspired teachers* and those who *have conversed with them*. The *inspired teachers* were the apostles and those that *conversed with them* were the Fathers succeeding them, as Athanasius writes elsewhere: "But our faith is right, and starts from the teaching of the Apostles and tradition of the fathers, being confirmed both by the New Testament and the Old" (NPNF 4:576-577).

Objection #75: "Concerning sola Scriptura, at least in the material sense, there is more unanimity than one would expect...Even some great Catholic theologians, such as Aquinas, can be cited in support of this position: "we believe the successors of the apostles and prophets only in so far as they tell us those things which the apostles and prophets have left in their writings..."[151]

Answer: As we have often found, some apologists "read into" an author what they want to see, extract quotes without providing the

[150] James White, *Sola Scriptura!* p. 50, from NPNF 4:66.

[151] Geisler and MacKenzie, pp. 33, 201. From *De Veritate* XIV, 10, ad 11.

context to the reader, and do not cite other statements from the author that would shed a different light on the apologists' conclusion. For example, Aquinas also said: "The formal object of faith is Primary Truth as manifested in Holy Scripture and in the teaching of the Church which proceeds from the Primary Truth. Hence, he who does not embrace the teaching of the Church as a divine and infallible law does not possess the habit of faith."[152] Thus one can easily see that not only does Aquinas direct his reader to the Church, but he also emphasizes that the Church houses the truth of Scripture, and that the Church, not just the Scripture, is a divine and *infallible* entity. This is quite different from the impression the present Protestant apologist conveys to an untrained reader.

Now, let's look more closely at the quote he chose from Aquinas. Does Aquinas say that he does not hold the Church as infallible or that he does not believe in Tradition? Certainly not. Aquinas is speaking only about one thing: that the Church's theologians must be faithful to Scripture, no more, no less. Aquinas, and the whole Catholic Church, would certainly condemn a Church theologian who said something in flat contradiction to Scripture. Consequently, if this is the best quote from Aquinas the apologist can muster to prove his point — a citation that he apparently feels is very important since he quotes it twice in his book— then we can safely conclude that Aquinas did not teach the Protestant doctrine of *sola scriptura*.

The apologist also quotes Aquinas as saying, "it is heretical to say that any falsehood whatsoever is contained either in the gospels or in any canonical Scripture."[153] Once again, Aquinas is not saying anything in regard to *sola scriptura*, but is merely extolling the inerrancy of Scripture.

---

[152] *Summa Theologica*, II-II, q. 5, a. 3.

[153] Geisler and MacKenzie, p. 201. From the *Commentary on the Book of Job* 13, lecture 1.

Chapter 6

What did the Protestant Reformers Teach about *Sola Scriptura*?

by Robert Fastiggi

We can understand the Protestant Reformation of the 16th century according to several characteristic principles, each beginning with the Latin word for "only." First, "Christ alone" (*solus Christus*) is the Savior; salvation comes by means of His "grace alone" (*sola gratia*) and is apprehended "by faith alone" (*sola fide*). Secondly, glory is to be given to God alone (*soli Deo gloria*), not to Mary, the angels or the saints. Finally, there is the belief that "Scripture alone" (*sola scriptura*) is the sole and sufficient rule of the Christian faith.

Christians of today who call themselves "Evangelical," "Reformed," or "Protestant" all accept the principle of *sola scriptura* as one of the defining characteristics of true Christianity. Individual churches and pastors often proclaim the "bible only" as the source of their teaching. To be called "bible-centered" or "bible-based" is, for many, the first sign of fidelity to the Christian message.

The multiplicity of denominations and sects all claiming to be "bible-based" shows that simply claiming the "bible only" as one's rule is no guarantee of uniform doctrine. The same Bible which persuaded Luther that Christ is really present "in, with and under" the bread and wine is the same Bible which persuaded Zwingli that Christ is only spiritually present in the sacrament. The Anabaptists, who denied the validity of infant baptism, read the same scriptures as the Calvinists, Lutherans and Anglicans who retained infant baptism. All this points to a need to understand what the original

Protestant Reformers taught about the Bible and how they regarded the Scriptures as the rule of faith.

Varieties of Protestantism

The Protestant Reformation was not monolithic. Although the Protestants shared a common conviction that Rome was in error, they were often in disagreement among themselves on a number of theological issues. Most historians divide the sixteenth century Protestants into four main groups: the Lutherans, the Calvinists, the Anglicans and the Radicals. As with all classifications, these are not perfect. For example, the Swiss reformer, Ulrich Zwingli (1484-1531) and the French reformer, Martin Bucer (1491-1551) cannot adequately be called "Calvinists" since they both developed their theologies prior to that of John Calvin (1509-1564) and they both, in fact, influenced his thought.

The Radical reformers were likewise a diverse group. There were those who rejected infant baptism (and thus were called the Anabaptists or "rebaptizers") like Menno Simons (1496-1561), Melchior Hoffman (1500-1543) and Thomas Müntzer (c. 1490-1525). There were also men like Juan de Valdes (1500-1541) and Sebastian Frank (1488-1542) who were called Spiritualists because they stressed the personal inspiration of the Holy Spirit. Finally, there were Rationalists like Michael Servetus (1511-1553) and Faustus Socinus (1539-1604) who denied the Trinity.

In light of this diversity within sixteenth century Protestantism, it is important to examine each movement separately. As we will see, all the Protestant groups emphasized the authority of Scripture, and some, quite explicitly, endorsed the principle of *sola scriptura*. We will also observe, however, that Protestants did not always follow this principle consistently and they often made implicit appeals to an authority other than Scripture.

Martin Luther and the Lutherans

Although the doctrine of *sola scriptura* has historical antecedents in theologians like John Wycliff (1320-1384) and John Hus (1369-1415), it is sixteenth century Protestantism which gives this principle its clearest and most enthusiastic endorsement.[1] In many respects, Martin Luther's famous answer given before the Diet of Worms on April 18, 1521 serves as a foundational articulation of the "Bible alone" principle:

> Your Imperial Majesty and Your Lordships demand a simple answer. Here it is, plain and unvarnished. Unless I am convicted of error by the testimony of Scriptures or (since I put no trust in the unsupported authority of Pope or of councils, since it is plain that they have often erred and often contradicted themselves) by manifest reasoning I stand convicted by the Scriptures to which I have appealed, and my conscience is taken captive by God's word, I cannot and will not recant anything, for to act against one's conscience is neither safe for us, nor open to us. On this I take my stand. I can do no other. God help me. Amen.[2]

This plea of Martin Luther (1483-1546) contains most of the basic elements of the Protestant *sola scriptura* principle. The authority of Scripture stands above that of the Pope and councils. The believer is held captive by God's Word, and no person can be said to be in error unless this can be manifestly demonstrated by biblical texts.

It is important, though, to see that Luther also appeals to two other sources of authority other than Scripture: namely, "manifest reasoning" and "conscience." Both of these, however, are quite

---

1 Whether Wycliff and Hus taught the principle of *sola scriptura* in the same manner as the sixteenth century Protestants is a matter of scholarly debate. The German scholar, H.G. Reventlow, has warned that equating Wycliff's position with that of Luther "would be to misunderstand Wycliff's attitude completely." H.G. Reventlow, *The Authority of the Bible and the Rise of the Modern World*, John Bowden, trans. (Philadelphia:Fortress Press, 1985), p. 32. Another German scholar, Bernhard Lohse, has written that: "Both the early and medieval church took the authority of Scripture for granted, although at certain points they did so in different ways. The principle of 'Scripture Alone' was never advocated before Luther, however." Bernhard Lohse, *Martin Luther: An Introduction to His Life and Work*, Robert C. Schultz, trans. (Philadelphia: Fortress Press, 1986)., p. 153.

2 Henry Bettenson, ed., *Documents of the Christian Church*, Second Edition (London: Oxford University Press, 1963), p. 199.

subjective in nature. It is Luther who must decide whether the "manifest reasoning" is convincing, and it is Luther who must decide how and in what way his conscience is taken captive by God's word. Thus, this foundational articulation of the Protestant *sola scriptura* principle contains inherent problems. Who is to decide whether arguments given from either Scripture or reason are persuasive? The ultimate arbiter of the meaning and authority of Scripture appears to be the subjective whims of the individual person rather than the Church Christ established.

Luther's articulation of the *sola scriptura* principle must be understood in the light of several theological tensions which underlie his writings. The first of these tensions is that between the Law and the Gospel, and the second is that between the Word of God and the Bible. For Luther, the essence of the Gospel is the doctrine of justification by means of faith alone. The Law of God has a civic function of restraining human wickedness. Its theological function, however, is to reveal the depth of our sinfulness and turn us towards Christ. All the parts of the Bible, therefore, which speak of the Law (whether in the Old or the New Testaments) must be understood in light of salvation through faith alone.

This first theological tension helps to explain why Luther believes that not all Scriptural books are equally authoritative. In his *Preface to the New Testament*, he establishes a "canon within the canon of scripture." He speaks of John's Gospel as "the one, fine, true, and chief gospel, and is far, far to be preferred over the other three and placed high above them."[3] In contrast to the traditional theological and liturgical priority given to the Gospels, Luther states that "the epistles of St. Paul and St. Peter far surpass the other three gospels, Matthew, Mark, and Luke."[4]

Ranking some scriptures above others, Luther asserts that "St. James' epistle is really an epistle of straw, compared to these others, for it has nothing of the nature of the gospel about it."[5] In another context, Luther makes it clear that he does not consider the

---

3 Timothy F. Lull, editor *Martin Luther's Basic Theological Writings* (Minneapolis: Fortress Press, 1989), p. 117.

4 Ibid.

5 Ibid.

Epistle of James "to be of apostolic authorship" because "in direct opposition to St. Paul and all the rest of the Bible, it ascribes justification to works..."[6] Luther's logic is that "what does not teach Christ is not apostolic, not even if taught by Peter or Paul."[7] For Luther, "the epistle of James... only drives you to the law and its works."[8] The author of this Epistle, moreover, "does violence to Scripture, and so contradicts Paul and all of Scripture."[9] Luther concludes by saying: "*I therefore refuse him a place among the true canon of my Bible*; but I would not prevent anyone placing him or raising him where he likes, for the epistle contains many excellent passages"[10] (emphasis mine).

We can see that the dialectical tension Luther created between the Law and the Gospel qualifies the *sola scriptura* doctrine. It is not simply the Bible which is the sole and sufficient rule of truth, but only those parts of the Bible which preach the Gospel (at least as Luther understands the Gospel). Thus, the whole of Scripture must be read through the lens of Luther's theological perspective. This makes it difficult to challenge Luther's theology on the basis of scriptural texts. Since those parts of the Bible which disagree with his theology are not deemed as authoritative as those which support his theology, Luther can dismiss those scriptures which do not teach his understanding of the Gospel. These lesser Scriptures, no doubt, would be, in Luther's mind, those that emphasize the Law rather than the Gospel.

Who, though, is to decide what the Gospel is? Luther's reasoning is circular. He claims that his understanding of the Gospel is correct because those Scriptures which support his understanding are those which are truly Gospel-oriented, and those scriptures which do not support his understanding are those which are not sufficiently Gospel-oriented. All this ultimately adds up to the con-

---

6 Martin Luther, "Preface to the Epistles of St. James and St. Jude," in John Dillenberger, editor *Martin Luther: Selections from His Writings* (Garden City, N.Y.: Doubleday Anchor, 1961), p. 35.

7 Ibid., p. 36.

8 Ibid.

9 Ibid.

10 Ibid.

clusion that whatever Luther believes is the true meaning of the Gospel is the true meaning of the Gospel.

The other theological tension we must investigate is that between the Word of God and the Bible. The contemporary Lutheran scholar, Jaroslav Pelikan, notes that when Luther speaks of "The Word of God," he sometimes means the scriptures but most of the time he is referring to Christ's message of salvation.[11] The Protestant historian, Justo Gonzalez, likewise observes that "the Word of God" for Luther could refer to the Scriptures, or "the eternal second Person of the Trinity" or "God's power as manifested in the creation of all things," or "the Incarnate Lord," or "the proclamation through which the Word in Scripture is actually heard by the believers."[12]

Luther articulates the distinction in these terms: "God and the Scriptures of God are two things, no less than the Creator and the creature are two things."[13] He also speaks of the Holy Scriptures as the cloths "in which the Christian faith lies wrapped up."[14] Passages such as these lead Bernhard Lohse to observe that Luther can describe the relationship between God's Word and the Bible in three ways: first, Luther "identifies the Bible and the Word of God;" Second, he identifies the Word as "the real content of the Bible" without strictly equating it with "the external form" of the scriptures; and, third, he can refer to "a dialectical relationship" between the Word and the Bible in a way analogous to the relationship of Creator and the creature.[15]

For Luther, the dialectic between the Word and the Bible enables him to place Christ at the center of Scripture. As he writes: "Take Christ out of the Scriptures, and what will you have left in

---

[11] Jaroslav Pelikan, *Luther's Works: Companion Volume: Luther, the Expositor* (St. Louis: Concordia Publishing House, 1959), pp. 66-67.

[12] Justo Gonzalez, *A History of Christian Thought, Vol. III From the Protestant Reformation to the Twentieth Century* (Nashville: Abingdon, 1975), p. 41.

[13] *The Bondage of the Will* in J. Pelikan et. al., editors *Luther's Works* , (henceforth LW) (St. Louis and Philadelphia: Concordia and Fortress Press, 1955-1986), vol. 33, p. 25.

[14] *The Gospel for Christmas Eve*; LW 52:21.

[15] Lohse, p. 156.

them?"[16] Hence, in Luther's mind, priority should be given to certain biblical books because some books show forth Christ more clearly. He points to "St. John's Gospel and his first epistle, St. Paul's epistles, especially Romans, Galatians and Ephesians, and St. Peter's first epistle" as "the books that show you Christ and teach you all that is necessary and salvatory for you to know, even if you were never to see or hear any other book or doctrine."[17] Here again we see that not all Scriptures are equal. Those that, in Luther's mind, manifest Christ and the Gospel most perfectly have priority over those that do not.

The dialectical relationship Luther perceives between God's Word and the biblical text qualifies his *sola scriptura* doctrine in a manner similar to the way his distinction between Law and the Gospel qualifies the doctrine. To Luther, when appealing to Scripture, it is not sufficient that a biblical text be cited. It must also be determined whether the biblical text adequately manifests God's Word. Here again, though, there is a problem. Who is to decide whether a given biblical text manifests God's Word more perfectly than another biblical text? We see again that Luther's approach to Scripture ultimately relies on a subjective criterion. It is *Luther's* theological perspective which is the ultimate standard of truth rather than the Scriptures themselves.

These theological considerations help us understand Luther's approach to the clarity of Scripture. Probably the most important text on this issue is Luther's *De servo arbitrio* (*On The Bondage of the Will*) which is written in 1525 as a response to the 1524 tract, *De libero arbitrio* (*On the Freedom of the Will*), written by Desiderius Erasmus (c.1469-1536). According to Erasmus, some passages of the Bible have "utmost clarity" such as those dealing with "the precepts for a morally good life."[18] However, "Holy Scripture contains numerous passages which have puzzled many, without ever anyone succeeding in completely clarifying them."[19]

16 *The Bondage of the Will*; LW 33:26

17 *Preface to the New Testament*; Lull, p. 117.

18 Ernst Winter, trans. and ed. *Erasmus-Luther: Discourse on Free Will* (New York: Frederick Ungar, 1961), pp. 9- 10.

19 Ibid., p. 9.

Luther's response to this is that "the Holy Spirit is no sceptic, and what He has written into our hearts are no doubts or opinions, but assertions, more certain and more firm than all human experience and life itself."[20]

Luther concedes that there are certain passages of Scripture which "are obscure and hard to elucidate, but that is due not to the exalted nature of their subject, but to our own linguistic and grammatical ignorance."[21] However, he maintains that, since the revelation of Christ, "the entire content of the Scriptures has now been brought to light, even though some passages which contain many unknown words remain obscure."[22] If people find the contents of Scripture obscure, Luther contends that this is due "not to any lack of clarity in Scripture, but to their own blindness and dullness, in that they make no effort to see truth which, in itself, could not be plainer."[23]

Luther goes on to make a distinction between the external perspicuity or clarity of Scripture and the internal perspicuity. As he sees it, the external clarity of Scripture must be affirmed. He maintains that "nothing whatsoever is left obscure or ambiguous, but that all that is in the Scripture is through the Word brought forth in the clearest light and proclaimed to the whole world."[24] However, the external clarity of the Bible is only perceived by those who have been given the gift of internal perspicuity by the Holy Spirit. As Luther writes: "the truth is that nobody who has not the Spirit of God sees a jot of what is in the Scriptures."[25] Those without the Spirit "can discuss and quote all that is in Scripture," but "they do not understand or really know any of it."[26] This is because "the Spirit is needed for the understanding of all Scripture and every part of Scripture."[27]

---

[20] Ibid., p. 103.

[21] *Bondage of the Will*; Dillenberger, p. 172.

[22] Ibid.

[23] Ibid., p. 173.

[24] Ibid., p. 175.

[25] Ibid., p. 174.

[26] Ibid.

[27] Ibid., pp. 174-175.

We now see another qualification to Luther's *sola scriptura* doctrine. All truths of the faith must be supported by the Scriptures, and "the teachings of the fathers are useful only to lead us to the Scriptures...and then we must hold to the Scriptures alone."[28] However, even though the Scriptures alone are the supreme authority, they themselves cannot be correctly understood unless a person is guided by the Holy Spirit. But, we ask, how do we know if someone has the Holy Spirit guiding him? Luther would simply respond by pointing to *his* correct understanding of the Scriptures. But this is just another way of saying that those who understand Scripture correctly are those who have the Holy Spirit. This, of course, leads Luther to conclude that those who do not understand Scripture (as he does) must not have the Holy Spirit. Thus, the ultimate norm for the possession of the Holy Spirit appears to be none other than one's agreement with Luther's theology.

Such a circular and subjective method helps to explain, at least in part, why Luther often lapses into acrimonious language when describing those who disagree with his interpretation of the Bible. Those who challenge his understanding of Scripture must be bereft of the Holy Spirit and enemies of God's Word. Thus, he laments that the fifth chapter of Matthew's Gospel "has fallen into the hands of the vulgar pigs and asses, the jurists and the sophists, the right hand of that jackass of a pope and of his mamelukes."[29] Out of "the beautiful rose" of this Scripture, "they have sucked and broadcast poison, covering up Christ with it and elevating and maintaining Antichrist."[30] Those theologians who maintain that 1 Cor. 13: 1ff. shows that faith, in order to be justifying, must be "formed and furnished with charity" are, according to Luther, "men without understanding" who can "see or understand nothing in Paul."[31] These theologians are promoting "a pernicious and pestilent gloss," "a most deadly and devilish poison," and, in the pro-

---

[28] "Answer to the SuperChristian, Superspiritual, and Superlearned Book of Goat Emser" in Hugh T. Kerr, Jr., ed. *A Compend of Luther's Theology* (Philadelphia: The Westminster Press, 1943), p. 14.

[29] *Preface to the Sermon on the Mount*; LW 21:3. Mamelukes were the military slaves of the Turkish Emperor.

[30] Ibid.

cess, they have "not only perverted the words of Paul, but have also denied Christ, and buried all his benefits."[32]

Of course, not all the members of the Lutheran movement wrote with such rhetorical acrimony, but in Luther a persistent pattern is present in which his opponents are portrayed as enemies of God, and those who challenge his understanding of the Bible oppose God's Word and are agents of the Devil and the Anti-Christ. All this demonstrates Luther's ultimate reliance on his own personal authority as a rule along with the rule of Scripture. Indeed, in the seventeenth-century, Lutheran Orthodoxy pointed to Revelation 14:6 as a prophecy of the divine mission of Luther: "Then I saw another angel flying in midheaven, with an eternal gospel to proclaim to those who dwell on earth, to every nation and tribe and tongue and people."[33] Bernhard Lohse observes that Lutheran theologians "ascribed to him the exercise of an almost infallible teaching office — comparable to the office that they denied to the pope."[34]

Luther himself says that, as a preacher, he has "the official responsibility" of defending God's word, and, therefore, he must rebuke "the pope, the bishops, the princes, and all the rest, who are persecuting the Gospel and trampling its poor adherents underfoot."[35] Furthermore, he must say to them:

> I am a preacher. I have to have teeth in my mouth. I have to bite and salt and tell them the truth. And if they refuse to hear, then in the name of God I have to excommunicate them, lock them out of heaven and consign them to the fire of hell, and turn them over to the devil.[36]

Thus, Luther has not only the authority to decide what the Scriptures teach, but he also has the authority to send to hell those who disagree with his interpretations — the very thing for which he castigated the Catholic Church.

---

[31] *Commentary on Galatians*; Dillenberger, pp. 115-116.

[32] Ibid.

[33] See Lohse, p. 203.

[34] Ibid.

[35] *The Sermon on the Mount*; LW 21:123-124.

[36] Ibid. p. 124.

The official statements of Lutheranism do not explicitly speak of Luther's "infallibility." *The Formula of Concord* (1577), however, does refer to "the Small and Large Catechisms of Dr. Luther" as "the Bible of the laity."[37] This can be understood as an implicit recognition of Luther's divine guidance in interpreting Scripture. Of course, *The Formula* also teaches and confesses "that the only rule and standard according to which at once all dogmas and teachers are to be esteemed and judged are nothing else than the prophetic and apostolic Scriptures of the Old and New Testament."[38]

The Formula does recognize writings other than Scripture as "witnesses" to the truth. Thus, the articles of the Apostles Creed, the Nicene Creed and the Athanasian Creed are considered "binding." Moreover, "The First and Unaltered Augsburg Confession... together with its Apology, and the Articles composed at Smalcald in the year 1577" are upheld as "the symbol of our time" in opposition to "the Papacy, and its false worship, idolatry, superstition, and against other sects."[39] Writings such as these, however, "should not be regarded as of equal authority with the Holy Scriptures, but should altogether be subordinated to them, and should not be received other or further than as witnesses."[40] These creeds and symbols, though, do provide a "direction" according to which "all doctrines should be adjusted, and that what is contrary thereto should be rejected and condemned as opposed to the unanimous declaration of our faith."[41]

The Lutheran articulation of *sola scriptura*, therefore, recognizes certain extra-biblical texts as providing a normative "direction" for the Christian faith. However, *The Formula of Concord* insists that "the Holy Scriptures alone remain the only judge, rule and standard, according to which, as the only test- stone, all dogmas should be discerned and judged, as to whether they be good or evil, right or wrong." The other authoritative symbols and writings

---

37 J. Mordon Melton, ed. *The Encyclopedia of American Religions: Religious Creeds* (Detroit: Gate Research Company, 1988), p. 70.

38 Ibid., pp. 69-70.

39 Ibid. p. 70.

40 Ibid.

41 Ibid.

"are not judges, as are the Holy Scriptures" but only "a witness and declaration of the faith, as to how at any time the Holy Scriptures have been understood and explained in the articles in controversy in the Church of God..."[42]

In the writings of Martin Luther and the Lutheran tradition, we see an appeal to the Bible as the only "judge, rule and standard" of the Christian faith. Luther's theology, however, exhibits a dialectic between (1) the Law and the Gospel, and (2) the Word and the written text which devolves into a recognition of some parts of the Bible as more evangelical and more expressive of God's Word than others. The true meaning of Scripture is only clear to those guided by the Holy Spirit, and, by implication, it is only Luther who is guided by the Holy Spirit while those who disagree with him are not. Thus, the Lutheran principle of *sola scriptura* is qualified by a theological tradition which ascribes a normative status not simply to Scripture but also to the *Lutheran* interpretation of Scripture.

The Calvinist/Reformed Understanding of Sola Scriptura

The Protestant Reformation in Switzerland and France was similar to the Lutheran Reformation in Germany, but it took on its own unique characteristics. Ulrich Zwingli (1484-1531) was a Swiss scholar who was influenced by Erasmus, but unlike him, Zwingli felt that the ecclesiastical and sacramental system of the Catholic Church was fundamentally flawed. Zwingli, like Luther, maintained that the Scriptures are the ultimate rule of Christian truth, and like Luther, he also believed that the "living Word of God" is more than just the written text. For Zwingli "the Word is mediated through the written documents, but it has its character and effectiveness as Word only in so far as it is directed by the Holy Spirit."[43]

Zwingli, like Luther, believed that an understanding of the external text of Scripture could only be achieved when the Holy Spirit

---

[42] Ibid.

[43] G.W. Bromiley, *Zwingli and Bullinger* (Philadelphia: The Westminster Press, 1953), p. 55.

provides "an internal apprehension of the divine teaching which the Scripture proclaims."[44] According to Zwingli, "everyone who approaches the Bible in prayer and in faith must inevitably come to the same general apprehension of [the Scripture's] truth..."[45] As Zwingli writes, "when the Word of God shines on the human understanding, it enlightens it in such a way that it understands and confesses the Word and knows the certainty of it."[46]

Zwingli's doctrine of the clarity of the Scriptures is similar to Luther's and has similar problems. While prayer, faith and the guidance of the Holy Spirit are necessary for a clear understanding of the Bible, we need to ask what happens when two men, both claiming to be guided by the Holy Spirit, come to different interpretations of the same biblical text. This, in fact, is what occurred at the famous Colloquy at Marburg (1529) when Luther and Zwingli (among others) could not come to an agreement on the meaning of the Eucharist as expressed in the New Testament.

For Zwingli, the key passage was John 6:63: "It is the spirit which gives life; the flesh is useless." For him, this established the truth of a figurative or spiritual presence of Christ in the Eucharist. As he told Luther: "This is the passage that will break your neck!"[47] For Luther, the words of Christ, "This is my body" (Mat. 26:26 and Luke 22:19) were sufficient to prove that Christ must be truly and bodily present in the Eucharist. Thus, he reminded Zwingli: "'This is my body!' Right here is our Scripture. You haven't torn it away from us like you promised to do. We need none other."[48] Thus, both men claimed to know the truth on the basis of the Bible, but different passages of the Bible led each man to a different conclusion. In the final analysis, it was agreed that "both sides should diligently pray to Almighty God that through his Spirit he might confirm us in the right understanding."[49]

---

44 Ibid., p. 56.

45 Ibid. p. 57.

46 *Clarity and Certainty of the Word of God*; Bromiley, p. 75.

47 Donald J. Ziegler, ed. Great Debates of the Reformation (New York: Random House, 1969), p. 86.

48 Ibid., 98.

49 LW 38:89.

The experience at Marburg presents a challenge to both Zwingli's and Luther's doctrine of the clarity of Scripture. The inability to reach consensus on the manner of Christ's presence in the Eucharist at the Colloquy could suggest several possibilities: 1) One side had the Holy Spirit guiding its interpretation of the Bible, and the other side did not. 2) Neither side had sufficient guidance from the Holy Spirit to correctly interpret the biblical text; 3) the Holy Spirit does not always provide sufficient clarity in interpreting a given Scriptural text. If possibility number one is true, then one branch of the Protestant Reformation was deluded. If number two is true, then both branches were deluded. If number three is true, then the doctrine of the clarity of Scriptures is proven false.

Some Protestants might suggest that the issue of Christ's presence in the Eucharist falls into the category of "adiaphora" or "a matter of indifference." If this were the case, however, we must ask why, at the Colloquy of Marburg, Luther and Zwingli, spent "a half day" arguing over the meaning of John 6:63 — "the flesh is of no avail."[50] Surely, the issue did not seem to be "a matter of indifference" to them. If the issue of the Eucharist were not of essential importance to the faith, why would it be cause for a division between the Lutheran and Reformed branches of the Reformation? A matter of indifference would not be a just reason for separate ecclesiastical communities.

Along with Zwingli, another theologian present at the Colloquy was Martin Bucer (1491-1551) who was dedicated to the cause of developing a mediating position acceptable to both the Lutheran and Swiss branches of Protestantism.[51] While Bucer can rightfully be described as a "scriptural theologian or biblicist,"[52] he also shows the influence of Stoic and Spiritualist thinking.[53] The Spiritualist tendency is most apparent in Bucer's acceptance of the three ages of the Spirit as predicted by the medieval monk, Joachim of Fiore (c.1132-1202). Following the Age of the Father (the Old Testament) and the Age of the Son (New Testament), there will come

---

50 LW, Companion Volume: Luther the Expositor, p. 65.
51 Gonzalez, p. 120.
52 Reventlow, p. 76.
53 See ibid., pp. 77-80.

the Age of the Spirit during which "the Spirit will take the place of the Law" and "the ceremonies and the outward word" will be rendered superfluous.

Although Bucer distanced himself from the Anabaptists and more radical Spiritualists, his approach to the Bible bears many similarities to theirs. He believed in a special illumination by the Holy Spirit which enables the elect to understand and interpret the Bible correctly. His emphasis on election developed into a major theme of Reformed theology which came to understand the Church as an invisible community of the elect. Bucer was also important for the development of Anglican theology since he moved to England in 1549 at the invitation of King Edward VI.

Without doubt, John Calvin (1509-1564) was the most influential of the Reformed theologians. In his *Institutes of the Christian Religion*, Vol. 1, chapters VI-IX, Calvin develops his main lines of argument for the authority of Scripture. In chapter VI, he demonstrates "the need of Scripture, as a guide and teacher in coming to know God as a creator."[54] His main point is that the knowledge of the divine given by means of the creation and the governance of the world is not sufficient to give man a true and saving knowledge of the living God. The human mind is easily prone to forget about God or to lapse into error. Therefore, God "has given the assistance of his Word," and "if we desire in earnest to a genuine contemplation of God," we must go to the Word "where the character of God... is described accurately and to the life... not by our own judgment, but by the standard of eternal truth."[55]

In chapter VII, Calvin argues that "the testimony of the Spirit" is "necessary to give full authority to Scripture" and that it is impious to maintain that "the credibility of scripture depends on the judgment of the Church."[56] He passionately reacts to the "pernicious error" which maintains that "Scripture is of importance only in so far as conceded to it by the suffrage of the Church; as if the eternal and inviolable truth of God could depend on the will of

---

54 John Calvin, *Institutes of the Christian Religion*, Vol. 1, trans. Henry Beveridge (London: James Clarke & Co., 1957), p. 64.

55 Ibid., pp. 66-67.

56 Ibid., p. 68.

men."[57] For Calvin, to maintain that "both the reverence which is due to Scripture and the books which are to be admitted into the canon" depend on "the determination of the Church" is "an insult to the Holy Spirit" and the opinion of "profane men."[58]

Calvin elaborates on this position by first quoting Ephesians 2:20 which says that the Church is "built on the foundation of the apostles and prophets." He then goes on to say that when the Church "receives [Scripture], and gives it the stamp of her authority, she does not make that authentic which was otherwise doubtful or controverted, but acknowledging it as the truth of God, she, as is duty bound, shows her reverence by an unhesitating assent."[59] How does the Church know that a given text is Scriptural? For Calvin, this is like asking: "How shall we learn to distinguish light from darkness, white from black, sweet from bitter?"[60] As he sees it, "Scripture bears upon the face of it as clear evidence of its truth, as white and black do of their color, sweet and bitter of their taste."[61]

There are several problems with Calvin's analysis. First, he sets the Church up against the Holy Spirit as if the leaders of the Church could not be guided by the divine Spirit in discerning the canon of Scripture. There appears to be little appreciation on the part of Calvin for the incarnational aspect of the Church as the Body of Christ animated by the Holy Spirit. This failure to appreciate the way God speaks through the mediation of the Church's leaders gives rise to his false dichotomy between "the will of men" and the will of the Holy Spirit.

Second, Calvin does not consider that in the early Church there were disputes as to whether certain writings (e.g. Hebrews, 2 Peter and Revelation) belonged in the New Testament canon.[62] Thus, it was not as simple as distinguishing light from darkness or black from white. Moreover, the rejection of the canonicity of the Letter

---

57 Ibid.

58 Ibid. pp. 68-69.

59 Ibid., p. 69.

60 Ibid.

61 Ibid.

62 See Harry Y. Gamble, "Canon: New Testament" in David Noel Freedman et. al., eds., *The Anchor Bible Dictionary*, Vol. 1 (New York: Doubleday, 1992), pp. 855-857.

of James by Calvin's fellow Protestant, Martin Luther, renders dubious his claim that Scripture bears upon itself the "clear evidence of its truth." We may further ask what is it about a writing like Paul's letter to Philemon that makes it so obviously canonical.

Finally, to say that the Church is "built upon the foundation of the apostles and prophets" (Eph. 2:20) in no way precludes the authority of the Church from establishing the canon of Scripture. Indeed, it is precisely because the Church is built on such a foundation that she can discern which books actually embody and express the deposit of faith handed on by the apostles. Once again, Calvin reduces decisions of the Church to "the will of men" without recognizing that the Holy Spirit speaks in and through the shepherds of the Church.

In his *Reply to Saldoleto*, Calvin does acknowledge that "ecclesiastical pastors" can speak with authority. However, obedience is due to a leader, such as the Pope, only "so long as he himself maintains his fidelity to Christ, and deviates not from the purity of the gospel."[63] Here again, though, a problem arises. Who is to say whether the Pope or any other Christian leader is being faithful to Christ and maintaining the purity of the Gospel? As with Luther, we find a subjective criterion at work.

Of course, Calvin does insist that an objective standard is being invoked: namely, the testimony of the Word and the Spirit. In chapter IX, book I of the *Institutes*, he criticizes "the fanatics" who place the inspiration of the Spirit above the authority of the Word. Describing such enthusiasts as "giddy men" and "miscreants,"[64] Calvin insists that "the Lord has so knit together the certainty of his word and his Spirit, that our minds are duly imbued with reverence for the word when the Spirit shining upon it enables us there to behold the face of God."[65]

As with Luther, Calvin maintains that the Holy Spirit bestows upon the faithful the correct understanding of Scripture. Once again, though, the question emerges: how are we to know who is illu-

63 John C. Olin, ed. *A Reformation Debate: Saldoleto's Letter to the Genevans and Calvin's Reply* (Grand Rapids, MI: Baker House, 1976), p. 77.

64 Calvin, *Institutes* I: IX; Beverdidge, p. 84.

65 Ibid., p. 86.

mined by the Holy Spirit? To reply that those who correctly understand the Scriptures are those who are illumined by the Holy Spirit is only to argue in a circle. Such an argument assumes that those who are illumined by the Spirit correctly understand the Scriptures. Ultimately, all that is being said is that those who are illumined by the Spirit are those who are illumined by the Spirit.

The major theses of the Calvinist understanding of *sola scriptura* are manifest in the various professions and statements of Reformed Protestantism. In the Belgic Confession of 1561, we find an affirmation of the Calvinist principle that the canonical books are to be received as "the regulation, foundation and confirmation of our faith" and that "all things contained within them" are to be believed "without any doubt."[66] Moreover, these books are to be received "as holy and canonical...not so much because the Church receives and approves them as such, but more especially because the Holy Spirit witnesses in our hearts that they are from God, and also because they carry the evidence thereof in themselves."[67] The Belgic Confession also maintains that the "Holy Scriptures fully contain the will of God, and that whatsoever man ought to believe unto salvation is sufficiently taught therein."[68] Thus, "no writings of men, however holy these men may have been" can be given "'equal value" with the "divine Scriptures," and ancient customs, "councils, decrees or statutes" can never be given "equal value with the truth of God."[69]

In the Second Helvetic Confession of the Hungarian Reformed Church, first promulgated in 1566, we find a similar affirmation of the principle of the sole sufficiency of Scripture as the rule of faith. It is stated that in the canonical books "the universal Church has the most complete exposition of all that pertains to a saving faith...and in this respect it is expressly commanded by God that nothing be either added to or taken from the same."[70] The Second Helvetic Confession goes beyond the Belgic Confession by providing a sec-

---

66 Melton, p. 163.
67 Ibid.
68 Ibid., p. 164.
69 Ibid.
70 Ibid., p. 184.

tion on "the True Interpretation of Scripture." Here the authors appeal to 2 Peter 1:20 as evidence that "the Holy Scriptures are not of private interpretation and thus we do not allow all possible interpretations."[71] But what interpretations are allowed? The authors are clear that those of "the Roman Church" cannot be tolerated:

> Nor consequently do we acknowledge as the true or genuine interpretation of the Scriptures what is called the conception of the Roman Church, that is, what the defenders of the Roman Church plainly maintain should be thrust upon all for acceptance. But we hold that the interpretation of the Scripture to be orthodox or genuine which is gleaned from the Scriptures themselves (from the matter of the language in which they were written, likewise according to the circumstances in which they were set down, and expounded in the light of like and unlike passages and of many clearer passages) and which agree with the rule of faith and love, and contributes much to the glory of God and man's salvation.[72]

Here we see an articulation of the Reformed principle that Scripture is to be interpreted in the light of Scripture itself and not by any other authority. Therefore, it is not permitted, "in controversies about religion or matters of faith, to urge our case with only the opinions of the fathers or decrees of councils; much less by received custom or by the large number of people who share the same opinion."[73] Who, then, is the judge? The authors are clear: "we do not admit any other judge than God himself who proclaims by the Holy Scriptures what is true, what is false, what is to be followed, or what to be avoided."[74] The authors also believe that nothing which contradicts the Scriptures can be followed since the "apostles did not contradict themselves in doctrine" and "apostolic men did not set forth things contrary to the apostles."[75]

Perhaps the clearest and most complete expression of the Calvinist/Reformed understanding of *sola scriptura* is to be found in

---

71 Ibid., p. 185.
72 Ibid.
73 Ibid., p. 186.
74 Ibid.
75 Ibid.

the Westminster Confession of Faith of 1648.[76] As in the Belgic and Second Helvitic Confessions, there is the articulation of the basic principle of the sole sufficiency of the Bible as the rule of faith:

> The whole counsel of God, concerning all things necessary for his own glory, man's salvation, faith and life, is either expressly set down in Scripture or by good and necessary consequence may be deduced from Scripture; unto which nothing at any time is to be added whether by new revelation of the Spirit, or the traditions of men.[77]

What the Westminster Confession adds to the other Reformed Confessions is a more detailed discussion of the role and importance of the Holy Spirit in the correct interpretation of Scripture. Thus, the authors acknowledge "the inward illumination of the Spirit of God to be necessary for the saving understanding of such things as are revealed in the Word."[78] They also point to "the Holy Spirit speaking in the Scripture" as "the Supreme Judge, by which all controversies of religion are to be determined, and all decrees of the councils, opinions of ancient writers, doctrines of men, and private spirits, are to be examined."[79]

How does the Holy Spirit guide Christians to the true understanding of the Bible? Here, as in the Second Helvitic Confession, there is the belief that the Scripture itself is its own rule of interpretation. As we read:

> The infallible rule of interpretation of Scripture is the Scripture itself; and therefore, when there is a question about the

---

[76] The importance of the Westminster Confession for the understanding of the Protestant principle of *sola scriptura* is evident in the way it is still cited by contemporary Reformed theologians. See John F. MacArthur, Jr., "The Sufficiency of the Written Word" in W. Robert Godfrey et. al. *Sola Scriptura! The Protestant Position on the Bible* (Morgan, PA: Soli Deo Gloria Publications, 1995), pp.166-167. See also James White, *The Roman Catholic Controversy: Catholics & Protestants—Do the Differences Still Matter?* (Minneapolis: Bethany House, 1996), pp. 60-61.

[77] Melton, p. 218.

[78] Ibid.

[79] Ibid.

> true and full sense of Scripture (which is not manifold but one), it must be searched and known by other places that speak more clearly.[80]

The Westminster Confession adds another distinction which the previous confessions did not address: namely, the distinction between those parts of Scripture whose meaning is clear and those parts whose meaning is not clear. We are told that:

> All things in Scripture are not alike plain in themselves, nor alike clear unto all; yet those things which are necessary to be known, believed and observed for salvation, are so clearly propounded and opened in some place of Scripture or other, that not only the learned but the unlearned, in a due sense of the ordinary means, may attain unto a sufficient understanding of them.[81]

This distinction between the things of Scripture necessary for salvation and the things which are not provides a Calvinist parallel to the Lutheran distinction between the Word of God and the written Bible. Perhaps the failure of Protestants to agree on all points of interpretation led the authors of the Westminster Confession to concede that not all things in the Bible are equally clear but only those "which are *necessary* to be known, believed, and observed for salvation"[82] (emphasis mine).

The Calvinist/Reformed articulation of *sola scriptura* has had an enormous influence on the history and character of the Protestant mind. In many ways, it is the defining characteristic of Protestantism itself. Because there is an emotional and intellectual investment in the truth of the *sola scriptura* principle, many Protestants do not adequately appreciate the intrinsic difficulties of the teaching. It is maintained that the canon of Scripture did not depend on the mediation of the Church but rather on the self-evident witness of the writings themselves to their status as the Word of God. This position, however, fails to do justice to the historical

[80] Ibid.
[81] Ibid.
[82] Ibid.

evidence, accepted today by both Protestant and Catholic scholars. It is now acknowledged that the New Testament canon was not stabilized until the late fourth century or early fifth century A.D.[83] It was not simply a case of spontaneous acceptance of certain texts as the Word of God by true Christians. Rather, the bishops and councils had to discern whether certain writings were in conformity with what the Church knew as the rule of faith. As one New Testament scholar observes:

> The criterion of orthodoxy signified that no document could be acknowledged as authoritative unless it conformed to, or at least did not contradict, what the church took to be its proper teaching. This presumes that the true faith of the church could be known independently of Scripture specifically in what was known as 'the rule of faith' (*regula fidei*), a traditional summary statement of the basic Christian confession. Hence there was no idea that Scripture was the sole repository of authoritative teaching. Rather, the authority of Scripture could be gauged against authoritative but unwritten tradition.[84]

If the leaders of the Church made use of authoritative unwritten tradition to decide what would count as authoritative written tradition (i.e. Scripture), then it is clear that the *sola scriptura* principle was not operative in the early Church. The Calvinist understanding of how the canon of Scripture was formed comes across as simplistic and naive in light of the historical evidence to the contrary.

In a similar manner, the Calvinist view of the clarity or perspicuity of Scripture has many problems, some of which have already been noted. To claim that the true understanding of the meaning of Scripture comes about by "the inward illumination of the Spirit of God" sounds persuasive to those who claim such an illumination for themselves. However, when a person claiming to be equally

---

[83] See Harry Y. Gamble, Jr. "Canon: New Testament" in David Noel Freedman et. al., eds. *The Anchor Bible Dictionary* (New York: Doubleday, 1992), Vol 1, pp. 855-856. According to an interview with the editor, this work is ecumenical in that it includes Jewish and Catholic authors, but its authorship is largely Protestant. Harry Gamble is an Episcopalian.

[84] Ibid., p. 858.

enlightened by the Holy Spirit, believes another interpretation to be true, problems invariably arise.

The matter does not seem to be resolved by the distinction of the Westminster Confession between the truths of Scripture necessary for salvation and those which are not. How are we to know which truths are *necessary* and which are indifferent? Inevitably, this position leads to the Lutheran tendency to reduce the saving message to a certain formula like justification by faith alone. Thus, an interpretive lens is placed over the Scriptures which enables the "true believer" to decide what passages contain those things "which are necessary to known, believed and observed for salvation."

The Anglican View of *Sola Scriptura*

As is well-known, the Church of England decided upon a political solution to the theological turmoil of the Reformation. The result was an attempt at a middle path or *via media* between "Roman" Catholicism and Protestantism. It was during the reign of Queen Elizabeth I (ruled 1558-1603) that the Church of England or Anglicanism took on its defining features. Probably the most complete statement of Anglican theology is to be found in the *Thirty-nine Articles of Religion.* These articles were heavily influenced by the thought of Thomas Cranmer (1489-1556), the Archbishop of Canterbury during the latter days of King Henry VIII and during the reign of Edward VI (ruled 1547-1553).[85]

Cranmer was the principal author of the first *English Book of Common Prayer* (1549), and his theology reveals definite influences of Protestant theologians like Luther, Calvin and Bucer. Thus, when the *Thirty-Nine Articles of Religion* were drawn up in 1563 and promulgated in their final form in 1571, there were many Protestant ideas present even though the Church of England was ostensibly trying to follow a middle path between Protestantism and "Roman" Catholicism. It is not surprising, therefore, to find the Protestant doctrine of *sola scriptura* making its way into Anglican

[85] As is well-known, Cranmer was executed in 1556 during the reign of Mary Tudor (Queen Mary I from 1553-1558) who tried to restore Catholicism in England.

thought. Even a theologian like John Jewel (1522-1571), who tried to root the Church of England in Patristic thought, believed that Scripture was to be the final arbiter of all theological disputes.[86]

It is in article six of the *Thirty-nine Articles of Religion* that the sole sufficiency of Scripture is taught:

> Holy Scriptures containeth all things necessary to salvation: so that whatsoever is not read therein, nor may be proved thereby, is not to be required of any man, that it should be believed as an article of the Faith, or be thought requisite or necessary to salvation.[87]

While the *Articles* say that doctrines must be proved from scripture, other sources of authority exist. The ancient creeds of the Christian faith, the Apostles, the Nicene and the Athanasian (included in the later version) "ought thoroughly to be received and believed: for they may be proved by most certain warrants of Holy Scripture."[88] The Church has the right to rule on matters of liturgy and doctrine, but it can never "ordain anything contrary to God's Word written" and it should never "enforce any thing to be believed for necessity of Salvation" that is not rooted in Scripture (article 20).[89]

What then is the binding force of Anglican liturgical practices which are judged as "not contrary to God's Word" but which might not be clearly established in the Bible? In article 34, we are told that "every particular or national Church hath authority to ordain, change and abolish, ceremonies or rites of the Church only by man's authority, so that all things be done to edifying."[90] Thus, there can be a legitimate diversity of liturgical traditions and ceremonies in different places and times. However, a warning is given to anyone who "willingly and purposely, doth openly break the traditions and ceremonies of the Church, which be not repugnant to the Word of

---

[86] See Gonzalez, Vol. III, pp. 168-169.
[87] Melton, p. 22.
[88] Ibid., p. 23.
[89] Ibid., p. 24.
[90] Ibid., p. 25.

God, and be ordained and approved by common authority."[91] Such a one "ought to be rebuked openly, (that others may fear to do the like,) as he that offendeth against the common order of the Church, and hurteth the authority of the Magistrate, and woundeth the consciences of the weak brethren."[92]

The Anglican solution was to uphold the principle of *sola scriptura* for matters of doctrine. Thus, no person could be required to believe in any article of faith which cannot be proved by Scripture. However, in matters of liturgical discipline, the national church has the authority to establish "traditions and ceremonies" which are not "repugnant to the Word of God." No one should presume the right to break or criticize these traditions since this offends "the common order of the Church" and injures "the authority of the Magistrate."

This, of course, was a political as well as a theological solution. The maintenance of outward ritual observance was a matter of civil order in a country with a national Church. It was clear, though, that not all people in England were satisfied with the Elizabethan settlement. The subsequent persecutions of the Baptists and "Roman" Catholics in England along with the Puritan upheavals show that political solutions to theological matters are not always felicitous.

The Anglican articulation of the *sola scriptura* doctrine is both like and unlike the Lutheran and Calvinist versions. On a theoretical level, it is very similar since article six upholds the principle that Scripture contains "all things necessary for salvation." It is also similar in subordinating all creeds and councils to the test of the written Word of God. However, because Anglicanism was upholding the idea of a national church, there was a greater emphasis on outward obedience and respect for the "common authority" of bishops and monarchs. External observance was, in many ways, more important than internal beliefs. The basic dogmas of the ancient creeds were, of course, to be believed, but there was a built-in mechanism for the toleration of differing opinions on the meaning of the Eucharist, the priesthood and the nature of justification. It

---

91 Ibid.

92 Ibid.

comes as no surprise, therefore, to find within the "Anglican Communion" a variety of theological opinions which give rise to both a "Protestant" branch and a "Catholic" branch within the same Church of England.[93]

Because of these factors, the Anglican version of *sola scriptura* never developed the type of "orthodoxy" found in Lutheranism and Calvinism which insists that certain doctrines like justification by faith alone or the predestination of the elect are to be found with pristine clarity in the Bible by those rightfully illumined by the Holy Spirit. As the Protestant scholars, Dillenberger and Welch observe:

> In sum, Anglicanism is best understood as a broad stream guided by a sense of order and tradition as guaranteed by the episcopacy and the Prayer Book. It asks no particular theological understanding, and has never been a theological church. Seldom has it had theological giants.[94]

Since the Anglican Church developed out of political and national concerns (in addition to the theological), there emerged a tendency to tolerate diverse theological opinions as long as the social order was not overturned. This attitude, eventually labeled Latitudinarianism, gave rise to a "softer" version of the *sola scriptura* doctrine. Scripture was upheld as the rule, but tradition and reason were also considered sources of authority. Among the Latitudinarians, there was a conscious effort to interpret revelation in the light of human reason. By the early eighteenth century, the evangelical witness of the faith had been severely weakened and

---

93 The "Catholic" side of Anglicanism was emphasized by the Oxford Movement of the 19th century. In the United States, certain parishes and dioceses are more Protestant and others more "Catholic." The "Catholic" Anglicans are often called "Anglo-Catholics." As one scholar notes: "Anglo-Catholics emphasize the seven sacraments, the Real Presence, fast and abstinence, auricular confession, prayers and requiem Masses for the dead, retreats, invocation of the saints. They say the rosary, make the sign of the cross, genuflect, address their priests as 'Father.'" William J. Whelan, *Separated Brethren* (Huntington, IN: Our Sunday Visitor, 1979), p. 55.

94 John Dillenberger and Claude Welch, *Protestant Christianity* (New York: Charles Scribner's Sons, 1954), p. 76.

the rise of the Wesleyan movement can be understood as "an attempt to recapture for the English church the living experience of redemption from sin."[95]

These observations point to the dangers of the Anglican solution. Any church which allows for state control of ecclesiastical matters runs the risk of having "what belongs to Caesar" interfere with "what belongs to God." Thus, conformity to dictates of the civil authority becomes as important (if not more important) than conformity to the teachings of the faith. Thus, lack of fidelity to civic order or treason becomes the ultimate heresy rather than denial of the truths of Christianity.

On the surface, the softer version of the *sola scriptura* doctrine appears to have some benefits. However, problems still remain. Nothing is to be required to be believed except those things which are found within scripture. But who is to decide what is found within or proved by Scripture? Of course, the Church of England did retain an episcopal hierarchy which theoretically had the right to decide on matters of doctrine. However, since there was ambiguity over the nature of episcopal authority,[96] the stage was set for individual Anglicans to receive the rulings of their bishops with an understandable degree of scepticism. Eventually, this led to a situation in which the outward observance of the civic religion could be retained while all types of free-thinking were developing. Given this context, it is no surprise that England became one of the centers of Deism and religious scepticism during the time of the Enlightenment.[97]

---

95 Ibid., p. 75.

96 Ibid., p. 76.

97 The forces which give rise to the Enlightenment are, admittedly, quite complex, and it would be wrong to see the Anglican solution as the only factor. According to Richard H. Popkin, the rise of scepticism during the 16th and 17th centuries was due to two interweaving factors: first, the revival of classical scepticism during the late Renaissance, and, second, the intellectual crisis of the Reformation over the norms of truth. See Richard H. Popkin, *The History of Scepticism from Erasmus to Spinoza* (Berkeley: University of California Press, 1979).

Sola Scriptura and the Radical Reformation

The radical reformers were those who went beyond the ideas of the Lutherans, the Calvinists and the Anglicans. Usually, historians point to three distinct groups of radical reformers: the Anabaptists, the Spiritualists and the Rationalists.[98] Further distinctions are also made between "early," "revolutionary" and "later" Anabaptists,[99] and it is likewise acknowledged that some Anabaptists also had spiritualist tendencies.[100] In light of the complex and varied nature of the radical reformation, it is not surprising that a number of views on *sola scriptura* are to be found.

The term "Anabaptist" is applied to those Protestant reformers who rejected infant baptism and insisted on the need for adults who were baptized as infants to be re-baptized as adults (hence the term Anabaptist which means "re-baptizer"). Later on, those who insisted on "believers' baptism" (as opposed to infant baptism) were simply called Baptists rather than Anabaptists.

In many respects, the original Anabaptists upheld the doctrine of *sola scriptura* in a manner similar to the Lutherans and the Calvinists. Thus, Conrad Grebel (c. 1498-1526), one of the original "Swiss Brethren" of Zurich, wrote to the radical German reformer, Thomas Müntzer, these words:

> Therefore we beg and admonish thee as a brother by the name, the power, the word, the spirit, and the salvation, which has come to all Christians through Jesus Christ our Master and Savior, that thou wilt take earnest heed to preach only the divine Word without fear, to set up and guard only divine institutions, to esteem as good and right only what may be found in pure and clear Scripture.[101]

This passage points to the authority and centrality of the Bible for the Anabaptist movement. Indeed, as Reventlow observes, the

---

98 See Gonzalez, vol. III, pp. 77-92.

99 Ibid., 78.

100 See Reventlow, pp. 53-56.

101 Angel Mergal and George Williams, ed. *Spiritual and Anabaptist Writers* (Philadelphia: The Westminster Press, 1957), p. 75.

Swiss Brethren and similar groups "had a much more rigorous principle of scripture than the mainstream Reformation...the Anabaptists were concerned to carry through consistently the demands of the New Testament, and especially of the Sermon on the Mount, as they understood them."[102] Menno Simons (1496-1561), the spiritual father of the Mennonites, believed in a literal observance of Christ's commands. This led him to reject the violence of revolutionary Anabaptists like Melchior Hoffman (c. 1500-1543) and to preach pacifism as the call of the Gospel.[103]

The original Anabaptists certainly appealed to the Bible as the rule of Christian truth, and when charges were made against them, "the whole of their argumentation" in refutation of such charges was "based on biblical texts."[104] However, it should be noted that the Anabaptists were an eclectic group. As George H. Williams notes, in their use of the Bible, "elements of several systems of interpretation— Catholic, normative Protestant, Spiritualist, and Rationalist — are to be found in their tracts and sermons alongside their more characteristic efforts."[105] Thus, there is a movement back and forth from the literal to the typological and allegorical interpretations. One group, known as the Sabbatarians, maintained that the sabbath law of the Old Testament was still binding.[106] However, the majority held to a "predominantly negative" attitude towards the Old Testament laws, choosing instead to uphold the law of Christ.[107]

On various doctrinal matters, the Anabaptists were in clear disagreement with the Lutherans and Calvinists. Regarding sin, grace and regeneration, the Anabaptists believed that, even after the fall, "man retained the capacity to prepare for grace," and, after the reception of grace, "there remained the need for ethical action to achieve Christian existence."[108] In contrast to Luther's denial of

---

102 Reventlow, p. 53.

103 See Gonzalez, vol. III, pp. 86-87.

104 Reventlow, p. 53.

105 George H. Williams, *The Radical Reformation* (Philadelphia: The Westminster Press, 1962), p. 830.

106 Reventlow, p. 63.

107 Ibid., p. 62.

108 See footnote 62 in Reventlow, p. 451.

free will, Balthazar Hubmaier (1481-1528) wrote: "Whoever denies the freedom of the human will, denies and rejects more than half of the Holy Scriptures."[109] Finally, the Anabaptists departed from the Lutherans and the Calvinists by rejecting infant baptism: As Menno Simons observed:

> Since, then, we do not find in all Scripture a single word by which Christ has ordained the baptism of infants, or that his apostles taught and practiced it, we say and confess rightly that infant baptism is but a human invention, an opinion of men, a perversion of the ordinance of Christ.[110]

The Anabaptists, of course, believed that the Holy Spirit was needed for the correct understanding of the Scriptures, and they were convinced that the Holy Spirit supported their interpretations. In a manner similar to the Lutherans and the Calvinists, they maintained that the "inner word" of the Holy Spirit enabled the believer to understand the meaning of "the outer word" of the written text.[111] The Anabaptists tried to hold these two in balance. However, the radical reformers known as the Spiritualists began to place so much emphasis on the Spirit that the written text became less important and (in some extreme cases) "completely superfluous."[112]

The transition from an Anabaptist to a Spiritualist perspective can be found in Hans Denck (c. 1495-1527) who, as George H. Williams notes, moved "from humanism through Lutheranism to Anabaptism and finally to evangelical Spiritualism."[113] In the final analysis, Denck believed that the Spirit can illuminate and save a person apart from the written Word. As he writes:

> I esteem the Holy Scriptures above all human treasure: yet not so much as I do the Word of God which is living, potent, eternal, free and independent of all the elements of this world:

---

[109] Harry Emerson Fosdick, ed. *Great Voices of the Reformation: An Anthology* (New York: Random House, 1952), p. 310.

[110] Ibid., p. 319.

[111] See Reventlow, p. 53.

[112] Ibid.

[113] Williams, *The Radical Reformation*, p. 150.

> for it is God Himself, it is Spirit and not letter, written without pen or paper so that it can never be blotted out. Therefore salvation is not bound up with the Scriptures, however good and useful they may be for that purpose. The reason is this. It is not possible for the Scriptures to make a bad heart good. But a good heart illumined with the light of God (a heart with a Divine spark in it) is improved by everything. The Scriptures are for the good and salvation of believers, but for unbelievers they are like everything else, only for their damnation. Therefore the elect of God can be saved without preaching and without Scriptures.[114]

This reliance on the Spirit ultimately led Denck to regard the sacraments as superfluous.[115] Like the written Word, the sacraments can be useful, but they are not where God is ultimately found. Rather, Denck writes: "See that you seek God where He is to be sought, in the temple and dwelling-place of the Divine glory, which is your heart and your soul."[116]

Andreas von Karlstadt (c. 1480-1541) and Thomas Müntzer (also spelled Münzer and Muentzer) (c. 1488-1525) were among the first Spiritualists in Germany, and they both became bitter enemies of Luther. Influenced by the Rhenish mystics, Karlstadt placed so much emphasis on the interior instructions of the Spirit that Scripture assumed a secondary role as simply the "outward witness" to the inner truth. Thus, he wrote that:

> As far as I am concerned I do not need the outward witness. I want to have the testimony of the Spirit within me, as it was promised by Christ... This is the way it was with the apostles, who were assured inwardly by the testimony of the Spirit, and who afterwards preached Christ outwardly, and reinforced by writings that Christ had to suffer for us.[117]

---

[114] Fosdick, pp. 300-301.

[115] Reventlow, p. 55.

[116] Fosdick, p. 302.

[117] *Vom greuliche Missbrauch des heiligen Abendmahls (On the Horrible Abuse of Holy Communion)*, in J. G. Walch, ed. *Luthers Werke* , henceforth Walch; (Halle, 1740-1753) XX, 2893; cited in George H. Williams, *The Radical Reformation*, p. 823.

Here we see that, for Karlstadt, the testimony of the Spirit has priority over the testimony of the written Word.

Thomas Müntzer had come under the influence of the three "Zwickau prophets," Nicholas Storch, Thomas Drechsel and Marcus Thomas Stubner who, among other things, claimed to receive "direct revelation in visions and dreams."[118] Known also as the Storchites and called the *Schwärmer* (fanatics) by Luther, the prophets of Zwickau repudiated infant baptism and preached about the rise of the Turk as Antichrist before the coming of the Millennium.[119] Although Müntzer did not accept all the beliefs of "the prophets," he was influenced by their apocalypticism and spiritualism, and he began to teach the necessity for each of the elect to receive a personal cross of suffering in order to experience the fullness of the Holy Spirit and true salvation. This emphasis on suffering would later take on a special note of militancy as Müntzer became a leader of the Peasants Revolt of 1524-1525 which eventually resulted in his own execution and the death (by some estimates) of more than 100,000 German peasants.[120]

In his approach to the Scriptures, Müntzer accepted the "Spiritualist hermeneutics" of the Storchites, and he, therefore, believed that both the Old and the New Testaments must be interpreted "in the Spirit."[121] He maintained that through a special charism, the man of God "comes into possession...of the key of David, whereby he can unlock the book of seven seals, the Bible, and discern the spirits."[122] Convinced that he possessed this special charism, Müntzer began to preach against infant baptism and to apply certain apocalyptic themes of the Bible to his own age. He eventually came to believe that the prophecy in Joel 2:27-32 and 3:1-4 about the outpouring of the Spirit applied to him and his followers. Thus, he felt inspired to predict "the imminent formation of a covenant of miners and magistrates as the realization of equality of possessions."[123]

---

118 Williams, *The Radical Reformation*, p. 46.

119 Ibid.

120 Justo Gonzalez, *The Story of Christianity*, Vol. 2 (New York: Harper & Row, 1984), p. 42.

121 Williams, *The Radical Reformation*, p. 48.

122 Ibid., p. 51.

123 Ibid., p. 55.

Although Müntzer made ample use of biblical texts for his views, he, like the other Spiritualists, believed that people could come to know the truth apart from Scripture. Thus, he wrote:

> If someone all his life long had neither heard nor seen the Bible, he can have a true Christian faith through the right teaching of the Spirit, such as was held by all those who wrote the scriptures without any books.[124]

Such a view placed him at odds with Luther, and Müntzer was fully aware of this. He began to condemn false religion of "the Wittenbergers" whom he referred to as "the scribes."[125] In 1524, he wrote to Frederick, the Elector of Saxony, referring to Luther and his followers "as godless theologians whom Satan drives to their downfall as before it was the monks and priests."[126] In this letter, he explains that: "I preach the sort of Christian faith that does not harmonize with Luther, but which is identical in all the hearts of elect upon earth (Psalm 67)..."[127] Müntzer concludes the letter by warning the Elector that if he does not come to his assistance, it will be said: "See, here is a man who was not willing to have God as his defence, but has abandoned himself to worldly arrogance."[128]

Müntzer was absolutely convinced that he was being led by the Holy Spirit, and he would often refer to himself as "the servant of God against the godless" and sign his letters as "Thomas Müntzer with the sword of Gideon" or "Thomas Müntzer with the hammer."[129] Such a confidence in one's special call from God can, of course, be very dangerous. One such danger occurs when two different men, each claiming to be divinely guided, find themselves at odds on matters of doctrine. This helps to explain why there was

---

[124] P. Kirn and G. Franz, ed. Thomas Müntzer, *Scriften und Briefe. Kritische Gesamtausgabe* (Guetesrslow,1968), p. 277; cited in Reventlow, pp. 64-65.

[125] See Reventlow, p. 64 and Williams, *The Radical Reformation*, p. 56.

[126] Katherine Leach, ed. *The German Reformation* (London: Macmillan Education, Ltd., 1991), p. 97.

[127] Ibid., pp. 97-98.

[128] Ibid., p. 98.

[129] Williams, *The Radical Reformation*, p. 76.

such bitter hatred between Müntzer and Luther. Herbert David Rix also takes note of the many common characteristics shared by the two rivals:

> Each has a radically egocentric nature, with no real insight into other human beings, and each man attempts to restate the Christian faith in the light of his own psychic problems. Each man has an uncontrollable drive to instil his views into as large a part of the human race as possible. Each man considers that he is the first in the history of Christendom since the days of the Apostles to discover the essential Christian message... Each uses Scripture as a taking-off point and there is only a difference of emphasis between the two on the role of the "Spirit" as the real source of his unparalleled understanding of the Christian faith.[130]

Since both Müntzer and Luther were convinced that they were being led by the Holy Spirit, each man also believed it was necessary to point out the errors of his opponent. This they often did more by means of invective than scholarly argumentation. Thus, Müntzer referred to Luther variously as "the Archheathen," "the Dragon," "Dr. Liar" and "the unspiritual, soft-living flesh of Wittenberg."[131] Not to be outdone, Luther, in a letter to Frederick of Saxony," called Müntzer "the Satan of Allstedt," and "a bad spirit."[132] He warned the Elector about the seditious plans of Müntzer "to betake himself to arms and set himself against the government, and forthwith raise a riot."[133] Thus, he urged Frederick "to act vigoursly" against the "storming and ranting" of Müntzer and his followers.[134] In a subsequent treatise, Luther implored the rulers "to stab, smite, and slay" as many rebels as

---

[130] Herbert David Rix, *Martin Luther: The Man and the Image* (New York: Irvington Publishers, 1983), p. 157.

[131] Williams, *The Radical Reformation*, p. 76 and Rix, p. 162. "Dr. Liar" (in German, *Doktor Lügner*) is an obvious play on *Doktor Luther*.

[132] Preserved Smith, *The Life and Letters of Martin Luther* (Boston: Houghton Mifflin, 1911), p.153.

[133] Ibid., p. 152.

[134] Ibid., p. 153.

possible and for each person "to avoid the peasants as he would the devil himself."[135]

Luther was able to win the favor of Frederick and the other nobles because they valued the support of the middle class more than that of the peasants. As Rix notes: "Luther's preaching had its strongest appeal to the middle class Germans, especially those with mild neurotic anxiety about their salvation, while Muentzer went after the uneducated proletariat — not many others would listen to him."[136] Luther was able to portray Müntzer and his followers as violent fanatics who claimed to "hear God speak to them immediately as to angels."[137] In this way, Luther showed his antipathy to those who upheld spiritual inspiration over the authority of the Bible. As he wrote: "they make nothing of the Scripture, which they call 'Bible-bubble-Babel'."[138]

The tendency to elevate the inspiration of the Spirit over the written Word gave way to an emphasis on interiority in Protestant reformers like Caspar Schwenckfeld (1489-1561) and Sebastian Frank (c. 1499-1542). In the latter, there developed the idea of an ongoing interior revelation which ultimately made all religious externals (such as the sacraments) superfluous.[139] With George Fox (1624-1691), the founder of the Quakers, the belief in the immediate inspiration by the Spirit ultimately led him to delegate Scripture to "a secondary rule, subordinate to the Spirit."[140] In a 1678 document entitled, *The Chief Principles of the Christian Religion as Professed by the People Called the Quakers*, Robert Barclay, a follower of Fox, explained the priority of the spiritual over the scriptural in these terms:

> Seeing no man knoweth the Father but the Son, and he to whom the Son revealeth Him; and seeing the revelation of the Son is in and by the Spirit; therefore the testimony of the

[135] Ibid, p. 163.

[136] Rix, p. 157. 17 Williams, *The Radical Reformation*, p. 76 and Rix, p. 162.

[137] Smith, p. 152.

[138] Ibid.

[139] See Gonzalez, vol. III, p. 90.

[140] Henry Bettenson, ed. *Documents of the Christian Church, Second Edition* (New York: Oxford University Press, 1963) p. 253.

> Spirit is that alone by which the true knowledge of God hath been, is and can only be revealed;...by the revelation of the same Spirit He hath manifested Himself all along unto the sons of men, both patriarchs, prophets and apostles...whether by outward voices and appearances, dreams, or inward manifestations of the heart...Moreover, these divine inward revelations, which we make absolutely necessary for the building up of true faith, neither do nor can contradict the outward testimony of the Scriptures, or right and sound reason. Yet from hence it will not follow, that these divine revelations are to be subjected either to the outward testimony of the Scriptures, or of the natural reason of man, as to a more noble or certain rule and touchstone; for this divine revelation and inward illumination, is that which is evident and clear of itself, forcing, by its own evidence and clearness, the well-disposed understanding to assent, irresistibly moving the same thereunto...[141]

Here we can see a nearly-complete departure from the Protestant principle of *sola scriptura.* Believing that ongoing, interior illuminations of the Holy Spirit were self-authenticating, the Quakers did not think such revelations needed to be subject to either the rule of Scripture or the standard of human reason. Of course, true revelations will not contradict Scripture and reason, but they are not subject to them since the interior is superior to the exterior. It is easy to suspect a high potential for delusion and abuse in such a system. Those who claim to receive interior revelations from the Holy Spirit become standards unto themselves. Ultimately, there is no concrete and objective standard of truth but only competing claims of subjective illuminations.

It was precisely these difficulties with subjective claims of spiritual illuminations which prompted the suppression of the Illuminists (*Alumbrados)* by the Spanish Inquisition in the late 15th and early 16th centuries. Yet the ideas of the "illumined ones" emerged once again in Protestant reformers like Juan de Valdes (1500-1541) and Bernardino Ochino (1487-1563). When rationalism combined with spiritualism, Protestants such as Michael Servetus (1511-1553)

---

[141] Ibid.

and Faustus Socinus (1539-1604) began to teach that the doctrine of the Trinity is not only anti-rational but also unsupported by Scripture.[142] Servetus was burned as a heretic in Calvin's Geneva, and Socinus fled to Poland.

After the execution of Servetus, one of Calvin's followers, Sebastian Castellio (c. 1509-1563), began to write and speak out against the persecution of heretics. Castellio believed that the meaning of the Bible was not always clear, and, therefore, toleration should be allowed for differing viewpoints. This, of course, ran against the Calvinist understanding of the clarity of the Scriptures, and Castellio was hounded and criticized by both Calvin and the other prominent teacher of Geneva, Theodore Beza (1519-1605).[143]

Castellio's book, *De arte dubitandi* (*On the Art of Doubting*) is a thoughtful book, but from the classical Protestant viewpoint, it is a complete surrender of the principle of *sola scriptura*. As Castellio writes:

> We have therefore established that the Scriptures, in their parts which are open to controversy, are truly obscure, and often they can be taken in two senses with equal probability: with the result that one has not been able to decide, even up to the present, after so many centuries, the majority of these controversies by appealing purely and simply to the words of the texts.[144]

Thus, Richard Popkin observes that Castellio came to believe that "we cannot resolve doubtful matters just by examining Scripture, as the Calvinists suggest, since there are many disputes about

---

[142] See Gonzalez, vol. III, pp. 91-92 and Williams, *The Radical Reformation*, pp. 605-635; on Servetus, also see Hanz- Jurgen Goertz, ed. *Profiles of Radical Reformers* (Scottdale, PA: Herald Press, 1982), pp. 247-254.

[143] Williams, *The Radical Reformation*, p. 630.

[144] Sébastien Castellio, *De L'Art de douter et de croire, d'ignorer et de savoir*, C. Baudouin, trans. (Geneva: Éditions Jeheber, 1953), p. 90. (my translation from the French which reads: Nous avons donc établi que les Ecritures, dans leurs parties sujette à controverse, sont vraiment obscures, et que souvent elles peuvent etre tirées dans les deux sens avec une égale probabilité: d'ou résulte qu'on n'a pu trancher, jusqu'à présent, après tant des siècles, la plupart de ces controverses en faisant appel purement et simplement aux termes des textes).

how to interpret the Bible, and Scripture is obscure on many points."[145] Castellio, however, was not led by this position to return to the Catholic faith. Instead, he preached a type of religious scepticism in which the quest for certainty would have to be abandoned. In this regard, he can be considered one of the fathers of "liberal Protestantism."[146]

With Castellio, the story of the Protestant reformers and *sola scriptura* comes full circle. It is amazing that within a generation after Luther's break with Rome, so many different theologies, movements and sects would emerge. Such tremendous diversity was understood by the great Catholic bishop from France, Jacques Bénigne Bossuet (1627-1704), as a sure sign of heresy. In his monumental study, *Histoire des variations des églises protestantes* ("History of the Variations of the Protestant Churches"), Bossuet notes that:

> The characteristic of the heretic, that is to say of someone who holds to a particular opinion, is the attachment to his own ideas; and the characteristic of the Catholic, that is to say of the universal, is to prefer the common opinion of the whole Church over his own opinions.[147]

The Problems with *Sola Scriptura*

This survey of what the Protestant Reformers taught about *sola scriptura* shows that there was neither absolute agreement on what this principle meant nor how it was to be applied. We have seen that although Scripture was often touted as the sole and sufficient rule of truth, there was invariably an appeal to something else — be it the need for the inward illumination of the Holy Spirit or the correct understanding of the Gospel. Moreover, we have seen that Protestants did not agree among themselves as to how to interpret the Bible, and when these conflicts emerged, they often resorted to vituperative attacks and insults as easily as rational discussions.

---

[145] Richard Popkin, *The History of Scepticism*, pp. 11-12.

[146] Ibid., p. 13.

[147] Jacques Bénigne Bossuet, *Histoire des variations des églises protestantes, Oeuvres completes de Bossuet*, F. Lachat, ed. (Paris, 1863), vol. XIV, p. 17. (my translation).

Luther, the grand champion of *sola scriptura*, ultimately was forced to set his own authority above Scripture when the Bible contradicted his position. As he wrote: "I am not put off at all by passages of Scripture, even if you were to produce six hundred in support of the righteousness of works and against the righteousness of faith, and if you were to scream that Scripture contradicts itself."[148] When protests were raised about his adding the word alone (*allein*) to his German translation of Rom. 3:28, he responded by saying: "If your Papist makes much useless fuss about the word *sola*, *allein*, tell him at once: 'Dr. Martin Luther will have it so.'"[149] This appeal to his own authority was consistent with his conviction that "in these matters of faith, to be sure, each Christian is for himself Pope and Church" (*in his enim, quae sunt fidei, quilibet Christianus est sibi Papa et Ecclesia).*[150]

The problems with each Christian being "for himself Pope and Church" are numerous. While Protestants, like Luther, might appeal to Scripture alone as their motto, it is also clear that they alone are the judges of what Scripture says. The attitude of the Protestants, according to Bossuet, was that "everything is so clear in Scripture, that one can find within it all that one needs to understand."[151] The danger, of course, is that one will find within Scripture exactly what one wants to find there. Thus, Luther is able to find in Jesus' blessing of "the pure of heart" in Mat. 5:8 material to attack monasticism which preaches a false view of the purity of the heart. As he writes:

---

[148] LW 26: 294 ff.

[149] Luther, "Send brief vom Dolmetshen" (in Plochman, et al.) Eds., *Luthers Werke* (Erlagen-Frankfort, 1827ff.), vol. LXV., p. 107ff. Cited in Philip Schaff's *History of the Christian Church* (Grand Rapids: Eerdmans, 1910) Vol. VII, p. 362.

[150] *D. Martin Luthers Werke: Kritische Gesamtausgabe* (Weimar: 1898; henceforth WA) 5:407, 35. It is clear that Luther believed his personal authority extended not only over matters of faith but of history as well. Thus, without any basis except his own authority, Luther was able to state that St. Francis faked his own stigmata: "He [Francis] printed them on himself by some sort of foolish devotion or, more likely, vainglory, by which he was able to flatter himself into believing he was so dear to Christ that He had even printed His wounds on his body" (LW 6:17, 142).

[151] Bossuet, vol. XIV, p. 292. The French reads: "...que tout est si clair dans L'Ecriture qu'il y entend tout ce qu'il faut entendre..."

> And you should realize that when a monk in the monastery is sitting in deepest contemplation, excluding the world from his heart altogether, and thinking about the Lord God the way he himself paints and imagines Him, he is actually sitting — if you will pardon the expression — in the dung, not up to his knees but up to his ears. For he is proceeding on his own ideas without the Word of God.[152]

A similar example of finding in Scripture what you want to find is noticed in Luther's exegesis of the famous parable of the last judgment of Matt. 25:31-46 in which Christ separates the sheep from goats. Instead of deeds of mercy as the norm for separating the sheep from the goats, Luther changes the norm to faith: "Christ will say to the pious and God-fearing: 'You came to me and believed in me...I will not cast you out,'" and to the goats Christ will say: "You did not want me and did not believe in me."[153] Thus, to avoid the obvious meaning that works of mercy (or the omission of them) are the standard of Christ's judgment, Luther had to change the meaning of the text to conform to his own theology of justification by faith alone.

Soon after *sola scriptura* became the doctrine of Protestantism, doctrinal chaos emerged. Some accepted infant baptism, and some denied it. Some believed in the real presence of Christ in the Eucharist, and some believed only in a spiritual or symbolic presence. Some began to teach that even the sacraments and the Bible could be ignored if one had been personally illumined by the Spirit. Finally, fundamental doctrines like the Trinity were denied, and people like Castellio threw in the towel and admitted that often the meaning of the Bible cannot be determined by the Bible alone.

Even Luther wound up attacking his own principles. The same man who claimed that every Christian is "Pope and Church" when it comes to matters of faith, sarcastically observed that: "Noblemen, townsmen, peasants, all classes understand the Evangelium better than I or St. Paul; they are now wise and think themselves more learned than all the ministers."[154] In the same vein, Luther

---

[152] LW 21:34.

[153] WA 33:90; cited in Rix, p. 147.

[154] Walch 14:1360; cited in Msgr. Patrick F. O'Hare, *The Facts about Luther* (Rockford, IL: Tan Books, 1987), pp. 208-209.

noted that: "There is no smearer but when he has heard a sermon or can read a chapter in German, makes a doctor of himself and crowns his ass and convinces himself that he knows everything better than all who teach him."[155]

Luther ultimately admitted that his great program of preaching the true Gospel did not make the people of his day more Christian. As he wrote:

> Since the downfall of Popery and the cessations of excommunications and spiritual penalties, the people have learned to despise the word of God. They no longer care for churches; they have ceased to fear and honor God... After throwing off the yoke of the Pope, everyone wishes to live as he pleases.[156]

All this shows that simply pointing people to the Bible is not enough to bring about true evangelization and conversion.

These observations demonstrate the problems and difficulties inherent in the *sola scriptura* doctrine. Of course, none of this is meant to disparage the authority of the Bible nor to deny that many Protestant men and women have led (and continue to lead) holy lives nourished by God's Sacred Word. Our concern has been to look at the teaching of *sola scriptura* objectively, in its historical setting, and to raise some critical questions as to its inner coherence and practicality as a theological and ecclesiological principle.

Our historical survey of what the Protestant reformers actually taught about *sola scriptura* has, I believe, established a number of valid points which must be considered by Christians of today:

1) Despite the claim that Scripture was the sole sufficient rule of faith, the Protestant reformers always appealed to some type of interior illumination by the Spirit as necessary for the correct understanding of the Word of God (and also what comprised the Word of God). To put this in scholastic language, they showed that the written texts themselves were only *materially* sufficient as a source of truth. There was still a need for a *formal* principle of sufficiency (such as the inner guidance of the Holy Spirit) to make the truths

[155] Walch 5:1652; O'Hare, p. 208.
[156] Walch 12:788.

of the scriptures discernable. The question of how one could know who had the guidance of the Holy Spirit was never answered to any degree of certitude and satisfaction.

2) The Protestant reformers soon discovered that the Scriptures were open to diverse interpretations. This led to tensions and divisions among the various groups of reformers. Such experience points to the difficulty with the claim that the true meaning of Scripture is clear to all "true believers," and it shows that *sola scriptura* was, and has been, a principle of disunity rather than unity among Christians. The existence of over 28,000 distinct Christian denominations in the world today is a direct result of the *sola scriptura* doctrine.[157]

3) Although Luther and the other Protestants saw themselves as "captive" to the Word of God, a close study shows that they often viewed the scriptural texts through the lens of their own theological doctrines and opinions. Luther was probably the most dramatic example in this regard since he was willing to use his own interpretive framework of justification by *faith alone* as a rationale for disparaging and even eliminating certain biblical texts as "unevangelical." Ultimately, the Bible could be cited as an authority only to the extent that it conformed to certain theological perspectives.

4) Despite the claim that the Bible was the sole, sufficient rule for matters of the faith, the Protestants (whether consciously or not) were always appealing to some other rule of authority. Luther came to rely on his own prophetic inspiration and, therefore, his judgments and interpretations became an authoritative rule (at least to himself and his close followers). The Calvinists and the Anglicans retained various forms of church structure and authority which provided them with something analogous to the hierarchical structure of Catholicism (even though they claimed the Bible as the ultimate court of appeal). The Anabaptists, the Spiritualists and the Rationalists of the Radical Reformation were more subjective or "spirit-

[157] See David B. Barret, ed. *World Christian Encyclopedia* (New York: Oxford University Press, 1982), p. 292.

based" in their search for authority, and this led many of them to abandon the *sola scriptura* doctrine altogether.

5) Whether intentionally or not, the Protestant doctrine of *sola scriptura* launched the West into an inevitable trajectory towards subjectivism and individualism. The dangers of chaos and self-delusion are always present when there is a break from an established authority on the basis of personal claims of knowledge or illumination. Only to a limited extent, can the words of the Bible serve as a "check" against unrestrained subjectivism. While adherence to the ancient creeds has helped to maintain some semblance of unity among the major Protestant denominations, the doctrine of *sola scriptura* has also opened the door to all types of aberrations. Groups like the Jehovah Witnesses who deny the Trinity and the divinity of Christ are a logical outcome of the "Bible only" philosophy. Contemporary secular forms of individualism and relativism can likewise be understood as part of the historical fallout of subjectivism spawned by the *sola scriptura* doctrine.

An objective study of history shows that the doctrine of *sola scriptura* has provided neither a clear nor a consistent rule for the Christian faith. The problems with the "Bible only" philosophy were perceived in the early Church by St. Vincent of Lérins, who, writing in the year 434, makes the following observation:

> Here someone may ask: since the canon of scriptures is complete, and is in itself adequate, why is there any need to join to its authority the understanding of the church? Because Holy Scripture, on account of its depth, is not accepted in a universal sense. The same statements are interpreted in one way by one person, in another sense by someone else, with the result that there seem to be as many opinions as there are people... Therefore, on account of the number and variety of errors, there is a need for someone to lay down a rule for the interpretation of the prophets and the apostles in such a way that it is directed by the rule of the catholic church.[158]

[158] Alister E. McGrath, ed. *The Christian Theology Reader* (Oxford, UK: Blackwell Publishers, Ltd, 1995),pp. 50-51.

Some Protestants might object that no system is perfect and that, in spite of its problems, an appeal to the Bible as the ultimate doctrinal authority is the best we can do. Such observations, however, fail to come to terms with, what for Christians, must be the ultimate test: namely, the will of Christ. Did Jesus intend to establish His Church on the basis of *sola scriptura*? Or did the Savior who said He would build His Church upon a certain rock and who gave to the man called Rock (*Petros*) the keys to the kingdom of heaven (Matt. 16:18-19) intend something other than a *sola scriptura* Church (or churches)? This is the question we must ask as we approach the dawn of the third millennium of the Christian era.

Chapter 7

What is Catholicism's Official Doctrine on Scripture and Tradition?

By Father Peter Stravinskas

To read some analyses of the Catholic position of the relationship between Scripture and Tradition, one could easily get the impression that it emerged "full-blown from the brow of Zeus" somewhere during the late Middle Ages. A more careful chronicling reveals something quite different.

From where did the Catholic approach to sacraments come? Authority? Community structure? All are grounded in our Jewish roots. And our notions of how Scripture and Tradition are related? Yes, also from Judaism. Nor should this surprise anyone for, as Pope Pius XI reminded us, we Catholics are by nature "religious Semites."[1]

The Lutheran scholar Kalfried Froehlich documents how the Jewish community inter-faced with the written Word of God under the influence of "the rabbis, the Qumran sect, and the various strands of Diaspora Judaism."[2] Interestingly, he makes the point that "at first the tradition of oral law had developed parallel to the transmission of Torah, but when its authority met with doubt, for example, among the Sadducees, the essential unity of Torah and tradition, written and oral law, had to be demonstrated."[3] Indeed, he

---

1 *La Documentation Catholique* 39, 1480.

2 Karlfried Froehlich, *Biblical Interpretation in the Early Church* (Philadelphia: Fortress Press, 1984), pp. 1-8.

3 Ibid., p. 3

goes so far as to note that "rabbinic exegetes claimed that both written and oral laws went back to God's revelation to Moses on Mount Sinai," with methods of interpretation designed and approved precisely to validate such an assertion.[4] Similarly, among the Qumran sectarians, we find that "the center of Scripture was moving away from the Torah to the prophets and to the revelational authority of the Teacher of Righteousness."[5] The pattern was likewise evident in Diaspora Judaism, from which came the Septuagint text and about which we learn that "for centuries the authority of the inspired Septuagint outweighed the authority of the Hebrew text among Jews of the Diaspora and Christians."[6] It is important to observe that the exegetical authority of scholars increased throughout the era of Diaspora Judaism, much of that period roughly contemporaneous with Jesus Himself (e.g., Philo, Hillel, Shammai); more to the point, we never encounter Jesus condemning such methods of scriptural interpretation. On the contrary, He urges His followers to heed the message of the scribes.[7]

The Reformed theologian A. Berkeley Mickelsen follows the exact same trajectory, all the while throwing it back further to the time of Ezra and further ahead into the sixth century A.D.[8] Yet another Calvinist seconds the historical outline given above, with the fascinating inclusion of an additional sect, the Karaites or the Beni Mikra, that is, the Sons of Reading, "so called because *their fundamental principle was to regard Scripture as the sole authority in matters of faith*"[9] (emphasis in original). He speaks of them as "the spiritual descendants of the Sadducees" and cites with approval their being dubbed "the Protestants of Judaism" by Farrar.[10] But, he observes, the mainstream approach held and grew into

4 Ibid.

5 Ibid., p. 5

6 Ibid., p. 7

7 Cf., Matthew 23:2.

8 A. Berkeley Mickelsen, *Interpreting the Bible* (Grand Rapids, Michigan: Eerdmans Publishing, 1974), pp. 20-30.

9 Louis Berkhof, *Principles of Biblical Interpretation* (Grand Rapids, Michigan: Baker Book House, 1962), p. 17.

10 Ibid., p. 16

movements of the late Middle Ages and Renaissance (e.g., Cabbalists, Spanish Jews).

Frederic Farrar, whom we just met briefly, provides a most detailed presentation of this whole situation in his 1885 Bampton Lectures. This Reformed scholar offers a history of interpretation in Judaism, viewing it with very negative lenses, almost to the point of being anti-Semitic. His animus is motivated as much by his anti-Catholicism as he attempts to show the continuity between Judaism and Catholicism, regarding this as evidence of the depravity of both. Nonetheless, he does bring forth riveting texts from Rabbinic Judaism on our topic, and so is worth quoting in large part. He writes:

> The Pentateuch was disparaged in comparison with the Mishna, the Mishna in comparison with the voluminous expansions of the Gemara. Supported by the False Decretals of Judaism which asserted that the Oral Law had been handed down by Mosaic succession through a chain of recipients, the Scribes proceeded to make disobedience to their decisions more perilous than disobedience to a moral commandment. 'The voice of the Rabbi is as the voice of God.' 'He who transgresses the words of the Scribes throws away his life.' 'Scripture is like water, the Mishna like wine; the Gemara like spiced wine.' 'The Scripture is as salt, the Mishna as pepper, the Gemara as spice.' 'There is no salvation,' said Rab, 'for the man who passes from the study of the Halakha to that of Scripture.' 'Men learned in Scripture are only as the tendrils of the vine; the Mishna students are the grapes; the students of the Gemara are the ripe clusters.' 'The study of Scripture is non-meritorious; the Gemara is an unapproachable virtue.' 'He who only studies the Scriptures is but an empty cistern.' 'Words of Scribes,' said Rabbi Johanan, 'are akin to words of the Law, and more beloved.'[11]

Farrar shows how the Jewish methods of interpretation began with Ezra and continued in increasingly dramatic force with each successive generation: Sopherim [BC 458-BC 320]; Chakhamim [BC 323-AD 13]; Tanaim [AD 13-AD 190]; Amoraim [AD 190-AD 498];

[11] Farrar, pp., 62-63.

Seboraim [AD 498-AD 689]; Gaonin [AD 689-AD 900], and so on into the thirteenth century of the Christian era. He summarizes it all thus: "...and indeed for twenty-two centuries the impulse given by Ezra continued to sway the course of Jewish thought."[12]

It is within this environment that Christianity breathed its first air — a context which needs to be appreciated in order to understand what became the Catholic position on Scripture and Tradition.

The Patristic and Medieval Periods

Since the patristic understanding of our question will be developed elsewhere in this volume, it is not necessary to survey the individual Fathers. Someone like Tertullian (ca. 200) could be taken as fairly typical as he "...argued that interpretation of Scripture must be ruled by the faith and teaching of the Church, the living tradition of the apostles passed on and guaranteed by the Church's teachers and bishops."[13] Irenœus adopted a similar position. Grant writes that in this Father of the Church:

> The Christian interpreter is no longer content to appeal only to his inspired intuition, as in the case of the writers of the New Testament, or to what is self-evidently rational (as the school of Alexandria was to appeal), but to an authority which is at once external and internal. The authority of the Church is external because it did not constitute the gospel; the gospel brought both the Scripture and the Church into existence. And yet it is internal, for the Scriptures are the Church's books, and the Church has been entrusted with the ministry of the gospel.[14]

Suffice it, then, to take Tavard's summary as accurate: "We are led by patristic theology to consider that there is a sense in which 'Scripture alone' is an authentic expression of Catholic

---

[12] Ibid., pp. 52-53.

[13] Phylis Bird, *The Bible as the Church's Book* (Phila, PA: Westminster Press, 1982), p. 41.

[14] Robert M. Grant, *A Short History of the Interpretation of the Bible* (New York: Macmillan, 1963), p. 73.

Christianity, inasmuch as, that is, the Scripture is, in the Church, the apostolic tradition and vice versa."[15] What does he mean? Very simply put, the patristic writers saw so intimate a union between Scripture and Tradition that they were virtually indistinguishable from one another.

Not surprisingly, then, do we find St. Thomas Aquinas coming up with a similar perspective. In the *Summa Theologica*, Aquinas speaks of "sacred doctrine" which, for him, includes both Scripture and the theology which grew up around it under the impulse of the Fathers and Doctors.[16] These two realities, however, go to form one unique reality, namely, "divine Revelation, in which Sacred Scripture, or Sacred Doctrine, is grounded."[17] The formula is clear for him: Sacred Scripture is identical with Sacred Doctrine. Tavard explains this position: "This inclusion of the Fathers within the body, if not the Canon, of Scripture, is consistent with the above-noted correlation of Scripture and Church."[18] Believers from the Early Church and the Middle Ages did not exhibit the same type of

---

15 Tavard, p. 11.

16 In an imaginative but theologically accurate conversation between Aquinas and Luther on the question of *sola Scriptura*, Peter Kreeft puts the following words into the mouth of the Angelic Doctor:

> *Sola scriptura* without one authoritative Church to interpret Scripture means that each pupil interprets the teacher's textbook in his own way, not the teacher's way, thus rendering the teacher superfluous. Eventually, there will be as many interpretations as pupils, in effect as many textbooks as pupils. Thus *sola Scriptura* undermines the authority of the very Scripture it exalts. The logical conclusion of private interpretation is private churches — eventually as many Protestantisms as Protestants.

Fifth, there is the causal argument. A fallible cause cannot produce an infallible effect. But the Church is the efficient cause of Scripture. She wrote it. She is also its formal cause: she defined its canon. Thus, if the Church is only fallible, her canon of Scripture is only fallible, and we do not know infallibly which books are Scripture, that is infallible. So again your sola Scriptura doctrine demeans the authority of the very Scripture you want to exalt. (*Ecumenical Jihad: Ecumenism and the Culture War* (San Francisco: Ignatius Press, 1996), p. 130).

17 *Summa Theologica*, P. I, q. I, a. 2, ad 2.

18 Tavard, p. 16.

skittishness about such a correlation as folks living under the sway of the Protestant Reformation, the Enlightenment or the modern era. Tavard goes on to note that, for the medievals, extension of Scripture to the Fathers and Doctors was normal and natural. Indeed, these holy men perceived it as "inseparable from the Bible itself. Both are to be read together. They stand or fall together. To trust the collective reading of Holy Writ does not amount to placing man-made traditions in the Holy of Holies. For this reading is itself the work of the Holy Ghost." He goes on:

> In other words, the Spirit is given in the Church for the understanding of Scripture. If Scripture is seen in the context of its spiritual reading, and not only as a material book, it evolves into a diptych wherein the Spirit of God inspires the understanding of the writings He Himself inspires. Because spirits are to be tested [1 John 4:1], no one can read alone. The total Scripture — comprising the written Word of God and commentaries flowing from that source — arises from the Church's total spiritual reliance upon her Lord.[19]

In a much more natural and organic view of things, Scripture and Church were regarded as closely intertwined, precisely due to the on-going presence of the Holy Spirit. Beyond that, no antagonism or dichotomy was seen between a so-called "institutional" Church and a Church of "the people." At this time, the Church is still very much the mother of her children, the members of the Church — the mother whose children are nourished by sacred doctrine at her abundant breasts.

With political developments in the secular sphere and corruption within the Church, confidence in such an ecclesial view declined — although it did not by any means evaporate. It is surely correct to assert, however, that "the fourteenth century introduced a cleavage between them [Church and Scripture]." With this unfolding, a wedge was driven between the voice of God coming to us from Scripture and that voice coming in and through the Church. Indeed, "more and more now, theologians introduce a *vel* or *aut* between arguments borrowed from Scripture and inspired by the

---

19 Ibid., pp. 19-20.

Church, as though it were possible for the former not to be included also under the latter heading."[20] All of which is to say that we are beginning to see the unraveling of the unity of Revelation.

Not everyone was affected by this developing consciousness. As eminent a thinker as Giovanni Pico della Mirandola was so impressed with the Jewish Cabala that he had come to believe that on Mount Sinai, the Almighty had given the Law to Moses in two parts, the one written which he passed on to the Israelites, the other spiritual [including proper interpretation] which God ordered him to hand on to seventy wise men to guard and pass it on to succeeding generations or guardians. Mirandola's fifteenth-century *Apologia* carried weight far beyond a passing interest in Jewish affairs. And even so marginal a figure as Erasmus, "in his desire to keep the Scriptures undefiled, so extols the work of spiritual interpretation and textual criticism, that Holy Writ cannot be understood apart from the reflections and efforts of post-apostolic centuries."[21]

The Reformation Theologians

It has become a truism that Luther, Calvin and the other Reformers espoused *sola Scriptura* in precisely the same manner as it has emerged in contemporary evangelical and fundamentalist Christian bodies. Granted, they did present the Bible as a "self-interpreting" document, and they certainly "set Scripture for the first time over against the Church and its teaching office, or at least alongside it, as an independent, and privileged, source of authority."[22] Perhaps more distinctive of their contribution, in contradistinction to the medieval period, was their insistence on a literal rather than an allegorical interpretation of the Word of God. But in this effort, they were not innovators, for St. Augustine had pressed for this approach nearly a millennium before. Indeed, Aquinas, consciously following Augustine's lead, teaches that any figurative interpretation has to flow from the literal and never be in contradiction to it.[23]

---

[20] Ibid., p. 22.

[21] Ibid., p. 77.

[22] Bird, p. 43.

[23] Augustine's *Epistula* xlviii, and *Summa Theologica*, I, 10, ad 1.

The Reformers, however, shifted the focus: to an emphasis on the sureness of the Word from a sureness of the Church. That having been said, however, Bird makes the point:

> Both Luther and Calvin remained in their understanding of Scripture closer to the long tradition that preceded them than to most later interpretation. While both rejected allegorical interpretation, they continued to read the Scriptures Christologically and to employ figuration and typology in their interpretation, especially of the Old Testament. They also continued to assume the coherence of Scripture and doctrine, though they shifted the emphasis to Scripture. It is that shift, however, which was all-important. It was the hallmark of the Reformation everywhere and it had far-reaching consequences.[24]

However, Luther cannot be brought to the side of those who would claim the "self-interpreting" nature of the Bible in any absolutist sense, for it is crucial to recall that Luther's version of *sola Scriptura* was much more nuanced. After all, it was he—and not the pre-Tridentine Catholic Church—who mandated a sermon at every service, precisely to interpret the Scripture for the congregation. And even more amazingly, it was he who proposed that preachers use prepared or "canned" sermons since so few men have the natural talents to preach well and wisely.[25]

The Council of Trent

The more extreme and vociferous echoes of Martin Luther's famous battle-cry of "sola Scriptura" were heard throughout the Church, and when the Church finally met in council at Trent, that issue was taken up. Rather than simply looking at the final conciliar document, it would be instructive for many reasons to review the theological debates that produced that document, not the least of which being that such a process will demonstrate that no single theory of divine Revelation dominated the Catholic landscape prior

[24] Bird, p. 44.
[25] Ibid., p. 45.

to Trent and indeed that none really did afterwards, either.[26] Granted, all the Catholic apologists were united in asserting that both Church and Scripture carried weight, but they were far from unanimous in explaining the relationship between the two.

The conciliar debate on this topic began on February 8, 1546, lasting until April 8 of the same year. Inexplicably, the theologians were remarkably quiet, with the majority of opinions being expressed by the bishops. Pietro Bertano, the Domincan Bishop of Fano, put the episcopal goal succinctly: "To formulate a dogma which would be directly contrary to the dogma of the Lutherans,"[27] that is, to argue against the exclusion of ecclesiastical traditions. The original aim was rather modest: to delineate the books which comprise the Bible and to address the abuses which had infringed on the use of these books. As can be seen, the Council Fathers thus were considering Scripture "in its strict canonical sense,"[28] that is, the "canon" or list of books deemed to be constitutive of the Sacred Scriptures. In response, however, the General Superior of the Servites alleged that this would be a waste of time since on that topic there was no substantive disagreement between Lutherans and Catholics, even though some of the Protestants did challenge the authorship of the Epistle to the Hebrews or the Epistle of James.[29]

One of the three papal legates, Cardinal del Monte, however, pressed for the canonical listing to occupy their attention for one general session and for another to be devoted to "ecclesiastical traditions."[30] Del Monte maintained that Revelation was a unified reality, coming to us in two sources, partly (Latin: *partim*) conveyed through the Old and New Testaments and partly (*partim*) "out of a

---

[26] For the discussion that follows, I am following closely the magisterial work of George Tavard in Chapter 12 of his *Holy Church or Holy Writ*. The reader should also refer to H. Schroeder's *Decrees and Canons of the Council of Trent.*

[27] The citations from the conciliar debates can be found in the *Gorresgesellschaft* edition of the diaries; the present quotation is found under the date of March 27, Vol. I, 39.

[28] Tavard, p. 196,

[29] February, 8, I, 29.

[30] February 12, V, 8.

simple transmission by hand."[31] What this meant in the concrete was the unity of the act of Revelation, coming through two secondary sources, namely, the canonical Scriptures and "the ecclesiastical tradition which is without Scripture."[32] To Del Monte's surprise, his proposal met with strong opposition: Most Council Fathers had no problem with handling Scripture and traditions[33] together, but the majority were adamant to exclude traditions that had not come from the apostles themselves. By February 18, Tradition had come to be limited to "apostolic traditions." This point of view gained ascendancy, so that the distinction between apostolic and post-apostolic traditions enabled the Council to focus its attention on apostolicity, whether biblical or extra-biblical — and that would become the hallmark of Revelation. This was further refined in such wise that apostolic traditions were binding, to the extent that they pertained to matters of faith, and not discipline. Beyond that, they were to be not only apostolic in origin, but handed down continuously to the present moment. In other words, simply identifying a teaching as having a foundation in the apostolic era was insufficient; it had to be demonstrated that that position was consistently and consciously transmitted ever since.

In direct conflict with the group holding the above position was a second group which, while not hostile to the binding authority of traditions, did not want to appear to put them on an equal footing with the Scriptures. The draft document came down on the side of the first group, but a furor erupted, with the result that on March 29 three questions were raised to determine the fate of the draft or any subsequent texts: a) "Is it enough to mention apostolic traditions? Or should the decree state that these traditions must be accepted?" Forty-four of 52 voters held for the latter; b) "Should the decree profess 'equal adhesion of faith' to Scripture and to traditions?" Thirty-three agreed with this proposition; c) "Should this

---

[31] I, 30. Editor's note: "by hand" meaning the preservation and handing down of tradition to successive generations.

[32] February 12, V, 8.

[33] It is important to notice that the plural form of the word "tradition" is used almost entirely throughout the discussion at Trent.

expression be softened as regards traditions concerning morals?" Thirty-three negatives were cast.[34]

On April 8, a final document was presented to the Council Fathers and unanimously passed — after two major changes were made to take account of the preliminary votes and the debates. First, traditions that were given "an equal adhesion of faith" had to "pertain either to faith or to behavior." Second, the partim/partim formula was dropped, so that we no longer read that the Gospel resides "partly" in the Scriptures and "partly" in the traditions; rather, the Gospel is contained in the Scriptures ***and*** in the traditions. The Catholic answer to Luther and others pressing for a sola Scriptura approach to divine Revelation came out in this way:

> ...this [Gospel] ... [is] the source at once of all saving truth and rules of conduct. [This council] clearly perceives that these truths and rules are contained in the written books and in the unwritten traditions, which, received by the Apostles themselves, the Holy Ghost dictating, have come down to us, transmitted as it were by hand ... it receives and venerates with a feeling of piety and reverence all the books both of the Old and New Testaments, since one God is the author of both; also morals, as having been dictated either orally by Christ or by the Holy Ghost, and preserved in the Catholic Church in unbroken succession.

As far as "private interpretation" goes, the Council had this to say:

> Furthermore, to check unbridled spirits, it decrees that no one relying on his own judgment shall, in matters of faith and morals pertaining to the edification of Christian doctrine, distorting the Holy Scriptures in accordance with his own conceptions, presume to interpret them contrary to the sense which holy mother Church, to whom it belongs to judge of their true sense and interpretation, has held and holds, or even contrary to the unanimous teaching of the Fathers, though such interpretations should never at any time be published.[35]

---

[34] Tavard, pp. 205-206.

[35] Schroeder, p. 17, 19.

What was the upshot of this decree? Tavard well summarizes it:

> Compared with pre-Tridentine theology, the decree of April 1546 makes it impossible to hold that new doctrines may still be revealed to the Church: The stress on apostolicity is too well marked to be compatible with such a view. It remains neutral on a notion of Tradition (in the singular), which would include Scripture and be identified with the life or conscience of the Church: The rationale of the Council precluded consideration of this problematic but did not gainsay the underlying theology. It finally respects the classical view: Scripture contains all revealed doctrine, and the Church's faith which includes apostolic traditions, interprets it.[36]

While Luther claimed to want the Gospel alone, his successors ended by opposing the Scriptures interpreted by the Church with a Gospel interpreted by Luther. Amazingly, we learn that as early as 1559, Nicholas von Armsdorf indicated that his teachings were based on those of "die heiligen Paulum und Lutherum," that is, "Saints (plural!) Paul and Luther."[37] Similarly as Catholics took their stand by councils, the Lutherans ended up grounding themselves in an ever-increasing number of confessional documents, like the 1580 *Book of Concord*, as well as the earlier 1531 *Apology of the Augsburg Confession* and the 1537 *Smalkald Articles*. Little by little, the Calvinists and Puritans engaged in like conduct. The Catholic response came to all this in the Counter-Reformation: Faced with a Protestant slogan of "Scripture alone," the Catholic apologists veered strongly toward "the Church alone," even though that was not the explicit teaching of Trent.

In a highly insightful conclusion to his work — and with noticeable irenicism, especially for 1959 — Tavard assesses the whole dynamic in this way:

> It therefore seems that the time may soon be ripe for a reassessment of the basic issue of 'Scripture alone.' If the lessons of history have any value, one point should become a

[36] Tavard, p. 209.

[37] Ibid., p. 96.

> common center of reference in such a reexamination. The dilemma that came to a head at the Reformation arose out of an artificial distinction between two God-given supernatural realities, Scripture and the Church. Since then, we have been struggling with a problematic of opposition, at a point where the old Church adhered to a problematic of inclusion.
>
> The secret of re-integration, or of Christian unity, or of a theology of ecumenism (whatever name we choose to give this) may lie in opening a way back to an inclusive concept of Scripture and of the Church. Scripture cannot be the Word of God once it has been severed from the Church which is the Bride and the Body of Christ. And the Church could not be the Bride and the Body, had she not received the gift of understanding the Word. These two phases of God's visitation of man are aspects of one mystery. They are ultimately one, though one in two. The Church implies the Scripture as the Scripture implies the Church.
>
> Who has beheld this oneness is blessed. For the whole mystery of the Church is open to him. The mind of man craves to tear apart what God has bound together. In Christ, however, God came to us in the partnership of the letter and the spirit, the Scripture and its understanding, the Book and the Church that reads it. Who does not separate them is blessed. For he has escaped the curse of St. John the Theologian: 'If any man shall take away from the words of the Book of this prophecy, God shall take away his part out of the Tree of Life and out of the Holy City which are described in this Book' [Revelation 22:19].
>
> The Book is the Word of God, and the City is the Church. The Book leads to the City. Yet the City is described in the Book. To prefer the one to the other amounts to renouncing both.[38]

Tavard's sensitive and intelligent plea found a hearing at the Second Vatican Council which, in turn, has found a hearing among

[38] Ibid., pp. 246-247.

sensitive and intelligent non-Catholic Christians. We now turn to that Council's formulations.

Vatican II on Scripture and Tradition

Between Trent and Vatican II, a great deal happened in the world and in the Church, not the least being the rise of intellectual currents like the Enlightenment, liberalism (in Protestantism) and modernism (in Catholicism). A rationalist philosopher like Thomas Hobbes had no more time for biblical theories which accorded infallibility to the Scriptures than for those which did likewise for the Church.[39] Interestingly enough, in assault after assault on the infallibility and inerrancy of the Scriptures, it was the authority of the Catholic Church which came to the rescue, with the teachings of the First Vatican Council (1870) and with papal decrees like *Lamentabili* (1907) and *Pascendi* (1907), as well as a host of documents from various Roman dicasteries and later popes. Protestantism's only defense against the demythologization efforts of a Bultmann was to take refuge in Fundamentalism. In that period between the Reformation and the twentieth century, the Catholic Church gradually developed a *modus vivendi* with some of the less extreme forms of biblical criticism and even developed an entire biblical movement of her own.

Of the sixteen documents which were promulgated by Pope Paul VI as a result of the Second Vatican Council, the Constitution on Divine Revelation (*Dei Verbum*) is one which is among the least known and appreciated at the popular level, however, it is among the most important since it is, in many ways, programmatic for all other aspects of life in the Church.

A bit of background on the document would be useful. All the topics which were to be presented for discussion at the Council were prepared for by means of preliminary drafts formulated by the Theological Commission. When the text relating to divine Revelation was presented to the Council Fathers, it met with severe

---

[39] For a good discussion of this whole era, see "The Rise of Rationalism" in Grant's *A Short History of the Interpretation of the Bible.*

criticism, so much so that Pope John XXIII took the unprecedented step of remanding it to the Commission for rewriting, which indeed happened. R.A.F. MacKenzie explains: "The original first chapter, 'Two Sources of Revelation' (namely, Scripture and Tradition), was replaced by two chapters, on Revelation itself and on its transmission, in which Scripture and Tradition were not explicitly distinguished as separate 'sources.'"[40] He goes on to note that "the treatment in general became less philosophical, more biblical and historical."[41] As can readily be seen, this is all quite germane to what occupies us in this present study.

Chapter I of the conciliar document begins with an analysis of the concept of Revelation itself, setting the tone for all that follows by the verbs chosen for the very first sentence, as it speaks of the Church "hearing the Word of God... and proclaiming it." The "hearing" dimension gives primacy to the Word, even as the "proclaiming" immediately sets the Church into the picture. Furthermore, the text is intent on demonstrating, from the outset, that there will be continuity between this conciliar constitution and its predecessors from the Councils of Trent and Vatican I.

In his commentary, then-Father Joseph Ratzinger shows how the drafters and the bishops were influenced by a philosophy and theology of personalism, whereby we consider how it is Almighty God Himself — as a Person — communicating with other persons which is the focus.[42] That is refined or clarified in the life and ministry of the God-Man, which becomes paradigmatic as Jesus' words and works, together, form Revelation. Thus, we find ourselves extricated from the dead-end battles pitting Scripture against Tradition, or vice-versa. In this way, we begin to realize that the "what" of Revelation is, in reality, a "Who." The language of the document confirms this intuition, as we read phrases like, "it pleased God," "addresses men," "moves among them," etc. That is summed up in the statement that "the most intimate truth which this revelation gives us about God and the salvation of man shines forth in Christ, *Who is Himself* both the mediator and the sum total of Rev-

40 R.A.F. MacKenzie, in Vorgrimler, p. 107.

41 Ibid.

42 Joseph Ratzinger, in Vorgrimler, commentary on chapter I, pp. 170ff.

elation" [emphasis added].[43] Which then leads to the question of "how" Revelation is communicated.

Chapter II is dedicated to "the transmission of divine Revelation." Articles 7 and 8 attempt to explain the history of this process, with particular emphasis placed on the apostolic and subapostolic Church. Article 9 then gives precision to it all, as Sacred Scripture is defined as "the speech of God as it is put down in writing under the breath of the Holy Spirit," while we are told that "Tradition transmits in its entirety the Word of God which has been entrusted to the apostles by Christ the Lord and the Holy Spirit."[44] For what purpose? Tradition,[45] we learn, transmits the Word of God "to the successors of the apostles so that, enlightened by the Spirit of truth, they may faithfully preserve, expound, and spread it abroad by their preaching."[46] With what result? The Church "does not derive her certainty about all revealed truths from the Holy Scriptures alone. Both Scripture and Tradition must be accepted and honored with equal sentiments of devotion and reverence." Therefore, "sacred Tradition and sacred Scripture make up a single sacred deposit of the Word of God, which is entrusted to the Church."[47] Thus, Scripture is placed within the framework of Tradition, for that is how it emerged, even as Tradition is shown completely in relation to Scripture. In this way, the two are not per-

[43] *Dei Verbum*, n. 2.

[44] Tradition here includes what Ratzinger terms "the totality of the presence of Christ in this world." The Council identifies three elements of this presence: teaching, life and worship.

[45] Already alluded to in n. 33 above, it is now worth taking account of Ratzinger's highlighting of the fact that whereas Trent spoke of Tradition only in the plural, Vatican II (except for one instance, and that is a scriptural citation) uses only the singular. He explains that Trent was confronted with a concrete question about specific ecclesiastical practices ("traditions"), while Vatican II was treating the matter in a more theoretical and theological fashion, thus enabling it to situate the discussion differently. Cf. Ratzinger, in Vorgrimler, p. 183.

[46] But Tradition is not a static reality, for as a living reality closely identified with the Church herself, we learn that Tradition "makes progress;" there is "a growth in insight," allowing the Church to "advance towards the plentitude of divine truth" (n. 8).

[47] *Dei Verbum*, n. 10.

ceived as antagonistic to each other since they are both witnesses to the one Word of God.[48]

Following the line of thought which slowly but surely emerged among the Fathers, MacKenzie explains that Revelation, "passed on orally... becomes tradition; recorded in writing, it becomes Scripture." He continues: "More precisely, Scripture *contains* Revelation, namely, in the form of a written record; but not all of Scripture *is* Revelation. Much of it is the record of Revelation's effects, of the human reactions to it, of men's faith or lack of it. All of Scripture is inspired, but not all is revealed" [emphasis in original]. Then zeroing in on how this problem was faced at Trent, our commentator observes:

> Similarly, tradition comes to include much that is only of human origin, however venerable and valuable. At the time of the Council of Trent, great difficulty was experienced in drawing a line between traditions which merely witnessed to ancient usages in the Church, and those which represented the revelation of Christ. Considerable progress has been made since then by theologians and Church historians in clarifying the point, but not all such questions are yet solved.[49]

Taking up the thorny matter of the "completeness" of the scriptural record, MacKenzie states the obvious, but something nonetheless hard for some to accept, that is, that although "the written record in the New Testament is vitally important — the permanent and unchanging testimony of the apostolic generation," it does not tell the full story, for "the New Testament writings do not claim to be — in fact obviously are not — a complete and balanced inventory of the early Church's beliefs."

At the same time, it is critical to assert that these writings do, in fact, "lay down what cannot be changed: the rule of faith as it was recorded, to which the Church is always bound, and which she can develop and expand but never falsify."[50] While holding the

[48] Interestingly enough, Scripture is defined ontologically, that is, according to what it is — the Word of God; Tradition, on the other hand, is defined functionally, according to what it *does*—hand on the Word of God.

[49] MacKenzie, pp. 108-109.

[50] Ibid., p. 109.

Revelation in written form as normative, reasonable men would be compelled to admit that "a written record is a dead letter, needing constant interpretation and commentary in succeeding ages." Why? Because as human experience and Christian history (Catholic, Orthodox and Protestant alike) amply demonstrate, "it [a solely written record] cannot of itself answer new questions, or explain what was once clear and has now become obscure." Therefore, "the writings transmitted in a living community, from one generation to another, are accompanied by a continuous tradition of understanding and explanation, which preserves and re-expresses their meaning, and which applies them, from time to time, to the solving of new problems."[51]

What is the mechanism for this on-going work of interpretation? The Council Fathers identify the Church's Magisterium or teaching authority, comprised of the college of bishops, presided over by the Bishop of Rome as their head.[52] And so, in Article 10 we find the conciliar Constitution propose the following: "But the task of giving an authentic interpretation of the Word of God, whether in its written form or in the form of Tradition, has been entrusted to the living teaching office of the Church alone. Its authority in this matter is exercised in the name of Jesus Christ." In a manner at once humble and realistic, the text proceeds: "Yet this Magisterium is not superior to the Word of God, but is its servant. It teaches only what has been handed on to it." How does this "work"? "At the divine command and with the help of the Holy Spirit, [the Magisterium] listens to this devotedly, guards it with dedication and expounds it faithfully. All that it proposes for belief as being divinely revealed is drawn from this single deposit of faith."[53]

Summing up the concrete and practical playing out of the doctrine, the document says:

---

51 Ibid.

52 It is interesting that the word "Magisterium" for centuries was not the theological "household word" in Catholic circles that it is today; ironically, students of the history of theology find its most frequent use in eighteenth- and nineteenth-century Lutheranism!

53 *Dei Verbum*, n. 11. This paragraph is thus completely in keeping with the teachings of Trent and Vatican I regarding any kind of private interpretation of Scripture which would go counter to the received Tradition [cf., DS 1507 and 3007].

> It is clear, therefore, that, in the supremely wise arrangement of God, sacred Tradition, sacred Scripture and the Magisterium of the Church are so connected and associated that one of them cannot stand without the others. Working together, each in its own way under the action of the one Holy Spirit, they all contribute effectively to the salvation of souls.[54]

MacKenzie summarizes the situation well when he speaks of how the Constitution stresses "the coordination and interplay of Scripture, Tradition and Magisterium." Appealing once more to human experience, he declares: "In whatever way the question of the separate values of the first two [Scripture and Tradition] may be answered in theory, in practice all three function together, and all are necessary for the Church's life."[55] this material is handily treated in the Catechism of the Catholic Church in five pages (nn. 80-100); the broader discussion is found in Chapter II of Part I of the Catechism under the heading of "God Comes to Meet Man," dealing with the fundamentals of divine Revelation and its transmission, along with a detailed presentation on the Sacred Scriptures (cf., nn. 50-141).

Conclusion

In discussions on Scripture and Tradition, one is often reminded of the classical debate: "Which came first? The chicken or the egg?" Both can touch off endless disputations and are largely irresolvable, but to make some sense of it all, we can resort to a temporal mode to find a way through the impasse.

Clearly, Tradition precedes Scripture from the point of view of time — and the Church precedes both, in that the writing of the New Testament did not begin until some fifteen to twenty years after the Pentecostal formation of the Church and may not have been completed until perhaps as late as A.D. 120. The Gospel message, then, was imparted through oral tradition first, and only later was it committed to written form. The means (whether oral or writ-

---

54 *Dei Verbum*, n. 10.

55 MacKenzie, p. 109.

ten), however, is in many ways secondary to the goal (Revelation) and to the receiver of the Revelation (God's people, the Church).

An example from American government might be instructive. The law of the land is found in the Constitution of the United States; it is normative for American life. However, it is not a self-interpreting document. On the contrary, it calls for detailed, professional interpretation from an entire branch of government dedicated to that purpose. Furthermore, when conflicting views do surface, standard procedures of jurisprudence require a return to the sources, in an effort to discover the mind of the people who produced the text.

With appropriate allowances made for divine workings in the case of Scripture, Tradition, and the Church, one finds many parallels that are useful. Scripture comes alive only in the life of the community that gave it birth and has ever since preached and proclaimed it. To remove Scripture from its moorings in the Church is to deny it genuine vitality. Scripture provides Tradition with a written record against which to judge its fidelity and thus serves as a safeguard. In the "balance of powers" (to have recourse again to the governmental analogy), Tradition is a defense against an unhealthy individualism that distorts the Bible through private interpretation at odds with the constant Tradition of the Church.

For Christians, the Bible is not Revelation in itself; for us, Revelation is a Person, not a book — no matter how holy. To worship a book is bibliolatry. A truly accurate and truly Christian perspective on Revelation takes all these seriously: God, the Church, the Church's Tradition, and the Church's Scriptures. The focus of our attention, however, is not the Church, the Scriptures or Tradition, but God. The other three are means given to us to arrive at our end — union with God.

Chapter 8

What did the Church Fathers Teach Concerning Scripture, Tradition, and Church Authority?

By Joseph Gallegos

> But beyond these [Scriptural] sayings, let us look at the very tradition, teaching, and faith of the Catholic Church from the beginning, which the Lord gave, the Apostles preached, and the Fathers kept. Upon this the Church is founded, and he who should fall away from it would not be a Christian, and should no longer be so called.
>
> **St. Athanasius**, *Ad Serapion* 1:28 (A.D. 360)

> The formal object of faith is Primary Truth as manifested in Holy Scripture and in the teaching of the Church which proceeds from the Primary Truth. Hence, he who does not embrace the teaching of the church as a divine and infallible law does not possess the habit of faith."
>
> **St. Thomas Aquinas**, *Summa Theologica* II-II, Q.5, A. 3

Introduction

This chapter will provide testimony from the Early Church Fathers regarding the rule of faith through the fifth century. The title *Church Father* was bestowed on those Catholic teachers in the ancient Church who transmitted the ecclesiastical faith to their spiritual sons and daughters. Irenaeus writes: "For when any person has been taught from the mouth of another, he is termed the son of him who instructs him, and the latter [is called] his father."[1] Clement of Alexandria writes: "Hence we call those who have instructed us, fathers."[2] We understand the *Church Fathers* have consisted of those men who during their lives combined these four marks: (1) orthodoxy in doctrine, (2) holiness in life, (3) Church approval and (4) antiquity. Today, this title has been bestowed on other writers who fulfilled only some of these marks (e.g., Tertullian, Eusebius of Caesarea, Origen). They are included because of the value of their service to the Catholic Church. The traditional mark of antiquity ends with St. John Damascene [A.D. 750] in the East and with St. Gregory the Great [A.D. 604] in the West. "[A]ssuredly it is incumbent on all Catholics who are anxious to approve themselves genuine sons of Mother Church, to adhere henceforth to the holy faith of the holy Fathers..."[3]

The Church Fathers, as the title claims, were first and foremost men of the Church who desired nothing more than to deliver and teach the traditional faith rather than their own understanding of the gospel. For example, Augustine writes:

> [T]he sentiments of the bishops who have gone before us, men who treated these divine words faithfully and memorably... what they found in the church, they held; what they had learned, they taught; what they had received from the fathers, this they delivered to the children.[4]

Cyril of Alexandria:

> As soon as he (Nestorius) had been ordained... he set himself eagerly to promulgate certain novel and unreasonable things, and which are far removed from that apostolic and evangelic faith, which our fathers ever preserved and handed down to us as a pearl of great price.[5]

---

1 Irenaeus, *Against Heresies*, 4, 41:2 (inter A.D. 180-199), ANF I:524.
2 Clement of Alexandria, *Stromata* 1:1 (post A.D. 202) ANF II:299.
3 Lerins, Vincent, *Commonitory,* 86 (c. A.D. 434) NPNF 2, XI:156.
4 Augustine, *Against Julian*, 2, 19:34 (c. A.D. 421) FOC I: 441.
5 Cyril of Alexandria, *To Coelestine*, Epistle 9 (A.D. 430) FOC I: 446.

From these kinds of statements it was simply not the desire of the Church Fathers to impart their own exegesis of Scriptures or to deliver novel doctrines on the basis of a private interpretation of the apostolic deposit. Instead, the Church Fathers, as the name implies, transmitted the same ecclesiastical faith that was bequeathed to them by their spiritual forefathers in the faith. Epiphanius in his work on heresies summarizes the role of the those who were called Fathers of the Church.

Epiphanius:

> Now of these which is wiser? This deceived man (Aerius) who has just now obtained notoriety, and who is still living; or they who were witnesses before us, who held before us the tradition in(or for) the church, and who themselves had received it from their fathers, whose fathers again had learnt it from their forefathers, even as the church, having received the true faith from its fathers, retains it, together with the traditions, even unto this day.[6]

In light of the emphasis on tradition, there are two recurring themes throughout the writings of the Church Fathers regarding the rule of faith. First, the Christian faith consists of a single deposit given to the Church. According to the Fathers, this deposit of faith can find its most perfect expression in the Sacred Scriptures. The second recurring theme is that in order to obtain a proper and full understanding of the Scriptures one must do so within the milieu of the Church and her unerring Tradition. In other words, the Scriptures are of no avail without the Church and her Tradition. Tradition according to the Fathers consisted of the entire deposit of faith which was "once for all delivered to the saints," a deposit which was not committed simply to a book to be broadcasted and understood by individuals on their own, but a deposit which was received by a teaching Church. It was the divine function of the Church to preach authoritatively and hand on this apostolic heritage. Tradition was the means of transmitting the entire apostolic faith.

---

6 Epiphanius, *Panarion*, 75 (inter A.D. 374-377) FOC I:433-434.

The Sufficiency of the Scriptures According to the Fathers

Some Protestant apologists have attempted to find the doctrine of *sola scriptura* in the Church Fathers by following either one of three approaches. First, they have provided a one-sided polemic regarding the Church Fathers and the authority of Scripture and Tradition. To illustrate this point, we will provide a dossier of quotations from the Fathers illustrating the authority of the Scriptures.

Ambrose [c.A.D. 339-397] "For how can we adopt those things which we do not find in the holy Scriptures?"[7]

Antony of Egypt [c.A.D. 250-356] "The Scriptures are enough for instruction..."[8]

Athanasius [c.A.D. 295-373] "[T]he sacred and inspired Scriptures are sufficient to declare the truth..."[9]

Augustine [A.D. 354-430] "[W]hat more can I teach you, than what we read in the Apostle? For holy Scripture setteth a rule to our teaching, that we dare not 'be wise more than it behoveth to be wise;'... Be it not therefore for me to teach you any other thing, save expound to you the words of the Teacher..."[10]

Chrysostom [inter A.D. 344/345-407] "Wherefore I exhort and entreat you all, disregard what this man and that man thinks about these things, and inquire from the Scriptures all these things; and having learnt what are the true riches, let us pursue after them that we may obtain also eternal good things..."[11]

---

7 Ambrose, *Duties of the Clergy*, I, 23:102 (c. A.D. 391) NPNF 2, X:18.

8 Antony, fragment in Athanasius' *Life of Antony*, 16 (inter A.D. 356-362) NPNF 2, IV:200.

9 Athanasius, *Against the Heathen*, 1:3 (c. A.D. 318) NPNF 2, IV:4.

10 Augustine, *The Good of Widowhood*, 2 (c. A.D. 414) NPNF I, III:442.

11 Chrysostom, *On 2nd Corinthians,* Homily 13 (c. A.D. 392) NPNF 1, XII:346.

Clement of Alexandria [c.A.D. 150-c.A.D. 216] "But those who are ready to toil in the most excellent pursuits, will not desist from the search after truth, till they get the demonstration from the Scriptures themselves."[12]

Cyril of Alexandria [d. A.D. 444] "Not all that the Lord did was written down, but only what was deemed sufficient, either from the point of view of morals, or from the point of view of dogmas..."[13]

Cyril of Jerusalem [c.A.D. 315-386] "For concerning the divine and holy mysteries of the Faith, not even a casual statement must be delivered without the Holy Scriptures; nor must we be drawn aside by mere plausibility and artifices of speech. Even to me, who tell thee these things, give not absolute credence, unless thou receive the proof of the things which I announce from the Divine Scriptures. For this salvation which we believe depends not on ingenious reasoning, but on demonstration of the Holy Scriptures."[14]

Gregory of Nyssa [c.A.D. 335-394] "Let the inspired Scripture, then, be our umpire, and the vote of truth will surely be given to those whose dogmas are found to agree with the Divine words."[15]

Hilary of Poitiers [c.A.D. 315-367/368] "Yet it is certainly by these same words of God [i.e. Scripture] that we must come to understand the things of God."[16]

Hippolytus of Rome [c.A.D. 170-235] "There is, brethren, one God, the knowledge of whom we gain from the Holy Scriptures and no other source."[17]

---

[12] Clement of Alexandria, *Stromata*, 7:16 (post A.D. 202)ANF, II:550.

[13] Cyril of Alexandria, *In Joann*, XII (ante A.D. 429) CON, 110.

[14] Cyril of Jerusalem, *Catechetical Lectures*, 4:17 (c. A.D. 350) NPNF 2, VII:23.

[15] Gregory of Nyssa, *On the Holy Spirit*, (c. A.D. 375)NPNF 2, V:327. This passage is found in Basil's Epistle 189 but is considered today to be a letter of Gregory of Nyssa.

[16] Hilary of Poitiers, *On the Trinity*, 4:14 (inter A.D. 356-359) NPNF 2, IX:75.

[17] Hippolytus of Rome, *Against the Heresy of one Noetus*, 9 (inter A.D. 200-210) ANF V:227.

Irenaeus [c.A.D 140-c.A.D. 202] "[B]eing most properly assured that the Scriptures are indeed perfect, since they were spoken by the Word of God and His Spirit..."[18]

Jerome [c.A.D. 347-420] "Ignorance of the Scriptures is Ignorance of Christ"[19]

Origen [c.A.D. 185-254] "For he knows that all Scripture is the one perfect and harmonized instrument of God, which from different sounds gives forth one saving voice to those willing to learn..."[20]

Tertullian [c.A.D. 160-post A.D. 220] "If it is nowhere written, then let it fear the woe which impends on all who add to or take away from the written word."[21]

Vincent of Lerins [d. ante A.D. 450] "Since the canon of Scripture is complete, and sufficient of itself for everything, and more than sufficient..."[22]

Passages like these can be multiplied without end from the Fathers. From these samples one may be tempted to conclude that the Fathers affirmed the doctrine of *sola scriptura.* But this is done by quoting only those passages which speak highly and eloquently on the authority of the Sacred Scriptures while downplaying or even ignoring passages from these same Fathers who speak just as highly about the authority of Tradition and the Church.

Such misrepresentation of the Fathers was a tactic often used in the early Church on various matters of the faith. For example, Athanasius had to contend with the Arians' misrepresentation of Church Fathers as they selected only certain passages that supported their particular doctrine.

---

18 Irenaeus, *Against Heresies*, 2, 28:2 (inter A.D. 180-199) ANF I:399.

19 Jerome, *Commentary in Isaiah* (inter A.D. 408-410), Prologue cited in *Vatican Collection: Vatican Council II*, vol.1, Austin Flannery, O.P., ed., (Boston:St. Paul, 1988) p. 764.

20 Origen, *Commentary on Matthew*, 2 (post A.D. 244) ANF X:413.

21 Tertullian, *Against Hermogenes*, 22 (inter A.D. 200-206) ANF III:490.

22 Vincent of Lerins, *Comminitory,* 2:5 (c. A.D. 434) NPNF 2, XI:132.

> Yes, he [Dionysius] wrote it, and we too admit that his letter runs thus. But just as he wrote this, he wrote also very many other letters, and they ought to consult those also; in order that the faith of the man may be made clear from them all, and not from this alone.[23]

Here we see Athanasius vindicating the faith of Dionysius, bishop of Alexandria [A.D. 233-265], by providing clear testimony from his other writings affirming Our Lord's deity alongside those passages plucked from their context by the Arians that seemed to downplay Our Lord's divinity. Similarly, alongside patristic passages we cited earlier that testify to the authority of the Sacred Scriptures, one can readily find equally authoritative testimony from these same Church Fathers on the authority of Tradition and Church, which we will show momentarily.

A second line of attack used by Protestant apologists is to redefine Tradition to mean only those teachings that have come down to us in unwritten form but are not contained in the Sacred Scriptures. The Church Fathers and the Catholic Church however, affirm that the entire deposit of faith was transmitted to the Church in its fullness through Tradition before the New Testament was written. Moreover, this Tradition was not retired or rendered useless after the canonization of the New Testament; rather, Tradition has been entrusted to the Church to hand down to subsequent generations of believers. In addition, these same Fathers affirm that the entire deposit of faith is found materially in the Scriptures. Hence, when a Church Father appeals to Tradition he will often appeal to a doctrine which was received through Tradition which is coincident in substance with the Scriptures. This leads us to a very crucial point:The Protestant apologist, not appreciating the full-orbed Catholic understanding of Tradition, makes frequently the misguided conclusion that a Church Father is appealing to the Scriptures when in reality that Church Father is actually appealing to a teaching received through Tradition. As is the case with all such arguments they are as easily destroyed as they are developed. The Catholic catechism states:

---

[23] Athanasius, *On the Opinion of Dionysius*, 4 (forte A.D. 350/351) NPNF 2, IV:177.

> And [Holy] *Tradition* transmits in its entirety the Word of God which has been entrusted to the apostles by Christ the Lord and the Holy Spirit. It transmits it to the successors of the apostles so that, enlightened by the Spirit of truth, they may faithfully preserve, expound, and spread it abroad by their preaching.[24]

The Fathers not only appealed to Tradition on matters of faith that were not explicit in the Scriptures (such as infant baptism and the deity of the Holy Spirit) but they also repaired to Tradition on doctrinal matters that were considered explicit in Scripture (such as the Incarnation) in order to prove their apostolicity and orthodoxy. The Fathers appealed to both the Scriptures and Tradition as coordinate and normative authorities.

A third approach, similar to the first, used by Protestant apologists is to confuse the material sufficiency of Scriptures with *sola scriptura*. The Catholic position allows for the material sufficiency of the Scriptures but denies its formal sufficiency. Hence, a Protestant case directed at proving a Father's belief in the material sufficiency of Scripture is innocuous, since Catholics too can affirm the material sufficiency of the Bible. Therefore, in order for Protestant apologists to *prove* that the Fathers affirmed *sola scriptura* (not simply material sufficiency) they must prove that the Fathers affirmed formal sufficiency. That is, they must show that the Fathers required no other normative authority (such as Tradition or a teaching Church) in order to interpret the Sacred text in an authoritative and orthodox manner. Hence, we must conclude:

> This addition need not mean that the truth of the gospel would be contained partially in Holy Scripture and partially in the Tradition. The [Tridentine] declaration can be understood as agreeing with the Fathers of the Church and the great theologians of the high Middle Ages in this way: Holy Scripture contains the whole faith in substance, but the faith must be grasped in its totality and fullness only in light of Tradition. So the Second Vatican Council teaches: 'The Church

---

[24] *Catechism of the Catholic Church: Liberia Editrice Vaticana* (Boston: St. Paul Books and Media, 1994) p. 26.

> does not draw her certainty about all revealed truths from the Holy Scriptures alone'[25]

The Fathers are consistent in their writings that the entire Christian faith is contained within the corpus of Sacred Scripture. The Fathers clearly understood Scripture as materially sufficient. However, these same Fathers write that Scripture must be understood and read within the context of the Church's Tradition. In other words, the Fathers assumed an authoritative Tradition and Church when they affirmed the sufficiency of Scripture.

The Church Fathers, particularly those Fathers who combated the various heresies, insisted that the heretics interpreted Sacred Scripture apart from mother Church and her Tradition. The main objective of this chapter is to show that the Fathers not only admitted Sacred Scripture in their rule, but also included an authoritative Tradition and the teaching Church. Let us begin our enquiry with the Apostolic period.

The Apostolic Fathers and Apologists

St. Ignatius, Bishop of Antioch [d. c. A.D. 110] [26]

> Stand fast, brethren, in the faith of Jesus Christ... Do ye all come together in common, and individually, through grace, in one faith... under the guidance of the Comforter, in obedience to the bishop and the presbytery with an undivided mind, breaking one and the same bread, which is the medicine of immortality, and the antidote which prevents us from dying...

The primary witnesses during this early period are Fathers such as Clement of Rome and St. Ignatius of Antioch, and the Apologists such as St. Justin Martyr and Theophilus of Antioch. This period is distinct from subsequent generations of the Church in two ways. First, it provides testimony from disciples who were personal hear-

---

[25] Jordan, Mark, ed., *A Catechism for Adults: The Church's Confession of Faith*, (San Francisco: Ignatius, 1987), p. 47.

[26] Ignatius of Antioch, *Epistle to the Ephesians*, 20 (c. A.D. 110) ANF I:57.

ers of the Apostles, or an acquaintance of a disciple of an Apostle. Secondly, during this period the New Testament had not been collated and canonized by the Church. The available Scripture (up to St. Irenaeus, Hippolytus and Theophilus of Antioch) were mainly comprised of the Septuagint version of the Old Testament.

It is from these Scriptures that the Apostolic Fathers and Apologists find the Christian message. It was clear from the writings during this period that the Scriptures were the property of the Church. The orthodox and authentic interpretation of the Old Testament Scripture centered on Jesus Christ. The gospel during this period was found implicitly in the Old Testament and later proclaimed explicitly by Christ and His Apostles. Hence, the rule of faith during this period included the Septuagint Scriptures and the teachings and doctrines inherited from Christ and His Apostles. The Old Testament was to be read and understood according to the Tradition inherited from Christ and His Apostles. Often when referring to the Apostolic deposit, the testimony during this period, did not make the distinction between the Apostolic writings or Apostolic Tradition. For example, **Clement of Rome** [reign. c.A.D. 91-c.A.D. 101] applies a traditional rule to an ethical issue. He writes:

> We are writing in this vein, dear friends, not only to admonish you but also to remind ourselves. For we are in the same arena and involved in the same struggle. Hence we should give up empty and futile concerns and turn to the glorious and holy rule of our tradition.[27]

Tradition is the body of beliefs and disciplines within the Church. Although the word "Tradition" was seldom used during this period, the concept of handing down teachings from Christ and His Apostles was affirmed.

Polycarp [A.D. 69/70-155/156], a disciple of John the Apostle, affirms that the Gospel message and the teachings of

---

[27] Clement of Rome, Pope, *1st Epistle to the Corinthians,* 7:2 (c. A.D. 96) as cited by Cyril C. Richardson, ed., *Early Christian Fathers*, (New York: Collier, 1970), pp. 46-47.

Christ and His Apostles have been handed down to the Church. He does this without making any distinction between the Apostolic writings or Traditions.

> Let us then serve Him in fear, and with all reverence, even as He Himself has commanded us, and as the apostles who preached the Gospel unto us, and the prophets who proclaimed beforehand the coming of the Lord [have alike taught us]... Wherefore, forsaking the vanity of many, and their false doctrines, let us return to the word which has been handed down to us from the beginning;[28]

During this period we also see testimony concerning the authority of the Church's magisterium. In the following quote **Clement** testifies to the authority of the episcopacy which is authenticated by Apostolic succession.

> Our apostles also knew, through our Lord Jesus Christ, and there would be strife on account of the office of the episcopate. For this reason, therefore, inasmuch as they had obtained a perfect fore-knowledge of this, they appointed those [ministers] already mentioned, and afterwards gave instructions, that when these should fall asleep, other approved men should succeed them in their ministry.[29]

Later on in his epistle Clement testifies to the unique authority placed in the See of Rome:

> The Church of God which sojourns in Rome to the Church of God which sojourns in Corinth... If anyone disobey the things which have been said by Him through us, let them know that they will involve themselves in transgression and in no small danger.[30]

---

[28] Polycarp, *Epistle to the Phillipians*, 6-7 (c. A.D 135) ANF I:34.

[29] Clement of Rome, Pope, *1st Epistle to the Corinthians,* 44:1-2 (c. A.D. 96) ANF I:17.

[30] Ibid., 1, 59:1, JUR, I:7, 12.

Theophilus [d. c.A.D. 185/191] makes an interesting comment regarding the authority of the Church and the doctrines of God. He affirms that the Church inherits these salvific doctrines, and those who wish to be saved must do so do through the refuge of the Church.

> And as in the sea there are islands, some of them habitable, and well-watered, and fruitful, with havens and harbours in which the storm-tossed may find refuge — so God has given to the world which is driven and tempest-tossed by sins, assemblies — we mean holy churches — in which survive the doctrines of the truth, as in the island-harbours of good anchorage; and into these run those who desire to be saved, being lovers of the truth, and wishing to escape the wrath and judgment of God.[31]

Most of our testimony in this period regarding the authority of the Church comes from the Ignatius of Antioch [d. c.A.D. 110]. Ignatius, the third bishop of Antioch, affirms the necessity of following the bishop. This is noted in three separate but related passages:

> Wherefore, as children of light and truth, avoid the dividing of your unity, and the wicked doctrine of the heretics, from whom 'a defiling influence has gone forth into all the earth.' But where the shepherd is, there do ye as sheep follow. For there are many wolves in sheep's clothing, who, by means of a pernicious pleasure, carry captive those that are running towards God; but in your unity they shall have no place.[32]

> Let governors be obedient to Caesar; soldiers to those that command them; deacons to the presbyters, as to high-priests; the presbyters, and deacons, and the rest of the clergy, together with all the people, and the soldiers, and the governors, and Caesar [himself], to the bishop; the bishop to Christ, even as Christ to the Father. And thus unity is preserved throughout.[33]

---

31 Theophilus of Antioch, *To Autolycus*, 2:14 (c. A.D. 181) ANF II:100.

32 Ignatius of Antioch, *Epistle to the Philadelphians*, 2 (c. A.D. 110) ANF I:79-80.

33 Ibid., 4, ANF I:81-82.

> Give heed to the bishop, and to the presbytery and deacons. But if ye suspect that I spake thus, as having learned beforehand the division caused by some among you, He is my witness, for whose sake I am in bonds, that I learned nothing of it from the mouth of any man. But the Spirit made an announcement to me, saying as follows: Do nothing without the bishop; keep your bodies as the temples of God; love unity; avoid divisions; be ye followers of Paul, and of the rest of the apostles, even as they also were of Christ.[34]

It is clear from these three passages that rule of faith during this early period includes obedience to the bishop particularly on matters of doctrine and discipline. Private judgment is simply not in the mind of the Church. Ignatius emphasizes the same point in his other epistle: "Look ye to the bishop, that God also may look upon you. I will be instead of the souls of those who are subject to the bishop, and the presbyters, and the deacons; with them may I have a portion in the presence of God!"[35]

In this often quoted passage **Ignatius** brings together the authority of the Church and the sacrament of the Eucharist.

> See that ye all follow the bishop, even as Jesus Christ does the Father, and the presbytery as ye would the apostles; and reverence the deacons, as being the institution of God. Let no man do anything connected with the Church without the bishop. Let that be deemed a proper Eucharist, which is [administered] either by the bishop, or by one to whom he has entrusted it. Wherever the bishop shall appear, there let the multitude [of the people] also be; even as, wherever Jesus Christ is, there is the Catholic Church. It is not lawful without the bishop either to baptize or to celebrate a love-feast; but whatsoever he shall approve of, that is also pleasing to God, so that everything that is done may be secure and valid.[36]

Ignatius writes as if he was anticipating those sects that would exclude an authoritative Church in their rule of faith.

[34] Ignatius of Antioch, *Epistle to the Philadelphians*, 7, ANF I:83.

[35] Ignatius of Antioch, *Epistle to Polycarp*, 6, ANF I:100.

[36] Ignatius of Antioch, *Epistle to the Smyraens*, 8, ANF I:89-90.

> Be ye subject to the bishop as to the Lord, for 'he watches for your souls, as one that shall give account to God.' Wherefore also, ye appear to me to live not after the manner of men, but according to Jesus Christ, who died for us, in order that, by believing in His death, ye may by baptism be made partakers of His resurrection. It is therefore necessary, whatsoever things ye do, to do nothing without the bishop.[37]

> And do ye reverence them as Christ Jesus, of whose place they are the keepers, even as the bishop is the representative of the Father of all things, and the presbyters are the sanhedrin of God, and assembly of the apostles of Christ.[38]

Lastly, during this period we also have direct testimony to the importance of teachings that were handed down not in letter but in unwritten means. For example, **Papias** [floruit c.A.D. 130] preserves a Tradition in the Church that provides us with the author of the second Gospel.

> This also the presbyter said: Mark, having become the interpreter of Peter, wrote down accurately, though not indeed in order, whatsoever he remembered. For he neither heard the Lord nor followed him, but afterward, as I said, he followed Peter, who adapted his teaching to the needs of his hearers, but with no intention of giving a connective account of the Lord's discourses, so that Mark committed no error while he thus wrote some things as he remembered them. For he was careful of one thing, not to omit any of the things which he had heard, and not to state any of them falsely.[39]

Elsewhere, Papias provides us an unwritten tradition regarding the first Gospel: "So then Matthew wrote the oracles in the Hebrew language, and every one interpreted them as he was able."[40]

---

[37] Ignatius of Antioch, *Epistle to the Trallians*, 2, ANF I:66.

[38] Ibid., 3, ANF I:67.

[39] Papias, fragment in Eusebius' *Ecclesiastical History*, 3, 39:15 (c.A.D. 130) NPNF 2, I:172-173.

[40] Papias, fragment in Eusebius' *Ecclesiastical History*, 3, 39:16, NPNF 2, I:173. Note also that Papias says Matthew was written in Hebrew, not Greek.

From this early period we clearly find a rule of faith consisting of the three-fold rule of faith: the Scriptures, Tradition and Church. The Apostolic Fathers viewed private interpretation and judgment as the root of heresy, evil, and dissension. Their rule of faith consisted of the Scriptures (the Old Testament) and the doctrines handed down from Our Lord and His Apostles. According to the Fathers of this period, the Church was given the Apostolic deposit to hand down, interpret and preserve. It is through this Church and nowhere else that one is saved. There is nothing in the writings of the Apostolic Fathers and the Apologists to suggest that the writers had only the Apostolic *writings* in mind when they referred to the Apostolic faith. In fact, it was the unwritten Tradition that preceded the written Tradition, hence the New Testament Scriptures were valued precisely because they enshrined the unwritten Tradition of the Apostles! Additionally, since the unwritten testimony preceded the canonization of the written it is logical to conclude that these writers simply had the general doctrines and teachings of the Church in mind which were found throughout the various ministrations of the early Church. Lastly, since the canon of the New Testament was only slowly being received by the Catholic Church as authoritative, post-apostolic Tradition was of inestimable value in preserving the authentic Apostolic message.

Fathers of the Second and Third Centuries

St. Irenaeus, Bishop of Lyons [41]

"It comes to this, therefore that these men [ie. the Gnostics] do now consent neither to Scripture nor to tradition."

The Fathers and the Gnostics

The latter part of the second century is marked by the first serious challenge to the Church's Tradition. First, the Apostles and their immediate disciples had passed away. No longer could anyone ap-

[41] Irenaeus, *Against Heresies*, 3, 2:2 (inter A.D. 180-199) ANF I:415.

peal to them personally. Secondly, Gnosticism challenged the canon of the Apostolic writings and the authority of the Church's Tradition. Marcion attempted to formulate his own version of the Scriptures, while Valentinus attempted to undermine the authentic interpretation of the Scriptures, both through a secret tradition claiming to have its source with the Apostles. Both of these heretical aberrations gave the impetus for the Church to fix and define the extent of the Apostolic writings and to establish the authenticity and apostolicity of the Church's Tradition. The Church was forced in a position to define precisely her rule of faith. The primary combatants of Gnosticism during this period were **Irenaeus** [c.A.D. 140-c.A.D. 202], bishop of Lyons, and **Tertullian** [c.A.D. 160-post A.D. 220] of Carthage. Both of these Church Fathers provided the first synthesis on the rule of faith. Tertullian's *Prescription* summarizes the Gnostic menacing attack on the Church's rule of faith.

> One man perverts the Scriptures with his hand, another their meaning by his exposition. For although Valentinus seems to use the entire volume, he has none the less laid violent hands on the truth only with a more cunning mind and skill than Marcion. Marcion expressly and openly used the knife, not the pen, since he made such an excision of the Scriptures as suited his own subject-matter. Valentinus, however, abstained from such excision, because he did not invent Scriptures to square with his own subject-matter, but adapted his matter to the Scriptures; and yet he took away more, and added more, by removing the proper meaning of every particular word, and adding fantastic arrangements of things which have no real existence.[42]

The Church's defense of its rule of faith and Tradition during this period inevitably raised the prestige and value of the Apostolic deposit to a level of supreme authority. According to the Fathers, the Scripture and Tradition were not so much two independent sources of revelation; rather, both were different ways in which the single deposit of faith was preserved and transmitted within the Church. In other words, Scripture and Tradition, ac-

---

[42] Tertullian, *On Prescription against the Heretics*, 38 (c. A.D. 200) ANF III:262.

cording to the Fathers, were essentially identical in content with varying degrees of explicitness. For example, **Hippolytus** of Rome [d. A.D. 235] considered the overall content of his great work on Church worship, order and sacraments as the expression of the Church's Tradition.

> [H]aving come to our most important topic, we turn to the subject of the Tradition which is proper for the Churches, in order that those who have been rightly instructed may hold fast to that tradition which has continued until now, and fully understanding it from our exposition may stand the more firmly therein.[43]

In addition, the distinction between Scripture(Old and New Testaments) and Sacred Tradition was being enhanced with the latter being elevated as the surest guide to interpreting the former. Lastly, it was the clear position of the Fathers, that the Church was the custodian and interpreter of this Apostolic deposit. Private judgment or a critical analysis of the Scripture/Creeds apart from the Church and her unerring Tradition were considered the tools of the heretics.

Irenaeus writes that the Gnostics read the Bible apart from the Church's Tradition. He affirms that without the Church's Tradition one can fabricate any doctrine from the letters of Sacred Scripture. Familiarity with the Apostolic teaching found in Tradition enable one to provide an authentic and proper understanding of Scripture and to discern between Apostolic teaching and teaching of men. Irenaeus often refers to this coordinate guide as the 'rule of truth', or as 'the preaching' or 'the faith'. The rule of faith for Irenaeus essentially consisted of a general body of doctrines that were taught by the Church which have Christ and His Apostles as their source. These doctrines consisted of such tenets as: One God the Father Almighty the Creator, Jesus Christ the Son of God, the Holy Spirit, the resurrection of the dead, the authoritative teach-

[43] Hippolytus of Rome, *The Apostolic Tradition*, 1(c. A.D. 215) as cited by Gregory Dix and Henry Chadwick, eds.,*The Treatise on the Apostolic Tradition of St. Hippolytus of Rome* (London: Alban, 1992), pp. 1-2.

ing Church, and other cardinal doctrines that would later be found in the Church's creeds.

Irenaeus provides a few analogies to demonstrate the necessity of holding fast to the rule of faith.

> By transferring passages, and dressing them up anew, and making one thing out of another, they succeed in deluding many through their wicked art in adapting the oracles of the Lord to their opinions. Their manner of acting is just as if one, when a beautiful image of a king has been constructed by some skillful artist out of precious jewels, should then take this likeness of the man all to pieces, should rearrange the gems, and so fit them together as to make them into the form of a dog or of a fox, and even that but poorly executed; and should then maintain and declare that this was the beautiful image of the king which the skillful artist constructed, pointing to the jewels which had been admirably fitted together by the first artist to form the image of the king, but have been with bad effect transferred by the latter one to the shape of a dog, and by thus exhibiting the jewels, should deceive the ignorant who had no conception what a king's form was like, and persuade them that that miserable likeness of the fox was, in fact, the beautiful image of the king. In like manner do these persons patch together old wives' fables, and then endeavour, by violently drawing away from their proper connection, words, expressions, and parables whenever found, to adapt the oracles of God to their baseless fictions. We have already stated how far they proceed in this way with respect to the interior of the Pleroma.[44]

Tertullian makes the same point in his treatise against the heretics of his day. He shows a couple of ways that heretics have perverted God's Word. The first method is to misrepresent God's Word by excising parts (e.g. Marcion) of the Sacred Text. The second method, a more serious offense according to Tertullian, is to interpret the Bible apart from the Church's Tradition. Hence, the her-

[44] Irenaeus, *Against Heresies*, 1, 8, ANF I:326.

etic, according to Tertullian, would interpret Scripture according to one's private understanding (Valentinus) and against the Church's Tradition. Tertullian refers to this ever-present guide as the 'rule of faith' (*regula fidei*).

According to Tertullian, like the Fathers before and after, the rule for recognizing the heretics' fables and the key to interpreting the Scriptures lies in the Church and her Tradition.

> From this, therefore, do we draw up our rule. Since the Lord Jesus Christ sent the apostles to preach, (our rule is) that no others ought to be received as preachers than those whom Christ appointed; for 'no man knoweth the Father save the Son, and he to whomsoever the Son will reveal Him.' Nor does the Son seem to have revealed Him to any other than the apostles, whom He sent forth to preach — that, of course, which He revealed to them. Now, what that was which they preached — in other words, what it was which Christ revealed to them — can, as I must here likewise prescribe, properly be proved in no other way than by those very churches which the apostles founded in person, by declaring the gospel to them directly themselves, both viva voce, as the phrase is, and subsequently by their epistles. If, then, these things are so, it is in the same degree manifest that all doctrine which agrees with the apostolic churches—those molds and original sources of the faith must be reckoned for truth, as undoubtedly containing that which the (said) churches received from the apostles, the apostles from Christ, Christ from God. Whereas all doctrine must be prejudged as false which savors of contrariety to the truth of the churches and apostles of Christ and God. It remains, then, that we demonstrate whether this doctrine of ours, of which we have now given the rule, has its origin in the Tradition of the apostles, and whether all other doctrines do not ipso facto proceed from falsehood. We hold communion with the apostolic churches because our doctrine is in no respect different from theirs. This is our witness of truth.[45]

[45] Tertullian, *On Prescription against the Heretics*, 21 (c. A.D. 200) ANF III:252-253.

During this period, several distinct themes concerning the rule of faith were synthesized and expressed by Irenaeus and Tertullian. First, like the Fathers of the previous generation, both affirmed the supreme authority of the Apostolic Tradition without making any distinction between their writings or their oral teachings. Apostolic Tradition simply meant the entire deposit of faith transmitted by Christ and His Apostles. Therefore, according to the Fathers, Scripture was contained within Tradition. Again, Tradition consisted materially of the Scriptures, creeds and confessions of the Church. Formally, Tradition consisted of the Church's understanding of the Sacred text and its interpretation of the various creeds and confessions of faith. In other words, the mere letter of the Sacred Text alone or the creed alone was insufficient. For the most part, both **Irenaeus** and **Tertullian** applied Tradition in this wider sense.

> Now all these [heretics] are of much later date than the bishops to whom the apostles committed the Churches; which fact I have in the third book taken all pains to demonstrate. It follows, then, as a matter of course, that these heretics aforementioned, since they are blind to the truth, and deviate from the [right] way, will walk in various roads; and therefore the footsteps of their doctrine are scattered here and there without agreement or connection. But the path of those belonging to the Church circumscribes the whole world, as possessing the sure tradition from the apostles, and gives unto us to see that the faith of all is one and the same, since all receive one and the same God the Father, and believe in the same dispensation regarding the incarnation of the Son of God, and are cognizant of the same gift of the Spirit, and are conversant with the same commandments, and preserve the same form of ecclesiastical constitution, and expect the same advent of the Lord, and await the same salvation of the complete man, that is, of the soul and body. And undoubtedly the preaching of the Church is true and steadfast, in which one and the same way of salvation is shown throughout the whole world. For to her is entrusted the light of God; and therefore the 'wisdom' of God, by means of which she saves all men, 'is declared in [its] going forth; it uttereth [its voice] faithfully in the streets, is preached on the tops of the walls, and speaks continually in the gates of the city.' For the Church preaches the truth

> everywhere, and she is the seven-branched candlestick which bears the light of Christ.[46]

> Such are the summary arguments which we use, when we take up arms against heretics for the faith of the gospel, maintaining both that order of periods, which rules that a late date is the mark of forgers, and that authority of churches which lends support to the tradition of the apostles; because truth must needs precede the forgery, and proceed straight from those by whom it has been handed on.[47]

On occasion, both **Irenaeus** and **Tertullian** specifically referred to Tradition as something distinct from Scripture. Tradition was applied in a narrow sense meaning those teachings (though coincident with the Scriptures) that have come down to us through unwritten means. This is especially true when a controversy arose about the interpretation of Scripture.

> For how stands the case? Suppose there arise a dispute relative to some important question among us, should we not have recourse to the most ancient Churches with which the apostles held constant intercourse, and learn from them what is certain and clear in regard to the present question? For how should it be if the apostles themselves had not left us writings? Would it not be necessary, [in that case] to follow the course of the tradition which they handed down to those to whom they did commit the Churches?[48]

> If, for these and other such rules, you insist upon having positive Scripture injunction, you will find none. Tradition will be held forth to you as the originator of them, custom as their strengthener, and faith as their observer. That reason will support tradition, and custom, and faith, you will either yourself perceive, or learn from some one who has.[49]

---

[46] Irenaeus, *Against Heresies*, 5, 20:1, ANF I:547-548.

[47] Tertullian, *Against Marcion*, 4:5, ANF III:351.

[48] Irenaeus, *Against Heresies*, 3, 4:1, ANF I:416-417. See also *Against Heresies*, 3, 4:2, ANF I:417; Tertullian, *The Crown*, 3, ANF III:94-95.

[49] Tertullian, *The Crown*, 4 (A.D. 211) ANF III:95.

Apart from this emphasis on Tradition as something distinct from Scripture, both **Irenaeus and Tertullian** affirmed that all of the Apostolic Tradition has also come down to us in writing. Both affirmed the material sufficiency of the Sacred Scriptures.

> We have learned from none others the plan of our salvation, than from those through whom the Gospel has come down to us, which they did at one time proclaim in public, and, at a later period, by the will of God, handed down to us in the Scriptures, to be the ground and pillar of our faith.[50]

> What, therefore, did not exist, the Scripture was unable to mention; and by not mentioning it, it has given us a clear proof that there was no such thing: for if there had been, the Scripture would have mentioned it.[51]

In spite of this elevation of Scripture, however, both would affirm that the letter of Scripture alone was insufficient in imparting its meaning. Something else was required, that is, the Church and her Tradition. Additionally, this Apostolic faith was given to the Church in its entirety through Scripture and her Tradition. The Church therefore was the sole custodian and preserver of the Apostolic deposit.

> Those, therefore, who desert the preaching of the Church, call in question the knowledge of the holy presbyters, not taking into consideration of how much greater consequence is a religious man, even in a private station, than a blasphemous and impudent sophist... It behooves us, therefore, to avoid their doctrines, and to take careful heed lest we suffer any injury from them; but to flee to the Church, and be brought up in her bosom, and be nourished with the Lord's Scriptures.[52]

Tertullian, in the following classic passage, declares that the Church 'alone' is the authentic custodian and interpreter of the Apostolic faith.

---

[50] Irenaeus, *Against Heresies*, 3,1:1, ANF I:414.
[51] Tertullian, *Against Hermogenes*, 20, ANF III:489.
[52] Irenaeus, *Against Heresies*, 5, 20:2, ANF I:548.

> Since this is the case, in order that the truth may be adjudged to belong to us, 'as many as walk according to the rule,' which the church has handed down from the apostles, the apostles from Christ, and Christ from God, the reason of our position is clear, when it determines that heretics ought not to be allowed to challenge an appeal to the Scriptures, since we, without the Scriptures, prove that they have nothing to do with the Scriptures. For as they are heretics, they cannot be true Christians, because it is not from Christ that they get that which they pursue of their own mere choice, and from the pursuit incur and admit the name of heretics. Thus, not being Christians, they have acquired no right to the Christian Scriptures; and it may be very fairly said to them, 'Who are you?'[53]

Irenaeus elsewhere goes even further by affirming that the bishops of the Catholic Church possess a particular 'charism' of truth.

> Wherefore it is incumbent to obey the presbyters who are in the Church,—those who, as I have shown, possess the succession from the apostles; those who, together with the succession of the episcopate, have received the certain gift of truth, according to the good pleasure of the Father. But [it is also incumbent] to hold in suspicion others who depart from the primitive succession, and assemble themselves together in any place whatsoever, [looking upon them] either as heretics of perverse minds, or as schismatics puffed up and self-pleasing, or again as hypocrites, acting thus for the sake of lucre and vainglory. For all these have fallen from the truth.[54]

It is obvious from these citations that the authentic and orthodox expositions of the Apostolic testimony are only to be found within the living teaching Church.

> Where, therefore, the gifts of the Lord have been placed, there it behooves us to learn the truth, [namely,] from those who possess that succession of the Church which is from the

---

[53] Tertullian, *On Prescription against the Heretics*, 37, ANF III:261.

[54] Irenaeus, *Against Heresies*, 4, 26:2, ANF I:497.

> apostles, and among whom exists that which is sound and blameless in conduct, as well as that which is unadulterated and incorrupt in speech. For these also preserve this faith of ours in one God who created all things; and they increase that love [which we have] for the Son of God, who accomplished such marvellous dispensations for our sake: and they expound the Scriptures to us without danger, neither blaspheming God, nor dishonouring the patriarchs, nor despising the prophets.[55]

> And then shall every word also seem consistent to him, if he for his part diligently read the Scriptures in company with those who are presbyters in the Church, among whom is the apostolic doctrine, as I have pointed out.[56]

> Our appeal, therefore, must not be made to the Scriptures; nor must controversy be admitted on points in which victory will either be impossible, or uncertain, or not certain enough. But even if a discussion from the Scriptures should not turn out in such a way as to place both sides on a par, (yet) the natural order of things would require that this point should be first proposed, which is now the only one which we must discuss: "With whom lies that very faith to which the Scriptures belong. From what and through whom, and when, and to whom, has been handed down that rule, by which men become Christians? For wherever it shall be manifest that the true Christian rule and faith shall be, there will likewise be the true Scriptures and expositions thereof, and all the Christian traditions.[57]

Tradition, according to **Irenaeus**, is authenticated and bound up by the succession of her bishops with the Apostles in contrast to heretical secret tradition (e.g. Gnosticism), which was alleged to have come from the Apostles.

> But, again, when we refer them to that tradition which originates from the apostles, [and] which is preserved by means

[55] Ibid., 4, 26:5, ANF I:498.
[56] Ibid., 4, 32:1, ANF I:506.
[57] Tertullian, *On Prescription against the Heretics*, 19, ANF III:251-252.

of the succession of presbyters in the Churches, they object to tradition, saying that they themselves are wiser not merely than the presbyters, but even than the apostles, because they have discovered the unadulterated truth... It comes to this, therefore that these men do now consent neither to Scripture nor to tradition.[58]

In this order, and by this succession, the ecclesiastical tradition from the apostles, and the preaching of the truth, have come down to us. And this is most abundant proof that there is one and the same vivifying faith, which has been preserved in the Church from the Apostles until now, and handed down in truth.[59]

From all such persons, therefore, it behooves us to keep aloof, but to adhere to those who, as I have already observed, do hold the doctrine of the apostles, and who, together with the order of priesthood (*presbyterii ordine*), display sound speech and blameless conduct for the confirmation and correction of others.[60]

Tertullian offers the same argument.

But if there be any (heresies) which are bold enough to plant themselves in the midst of the apostolic age, that they may thereby seem to have been handed down by the apostles, because they existed in the time of the apostles, we can say: Let them produce the original records of their churches; let them unfold the roll of their bishops, running down in due succession from the beginning in such a manner that [that first bishop of theirs] bishop shall be able to show for his ordainer and predecessor some one of the apostles or of apostolic men, — a man, moreover, who continued steadfast with the apostles. For this is the manner in which the apostolic churches transmit their registers: as the church of Smyrna, which records that Polycarp was placed therein by

58 Irenaeus, *Against Heresies*, 3, 2:2 ANF I:415.
59 Ibid., 3, 3:3 ANF I:416.
60 Ibid., 4, 26:4 ANF I:497.

> John; as also the church of Rome, which makes Clement to have been ordained in like manner by Peter. In exactly the same way the other churches likewise exhibit (their several worthies), whom, as having been appointed to their episcopal places by apostles, they regard as transmitters of the apostolic seed. Let the heretics contrive something of the same kind. For after their blasphemy, what is there that is unlawful for them (to attempt)? But should they even effect the contrivance, they will not advance a step. For their very doctrine, after comparison with that of the apostles, will declare, by its own diversity and contrariety, that it had for its author neither an apostle nor an apostolic man; because, as the apostles would never have taught things which were self-contradictory, so the apostolic men would not have inculcated teaching different from the apostles, unless they who received their instruction from the apostles went and preached in a contrary manner. To this test, therefore will they be submitted for proof by those churches, who, although they derive not their founder from apostles or apostolic men (as being of much later date, for they are in fact being founded daily), yet, since they agree in the same faith, they are accounted as not less apostolic because they are akin in doctrine. Then let all the heresies, when challenged to these two tests by our apostolic church, offer their proof of how they deem themselves to be apostolic. But in truth they neither are so, nor are they able to prove themselves to be what they are not. Nor are they admitted to peaceful relations and communion by such churches as are in any way connected with apostles, inasmuch as they are in no sense themselves apostolic because of their diversity as to the mysteries of the faith.[61]

In addition to the general argument based on apostolic succession, **Irenaeus** offered a shortcut to this argument by referring to the greatest See of all, the Roman See.

> Since, however, it would be very tedious, in such a volume as this, to reckon up the successions of all the Churches, we do put to confusion all those who, in whatever manner, whether by an evil self-pleasing, by vainglory, or by blindness and perverse opinion, assemble in unauthorized meetings; [we do

> this, I say,] by indicating that tradition derived from the apostles, of the very great, the very ancient, and universally known Church founded and organized at Rome by the two most glorious apostles, Peter and Paul; as also [by pointing out] the faith preached to men, which comes down to our time by means of the successions of the bishops. For it is a matter of necessity that every Church should agree with this Church, on account of its preeminent authority, that is, the faithful everywhere, inasmuch as the apostolical tradition has been preserved continuously by those [faithful men] who exist everywhere.[62]

Authentic Apostolic Tradition, according to **Irenaeus**, is one that is plain and public in contrast to the secret tradition of the Gnostics: "His testimony, therefore, is true, and the doctrine of the apostles is open and steadfast, holding nothing in reserve; nor did they teach one set of doctrines in private, and another in public."[63]

Both **Irenaeus** and **Tertullian** affirmed, almost as if they were anticipating the novel concept of *sola scriptura*, that the fatal flaw of the Gnostic heretics was the abandonment of the Church's rule of faith when interpreting the Scriptures. Private interpretation and judgment were considered the play tools of the Gnostic heretics that lead to division and dissension. Not surprisingly, what they say of the sects in their day can equally apply to denominational sects in our day:

> When, however, they are confuted from the Scriptures, they turn round and accuse these same Scriptures, as if they were not correct, nor of authority, and [assert] that they are ambiguous, and that the truth cannot be extracted from them by those who are ignorant of tradition.[64]

> Alienated thus from the truth, they do deservedly wallow in all error, tossed to and fro by it, thinking differently in regard to the same things at different times, and never attaining to a

61 Tertullian, *On Prescription against the Heretics*, 32, ANF III:258.
62 Irenaeus, *Against Heresies*, 3, 3:2, ANF I:415-416.
63 Ibid., 3, 15:1, ANF I:439.
64 Ibid., 3, 2:1 ANF I:415.

> well-grounded knowledge, being more anxious to be sophists of words than disciples of the truth. For they have not been founded upon the one rock, but upon the sand, which has in itself a multitude of stones.[65]

> We, however, are not permitted to cherish any object after our own will, nor yet to make choice of that which another has introduced of his private fancy. In the Lord's apostles we possess our authority; for even they did not of themselves choose to introduce anything, but faithfully delivered to the nations (of mankind) the doctrine which they had received from Christ...[66] "Where diversity of doctrine is found, there, then, must the corruption both of the Scriptures and the expositions thereof be regarded as existing."[67]

Following the authentic Apostolic Tradition, the faith expressed within the various Sees and cities of the Church is one and the same, in contrast to the dissension and division of the Gnostic faith traditions.

> As I have already observed, the Church, having received this preaching and this faith, although scattered throughout the whole world, yet, as if occupying but one house, carefully preserves it. She also believes these points [of doctrine] just as if she had but one soul, and one and the same heart, and she proclaims them, and teaches them, and hands them down, with perfect harmony, as if she possessed only one mouth. For, although the languages of the world are dissimilar, yet the import of the tradition is one and the same. For the Churches which have been planted in Germany do not believe or hand down anything different, nor do those in Spain, nor those in Gaul, nor those in the East, nor those in Egypt, nor those in Libya...[68]

> Grant, then, that all have erred; that the apostle was mistaken in giving his testimony; that the Holy Ghost had no such

---

65 Ibid., 3, 24:2 ANF I:458.

66 Tertullian, *On Prescription against the Heretics*, 6, ANF III:245-246.

67 Tertullian, *On Prescription against the Heretics*, 38, ANF III:261.

68 Irenaeus, *Against Heresies*, 1, 10:2, ANF I:331.

> respect to any one (church) as to lead it into truth, although sent with this view by Christ, and for this asked of the Father that He might be the teacher of truth; grant, also, that He, the Steward of God, the Vicar of Christ, neglected His office, permitting the churches for a time to understand differently, (and) to believe differently, what He Himself was preaching by the apostles — is it likely that so many churches, and they so great, should have gone astray into one and the same faith? No casualty distributed among many men issues in one and the same result. Error of doctrine in the churches must necessarily have produced various issues. When, however, that which is deposited among many is found to be one and the same, it is not the result of error, but of tradition. Can any one, then, be reckless enough to say that they were in error who handed on the tradition?[69]

Origen [c.A.D. 185-254]

One of the most prolific writers of the third century is Origen of Alexandria. Like the Fathers before him, he testifies in his dogmatic treatise on the Christian faith of the necessity of holding fast to the traditional faith of the Church. This faith is transmitted and preserved through orderly succession from the apostles.

> Since many, however, of those who profess to believe in Christ differ from each other, not only in small and trifling matters, but also on subjects of the highest importance, as, e.g., regarding God, or the Lord Jesus Christ, or the Holy Spirit; and not only regarding these, but also regarding others which are created existences, viz., the powers and the holy virtues; it seems on that account necessary first of all to fix a definite limit and to lay down an unmistakable rule regarding each one of these, and then to pass to the investigation of other points. For as we ceased to seek for truth (notwithstanding the professions of many among Greeks and Barbarians to make it known) among all who claimed it for erroneous opinions, after we had come to believe that Christ was the Son of God, and were persuaded that we must learn it from Himself;

[69] Tertullian, *On Prescription against the Heretics*, 28, ANF III:256.

> so, seeing there are many who think they hold the opinions of Christ, and yet some of these think differently from their predecessors, yet as the teaching of the Church, transmitted in orderly succession from the apostles, and remaining in the Churches to the present day, is still preserved, that alone is to be accepted as truth which differs in no respect from ecclesiastical and apostolical tradition.[70]

In a later chapter Origen replays the consistent theme of the Fathers, that is, one must interpret the Sacred Text according to the ecclesiastical standard established in Tradition, one which is authenticated by the order of succession from the apostles.

> Now the cause, in all the points previously enumerated, of the false opinions, and of the impious statements or ignorant assertions about God, appears to be nothing else than the not understanding the Scripture according to its spiritual meaning, but the interpretation of it agreeably to the mere letter. And therefore, to those who believe that the sacred books are not the compositions of men, but that they were composed by inspiration of the Holy Spirit, agreeably to the will of the Father of all things through Jesus Christ, and that they have come down to us, we must point out the ways (of interpreting them) which appear (correct) to us, who cling to the standard of the heavenly Church of Jesus Christ according to the succession of the apostles.[71]

Clement of Alexandria [c.A.D. 150-c.A.D. 216]

Clement of Alexandria applies the same methodology regarding the interpretation of the Scriptures. According to Clement, one must read the Scriptures within the milieu of the rule of faith ('canon of truth') which has been handed down from the Apostles to the Church.

> The liars, then, in reality, are not those who for the sake of the scheme of salvation conform, nor those who err in minute points, but those who are wrong in essentials, and reject the

[70] Origen, *On First Principles*, 1, Preface: 2 ANF IV:239.

[71] Ibid., 4, 1:9 ANF IV:357.

> Lord, and as far as in them lies deprive the Lord of the true teaching; who do not quote or deliver the Scriptures in a manner worthy of God and of the Lord; for the deposit rendered to God, according to the teaching of the Lord by His apostles, is the understanding and the practice of the godly tradition. 'And what ye hear in the ear' — that is, in a hidden manner, and in a mystery (for such things are figuratively said to be spoken in the ear) — 'proclaim,' He says, 'on the housetops,' understanding them sublimely, and delivering them in a lofty strain, and according to the canon of truth explaining the Scriptures;[72]

Similarly, as with the Fathers before and after, Clement finds that the fundamental error of the heretic is that he doesn't apply the Church's inerrant Tradition when interpreting the Scriptures. Instead, the heretic selects and interprets the passages of the Sacred Text according to his own judgment and desires apart from the traditional truth contained in the Church.

> There being demonstration, then, it is necessary to condescend to questions, and to ascertain by way of demonstration by the Scriptures themselves how the heresies failed, and how in the truth alone and in the ancient Church is both the exactest knowledge, and the truly best set of principles.[73]

> For those are slothful who, having it in their power to provide themselves with proper proofs for the divine Scriptures from the Scriptures themselves, select only what contributes to their own pleasures. And those have a craving for glory who voluntarily evade, by arguments of a diverse sort, the things delivered by the blessed apostles and teachers, which are wedded to inspired words; opposing the divine tradition by human teachings, in order to establish the heresy.[74]

Cyprian [c.A.D. 200/210-258]

Cyprian of Carthage offers a great deal of testimony regarding the teaching authority of the Church. In many of his writings, he

---

[72] Clement of Alexandria, *Stromata*, 6:15 (post A.D. 202) ANF II:509.

[73] Ibid., 7:15, ANF II:550.

[74] Ibid., 7:16 ANF II:553-554.

affirms the magisterial authority of the episcopacy and their responsibility to preserve the Tradition of the Church and the faith of their flocks. Cyprian holds that one must adhere to the Church's Tradition, which has its root in Christ and His Apostles, in order to be kept from evil.

> Cyprian to Caecilius his brother, greeting. Although I know, dearest brother, that very many of the bishops who are set over the churches of the Lord by divine condescension, throughout the whole world, maintain the plan of evangelical truth, and of the tradition of the Lord, and do not by human and novel institution depart from that which Christ our Master both prescribed and did; yet since some, either by ignorance or simplicity in sanctifying the cup of the Lord, and in ministering to the people, do not do that which Jesus Christ, our Lord and God, the founder and teacher of this sacrifice, did and taught, I have thought it as well a religious as a necessary thing to write to you this letter, that, if any one is still kept in this error, he may behold the light of truth, and return to the root and origin of the tradition of the Lord.[75]

In one of his more famous sayings Cyprian writes: "He can no longer have God for his Father, who has not the Church for his mother."[76]

Prior to controversy with Pope Stephen [reign A.D. 254-257] regarding heretical baptism, we find **Cyprian** testifying to the unique magisterial authority of the See of Rome:

> Some persons, however, sometimes disturb men's minds and spirits by their words, in that they relate things otherwise than is the truth. For we, who furnish every person who sails hence with a plan that they may sail without any offence, know that we have exhorted them to acknowledge and hold the root and matrix of the Catholic Church.[77]

---

[75] Cyprian, *Epistle To Caecilius*, 62 (63), 1 (A.D. 253) ANF V:358-359.

[76] Cyprian, *The Unity of the Church*, 6 (A.D. 251/256) ANF V:423.

[77] Cyprian, *Epistle To Pope Cornelius*, 44 (48):3 (A.D. 251) ANF V:322.

> And he says to him again after the resurrection, 'Feed my sheep.' It is on him that he builds the Church, and to him that he entrusts the sheep to feed. And although he assigns a like power to all the apostles, yet he founded a single Chair, thus establishing by his own authority the source and hallmark of the (Church's) oneness. No doubt the others were all that Peter was, but a primacy is given to Peter, and it is (thus) made clear that there is but one flock which is to be fed by all the apostles in common accord. If a man does not hold fast to this oneness of Peter, does he imagine that he still holds the faith? If he deserts the Chair of Peter upon whom the Church was built, has he still confidence that he is in the Church? This unity firmly should we hold and maintain, especially we bishops, presiding in the Church, in order that we may approve the episcopate itself to be the one and undivided.[78]

During this period arose one of the first doctrinal challenges of the Church in which there was no clear answer in Scripture. The question the Church had to answer: If an officially branded heretic baptizes another person, is that baptism valid? In this case the Church appeals to Tradition in order to substantiate the validity of such a baptism. Cyprian held that baptism given by heretics was invalid, while Pope Stephen held the opposite view. What is interesting to note here is that both Cyprian and Pope Stephen, like good Church men, appealed to Tradition and not to their own private judgment, in order to substantiate their claim. Protestant writers have often used Cyprian's decision in denying the validity of baptism done through the ministry of a heretic as an attempt to resist and therefore deny the validity of Tradition all together. Cyprian writes:

> He [Pope Stephen] forbade one coming from any heresy to be baptized in the Church; that is, he judged the baptism of all heretics to be just and lawful. And although special heresies have special baptisms and different sins, he, holding communion with the baptism of all, gathered up the sins of all, heaped together into his own bosom. And he charged that

[78] Cyprian, *The Unity of the Church*, 4-5 (Primacy Text, A.D. 251/256) NE 228-229.

> nothing should be innovated except what had been handed down; as if he were an innovator, who, holding the unity, claims for the one Church one baptism; and not manifestly he who, forgetful of unity, adopts the lies and the contagions of a profane washing. Let nothing be innovated, says he, nothing maintained, except what has been handed down. Whence is that tradition?[79]

Thus, whatever the nature of **Cyprian's** contention, it is clear that Pope Stephen is imparting a teaching not of his own devise but one that he judges as inherited without innovation from the Church. Cyprian counters with:

> And this it behooves the priests of God to do now, if they would keep the divine precepts, that if in any respect the truth have wavered and vacillated, we should return to our original and Lord, and to the evangelical and apostolical tradition; and thence may arise the ground of our action, whence has taken rise both our order and our origin.[80]

Obviously, both Cyprian and Stephen appealed to Tradition in order to prove the universality and apostolicity of their beliefs. We have discovered, however, that Cyprian was appealing to a teaching mainly held in Africa, which was no older than the second century. We assume that had Cyprian known the true tradition he would have accepted it in lieu of his personal beliefs. The mere fact that he appealed to Tradition shows that his criterion for truth was not determined by *sola scriptura*. More importantly, the case of Cyprian shows that when Tradition and Scripture are obscure, the Church had a third authority on which to depend—its own magisterium. Pope Stephen's decision would not be the last papal edict which determined between two options the doctrine of the universal church. Thus, today, almost two thousand years later, Pope Stephen's decision to affirm the validity of baptism by heretics stands as the unalterable position of the Catholic Church. In effect, Pope Stephen helped establish the Tradition of the Church.

---

79 Cyprian, *Epistle To Pompey*, 73 (74):2 (A.D. 256) ANF V:386.

80 Cyprian, *Epistle to Pompey*, 73 (74):9-10 (A.D. 256) ANF V:389.

In sum, the Fathers of this period affirmed, with greater clarity and force than in the previous period, that both Scripture and Tradition are included in the rule of faith of the Church. Like the Fathers before them, Scripture and Tradition were essentially the same in content. Tradition was utilized not so much to supply material truths not contained in the Bible, but as the surest way in interpreting the Sacred text. In other words, the Fathers held that the Bible was materially sufficient but formally insufficient. That is, Scripture contained, at least implicitly, all the doctrines of the Catholic faith necessary for salvation. However, they also affirmed that the Scriptures are incapable apart from Tradition and Church, of communicating its true and intended meaning. The Fathers consistently taught that private interpretation was the play tool of the heretics. Moreover, these same Fathers did not affirm any old tradition allegedly coming from the Apostles, but a Tradition that was public and guaranteed by the Church whose Bishops succeeded from the Apostles themselves. Lastly, we see in this period a growing recognition of the magisterial authority of the Church with a particular emphasis on the Apostolic See of Rome.

Fathers of the Fourth and Fifth Centuries (Classical Period)

St. Epiphanius, Bishop of Salamis[81]

"Apostolic traditions, holy scriptures and successions of teachers have been made our boundaries and foundations for the upholding of our faith, and God's truth has been protected in every way. No one need be deceived by worthless stories."

This is the period of the first four Ecumenical Councils, which served as the foundation of subsequent Councils. During this time, the Church was attacked by several major heresies. They include Eastern heresies such as Arianism, Nestorianism, Sabellianism and Monophystism and Western heresies such as Pelagianism and

[81] Epiphanius, *Panarion*, 55 (inter A.D. 374-377) as cited by Frank Williams, trans.,*The Panarion of Epiphanius of Salamis* (New York: E. J. Brill, 1987) vol. 2, p. 80.

Donatism. In response to these heresies the Church produced theological giants to combat them. From this period alone we inherit seven of the eight 'great' Fathers of the Catholic Church. From the West: St. Jerome [d. A.D. 420], St. Ambrose [d. A.D. 397], and St. Augustine [d. A.D. 430]. From the East: St. Athanasius [d. A.D. 373], St. Basil [d. A.D. 379], St. Gregory of Nazianzen [d. c.A.D.389] and St. John Chrysostom [d. A.D. 407]. During this time the Church canonized the 73 books of Scripture; the ecclesiastical canons governing the practice and disciplines of the Church took shape; and the Church's liturgy was well in place. In sum, the Church had assumed all its fundamental features.

During this period, the testimony of 'Sacred Tradition' became more defined and explicit. Although the Church understood Tradition as originating from the single deposit of faith given to the Apostles, which was transmitted to the Church through written and unwritten means, it also included the Church's progressive witness and understanding of this single deposit of faith through the subsequent generations of the Church. Hence, appeals to the authority of the Church Fathers became increasingly prevalent during this period as a particular argument from Tradition. In fact, frequent citations from the early Church Fathers regarding a particular doctrinal matter are common throughout this golden age.

The rule of faith for the Church Fathers during this period remained the same as it was for the Fathers of the first three centuries. First, the Fathers affirmed a material sufficiency of the Sacred Scriptures. Second, if it is possible to point to a single consistent position espoused by these Fathers, it is the fact that Scripture, Tradition and Church are inseparably linked. All the Fathers consistently affirm that Scripture can be correctly interpreted and understood only within the milieu of the Church and her Tradition.

Athanasius [c.A.D. 295-373], the Patriarch of Alexandria and one of the main defenders of the Nicene faith, will be our primary model and guide during this period. Athanasius, like the Fathers before and after him, affirmed the three-fold pillars of the Catholic rule of faith: Scripture, Tradition, and Church. First, Athanasius affirms the primacy and the authority of Holy Scripture and the material sufficiency of the Scriptures. But Athanasius also affirms particularly in his polemical writings against the Arians, the necessity of a teaching Church and the coordinate deposit of faith found in Tradition in order to obtain the fullness of God's Word without distortion or error. In his controversies with the Arian factions, Athanasius assumed a Tradition which is substantive in content, authoritative, and able to provide the true and orthodox understanding of the Scriptures.

Athanasius: Defense According to the Catholic Rule of Faith

In his controversies with the Arians, Athanasius starts by providing an exposition of traditional Catholic doctrine, then creates support for the doctrine primarily from Scripture by applying ecclesiastical Tradition as the rule for interpretation. For example, Athanasius points out that the Arians focus only on those passages that seem to downplay Our Lord's divinity and therefore they concluded wrongly that He was not divine. Let us observe Athanasius' logical argumentation. He writes: "This then is what happens to God's enemies the Arians; for looking at what is human in the Saviour, they have judged Him to be a creature."[82] Then he goes on to quote a passage that is misinterpreted by the Arians and used to equate Our Lord as a creature. "But for them, learn they, however tardily, that 'the Word made flesh;"[83] Then he continues to show that he does not rely on the force of this passage alone in order to interpret it in an orthodox and pious manner. "[A]nd let us, retaining the general scope of the faith, acknowledge that what they interpret ill, has a right interpretation."[84] In other words, Athanasius interprets the Sacred Text in accordance with the traditional doctrine of the Incarnation.

Elsewhere, Athanasius argues in the same vein. In his defense of the divinity of the Holy Spirit, Athanasius provides a dossier of passages from the Bible that justifies the doctrine of the Holy Spirit's divinity.

---

82 Athanasius, *Discourses Against the Arians*, 3:35 (inter A.D. 358-362) NPNF 2, IV:413.

83 Ibid.

84 Ibid.

> These sayings concerning the Holy Spirit, by themselves alone, show that in nature and essence he has nothing in common with or proper to creatures, but is distinct from things originating, proper to, and not alien from, the Godhead and essence of the Son; in virtue of which essence and nature he is of the Holy Triad.[85]

Following his appeal to Scripture **Athanasius** explains that he does not rely on the inherent force of the Scriptural passages alone to provide their meaning. Athanasius affirms that although the various passages of Scripture justify the doctrine of the Holy Spirit, the traditional faith obliges him to interpret the text in a certain way.

> But beyond these [Scriptural] sayings, let us look at the *very tradition, teaching and faith* of the Catholic Church from the beginning, which the Lord gave, the Apostles preached, and the Fathers kept. Upon this the Church is founded, and he who should fall away from it should not be a Christian, and should no longer be so called. There is, then, a Triad, holy and complete, confessed to be God in Father, Son, and Holy Spirit, having nothing foreign or external mixed with it, not composed of one that creates and one that is originated, but all creative; and is consistent and in nature indivisible, and its activity is one.[86]

According to Athanasius, Tradition is substantive in content and authoritative. He receives these ecclesiastical doctrines through Tradition and it is within this traditional milieu that the Scriptures are to be understood. The Arians believed that Christ was 'not begotten' (as the Nicene formula states) but was 'made.' In a very clever argument, and one that explicitly shows Athanasius' reliance on Tradition, he extracts from Scripture an argument that seems to support the 'Arian position. He writes:

---

85 Athanasius, *Four Letters to Serapion of Thmuis*, 1:27 (A.D. 359-360) as cited by C. R. B. Shapland, trans., *The Letters of St. Athanasius: Concerning the Holy Spirit* (New York: Philosophical Library, 1951), p. 133.

86 Ibid., 1:28, pp. 133-135.

> For as Solomon, though a son, is called a servant, so, to repeat what was said above, although parents call the sons springing from themselves 'made' and 'created' and 'becoming,' for all this they do not deny their nature. Thus Hezekiah, as it is written in Isaiah, said in his prayer, 'From this day I will make children, who shall declare Thy righteousness, O God of my salvation.' He then said, 'I will make;' but the Prophet in that very book and the Fourth of Kings, thus speaks, 'And the sons who shall come forth of thee.' He uses then 'make' for 'beget' and he calls them who were to spring from him, 'made, and no one questions whether the term has reference to a natural offspring.[87]

Hence, Scripture at least in this instance, justifies his use of the word 'made' with 'begotten.' But immediately following, Athanasius concludes with his recurring theme of applying Tradition to his understanding of the Scriptures.

> For *nature* and *truth* draw their meaning to themselves. This being so, when persons ask whether the Lord is a creature or work, it is proper to ask of them this first, whether He is Son and Word and Wisdom.[88]

In other words, the *nature* of Christ is determined by the doctrinal *truth* of the Incarnation. Hence, traditional doctrine of the Incarnation commands him to interpret the word 'made' to mean divine generation. Again, Athanasius considers Tradition the rule of interpretation. These few examples illustrate what is meant when Athanasius refers to an 'orthodox' or 'pious' or 'good' understanding of the Sacred Text. That is, Scripture is to be interpreted within the background of the Church's Tradition in contrast to the private judgments of heretics.

The Nicene Creed

In order to safeguard the doctrine of Our Lord's divinity the Church Fathers formulated a non-scriptural test rather than apply a

---

[87] Athanasius, *Discourses Against the Arians*, 2:4, NPNF 2, IV:350.

[88] Ibid., 2:4-5, NPNF 2, IV:350.

passage from Scripture. The Fathers at Nicea recognized the futility of applying a Scriptural test since the Arian exegetes had their own interpretation of the various passages which had bearing on Our Lord's divinity. In fact, as soon as a passage from Scripture which supported the divinity of Christ, a slew of 'nods' and 'winks' from the Arian side came forth, conveying the fact that they had their own interpretation. Athanasius gives us a view of the scene:

> Again, when the Bishops said that the Word must be described as the True Power and Image of the Father, in all things exact and like the Father, and as unalterable, and as always, and as in Him without division (for never was the Word not, but He was always, existing everlastingly with the Father, as the radiance of light), Eusebius and his fellows endured indeed, as not daring to contradict, being put to shame by the arguments which were urged against them; but withal they were caught whispering to each other and winking with their eyes, that 'like,' and 'always,' and 'power,' and 'in Him,' were, as before, common to us and the Son, and that it was no difficulty to agree to these. As to 'like,' they said that it is written of us, 'Man is the image and glory of God:' 'always,' that it was written, 'For we which live are always:' 'in Him,' 'In Him we live and move and have our being:' 'unalterable,' that it is written, 'Nothing shall separate us from the love of Christ:' as to 'power,' that the caterpillar and the locust are called 'power' and 'great power,' and that it is often said of the people, for instance, All the power of the Lord came out of the land of Egypt: and there are others also, heavenly ones, for Scripture says, The Lord of powers is with us, the God of Jacob is our refuge...' therefore the Council, as understanding this, suitably wrote 'one in essence, 'that they might both defeat the perverseness of the heretics, and shew that the Word was other than originated things.[89]

It was readily apparent to the **Fathers at Nicea** that Scripture by itself was insufficient for safeguarding and defining the faith. In other words, the Fathers concluded that Scripture was *formally* in-

---

[89] Athanasius, *Defence of the Nicene Definition*, 20 (A.D. 350/351) NPNF 2, IV:163-164.

sufficient. In order to safeguard the faith, more exact distinct terms were required than what could be garnered from Scripture.

> Yes, it behooved, say I too; for the tokens of truth are more exact as drawn from Scripture, than from other sources; but the ill disposition and the versatile and crafty irreligion of Eusebius and his fellows, compelled the Bishops [at Nicea], as I said before, to publish [i.e. the non-scriptural phrase 'one in essence'] *more distinctly* the terms which overthrew their irreligion.[90]

> For whereas they contrive to put sophistical construction on all other words at their will, this phrase only [i.e. homoousion], as detecting their heresy, do they dread; which the Fathers set down as a *bulwark* against their irreligious notions once and for all.[91]

In order to preserve the true meaning of Scripture, something else was required other than Scripture. That is why Athanasius does not hesitate to affirm the absolute authority and sufficiency of the Church at Council and her profession of faith contained in the Nicene creed: "The confession arrived at Nicea was, we say more, *sufficient* and enough by itself, for the subversion of all irreligious heresy, and for the security and furtherance of the doctrine of the Church."[92] "For this Synod of Nicaea is in truth a proscription of every heresy."[93]

It was painfully obvious to all involved that Scripture was insufficient to combat the Arian party since they could quote Scripture to their own ends. It became clear that the only way to squash the Arian doctrine was to formulate a statement of faith that would not be reinterpreted by the Arians. In sum, the Fathers at Nicea considered only one question in defining the faith. The question was not how they personally interpreted the Bible; rather, was this

---

[90] Ibid., 32, NPNF 2, IV:172.

[91] Athanasius, *Councils of Ariminum and Seleucia*, 45 (A.D. 361/362) NPNF 2, IV:474.

[92] Athanasius, *To the Bishops of Africa*, 1 (inter A.D. 368-372) NPNF 2, IV:489.

[93] Ibid., 11, NPNF 2, IV:494.

the teaching that was handed down from my teachers? The Fathers would not budge from their single obligation to the Church. The Fathers did not consider themselves as private exegetes but as witnesses to the faith. They received and they transmitted. This is the essence of Tradition. It was the essence behind a new and non-Scriptural term, *homoousion*, through which its champions (Athanasius 'contra mundum,' Marcellus of Ancrya, and Pope Julius) orthodoxy at last triumphed.

In a larger sense, Tradition for Athanasius consisted materially of the Christian faith which was deposited by Christ and His Apostles. This Tradition included such things as the instruction he received at school, the catechesis he received in the Church, the ecumenical faith espoused by the Christian people, the faith of the Fathers at Nicea and the writings of the saints of the Church.

In the following section, we will examine the Fathers' appeal to the various monuments of Tradition, and to the various organs of the teaching Church. Additionally, through the eyes of the Fathers we will examine the heretic's use of Scripture.

Augustine versus Maximinus the Arian

The debate between Maximinus, a staunch defender of the Arian heresy, and Augustine, the orthodox bishop of Hippo [A.D. 354-430], provides us with a classic example how the Catholic rule of faith contrasts with the concept of *sola scriptura*. Maximinus was one of the most formidable opponents that Augustine had ever faced in debate. Maximinus insisted on adhering to Scripture alone throughout the debate. He did not allow traditional formulas such as the Nicaean Creed or 'homoousion,' since he did not find these in Scripture. Therefore, the oral debate between Maximinus and Augustine was based on Scripture, since this was the only common authority between them. In the debate and his follow-up replies, Augustine imparted the ecclesiastical understanding of Scripture and never wavered from the traditional Catholic faith. Not surprisingly, Maximinus imparted his own Arian understanding of Scriptures and rejected Catholic tradition. Maximinus not only exhibited a great facility in handling Scripture, he also possessed great oratory skills. His deftness in Scripture allowed him to defeat

Heraclius, a disciple of Augustine, in debate. This defeat brought the bishop of Hippo out of retirement to debate Maximinus. The first series of passages below are from Maximinus. These passages clearly show Maximinus' insistence and reliance on Scripture alone, apart from any traditional landmark. He even appeals to 2 Timothy 3:16, a favorite passage often used by Protestant apologists today, in defending the concept of scripture alone.[94] Maximinus writes:

> If you produce from the divine scriptures something that we all share, we shall have to listen. But those words which are not found in the scriptures are under no circumstance accepted by us, especially since the Lord warns us, saying, 'In vain they worship me, teaching human commandments and precepts'(Mt 5:19)[95]
>
> "I state this on the basis of the scriptures. At your bidding, I will follow up with testimonies [from the scriptures]"[96]
>
> "But if one uses some literary skill or cleverness of mind and makes up words which the holy scriptures do not contain, they are both idle and superfluous."[97]
>
> "And I profess in accord with the statement of the divine scriptures..."[98]
>
> "After all, we are protected not by mere talk, but by the testimonies of the divine scriptures."[99]
>
> "We believe the scriptures, and we venerate the divine scriptures. We do not want a single particle of a letter to perish, for we fear the threat that is stated in these divine scriptures, 'Woe to those who take away or add!' (Dt 4:2)."[100]

---

94 See Robert Sungenis, chapter 4, in this volume for a thorough discussion of 2 Timothy 3:16-17.

95 Maximinus, *Debate with Maximinus*, 1 (c.A.D. 428) AAOH 188.

96 Ibid., 4, AAOH 189.

97 Ibid., 13 AAOH 196.

98 Ibid., 13 AAOH 197.

99 Ibid., 15:1 AAOH 202.

100 Ibid., 15:13 AAOH 208.

"'All divinely inspired scripture is useful for teaching (2 Tm 3:16). For that reason, 'not one least letter or one particle of a letter will pass away (Mt 5:18). The Lord said, 'Heaven and earth will pass away, but my words will not pass away.'(Mt 24:35)."[101]

"We ought to accept all the things that are brought forth from the holy scriptures with full veneration. The divine scripture has not come as a source of our instruction so that we might correct it. How I wish that we may prove to be worthy disciples of the scriptures!"[102]

"The truth is not obtained by argumentation, but is proved by certain testimonies [ie. the Scriptures]."[103]

"[T]hat, if you state this [ie. the doctrine of the Trinity] from the divine scriptures, if you produce any passage of scripture, we are eager to be found disciples of the divine scriptures."[104]

In contrast, **Augustine** provides the correct perspective on Scripture as it balanced with the Church's interpretation of Scripture.

Thus, you have professed that Christ was defiled by flesh. But I say — indeed, the Catholic faith which I hold with the Church of Christ say s— that our Lord Jesus Christ became flesh in such a way that he suffered no contamination from the human race and from human flesh... [105]

Hold with the Catholic Church the correct faith; do not be ashamed to correct the incorrect faith. Hold with the Catholic Church that the Father is not the Son and that the Son is not the Father, but that the Father is God and the Son is God, though the two together are not two gods... [106]

---

[101] Ibid., 15:16 AAOH 213.
[102] Ibid., 15:20 AAOH 214.
[103] Ibid., 15:21 AAOH 215.
[104] Ibid., 15:26 AAOH 219.
[105] Ibid., 14 AAOH 198.
[106] Augustine, *Answer to Maximinus*, 1:1 (c.A.D. 428) AAOH 246.

> But whoever of us has learned according to the correct faith that the Trinity is our one Lord God has every confidence that we serve the Lord God alone, when we serve the Trinity alone with the service we owe to God.[107]

> The Father and the Son are, then, of one and the same substance. This is the meaning of that *"homoousios"* that was confirmed against the Arian heretics in the Council of Nicaea by the Catholic fathers with the authority of truth and the truth of authority.[108]

> If the depth of this great mystery which we read in the Letter of John can be explained and understood in some other way in accord with the Catholic faith, that neither confuses nor divides the Trinity... we should on no account reject it.[109] "As a Catholic you would understand that Christ was seen on earth and lived among human beings in the form of the servant..."[110]

Heretics and Private Interpretation

In contrast to the traditional sense, the rule of faith of the early heretics, such as the Arians, was marked by a private understanding of the Bible. Athanasius consistently contrasts the traditional faith of the Church with the isolated opinions of the Arians:

> But since they allege the divine oracles and force on them a misinterpretation, according to their private sense, it becomes necessary to meet them just so far as to vindicate these passages, and to shew that they bear an orthodox sense, and that our opponents are in error.[111]

> For being forced from the conceptions or rather misconceptions of their own hearts, they fall back upon passages of divine Scripture, and here too from want of understanding, ac-

[107] Ibid., 2:1 AAOH 274.
[108] Ibid., 2:14, 3 AAOH 281.
[109] Ibid., 2:22, 3 AAOH 308.
[110] Ibid., 2:26, 13 AAOH 328.
[111] Athanasius, *Discourses Against the Arians*, I:37, NPNF 2, IV: 327-328.

> cording to their wont, they discern not their meaning; but laying down their own irreligion as a sort of canon of interpretation, they wrest the whole of the divine oracles into accordance with it.[112]

> These passages they brought forward at every turn, mistaking their sense, under the idea that they proved that the Word of God was a creature and work and one of things originate; and thus they deceive the thoughtless, making the language of Scripture their pretence, but instead of the true sense sowing upon it the poison of their own heresy.[113]

> "However here too they (the Arians) introduce their private fictions..."[114]

Likewise **Basil** [c.A.D. 330-379], writing to the women of Canonica, affirms the ecclesiastical faith of the Fathers at Nicea and denigrates the use of private judgment: "To refuse to follow the Fathers, not holding their declaration of more authority than one's own opinion, is conduct worthy of blame, as being brimful of self-sufficiency."[115]

In **Gregory of Nyssa's** [c.A.D. 335-394] defense of the Holy Trinity he contrasts Eunomius' private and wayward opinions with the universal and orthodox faith of the Catholic Church:

> If then the expressions of Eunomius are meant in accordance with the mind of the Psalmist, they are a testimony to the Divinity of the Holy Ghost: but if they are opposed to the word of prophecy, then by this very fact a charge of blasphemy lies against Eunomius, because he sets up his own opinions in opposition to the holy prophets.[116]

---

[112] Ibid., I:52, NPNF 2, IV:337.
[113] Ibid., I:53, NPNF 2, IV:337.
[114] Ibid., III:10, NPNF 2, IV:399.
[115] Basil, *Epistle To the Canonicae*, 52:1 (A.D. 370) NPNF 2, VIII:155.
[116] Gregory of Nyssa, *Against Eunomius* ,2:15 (inter A.D. 380-384) NPNF 2, V:133.

> Who knows not that what separates the Church from heresy is this term, 'product of creation,' applied to the Son? Accordingly, the doctrinal difference being universally acknowledged, what would be the reasonable course for a man to take who endeavors to show that his opinions are more true than ours?[117]

Heretics and the Rejection of the Rule of Faith

As a consequence of interpreting the Scriptures according to their own devices, heretics have created doctrinal errors and made shipwreck of their faith. In short, according to **Athanasius**, the heretics from the very first, have committed a fatal flaw by abandoning the rule of faith, which consisted of Scripture, Tradition and Church.

> [I]f we now consider the scope of that faith which we Christians hold, and using it as a rule, apply ourselves, as the Apostle teaches to the reading of inspired Scripture. For Christ's enemies, being ignorant of this scope, have wandered from the way of truth, and have stumbled on a stone of stumbling, thinking otherwise than they should think.[118] "[L]et us, retaining the general scope of the faith, acknowledge that what they interpret ill, has a right interpretation."[119]

> But after him [the devil] and with him are all inventors of unlawful heresies, who indeed refer to the Scriptures, but do not hold such opinions as the saints have handed down, and receiving them as the traditions of men, err, because they do not rightly know them nor their power.[120]

> [A]nd it is seemingly and most irreligious when Scripture contains such images, to form ideas concerning our Lord from others which are neither in Scripture, nor have any religious

---

[117] Ibid., 4:6, NPNF 2, V:162.

[118] Athanasius, *Discourses Against the Arians*, III: 28 (inter A.D. 358-362) NPNF 2, IV:409.

[119] Ibid., III:35, NPNF 2, IV:413.

[120] Athanasius, *Festal Letters*, 2:6 (A.D. 300) NPNF 2, IV:511.

> bearing. Therefore let them tell us from what teacher or by what tradition they derived these notions concerning the Saviour?... But they seem to me to have a wrong understanding of this passage also; for it has a religious and very orthodox sense, which had they understood, they would not have blasphemed the Lord of glory[121]

This authoritative Tradition is so fundamental to **Athanasius'** rule of faith that he begins and ends his discourses against the Arians with this central theme. At the beginning of his first discourse he writes: "This then I consider the sense of this passage, and that, a very ecclesiastical sense."[122] At the end of his third discourse he writes: "Had Christ enemies thus dwelt on these thoughts, and recognized the ecclesiastical scope and an anchor for the faith, they would not have made shipwreck of the faith..."[123]

Similarly, Gregory of Nyssa asserts that Eunomius and his disciples have abandoned the faith of the evangelists, apostles and the fathers of the Church.

> [F]or it is enough for proof of our statement, that the tradition has come down to us from our Fathers, handed on, like some inheritance, by succession from the Apostles and the saints who came after them. They, on the other hand, who change their doctrines to this novelty, would need the support of their arguments in abundance, if they were about to bring over to their views, not men light as dust, and unstable, but men of weight and steadiness: but so long as their statement is advanced without being established, and without being proved, who is so foolish and so brutish as to account the teaching of the evangelists and apostles, and of those who successively shone like lights in the churches, of less force than this undemonstrated nonsense.[124]

---

[121] Athanasius, *Defence of the Nicene Definition*, 12-13 (A.D. 350/351) NPNF 2, IV:158.

[122] Athanasius, *Discourses Against the Arians*, I:44, NPNF 2, IV:331.

[123] Ibid., III:58, NPNF 2, IV:425.

[124] Gregory of Nyssa, *Against Eunomius*, 4:6 (inter A.D. 380-384) NPNF 2, V:163.

In **Basil's** defense of the Holy Spirit's divinity he equates the perversion of truth with abandoning the Church's Tradition.

> Can I then, perverted by these men's seductive words, abandon the tradition which guided me to the light, which bestowed on me the boon of the knowledge of God, whereby I, so long a foe by reason of sin, was made a child of God? But, for myself, I pray that with this confession I may depart hence to the Lord, and them I charge to preserve the faith secure until the day of Christ, and to keep the Spirit undivided from the Father and the Son, preserving, both in the confession of faith and in the doxology, the doctrine taught them at their baptism.[125]

Augustine offers the identical argument when discussing the fundamental flaw of various heretical traditions.

> For heresies, and certain tenets of perversity, ensnaring souls and hurling them into the deep, have not sprung up except when good Scriptures are not rightly understood, and when that in them which is not rightly understood is rashly and boldly asserted. And so, dearly beloved, ought we very cautiously to hear those things for the understanding of which we are but little ones, and that, too, with pious heart and with trembling, as it is written, holding this rule of soundness, that we rejoice as in food in that which we have been able to understand, according to the faith with which we are imbued;[126]

Dissension and Division

As a consequence of abandoning the Church and her Tradition, heretics have always dissented and divided among themselves. This is pointed out frequently by the Fathers. Athanasius writes: "For they dissent from each other, and, whereas they have revolted

[125] Basil, *On the Spirit*, 10:26 (A.D. 375) NPNF 2, VIII:17.

[126] Augustine, *On the Gospel of John*, Homily XVIII:1 (A.D. 416 et 417) NPNF I, VII:117.

from their fathers, are not of one and the same mind, but float about with various discordant changes."[127]

Socrates [c.A.D 380-post A.D. 439] records Emperor Theodosius' [A.D. 346/347-395] reaction to the various sects and heresies of his day. Theodosius clearly affirmed that the divisiveness and dissension of the heretics was due to their repudiation of the traditional teaching preserved and passed down by the Church Fathers.

> For a division was caused among them as some acquiesced in the reasonableness of the emperor's proposition while others shrunk from it, conscious that it was by no means favorable to their interests: so that all being variously affected towards the writings of the ancients, they could no longer agree among themselves, dissenting not only from other sects, but those of the same sect differing from one another.[128]

Ephraem [c.A.D. 306-373] of Syria, in his commentary on the Scriptures, contrasts the unity of faith of mother Church with the proliferation of heretical faith traditions: "For all heresies delight in division; on the other hand, the true mother, and the alone church of Christ, avoids dissensions and schisms, 'careful to keep the unity of the Spirit in the bond of peace.'"[129]

Interpretation According to the Ecclesiastical Sense

Athanasius affirms that some passages, in spite of their apparent Arian meaning, bear a *religious*, a *pious*, an *ecclesiastical*, an *orthodox*, or a *good* sense. In other words, one must interpret the Sacred Text according to the ecclesiastical rule and not according to one's own understanding: "But this is no sentiment of the Church, but of the Samosatene and of the present Jews."[130]

---

[127] Athanasius, *Councils of Ariminum and Seleucia*, 14 (A.D. 361/362) NPNF 2, IV:457.

[128] Socrates, *Ecclesiastical History*, 5:10 (A.D. 439),in NPNF 2,II:123.

[129] Ephraem, *Commentary on Sacred Scripture* (ante A.D. 373) FOC I:163-164.

[130] Athanasius, *Discourses Against the Arians*, I:38, NPNF 2,IV:328.

"This then I consider the sense of this passage, and that, a very ecclesiastical sense."[131]

> Scarcely, however, did they begin to speak, when they were condemned, and one differed from another; then perceiving the straits in which their heresy lay, they remained dumb, and by their silence confessed the disgrace which came upon their heterodoxy. On this the Bishops, having negatived the terms they had invented, published against them the sound and ecclesiastical faith... [132]

Augustine applies the same ecclesiastical standard when determining matters of faith:

> It is obvious; the faith allows it; the Catholic Church approves; it is true."[133] "[L]et the reader consult the rule of faith which he has gathered from the plainer passages of Scripture, and from the authority of the Church, and of which I treated at sufficient length when I was speaking in the first book about things."[134] Basil contrasts ecclesiastical understanding with the private judgment: "[N]or do I venture to propound the outcome of my own intelligence, lest I make the words of true religion merely human words; but what I have been taught by the holy Fathers, that I announce to all who question me.[135]

The Rule of Faith: Scripture and Tradition

The rule of faith during the post-Nicene period is essentially the same as the ante-Nicene. It consisted of Scripture, Tradition and Church. The Fathers did not set Scripture against Tradition, nor did they ask which authority was greater. Instead, the Fathers consistently linked Scripture and Tradition together, showing how the apostolic heritage is communicated to the Church. For them, Scripture and Tradition were two modes or mediums in transmit-

[131] Ibid., I:44, NPNF 2, IV:331.
[132] Athanasius, *Defence of the Nicene Definition*, 3, NPNF 2, IV:152.
[133] Augustine, *Sermons*, 117:6 (inter .A.D. 391-430) ENO 135.
[134] Augustine, *On Christian Doctrine*, 3,2:2 (A.D. 397) NPNF I, II:557.
[135] Basil, *To the Church of Antioch*, Epistle 140:2 (A.D. 373) NPNF 2, VIII:204.

ting the single deposit of faith. The Fathers believed that all apostolic teachings are contained within Scripture and Tradition. The content of Tradition is coincident with Scripture, differing primarily in its degree of explicitness and mode of transmission. Athanasius, in this magisterial passage, summarizes the rule of faith of the Catholic Church following a host of Scriptural passages affirming the deity of the Holy Spirit.

> But beyond these sayings [i.e. Scripture], let us look at the very tradition, teaching, and faith of the Catholic Church from the beginning which the Lord gave, the Apostles preached, and the Fathers kept. Upon this the Church is founded, and he who should fall away from it would not be a Christian, and should no longer be so called.[136]

Basil, in his defense of the Holy Spirit's deity, affirms, in this classic passage the necessity of holding fast to both Scripture and the Church's Tradition.

> Of the dogmas and kerygmas preserved in the Church, some we possess from written teaching and others we receive from the tradition of the Apostles, handed on to us in mystery. In respect to piety both are of the same force. No one will contradict any of these, no one, at any rate, who is even moderately versed in matters ecclesiastical. Indeed, were we to try to reject unwritten customs as having no great authority, we would unwittingly injure the Gospel in its vitals; or rather, we would reduce kerygma to a mere term.[137]

Likewise, **John Chrysostom** [inter A.D. 344/345-407], as if to anticipate the claims of *sola scriptura*, appeals to 2 Thess. 2:15 in defending the coordinate authority of the Church and her inerrant Tradition.

---

136 Athanasius, *Four Letters to Serapion of Thmuis*, 1:28 (A.D. 359-360) as cited by C. R. B. Shapland, trans., *The Letters of St. Athanasius: Concerning the Holy Spirit* (New York:Philosophical Library, 1951) pp. 133-134.

137 Basil, *On the Spirit*, 27:66 (A.D. 375) JUR, II:18-19.

> 'So then, brethren, stand fast, and hold to the traditions which ye were taught, whether by word, or by Epistle of ours.' Hence it is manifest, that they did not deliver all things by Epistle, but many things also unwritten, and in like manner both the one and the other are worthy of credit. Therefore let us think the tradition of the Church also worthy of credit. It is a tradition, seek no farther.[138]

Cyril of Alexandria [d. A.D. 444], in his letter to John of Antioch also testifies to the complementary authorities of Scripture and Tradition: "[W]e give thanks to God, the Saviour of the world, rejoicing with one another that our Churches, both ours and yours, hold a faith in accordance with the divinely inspired Scriptures and with the tradition of our holy Fathers."[139]

Epiphanius [c.A.D. 315-403], in his treatise against all heresies, appeals to 1 Cor. 11:2, a passage often cited by Catholic apologists, in support of Scripture and Tradition.

> However, none of the sacred words need an allegorical interpretation of their meaning; they need examination, and the perception to understand each proposition's force. But tradition must be used too, for not everything is available from the sacred scripture. Thus the holy apostles handed some things down in scripture but some in traditions, as St. Paul says, 'As I delivered the tradition to you,' and elsewhere, 'So I teach, and so I have delivered the tradition in the churches,' and, 'If ye keep the tradition in memory, unless ye believed in vain.'[140]

Pope Leo the Great [reigned A.D. 440-461], while commenting on the faith of the Alexandrian Church, affirms the necessity of holding fast to Scripture and the teaching passed down by the Church Fathers: "[W]e commend you for holding fast that teach-

---

[138] Chrysostom, John, *On the 2nd Epistle to the Thessalonians*, Homily 4:2 (inter A.D. 398-404) NPNF I, XIII:390.

[139] Cyril of Alexandria, *Epistle to John of Antioch*, 39 (A.D. 433) CCC, 315.

[140] Epiphanius, *Panarion*, 61 (inter A.D. 374-377) as cited by Frank Williams, trans., *The Panarion of Epiphanius of Salamis* (New York: E. J. Brill, 1987) vol. 2, p. 119.

ing which has come down to us from the Blessed Apostles and the holy Fathers."[141]

Theodoret of Cyrus [c.A.D. 393-c.A.D. 466] refers to the two-fold guide of the Church as the basis for combating heresies and the instrument that maintains the faith undefiled.

> [B]ut up to now I have ever kept the faith of the apostles undefiled... So have I learnt not only from the apostles and prophets but also from the interpreters of their writings, Ignatius, Eustathius, Athanasius, Basil, Gregory, John, and the rest of the lights of the world; and before these from the holy Fathers in council at Nicaea, whose confession of the faith I preserve in its integrity, like an ancestral inheritance, styling corrupt and enemies of the truth all who dare to transgress its decrees. I invoke your greatness, now that you have heard from me in these terms, to shut the mouths of my calumniators.[142]

Augustine, in his discussion of Christ's death and resurrection, refers to the authority of Scripture, Tradition and the Church.

> But those reasons which I have here given, I have either gathered from the authority of the church, according to the tradition of our forefathers, or from the testimony of the divine Scriptures, or from the nature itself of numbers and of similitudes. No sober person will decide against reason, no Christian against the Scriptures, no peaceable person against the church.[143]

Tradition: Appeal to the Church Fathers

As we have seen, Tradition has various monuments by which the apostolic faith is transmitted to subsequent generations of the Church. The appeal to the Church Fathers found increased recognition and use during this period. **Athanasius**, commenting on the

---

[141] Leo the Great, Pope, *To Proterius*, Epistle 129:1 (inter A.D. 442-460) NPNF 2, XII:96.

[142] Theodoret of Cyrus, *To Florentius*, Epistle 89 (ante A.D. 466) NPNF 2, III:283.

[143] Augustine, *On the Trinity*, 4, 6:10 (inter A.D. 400-416) NPNF I, III:75.

pedigree of faith that has come down to us through the Fathers, writes: "But our faith is right, and starts from the teaching of the Apostles and tradition of the fathers, being confirmed both by the New Testament and the Old."[144]

> For, what our fathers have delivered, this is truly doctrine; and this is truly the token of doctors, to confess the same thing with each other, and to vary neither from themselves nor from their fathers... Thus the Greeks, as not witnessing to the same doctrines, but quarreling one with another, have no truth of teaching; but the holy and veritable heralds of truth agree together, and do not differ... preaching the same Word harmoniously.[145]

> See, we are proving that this view has been transmitted from father to father, but ye, O modern Jews and disciples of Caiaphas, how many fathers can ye assign to your phrases? Not one of the understandings and wise; for all abhor you, but the devil alone; none but he is your father in this apostasy, who both in the beginning sowed you with the seed of this irreligion, and now persuades you to slander the Ecumenical Council, for committing to writing, not your doctrines, but that which from the beginning those who were eyewitnesses and ministers of the Word have handed down to us. For the faith which the council has confessed in writing, that is the faith of the Catholic Church; to assert this, the blessed Fathers so expressed themselves while condemning the Arian heresy...[146] "For it is right and meet thus to feel, and to maintain a good conscience toward the Fathers, if we be not spurious children, but have received the traditions from them, and the lessons of religion at their hands."[147]

Augustine appeals to the writings and faith of the Church Fathers in support of the Catholic doctrines concerning grace.

---

144 Athanasius, *To Adelphius*, Epistle 60:6 (A.D. 370/371) NPNF 2, IV:576-577.
145 Athanasius, *Defence of the Nicene Definition*, 4 (A.D. 350/351) NPNF 2, IV:153.
146 Athanasius, *Defence of the Nicene Definition*, 27 NPNF 2, IV:168-169.
147 Athanasius, *Councils of Ariminum and Seleucia*, 47 NPNF 2, IV:475.

> Holy and blessed priests, widely reknowned for their diligence in divine eloquence, Irenaeus, Cyprian, Reticius, Olympius, Hilary, Ambrose, Gregory, Innocent, John, Basil — and whether you like it or not, I will add the presbyter Jerome, while omitting those who are still alive — have pronounced against you their opinion about original sin in the guilty succession of all men... What they found in the Church, they kept; what they learned, they taught; what they received from the fathers, they handed on to the sons. We were never involved with you before these judges; but our case has been tried before them. Neither we nor you were known to them; we but recite their judgments delivered in our favor against you.[148]

Basil appeals to the faith of the Church Fathers in defending the deity of the Holy Spirit.

> The one aim of the whole band of opponents and enemies of 'sound doctrine' is to shake down the foundation of the faith of Christ by leveling apostolic tradition with the ground, and utterly destroying it. So like the debtors — of course bona fide debtors — they clamour for written proof, and reject as worthless the unwritten tradition of the Fathers.[149]

> Wherefore we too are undismayed at the cloud of our enemies, and, resting our hope on the aid of the Spirit, have, with all boldness, proclaimed the truth. Had I not so done, it would truly have been terrible that the blasphemers of the Spirit should so easily be emboldened in their attack upon true religion, and that we, with so mighty an ally and supporter at our side, should shrink from the service of that doctrine, which by the tradition of the Fathers has been preserved by an unbroken sequence of memory to our own day.[150]

Cyril of Alexandria, in his controversies with Nestorius often appealed to the writings of the Church Fathers.

---

148 Augustine, *Against Julian*, 2, 10:33 (c. A.D. 421) JUR III:144.

149 Basil, *On the Spirit*,10:25 (A.D. 375),in NPNF 2, VIII:16.

150 Ibid., 30:79, NPNF2,VIII:50.

> But I make no great account of these matters lest I should stretch the measure of my littleness beyond my Lord and Master, or even beyond the Fathers... And in this we shall succeed, if, betaking ourselves to the statements of the holy Fathers, we are careful to esteem them highly, and, proving ourselves whether we be in the faith, as it is written, thoroughly conform our own beliefs to their sound and unexceptionable doctrines.[151]

> To these things we have been taught to assent by the holy Apostles and Evangelists, and by all the inspired Scripture, and from the true confession of the blessed Fathers. To all of them it behooves thy Religiousness also to assent and consent without dissimulation of any sort.[152]

Epiphanius in his great work against heresies, refers to the authority of the Fathers.

> [The Antiochians] confess that Father, Son, and Holy Spirit are consubstantial, three Persons, one substance, one God, because that faith is true which is handed down by those who came first, that faith which is both prophetic and evangelic and apostolic, that faith which our fathers and bishops confessed, when they met in the Synod of Nicaea in the presence of Constantine, the great and blessed king.[153]

Athanasius chronicles the fact that Eusebius of Ceasarea believed that the Nicene faith was the faith of the Church and her Fathers. Elsewhere, Eusebius affirms that the authentic faith has come to him through the tradition of the Fathers. "...Eusebius of Ceasarea in Palestine sent to his Church a letter, saying that this was the Church's faith, and the tradition of the Fathers"[154] "[A]nd besides these, Phillip... and finally Irenaeus. From them has come

---

[151] Cyril of Alexandria, *Second Letter to Nestorius*, Epistle 4 (A.D. 430) CCC, 295.

[152] Cyril of Alexandria, *Third Letter to Nestorius*, Epistle 17 (A.D. 430) CCC,306.

[153] Epiphanius, *Panarion*, 73:34 (inter A.D. 374-377) JUR, II:75.

[154] Athanasius, *Defence of the Nicene Definition*, 3 NPNF 2, IV:152.

down to us in writing, the sound and orthodox faith received from apostolic tradition."[155]

Gregory of Nazianzus [c.A.D. 330-c.A.D. 389] repeats the same theme: "My sheep hear my voice, which I have heard from the oracles of God, which I have been taught by the Holy Fathers, which I have taught alike on all occasions, not conforming myself to the opportune, and which I will never cease to teach; in which I was born, and in which I will depart."[156]

Gregory of Nyssa affirms the necessity of preserving the tradition of the Fathers. "[I]f our reasoning be found unequal to the problem, we must keep for ever, firm and unmoved the tradition which we received by succession from the fathers..."[157]

Hilary of Poitiers [c.A.D. 315-367/368] makes the same assertion.

> We must not depart from the creed received... and we shall not depart from the faith which we have received, through the prophets, from God the Father, through Christ our Lord, thanks to the teaching of the Holy Spirit, in the Gospels as well as in the writings of the Apostles; the faith established by the Tradition of the Fathers, following succession of the Apostles until its formulation at Nicaea, drawn up against the heresy, which arose at this time, and this formulation will remain. To all this, we believe that nothing must be added nor, obviously, can anything be taken away. We want no novelties introduced. The words, inscribed in our minds from the many passages in the holy Scriptures, as well as the reality of 'substance, 'must remain unshaken. The Catholic Church has never stopped confessing and professing this doctrine in accord with the divine teaching.[158]

---

[155] Eusebius, *Ecclesiastical History*, 4:21 (inter A.D. 300-325) NPNF 2, I:197-198.

[156] Gregory of Nazianzus, *Against the Arians*, Oration 33:15 (A.D. 380) NPNF 2, VII:333.

[157] Gregory of Nyssa, *That there are not three Gods* (A.D. 375) NPNF 2, V:331.

[158] Hilary of Poitiers, *Ex Oper. Hist. Fragment*, 7:3 (inter A.D. 353-368) ENO, 100-101.

Jerome [c.A.D. 347-420], in a letter to a friend, witnesses to the necessity of holding fast to the faith of the Church Fathers and comments on the pristine faith of the Roman Church.

> I thank you for your reminder concerning the canons of the Church. Truly, 'whom the Lord loveth he chasteneth, and scourgeth every son whom he receiveth.' Still I would assure you that nothing is more my aim than to maintain the rights of Christ, to keep to the lines laid down by the fathers, and always to remember the faith of Rome; that faith which is praised by the lips of an apostle, and of which the Alexandrian church boasts to be a sharer.[159]

Pope Leo the Great, in his discussions with the bishop of Alexandria, reinforces the importance of holding fast to the Traditions of the Fathers in order to safeguard the faith.

> You do right, brother, to be displeased at their stubbornness, and we commend you for holding fast that teaching which has come down to us from the blessed Apostles and the holy Fathers... And you must so diligently exhort the laity and clergy and all the brotherhood to advance in the Faith as to show that you teach nothing new but instil into all men's breasts those things, which the Fathers of revered memory have with harmony of statement taught, and with which in all things our epistle agrees. And this must be shown not only by your words but also by the actually reading aloud of previous statements, that God's people may know that what the Fathers received from their predecessors and handed on to their descendants, is still instilled into them in the present day. And to this end, when the statements of the aforesaid priests have first been read, then lastly let my writings also be recited, that the ears of the faithful may attest that we preach nothing else than what we received from our forefathers. And because their understandings are but little practiced in discerning these things, let them at least learn from the letters of the Fathers, how ancient this evil is, which is now condemned by us in Nestorius as well as in Eutyches, who have both been ashamed

[159] Jerome, *To Theophilus*, Epistle 63:2 (c. A.D. 397) NPNF 2, VI:134.

> to preach the gospel of Christ according to the Lord's own teaching. Accordingly, both in the rule of Faith and in the observance of discipline, let the standard of antiquity be maintained throughout... [160]

Theodoret of Cyrus often refers to the authority and consensus of faith of the Church Fathers in his writings.

> This is the doctrine delivered to us by the divine prophets; this is the doctrine of the company of the holy apostles; this is the doctrine of the great saints of the East and of the West; of the far-famed Ignatius, who received his archpriesthood by the right hand of the great Peter, and for the sake of his confession of Christ was devoured by savage beasts; and of the great Eustathius, who presided over the assembled council, and on account of his fiery zeal for true religion was driven into exile. This doctrine was preached by the illustrious Meletius, at the cost of no less pains, for thrice was he driven from his flock in the cause of the apostles' doctrines; by Flavianus, glory of the imperial see; and by the admirable Ephraim, instrument of divine grace, who has left us in the Syriac tongue a written heritage of good things; by Cyprian, the illustrious ruler of Carthage and of all Libya, who for Christ's sake found a death in the fire; by Damasus, bishop of great Rome, and by Ambrose, glory of Milan, who preached and wrote it in the language of Rome. The same was taught by the great luminaries of Alexandria, Alexander and Athanasius, men of one mind, who underwent sufferings celebrated throughout the world. This was the pasture given to their flocks by the great teachers of the imperial city, by Gregory, shining friend and supporter of the truth; by John, teacher of the world, by Atticus, their successor alike in see and in sentiment. By these doctrines Basil, great light of the truth, and Gregory sprung from the same parents, and Amphilochius, who from him received the gift of the high-priesthood, taught their contemporaries, and have left the same to us in their writings for a goodly heritage. Time would fail me to tell of Polycarp, and Irenaeus, of Methodius

---

160 Leo the Great, *To Proterius-Bishop of Alexandria*, Epistle 129 (A.D. 454) NPNF 2, XII:96.

and Hippolytus, and the rest of the teachers of the Church. In a word I assert that I follow the divine oracles and at the same time all these saints.[161]

Tradition: Catechesis and Preaching

Catechesis and ecclesiastical preaching of the faith are additional monuments of Tradition. Athanasius cites them as coordinate authorities in his controversies with the Arians.

> For who was ever yet a hearer of such a doctrine? or whence or from whom did the abettors and hirelings of the heresy gain it? who thus expounded to them when they were at school? who told them, 'Abandon the worship of the creation, and then draw near and worship a creature and a work?' But if they themselves own that they have heard it now for the first time, how can they deny that this heresy is foreign, and not from our fathers?[162]

> [W]ho heard in his first catechizing, that God has a Son and has made all things by His proper Word, but understood it in that sense in which we now mean it? Who on the rise of this odious heresy of the Arians, was not startled at what he heard, as strange... However here too they [the Arians] introduce their private fictions, and contend that the Son and the Father are not in such wise 'one,' or 'like,' as the Church preaches, but as they themselves would have it.[163]

Similarly, **John Cassian** [c.A.D. 360-c.A.D. 435] asserts the authority of the faith handed down through catechetical instruction and contrasts the catechetical faith with the heresies of Arius and Sabellius.

> If you were an assertor of the Arian or Sabellian heresy, and did not use your own creed, I would still confute you by the authority of the holy Scriptures; I would confute you by the

161 Theodoret of Cyrus, *To the Monks*, Epistle 151 (A.D. 431) NPNF 2, III:332.
162 Athanasius, *Discourses Against the Arians*, I:8, NPNF 2, IV:310.
163 Ibid., 3:10, NPNF 2, IV:399.

> words of the law itself; I would refute you by the truth of the Creed which has been approved throughout the whole world. I would say that, even if you were void of sense and understanding, yet still you ought at least to follow universal consent: and not to make more of the perverse view of a few wicked men than of the faith of all the Churches: which as it was established by Christ, and handed down by the apostles ought to be regarded as nothing but the voice of the authority of God, which is certainly in possession of the voice and mind of God. And what then if I were to deal with you in this way? What would you say? What would you answer? Would it not, I adjure you, be this: viz., that you had not been trained up and taught in this way: that something different had been delivered to you by your parents, and masters, and teachers. That you did not hear this in the meeting place of your father's teaching, nor in the Church of your Baptism: finally that the text and words of the Creed delivered and taught to you contained something different.[164]
>
> Therefore, as I said above, if you had been a follower and assertor of Sabellianism or Arianism or any heresy you please, you might shelter yourself under the example of your parents, the teaching of your instructors, the company of those about you, the faith of your creed. I ask, O you heretic, nothing unfair, and nothing hard. As you have been brought up in the Catholic faith, do that which you would do for a wrong belief. Hold fast to the teaching of your parents. Hold fast the faith of the Church: hold fast the truth of the Creed: hold fast the salvation of baptism.[165]

Tradition: The Scope of Faith

In **Athanasius**' three discourses against the Arians, he refers to the 'ecclesiastical scope' as one of the keys to interpreting Scripture. The ecclesiastical scope refers to the ecumenical voice and doctrines held by the Catholic faithful. The 'ecclesiastical scope'

---

[164] Cassian, John, *Incarnation of the Lord*, 6:5 (c. A.D. 429/430) NPNF 2, XI:593.

[165] Cassian, John, *Incarnation of the Lord*, 6:5 (c. A.D. 429/430) NPNF 2, XI:593-594.

in the following passages specifically refers to the Catholic doctrine of the Incarnation.

> Now the scope and character of Holy Scripture, as we have often said, is this — it contains a double account of the Saviour; that He was ever God, and is the Son, being the Father's Word and Radiance and Wisdom; and that afterwards for us He took flesh of a Virgin, Mary Bearer of God, and was made man.[166]

Where is this scope found? First in Sacred Scripture. "And this scope is to be found throughout inspired Scriptures..."[167]

Second Athanasius finds this scope in the ecclesiastical and ecumenical faith of the Church, a monument of Tradition. The Arians, Athanasius insists, have abandoned the traditional doctrine of the Incarnation and have interpreted the Sacred Text according to their own understanding and judgment.

> Now what has been briefly said above may suffice to shew their misunderstanding of the passages they then alleged; and that of what they now allege from the Gospels they certainly give an unsound interpretation, we may easily see, if we now consider the scope of that faith which we Christians hold, and using it as a rule, apply ourselves, as the Apostle teaches, to the reading of inspired Scripture. For Christ's enemies, being ignorant of this scope, have wandered from the way of truth, and have stumbled on a stone of stumbling, thinking otherwise than they should think.[168]

This is Athanasius' pattern of argument and debate. He starts with the traditional doctrine of the Catholic Church as his foundation, and then vindicates those passages the Arians misinterpret. If one interprets a Scriptural passage within the context of the Church's traditional doctrines, such as the Incarnation, one will be able to distinguish between an orthodox and a heterodox interpretation.

---

166 Athanasius, *Discourses Against the Arians*, 3:29 NPNF 2, IV:409.
167 Ibid., 3:29, NPNF 2, IV:409.
168 Athanasius, *Discourses Against the Arians*, 3:28, NPNF 2, IV:409.

"But for them, learn they, however tardily, that 'the Word became flesh;' and let us, retaining the general scope of the faith, acknowledge that what they interpret ill, has a right interpretation."[169]

Athanasius ends his final discourse by reiterating a theme of the Fathers: Those who abandon the traditional doctrine of the Church will inevitably misinterpret the Scriptures and eventually apostasize. "Had Christ enemies thus dwelt on these thoughts, and recognized the ecclesiastical scope and an anchor for the faith, they would not have made shipwreck of the faith..."[170]

Hilary takes a similar course in his treatise against the Arian heresy: "And, O wretched heretic! you turn the weapons granted to the Church against the Synagogue, against belief in the Church's preaching, and distort against the common salvation of all the sure meaning of a saving doctrine."[171]

In the same vein as St. Athanasius, **Hilary of Poitiers** asserts that if heretics had held fast to the doctrine of the Incarnation, they would have interpreted "The Lord created me for the beginning of his ways" (Prov. 8:22 LXX) in an orthodox and pious manner: "Learn at last, heretic, from the revelation of Catholic teaching, what is the meaning of the saying that Christ was created for the beginning of the ways of God and for His works; and be taught by the words of Wisdom itself the folly of your impious dulness."[172]

Tradition: Lex Orandi, Lex Credendi[173]

During this period the Fathers often appealed to Traditions which had no explicit Scriptural support. The majority of these unwritten Traditions consisted of ecclesiastical practices which included such things as the blessing of the baptismal water, the blessing of the oil for anointing, renunciation of Satan and his angels during the baptismal rite, turning to the East for prayer, sign of the cross and the triple immersion of baptism. Protestants have

---

[169] Ibid., 3:35 NPNF 2, IV:413.
[170] Ibid., 3:58, NPNF 2, IV:425.
[171] Hilary of Poitiers, *On the Trinity*, 12:36 (inter A.D. 356-359) NPNF 2, IX:227.
[172] Ibid., 12:44, NPNF 2, IX:229.
[173] Lex Orandi, Lex Credendi [the rule of prayer is the rule of belief]

often made light of these unwritten Traditions and downplayed their authority since they only refer to ecclesiastical disciplines and practices and not doctrines. The Church Fathers however, often proved the orthodoxy of a doctrine on the basis of Church life and practice. The practice of supporting theological principles on the basis of worship and prayer life of the Church became popular during this period. The phrase, lex orandi, lex credendi' means 'the rule of prayer is the rule of belief.' In other words, practice and worship within the Church helps facilitate doctrinal definition. **Athanasius** and Basil provide the classic examples of applying the rule of practice and worship in defending the divinity of Christ and of the Holy Spirit respectively.

> But if the whole earth hymns the Framer and the Truth, and blesses, and fears it, and its Framer is the Word, and He Himself says, 'I am the Truth,' it follows that the Word is not a creature, but alone proper to the Father, in whom all things are disposed, and He is celebrated by all, as Framer; for 'I was by Him disposing;' and 'My Father worketh hitherto, and I work.' And the word 'hitherto shows His eternal existence in the Father as the Word; for it is proper to the Word to work the Father's works and not to be external to Him.[174]

This rule of practice and worship was one of the most important and formidable arguments on behalf of Christ's divinity. Athanasius applied the rule of worship when he contrasted the Arian doctrine of Christ with the regenerative sacrament of Baptism. Athanasius argued that Christ is divine since the salvific sacrament of baptism calls out the name of the Father, Son and Holy Spirit. In other words, the source of grace and power of the sacrament of baptism was God, not a creature: "If the Word were a creature, He would not assume the created body to quicken it. For what help can creatures derive from a creature that itself needs salvation."[175]

In addition, the Church's prayer life and liturgy included prayers of worship to Christ as God. In fact, Athanasius insisted

---

174 Athanasius, *Discourses Against the Arians*, 2:20 (inter A.D. 358-362) NPNF 2, IV:359.

175 Athanasius, *To Adelphius*, Epistle 60:8 (A.D. 370/371) NPNF 2, IV:577.

that one of the flaws of the Arian heresy is that it would make the faithful guilty of worshiping a creature: "We do not worship a creature. Far be the thought. For such an error belongs to the heathens and Arians. But we worship the Lord of Creation, Incarnate, the Word of God."[176]

Similarly, Basil applied the same traditional argument in defending the divinity of the Holy Spirit.

> In answer to the objection that the doxology in the form 'with the Spirit' has no written authority, we maintain that if there is not other instance of that which is unwritten, then this must not be received. But if the great number of our mysteries are admitted into our constitution without written authority, then, in company with the many others, let us receive this one. For I hold it apostolic to abide also by the unwritten traditions. 'I praise you,' it is said, 'that ye remember me in all things, and keep the ordinances as I have delivered them to you;' and 'Hold fast the traditions which ye have been taught whether by word, or our Epistle.' One of these traditions is the practice which is now before us, which they who ordained from the beginning, rooted firmly in the churches, delivering it to their successors, and its use through long custom advances pace by pace with time. If, as in a Court of Law, we were at a loss for documentary evidence, but were able to bring before you a large number of witnesses, would you not give your vote for our acquittal? I think so; for 'at the mouth of two or three witnesses shall the matter be established.' And if we could prove clearly to you that a long period of time was in our favour, should we not have seemed to you to urge you with reason that this suit ought not to be brought into court against us? For ancient dogmas inspire a certain sense of awe, venerable as they are with hoary antiquity.[177]

Basil's primary basis for the defense of the Holy Spirit's divinity was the unwritten Tradition expressed in liturgy of the Church rather than Scripture. This Tradition consisted of the liturgical phrase 'Glory be to the Father with the Son together with the Holy Ghost.'

---

[176] Ibid., 60:3, NPNF 2, IV:575.

[177] Basil, *On the Spirit*, 29:71 (A.D. 375) NPNF 2, VIII:44-45.

This doxology is not in Scripture, though the teaching is coincident with it, and provides Basil with his central argument for the deity of the Holy Spirit.

Athanasius extended the traditional argument in his defense of the Holy Spirit's deity. He affirms the Holy Spirit's nature must be consubstantial with the Father and the Son, since the Holy Spirit conjoins with the Father and the Son in the most solemn sacrament of baptism.

> If you divide and alienate the Spirit from the Godhead, you have not that which is 'in all'; and, if you think like this, the rite of initiation which you reckon to perform is not entirely into the Godhead. For with the Godhead there is mixed a creature; and, like the Arians and the heathen, you too confess creation to be divine together with God who made it through his own Word... Such are your rites and those of the Arians, who dispute about the Godhead and serve creatures before God who created all things.[178]

In addition to unwritten Traditions relating to Church custom and practice, the Church Fathers appealed to such Traditions in direct support of doctrines. For example, Augustine appeals to an unwritten tradition in support of validity of heretical baptism and infant baptism.

> For this question of baptism... not repeating what was already given, even in the case of schismatics and heretics... And this custom, coming, I suppose, from apostolical tradition (like many other things which are held to have been handed down under their actual sanction, because they are preserved throughout the whole Church, though they are not found either in their letters, or in the Councils of their successors) — this most wholesome custom...[179]

---

[178] Athanasius, *Four Letters to Serapion of Thmuis*, 1:29 (A.D. 359-360) as cited by C. R. B. Shapland, trans., The Letters of St. Athanasius: Concerning the Holy Spirit ,(New York: Philosophical Library, 1951) pp. 137-139.

[179] Augustine, *On Baptism Against the Donatists*, 2,7:12 (A.D. 400) NPNF I, IV:430.

> And if any one seek for divine authority in this matter [i.e. infant baptism], though what is held by the whole Church, and that not as instituted by Councils, but as a matter of invariable custom, is rightly held to have been handed down by apostolical authority...[180]

Augustine determines apostolic truth on the basis of ecumenical faith rather than on the basis of Scripture alone.

> As to those other things which we hold on the authority, not of Scripture, but of tradition, and which are observed throughout the whole world, it may be understood that they are held as approved and instituted either by the apostles themselves, or by plenary Councils, whose authority in the Church is most useful...[181]

Jerome affirms the same regarding the authority of ecumenical belief. Tradition for Jerome, is substantive and normative in authority, which is able to determine the apostolic faith and discipline for the Church.

> Don't you know that laying on hands after baptism and then the invocation of the Holy Spirit is a custom of the Church? Do you demand Scripture proof? You may find it in Acts of the Apostles. And even if it did not rest on the authority of the Scripture the consensus of the whole world in this respect would have the force of command.[182]

Likewise, **John Chrysostom** appeals to an unwritten Tradition as a basis for the doctrine of intercessory prayers for the dead: "Not in vain did the Apostles order that remembrance should be made of the dead in the dreadful Mysteries."[183]

These are just a few of the many examples in which the Fathers affirmed the authority of Tradition when no explicit support

---

[180] Ibid., 4, 24:31, NPNF I, IV:461.

[181] Augustine, *To Januarius*, Epistle 54:1, NPNF I, I:301.

[182] Jerome, *The Dialogue Against the Luciferians*, 8 (c. A.D. 379) NPNF 2, VI:324.

[183] Chrysostom, John, *On Phillippians*, Homily 3, Vol. 24 (inter A.D. 398-404) NPNF I:XIII:197.

in Scripture existed. Many, if not most, of these unwritten Traditions refer to ecclesiastical practices. However, the Church Fathers often used these unwritten ecclesiastical practices of the Church in determining the authenticity and apostolicity of a doctrine.

The Church: The Custodian and Interpreter of the Scriptures

According to the Fathers, Christ entrusts the entire deposit of faith to the Church and the responsibility for interpreting it in an orthodox and authoritative manner. Therefore, in order to understand Scripture fully and without error one must read it according to the Church's preaching and teaching. Athanasius knows no other method of interpreting the Scriptures than applying this ecclesiastical rule in contrast to the heretics private judgment. In short, according to the Fathers, if one wants to know the orthodox and authentic understanding of the Sacred Text one must appeal to the Catholic Church.

> [A]ll who are to be found anywhere of orthodox sentiments, and maintaining the doctrine of the Catholic Church, which was delivered to them from the Fathers."[184] "However here too they [i.e. the Arians] introduce their private fictions, and contend that the Son and the Father are not in such wise 'one,' or 'like,' as the Church preaches, but as they themselves would have it."[185] "[W]e are content with the fact that this is not the teaching of the Catholic Church, nor did the Fathers hold this."[186] "But the sectaries, who have fallen away from the teaching of the Church, and made shipwreck concerning the faith...[187]

Ambrose [c.A.D. 339-397] applies the same ecclesiastical rule and affirms that the Church is the possessor and teacher of the

[184] Athanasius, *Defence Against the Arians*, 37, NPNF 2, IV:120.

[185] Athanasius, *Discourses Against the Arians*, III:10 (inter A.D. 358-362), NPNF 2, IV:399.

[186] Athanasius, *To Epictetus*, Epistle 59:3 (A.D. 370/371) NPNF 2, IV:571.

[187] Athanasius, *Against the Heathens*, 6 (c.A.D. 318) NPNF 2, IV:6-7.

apostolic faith: "Wherefore all other generations are strangers to truth; all the generations of heretics hold not the truth: the church alone, with pious affection, is in possession of the truth."[188]

Basil, in sharp contrast with the heretics, asserts that one is outside the salvific arms of mother Church if one's faith is not in line with the Church's faith.

> [C]onsidering myself bound to follow the high authority of such a man and of those who made the rule, and with every desire on my part to win the reward promised peacemakers, did enroll in the lists of communicants all who accepted that creed. [The fair thing would be to judge of me, not from one or two who do not walk uprightly in the truth, but from the multitude of bishops throughout the world, connected with me by the grace of the Lord...] you may learn that we are all of one mind and of one opinion. [Whoso shuns communion with me, it cannot escape your accuracy, cuts himself off from the whole Church...][189]

Similarly, **Cyril of Jerusalem** [c.A.D. 315-386], in his lectures on the faith, affirms the coordinate authority of the Church: "But in learning the Faith and in professing it, acquire and keep that only, which is now delivered to thee by the Church, and which has been built up strongly out of all the Scriptures."[190]

Gregory of Nyssa contrasts the Church's authority with private understanding and judgment: "[S]eeing, I say, that the Church teaches this in plain language, that the Only-begotten is essentially God, very God of the essence of the very God, how ought one who opposes her decisions to overthrow the preconceived opinion?"[191]

Hilary of Poitiers asserts that one will not understand the meaning of God's Word apart from the guidance of mother Church: "[T]hey who are placed without the Church, cannot attain to any

---

188 Ambrose, *Commentary of Psalm* 118, 19 (inter A.D. 387-388) FOC I:71.

189 Basil, *To Neocaesareans*, Epistle 204:6-7 (A.D. 375) NPNF 2, VIII:245.

190 Cyril of Jerusalem, *Catechetical Lectures*, 5:12 (c. A.D. 350) NPNF 2, VII:32.

understanding of the divine word. For the ship exhibits a type of Church, the word of life placed and preached within which, they who are without, and lie near like barren and useless sands, cannot understand."[192]

Augustine affirmed the authority of the Church throughout his controversies with the Pelagian, Manichean, and Donatist heresies.

> The epistle begins thus: 'Manichaeus, an apostle of Jesus Christ, by the providence of God the Father. These are the wholesome words from the perennial and living fountain.' Now, if you please, patiently give heed to my inquiry. I do not believe Manichaeus to be an apostle of Christ. Do not, I beg you, be enraged and begin to curse. For you know that it is my rule to believe none of your statements without consideration. Therefore I ask, who is this Manichaeus? You will reply, An Apostle of Christ. I do not believe it. Now you are at a loss what to say or do; for you promised to give knowledge of truth, and here you are forcing me to believe what I have no knowledge of. Perhaps you will read the gospel to me, and will attempt to find there a testimony to Manichaeus. But should you meet with a person not yet believing in the gospel, how would you reply to him were he to say, I do not believe? For my part, I should not believe the gospel except moved by the authority of the Catholic Church. So when those on whose authority I have consented to believe in the gospel tell me not to believe in Manichaeus, how can I but consent?[193]

The Church and The Canon of the New Testament

It was the Church who decided which books were and were not included in the canon of Scripture. The Church recognized the authenticity of a New Testament book primarily on the basis of its apostolicity. This was determined through certain criteria. First, the work had to be ascribed to an apostle or a disciple of an apostle. The ascription was first determined by the internal evidence, but

---

[191] Gregory of Nyssa, *Against Eunomius*, 4:6 (inter A.D. 380-384) NPNF 2, V:163.
[192] Hilary of Poitiers, *On Matthew*, Homily 13:1 (inter A.D. 353-355) FOC I:347.
[193] Augustine, *Against the Epistle of Manichaeus*, 5:6 (A.D. 397) NPNF I, IV:131.

ultimately through tradition, particularly the beliefs of the major Sees. Secondly, the mark of apostolicity was simply not a matter of historical research; rather, it had to be recognized by the Catholic Church in its everyday prayer, practice and worship.

Cyril of Jerusalem discusses where one finds the authentic canon of the Bible in his lectures on the faith: "Learn also diligently, and from the Church, what are the books of the Old Testaments, and what those of the New."[194]

Likewise, **Athanasius** hands down the canon as given to him by the Church and her fathers in the faith.

> I beseech you to bear patiently, if I also write, by way of remembrance, of matters with which you are acquainted, influenced by the need and advantage of the Church. In proceeding to make mention of these things [the canon], I shall adopt, to comment my undertaking, the pattern of Luke... to reduce into order for themselves the books termed apocryphal, and to mix them up with the divinely inspired Scripture, concerning which we have been fully persuaded, as they who from the beginning were eyewitnesses and ministers of the Word, delivered to the fathers; it seemed good to me also, having been urged thereto by true brethren, and having learned from the beginning, to set before you the books included in the Canon...[195]

Pope Damasus and the Council of Rome in the fourth century accept only the canon which was received by the Catholic Church: "Likewise it has been said: Now indeed we must treat of the divine Scriptures, what the universal Catholic Church accepts and what she ought to shun."[196]

---

[194] Cyril of Jerusalem, *Catechetical Lectures*, 4:33 (A.D. 350) NPNF 2, VII:26.

[195] Athanasius, *Festal Letters*, 39 (A.D. 367) NPNF 2, IV:551-552.

[196] Council of Rome-Decree of Pope Damasus, *The Canon of Scripture* (A.D. 382) as cited by Henry Denzinger, *The Sources of Catholic Dogma*, Roy J. Deferrari, trans. (St. Louis: Herder, 1957) p. 33.

Augustine and **Cyril of Alexandria** make similar remarks regarding the Church and the canon of the Bible: "The authority of our books [Scriptures], which is confirmed by agreement of so many nations, supported by a succession of apostles, bishops, and councils, is against you."[197] "The book of the Apocalypse which John the wise wrote, and which has been honoured by the approval of the fathers."[198]

The acts of the **Council of Toledo** and **Carthage** echo the same belief: "If any one shall say, or shall believe, that other Scriptures, besides those which the Catholic church has received, are to be esteemed of authority, or to be venerated, let him be anathema."[199] "Item, that besides the Canonical Scriptures nothing be read in the church under the name of divine Scripture. But the Canonical Scriptures are as follows: Genesis... The Revelation of John... for these are the things which we have received from our fathers to be read in the church."[200]

Magisterial Authority and Apostolic Succession

The Fathers anticipated that the Church's Tradition as well as her Scriptures would be misunderstood and misinterpreted. According to the Fathers, the Church, through her authentic succession from the apostles alone possesses, the teaching authority to interpret and hand-on the deposit of faith in fullness and without error. Athanasius confirms the apostolic authority of the bishopric in a letter urging a friend not to refuse the episcopal office.

> And before you had received the grace of the episcopate, no one knew you; but after you became one, the laity expected you to bring them food, namely instruction from the Scriptures... For if all were of the same mind as your present advis-

---

197 Augustine, *Reply to Faustus the Manichaean*, 13:5 (c.A.D. 400) NPNF I, IV:201.

198 Cyril of Alexandria, *Worship and Adoration in Spirit and in Truth*, 5 (inter A.D. 423-425) FOC, I: 445.

199 Council of Toledo, *Canon 12* (A.D. 400) FOC, I:335.

200 Council of Carthage, *African Code*, Canon 24 (A.D. 419) NPNF 2, XIV:453-454. The African code contains all 73 books that appear in the Catholic Bible.

> ers, how would you have become a Christian, since there would be no bishops? Or if our successors are to inherit the state of mind, how will the Churches be able to hold together?[201]

Augustine, in a letter to Fortunatus, contrasts the Donatist ecclesiology with Apostolic succession.

> For if the lineal succession of bishops is to be taken into account, with how much more certainty and benefit to the Church do we reckon back till we reach Peter himself, to whom, as bearing in a figure the whole Church, the Lord said: 'Upon this rock will I build my Church, and the gates of hell shall not prevail against it!' The successor of Peter was Linus, and his successors in unbroken continuity were these: Clement, Anacletus... Sylvester, Marcus, Julius, Liberius, Damasus, and Siricius, whose successor is the present Bishop Anastasius. In this order of succession no Donatist bishop is found.[202]

Basil comments on Athanasius' insistence of adhering to the faith passed on by the bishops at Nicea: "[A]nyone... accepting the Nicene Creed, is to be received without hesitation and difficulty, citing in support of his opinion the unanimous assent of the bishops of Macedonia and Asia..."[203]

Jerome describes the august responsibility and authority of the ministerial priesthood.

> Far be it from me to censure the successors of the apostles, who with holy words consecrate the body of Christ, and who make us Christians. Having the keys of the kingdom of heaven, they judge men to some extent before the day of judgment, and guard the chastity of the bride of Christ.[204]

Gregory of Nazianzus, during his discourse on St. Athanasius, comments on apostolic succession.

---

201 Athanasius, *To Dracontius*, Epistle 49:2,4 (c.A.D. 355) NPNF 2, IV:558.
202 Augustine, *To Fortunatus*, Epistle 53:2(A.D. 400) NPNF I, I:298.
203 Basil, *To Neocaesareans*, Epistle 204:6 (A.D. 375) NPNF 2, VIII:245.
204 Jerome, *To Heliodorus*, Epistle 14:8 (c.A.D. 374) NPNF 2, VI:16.

> Thus, and for these reasons, by the vote of the whole people, not in evil fashion which has since prevailed, nor by means of bloodshed and oppression, but in an apostolic and spiritual manner, he is led up to the throne of St. Mark, to succeed him in piety, no less than in office; in the latter indeed at a great distance from him, in the former, which is the genuine right of succession, following him closely. For the unity in doctrine deserves unity in office; and a rival teacher sets up a rival throne; the one is a successor in reality, the other but in name. For it is not the intruder, but he whose rights are intruded upon, who is the successor, not the lawbreaker, but the lawfully appointed, not the man of contrary opinions, but the man of the same faith; if this is not what we mean by successor, he succeeds in the same sense as disease to health, darkness to light, storm to calm, and frenzy to sound sense.[205]

Magisterial Authority and The Councils

During this period, the magisterium as expressed through ecumenical council, was considered an infallible and authoritative instrument of the Church whose decisions on matters of the faith were binding on the consciences of all Christians. The Council did not consider itself as transmitting new or innovative truths but as transmitting, without error, the Apostolic faith once delivered to the Saints, under the protection and guidance of the Holy Spirit. **Athanasius** expresses the unimpeachable authority of the ecumenical council at Nicea throughout his writings.

> As to the Nicene Council, it was not a common meeting, but convened upon a pressing necessity, and for a reasonable object... 'Thus believes the Catholic Church;' and thereupon they confessed how they believed, in order to shew that their own sentiments were not novel, but Apostolical; and what they wrote down was no discovery of theirs, but is the same as was taught by the Apostles.[206]

---

[205] Gregory of Nazianzus, *Orations*, 21 (c.A.D. 379) NPNF 2, VII:271.

[206] Athanasius, *Councils of Ariminum and Seleucia*, 5 (A.D. 361/362) NPNF 2, IV:452-453.

In another place, Athanasius emphasizes the divine influence and authority of the Council of Nicea: "But the word of the Lord which came through the ecumenical Synod at Nicea, abides forever.[207] "Are they not then committing a crime in their very thought to gainsay so great and ecumenical a Council?"[208]

Ambrose [c.A.D. 339-397] repeats the same sentiment: "I follow the teaching of the Council of Nicaea, from which neither death nor sword shall ever separate me."[209]

In his letter to Januarius, **Augustine** affirms the authority of Tradition, as expressed by an ecumenical council on matters of faith not explicit in Scripture:

> As to those other things which we hold on the authority, not of Scripture, but of tradition, and which are observed throughout the whole world, it may be understood that they are held as approved and instituted either by the apostles themselves, or by plenary Councils, whose authority in the Church is most useful... [210]

In this pastoral letter to the bishop of Antioch, **Pope Leo the Great** affirms the inviolate nature of the Nicaean Council.

> [M]y respect for the Nicene canons is such that I never have allowed nor ever will the institutions of the holy Fathers to be violated by any innovation. For different sometimes as are the deserts of individual prelates, yet the rights of their Sees are permanent: and although rivalry may perchance cause some disturbance about them, yet it cannot impair their dignity... But at the present time let it be enough to make a general proclamation on all points, that if in any synod any one makes any attempt upon or seems to take occasion of wresting an advantage against the provisions of the Nicene can-

[207] Athanasius, *To the Bishops of Africa*, 2 (inter A.D. 368-372) NPNF 2, IV:489.
[208] Athanasius, *Defence of the Nicene Definition*, 4 (A.D. 350/351) NPNF 2, IV:152.
[209] Ambrose, *To Emperor Valentinian*, Epistle 21:14 (A.D. 386) JUR II:147.
[210] Augustine, *To Januarius*, Epistle 54:1 (A.D. 400) NPNF I:I:300.

> ons, he can inflict no discredit upon their inviolable decrees: and it will be easier for the compacts of any conspiracy to be broken through than for the regulations of the aforesaid canons to be in any particular invalidated.[211]

The force behind the creeds and canons of the ecumenical councils is traditional apostolic truth and the Church's divine authority. The Fathers in Council considered themselves the official custodians of the Church and expositors of Scripture and Tradition. According to the Fathers, the Church is a visible, authoritative and hierarchical body, whose decisions on matters of faith are binding on the consciences of the faithful. The Church is the 'ark of Noah,' outside of which there is no salvation. Various statements from the councils confirm this belief:

Council of Nicea I [A.D. 325] "[T]hese the Catholic and apostolic Church anathematizes."[212]

Council of Constantinople I [A.D. 381] "We believe... in one holy Catholic and apostolic Church."[213]

Council of Ephesus [A.D. 431] "When these things had been read, the holy Synod decreed that it is unlawful for any man to bring forward, or to write, or to compose a different Faith as a rival to that established by the Holy Fathers assembled with the Holy Ghost in Nicaea."[214]

Council of Chalcedon [A.D. 451] "These things, therefore, having been expressed by us with the greatest accuracy and attention, the holy Ecumenical Synod defines that no one shall be suffered to bring forward a different faith, nor to write, nor to put together, nor to excogitate, nor to teach it to others. But such as dare either to put together another faith or to bring forward or to

---

211 Leo the Great, Pope, *To Maximus: Bishop of Antioch* (A.D. 453) Epistle 119:3-4, NPNF 2, XII:86.

212 *Creed of Nicaea* (A.D. 325) ECC 216.

213 *Creed of Constantinople* (A.D. 381) ECC 298.

214 Council of Ephesus, *Canon VII* (A.D. 431) NPNF 2, XIV:231.

teach or to deliver a different Creed to such as wish to be converted to the knowledge of the truth from the Gentiles, or Jews or any heresy whatever, if they be Bishops or clerics let them be deposed, the Bishops from the Episcopate, and the clerics from the clergy; but if they be monks or laics: let them be anathematized... this is the faith of the Apostles: by this we all stand: thus we all believe."[215]

Magisterial Authority and the See of Rome[216]

During the post-Nicene period, there was a growing recognition of the authority of the See of Rome. Rome viewed herself, as did other Sees, as the mouthpiece and primary expositor of the faith for the One Holy Catholic and Apostolic Church. For example, **Athanasius** preserves Pope Julius' [reigned A.D. 337-352] letter (to the Eusebian faction) which contained the orthodoxy of the Nicene faith and Rome's vindication of Athanasius, as the most important document of defense against the Arians (chapters 20-35 in *Defence Against the Arians*).

> Julius to the beloved brethren... I must inform you that although I alone wrote, yet the view I expressed is not only mine... Supposing, as you assert, that there was some charge against them [Athanasius & Marcellus], the case ought not to have been conducted thus, but according to ecclesiastical canon. You should have written to us all, so that justice might be determined by all. For the sufferers were bishops, and prominent churches, which the apostles themselves had governed. And why were we [Church of Rome] not written to especially about the church of the Alexandrians? Are you ignorant that the custom was first to write to us, and then for

---

215 Council of Chalcedon, *Session V* (A.D. 431) NPNF 2, XIV:265.

216 For a more thorough discussion on the primacy of the See of Peter in Patristic thought see Abbot John Chapman, O. S. B., *Studies on the Early Papacy* (New York: Benzinger, 1928) and *Bishop Gore and Catholic Claims* (New York: Longmans, 1905); James T. Shotwell and L. R. Loomis *The See of Peter* (New York: Columbia, 1927); E. Giles *Documents Illustrating Papal Authority A.D. 96-454* (London: SPCK, 1952); and S. Butler, N. Dahlgren, and D. Hess, *Jesus, Peter & the Keys* (Santa Barbara: Queenship, 1996).

> justice to be determined from here? ...I beseech you, readily bear with me: what I write is for the common good. For what we have received from the blessed apostle Peter, that I point out to you... [217]

In addition, Athanasius attended and sanctioned the deliberations of the Council of Sardica that confirmed various aspects of the primacy of the Roman See. Athanasius, throughout his writings, refers to the meeting at Sardica as "the great Council" *(Defense Against the Arians* 1) or "the Holy Synod" (*Letter to the People of Antioch* 5) assembled at Sardica.

Council of Sardica [A.D. 343/343] "Bishop Hosius said: This also it is necessary to add — that no bishop pass from his own province to another province in which there are bishops, unless indeed he be called by his brethren, that we seem not to close the gates of charity. And this case likewise is to be provided for, that if in any province a bishop has some matter against his brother and fellow-bishop, neither of the two should call in as arbiters bishops from another province. But if perchance sentence be given against a bishop in any matter and he supposes his case to be not unsound but good, in order that the question may be reopened, let us, if it seem good to your charity, honour the memory of Peter the Apostle, and let those who gave judgment write to Julius, the bishop of Rome, so that, if necessary, the case may be retried by the bishops of the neighbouring provinces and let him appoint arbiters; but if it cannot be shown that his case is of such a sort as to need a new trial, let the judgment once given not be annulled, but stand good as before."[218]

"Bishop Gaudentius said: If it seems good to you, it is necessary to add to this decision full of sincere charity which thou hast pronounced, that if any bishop be deposed by the sentence of these neighbouring bishops, and assert that he has fresh matter in defense, a new bishop be not settled in his see, unless the bishop of Rome judge and render a decision as to this."[219]

---

[217] Julius, Pope, *To the Eusebians* (A.D. 340) in Athanasius' *Defence Against the Arians*, 20, 26, 35 (A.D. 347) GILES, 96-98.

[218] Council of Sardica, *Canon III* (A.D. 343/344) NPNF 2, XIV:416-417.

"Bishop Hosius said: Decreed, that if any bishop is accused, and the bishops of the same region assemble and depose him from his office, and he appealing, so to speak, takes refuge with the most blessed bishop of the Roman church, and he be willing to give him a hearing, and think it right to renew the examination of his case, let him be pleased to write to those fellow-bishops who are nearest the province that they may examine the particulars with care and accuracy and give their votes on the matter in accordance with the word of truth. And if any one require that his case be heard yet again, and at his request it seem good to move the bishop of Rome to send presbyters *a latere*, let it be in the power of that bishop, according as he judges it to be good and decides it to be right — that some be sent to be judges with the bishops and invested with his authority by whom they were sent. And be this also ordained. But if he think that the bishops are sufficient for the examination and decision of the matter let him do what shall seem good in his most prudent judgment. The bishops answered: What has been said is approved."[220]

The orthodox bishops in communion with Athanasius at Sardica, presided by Hosius with the papal legates, wrote the following letter to Pope Julius:

> What we have always believed, that we now know, for experience is proving and confirming for each of us what he has heard with his ears. It is true what the Apostle Paul, the most blessed teacher of the Gentiles, said of himself: 'Do ye seek a proof of him who speaks in me?' For, since the Lord Christ dwelt in him, there can be no doubt that the Spirit spoke by through his soul and animated the instrument of his body. And thus you, dearly beloved brother, though distant in body, have been with us in unison of mind and will. The reason for your absence was both honorable and imperative, that the schismatic wolves might not rob and plunder by stealth nor the heretical dogs bark madly in the rapid fury nor the very serpent, the devil, discharge his blasphemous venom. So it seems to us right and altogether fitting that priests of the Lord

[219] Council of Sardica, *Canon IV*, NPNF 2, XIV:418.
[220] Council of Sardica, *Canon V*, NPNF 2,XIV:419.

> from each and every province should report to their head, that is, to the See of Peter, the Apostle.[221]

In short, there was no question in the minds of the orthodox bishops that the Bishop of Rome could summon a bishop to Rome (even the great Patriarch of Alexandria); could order a Council to be held; could restore a bishop to his See; and could nullify the acts and canons of a Council, however large, if the Pope had sufficient justification.

Ambrose in a synodal letter to Pope Siricius [reigned A.D. 384-399] testifies to the immaculate faith and authority of the Roman Church.

> But if they will not believe the doctrines of the priests, let them believe Christ's oracles, let them believe the admonitions of angels who say, "For with God nothing is impossible." Let them believe the apostles' creed which the Roman church has always kept undefiled... And so you are to know that Jovinian, Auxentius [etc.], whom your holiness has condemned, have also been condemned by us, according to your judgement.[222]

Augustine also affirms the primacy of the Roman See. "[T]o the Roman Church, in which the supremacy of an apostolic chair has always flourished..."[223]

In his famous sermon against Pelagianism, Augustine affirms the right of the Roman See to judge doctrinal matters conclusively.

> My brethren, have compassion with me. When you find such men, do not hide them; have no misdirected mercy. Refute those who contradict, and those who resist bring to us. For already two councils on this question have been sent to the

---

221 Council of Sardica, *To Pope Julius* (A.D. 342) as cited by James T. Shotwell and Louise Ropes Loomis *The See of Peter* (New York: Columbia, 1927) pp. 527-528.

222 Ambrose, *To Sircius*, Epistle 42:5 (A.D. 391) GILES, p. 147.

223 Augustine, *To Glorius, et.al.*, Epistle 43 (A.D. 397) NPNF I, I:278.

> apostolic see [i.e. Rome];and replies have also come from there. The cause is finished; would that error might sometime be finished also![224]

John Chrysostom, in his homily on the Epistle to the Romans, praises the authority of the Roman Church on the basis of two most glorious Apostles, Peter and Paul.

> I love Rome even for this, although indeed one has other grounds for praising it, both for its greatness, and its antiquity, and its beauty, and its populousness, and for its power, and its wealth, and for its successes in war. But I let all this pass, and esteem it blessed on this account, that both in his lifetime he wrote to them, and loved them so, and talked with them whiles he was with us, and brought his life to a close there. Wherefore the city is more notable upon this ground, than upon all others together. And as a body great and strong, it hath as two glistening eyes the bodies of these Saints. Not so bright is the heaven, when the sun sends forth his rays, as is the city of Rome, sending out these two lights into all parts of the world. From thence will Paul be caught up, from thence Peter. Just bethink you, and shudder at the thought of what a sight Rome will see, when Paul ariseth suddenly from that deposit, together with Peter, and is lifted up to meet the Lord. (1 Thess. iv. 17.) What a rose will Rome send up to Christ! (Is. xxxv. 1) what two crowns will the city have about it! what golden chains will she be girded with! what fountains possess! Therefore I admire the city, not for the much gold, not for the columns, not for the other display there, but for these pillars of the Church.[225]

Council of Ephesus [A.D. 431] "And all the most reverend bishops at the same time cried out. This is a just judgment. To Coelestine [Pope, reign A.D. 422-432], a new Paul! To Cyril a new Paul! To Coelestine the guardian of the faith! To Coelestine of one mind with the synod! To Coelestine the whole Synod offers its

---

224 Augustine, *Sermons,*131:10 (A.D. 417) GILES,204. The paradigm "Rome has spoken, case is closed" is derived from this sermon.

225 Chrysostom, John, *On Romans*, Homily 32 (A.D. 391) NPNF I, XI:561-562.

thanks! One Coelestine! One Cyril! One faith of the Synod! One faith of the world! ...Arcadius ... said: ...Wherefore we desire to ask your blessedness, that you command that we taught what has been already decreed by your holiness... Theodotus ... said: The God of the whole world has made manifest the justice of the judgment pronounced by the holy Synod by the writings of the most religious bishop Coelestine, and by the coming of your holiness. For ye have made manifest the zeal of the most holy and reverend bishop Coelestine, and his care for the pious faith. And since very reasonably your reverence is desirous of learning what has been done from the minutes of the acts concerning the deposition of Nestorius your reverence will be fully convinced of the justice of the sentence, and of the zeal of the holy Synod, and the symphony of the faith which the most pious and holy bishop Coelestine has proclaimed with a great voice, of course after your full conviction, the rest shall be added to the present action."[226]

"Philip, presbyter and legate of the Apostolic See, said: 'There is no doubt, and in fact it has been known in all ages, that the holy and most blessed Peter, prince and head of the apostles, pillar of the faith, and foundation of the Catholic Church, received the keys of the kingdom from our Lord Jesus Christ, the Saviour and Redeemer of the human race, and that to him was given the power of loosing and binding sins: Our holy and most blessed Pope Celestine the bishop is according to due order his successor and holds his place... Accordingly the decision of all churches is firm, for the priests of the eastern and western churches are present... Wherefore Nestorius knows that he is alienated from the communion of the priests of the Catholic Church."[227]

Council of Chalcedon [A.D. 451] "After the reading of the foregoing epistle [i.e. the *Tome of Pope Leo*], the most reverend bishops cried out: This is the faith of the fathers, this is the faith of the Apostles. So we all believe, thus the orthodox believe. Anathema to him who does not thus believe. Peter has spoken thus through Leo [reigned A.D. 440-461]. So taught the Apostles. Piously and

---

[226] Council of Ephesus, *Session II* (A.D. 431) NPNF 2, XIV:222-223.

[227] Council of Ephesus, *Session III* (A.D. 431) GILES p. 252.

truly did Leo teach, so taught Cyril. Everlasting be the memory of Cyril. Leo and Cyril taught the same thing, anathema to him who does not so believe. This is the true faith. Those of us who are orthodox thus believe. This is the faith of the fathers. Why were not these things read at Ephesus [i.e. at the heretical synod held there]? These are the things Dioscorus hid away."[228]

"Wherefore the most holy and blessed Leo, archbishop of the great and elder Rome, through us, and through this present most holy synod together with the thrice blessed and all-glorious Peter the Apostle, who is the rock and foundation of the Catholic Church, and the foundation of the orthodox faith, hath stripped him of the episcopate, and hath alienated from him all hieratic worthiness. Therefore let this most holy and great synod sentence the before mentioned Dioscorus to the canonical penalties."[229]

"The great and holy and universal Synod... in the metropolis of Chalcedon... to the most holy and blessed archbishop of Rome, Leo... being set as the mouthpiece unto all of the blessed Peter, and imparting the blessedness of his Faith unto all... and besides all this he [Dioscorus] stretched forth his fury even against him who had been charged with the custody of the vine by the Savior, we mean of course your holiness..."[230]

Optatus of Milevis [c.A.D. 320-c.A.D. 385], in his treatise against the Donatist Churches, affirms the primacy of Peter the Apostle and the See of Rome.

> So we have proved that the Catholic Church is the Church which is diffused throughout the world. We must now mention its ornaments... For one who knows, to err is sin; those who do not know may sometimes be pardoned. You cannot deny that you know that upon Peter in the city of Rome was conferred the episcopal chair, on which sat Peter, the head of all the apostles, whence he was called Cephas, that in this one chair unity should be preserved by all, lest the other

[228] Council of Chalcedon, *Session II* (A.D. 451) NPNF 2, XIV:259.
[229] Ibid., NPNF 2, XIV:259-260.
[230] Leo the Great, Pope, *Chalcdeon to Pope Leo*, Epistle 98:1-2 (A.D. 451) NPNF 2, XII:72.

> apostles might uphold each for himself separate chairs, so that he who should set up a second chair, against the unique chair, would already be a schismatic and a sinner. Well, then on the one chair, which is the first of the endowments, Peter sat first, to whom succeeded Linus; to Linus succeeded Clement... Damasus; to Damasus Siricius, who to-day is our colleague, and he, with the whole world, agrees with us in one bond of communion through intercourse of letter of peace.[231]

In this famous letter to Pope Damasus [reigned A.D. 366-384], **Jerome** begs the Pope for a decision to determine the proper claimant of the Eastern Patriarchal See of Antioch:

> Yet, though your greatness terrifies me, your kindness attracts me. From the priest I demand the safe-keeping of the victim, from the shepherd the protection due to the sheep. Away with all that is overweening; let the state of Roman majesty withdraw. My words are spoken to the successor of the fisherman, to the disciple of the cross. As I follow no leader save Christ, so I communicate with none but your blessedness, that is with the chair of Peter. For this, I know, is the rock on which the church is built! This is the house where alone the paschal lamb can be rightly eaten. This is the ark of Noah, and he who is not found in it shall perish when the flood prevails. But since by reason of my sins I have betaken myself to this desert which lies between Syria and the uncivilized waste, I cannot, owing to the great distance between us, always ask of your sanctity the holy thing of the Lord. Consequently I here follow the Egyptian confessors who share your faith, and anchor my frail craft under the shadow of their great argosies. I know nothing of Vitalis; I reject Meletius; I have nothing to do with Paulinus. He that gathers not with you scatters; he that is not of Christ is of Antichrist.[232]

Jerome, in a letter to a woman in Rome, contrasts private understanding of the faith with the inerrant faith of the Roman See.

---

[231] Optatus of Mileve, *The Schism of Donatists*, 2:2-3 (c. A.D. 367) GILES p. 118.

[232] Jerome, *To Pope Damasus*, Epistle 15:2 (c. A.D. 376) NPNF 2, VI:18-19.

> I have all but passed over the most important point of all. While you were still quite small, bishop Anastasius [reigned A.D. 399-401] of holy and blessed memory ruled the Roman church. In his days a terrible storm of heresy came from the East and strove first to corrupt and then to undermine that simple faith which an apostle has praised. However the bishop, rich in poverty and as careful of his flock as an apostle, at once smote the noxious thing on the head, and stayed the hydra's hissing. Now I have reason to fear — in fact a report has reached me to this effect that the poisonous germs of this heresy still live and sprout in the minds of some to this day. I think, therefore, that I ought to warn you, in all kindness and affection, to hold fast the faith of the saintly Innocent [reigned A.D. 401-417], the spiritual son of Anastasius and his successor in the apostolic see; and not to receive any foreign doctrine, however wise and discerning you may take yourself to be.[233]

Representing Gaul, **Prosper of Aquitaine** [d. A.D. 455] affirms the primacy of the Roman See: "First to hew down the oncoming scourge was Rome, the see of Peter, which, having been made capital of the world's pastoral office, holds by religion whatever it does not hold by arms."[234]

Possidius [floruit A.D. 437] summarizes the role of the Roman See in the Pelagian controversy.

> And since these heretics were trying to bring the apostolic see round to their view, African councils of holy bishops also did their best to persuade the holy Pope of the city (first the venerable Innocent, and afterwards his successor Zosimus) that this heresy was to be abhorred and condemned by the catholic faith. And these bishops of so great a see successively branded them, and cut them off from the members of the Church, giving letters to the African Churches in the West, and to the Churches of the East, and declared that they were to be anathematized and avoided by all catholics. The judgment pronounced upon them by the Catholic Church

[233] Jerome, *To Demetrius*, Epistle 130:16 (A.D. 414) NPNF 2, VI:269.
[234] Prosper of Aquitaine, *Poem on the Ungrateful*, I:39 (A.D. 429) GILES p. 261.

> of God was heard and followed also by the most pious Emperor Honorius... [235]

This concludes the testimony from this golden period. Next, the classic expression for the Church's rule of faith is expressed by Vincent of Lerins. Vincent of Lerins' *Commonitories* is considered a pinnacle in the development of the Church's rule of faith during this period.

Towards Synthesis

St. Vincent of Lerins[236]: "Quod ubique, quod semper, quod ab omnibus."

Vincent of Lerins' [d. ante A.D. 450] *Commonitories* will serve as our final witness providing the clearest expression of the rule of faith. The *Commonitory* is a procedure or rule for determining orthodox Catholic doctrine. In his work, Vincent catalogs and examines the faith of the Fathers and the Church for the first five centuries. Simply stated, the rule of faith according to Vincent of Lerins consists of reading and interpreting Sacred Scripture within the framework of the Church and her unerring Tradition.

> I have often then inquired earnestly and attentively of very many men eminent for sanctity and learning, how and by what sure and so to speak universal rule I may be able to distinguish the truth of Catholic faith from the falsehood of heretical pravity; and I have always, and in almost every instance, received an answer to this effect: That whether I or any one else should wish to detect the frauds and avoid the snares of heretics as they rise, and to continue sound and complete in the Catholic faith, we must, the Lord helping, fortify our own belief in *two* ways; first, by the authority of the *Divine Law, and then, by the Tradition of the Catholic Church.*[237]

---

235 Possidius, *Life of Augustine*, 18 (A.D. 437) GILES p. 265-266.

236 Universality, antiquity, consent. Vincent of Lerins, *Commonitory*, 2:6 (c.A.D. 434), NPNF 2, XI:132.

237 Vincent of Lerins, *Commonitory*, 2:4 (c. A.D. 434) NPNF 2, XI:132.

In other words, private interpretation of Sacred Scripture, apart from the understanding and faith of the Church, is not the method for discovering orthodox doctrine.

> But some one will ask, How is it then, that certain excellent persons, and of position in the Church, are often permitted by God to preach novel doctrines to Catholics? A proper question, certainly, and one which ought to be very carefully and fully dealt with, but answered at the same time, *not* in reliance upon *one's own ability*, but by the authority of the divine Law, *and* by appeal to the Church's determination.[238]

Vincent, like the Fathers before and after him, affirms the sufficiency of Scripture, but only in so far as one interprets the Sacred Text according to the Church's unerring Tradition.

> But here some one perhaps will ask, Since the canon of Scripture is complete, and sufficient of itself for everything, and more than sufficient, what need is there to join with it the authority of the Church's interpretation? For this reason — because, owing to the depth of Holy Scripture, all do not accept it in one and the same sense, but one understands its words in one way, another in another; so that it seems to be capable of as many interpretations as there are interpreters. For Novatian expounds it one way, Sabellius another, Donatus another, Arius, Eunomius, Macedonius, another, Photinus, Apollinaris, Priscillian, another, Iovinian, Pelagius, Celestius, another, lastly, Nestorius another. Therefore, it is very necessary, on account of so great intricacies of such various error, that the *rule for the right understanding* of the prophets and apostles should be fr*amed in accordance with the standard of Ecclesiastical and Catholic interpretation*.[239]

Following this Vincent affirms the normative authority of the traditional faith with his classic canon: "This rule we shall observe if we follow *universality*, *antiquity*, *consent*."[240]

---

[238] Vincent of Lerins, *Commonitory*, 10:27 (c. A.D. 434) NPNF 2, XI:137-138.
[239] Ibid., 2:5 (c. A.D. 434) NPNF 2, XI:132.
[240] Ibid., 2:6 (c. A.D. 434) NPNF 2, XI:132.

As attractive as this simple formula may seem, nevertheless, it requires and anticipates an authority to apply and measure its three marks. How much antiquity is required? How is consensus measured? How broad is the requirement to fulfill the mark of universality? Vincent answers the question by including the magisterial authority of the Church in the rule of faith. In particular, Vincent appeals to the witness of the Church Fathers, the faith and canons of the Ecumenical Councils, and the authority vested in the Apostolic See of Rome: "[B]ut adhering to the decrees and definitions of the universal priesthood of the Holy Church, the heirs of the Apostolic and Catholic truth, they [i.e. the martyrs] chose rather to deliver up themselves than to betray the faith of universality and antiquity."[241]

> Examples there are without number: but to be brief, we will take one, and that, in preference to others, from the Apostolic See, so that it may be clearer than day to every one with how great energy, with how great zeal, with how great earnestness, the blessed successors of the blessed apostles have constantly defended the integrity of the religion which they have once received... Pope Stephen of blessed memory, Prelate of the Apostolic See... laid down this rule: 'Let there be no innovation — nothing but what has been handed down.'[242]

> But yet that nothing might be wanting to such completeness of proof, we added, at the close, the twofold authority of the Apostolic See, first, that of holy Pope Sixtus, the venerable prelate who now adorns the Roman Church; and secondly that of his predecessor, Pope Celestine of blessed memory, which same we think it necessary to insert here also.[243]

> But the Church of Christ, the careful and watchful guardian of the doctrines deposited in her charge, never changes anything in them, never diminishes, never adds, does not cut off what is necessary, does not add what is superfluous, does not lose her own, does not appropriate what is another's, but while

---

[241] Ibid., 5:14 NPNF 2, XI:134.

[242] Ibid., 6:15-16 NPNF 2, XI:135.

[243] Ibid., 32:84 NPNF 2, XI:155.

> dealing faithfully and judiciously with ancient doctrine, keeps this one object carefully in view,—if there be anything which antiquity has left shapeless and rudimentary, to fashion and polish it, if anything already reduced to shape and developed, to consolidate and strengthen it, if any already ratified and defined to keep and guard it. Finally, what other object have Councils ever aimed at in their decrees, than to provide that what was before believed in simplicity should in future be believed intelligently, that what was before preached coldly should in future be preached earnestly, that what was before practiced negligently should thenceforward be practiced with double solicitude? This, I say, is what the Catholic Church, roused by the novelties of heretics, has accomplished by the decrees of her Councils — this, and nothing else — she has thenceforward consigned to posterity in writing what she had received from those of olden times only by tradition, comprising a great amount of matter in a few words, and often, for the better understanding, designating an old article of the faith by the characteristic of a new name.[244]

> [E]arnestly to be held in view by those who would keep clear of heresy: first they should ascertain whether any decision has been given in ancient times as to the matter in question by the whole priesthood of the Catholic Church, with the authority of a General Council: and, secondly, if some new question should arise on which no decision has been given, they should then have recourse to the opinions of the holy Fathers... this ought to be accounted the true and Catholic doctrine of the Church, without any doubt or scruple.[245]

Vincent repeats another favorite theme of the Fathers concerning the purpose of an Ecumenical Council. The Fathers' main objective during an Ecumenical Council was not to impose their own understanding of Scripture or even to transmit their own doctrinal synthesis based on deductive arguments, rather the Fathers' main goal was a simple one; to transmit the same faith they received from their teachers. They received and they transmitted.

---

[244] Ibid., 23:59 NPNF 2, XI:148-149.
[245] Ibid., 29:77 NPNF 2, XI:153-154.

> Next we expressed our admiration of the humility and sanctity of that Council, such that, though the number of priests was so great, almost the more part of them metropolitans, so erudite, so learned, that almost all were capable of taking part in doctrinal discussions, whom the very circumstance of their being assembled for the purpose, might seem to embolden to make some determination on their own authority, yet they innovated nothing, presumed nothing, arrogated to themselves absolutely nothing, but used *all possible care to hand down nothing to posterity but what they had themselves received from their Fathers*. And not only did they dispose satisfactorily of the matter presently in hand, but they also set an example to those who should come after them, how they also should adhere to the determinations of sacred antiquity, and condemn the devices of profane novelty.[246]

Vincent knows of no other sense of Scripture than the one bequeathed to him by the Church. A private reading and judgment of Scripture is the tool of heretics.

> Accursed then be Photinus, who does not receive the Trinity complete... Accursed be Apollinaris, who affirms that the Godhead of Christ is marred by conversion... Accursed be Nestorius who denies God was born of a virgin... [247]

In contrast, Vincent continues:

> But blessed be the Catholic Church, which worships one God in the completeness of the Trinity... Blessed, I say, be the Church, which believes that in Christ there are two true and perfect substances but one Person... Blessed, I say, be the Church, which understands God to have become Man... Blessed, I say, be the Church, which declares this unity of Person... [248]

---

[246] Ibid., 31:82 NPNF 2, XI:155.
[247] Ibid., 16:41 NPNF 2, XI:143.
[248] Ibid., 16:41 NPNF 2, XI:143.

Elsewhere, Vincent points out that even great lights as Origen have fallen by interpreting Scripture according to their own critical mind and not according to the mind of the Church.

> What shall I say more? The result was that very many were led astray from the integrity of the faith, not by any human excellencies of this so great man, this so great doctor, this so great prophet, but, as the event showed, by the too perilous trial which he proved to be. Hence it came to pass, that this Origen, such and so great as he was, wantonly *abusing the grace of God, rashly following the bent of his own genius*, and placing overmuch confidence in himself, making light account of the ancient simplicity of the Christian religion, *presuming that he knew more than all the world besides, despising the traditions of the Church and the determinations of the ancients*, and interpreting certain passages of Scripture in a novel way, deserved for himself the warning given to the Church of God, as applicable in his case as in that of others, "If there arise a prophet in the midst of thee, '... thou shalt not hearken to the words of that prophet...' because the Lord your God doth make trial of you, whether you love Him or not." Truly, thus of a sudden to seduce the Church which was devoted to him, and hung upon him through admiration of his genius, his learning, his eloquence, his manner of life and influence, while she had no fear, no suspicion for herself — thus, I say, to seduce the Church, slowly and little by little, from the old religion to a new profaneness, was not only a trial, but a great trial.[249]

According to Vincent, a heretic's fatal flaw consists of denying the normative authority of Tradition:

> [A]ll heresies, that they evermore delight in profane novelties, scorn the decisions of antiquity, and ... make shipwreck of the faith. On the other hand, it is the sure characteristic of Catholics to keep that which has been committed to their trust by the holy Fathers... [250]

---

249 Ibid., 17:44 NPNF 2, XI:144-145.
250 Ibid., 24:63 NPNF 2, XI:150.

In summary, Vincent summarizes the faith of the Church and her Fathers, contrasting the private prescription of the heretics with the antidote found in Catholic rule of faith: Scripture and Tradition.

> But it will be said, If the words, the sentiments, the promises of Scripture, are appealed to by the Devil and his disciples, of whom some are false apostles, some false prophets and false teachers, and all without exception heretics, what are Catholics and the sons of Mother Church to do? How are they to distinguish truth from falsehood in the sacred Scriptures? They must be very careful to pursue that course which, in the beginning of this *Commonitory*, we said that holy and learned men had commended to us, that is to say, they *must interpret the sacred Canon according to the traditions of the Universal Church...* [251]

The message of Vincent of Lerins, which represents the faith of the Fathers, is simple, clear and brief. A private reading and interpretation of Scripture breeds division, dissension, and heresy. The Scriptures require the Church and her unerring Tradition in order to know God's Word in its fullness and without error. The Church not only provides a magisterial role in providing the orthodox understanding of Scripture, but also plays an equally regulative role with the various monuments of Tradition. Heretics not only have asserted their private interpretation of Scripture, but they have also shown their misunderstanding of the witness of Tradition.

Summary

The concept of *sola scriptura* was never in the minds of the Church Fathers. A convert from Anglicanism to Catholicism, **John Henry Cardinal Newman**, succinctly summarizes and critiques Protestant attempts to deny the testimony of the historic church:

> History is not a creed or a catechism, it gives lessons rather than rules; still no one can mistake its general teaching in this matter, whether he accept it or stumble at it. Bold outlines

[251] Ibid., 27:70 NPNF 2, XI:152.

> and broad masses of color rise out of the records of the past. They may be dim, they may be incomplete; but they are definite. And this one thing at least is certain; whatever history teaches, whatever it omits, whatever it exaggerates or extenuates, whatever it says and unsays, at least the Christianity is not Protestantism. If ever there were a safe truth, it is this. And Protestantism has ever felt it so. I do not mean that every writer on the Protestant side has felt it; for it was fashion at first, at least as a rhetorical argument against Rome, to appeal to past ages, or to some of them; but Protestantism, as a whole, feels it, and has felt it. This is shown in the determination already referred to of *dispensing with historical Christianity* altogether, and forming a Christianity from the *Bible alone*: men never would have put it aside, unless they had despaired of it. It is shown by the long neglect, which prevails even in the English Church. Our popular religion scarcely recognizes the fact of the twelve long ages which lie between the Councils of Nicea and Trent, except as affording one or two passages to illustrate its wild interpretations of certain prophesies of St. Paul and St. John. It is melancholy to say it, but the chief, perhaps the only English writer who has any claim to be considered an ecclesiastical historian, is the unbeliever Gibbon. To be deep in history is to cease to be a Protestant.[252]

This passage is just as relevant and telling now as it was in the 19th century. Protestant apologists who have attempted to discover the novel concept of *sola scriptura* within the faith of the Church Fathers have either not probed *deep* enough into history, and therefore have misunderstood the faith of the Fathers, or it is also possible that, they are so blinded by their anti-Catholic zeal that they substitute misrepresentations, strawmen and historical anachronisms for scholarship. In contrast the judgments of some astute non-Catholic scholars are more sobering:

> Meanwhile another position was beginning to take shape and become articulate. Along with the total commitment to the Scriptures as the norm of all doctrine, a new and clear con-

[252] Newman, John Henry, *Development of Christian Doctrine* (Notre Dame: University of Notre Dame, 1989) pp.7-8.

viction concerning the authority of oral Tradition began to develop. This oral Tradition, handed down from generation to generation and going back through the apostles directly to Christ, in no way conflicted with the Scriptures. But it did aid the church in interpreting the Scriptures and particularly summarizing the Christian faith and thus protecting Christians against the aberrations of the Gnostics and other heretics... Thus for all practical purposes we have at the turn of the third century a kind of two-source doctrine of authority in the church, with both the New Testament and the rule of faith thought to be eminently apostolic... Thus two revelatory authorities, identical in content, complemented and authenticated each other. This position was held in a variety of forms from the third century until the time of the reformation, and it continued after that time in the Roman Catholic Church." **Robert Preus** [253]

Throughout the whole period Scripture and tradition ranked as complementary authorities, media different in form, but coincident in content. To inquire which counted as superior or more ultimate is to pose the question in misleading and anachronistic terms. If Scripture was abundantly sufficient in principle, tradition was recognized as the surest clue to its interpretation, for in tradition the Church retained, as a legacy from the apostles, which was embedded in all the organs of her institutional life, an unerring grasp of the real purport and meaning of the revelation to which Scripture and tradition alike bore witness. **J.N.D. Kelly** [254]

The church view respecting the sources of Christian theology and the rule of faith and practice remains as it was in the previous period, except that it is further developed in particulars. The divine Scriptures of the Old and New Testaments, as opposed to human writings; and the oral tradition or living faith of the catholic church from the apostles down, as op-

---

[253] Preus, Robert "The View of the Bible held by the Church: Early Church through Luther" in *Inerrancy*, Norman Geisler, ed., (Grand Rapids: Zondervan, 1980) pp. 359-360.

[254] Kelly, J. N. D. *Early Christian Doctrines* (San Francisco: Harper & Row, 1978) pp. 47-48.

posed to the varying opinions of the heretical sects — together form the one infallible source and rule of faith. Both are vehicles of the same substance: the saving revelation of God in Christ; with this difference in form and office, that the church tradition determines the canon, furnishes the key to the true interpretation of the Scriptures, and guards them against heretical abuse. **Philip Schaff** [255]

By the fourth and fifth centuries the principle of the Bible as the primary norm and authority in the church was well established... And yet there existed a body of tradition outside the Bible which was equally authoritative, because it was considered apostolic and in harmony with the Scriptures... The primary criterion of orthodoxy in the ancient church was that of apostolicity, as reflected in the church's apostolic liturgy, apostolic succession, apostolic witness (the New Testament), and the Apostles Creed. **Carl Volz** [256]

Scripture, it is true, was sometimes treated as a set of propositional statements from which the truth could be read off by a process of deductive logic. But Scripture was never the sole court of appeal. The living tradition of the Church included not only the historical facts recorded in Scripture but also the continuing and contemporary experience of Christians. **Maurice Wiles** [257]

Clearly it is an anachronism to superimpose upon the discussions of the second and third centuries categories derived from the controversies over the relation of Scripture and tradition in the sixteenth century, for 'in the ante-Nicene Church... there was no notion of Sola Scriptura, but neither was there a doctrine of traditio sola...' The term 'rule of faith' or 'rule of truth' did not always refer to such creeds and confessions,

---

[255] Schaff, Philip. *History of the Christian Church*, 3 vols (AP&A) I:3, 248-249.

[256] Volz, Carl, A. *Faith and Practice in the Early Church* (Minneapolis: Augsburg, 1983) pp. 147-150.

[257] Wiles, Maurice, *The Making of Christian Doctrine: A Study in the Principles of Early Doctrinal Development* (London: Cambridge, 1967) p. 160.

[258] Pelikan, Jaroslav *The Christian Tradition: A History of the Development of Doctrine*, vol. 1, (Chicago: UCP: 1971) pp. 115,117.

and seems sometimes to have meant the 'tradition,' sometimes the Scriptures, sometimes the message of the gospel.
Jaroslav Pelikan [258]

Vincent of Lerins:[259] "[I]t is therefore necessary that the interpretation of the divine Scripture *should be ruled* according to the one standard of the Church's belief..."

[259] Vincent of Lerins, *Commonitory*, 76 NPNF 2, XI:153.

Appendix 1

A Dossier Illustrating the Authority of Tradition and Church[1]

Alexander of Alexandria [d.A.D. 328]

"Who will not either that any of the ancients should be compared with them, or suffer that any of those whom, from our earliest years, we have used as instructors should be placed on a level with them. Nay, and they do not think that any of all those who are now our colleagues, has attained even to a moderate amount of wisdom; boasting themselves to be the only men who are wise and divested of worldly possessions, the sole discoverers of dogmas, and that to them alone are those things revealed which have never before come into the mind of any other under the sun. Oh, the impious arrogance! Oh, the immeasurable madness! Oh, the vainglory befitting those that are crazed! Oh, the pride of Satan which has taken root in their unholy souls. The religious perspicuity of the ancient Scriptures caused them no shame, nor did the consentient doctrine of our colleagues concerning Christ keep in check their audacity against Him. Their impiety not even the demons will bear, who are ever on the watch for a blasphemous word uttered against the Son... Concerning whom we thus believe, even as the Apostolic Church believes... And besides the pious opinion concerning

---

1 For a detail description of the lives and works of the Church Fathers see Quasten J. *Patrology*, 4 volumes, (Westminster, MD: Christian Classics, 1953-1986).

the Father and the Son, we confess to one Holy Spirit, as the divine Scriptures teach us; who hath inaugurated both the holy men of the Old Testament, and the divine teachers of that which is called the New. And besides, also, one only Catholic and Apostolic Church, which can never be destroyed, though all the world should seek to make war with it; but it is victorious over every most impious revolt of the heretics who rise up against it. For her Goodman hath confirmed our minds by saying, 'Be of good cheer, I have overcome the world.' After this we know of the resurrection of the dead, the first-fruits of which was our Lord Jesus Christ, who in very deed, and not in appearance merely, carried a body, of Mary Mother of God, who in the end of the world came to the human race to put away sin, was crucified and died, and yet did He not thus perceive any detriment to His divinity, being raised from the dead, taken up into heaven, seated at the right hand of majesty. These things in part have I written in this epistle, thinking it burdensome to write out each accurately, even as I said before, because they escape not your religious diligence. Thus do we teach, thus do we preach. These are the apostolic doctrines of the Church, for which also we die, esteeming those but little who would compel us to forswear them, even if they would force us by tortures, and not casting away our hope in them."[2]

Ambrose [c.A.D. 339-397]

"Who amongst us will dare to re-open (or, abandon) that sacerdotal book [the decrees of the council of Nicaea], sealed by confessors, and long since consecrated by the martyrdom of many? which book they were driven to re-open, did afterwards seal, and condemn the cheat practiced on them: they who dared not violate it were confessors and martyrs. How can we deny the faith of those whose victory we openly celebrate?"[3]

---

2 Alexander of Alexandria, *Epistles on the Arian Heresy*, 10, 12, 13 (A.D. 321) ANF, VI:294-296.

3 Ambrose, *The Faith*, 3, 15:128 (A.D. 378-380) FOC I:435.

"How is it then that the name of the council of Nicaea is put forward, and novelties are brought in, which were never thought of by our predecessors?"[4]

"Neither have we innovated anything; but guarding what was settled by Athanasius of holy memory, — who was as it were a pillar of the faith, — and what was defined in the councils held by our fathers of the old holiness, we tear not up the landmarks which our fathers have set, nor violate the rights of an hereditary communion."[5]

"As the kingdom of God is not in words, but in power; if a word gives offence, appeal to the power of the profession (of faith).The profession of faith is the declaration which we hold as handed down from our predecessors against the Sabellians and Arians."[6]

"Stand, therefore in the church; stand where I have appeared to thee; there I am with thee. Where the church is, there is the most secure resting-place (or harbour) for thy mind."[7]

"The traditions of the Scriptures are his body; the Church is his body."[8]

Anastasius, Pope [regn. 399-401]

"This, then, is my opinion, that the reading of this (Rufinus' translation from Origen), has made it clear to the inhabitants of this city, that the author (Origen), by throwing a kind of dark cloud over pure minds, had in view, by his turnings and windings, to destroy the faith of the apostles, which has been confirmed also by

---

4 Ambrose, *The Mystery of the Lord's Incarnation*, 6:52, FOC I:435.

5 Ambrose, *To Theodosius*, Epistle 14, FOC I:435.

6 Ambrose,*To Sabinus*, Epistle 48 (c.A.D. 390) FOC I:435.

7 Ambrose, *To the Church of Vercelli*, Epistle 63, FOC I:72.

8 Ambrose, *Commentary on the Gospel of Luke*, 6:33 (c.A.D. 389),as cited by George H. Tavard *Holy Writ or Holy Church* (London: Burns & Oates, 1959) p. 9.

the tradition of the fathers... If the translator of so many evil things coincide in them, and bring them forward as matters to be read by the people, he has effected nothing as the result of his labour, but by the judgment of his individual understanding, to (try to) subvert on the ground of an unprecedented assertion, things which have been held, amongst Catholic Christians with true faith, as the alone (true), as primitive, from the time of the apostles until now. Far be this from the Catholic discipline of the Roman Church."[9]

Andrew of Caesarea [5th Cent.]

"Now I think it superfluous to treat at length of the credibility and authority of this book (the Apocalypse). For it is well known that those blessed men and fathers of ours, Gregory the Theologian, Cyril of Alexandria, and others more ancient that they, as Papias, Irenaeus, Methodius, and Hippolytus, have, on more than one occasion declared it to be divine and deserving credit, and we have, on account of what is contained in their works, come to this same conclusion."[10]

Aphraates [c.A.D. 280 post A.D. 345]

"These things I have written according to what I have attained to. But if anyone shall read these dicourses, and find words that do not agree with his thought, he ought not to scorn them; because whatsoever is written in these chapters was not written according to the thought of one man, nor for the persuasion of one reader; but according to the thought of all the Church, and for the persuasion of all faith."[11]

Apostolic Constitutions [c.A.D. 400]

"The bishop, he is the minister of the word, the keeper of knowledge, the mediator between God and you in those things which

---

9 Anastasius, Pope, *To John of Jerusalem*, Epistle 1 (A.D. 401) FOC I:441-442.

10 Andrew of Caesarea, *Commentary on Revelation* [5th Cent],in FOC I:444-445.

11 Aphraates, *Demonstrations*, 22:26 (inter A.D. 336-345) NPNF 2, XIII:411.

pertain to his worship; he is the teacher of piety; he is, after God, your father, who has regenerated you by water and the Spirit unto the adoption of sons. He is your ruler, and he is your king and potentate; he is, next after God, your earthly God, who has a right to receive honour from you; for of him, and of such as he, God has said, 'I have said ye are gods, and all of you sons of the Most High' (Ps. lxxxi. 6); 'and you shall not speak evil of the gods' (Exod. xxii. 28.) For let the bishop preside over you, as one honoured with the dignity of God, with which he rules the clergy, and governs all the people."[12]

Arnobius, Junior [d. post A.D. 451]

"Serapion, (the heretic) said: 'I confess that I hold his (St. Augustine's) statement as so assured, that the man who should think any declaration of his deserving of reprehension, would, out of his own mouth, prove himself to be a heretic.' Arnobius replied: 'You have expressed my sentiment, for what I now produce from him I so believe, and hold, and defend, as though it were the most sacred writings of the Apostles."[13]

"Wherefore because that they are without the church, wandering about amongst creatures little and great, they meet with a dragon, that so makes sport of them, as that they fancy that they are wiser than the Catholics; and, according to their own fancies, they meet with the destruction of eternal death, when they have sunk into the depths."[14]

Athanasius [c.A.D. 295-373]

"Let these unlearned persons cease such misrepresentations, but let them learn from the example of the Fathers; and let them read the Scriptures."[15]

---

[12] *Apostolic Constitutions*, 2:26 (c.A.D. 400) FOC I:39-40.

[13] Arnobius, Junior, *Debate between Arnobius and Serapion* (ante A.D. 451) FOC I:456-457.

[14] Arnobius, Junior, *Commentary on Psalms*, 103 FOC I:118.

[15] Athanasius, *Defence Before Constantius*, 18 (A.D. 357) NPNF 2, IV:245.

"[H]old fast, every one, the faith we have received from the Fathers, which they assembled at Nicaea... And however they [the Arians] may write phrases out of the Scripture, endure not their writings; however they may speak the language of the orthodox, yet attend not to what they say; for they speak not with an upright mind, but putting on such language like sheep's clothing, in their hearts they think with Arius, after the manner of the devil, who is the author of all heresies. For he too made use of the words of Scripture, but was put to silence by our Saviour... Had these expositions of theirs[the Arians] proceeded from the orthodox, from such as the Great Confessor Hosius... Bishops of the East, or Julius and Liberius of Rome... Basil [and a host of other Fathers]... — there would have been nothing to respect in their statements, for the character of apostolic men is sincere and incapable of fraud."[16]

"But ye are blessed, who by faith are in the Church, dwell upon the foundations of the faith, and have full satisfaction, even the highest degree of faith which remains among you unshaken. For it has come down to you from Apostolic tradition..."[17]

"Accordingly we too, according to your confession of faith, desire to hold the Apostolic tradition, and to live according to the commands of the divine law..."[18]

"[A]nd in dizziness about the truth, are full set upon accusing the Council, let them tell us what are the sort of Scriptures from which they have learned , or who is the Saint by whom they have been taught..."[19]

"And he [the Arian] who holds these, contradicts the Council; but he who does not hold with Arius, must needs hold and intend the decisions of the Council, suitably regarding them to signify the

---

[16] Athanasius, *To the Bishops of Egypt*, 8 (A.D. 356) NPNF 2, IV:227.

[17] Athanasius, *Fragment* (c.A.D 357) NPNF 2, IV:551.

[18] Athanasius, *Second Letter to Lucifer*, Epistle 51 NPNF 2, IV:561-562.

[19] Athanasius, *Defence of the Nicene Definition*, 18 NPNF 2, IV:161.

relation of the radiance to the light, and from thence gaining the illustration to the truth."[20]

"Such then, as we confess and believe, being the sense of the Fathers..."[21]

"[B]ut do you, remaining on the foundation of the Apostles, and holding fast the traditions of the Fathers, pray that now at length all strife and rivalry may cease, and the futile questions of the heretics may be condemned..."[22]

"For although the sacred and inspired Scriptures are sufficient to declare the truth — while there are other works of our blessed teachers compiled for this purpose, if he meet with which a man will gain knowledge of the interpretation of the Scriptures, and be able to learn what he wishes to know — still, as we have not at present in our hands the compositions of our teachers, we must communicate in writing to you what we learned from them..."[23]

"But that the soul is made immortal is a further point in the Church's teaching which you must know..."[24]

"[H]e had not received his ordination according to ecclesiastical rule, nor had been called to be Bishop by apostolic tradition..."[25]

Antony of Egypt [c.A.D. 251-356]

"Wherefore keep yourselves all the more untainted by them, and observe the traditions of the fathers, and chiefly the holy faith

---

20 Athanasius, *Defence of the Nicene Definition*, 20 NPNF 2, IV:164.

21 Athanasius, *Councils of Arminum and Seleucia*, 48(A.D. 361/362) NPNF 2, IV:475.

22 Athanasius, *Councils of Arminum and Seleucia*, 54 (A.D. 361/362) NPNF 2, IV:479.

23 Athanasius, *Against the Heathen*, 1:3 (c.A.D. 318) NPNF 2, IV:4.

24 Athanasius, *Against the Heathen*, 33:1 NPNF 2, IV:21.

25 Athanasius, *History of the Arians*, 14 (A.D. 358) NPNF 2, IV:274.

in our Lord Jesus Christ, which you have learned from the Scripture, and of which you have often been put in mind by me."[26]

Augustine [A.D. 354-430]

"It is not to be doubted that the dead are aided by prayers of holy church, and by the salutary sacrifice, and by the alms, which are offered for their spirits; that the Lord may deal with them more mercifully than their sins have deserved. For this, which has been handed down by the Fathers, the universal church observes."[27]

"For in the Catholic Church, not to speak of the purest wisdom, to the knowledge of which a few spiritual, men attain in this life, so as to know it, in the scantiest measure, indeed, because they are but men, still without any uncertainty (since the rest of the multitude derive their entire security not from acuteness of intellect, but from simplicity of faith) — not to speak of this wisdom, which you do not believe to be in the Catholic Church, there are many other things which most justly keep me in her bosom. The consent of peoples and nations keeps me in the Church; so does her authority, inaugurated by miracles, nourished by hope, enlarged by love, established by age. The succession of priests keeps me, beginning from the very seat of the Apostle Peter, to whom the Lord, after His resurrection, gave it in charge to feed His sheep, down to the present episcopate. And so, lastly, does the name itself of Catholic, which, not without reason, amid so many heresies, the Church has thus retained; so that, though all heretics wish to be called Catholics, yet when a stranger asks where the Catholic Church meets, no heretic will venture to point to his own chapel or house. Such then in number and importance are the precious ties belonging to the Christian name which keep a believer in the Catholic Church, as it is right they should, though from the slowness of our understanding, or the small attainment of our life, the truth

---

[26] Antony of Egypt, fragment in Athanasius' *Life of Antony*, 89 (c.A.D. 357) NPNF 2, IV:220.

[27] Augustine, *Sermons*, 172 (inter A.D. 391-430) FOC I: 439.

may not yet fully disclose itself. But with you, where there is none of these things to attract or keep me, the promise of truth is the only thing that comes into play. Now if the truth is so clearly proved as to leave no possibility of doubt, it must be set before all the things that keep me in the Catholic Church; but if there is only a promise without any fulfillment, no one shall move me from the faith which binds my mind with ties so many and so strong to the Christian religion."[28]

"...If I must believe without knowing, why should I not prefer to believe those things which have wide-spread notoriety from the consent of learned and unlearned, and which among all nations are established by the weightiest authority?"[29]

"What authority will you quote against this? Perhaps some book of Manichaeus, where it is denied that Jesus was born of a virgin. As, then, I believe your book to be the production of Manichaeus, since it has been kept and handed down among the disciples of Manichaeus, from the time when he lived to the present time, by a regular succession of your presidents, so I ask you to believe the book which I quote to have been written by Matthew, since it has been handed down from the days of Matthew in the Church, without any break in the connection between that time and the present. The question then is, whether we are to believe the statements of an apostle who was in the company of Christ while He was on earth, or of a man away in Persia, born long after Christ. But perhaps you will quote some other book bearing the name of an apostle known to have been chosen by Christ; and you will find there that Christ was not born of Mary. Since, then, one of the books must be false, the question in this case is, whether we are to yield our belief to a book acknowledged and approved as handed down from the beginning in the Church founded by Christ Himself, and maintained through the apostles and their successors in an unbroken connection all over the world to the present day; or to a book which this Church condemns as unknown, and which,

28 Augustine, *Against the Epistle of Manichaeus*, 4:5 (A.D. 397) NPNF I, IV:130.

29 Ibid.,14:18 NPNF I, IV:136.

moreover, is brought forward by men who prove their veracity by praising Christ for falsehood."[30]

"...I close with a word of counsel to you who are implicated in those shocking and damnable errors, that, if you acknowledge the supreme authority of Scripture, you should recognise that authority which from the time of Christ Himself, through the ministry of His apostles, and through a regular succession of bishops in the seats of the apostles, has been preserved to our own day throughout the whole world, with a reputation known to all."[31]

"To be sure, although on this matter, we cannot quote a clear example taken from the canonical Scriptures, at any rate, on this question, we are following the true thought of Scriptures when we observe what has appeared good to the universal Church which the authority of these same Scriptures recommends to you; thus, since Holy Scripture cannot be mistaken, anyone fearing to be misled by the obscurity of this question has only to consult on this same subject this very Church which the Holy Scriptures point out without ambiguity. Do you hesitate to believe that the Church which is spread throughout the great masses of the people in all nations has Scripture to recommend it...?"[32]

"Will you, then, so love your error, into which you have fallen through adolescent overconfidence and human weakness, that you will separate yourself from these leaders of Catholic unity and truth, from so many different parts of the world who are in agreement among themselves on so important a question, one in which the essence of the Christian religion involved...?"[33]

"And if any one seek for divine authority in this matter, though what is held by the whole Church, and that not as instituted by

---

[30] Augustine, *Reply to Faustus the Manichaean*, 28:2 (c.A..D. 400) NPNF I, IV:325.

[31] Ibid., 33:9 NPNF I, IV:345.

[32] Augustine, *Against Cresconius*, I:33 (c.A..D. 406) ENO 134.

[33] Augustine, *Against Julian*, I,7:34 (c.A..D. 421) ENO 136.

Councils, but as a matter of invariable custom, is rightly held to have been handed down by apostolical authority, still we can form a true conjecture of the value of the sacrament of baptism in the case of infants..."[34]

"'The apostles,' indeed, 'gave no injunctions on the point;' but the custom, which is opposed to Cyprian, may be supposed to have had its origin in apostolic tradition, just as there are many things which are observed by the whole Church, and therefore are fairly held to have been enjoined by the apostles, which yet are not mentioned in their writings."[35]

"The Christians of Carthage have an excellent name for the sacraments, when they say that baptism is nothing else than 'salvation,' and the sacrament of the body of Christ nothing else than 'life.' Whence, however, was this derived, but from that primitive, as I suppose, and apostolic tradition, by which the Churches of Christ maintain it to be an inherent principle, that without baptism and partaking of the supper of the Lord it is impossible for any man to attain either to the kingdom of God or to salvation and everlasting life?"[36]

"God has placed this authority first of all in his Church."[37]

"[F]rom whatever source it was handed down to the Church — although the authority of the canonical Scriptures cannot be brought forward as speaking expressly in its support..."[38]

"The custom of Mother Church in baptizing infants certainly not to be scorned, nor is it to be regarded in any way as superflu-

---

[34] Augustine, *On Baptism Against the Donatists*, 4, 24:31 (A.D. 400) NPNF I, IV:461.

[35] Ibid., 5, 23:31, NPNF I, IV:475.

[36] Augustine, *On Forgiveness of Sins and Baptism*, 1:34 (A.D. 412) NPNF I, V:28.

[37] Augustine, *Explanations of the Psalms*, Tract 103:8, PL 37:520-521 (inter A.D. 391-430) CON 392.

[38] Augustine, *To Evodius of Uzalis*, Epistle 164:6 (A.D. 414) NPNF I, I:516.

ous, nor is it to be believed that its tradition is anything except Apostolic."[39]

"And thus a man who is resting upon faith, hope and love, and who keeps a firm hold upon these, does not need the Scriptures except for the purpose of instructing others. Accordingly, many live without copies of the Scriptures, even in solitude, on the strength of these three graces."[40]

"Now, in regard to the canonical Scriptures, he must follow the judgment of the greater number of catholic churches; and among these, of course, a high place must be given to such as have been thought worthy to be the seat of an apostle and to receive epistles."[41]

"This fellow, of course, set forth proofs from the apocryphal writings written under the names of Andrew and John. If they were theirs, they would have been accepted by the Church, which continues from their times right up to ours and beyond through the certain succession of bishops and offers to God in the body of Christ the sacrifice of praise..."[42]

Basil [c.A.D. 330-379]

"It remains then for them to assert that, by means of words, they have discovered the substance of his divinity. Where are these words? In what part of Scripture are they set down? By which of the saints have they been handed down?"[43]

"Let tradition shame thee from separating the Holy Ghost from the Father and Son. Thus did the Lord teach, apostles preach, fa-

---

39 Augustine, *The Literal Interpretation of Genesis*, 10,23:39 (inter A.D. 401-415) JUR III:86.

40 Augustine, *On Christian Doctrine*, I, 39:43 (A.D. 397) NPNF I, II:534.

41 Ibid., 2, 8:12 NPNF I, II:538.

42 Augustine, *Answer to an enemy of the Law and the Prophets*, 20:39 (c. A.D. 419) as cited by Roland J. Tske, trans., John E. Rotelle, ed., *Arianism and Other Heresies* (Hyde Park: New City Press, 1995). p. 383.

43 Basil, *Against Eunomius*, 1:12 (inter A.D. 363-365) FOC I: 425.

thers preserve, martyrs confirm. Let it suffice thee to speak as thou has been taught, and let me not hear these sophisms."[44]

"Let us now investigate what are our common conceptions concerning the Spirit, as well those which have been gathered by us from Holy Scripture concerning It as those which have received from the unwritten tradition of the Fathers." [45]

"Time will fail me if I attempt to recount the unwritten mysteries of the Church. Of the rest I say nothing; but of the very confession of our faith in Father, Son, and Holy Ghost, what is the written source?"[46]

"While the unwritten traditions are so many, and their bearing on 'the mystery of godliness' is so important, can they refuse to allow us a single word which has come down to us from the Fathers — which we found, derived from untutored custom, abiding in unperverted churches — a word for which the arguments are strong, and which contributes in no small degree to the completeness of the force of the mystery?"[47]

"For all these reasons I ought to have kept silence, but I was drawn in the other direction by love, which 'seeketh not her own,' and desires to overcome every difficulty put in her way by time and circumstance... Wherefore we too are undismayed at the cloud of our enemies, and, resting our hope on the aid of the Spirit, have, with all boldness, proclaimed the truth. Had I not so done, it would truly have been terrible that the blasphemers of the Spirit should so easily be emboldened in their attack upon true religion, and that we, with so mighty an ally and supporter at our side, should shrink from the service of that doctrine, which by the tra-

---

[44] Basil, *Against the Sabellians, Arians, and Anomoeans*, Homily 24:6 (ante A.D. 379) FOC I:425-426.

[45] Basil, *On the Spirit*, 9:22 (A.D. 375) NPNF 2, VIII:15.

[46] Ibid., 27:67 NPNF 2, VIII:43.

[47] Ibid., 27:67 NPNF 2, VIII:43.

dition of the Fathers has been preserved by an unbroken sequence of memory to our own day."[48]

"[W]e do not speak of the Holy Ghost as unbegotten, for we recognise one Unbegotten and one Origin of all things, the Father of our Lord Jesus Christ: nor do we speak of the Holy Ghost as begotten, for by the tradition of the faith we have been taught one Only-begotten..."[49]

"[A]nd I have not allowed my judgment concerning them to rest wholly with myself, but have followed the decisions given about them by our Fathers."[50]

Boniface, Pope [regn. A.D. 418-422]

"So it is clear that this church is to all churches throughout the world as the head is to the members, and that whoever separates himself from it becomes an exile from the Christian religion, since he ceases to belong to its fellowship."[51]

Caius [floruit c.A.D. 198-217]

"In a laborious work by one of these writers against the heresy of Artemon, which Paul of Samosata attempted to revive again in our day, there is an account appropriate to the history which we are now examining. For he criticises, as a late innovation, the above-mentioned heresy which teaches that the Saviour was a mere man, because they were attempting to magnify it as ancient? Having given in his work many other arguments in refutation of their blasphemous falsehood, he adds the following words:

---

48 Ibid., 30:79 NPNF 2, VIII:50.

49 Basil, *Transcript of Faith*, Epistle 125:3 (A.D. 373) NPNF 2, VIII:195.

50 Basil, *To the Neocaearcans*, Epistle 204:6 (A.D. 375) NPNF 2, VIII:245.

51 Boniface, Pope, *To the Bishops of Thessalonica*, Epistle 14 (A.D. 422) GILES 230.

'For they say that all the early teachers and the apostles received and taught what they now declare, and that the truth of the Gospel was preserved until the times of Victor, who was the thirteenth bishop of Rome from Peter, but that from his successor, Zephyrinus, the truth had been corrupted. And what they say might be plausible, if first of all the Divine Scriptures did not contradict them. And there are writings of certain brethren older than the times of Victor, which they wrote in behalf of the truth against the heathen, and against the heresies which existed in their day. I refer to Justin and Miltiades and Tatian and Clement and many others, in all of whose works Christ is spoken of as God. For who does not know the works of Irenaeus and of Melito and of others which teach that Christ is God and man? And how many psalms and hymns, written by the faithful brethren from the beginning, celebrate Christ the Word of God, speaking of him as Divine. How then since the opinion held by the Church has been preached for so many years, can its preaching have been delayed as they affirm, until the times of Victor? And how is it that they are not ashamed to speak thus falsely of Victor, knowing well that he cut off from communion Theodotus, the cobbler, the leader and father of this God-denying apostasy, and the first to declare that Christ is mere man? For if Victor agreed with their opinions, as their slander affirms, how came he to cast out Theodotus, the inventor of this heresy?'"[52]

Capreolus of Carthage [5th Cent.]

"Again, as an example to posterity — that what is now defined relative to Catholic faith may be for ever firmly received, those matters which have already been defined by the Fathers, must be preserved inviolate. Since whoso would fain that what he has defined concerning the right ordering of faith should continue for ever, must needs confirm his sentiments, not by his private authority, but also by the judgment of the more ancient (Fathers); so that, in this manner, proving that what he asserts is, both by the decisions of the ancient and of the moderns, the alone truth of the Catho-

[52] Caius, *fragment in Eusebius' Ecclesiastical History*, 5:28 (c.A.D. 198-217) NPNF 2, I:246-247 or ANF V:601.

lic church — a truth descending from the past ages even to the present, or our days, in simple purity and invincible authority..."[53]

John Cassian [c.A.D. 360-c.A.D. 435]

"Art thou then the reformer of the early prelates [i.e. the Church Fathers]? dost thou condemn the ancient priests? art thou more excellent than Gregory? more to be followed than Nectarius; to be preferred before John, and all the priests of the eastern churches — priests who, though they have not the same reputation as those whom I have named, are of the same faith. And this, as far as regards this matter, is sufficient; because when it is a question about faith, all men are the same as the greatest, in that they are united in fellowship with the greatest."[54]

Celestine, Pope [regn. A.D. 422-432]

"Whereas certain persons, who pride themselves in the name of Catholic, continuing in the condemned opinions, or wickedness, of these heretics (Pelagius, &c.), presume to argue against the pious defenders of the faith, and while they do not hesitate to anathematize Pelagius and Coelestius, yet traduce our teachers as though they had exceeded the requisite bounds, and profess that they do nothing more than follow and approve what the most holy see of Peter has, through the ministry of its prelates, decreed and taught against the enemies of the grace of God, it became necessary to enquire diligently what the rulers of the church of Rome have decided on this heresy, in their days. [He then cites Innocent, Zosmius, and others; and proceeds to another source of evidence, the Liturgy]. Besides these inviolable decisions of the apostolic see... let us look to the sacraments of the sacredotal supplications, which, (sacraments, or mysteries) transmitted by the apostles, are uniformly celebrated in the whole world and in all the Catholic church, that so the law of praying may establish the law of believing."[55]

---

[53] Capreolus of Carthage, *To the Council of Ephesus* (A.D. 431) FOC I:101.
[54] Cassian, John, *The Incarnation of Christ*, 7 (c.A.D. 429/430) FOC I: 450-451.
[55] Celestine, Pope, *To the Bishops of Gaul*, Epistle 21 (A.D. 431) FOC I:443-444.

"Justly does the blame touch us, if by silence we foster error; therefore let such men be corrected ; let them not have liberty to speak at their pleasure. Let novelty cease, if the matter be so, to molest antiquity; let restlessness cease to trouble the peacefulness of the churches."[56]

Chrysostom, John [inter A.D. 344/345-407]

"'That ye remember me in all things and hold fast the traditions, even as I delivered them to you.' It appears then that he used at that time to deliver many things also not in writing, which he shows too in many other places. But at that time he only delivered them, whereas now he adds an explanation of their reason..."[57]

"Not by letters alone did Paul instruct his disciple in his duty, but before by words also which he shows, both in many other passages, as where he says, 'whether by word or our Epistle' (2 Thess. ii. 15), and especially here. Let us not therefore suppose that anything relating to doctrine was spoken imperfectly. For many things he delivered to him without writing. Of these therefore he reminds him, when he says, 'Hold fast the form of sound words, which thou hast heard of me.'"[58]

"We may answer, that what is here written, was sufficient for those who would attend, and that the sacred writers ever addressed themselves to the matter of immediate importance, whatever it might be at that time: it was no object with them to be writers of books: in fact, there are many things which they have delivered by unwritten tradition. Now while all that is contained in this Book is worthy of admiration, so is especially the way the Apostles have of coming down to the wants of their hearers: a condescension suggested by the Spirit who has so ordered it, that the subject on which they

---

[56] Ibid., Epistle 21 FOC I:386.

[57] Chrysostom, John, *On First Corinthians*, Homily 26 (c.A.D. 392) NPNF I, XII:149.

[58] Chrysostom, John, *On Second Timothy*, Homily 3 (inter A.D. 393-397) NPNF I, XIII:484.

chiefly dwell is that which pertains to Christ as man. For so it is, that while they discourse so much about Christ, they have spoken but little concerning His Godhead: it was mostly of the Manhood that they discoursed, and of the Passion, and the Resurrection, and the Ascension."[59]

"Here is forethought for providing a teacher; here was the first who ordained a teacher. He did not say, 'We are sufficient.' So far was he beyond all vain-glory, and he looked to one thing alone. And yet he (Peter) had the same power to ordain as they all collectively. But well might these things be done in this fashion, through the noble spirit of the man, and because prelacy then was not an affair of dignity, but of provident care for the governed. This neither made the elected to become elated, for it was to dangers that they were called, nor those not elected to make a grievance of it, as if they were disgraced. But things are not done in this fashion now; nay, quite the contrary. For observe, they were an hundred and twenty, and he asks for one out of the whole body with good right, as having been put in charge of them: for to him had Christ said, 'And when thou art converted, strengthen thy brethren.' (Luke xxii. 32)"[60]

Clement of Alexandria [c.A.D. 150-c.A.D. 216]

"Well, they preserving the tradition of the blessed doctrine derived directly from the holy apostles, Peter, James, John, and Paul, the sons receiving it from the father (but few were like the fathers), came by God's will to us also to deposit those ancestral and apostolic seeds. And well I know that they will exult; I do not mean delighted with this tribute, but solely on account of the preservation of the truth, according as they delivered it."[61]

"'But all things are right,' right says the Scripture, 'before those who understand' that is, those who receive and observe, accord-

---

[59] Chrysostom, John, *On Acts of the Apostles*, Homily 1 (A.D. 388) NPNF I, XI:2.
[60] Chrysostom, John, *On Acts of the Apostles*, Homily 3 (A.D. 388) NPNF I, XI:20.
[61] Clement of Alexandria, *Stromata*, 1:1 (post A.D. 202) ANF II:301.

ing to the ecclesiastical rule, the exposition of the Scriptures explained by Him; and the ecclesiastical rule is the concord and harmony of the law and the prophets in the covenant delivered at the coming of the Lord."[62]

"Those, then, that adhere to impious words, and dictate them to others, inasmuch as they do not make a right but a perverse use of the divine words, neither themselves enter into the kingdom of heaven, nor permit those whom they have deluded to attain the truth. But not having the key of entrance, but a false (and as the common phrase expresses it), a counterfeit key (antikleis), by which they do not enter in as we enter in, through the tradition of the Lord, by drawing aside the curtain; but bursting through the side-door, and digging clandestinely through the wall of the Church, and stepping over the truth, they constitute themselves the Mystagogues of the soul of the impious."[63]

Clement of Rome, Pope [regn. c.A.D. 91-c.A.D. 101]

"The apostles have preached the Gospel to us from the Lord Jesus Christ; Jesus Christ [has done so] from God. Christ therefore was sent forth by God, and the apostles by Christ. Both these appointments, then, were made in an orderly way, according to the will of God. Having therefore received their orders, and being fully assured by the resurrection of our Lord Jesus Christ, and established in the word of God, with full assurance of the Holy Ghost, they went forth proclaiming that the kingdom of God was at hand. And thus preaching through countries and cities, they appointed the first-fruits [of their labours], having first proved them by the Spirit, to be bishops and deacons of those who should afterwards believe. Nor was this any new thing, since indeed many ages before it was written concerning bishops and deacons. For thus saith the Scripture in a certain place, 'I will appoint their bishops in righteousness, and their deacons in faith.'"[64]

---

[62] Ibid., 6:15 ANF II:509.

[63] Ibid., 7:17 ANF II:554.

[64] Clement of Rome, *1st Epistle to the Corinthians*, 42 (c.A.D. 96) ANF I:16.

"Our apostles also knew, through our Lord Jesus Christ, and that there would be strife on account of the office of the episcopate. For this reason, therefore, inasmuch as they had obtained a perfect fore-knowledge of this, they appointed those [ministers] already mentioned, and afterwards gave instructions, that when these should fall asleep, other approved men should succeed them in their ministry."[65]

"Accept our counsel, and you will have nothing to regret."[66]

Clement-Pseudo-Homilies

"Knowing, my brother, your eager desire after that which is for the advantage of us all, I beg and beseech you not to communicate to any one of the Gentiles the books of my preachings which I sent to you, nor to any one of our own tribe before trial; but if any one has been proved and found worthy, then to commit them to him, after the manner in which Moses delivered his books to the Seventy who succeeded to his chair. Wherefore also the fruit of that caution appears even till now. For his countrymen keep the same rule of monarchy and polity everywhere, being unable in any way to think otherwise, or to be led out of the way of the much-indicating Scriptures. For, according to the rule delivered to them, they endeavour to correct the discordances of the Scriptures, if any one, haply not knowing the traditions, is confounded at the various utterances of the prophets. Wherefore they charge no one to teach, unless he has first learned how the Scriptures must be used."[67]

"Therefore, that no such thing may happen, for this end I have prayed and besought you not to communicate the books of my preaching which I have sent you to any one, whether of our own nation or of another nation, before trial; but if any one, having been tested, has been found worthy, then to hand them over to him, according to the initiation of Moses, by which he delivered his books

65 Clement of Rome, *1st Epistle to the Corinthians*, 44 (c.A.D. 96) ANF I:17.
66 Ibid., 58 JUR I:12.
67 Clement-Pseudo, *Epistle of Peter to James*, I,ANF VIII:215.

to the Seventy who succeeded to his chair; in order that thus they may keep the faith, and everywhere deliver the rule of truth, explaining all things after our tradition; lest being themselves dragged down by ignorance, being drawn into error by conjectures after their mind, they bring others into the like pit of destruction. "[68]

Constantine, The Emperor
[c.A.D. 274-337, regn A.D. 306-337]

"While more than three hundred bishops remarkable for their moderation and intellectual keenness, were unanimous in their confirmation of one and the same faith, which according to the truth and legitimate construction of the law of God can only be the faith; Arius alone beguiled by the subtlety of the devil was discovered to be the sole disseminator of this mischief, first among you, and afterward with unhallowed purposes among others also. Let us therefore embrace that doctrine which the Almighty has presented to us: let us return to our beloved brethren from whom an irreverent servant of the devil has separated us: let us go with all speed to the common body and our own natural members. For this is becoming your penetration, faith and sanctity; that since the error has been proved to be due to him who is an enemy to the truth, ye should return to the divine favor. For that which has commended itself to the judgment of three hundred bishops cannot be other than the doctrine of God; seeing that the Holy Spirit dwelling in the minds of so many dignified persons has effectually enlightened them respecting the Divine will."[69]

Council of Ancyra [A.D. 358]

"We, therefore, beseech you, most honoured lords, and fellow-ministers, praying you that your delight be in the faith transmitted by the fathers, and that you would signify that you think harmoniously with what we have believed; that so they who pre-

---

68 Clement-Pseudo, *Epistle of Peter to James*, 3, ANF VIII:215.

69 Constantine, Emperor, fragment in Socrates' *Ecclesiastical History*, I:9, NPNF 2, II:13-14.

sume to introduce this ungodliness, being fully certified that, having received the faith as an inheritance, from the times of the apostles, through the fathers who have been in the period intermediate between those and our days, we guard it; and either filled with shame they will be corrected, or preserving they will be proscribed from the church."[70]

Council of Arles [A.D. 314]

"We also agreed to write first to you who hold the greater dioceses, that by you especially they (the Council) should be brought to the knowledge of all."[71]

"In the first place, concerning the observance of Easter, it shall be observed by us on one day and at one time, throughout the world, when you [Pope Sylvester], according to custom, direct letters to all."[72]

Council of Constantinople II [A.D. 553]

"We confessed that we hold, preserve, and declare to the holy churches that confession of faith which the 318 holy Fathers more at length set forth, who were gathered together at Nice, who handed down the holy mathema or creed. Moreover, the 150 gathered together at Constantinople set forth our faith, who followed that same confession of faith and explained it. And the consent of 200 holy fathers gathered for the same faith in the first Council of Ephesus. And what things were defined by the 630 gathered at Chalcedon for the one and the same faith, which they both followed and taught. And all those who from time to time have been condemned or anathematized by the Catholic Church, and by the aforesaid four Councils, we confessed that we hold them condemned and anathematized."[73]

---

[70] Council of Ancyra, *Synodal Epistle* (A.D. 358) FOC I:273.

[71] Council of Arles, *To Pope Sylvester* (A.D. 314) GILES 89.

[72] Council of Arles, *Canons*, 1, GILES 90.

[73] Council of Constantinople II, *Sentence of the Synod* (A.D. 553) NPNF 2, XIV:307.

Council of Constantinople III [A.D. 681]

"The holy and Ecumenical Synod further says, this pious and orthodox Creed of the Divine grace would be sufficient for the full knowledge and confirmation of the orthodox faith."[74]

Council of Milevis [A.D. 416]

"That which the apostle says, 'By one man sin entered the world, and by sin death: and so death passed upon all men in whom all have sinned' Rom.v.), is not to be understood otherwise than as the Catholic Church, spread everywhere, has always understood it. For on account of this rule, even infants, who could not as yet commit any sins of themselves, are therefore truly baptized for the remission of sins, that what they derived from generation may be cleansed in them by regeneration."[75]

Council of Nicea II [A.D. 787]

"We, continuing in the regal path, and following the divinely inspired teaching of the Holy Fathers, and the tradition of the Catholic Church... For thus the doctrine of our Holy Fathers, that is, the tradition of the Catholic Church which has received the Gospel from and even to the end of the world is strengthened. Thus we follow Paul, who spoke in Christ (2 Cor 2:17), and all the divine apostolic group and the paternal sanctity keeping the traditions (2 Thess 2:15) which we have received."[76]

"If anyone rejects all ecclesiastical tradition either written or not written... let him be anathema."[77]

---

74 Council of Constantinople III, *Definition of Faith*, Session 18 (A.D. 680-681) NPNF 2, XIV:344.

75 Council of Milevis, *Canon 2* (A.D. 416) FOC I:352.

76 Council of Nicea II, *Definition of the Sacred Images and Tradition*, Act 7:1-2 (A.D. 787) as cited by Henry Denzinger, *The Sources of Catholic Dogma*, Roy J. Deferrari, trans., (St. Louis: Herder, 1957) pp. 121-122.

77 Council of Nicea II, *Images, the Humanity of Christ, Tradition*,Act 8 (A.D. 787) Denzinger, p.123.

Council of Rome [A.D. 494]

"We have also thought that it ought to be noticed, that although the Catholic churches, spread over the world, be the one bridal chamber as it were of Christ, yet has the Roman church been, by certain synodal constitutions, raised about the rest of the churches; yea, also, by the evangelical voice of the Saviour did it obtain the primacy. 'Thou art Peter, and upon this rock, &c.' (Matt xvi.) ... The first see, therefore, of the apostle Peter, is the Roman Church."[78]

Cyprian [c.A.D. 200/210-258]

"After such things as these, moreover, they still dare — a false bishop having been appointed for them by heretics — to set sail and bear letters from schismatic and profane persons to the throne of Peter, and to the chief church whence priestly unity takes its source; and not to consider that these were the Romans whose faith was praised in the preaching of the apostle, to whom faithlessness could have no access."[79]

Regarding heretical baptism:

"For if we return to the head and source of divine tradition, human error ceases... And this it behoves the priests of God to do now, if they would keep the divine precepts, that if in any respect the truth have wavered and vacillated, we should return to our original and Lord, and to the evangelical and apostolical tradition; and thence may arise the ground of our action, whence has taken rise both our order and our origin."[80]

Cyril of Alexandria [d. A.D. 444]

"I am filled with wonder that certain persons doubt whether the blessed Virgin ought to be called Mother of God, or not ... This

[78] Council of Rome (A.D. 494) FOC I:327-328.
[79] Cyprian, *To Pope Cornelius*, Epistle 54 (59):14 (A.D. 252) ANF V:344.
[80] Cyprian, *To Pompey*, Epistle 73 (74):10 (A.D. 256) ANF V:389.

faith the divine disciples have handed down to us, although they may not indeed make mention of the word (theotokos):so to think have we been taught by the holy fathers."[81]

"But 'continue thou', as St. Paul says, 'in those things which thou has learned'; avoiding foolish logomachies and repudiating the old-wives' words of heretics, and rejecting idle fables, hold fast the faith in simplicity of mind; establishing the tradition of the church as a foundation, in the inmost recesses of thy heart, hold the doctrines which are well-pleasing unto God."[82]

"[H]ave a faith that corresponds with the divine Scriptures, and with the tradition of our holy fathers."[83]

"Our sentiments, therefore, concerning our Lord's incarnation, are those which were entertained by the holy fathers before us: for when reading their works we so regulate our mind that it follow in their traces, and bring nothing new to the orthodox doctrines."[84]

"Those things are orthodox and irreprehensible which agree with the divine writings and with the faith which has been set down by our holy fathers."[85]

"We describe as sources of the Saviour the holy prophets, the evangelists and the apostles; being all filled with the Holy Spirit, they are like rivers pouring out on this world the waters of a saving doctrine which comes from heaven; they make the earth rejoice."[86]

---

[81] Cyril of Alexandria, *To the Monks of Egypt*, Epistle 1 (inter A.D. 423/431) FOC I: 445.
[82] Cyril of Alexandria, *Festal Letters*, Homily 8 (A.D. 414-442) FOC I: 446-447.
[83] Ibid., Homily 8 FOC I: 447.
[84] Cyril of Alexandria, *Ad Successum* (ante A.D. 444) FOC I: 447.
[85] Cyril of Alexandria, *Ad Theognos*. (ante A.D. 444) FOC I: 447.
[86] Cyril of Alexandria, *Memorials on the True Faith*, PG 76:1337 (A.D. 430) CON 43.

Cyril of Jerusalem [c.A.D. 315-386]

"Attend closely to the catechisings, and though we should prolong our discourse, let not thy mind be wearied out... Let me give this charge also. Study our teachings and keep them forever."[87]

"We have need therefore of divine grace, and of a sober mind, and of eyes that see, lest from eating tares as wheat we suffer harm from ignorance, and lest from taking the wolf to be a sheep we become his prey, and from supposing the destroying Devil to be a beneficent Angel we be devoured: for, as the Scripture saith, he goeth about as a roaring lion, seeking whom he may devour. This is the cause of the Church's admonitions, the cause of the present instructions, and of the lessons which are read."[88]

"For the method of godliness consists of these two things, pious doctrines, and virtuous practice: and neither are the doctrines acceptable to God apart from good works, nor does God accept the works which are not perfected with pious doctrines. For what profit is it, to know well the doctrines concerning God, and yet to be a vile fornicator? And again, what profit is it, to be nobly temperate, and an impious blasphemer? A most precious possession therefore is the knowledge of doctrines: also there is need of a wakeful soul, since there are many that make spoil through philosophy and vain deceit. The Greeks on the one hand draw men away by their smooth tongue, for honey droppeth from a harlot's lips: whereas they of the Circumcision deceive those who come to them by means of the Divine Scriptures, which they miserably misinterpret though studying them from childhood to all age, and growing old in ignorance. But the children of heretics, by their good words and smooth tongue, deceive the hearts of the innocent, disguising with the name of Christ as it were with honey the poisoned arrows of their impious doctrines: concerning all of whom together the Lord saith, Take

[87] Cyril of Jerusalem, *Catechetical Lectures*, Protocatechesis 10-11 (A.D. 350) NPNF 2, VII:3.

[88] Cyril of Jerusalem, *Catechetical Lectures*, 4:1 NPNF 2, VII:19.

heed lest any man mislead you. This is the reason for the teaching of the Creed and for expositions upon it."[89]

"Study earnestly these only which we read openly in the Church. Far wiser and more pious than thyself were the Apostles, and the bishops of old time, the presidents of the Church who handed down these books. Being therefore a child of the Church, trench thou not upon its statutes."[90]

"These mysteries which the Church now explains to thee who art passing out of the class of Catechumens, it is not the custom to explain to heathen."[91]

"Of these things the Church admonishes and teaches thee, and touches mire, that thou mayest not be bemired: she tells of the wounds, that thou mayest not be wounded."[92]

"Make thou thy fold with the sheep: flee from wolves: depart not from the Church."[93]

"But the Divine Scriptures and the doctrines of the truth know but One God..."[94]

"These things I say to you because of the following context of the Creed, and because we say, WE BELIEVE IN ONE GOD, THE FATHER ALMIGHTY, MAKER OF HEAVEN AND EARTH, AND OF ALL THINGS VISIBLE AND INVISIBLE; in order that we may remember that the Father of our Lord Jesus Christ is the same as He that made the heaven and the earth, and that we may make ourselves safe against the wrong paths of the godless heretics, who have dared to speak evil of the All wise Artificer of all

89 Ibid., 4:2 NPNF 2, VII:19.
90 Ibid., 4:35 NPNF 2, VII:27.
91 Ibid., 6:29 NPNF 2, VII:42.
92 Ibid., 6:34 NPNF 2, VII:43.
93 Ibid., 6:36 NPNF 2, VII:43.
94 Ibid., 8:4 NPNF 2, VII:48.

this world, men who see with eyes of flesh, but have the eyes of their understanding blinded."[95]

"The course of instruction in the Faith would lead me to speak of the Ascension also; but the grace of God so ordered it, that thou heardest most fully concerning it, as far as our weakness allowed, yesterday, on the Lord's day; since, by the providence of divine grace, the course of the Lessons in Church included the account of our Saviour's going up into the heavens; and what was then said was spoken principally for the sake of all, and for the assembled body of the faithful, yet especially for thy sake."[96]

"Now these things we teach, not of our own invention, but having learned them out of the divine Scriptures used in the Church... And that this kingdom is that of the Romans, has been a tradition of the Church's interpreters."[97]

"But since concerning spirit in general many diverse things are written in the divine Scriptures, and there is fear lest some out of ignorance fall into confusion, not knowing to what sort of spirit the writing refers; it will be well now to certify you, of what kind the Scripture declares the Holy Spirit to be. For as Aaron is called Christ, and David and Saul and others are called Christs, but there is only one true Christ, so likewise since the name of spirit is given to different things, it is right to see what is that which is distinctively called the Holy Spirit. For many things are called spirits."[98]

"But lest any from lack of learning, should suppose from the different titles of the Holy Ghost that these are divers spirits, and not one and the self-same, which alone there is, therefore the Catholic Church guarding thee beforehand hath delivered to thee in the profession of the faith, that thou 'BELIEVE IN ONE HOLY GHOST THE COMFORTER, WHO SPAKE BY THE PROPH-

---

95 Ibid., 9:4 NPNF 2, VII:51-52.
96 Ibid., 14:24 NPNF 2, VII:100-101.
97 Ibid., 15:13 NPNF 2, VII:108.
98 Ibid., 16:13 NPNF 2, VII:118.

ETS;' that thou mightest know, that though His names be many, the Holy Spirit is but one — of which names, we will now rehearse to you a few out of many."[99]

"In the power of the same Holy Spirit Peter also, the chief of the Apostles and the bearer of the keys of the kingdom of heaven..."[100]

"[Y]et the arrangement of articles in the Faith, if religiously understood, disproves the error of Sabellius also."[101]

"Faith therefore in the Resurrection of the dead, is a great commandment and doctrine of the Holy Catholic Church; great and most necessary, though gainsaid by many, yet surely warranted by the truth. Greeks contradict it, Samaritans disbelieve it, heretics mutilate it; the contradiction is manifold, but the truth is uniform."[102]

"It is called Catholic then because it extends over all the world, from one end of the earth to the other; and because it teaches universally and completely one and all the doctrines which ought to come to men's knowledge, concerning things both visible and invisible, heavenly and earthly; and because it brings into subjection to godliness the whole race of mankind, governors and governed, learned and unlearned; and because it universally treats and heals the whole class of sins, which are committed by soul or body, and possesses in itself every form of virtue which is named, both in deeds and words, and in every kind of spiritual gifts."[103]

"[T]he Catholic Church. For this is the peculiar name of this Holy Church, the mother of us all, which is the spouse of our Lord Jesus Christ, the Only-begotten Son of God (for it is written, As Christ also loved the Church and gave Himself for it, and all the

---

[99] Ibid., 17:3 NPNF 2, VII:124.
[100] Ibid., 17:27 NPNF 2, VII:130.
[101] Ibid., 17:34 NPNF 2, VII:132.
[102] Ibid., 18:1 NPNF 2, VII:134.
[103] Ibid., 18:23 NPNF 2, VII:139-140.

rest,) and is a figure and copy of Jerusalem which is above, which is free, and the mother of us all; which before was barren, but now has many children."[104]

"In this Holy Catholic Church receiving instruction and behaving ourselves virtuously, we shall attain the kingdom of heaven, and inherit ETERNAL LIFE..."[105]

"Having been sufficiently instructed in these things, keep them, I beseech you, in your remembrance; that I also, unworthy though I be, may say of you, Now I love you, because ye always remember me, and hold fast the traditions, which I delivered unto you. And God, who has presented you as it were alive from the dead, is able to grant unto you to walk in newness of life: because His is the glory and the power, now and for ever. Amen."[106]

"Hold fast these traditions [i.e. the doctrines regarding the Mass] undefiled and, keep yourselves free from offence. Sever not yourselves from the Communion; deprive not yourselves, through the pollution of sins, of these Holy and Spiritual Mysteries."[107]

Damasus, Pope [regn. A.D. 366-384]

"We believe that we, priests of God, by whom it is right for the rest to be instructed, are holding and teaching our people the Holy Creed which was founded on the teaching of the Apostles, and in no way departs from the definition of the Fathers."[108]

Didache [c.A.D. 140]

"Accordingly, elect for yourselves bishops and deacons, men who are an honor to the Lord, of gentle disposition, not attached

---

[104] Ibid., 18:26 NPNF 2, VII:140.
[105] Ibid., 18:28 NPNF 2, VII:141.
[106] Cyril of Jerusalem, *Catechetical Lectures*, Mystagogical Catechesis 2:8 (A.D. 350) NPNF 2, VII:148.
[107] Ibid., 5:23 NPNF 2, VII:157.
[108] Damasus, Pope, *Synodal Act of Damasus*, Epistle 1 (A.D. 371) NPNF 2, III:83.

to money, honest and well-tried; for they, too, render the sacred service of the prophets and teachers. Do not, then, despise them; after all, they are your dignitaries together with the prophets and teachers."[109]

Didymus of Alexandria, The Blind [c.A.D. 313-c.A.D. 398]

"For it is a natural consequence that they who have separated themselves from the assembly of the faithful are antichrists. For how can they help but be antichrists, they who hold opinions opposite to those which the church of Christ confesses."[110]

Diodorus [4th Cent.]

"And, in sooth, in what he [Manes] has said, there were some things which are part of our faith, but others of his assertions were widely different from what comes down to us from the tradition of the fathers. For he gave some interpretations quite opposite to ours..."[111]

Ephraem [c.A.D. 306-373]

"Be firmly persuaded of this, not as an opinion, but as truth, that whatsoever has been transmitted, whether in writing only or by word of mouth — and by consequence the divine names and apellations — is directed to this end, that we may have life, and may have it more abundantly."[112]

"While (the sects) mutually refute and condemn each other, it has happened to truth as to Gideon; that is, while they fight against each other, and fall under wounds mutually inflicted, they crown her. All the heretics acknowledge that there is a true Scripture. Had they all falsely believed that none existed, some one might reply

---

[109] Didache, 15 (c.A.D. 140) ACW 6:24.
[110] Didymus of Alexandria, *Commentary on 1st John* (ante c.A.D. 398) FOC I:54.
[111] Diodorus, *To Bishop Archelaus* (4th Cent.) FOC I:372.
[112] Ephraem, *Adv. Scrutat.* (ante A.D. 373) FOC I:420.

that such Scripture was unknown to them. But now that they have themselves taken away the force of such plea, from the fact that they have mutilated the very Scriptures. For they have corrupted the sacred copies; and words which ought to have but one interpretation, they have wrested to strange significations. Whilst, when one of them attempts this, and cuts off a member of his own body, the rest demand and claim back the severed limb... It is the church which perfect truth perfects. The church of believers is great, and its bosom most ample; it embraces the fulness (or, the whole) of the two Testaments."[113]

Epiphanius of Salamis [c.A.D. 315-403]

"The Scripture is in every way true. But there needs wisdom to know God, to believe him and his words, and what he has vouchsafed unto us... For every heresy is a deceiver, not having received the Holy Ghost, according to the tradition of the fathers in the holy Catholic church of God."[114]

"For they [Encratites] do not teach as the church does; their message does not accord with the truth."[115]

"For the boundaries have been fixed for us, and foundations laid, and we have the dwelling-place of faith, and traditions of the apostles, and sacred Scriptures, and successions of doctrine, and on every side has God's truth been secured; and let none of us be led astray by empty fables."[116]

"Thus these people [Audians] also, who are so contentious on this point, have stepped outside of the church's tradition on the subject, the tradition which holds that every human being is in the image."[117]

---

[113] Ephraem, *Adv. Haeres*. (ante A.D. 373) FOC I:377-378.
[114] Epiphanius, *The Well Anchored Man*, 63 (A.D. 374) FOC I:348.
[115] Epiphanius, *Panarion,* 47 (inter A.D. 374-377) PAN 168.
[116] Ibid., 55 FOC I:433.
[117] Ibid., 70 PAN 272.

"It is rather that the man could have been of the greatest benefit to us, [having excelled] those in this world [on account of his training] and his love, if his views had entirely agreed with those held by God's holy church everywhere, and had he not introduced a foreign doctrine."[118]

"We advised and urged him to assent to the faith of the holy church and to leave outside the doctrine causing contention."[119]

Eusebius [c.A.D. 263-340]

"But we have nevertheless felt compelled to give a catalogue of these also, distinguishing those works which according to ecclesiastical tradition are true and genuine and commonly accepted..."[120]

"We have received from tradition that we are to assemble on that day [Sunday]."[121]

"Which things being shortly propounded to the Galatians, out of their own epistle, namely, the saving faith which gives us the mystical regeneration in the name of the Father, and of the Son, and of the Holy Ghost; and besides the divine (traditions) which are written, the catholic church of God, which is from one end of the earth to the other, seals to us the testimonies of Scripture, by tradition which is not written."[122]

"And what they say might be plausible, if first of all the Divine Scriptures did not contradict them. And there are writings of certain brethren older than the times of Victor, which they wrote in behalf of the truth against the heresies."[123]

---

[118] Ibid., 77 PAN 342.

[119] Ibid., 77 PAN 343.

[120] Eusebius, *Ecclesiastical History*, 3, 26 (inter A.D. 300-325) NPNF 2, I:157.

[121] Eusebius, *Commentary on the Psalms*, 91 (ante A.D. 340) FOC I:413.

[122] Eusebius, *Against Marcellus*, 1:1 (ante A.D. 340) as cited by George Peck, *Rule of Faith* (New York: Carlton, 1844) p. 164.

[123] Eusebius, *Ecclesiastical History*, 5:28 NPNF 2, I:246-247.

Faustinus [4th Cent.]

"I will declare of the Holy Ghost that he is fully God and Lord, thus taught by ecclesiastical men who have preceded me; who, themselves also, having been previously instructed in the testimonies of the divine Scriptures by apostolic men, have delivered them to their successors."[124]

Felix III (II), Pope [regn. A.D. 483-492]

"This (heretic) has dared to say that we ought not to call Christ the Son of God, though this be agreeable to the divine appointment of the Saviour, and the tradition of the divine Scriptures, and the exposition of the fathers."[125]

Firmilian [A.D. d. 268]

Commenting on heretical baptism:

"And this indeed you Africans are able to say against Stephen, that when you knew the truth you forsook the error of custom. But we join custom to truth, and to the Romans' custom we oppose custom, but the custom of truth; holding from the beginning that which was delivered by Christ and the apostles. Nor do we remember that this at any time began among us, since it has always been observed here, that we knew none but one Church of God, and accounted no baptism holy except that of the holy Church."[126]

Gaudentius of Brescia [d. c.A.D. 410]

"It is certain that all men of that age perished in the deluge, save those who were found worthy to be within the ark, which was a type of the church. For in like manner also now, they cannot be

[124] Faustinus, *On the Trinity*, 7:3 (c.A.D. 385) FOC I:431.
[125] Felix III (II), Pope, *To Emperor Zeno* (ante A.D. 492) FOC I:357.
[126] Firmilian, *To Cyprian*, Epistle 74 (75):19 (A.D. 256) ANF V:395.

anywise saved who are aliens from the apostolic faith, and from the Catholic church."[127]

Gelasius, Pope [regn. A.D. 492-496]

"If then you adhere to the ancient faith, and which has been transmitted to us by the holy fathers; if your sentiments, like ours, correspond with those which they entertained concerning the Incarnation of the Lord our Saviour, and if you in nothing deviate from the doctrine of the universal church... this faith let us mutually hold in sincerity of mind and truth of heart, and there is peace. Let us also keep inviolate the rules which the church has received from those same fathers, and there is peace. Let this be a thing certain and fixed, and there is no discord."[128]

Gelazius of Cyzicus [5th Cent.]

"This is the apostolic and unspotted faith of the church, which (faith) delivered from heaven by the Lord himself through the apostles, the church reverences (as) transmitted from father to son, and retains it now and for evermore, the Lord saying to his disciples, 'Going teach all nations...' It has seemed good to us all together that the word 'consubstantial' ought to be defined in the Catholic faith, in the same way as our holy fathers, who have lived since the apostles, have delivered this faith."[129]

Gregory of Nazianzus [c.A.D. 330-c.A.D. 389]

"I never have and never can honour anything above the Nicene Faith, that of the Holy Fathers who met there to destroy that Arian heresy..."[130]

---

[127] Gaudentius, *Sermon 8* (ante c.A.D. 410) FOC I:176-177.
[128] Gelasius, Pope, *Suppl. Acacian.* (ante A.D. 496) FOC I:457.
[129] Gelazius of Cyzicus, *History of the Council of Nicea* (A.D. 476) FOC I:457-458.
[130] Gregory of Nazianzus, *To Cledonius*, Epistle 102 (A.D. 382) NPNF 2, VII:443.

"May we, to the last breath of life confess with great confidence that excellent deposit of the holy fathers who were nearest to Christ, and the primitive faith; that confession which we imbibed from our infancy; which we first uttered; and with which may we depart this life."[131]

"I desire to learn what is this fashion of innovation in things concerning the Church... But since our faith has been proclaimed, both in writing and without writing, here and in distant parts, in times of danger and of safety, how comes it that some make such attempts, and that others keep silence?"[132]

Gregory of Nyssa [c.A.D. 335-394]

"And yet if those had been the more appropriate names, the Truth Himself would not have been at a loss to discover them, nor those men either, on whom successively devolved the preaching of the mystery, whether they were from the first eye-witnesses and ministers of the Word, or, as successors to these, filled the whole world with the Evangelical doctrines, and again at various periods after this defined in a common assembly the ambiguities raised about the doctrine; whose traditions are constantly preserved in writing in the churches."[133]

"The doctrine of the true faith is clear in the first tradition we receive, in accordance with the Lord's wish, in the bath of the new birth."[134]

Hegesippus [floruit c.A.D. 180]

"Hegesippus in the five books of Memoirs which have come down to us has left a most complete record of his own views. In them he states that on a journey to Rome he met a great many

[131] Gregory of Nazianzus, *Orations*, 6 (ante A.D. 389) FOC I: 422.
[132] Gregory of Nazianzus, *To Cledonius*, Epistle 101 (A.D. 382) NPFN 2, VII:439.
[133] Gregory of Nyssa, *Against Eunomius*, I:13 (inter A.D. 380-384) NPNF 2, V:50.
[134] Gregory of Nyssa, *Epistles*, 24 (ante A.D. 394) PG 46:1088D, CON 29.

bishops, and that he received the same doctrine from all. It is fitting to hear what he says after making some remarks about the epistle of Clement to the Corinthians. His words are as follows: 'And the church of Corinth continued in the true faith until Primus was bishop in Corinth. I conversed with them on my way to Rome, and abode with the Corinthians many days, during which we were mutually refreshed in the true doctrine. And when I had come to Rome I remained there until Anicetus, whose deacon was Eleutherus. And Anicetus was succeeded by Soter, and he by Eleutherus. In every succession, and in every city that is held which is preached by the law and the prophets and the Lord.'"[135]

Hilary of Poitiers [c.A.D. 315-367/368]

"The reason why the Lord sat in the ship, and the crowds stood without, is derived from the subject-matter. For he was about to speak in parables; and by this kind of action he signifies that they who are placed without the church, cannot attain to any understanding of the divine word. For the ship exhibits a type of the church, the word of life placed and preached within which, they who are without, and lie near like barren and useless sands, cannot understand."[136]

Hippolytus of Rome [c.A.D.170-235]

"But we, as being their successors, and as participators in this grace, high-priesthood, and office of teaching, as well as being reputed guardians of the Church, must not be found deficient in vigilance, or disposed to suppress correct doctrine... they have endeavoured to establish their tenets, taking nothing from the holy Scriptures — nor is it from preserving the succession of any saint that they have hurried headlong into these opinions..."[137]

---

[135] Hegesippus, fragment in Eusebius' *Ecclesiastical History*, 4:22 (c. A.D. 180) NPNF 2, I:198-199.

[136] Hilary of Poitiers, *Commentary On Matthew*, 13 (c. A.D. 353-355) FOC I:347.

[137] Hippolytus of Rome, *Refutation of All Heresies*, 1:Preface (post A.D. 222) ANF V:10.

"When the blessed presbyters heard this, they summoned him before the Church, and examined him. But he denied at first that he held such opinions. Afterwards, however, taking shelter among some, and having gathered round him some others who had embraced the same error, he wished thereafter to uphold his dogma openly as correct. And the blessed presbyters called him again before them, and examined him. But he stood out against them, saying, 'What evil, then, am I doing in glorifying Christ?' And the presbyters replied to him, 'We too know in truth one God; we know Christ; we know that the Son suffered even as He suffered, and died even as He died, and rose again on the third day, and is at the right hand of the Father, and cometh to judge the living and the dead. And these things which we have learned we allege.' Then, after examining him, they expelled him from the Church. And he was carried to such a pitch of pride, that he established a school."[138]

"Let us believe then, dear brethren, according to the tradition of the apostles, that God the Word came down from heaven, (and entered) into the holy Virgin Mary, in order that, taking the flesh from her, and assuming also a human, by which I mean a rational soul, and becoming thus all that man is with the exception of sin..."[139]

Hosius [c.A.D. 256-c.A.D. 375]

God has put into your hands the kingdom; to us He has entrusted the affairs of His Church; and as he who would steal the empire from you would resist the ordinance of God, so likewise fear on your part lest by taking upon yourself the government of the Church, you become guilty of a great offence."[140]

---

[138] Hippolytus of Rome, *Against the Heresy of one Noetus*, 1 (inter A.D. 200-210) ANF V:223.

[139] Hippolytus of Rome, *Against the Heresy of one Noetus*, 17 (inter A.D. 200-210) ANF V:230.

[140] Hosius, *To Emperor Constantius*, fragment in Athanasius' *History of the Arians* 44 (A.D. 356) NPNF 2, IV:286.

Ignatius of Antioch [d. c.A.D. 110]

"It is therefore befitting that you should in every way glorify Jesus Christ, who hath glorified you, that by a unanimous obedience 'ye may be perfectly joined together in the same mind and in the same judgment, and may all speak the same thing concerning the same thing, and that, being subject to the bishop and the presbytery, ye may in all respects be sanctified."[141]

"The more, therefore, you see the bishop silent, the more do you reverence him. For we ought to receive every one whom the Master of the house sends to be over His household, as we would do Him that sent him. It is manifest, therefore, that we should look upon the bishop even as we would look upon the Lord Himself, standing, as he does, before the Lord."[142]

"Since therefore I have, in the persons before mentioned, beheld the whole multitude of you in faith and love, I exhort you to study to do all things with a divine harmony, while your bishop presides in the place of God, and your presbyters in the place of the assembly of the apostles, along with your deacons, who are most dear to me, and are entrusted with the ministry of Jesus Christ. He, being begotten by the Father before the beginning of time, was God the Word, the only-begotten Son, and remains the same for ever; for 'of His kingdom there shall be no end,' says Daniel the prophet. Let us all therefore love one another in harmony, and let no one look upon his neighbour according to the flesh, but in Christ Jesus. Let nothing exist among you which may divide you; but be ye united with your bishop, being through him subject to God in Christ."[143]

"Study, therefore, to be established in the doctrines of the Lord and the apostles, that so all things, whatsoever ye do, may prosper, both in the flesh and spirit, in faith and love, with your most admirable bishop, and the well-compacted spiritual crown of your

---

[141] Ignatius of Antioch, *Epistle to the Ephesians*, 2 (c. A.D. 110) ANF I:50.
[142] Ibid., 6, ANF I:51.
[143] Ignatius of Antioch, *Epistle to the Magnesians*, 6 (c. A.D. 110) ANF I:61.

presbytery, and the deacons who are according to God. Be ye subject to the bishop, and to one another, as Christ to the Father, that there may be a unity according to God among you."[144]

"When I heard some saying, If I do not find it in the ancient Scriptures [ie. OT], I will not believe the Gospel; on my saying to them, It is written, they answered me, That remains to be proved. But to me Jesus Christ is in the place of all that is ancient: His cross, and death and resurrection, and the faith which is by Him are undefiled monuments of antiquity..."[145]

Innocent, Pope [regn. A.D. 401-417]

"If the priests of the Lord but desired to guard entire the ecclesiastical constitutions transmitted by the blessed apostles, there would be no diversity, no variety in ordination and consecrations... On these we send you replies, not as thinking you any respect ignorant, but that you may regulate your people with greater authority; or, should any have gone aside from the institutions of the Roman Church, that you may either yourself admonish them, or not delay to point them out to us, that we may know who they are who either introduce novelties, or who think that the custom of any other church, but that of Rome, is to be followed."[146]

Irenaeus [c.A.D. 140-c.A.D. 202]

"For even creation reveals Him who formed it, and the very work made suggests Him who made it, and the world manifests Him who ordered it. The Universal Church, moreover, through the whole world, has received this tradition from the apostles."[147]

"It is within the power of all, therefore in every Church, who may wish to see the truth, to contemplate clearly the tradition of

[144] Ibid., 13 ANF I:64.
[145] Ignatius of Antioch, *Epistle to the Philadelphians*, 8 (c. A.D. 110), ANF I:84.
[146] Innocent, Pope, *To Decentius-Bishop of Gubbio*, Epistle 25 (A.D. 416) FOC I:442-443.
[147] Irenaeus, *Against Heresies*, 2, 9:1 (inter A.D. 180-199) ANF I:369.

the apostles manifested throughout the whole world; and we are in a position to reckon up to those who were by the apostles instituted bishops in the Churches, and [to demonstrate] the succession of these men down to our own times; those who neither taught nor knew of anything like what these [heretics] rave about. For if the apostles had known hidden mysteries, which they were in the habit of imparting to 'the perfect' apart and privily from the rest, they would have delivered them especially to those to whom they were also committing the Churches themselves."[148]

"But Polycarp also was not only instructed by apostles, and conversed with many who had seen Christ, but was also, by apostles in Asia, appointed bishop of the Church in Smyrna, whom I also saw in my early youth, for he tarried [on earth] a very long time, and, when a very old man, gloriously and most nobly suffering martyrdom, departed this life, having always taught the things which he had learned from the apostles, and which the Church has handed down, and which alone are true."[149]

"Since, therefore, the tradition from the apostles does thus exist in the Church, and is permanent among us, let us revert to the Scriptural proof furnished by those apostles who did also write the Gospel, in which they recorded the doctrine regarding God, pointing out that our Lord Jesus Christ is the truth, and that no lie is in Him."[150]

"True knowledge is [that which consists in] the doctrine of the apostles, and the ancient constitution of the Church throughout all the world, and the distinctive manifestation of the body of Christ according to the successions of the bishops, by which they have handed down that Church which exists in every place, and has come even unto us, being guarded and preserved without any forging of Scriptures, by a very complete system of doctrine, and neither receiving addition nor [suffering] curtailment [in the truths which she believes]; and [it consists in] reading [the word of God] with-

[148] Ibid., 3,3:1 ANF I:415.
[149] Ibid., 3,3:4 ANF I:416.
[150] Ibid., 3, 5:1 ANF I:417.

out falsification, and a lawful and diligent exposition in harmony with the Scriptures, both without danger and without blasphemy; and [above all, it consists in] the pre-eminent gift of love, which is more precious than knowledge, more glorious than prophecy, and which excels all the other gifts [of God]."[151]

"Then I have pointed out the truth, and shown the preaching of the Church, which the prophets proclaimed (as I have already demonstrated), but which Christ brought to perfection, and the apostles have handed down, from whom the Church, receiving [these truths], and throughout all the world alone preserving them in their integrity (bene), has transmitted them to her sons. Then also — having disposed of all questions which the heretics propose to us, and having explained the doctrine of the apostles, and clearly set forth many of those things which were said and done by the Lord in parables — I shall endeavour, in this the fifth book of the entire work which treats of the exposure and refutation of knowledge falsely so called, to exhibit proofs from the rest of the Lord's doctrine and the apostolical epistles: [thus] complying with thy demand, as thou didst request of me (since indeed I have been assigned a place in the ministry of the word); and, labouring by every means in my power to furnish thee with large assistance against the contradictions of the heretics, as also to reclaim the wanderers and convert them to the Church of God, to confirm at the same time the minds of the neophytes, that they may preserve stedfast the faith which they have received, guarded by the Church in its integrity, in order that they be in no way perverted by those who endeavour to teach them false doctrines, and lead them away from the truth."[152]

"In the letter to Florinus, of which we have spoken, Irenaeus mentions again his intimacy with Polycarp, saying: 'These doctrines, O Florinus, to speak mildly, are not of sound judgment. These doctrines disagree with the Church, and drive into the greatest impiety those who accept them. These doctrines, not even the heretics outside of the Church, have ever dared to publish. These doc-

[151] Ibid., 4, 33:8 ANF I:508.
[152] Ibid., 5, Preface ANF I:526.

trines, the presbyters who were before us, and who were companions of the apostles, did not deliver to thee. For when I was a boy, I saw thee in lower Asia with Polycarp, moving in splendor in the royal court, and endeavoring to gain his approbation. I remember the events of that time more clearly than those of recent years. For what boys learn, growing with their mind, becomes joined with it; so that I am able to describe the very place in which the blessed Polycarp sat as he discoursed, and his goings out and his comings in, and the manner of his life, and his physical appearance, and his discourses to the people, and the accounts which he gave of his intercourse with John and with the others who had seen the Lord. And as he remembered their words, and what he heard from them concerning the Lord, and concerning his miracles and his teaching, having received them from eyewitnesses of the 'Word of life, ' Polycarp related all things in harmony with the Scriptures.'"[153]

Isaias, Abbot [4th Cent.]

"Do not, even for the sake of defending the faith, converse with heretics, for fear lest their words instil their venom into thy mind. If thou meet with a book said to be by one of the heretics, read it not, lest it fill thy heart with deadly poison; but so continue in that doctrine which thou hast learnt in holy church, as neither to add or to take from it."[154]

Isidore of Pelusium [c.A.D. 360-c.A.D. 435]

"Every writing which has for its aim true religion is commendable, very beautiful, and deserving of praise. But the sacred volumes, which contain the testimonies of the divine writings, are steps whereby to ascend unto God. All those books, therefore, that are set before thee in the church of God, receive as tried gold, they have been tried in the fire by the divine Spirit of the truth. But leave aside those which are scattered about without that church —

---

[153] Irenaeus, fragment in Eusebius' *Ecclesiastical History*, 5:20 (ante A.D. 202) NPNF 2, I:238-239.

[154] Isaias, Abbot, *Discourse 4* (4th Cent.) FOC I:62.

even though they may contain something persuasive to holiness — to be sought after and kept by those who are free from conflicts like thine."[155]

"We ought not follow the decisions of men labouring under such disorders, but to derive our demonstrations from the judgment of men free from all disorder, and cleave to the holy synod which assembled at Nicaea, nothing adding (thereto), nothing diminishing; for that synod being divinely inspired, taught the true doctrine."[156]

Jerome [c.A.D 347-420]

"About this corn and wine (the Eucharist) heretics are torn in pieces, and build unto themselves divers tabernacles; or in fact they are cut off from the body of the church, and affect to mediate and to muse on the law of the Lord. But doing this they withdraw from the Lord who taught them in the church, and gave them strength to fight against the enemy. But they thought evil against the Lord, raising up most impious heresies, and have retrograded unto the condition of the Gentiles, so as to be without the knowledge and the yoke of God..."[157]

"They shall not fall 'who have their abode in the universe, and their resting-place in the church which is the abode of the Father, and Son, and Holy Ghost."[158]

"And let them not flatter you themselves if they think they have Scripture authority for their assertions, since the devil himself has quoted Scripture texts, and the essence of the Scriptures is not the letter, but the meaning. Otherwise, if we follow the letter, we too can concoct a new dogma and assert that such persons as wear shoes and have two coats must not be received into the Church."[159]

---

[155] Isidore of Pelusium, *Epistle* I:369 (inter A.D. 393-433) FOC I:85-86.
[156] Isidore of Pelusium, *Epistle* 4:99 FOC I:466.
[157] Jerome, *Commentary in Hosea* (A.D. 406) FOC I:74.
[158] Jerome, *Commentary in Isaiah* (inter A.D. 408-410) FOC I:73-74.
[159] Jerome, *Dialogue against the Luciferians*, 28 (A.D. 379/382) NPNF 2, VI:334.

"I meantime keep crying: 'He who clings to the chair of Peter is accepted by me.' Meletius, Vitalis, and Paulinus all profess to cleave to you, and I could believe the assertion if it were made by one of them only. As it is, either two of them or else all three are guilty of falsehood. Therefore I implore your blessedness, by our Lord's cross and passion, those necessary glories of our faith, as you hold an apostolic office, to give an apostolic decision. Only tell me by letter with whom I am to communicate in Syria, and I will pray for you that you may sit in judgment enthroned with the twelve; that when you grow old, like Peter, you may be girded not by yourself but by another, and that, like Paul, you may be made a citizen of the heavenly kingdom. Do not despise a soul for which Christ died."[160]

"These instances have been just touched upon by me (the limits of a letter forbid a more discursive treatment of them) to convince you that in the holy scriptures you can make no progress unless you have a guide to shew you the way."[161]

"My resolution is, to read the ancients, to try everything, to hold fast what is good, and not to recede from the faith of the Catholic Church."[162]

Julius, Pope [regn. A.D. 337-352]

"Not so have the constitutions of Paul, not so have the traditions of the Fathers directed; this is another form of procedure, a novel practice. I beseech you, readily bear with me: what I write is for the common good. For what we have received from the blessed Apostle Peter, that I signify to you..."[163]

[160] Jerome, *To Pope Damasus*, Epistle 16 (A.D. 377/378) NPNF 2, VI:20.

[161] Jerome, *To Paulinus*, Epistle 53 (A.D. 394) NPNF 2, VI:98.

[162] Jerome, *To Minervius and Alexander*, Epistle 119 (A.D. 406) FOC I:73.

[163] Julius, Pope, *To the Eusebians*, fragment in Athanasius' *Defence Against the Arians* 35 (A.D. 340) NPNF 2, IV:118.

Justin Martyr [A.D. 100/110-c.A.D. 165]

"And that it was foreknown that these infamous things should be uttered against those who confessed Christ, and that those who slandered Him, and said that it was well to preserve the ancient customs, should be miserable, hear what was briefly said by Isaiah; it is this: 'Woe unto them that call sweet bitter, and bitter sweet.'"[164]

"For with what reason should we believe of a crucified man that He is the first-born of the unbegotten God, and Himself will pass judgment on the whole human race, unless we had found testimonies concerning Him published before He came and was born as man, and unless we saw that things had happened accordingly — the devastation of the land of the Jews, and men of every race persuaded by His teaching through the apostles, and rejecting their old habits, in which, being deceived..."[165]

Lactantius [c.A.D. 250-post A.D. 317]

"Whilst some there have been, not learned enough in the heavenly writings, who, unable to reply to their opponents, when they objected that is was both impossible and unbecoming that God should be enclosed within a woman's womb... have been perverted from the right path, and have corrupted the heavenly writings, so far as to fashion for themselves a new doctrine without any root or firmness: whilst some, enticed away by the predictions of false prophets, who have been, both by Him and by the true prophets, foretold, have fallen away from God's doctrine, and abandoned the true tradition... The Catholic church is therefore the only one that retains the true worship. This is the source of truth; this is the dwelling-place of faith; this is the temple of God, which whosoever en-

---

[164] Justin Martyr, *The First Apology of Justin*, 49 (inter A.D. 148-155) ANF I:179.
[165] Ibid., 53 ANF I:180.

ters not, or from which whosoever departs, he is an alien from the hope of life, and eternal salvation."[166]

Leo the Great, Pope [regn. A.D 440-461]

"It is not to be doubted that every Christian observance is taught of God, and whatsoever has been received by the church as a customary devotion is derived from apostolic tradition, and from the teaching of the Holy Spirit, who now also presides over the hearts of the faithful by his own appointments, that so all men may both obediently observe and wisely understand them."[167]

"That man perishes by his own obstinacy, and by his own madness withdraws from Christ, who follows that impiety by which he knows that many before him have perished; and who thinks that is for him religious and Catholic, which, by the judgment of the holy fathers, it is well known has been condemned, both in the perfidy of Photinus, and in the folly of Manichaeus, and in the madness of Apollinaris."[168]

"[H]e never ought to have departed from the catholic tradition, but to have preserved in the same belief as is held by all."[169]

"But because both we and our blessed fathers, whose teaching we revere and follow, are in concord on the one Faith... But if any dissent from the purity of our Faith and from the authority of the Fathers, the Synod which has met at Rome for that purpose joins with me in asking your clemency to permit a universal council within the limits of Italy..."[170]

---

[166] Lactantius, *Divine Institutions*, 4:30 (inter A.D. 304-310) FOC I:44-45.

[167] Leo the Great, *Sermons*, 79 (ante A.D. 461) FOC I:453-454.

[168] Ibid., 96 FOC I: 454.

[169] Leo the Great, *To Flavian-Bishop of Constantinople*, Epistle 27 (A.D. 449) NPNF 2, XII:38.

[170] Leo the Great, *To Theodosius Augustus*, Epistle 69 (A.D. 450) NPNF 2, XII:63-64.

Liberius, Pope [regn. A.D. 352-366]

"This is no ecclesiastical Canon; nor have we transmitted to us any such tradition from the Fathers, who in turn received from the great and blessed Apostle Peter."[171]

Lucifer of Cagliari [d. c.A.D. 371]

"The Holy Spirit, the Comforter, who was in the prophets, remained also in the apostles, which same Holy Spirit, the Comforter, since he is in God's church, and you have been placed without the church, He abides not in you, who are thereby proved to have the spirit of antichrist, which unclean spirit, for fear lest you should see what we now urge upon you, spreads the blinding, darkness of error over your heretical hearts."[172]

"Cease, Constantius, to persecute the house of God... Proclaim thyself Christian; execrate with us the mob of Arians brought together by the devil's trickery; believe as we believe, we, who are, by succession from the blessed apostles, bishops; confess as we and they have confessed, the only Son of God, and thus shalt thou obtain forgiveness for thy numerous crimes."[173]

Methodius [d. c.A.D. 311]

"'Arise, shine; for thy light is come, and the glory of the Lord is risen upon thee. For, behold, the darkness shall cover the earth, and gross darkness the people: but the Lord shall arise upon thee, and His glory shall be seen upon thee...' It is the Church whose children shall come to her with all speed after the resurrection, running to her from all quarters. She rejoices receiving the light

---

[171] Liberius, Pope, *To Eusebius*, fragment in Athanasius' *History of the Arians* 36 (ante A.D. 366) NPNF 2, IV:282.

[172] Lucifer of Cagliari, *De non parcendo in Deum delinquentibus*, 37 (ante c.A.D. 371) FOC I:53-54.

[173] Lucifer of Cagliari, *Pro Sancto Athanasio*, 1:33 (ante c.A.D. 371) FOC I:274.

which never goes down, and clothed with the brightness of the Word as with a robe... Come, then, let us go forward in our discourse, and look upon this marvelous woman as upon virgins prepared for a marriage, pure and undefiled, perfect and radiating a permanent beauty, wanting nothing of the brightness of light; and instead of a dress, clothed with light itself; and instead of precious stones, her head adorned with shining stars. For instead of the clothing which we have, she had light; and for gold and brilliant stones, she had stars; but stars not such as those which are set in the invisible heaven, but better and more resplendent, so that those may rather be considered as their images and likenesses."[174]

Nilus of Ancrya [d. c.A.D. 430]

"You asked me by your letter, whether we ought to believe that the Holy Ghost is consubstantial with the Father and the Son. So we hold, and believe, having been taught by the divine fathers."[175]

Optatus of Milevis [c.A.D. 320-c.A.D. 385]

"But you say that you have a certain share in the city of Rome. This is a branch of your error, shooting forth falsehood, not from the root of truth. In fact, if Macrobius be asked what chair he fills in that city, can he answer, 'Peter's chair?' ...Whence he that holds one, must needs hold all, as each cannot be separated from the rest. Add to this, that we are in possession, not of one (of these marks), but we have them as properly ours. Of the aforesaid marks, then, the chair is, as we have said, the first, which we have proved is ours through Peter, and this first mark carries with it the angel (jurisdiction)."[176]

---

174 Methodius, *Banquet of the Ten Virgins*, 8:5 (ante A.D. 300) ANF VI:336.

175 Nilus of Ancrya, *Epistle* 2:210 (ante A.D. 430) FOC I:444.

176 Optatus of Milevis, *The Schism of the Donatists*, 2:4, 6 (c. A.D. 367) FOC I:315-317.

Origen [c.A.D. 185-254]

"We are not to credit these men, nor go out from the first and the ecclesiastical tradition; nor to believe otherwise than as the churches of God have by succession transmitted to us."[177]

"But now according to our ability let us make investigation also into the things that are stored up in it. In this place it does not appear to me that by Elijah the soul is spoken of, lest I should fall into the dogma of transmigration, which is foreign to the church of God, and not handed down by the Apostles, nor anywhere set forth in the Scriptures;"[178]

"Let Basilades, and whosoever agrees with him, be left in their impiety. But for us, let us turn to the meaning of the apostle, according to the piety of ecclesiastical doctrine."[179]

"The Church received from the Apostles the tradition of giving Baptism even to infants."[180]

"If, therefore, any church holds this epistle (Hebrews) as Paul's, let it receive praise on this account. For the ancients have not rashly transmitted it as Paul's."[181]

"Among the four Gospels, which are the only indisputable ones in the Church of God under heaven, I have learned by tradition..."[182]

"Wherefore, do thou too try, oh hearer, to have thine own well, and thine own spring, that thou too, when thou shalt take hold of a book of the Scriptures, mayest begin, even from thine own under-

---

[177] Origen, *Commentary on Matthew* (post A.D. 244) FOC I:407.
[178] Origen, *Commentary on Matthew*, 13:1 ANF X:474.
[179] Origen, *Commentary on Romans*, 5 FOC I:346.
[180] Origen, *Commentary on Romans*, 5 JUR I:209.
[181] Origen, *Fragment in Pamphilus' Apology for Origen* (ante A.D. 254) FOC I:407.
[182] Origen, *Fragment in Eusebius' Ecclesiasitcal History*, 6:25 (post A.D. 244) NPNF 2, I:273.

standing, to produce some meaning; and, according to those things which thou hast learned in the church, do thou too try to drink from the spring of thine ability."[183]

"When heretics show us the canonical Scriptures, in which every Christian believes and trusts, they seem to be saying: 'Lo, he is in the inner rooms [ie., the word of truth]' (Matt 24.6). But we must not believe them, nor leave the original tradition of the Church, nor believe otherwise than we have been taught by the succession in the Church of God." [184]

"The true disciple of Jesus is he who enters the house, that is to say, the Church. He enters it by thinking as the Church does and living as she does;this is how he understands her Word. The key to the Scriptures must be received from the tradition of the Church, as from the Lord himself"[185]

"But as the preaching of the Church includes a belief in a future and just judgment of God, which belief incites and persuades men to a good and virtuous life, and to an avoidance of sin by all possible means."[186]

Pacian of Barcelona [d. inter A.D. 379-392]

"What! is the authority derived from apostolic men, from the priests, from the most blessed martyr and doctor, Cyprian, of slight weight with us?... What say you to the numerous priests on this same side, whom one and the same peace firmly united, throughout the whole world... What to so many aged bishops, and martyrs, and confessors? Say, if they were not authorities enough for taking this name (Catholic), are we sufficient for rejecting it? And shall

---

[183] Origen, *Homilies On Genesis*, 12 (ante A.D. 232) FOC I:28.

[184] Origen, *Homilies on Matthew*, Homily 46, PG 13:1667 (ante A.D. 254) CON 392.

[185] Origen, as cited by Yves Congar, *The Meaning of Tradition* (New York: Hawthorn, 1964) p. 83.

[186] Origen, *On First Principles*, 3, 1:1 (inter A.D. 220-230) ANF IV:302.

the fathers rather follow our authority; and the antiquity of saints give way to be amended (by us); and times, grown rank with vice, pluck out the gray hairs of apostolic age? And yet, my brother, fret not yourself: Christian is my name, but Catholic my surname."[187]

Pamphilus of Caesarea [c.A.D. 240-c.A.D. 309]

"These remarks (he alludes to the extract referred to) are made by Origen... to show what has been manifestly handed down in the public teaching of the church, and what has not been clearly defined... But in every case, he bears in mind his own declaration — the one made above, wherein he says that, that alone is to be received and believed as truth, which in nothing is opposed to the apostolic and ecclesiastical dogmas."[188]

Papias [floruit c.A.D. 130]

"But I shall not hesitate also to put down for you along with my interpretations whatsoever things I have at any time learned carefully from the elders, and carefully remembered guaranteeing their truth. For I did not, like the multitude, take pleasure in those that speak much, but in those that teach the truth; not in those that relate strange commandments, but in those that deliver the commandments given by the Lord to faith, and springing from the truth itself. If, then, any one came, who had been a follower of the elders, I questioned him in regard to the words of the elders — what Andrew or what Peter said, or what was said by Philip, or by Thomas, or by James, or by John, or by Matthew, or by any other of the disciples of the Lord, and what things Aristion and the presbyter John, the disciples of the Lord, say. For I did not think that what was to be gotten from the books would profit me as much as what came from the living and abiding voice."[189]

---

[187] Pacian of Barcelona, *To the Novationist Sympronian*, Epistle 1 (inter c.A.D. 375-392) FOC I:300.

[188] Pamphilus of Caesarea, *Apology for Origen* (ante c.A.D. 309) FOC I:41.

[189] Papias, fragment in Eusebius' *Ecclesiastical History*, 3, 39:1-4 (c. A.D. 130) NPNF 2, I:170-171.

Paulinus the Deacon [floruit c.A.D. 380-418]

"I beseech justice of your blessedness, Lord Zosmius, venerable Pope. The true faith is never disturbed, certainly not in the apostolic church, in which the teachers of false faith are as truly punished as they are easily discovered, that they may die in the evils they have committed, unless they correct them so that in them may be that true faith which the apostles taught, and which the Roman church holds, together with all the doctors of the catholic faith."[190]

Paulinus of Nola [c.A.D. 353-A.D. 431]

"This privilege Catholic love alone has a right to claim for itself; she, that is 'the alone one, and the perfect one to her one bridegroom (Cant. vi. 8) takes the kisses of truth from the Word Himself, that she may not be defiled by the venom of heretical deceitfulness, as though by incestuous kisses from a stranger's lips."[191]

Paulus Orosius [floruit c.A.D. 415]

"The Fathers with one accord, and the Martrys, who are now at rest, Cyprian, Hilary, and Ambrose, as also they who are still in the flesh, and are the pillars and supports of the Catholic church, Aurelius, Augustin, Jerom[e], have already in their highly-approved writings, published much against this wicked heresy (Pelagianism), though without specifying the names of heretics... The Fathers whom the universal church throughout the world approves, to whose communion it is a matter of rejoicing with you that we adhere, have decreed that these dogmas are damnable. It becomes us to obey, when they adjudge. Why ask the children what their sentiments are, when you hear what the Fathers decided?"[192]

---

[190] Paulinus the Deacon, *Against Caelestius-To Pope Zosmius*, 1 (A.D. 417) GILES 209.

[191] Paulinus of Nola, *To Sulpicius Severus*, Epistle 4 (ante A.D. 431) FOC I:86.

[192] Paulus of Orosius, *De Arbitrii Libert.* (A.D. 415) FOC I:86-87.

Peter Chrysologus [c.A.D. 400-c.A.D.454]

"I believe... in the Holy Catholic church. Because the church is in Christ, and Christ is in the church: whoso, therefore, acknowledges the church, has confessed that he has believed in the church."[193]

Philastrius of Brescia [d. A.D. 387]

"There is also a heresy called the apocryphal, or the secret, which receives only the prophets and the apostles, and not the canonical writings, to wit the law and the prophets, both the Old and the New Testament... It has been ordained by the apostles and their successors, that nothing be read in the Catholic church, except the law, and the prophets, and the gospels, &c."[194]

Phoebadius of Agen [floruit A.D. 357]

"For, what cause, or reason is there why what has been handed down to all churches to be believed and taught, and which the apostolic men, our fathers, purified by the Holy Spirit, from a Catholic motive, set down — as a kind of barrier in defence of the truth, by which they might obstruct every approach to pestilential doctrine — in opposition to all heresies, and especially the Arian, should now be the object of no small labour and striving, that it may be removed, on part of those who are favourable to what has condemned the Arian defilement."[195]

Polycarp [A.D. 69/70-155/156]

"Wherefore, it is needful to abstain from all these things, being subject to the presbyters and deacons, as unto God and Christ. The virgins also must walk in a blameless and pure conscience."[196]

---

[193] Peter Chrysologus, *De Symbolo*, Sermon 62 (post A.D. 432) FOC I:111.

[194] Philastrius of Brescia, *The Heresies*, 60 (ante A.D. 387) FOC I:280.

[195] Phoebadius of Agen, *The Orthodox Faith against the Arians*, 1 (A.D. 357/358) FOC I:461.

[196] Polycarp, *To the Phillipians*, 5 (c. A.D. 135) ANF I:34.

Prosper of Aquitaine [d. post A.D. 455]

"Out of Jerusalem there is no blessing. For no one is sanctified save he who is united to the church, which is the body of Christ."[197]

Serapion of Antioch [floruit c.A.D. 200]

"For we, brethren, receive both Peter and the other apostles as Christ; but we reject intelligently the writings falsely ascribed to them [i.e. Gospel of Peter], knowing that such were not handed down to us."[198]

"That you may see the doings of this lying band of the new prophecy [Montanism], so called, are an abomination to all the brotherhood throughout the world..."[199]

Siricius, Pope [regn. A.D. 384-399]

"Wherefore following the precept of the apostle, know that it was the unanimous opinion, as well of all our priests and deacons, as also of all the clergy, that seeing that these men have taught otherwise than we have received, they ought, Jovinian, that is, Auxentius, &c., both by the divine sentence, and our judgment, to be for ever condemned to be without the pale of the church."[200]

Socrates Scholastikos [c.A.D. 380-post A.D. 439]

"As soon as Eusebius reached Alexandria, he in concert with Athanasius immediately convoked a Synod. The bishops assembled on this occasion out of various cities, took into consideration many subjects of the utmost importance. They asserted the divinity of

---

197 Prosper of Aquitaine, *Explanation of the Psalms*, 147 (post A.D. 431 ante A.D. 449) FOC I:89.

198 Serapion of Antioch, *On the Gospel of Peter*, fragment in *Eusebius' Ecclesiastical History* 6:12 (c.A.D. 200) NPNF 2, I:258.

199 Serapion of Antioch, fragment in Eusebius' *Ecclesiastical History* 5:19 (c.A.D. 200) NPNF2, I:237.

200 Sircius, Pope, *To the African Bishops*, Epistle 5 (ante A.D. 399) FOC I:431-432.

the Holy Spirit and comprehended him in the consubstantial Trinity: they also declared that the Word in being made man, assumed not only flesh, but also a soul, in accordance with the views of the early ecclesiastics. For they did not introduce any new doctrine of their own devising into the church, but contented themselves with recording their sanction of those points which ecclesiastical tradition has insisted on from the beginning, and wise Christians have demonstratively taught."[201]

Stephen I, Pope [regn. A.D. 254-257]

"If any one, therefore, come to you from any heresy whatever, let nothing be innovated (or done) which has not been handed down, to wit, that hands be imposed on him for repentance;"[202]

Tertullian [c.A.D. 160-post A.D. 220]

"You lay down a prescription that this faith has its solemnities 'appointed' by the Scriptures or the tradition of the ancestors; and that no further addition in the way of observance must be added, on account of the unlawfulness of innovation. Stand on that ground, if you can... Besides, throughout the provinces of Greece there are held in definite localities those councils gathered out of the universal Churches, by whose means not only all the deeper questions are handled for the common benefit, but the actual representation of the whole Christian name is celebrated with great veneration."[203]

"After such a fashion as this, I suppose you have had, O Marcion, the hardihood of blotting out the original records (of the history) of Christ that His flesh may lose the proofs of its reality. But, prithee, on what grounds (do you do this)? Show me your authority. If you are a prophet, foretell us a thing; if you are an apostle, open your message in public; if a follower of apostles,

---

201 Socrates, *Ecclesiastical History*, 3:7 (c.A.D. 439) NPNF 2, II:81.

202 Stephen, Pope, fragment in Cyprian's *Epistle To Pompey*, 73 (74):1 (A.D. 256) ANF, V:386.

203 Tertullian, *On Fasting*, 13 (c.A.D. 208) ANF IV:111.

side with apostles in thought; if you are only a (private) Christian, believe what has been handed down to us: if, however, you are nothing of all this, then (as I have the best reason to say) cease to live... Now that which had been handed down was true, inasmuch as it had been transmitted by those whose duty it was to hand it down. Therefore, when rejecting that which had been handed down, you rejected that which was true. You had no authority for what you did."[204]

"As for us, although we must still seek, and that always, yet where ought our search to be made? Amongst the heretics, where all things are foreign and opposed to our own verity, and to whom we are forbidden to draw near?... No man gets instruction from that which tends to destruction. No man receives illumination from a quarter where all is darkness. Let our 'seeking, ' therefore be in that which is our own, and from those who are our own: and concerning that which is our own — that, and only that, which can become an object of inquiry without impairing the rule of faith."[205]

"Now, with regard to this rule of faith — that we may from this point acknowledge what it is which we defend — it is, you must know, that which prescribes the belief that there is one only God, and that He is none other than the Creator of the world, who produced all things out of nothing through His own Word, first of all sent forth; that this Word is called His Son, and, under the name of God, was seen 'in diverse manners' by the patriarchs, heard at all times in the prophets, at last brought down by the Spirit and Power of the Father into the Virgin Mary, was made flesh in her womb, and, being born of her, went forth as Jesus Christ; thenceforth He preached the new law and the new promise of the kingdom of heaven, worked miracles; having been crucified, He rose again the third day; (then) having ascended into the heavens, He sat at the right hand of the Father; sent instead of Himself the Power of the Holy Ghost to lead such as believe; will come with glory to take the saints to the enjoyment of everlasting life and of

[204] Tertullian, *On the Flesh of Christ*, 2 ANF III:522.
[205] Tertullian, *On Prescription against the Heretics*, 12, ANF III:249.

the heavenly promises, and to condemn the wicked to everlasting fire, after the resurrection of both these classes shall have happened, together with the restoration of their flesh. This rule, as it will be proved, was taught by Christ, and raises amongst ourselves no other questions than those which heresies introduce, and which make men heretics."[206]

"'Thy faith,' He says, 'hath saved thee' not observe your skill in the Scriptures. Now, faith has been deposited in the rule; it has a law, and (in the observance thereof) salvation. Skill, however, consists in curious art, having for its glory simply the readiness that comes from knack. Let such curious art give place to faith; let such glory yield to salvation. At any rate, let them either relinquish their noisiness, or else be quiet. To know nothing in opposition to the rule (of faith), is to know all things."[207]

"We are therefore come to (the gist of) our position; for at this point we were aiming, and for this we were preparing in the preamble of our address (which we have just completed) — so that we may now join issue on the contention to which our adversaries challenge us. They put forward the Scriptures, and by this insolence of theirs they at once influence some. In the encounter itself, however, they weary the strong, they catch the weak, and dismiss waverers with a doubt. Accordingly, we oppose to them this step above all others, of not admitting them to any discussion of the Scriptures. If in these lie their resources, before they can use them, it ought to be clearly seen to whom belongs the possession of the Scriptures, that none may be admitted to the use thereof who has no title at all to the privilege."[208]

"Immediately, therefore, so did the apostles, whom this designation indicates as 'the sent.' Having, on the authority of a prophecy, which occurs in a psalm of David, chosen Matthias by lot as the twelfth, into the place of Judas, they obtained the promised

---

[206] Ibid., 13 ANF III:249.
[207] Ibid., 14 ANF III:250.
[208] Ibid., 15 ANF III:250.

power of the Holy Ghost for the gift of miracles and of utterance; and after first bearing witness to the faith in Jesus Christ throughout Judaea, and founding churches (there), they next went forth into the world and preached the same doctrine of the same faith to the nations. They then in like manner rounded churches in every city, from which all the other churches, one after another, derived the tradition of the faith, and the seeds of doctrine, and are every day deriving them, that they may become churches. Indeed, it is on this account only that they will be able to deem themselves apostolic, as being the offspring of apostolic churches. Every sort of thing must necessarily revert to its original for its classification. Therefore the churches, although they are so many and so great, comprise but the one primitive church, (rounded) by the apostles, from which they all (spring). In this way all are primitive, and all are apostolic, whilst they are all proved to be one, in (unbroken) unity, by their peaceful communion, and title of brotherhood, and bond of hospitality — privileges which no other rule directs than the one tradition of the selfsame mystery."[209]

"Not so; for in all cases truth precedes its copy, the likeness succeeds the reality. Absurd enough, however, is it, that heresy should be deemed to have preceded its own prior doctrine, even on this account, because it is that (doctrine) itself which foretold that there should be heresies against which men would have to guard! To a church which possessed this doctrine, it was written — yea, the doctrine itself writes to its own church — 'Though an angel from heaven preach any other gospel than that which we have preached, let him be accursed.'[210]

"Come now, you who would indulge a better curiosity, if you would apply it to the business of your salvation, run over the apostolic churches, in which the very thrones of the apostles are still pre-eminent in their places, in which their own authentic writings are read, uttering the voice and representing the face of each of them severally. Achaia is very near you, (in which) you find Corinth.

[209] Ibid., 20 ANF III:252.
[210] Ibid., 29 ANF III:256-257.

Since you are not far from Macedonia, you have Philippi; (and there too) you have the Thessalonians. Since you are able to cross to Asia, you get Ephesus. Since, moreover, you are close upon Italy, you have Rome, from which there comes even into our own hands the very authority (of apostles themselves). How happy is its church, on which apostles poured forth all their doctrine along with their blood! where Peter endures a passion like his Lord's! where Paul wins his crown in a death like John's!"[211]

"But what shall I say concerning the ministry of the word, since they make it their business not to convert the heathen, but to subvert our people? This is rather the glory which they catch at, to compass the fall of those who stand, not the raising of those who are down. Accordingly, since the very work which they purpose to themselves comes not from the building up of their own society, but from the demolition of the truth, they undermine our edifices, that they may erect their own. Only deprive them of the law of Moses, and the prophets, and the divinity of the Creator, and they have not another objection to talk about. The consequence is, that they more easily accomplish the ruin of standing houses than the erection of fallen ruins. It is only when they have such objects in view that they show themselves humble and bland and respectful. Otherwise they know no respect even for their own leaders. Hence it is [supposed] that schisms seldom happen among heretics, because, even when they exist, they are not obvious. Their very unity, however, is schism. I am greatly in error if they do not amongst themselves swerve even from their own regulations, forasmuch as every man, just as it suits his own temper, modifies the traditions he has received after the same fashion as the man who handed them down did, when he moulded them according to his own will. The progress of the matter is an acknowledgment at once of its character and of the manner of its birth. That was allowable to the Valentinians which had been allowed to Valentinus; that was also fair for the Marcionites which had been done by Marcion — even to innovate on the faith, as was agreeable to their own pleasure. In

[211] Ibid., 36 ANF III:260.

short, all heresies, when thoroughly looked into, are detected harbouring dissent in many particulars even from their own founders. The majority of them have not even churches. Motherless, houseless, creedless, outcasts, they wander about in their own essential worthlessness."[212]

"[S]o that no other teaching will have the right of being received as apostolic than that which is at the present day proclaimed in the churches of apostolic foundation. You will, however, find no church of apostolic origin but such as reposes its Christian faith in the Creator. But if the churches shall prove to have been corrupt from the beginning, where shall the pure ones be found? Will it be amongst the adversaries of the Creator? Show us, then, one of your churches, tracing its descent from an apostle, and you will have gained the day."[213]

"[T]hat is from the beginning which has the apostles for its authors, then it will certainly be quite as evident, that that comes down from the apostles, which has been kept as a sacred deposit in the churches of the apostles... For although Marcion rejects his Apocalypse, the order of bishops (thereof), when traced up to their origin, will rest on John as their author..."[214]

"An easy thing it is at once to demand where it is written that we should not be crowned. But is it written that we should be crowned? Indeed, in urgently demanding the warrant of Scripture in a different side from their own, men prejudge that the support of Scripture ought no less to appear on their part. For if it shall be said that it is lawful to be crowned on this ground, that Scripture does not forbid it, it will as validly be retorted that just on this ground is the crown unlawful, because the Scripture does not enjoin it. What shall discipline do? Shall it accept both things, as if neither were forbidden? Or shall it refuse both, as if neither were enjoined? But

---

212 Ibid., 42 ANF III:263-264.
213 Tertullian, *Against Marcion*, I:21 (inter A.D. 207-212) ANF III:286.
214 Ibid., 4:5 ANF III:349-350.

'the thing which is not forbidden is freely permitted' should rather say that what has not been freely allowed is forbidden."[215]

"In the course of time, then, the Father forsooth was born, and the Father suffered, God Himself, the Lord Almighty, whom in their preaching they declare to be Jesus Christ. We, however, as we indeed always have done (and more especially since we have been better instructed by the Paraclete, who leads men indeed into all truth), believe that there is one only God, but under the following dispensation, or oikonomia, as it is called, that this one only God has also a Son, His Word, who proceeded from Himself, by whom all things were made, and without whom nothing was made. Him we believe to have been sent by the Father into the Virgin, and to have been born of her — being both Man and God, the Son of Man and the Son of God, and to have been called by the name of Jesus Christ; we believe Him to have suffered, died, and been buried, according to the Scriptures, and, after He had been raised again by the Father and taken back to heaven, to be sitting at the right hand of the Father, and that He will come to judge the quick and the dead; who sent also from heaven from the Father, according to His own promise, the Holy Ghost, the Paraclete, the sanctifier of the faith of those who believe in the Father, and in the Son, and in the Holy Ghost. That this rule of faith has come down to us from the beginning of the gospel, even before any of the older heretics, much more before Praxeas, a pretender of yesterday, will be apparent both from the lateness of date which marks all heresies, and also from the absolutely novel character of our new-fangled Praxeas. In this principle also we must henceforth find a presumption of equal force against all heresies whatsoever — that whatever is first is true, whereas that is spurious which is later in date. But keeping this prescriptive rule inviolate, still some opportunity must be given for reviewing (the statements of heretics), with a view to the instruction and protection of divers persons; were it only that it may not seem that each perversion of the truth is condemned without examination, and simply prejudged; especially in the case of this heresy, which supposes itself to possess the pure truth, in thinking

---

[215] Tertullian, *The Chaplet, the Soldier's Crown*, 2 (A.D. 211) ANF III:94.

that one cannot believe in One Only God in any other way than by saying that the Father, the Son, and the Holy Ghost are the very selfsame Person."[216]

"But I must take some further pains to rebut their arguments, when they make selections from the Scriptures in support of their opinion, and refuse to consider the other points, which obviously maintain the rule of faith without any infraction of the unity of the Godhead... But in their contention they only act on the principle of all heretics. For, inasmuch as only a few testimonies are to be found (making for them) in the general mass, they pertinaciously set off the few against the many, and assume the later against the earlier. The rule, however, which has been from the beginning established for every case, gives its prescription against the later assumptions, as indeed it also does against the fewer."[217]

"[W]hether there is room for maintaining that the Paraclete has taught any such thing as can either be charged with novelty, in opposition to catholic tradition, or with burdensomeness, in opposition to the 'light burden' of the Lord. Now concerning each point the Lord Himself has pronounced. For in saying, 'I still have many things to say unto you, but ye are not yet able to bear them: when the Holy Spirit shall be come, He will lead you into all truth,' He sufficiently, of course, sets before us that He will bring such (teachings) as may be esteemed alike novel, as having never before been published, and finally burdensome, as if that were the reason why they were not published. 'It follows,' you say, 'that by this line of argument, anything you please which is novel and burdensome may be ascribed to the Paraclete, even if it have come from the adversary spirit.' No, of course. For the adversary spirit would be apparent from the diversity of his preaching, beginning by adulterating the rule of faith, and so (going on to) adulterating the order of discipline; because the corruption of that which holds the first grade, (that is, of faith, which is prior to discipline,) comes first. A man must of necessity hold heretical views of God first,

[216] Tertullian, *Against Praxeas*, 2 (post A.D. 213) ANF III:598.
[217] Ibid., 20 ANF III:615.

and then of His institution. But the Paraclete, having many things to teach fully which the Lord deferred till He came, (according to the pre-definition), will begin by bearing emphatic witness to Christ, (as being) such as we believe (Him to be), together with the whole order of God the Creator, and will glorify Him, and will 'bring to remembrance' concerning Him. And when He has thus been recognised (as the promised Comforter), on the ground of the cardinal rule, He will reveal those 'many things' which appertain to disciplines..."[218]

Theodoret of Cyrus [c.A.D. 393-c.A.D 466]

"'Therefore, brethren, standfast, and hold the traditions which you have learned, &c.' (ii Thess 2:15). Have as a rule of doctrine the words which we have delivered unto you, which both when present we have preached, and when absent we have written to you."[219]

"His (Nestorius) first attempt at innovation was, that the holy Virgin, who bore the Word of God, who took flesh of her, ought not to be confessed to be the mother of God, but only the mother of Christ; though of old, yea from the first, the preachers of the orthodox faith taught, agreeably to the apostolic tradition, that the mother of God. And now let me produce his blasphemous artifice and observation unknown to any one before him."[220]

"But the colophon of our union is our harmony in faith; our refusal to accept any spurious doctrines; our preservation of the ancient and apostolic teaching, which has been brought to you by hoary wisdom and nurtured by virtue's hardy toil."[221]

---

[218] Tertullian, *Monogamy*, 2, ANF IV:59-60. Here Tertullian, a Montanist, argues against the traditional argument and for novelty.

[219] Theodoret of Cyrus, *Interpretation of the 14 Epistles of Paul*, On 2 Thessalonians (ante A.D. 466) FOC I:448.

[220] Theodoret of Cyrus, *Compendium of Heretics' Fables*, 12 (c. A.D. 453) FOC I:449.

[221] Theodoret of Cyrus, *To the Clergy of Beroea*, Epistle 75 NPNF 2, III:272.

"These lessons we have learnt alike from the holy Scripture and from the holy Fathers who have expounded it, Alexander and Athanasius, loud voiced heralds of the truth, who have been ornaments of your apostolic see; from Basil and from Gregory and the rest of the lights of the world..."[222]

"I hope then that your piety will deign, if there really are any, though I cannot believe it, who disobey the apostolic doctrines to close their mouths, to rebuke them as the laws of the Church require, and teach them to follow the footsteps of the holy Fathers and preserve undefiled the faith laid down at Nicaea in Bithynia by the holy and blessed Fathers, as summing up the teaching of Evangelists and Apostles."[223]

"I follow the laws and rules of the apostles. I test my teaching by applying to it, like a rule and measure, the faith laid down by the holy and blessed Fathers at Nicaea. If any one maintain that I hold any contrary opinion, let him accuse me face to face; let him not slander me in my absence."[224]

"They [Church Fathers] are successors of the divine apostles; some even of those apostles were privileged to hear the holy voice and see the goodly sight. The majority of them too were adorned with the crown of martyrdom. Does it seem right for you to wag the tongue of blasphemy against them?"[225]

"Now I will show you that in their own writings the holy Fathers have held the opinions we have expressed. Of the witnesses I shall bring forward some took part in that great Council; some flourished in the Church after their time; some illuminated the world long before. But their harmony is broken neither by difference of periods nor by diversity of language; like the harp their strings are

---

222 Theodoret of Cyrus, *To Dioscorus-Archbishop of Alexandria*, Epistle 83 NPNF 2, III:280.

223 Theodoret of Cyrus, *To the Bishops of Cilicia*, Epistle 84 NPNF 2, III:280-281.

224 Theodoret of Cyrus, *To Lupicinus*, Epistle 90 NPNF 2, III:283.

225 Theodoret of Cyrus, *Eranistes*, 1 (A.D. 447/451) NPNF 2 III:182.

several and separate but like the harp they make one harmonious music... Now; open your ears and receive the streams that flow from the spiritual springs."[226]

Theodotus of Ancrya [floruit A.D. 429]

"This also did the Fathers, who received from the Apostles the mystery of the incarnation (economy), teach. Thus also did the three hundred and eighteen fathers, assembled at Nicaea, decree, concerning the Only-Begotten... These are the Fathers [of Nicaea] words, which lay down for us the faith regarding the Only-Begotten, guiding light, as a rule, every human thought. For, as a rule corrects the senses that are being deceived as to the straightness of a line, proving it to be crooked, so does this statement correct the designs of men who seek to pervert our faith by their fancies. Let us follow these (Fathers), believing their words, not weaving doubtful questions. For these men say, 'we believe,' not 'we adduce demonstrations by reasonings...' For we correct not (or enquire not into) the things that have been already believed by the Fathers, but confess that these things were so done of God, faith confirming our understanding."[227]

"I have thus laid before you a sufficient refutation of the errors of these men, not from my own resources, and from myself, but, both out of the divine Scripture, and from the faith set down by the holy fathers who assembled at Nicaea."[228]

Theophilus of Alexandria [d. A.D. 412]

"Since he has strayed away into a different path from that pointed out by the rules of the apostles, he is, as a man, unworthy and profane, cast forth from the choir of Christ, and from the fellowship of his mysteries; and striving, as he does, to join the tattered and antiquated rags of the philosophers to the new and firm

[226] Ibid., 3 NPNF 2, III:234.
[227] Theodotus of Ancrya, *Expos. Symbol.*, 8, 9, 11 (A.D. 429) FOC I:99.
[228] Ibid., 24, FOC I:352.

garment of the church, and to unite the true with the false, he is driven far away from the fathers and elders who founded the church of the Saviour."[229]

Vincent of Lerins [d. ante A.D. 450]

"This being the case, he is the true and genuine Catholic who loves the truth of God, who loves the Church, who loves the Body of Christ, who esteems divine religion and the Catholic Faith above every thing, above the authority, above the regard, above the genius, above the eloquence, above the philosophy, of every man whatsoever; who sets light by all of these, and continuing steadfast and established in the faith, resolves that he will believe that, and that only, which he is sure the Catholic Church has held universally and from ancient time; but that whatsoever new and unheard-of doctrine he shall find to have been furtively introduced by some one or another, besides that of all, or contrary to that of all the saints, this, he will understand, does not pertain to religion, but is permitted as a trial, being instructed especially by the words of the blessed Apostle Paul, who writes thus in his first Epistle to the Corinthians, 'There must needs be heresies, that they who are approved may be made manifest among you:' as though he should say, This is the reason why the authors of Heresies are not forthwith rooted up by God, namely, that they who are approved may be made manifest that is, that it may be apparent of each individual, how tenacious and faithful and steadfast he is in his love of the Catholic faith."[230]

"And if one should ask one of the heretics who gives this advice, How do you prove? What ground have you, for saying, that I ought to cast away the universal and ancient faith of the Catholic Church? he has the answer ready, "For it is written;" and forthwith he produces a thousand testimonies, a thousand examples, a thousand authorities from the Law, from the Psalms, from the apostles, from the Prophets, by means of which, interpreted on a new and

---

229 Theophilus of Alexandria, *Festal Letters*, 9 (ante A.D. 412) FOC I:432-433.
230 Vincent of Lerins, *Commonitory*, 20:48 (c. A.D. 434) NPNF 2, XI:146.

wrong principle, the unhappy soul may be precipitated from the height of Catholic truth to the lowest abyss of heresy."[231]

Victor of Vita [d. A.D. 490]

"If the king wish to know our faith, which is the one, true faith, let him send to his friends, and I too will write to my brethren, that my fellow-bishops may come — men who may be able, with me, to demonstrate to you our common faith; and especially the Roman church, which is the head of all the churches.., If he wish to know the true faith, let him write to his friends that they may direct our Catholic bishops, and I will write to my fellow-bishops, because the cause of the whole Catholic church is one."[232]

Xistus III, Pope [regn. A.D. 432-440]

"Wherefore, because the faith, as the apostle says, 'is one', that faith which has triumphantly prevailed, let us believe what it behoves us to teach, and teach what it behoves us to hold. Let nothing further be allowed to novelty, because it is fitting that nothing be added to antiquity. Let not the belief of our ancestors be troubled by any admixture of filth."[233]

---

[231] Vincent of Lerins, *Commonitory*, 26:69 (c. A.D. 434) NPNF 2, XI:151.

[232] Victor of Vita, *History of the Persecutions under the Vandals*, 3 (ante A.D. 490) FOC I:328.

[233] Xistus III, Pope, *To John of Antioch*, Epistle 8 (ante A.D. 440) FOC I:185-186.

Appendix 2

Excursus on Matthew 15:1-20 and Mark 7:1-23

by Rev. Mitchell Pacwa

In the controversy of Mark 7:1-23, Jesus takes on two issues: He attacks the Pharisees and Scribes for placing the oral tradition on the same level as the written Law and He abrogates the dietary laws in Leviticus. He interprets the quote from Isaiah 29 as an attack on human tradition, a tradition which is against God's law. By this He implies that the Oral Torah is merely human tradition. However, Matthew 15:1-20 is structured a bit differently. Matthew places the quote from Isaiah 29:13 at the end of the paragraph and puts the Korban illustration at the beginning. While Mark has, "You no longer permit him to do anything for his father," Matthew reads, "You say...He need not honor his father." This makes the oral tradition run counter to the Fourth Commandment to honor one's father and mother, and therefore the tradition is void. The Isaiah 29 passage is not so strong in its present position. The Pharisees' tradition which contradicts the law at Sinai will be rooted out, but that does not destroy one's confidence in the authority of the Oral Torah. Also, while Mark 7:19 mentions, "Thus He declared all foods clean," Matthew does not mention this issue.[1]

---

[1] David Hill, *The Gospel of Matthew*, The New Century Bible Commentary, Gen. Ed. Matthew Black, (Grand Rapids, Michigan: Wm. B. Eerdmans Publishing Company, 1972).

There is no time reference to connect this section of Matthew with the immediate context. Perhaps there is significance in the mention of a stay near Gennesaret in Matt. 14:34, a small fertile plain NW of the Lake, between Capernaum and Tiberias, and a Roman town built on the site of ancient Chinnereth (cf., Dt. 3:17). Jesus had healed large numbers of people at Gennesaret (14:34-36) and many people were touching Him. Pharisees and Essenes considered it an abomination to be touched by large groups of people. This coincides with the following accounts in Matthew 15 regarding discussions of purity and impurity. Perhaps Gennesaret was a natural scene for an encounter with officials from Jerusalem.[2] Jesus is the focus of this passage, but a problem is raised in regard to His disciples' behavior. This would reflect the debate between the Matthean Church and Judaism between 80-90 AD.[3]

Mark's material is rearranged, omitting the two verses explaining the customs of the Jews regarding washing. This explanation would not be necessary for Matthew, while Mark's Gentile audience would need it. In 15:12-14, Matthew inserts the issue regarding the blind leaders of the blind (cf. Luke 6:39). This last addition does not make the pericope an attack on the Pharisees, but rather on the oral tradition.[4]

While in Mark Jesus annuls the written Law about clean and unclean (Mk. 7:19), Matthew does not include these words or their intent. Matthew ends the section with the words, "to eat with unwashed hands does not defile a man," a line which is not in Mark. The effect of these differences is that Mark makes the whole passage revolve around the question of the oral tradition rather than the written Law, which says nothing about washing hands.[5]

Regarding Matt. 15:2, Josephus calls it "the tradition of the fathers."[6] The act of washing the hands was meant to remove ceremonial defilement caused by contact with things unclean. Ablu-

---

2 Hill, p. 249.

3 Ibid., pp. 249-250.

4 G. D. Kilpatrick, *The Origins of the Gospel According to St. Matthew*, Oxford, 1946, p. 108. Hill, p. 250.

5 Hill, p. 250.

6 Ibid.,

tions were part of the faith and early religion of Israel (cf., Ex. 30:8ff; Dt. 21:6) and were common among the Qumran sectaries 1QS v. 13-14 in the *Manual of Discipline*.[7]

> No one is permitted to go into the water to obtain the purity of holy men. For men cannot be purified except they repent their evil. God regards as impure all that transgress His word. No one is to have any association with such a man either in work or in gods, lest he incur the penalty of prosecution. Rather is he to keep away from such a man in every respect, for Scripture says: 'Keep away from every false thing' [Ex. 23.7][8] (*Manual of Discipline*).

Berakoth 8:1 introduces a discussion on how "the School of Shammai and the School of Hillel differ in what concerns a meal." (8:2) The School of Shammai says: 'They wash the hands and then mix the cup.' And the School of Hillel says: 'They mix the cup and then wash the hands.' (8:3) "The School of Shammai says: 'A man wipes his hands with a napkin and lays it on a table.' And the School of Hillel says: '[He lays it] on the cushion.' (8:4) "The School of Shammai says: 'They sweep up the room and then wash the hands.' And the School of Hillel says: 'They wash the hands and then sweep up the room.'

Hagigah 2:5 (The Festal Offering), records: "For [the eating of food that is] unconsecrated of [Second] Tithe or Heave-offering, the hands need but to be rinsed; and for Hallowed Things they need to be immersed; and what concerns the Sin-offering water, if a man's hands are unclean his whole body is deemed unclean." The Hallowed Things are those which need to be offered in the Temple, are devoted to the altar and may only be consumed within the court of the Temple.[9] The immersion has to be performed in a valid Immersion-pool containing forty seahs of undrawn water, as described in tractate Miqwaoth.[10]

---

7 Ibid., p. 251.

8 Gaster, p. 53.

9 Danby, n. 16, p. 213.

10 Ibid., n. 17.

Eduyoth 5:6 (Testimonies) records: "But whom did they put under a ban? Eleazar b. Enoch, because he threw doubt on [the teaching of the Sages concerning] the cleansing of hands." This teaching was also found in Yadaim 3:2.

Aboth 3:14 R. Akiba (b. C. 50 AD, died 135) said: "Jesting and levity accustom a man to lewdness. The tradition is a fence around the Law; Tithes are a fence around riches; vows are a fence around abstinence; a fence around wisdom is silence."

Yadaim 1:1 "[To render the hands clean] a quarter-*log* or more [of water] must be poured over the hands [to suffice] for one person or even for two; a half-*log* or more [suffices] for three persons or for four; one *log* or more suffices for five or for ten or for a hundred. R. Jose says: Provided that for the last among them there remains not less than a quarter-*log*. More water may be added to the second [water that is poured over the hands], but more may not be added to the first." A quarter-*log* equals the bulk of an egg and a half.

> The custom was to give the hands a double rinsing; if for the second rinsing the remaining water was not enough to reach the wrist, more water may be added to the residue of the first quantity, but if there was not enough to reach the wrist at the first rinsing, the water may not be added to, but a fresh quarter-*log's* supply must be used.[11]

According to Yadaim 1:2: "The water may be poured over the hands out of any vessel, even from vessels made from cattle-dung or vessels of stone or vessels of [unbaked] clay. It may not be poured over the hands out of the sides of [broken] vessels or out of the flanks of a ladling jar or out of the plug of a jar, nor may a man pour it over his fellow's hands out of his cupped hands..." (2:3) "The hands are susceptible to uncleanness, and they are rendered clean [by the pouring over them of water] up to the wrist. Thus if a man had poured the first water up to the wrist and the second water beyond the wrist, and the water flowed back to the hand, the hand becomes clean; but if he poured both the first water and the second beyond the wrist, and the water flowed back to the hand, the hand

[11] Ibid., n. 9, 10, p. 778.

remains unclean. If he poured the first water over the one hand alone and then bethought himself and poured the second water over both hands, they remain unclean. If he poured the first water over both hands and then bethought himself and poured the second water over the one hand, his one hand [alone] is clean. If he had poured the water over the one hand and rubbed it on the other, it becomes unclean; but if he rubbed it on his head or on the wall [to dry it] it remains clean. The water may be poured over [the hands of] four or five persons side by side or one above the other, provided that they lie but loosely together so that the water may flow between them."

Regarding Matt. 15:5, in Nedarim 1:2 the Mishnah mentions declaring something Korban, that is an Offering which is forbidden for common use because it must be used as a Temple offering.[12] In his Appendix I, Danby defines Korban and Konam, its substitute word, as "(lit. 'an offering,' i.e. sacred as an offering dedicated to the Temple), the usual term introducing a vow to abstain from anything, or to deny another person the use of anything."[13] Nedarim 1:3-4 states: "If a man said, 'May what I eat of thine be the *Korban*' or 'as a *Korban*,' or 'a *Korban*,' it is forbidden to him. [If he said,] 'For *Korban*! I will not eat of thine,' R. Meir declares it forbidden." Nedarim 2:2 states: "[If he said,] *Korban*! If I eat of thine,' or '*Korban*! If I eat not of thine,' or 'No *Korban*! If I eat of thine,' he is not thereby bound." Nedarim 3:1-4, 10-11; 4:1-7; 5:6; 9:1, 4 also expounds on the Korban rules and exceptions.

Baba Kamma 9:10 states: "If a man said to his son, "*Konam* be any benefit thou hast of mine!' and he died, the son may inherit from him; [but if moreover he said] 'both during my life and at my death!' when he died the son may not inherit from him and he must restore [what he had received from his father at any time] to the father's sons of brothers; and if he has naught [wherewith to repay] he must borrow and the creditors come and exact payment."

Shebiith 10:3 (The Seventh Year), states: "[A loan secured by] a *prozbul* is not canceled [by the Seventh Year]. This is one of the things that Hillel the Elder ordained. When he saw that the people refrained from giving loans to one another and transgressed what

[12] Danby, n 6, p. 264
[13] Ibid., p. 794.

is written in the Law, *Beware that there be not a base thought in thine heart...*(Deut. 15:9), Hillel ordained the *prozbul*."

The term *prozbul* is an abbreviation which means, "for the will of the one's willing." According to Deut. 15:2, all loans were remitted in the seventh year. To prevent this from leading to fraud or oppression (Deut. 15:9), Hillel enacted the rule of the *prozbul*, which was a declaration made before a court of law by a creditor, and signed by witnesses, to the effect that the loan in question would not be remitted under the terms of the Seventh-Year law.[14]

Mark 7:1-23

7:1-23 is the final encounter between Jesus and His Jewish adversaries in Galilee. Their opposition and misunderstanding are in sharp contrast to the faith of the Syro-Phoenician woman in 7:24-30 and the spread of the Gospel in the Decapolis (7:31-37).[15]

The two foci of the text are defilement (7:15) and tradition (7:9, 13). The question by the Scribes and Pharisees about the disciples' omission of hand washing deals with both issues (7:5).[16] Jesus makes the relationship between Scripture and tradition the main issue, with the question of defilement as a specific example of the issue, as seen in the hand washing and kosher laws about eating.[17] Mark 7:3-4 lists laws meant to put a fence around Torah to protect it from inadvertent violations. Jesus carefully distinguishes between the law and the fence around it.

The case law is called "tradition of the elders," "tradition of men" and "your tradition" and these synonymous terms are equated to the precepts of men in Isaiah 29:13 (Mk. 7:7). Jesus opposes this "tradition of the elders." Jesus speaks positively of "commandment of God" and "word of God" to refer to the Torah. He specifically cites Ex. 20:12 and 21:17 in favor of honoring mother and father. Jesus does not attack the Law but upholds it over against the tradition that would be used to subvert these commands. Neither

---

[14] Ibid., pp. 795-796.

[15] Lamar Williamson, Jr., Mark, (Atlanta: John Knox Press, 1983), p. 133.

[16] Ibid.

[17] Ibid., p. 134

does Jesus abolish the concept of defilement or the "clean/unclean" distinction. He reinterprets the latter in light of the ethical principles of uncleanness and rejects the Pharisaic ritual understanding. Jesus sweeps away Jewish dietary laws (7:15) while affirming ethical values (7:21-23). The criterion is fidelity to the intent of God's commandment mediated through Scripture.[18]

Though Mark gives no spatial or temporal contexts for this event, he may have had two reasons to place it here. First, after stories of ministerial success (6:31-34, 54-56), and a passage about Jesus' true power and glory (6:30-52), Mark reminds readers that the blindness and pride of men, especially of the Jewish authorities, would bring Jesus' ministry to an ignominious end.[19] Second, the message of emancipation from Jewish particularism is a fitting prelude to the account of Jesus' ministry on Gentile soil (7:24ff).[20]

The mention of the leaders of Jewish thought coming from Jerusalem is a trait which indicates their more or less official status and hints at the serious consequences of the debate.[21]

The question of washing the hands is only a peg on which to question why the disciples do not conform their whole lives to the demands of the Pharisees' code. The purpose of the oral tradition was to ensure the full observance of the written law by prescribing its detailed application, settling disputed points of interpretation, and reconciling apparent inconsistencies.[22]

Regarding Mark 7:2-4, some experts in Mishnah and Talmud claim Talmudic evidence shows that at the time of Jesus, only priests had the obligation of the ritual washing of hands before meals. The ordinary layman, including Scribe and Pharisee, was not concerned about religious defilement unless he was about to enter the Temple and make a sacrifice. The lateness of these Jewish sources detracts from their value as evidence during the time of Jesus. All scholars agree that by 100 A.D. ritual washing became obligatory for all.

---

18 Ibid.

19 D. E. Nineham, *The Gospel of St. Mark*, The Pelican New Testament Commentaries, (Harmondsworth, Middlesex, England: Penguin Books, Ltd., 1963).

20 Ibid., p. 188

21 Ibid.

22 Ibid., pp. 188-189.

However, such a change would not have come about suddenly. Perhaps a move in that direction had begun during the life of Jesus.[23] A. Buchler suggests that Jews living in the Diaspora may have needed to take more care about washing things bought in the market because of the easy contact with Gentiles. However, none of these questions affect the logic of the passage (7:1-13) regarding the relationship between Scripture and tradition.[24]

Mark 7:3-4 is a redactional note to explain to Gentile readers the variety of washings (Greek: baptismous), of foods and vessels which the Pharisees hold as the tradition of the elders. For this reason the Pharisees and Scribes asked Jesus why His disciples do not follow the tradition of the elders but eat food with unclean, i.e., common or defiled (koinos) hands. In fact, Mark 7:3 literally says, "For the Pharisees and all the Jews do not eat unless they wash the hands with the fist." Without knowing their tradition, the meaning of the phrase, "with the fist," is lost to modern readers. Some possibilities are suggested: washing the hands up to the wrist; using a fistful of water to wash the hands; or rotating the hand in the fist.[25] However, the precise meaning is unknown without having the living tradition to explain it. Such a problem of interpretation points out the need for the oral tradition to explain the words of the written tradition.

The scribe was a "man learned in the Torah," a "rabbi," or an "ordained theologian." Josephus called them "exegetes of the customs of the law" (Ant. 17, 149) and "priestly scribes" (Jewish Wars, 6, 291). In the period of the kings, the scribe was a court official. From the post-exilic time, as witnessed in Ezra 7:6, 11, 12-26, Nehemiah, 1 Chronicles and Sirach, the scribe was someone learned in the Torah. After the destruction of Jerusalem, the term "scribe" is no longer used, except in the New Testament. Jewish authors call rabbis of their day "the sages" while the earlier rabbis are referred to as "scribes," as are the biblical instructors and secretaries in everyday life.

---

[23] Ibid., p. 193.

[24] Ibid.

[25] Eduard Schweizer, *The Good News According to Mark*, trans. Donald H. Madvig, (Atlanta: John Knox, 1970), p. 148.

Rabbis were a closed order of fully qualified scholars, who by ordination had received the official spirit of Moses, mediated by succession, and thereby became scribes. Their high reputation among the people came from their knowledge of the Torah and the oral tradition, plus esoteric doctrines about the origin of the cosmos and its end in the eschaton. They were considered the direct successors of the prophets; men who knew God's will and proclaimed it in instruction, judgment and teaching. Most of the Pharisees were people without theological mastery. The accusations against the scribes by Christ refer to the theological learning of the scribes and the social claims and privileges which resulted from their positions as learned men.[26] Matthew shows sympathy for the scribes by the omission or the change of their name in two-thirds of the hostile Marcan references. He leaves them in when they are essential to a legal controversy, and in the two prophecies of the Passion.[27]

Sayings About the Scribes from the Mishnah

Orlah, 3:9 concludes the section on Orlah (The Fruit of Young Trees) by distinguishing: "New Produce is forbidden by the Law everywhere; the Law of Orlah is Halakhah, and the law of Diverse Kinds is from the words of the Scribes."

Yebamoth (Sisters-in-law) deals with the levirate marriage law of Deut. 25:5-10 and the halitzah, the "drawing off of the shoe" in the case of refusal to marry the widow (Dt. 25:9-10). Yebamoth 2:3, 4 mentions the Scribes as providing ordinances to exempt from halitzah or the levirate marriage in the cases of a widow marrying a High Priest, or a divorced woman marrying a common priest, or a bastard woman or a Nethinah (descendent of the Gibeonites) marrying an Israelite, or an Israelite woman marrying a bastard or Nethin man. In 9:3 the Scribes forbid marriage to someone of the second degree of kinship.

Sanhedrin 11:3 states: "Greater stringency applies to [the observance of] the words of the Scribes than to [the observance of] the

[26] See Joachim Jeremias on "grammateus" in *Theological Dictionary of the New Testament,* ed. Gerhard Kittel, tr. Geoffrey W. Bromiley, Vol. I, (Grand Rapids, Michigan: Wm. B. Eerdmans Publishing Company, 1964), pp. 740-742.

[27] Goulder, p. 15.

words of the [written] Law. If a man said, 'There is no obligation to wear phylacteries' so that he transgresses the words of the Law, he is not culpable; [but if he said], 'There should be in them five partitions,' so that he adds to the words of the Scribes, he is culpable."

Kelim 13:7 (Vessels), in a section concerned with the susceptibility of wooden pitch-forks, winnowing-fans and rakes with broken and then repaired parts, states: "R. Joshua said, The Scribes have invented a new thing, and I cannot make answer [to them that would gainsay them]." This is repeated in Tebul Yom 4:6.

Parah 11:5 (The Red Heifer), states: "Whosoever according to the words of the Scribes requires immersion, conveys uncleanness to Hallowed Things and renders Heave-offering invalid; but common food and [Second] Tithe are permitted to him." This refers to those who eat or drink what is unclean or to vessels that have touched unclean liquids, and the hands. Parah 11:6 states: "Whosoever, whether according to what is prescribed in the Law or according to the words of the Scribes, requires immersion, conveys uncleanness, whether by contact or by carrying, to the Sin-offering water and to the ashes of the Sin-offering." These laws deal with some of the washings (Greek "baptisms") mentioned in Mark 7.

Yadaim 3:2, (a tractate dealing with the second-grade uncleanness), states: "Whatsoever renders Heave-offering invalid can convey second-grade uncleanness to the hands; the one hand can render the other unclean. So. R. Joshua. But the Sages say: 'That which suffers second-grade uncleanness to aught else.' He said to them, 'But do not the Holy Scriptures, which suffer second-grade uncleanness, render the hands unclean?' They answered, 'Ye may infer nothing about the words of the Law from the words of the Scribes and nothing about the words of the Scribes from the words of the Law, and nothing about the words of the Scribes from [other] words of the Scribes.'"

In Mark 7:6-8 Jesus applies Isaiah 29:13 to mean that the Pharisees follow their oral tradition at the expense of the written Law, even with the express purpose of having an excuse to disobey it. One problem is that this interpretation depends on the Septuagint translation of Isaiah 29:13. It is not very likely that Jesus quoted the Greek version to a Palestinian audience. Another problem is that the Pharisees saw the oral law not as a way to evade it but on the contrary to fulfill it more completely and exactly.[28] Here, Christ does not reprove individuals so much as the basic principle of legalism as pseudo-holiness. Matthew uses the term hypocrite very freely and it is used in the Didache 8:1-2.[29] Mark 7:7 quotes Isaiah 29:13, which is a prophetic criticism of superficial piety.[30]

In the controversy of this section, Jesus takes on two issues: He attacks the Pharisees and Scribes for placing the oral tradition on the same level as the written Law and He abrogates the dietary laws in Leviticus. He interprets the quote from Isaiah 29 as an attack on human tradition as against God's law. By this He implies that the Oral Torah is merely human tradition.[31]

Since the quote of Isaiah 29:13 is from the LXX, and only the LXX has relevance to the point of this passage, perhaps this was a text used by the early Christians in their polemic against the Jews (Col. 2:8f; Titus 1:14). St. Mark may have heard about the text in that environment and came to use it here. Yet, the style of speech and the issue is entirely Jesus' style.[32]

Some passages in the New Testament use "tradition" to refer to the basic teachings of the Gospel (e.g. 1 Cor. 11:2; 15:3; 2 Thess 2:15; 3:6). All interpreters of Scripture are guardians and passers-on of tradition. Jesus' attack in the present text is against "*your* tradition which you hand on" (7:13 TEV). The problem addressed is tradition alienated from the word of God. By emphasizing the secondary place of human traditions and the primary place of the commandment of God, this text calls us beyond arguments over what is old and what is new to a concern for what is vital."[33]

In Mark 7:11, Korban is what a person says when dedicating an object to God so as to withdraw it from ordinary use without handing it over directly to the Temple treasury.[34] Regarding Mark 7:9-13, later Jewish commentators agreed with Jesus' point about

---

28 Nineham, pp. 189-190.
29 Schweizer, p. 148.
30 Ibid.
31 Goulder, p. 19.
32 Nineham, p. 194.
33 Williamson, p. 136.
34 Schweizer, p. 149.

the case of something directed to parents vs. Korban. Not enough is known about the Korban practice being criticized here. What seems to be meant is that a man can evade his obligation to his parents by vowing to give the Temple treasury (either actually or by legal fiction) the earnings that might otherwise have been available for their support. It is possible that if a man informed his parents with a solemn vow that anything they might have hoped to get from him was henceforth *for them* as though it had been dedicated to the Temple, it was withheld to prevent the parents touching it, although the son retained it none the less. But the word Korban was used without stress on its literal meaning, rather as a simple formula for a particular oath or vow. Jesus may have had in mind a man who, using the solemn Korban oath, swore (perhaps in a fit of passion) that he would not support his parents. If the rabbis upheld this oath, it was a handle for the evasion of a fundamental duty.

Mark 7:14 marks a break in the section as Jesus summons a new audience. The subsequent comment is only very loosely related to the Pharisees' question or to Jesus' two replies to it. The comment is very radical, and is along the lines of the prophetic tradition, undercutting the basis for a large part of the written Law on kosher foods. While this comment of Christ teaches that the only type of cleanness which matters for religion is moral cleanness, the written Law maintains that ritual cleanness is of vital importance in God's eyes. Jesus' statement emancipates people from obedience to large parts of the written Law, precisely at a point where He is attacking the Pharisees for not taking the written Law seriously enough. For this reason, some commentators see this as not an authentic saying of Christ but an invention of a "liberalizing" party in the early Church. However, B. H. Branscomb in the Moffatt Commentaries and Nineham consider the saying to be authentic, though the original statement may have been less sweeping. Just as Christ never abrogated the Sabbath and its laws, He did ignore and reject the laws about Sabbath work on occasions when human needs were at stake.[35]

Mark 7:15 is represented as a parable in the Marcan sense of an obscure utterance which can only be interpreted by those who

[35] Nineham, p. 191.

have the key to it, as in Mk. 4:10, 34. For this reason, here, too, the disciples go off with Jesus privately to learn the key to this saying in 7:18-19 and in 20-23. The catalogue of sins is similar to St. Paul's lists, suggesting the influence of the Hellenistic world. However, such lists were not unknown among Jews.

Mark 7:16 states: "If any man has ears to hear, let him hear." This is the reading of the Western, Caesarean, Syriac and Byzantine texts and of some Egyptian manuscripts. It could have dropped out of a precursor of the Vaticanus and Sinaiticus manuscripts by assimilation to Matthew 15, where it is apparently missing.[36]

Mark 7:19 states: "Thus He declared all foods clean." This may be the background of Romans 14:14, where St. Paul says, "I know and am persuaded in the Lord Jesus that nothing is unclean in itself."[37]

In Mark 7:22 Jesus warns against the evil eye which defiles a man from his heart. Prov. 22:9 speaks of the generous man as the "good of eye." Matt. 6:22 speaks of the eye as the lamp of the body, and the generous eye makes the whole body ful of light.[38]

Pirke Aboth 2:9 R. Johannan b. Zakkai said: "Go forth and see which is the good way to which a man should cleave. R. Eliezer [b. Hyrcanus] said, A good eye. R. Joshua said, A good companion. R. Jose said, A good neighbor. R. Simeon said, One that sees what will be. R. Eleazar said, A good heart. He said to them: I approve the words of Eleazar b. Arak more than your words, for in his words are your words included. He said to them: Go forth and see which is the evil way which a man should shun. R. Eliezer said, An evil eye. R. Joshua said, An evil companion. R. Jose said, An evil neighbor. R. Simeon said, He that borrows and does not repay. He that borrows from a man is as one that borrows from God, for it is written, *The wicked borroweth and* payeth not again but the righteous dealeth graciously and giveth [Ps. 37:21]. R. Eleazar said, An evil heart. He said to them, I approve the words of Eleazar b. Arak more than your words for in his words are your words included."

---

36 Goulder, p. 379.

37 Ibid., p. 147.

38 Ibid., p. 302.

Pirqe Aboth 2:11 R. Joshua said: "The evil eye and the evil nature and hatred of mankind put a man out of the world." Pirqe Aboth 5:19: "He in whom are these three things is of the disciples of Abraham our father; but [he in whom are] three other things is of the disciples of Balaam the wicked. A good eye and a humble spirit and a lowly soul — [they in whom are these] are of the disciples of Abraham our father. An evil eye, a haughty spirit, and a proud soul — [they in whom are these] are of the disciples of Balaam the wicked."

In Mark 7:21-22, the list of vices corresponds with similar compilations which probably arose in Hellenistic Judaism (cf. E.g. Romans 1:29-31; Gal. 5:19-21; Col. 3:5,8; 1 Tim. 1:9-10; 2 Tim. 3:2-5). "Doing evil" is placed alongside covetousness here and in Rom. 1:29, too.[39]

The evil eye in a Jewish context meant envy, but if the list is from a Gentile provenance, it may mean the malevolent glance which casts a spell.[40]

---

[39] Scweizer, p. 150.

[40] Nineham, pp. 196-197.

Appendix 3

A Formal Debate on *Sola Scriptura*

During 1997, two debates occurred between Catholic spokesman **Patrick Madrid**, editor-in-chief of the Catholic apologetic magazine *Envoy*, and Protestant spokesman **Douglas Jones**, editor-in-chief of the Protestant/Reformed magazine *Credenda/Agenda.* We have recorded those debates in this appendix. The first debate was published in *Credenda/Agenda*, while the second was published in *Re:generation Quarterly* (Vol. 3, Num. 3).

As we record these debates, our editor, **Robert Sungenis**, will offer comments to help the reader follow the course of the debate; the arguments being proposed by each participant; and additional critique of the position advanced by Douglas Jones. These editorial comments will be confined to the footnotes. Here is the debate:

Douglas Jones: Many modern evangelicals and Roman Catholics haggle over the Anabaptistic notion of *solo* rather than *sola Scriptura.* The classical Protestant notion of that doctrine was never intended as a condemnation of tradition or a denigration of the authority of the Church. Both Scripture and the Church are genuinely authoritative norms, not mere advisory boards. Protestants maintain that Scripture is the ultimate authority, with the Church serving as a subordinate, though real, authority. In practice, conservative Roman Catholicism reverses this hierarchy, necessitating an infallible Church. The debate with Rome over *sola Scriptura* really turns on the question of Rome's claim to infallibility. If it can't justify that claim, then *sola Scriptura* takes the day rather easily.[1]

Patrick Madrid: Since you concede that the Church is "genuinely authoritative," not a mere advisory board, I have this debate already half won. The other half will be to demonstrate that this means Scripture is not sufficient in se for all matters of doctrine. For if, to be correctly interpreted, Scripture needs a magisterial Church (as I believe Christ intended), then *sola Scriptura*, as promulgated by the Westminster Confession, is an erroneous concept. "Geneva" asserts: "The only infallible rule of interpretation of Scripture is the Scripture itself (WCF I, 9)." Rome responds: "Tradition, Sacred Scripture and the teaching authority of the Church... are so

---

1 Essentially, Jones claims that Madrid's argument must center on defending church infallibility rather than on critiquing *sola scriptura*. If Madrid cannot do this, Jones asserts that he wins the debate by default. Although it is true that the Catholic apologetic must eventually defend church infallibility, it certainly does not have to be nor should it be the focus of Madrid's approach. Jones is attempting to make the debate an issue of biblical infallibility versus church infallibility, but not only is this too simplistic, it also distorts the main issue of the debate, i.e., the validity or invalidity of *sola scriptura* itself. Jones's position implicitly, but wrongly, equates (A) Scripture's inerrancy with (B) *sola scriptura*. No faithful Catholic would ever question inerrancy, but he would not conclude that inerrancy necessitates a belief in *sola scriptura*, even if the Church were not infallible. If *sola scriptura* purports to provide the Christian with correct answers to questions of faith and morals (we will call this goal C), then when we consider that one must first interpret Scripture correctly to arrive at correct answers, the main question that Jones must address is *not* how he gets from A to B, but how he gets from A to C. In addition, Jones' definition of *sola scriptura*, which he later specifies in the second debate as "...the classical Protestant view with deep medieval and patristic roots, namely the teaching that Scripture is the only infallible and supreme criterion of truth" simply does not have the so-called "roots" that he claims it has. Our challenge to Jones is to produce just one recognized patristic witness that understood Scripture as the "only infallible criterion of truth." Although the Fathers certainly recognized that Scripture was infallible, none of them ever said it was the ***only*** infallible truth.

linked and joined together that one cannot stand without the others" (Dei Verbum 10).[2]

Douglas Jones: Notice, though, what you do here. You have to treat the classical Protestant teaching on the genuine authority of the Church (potestas ordinis) as though it were a modern "concession." But classical Protestants never held to such Anabaptistic views as you suppose. Connected to this, your third sentence assumes that genuine spiritual authority requires infallibility. This is clearly false, though. We would agree that parents have genuine spiritual authority without being infallible. Isn't it a non sequitur, then, for Rome to insist the Church must be infallible to be authoritative? If you want to undermine the classical view, you need to criticize, not sole sufficiency, but the claim that Scripture alone is the ultimate and infallible norm.[3]

Patrick Madrid: Stop flailing at the poor Anabaptists. It remains for you to make good the WCF's claim that "the only infallible rule of interpretation of Scripture is the Scripture itself." Where does Scripture teach that? Which pre-Reformation Church council or creed taught that? Scripture doesn't and the Church never did.

---

2 Madrid is attempting to corner Jones by showing that if Jones admits to a "genuinely authoritative" Church then this substantially weakens the *sola scriptura* position, since the Scripture's interpretation is subject to the authority of the Church. Having pointed this out, Madrid feels that he can move on to the next issue, that is, Scripture's inherent insufficiency to address, let alone decide, all matters of doctrine.

3 Jones says several things here. In order to distinguish himself from the anti-Church/antiestablishment mentality of the sixteenth century Anabaptists, Jones tries to assert a healthy understanding of Church authority, and thereby claims to satisfy Madrid's emphasis on the necessity of the Church, but he does so without conceding to Madrid the dimension of infallibility. His example, that parental authority does not necessitate that the parent be infallible, seems appropriate and to the point. By posing this seemingly logical answer, Jones tries to force Madrid back to explaining why Scripture's infallibility does not necessitate a belief in *sola scriptura*, rather than allow Madrid to attack *sola scriptura* on the basis that Scripture is not sufficient to answer all matters of doctrine.

(Historically, the "classical" view is Rome's, not Geneva's.) The "parent/child" analogy doesn't obtain. One needn't assume the need for an infallible Church. I recognize this as Christ's intention (viz. the historical and scriptural evidence). And you've just demonstrated why Scripture requires an infallible Church, by claiming the Anabaptist view is "incorrect." The Anabaptists sure think it's what Scripture teaches. Who decides? Aren't they just being consistent with the WCF claim?[4]

Douglas Jones: Flailing Anabaptists must remain an important hobby, especially since Rome tries to force everyone into an individualistic mold. For example, you read your cite of the WCF as claiming that only individuals can infallibly interpret Scripture, a position rejected by the Westminster divines and the Reformers. The Church has genuine interpretive authority like a supreme court, but Rome's novelty is to insist that this authority must be infallible. That runs contrary to Scriptural descriptions of an authoritative Church which in abnormal times may teach falsehood (Jer.

---

4 Madrid strikes a crucial blow here — a blow from which Jones never really recovers during the remainder of the debate. By the mere mention of another rival denomination, the Anabaptists, that disagrees with Jones's view of Scripture and authority, Madrid shows implicitly that a more controlling authority is needed to preserve doctrinal purity than Jones' concept of authority, however "genuine" he believes it to be. In addition, Madrid appeals to Scripture and history and posits that they offer no support for the concept of *sola scriptura*. Madrid also claims that Jones's attempt to support the Protestant position by contrasting infallible divine authority with fallible parental authority is not valid in this debate because although Jones' estimation of parental authority is correct, still, parents are not identical with the Church. What Madrid means is this: parents, though they make decisions on faith and morals for their children, do so not only by their own reasoning abilities but primarily under the guidance of the Church. Parents themselves are not infallible, yet they can give trustworthy guidance to their children only because an infallible Church tells them the right answers to crucial questions, especially in difficult areas of life whose solutions are not immediately apparent. In this way, the parents, though fallible in their nature, can provide infallible truth for their children. In other words, parents have their own authority but they themselves are subject to and derive authority from the Church.

6:13; 14:14; Is. 29:10; Ez. 22:25; 2 Pet. 2:2; Acts 20:29; 1 Tim. 4:1). You ask "who decides?" The answer does require authority, but how does it require infallibility?[5]

---

5 Perhaps sensing that Madrid is correct about the Anabaptists, Jones inadvertently concedes Madrid's point by having no ready reply to it except sarcastically to label the attack on Anabaptism a "hobby," which, if anything, only reinforces Madrid's point. Jones introduces Catholicism's claim to infallibility as a "novelty," which, he says, runs contrary to instances in Scripture in which the Church has taught falsehood. Notice that Jones's accusation of "novelty" is not based on the history of Christendom (possibly because it is obvious even to him that the Church, for sixteen centuries prior to the Reformation, believed in the Church's infallibility), but on his interpretation of Scripture. In other words, Catholicism has a "novel" interpretation of Scripture compared to his "true" interpretation. This implicitly strikes a blow to Jones's position simply because Jones must answer (but does not) where the true novelty lies when those in later centuries who claim the correct interpretation are suddenly found overturning sixteen centuries of consistent interpretation. Of course, this *overturning* of interpretations is precisely the history of Protestantism from its very beginning — each denomination *overturning* the interpretation, whether great or small, of a previous denomination. But more importantly, the Scriptures that Jones chooses to prove his accusation of "novelty" he, ironically, wrongly interprets (notice that we are disagreeing with Jones's interpretation, further demonstrating that Scripture is insufficient to resolve this issue). The verses he chooses (Jr. 6:13; 14:14...Acts 20:29; 1 Tim. 4:1) fail to prove that the Church cannot preserve infallible doctrine in the midst of apostate members. For example, even Jones's use of Paul's warning to Timothy in 1 Tim. 4:1 that "some would depart from the faith" implies that at least some faithful individuals will remain in the Church and will identify those departing as apostates. Paul indicates this himself by saying only "some" would depart, not the whole Church. Jeremiah 6:13, and other such verses, convey the same truth. The mere fact that the Lord chose Jeremiah to write the truth concerning the apostates of his day shows that there are some left, like Jeremiah, who preserve the truth of God. In fact, so well did he preserve the truth that even after 70 years of domination in the foreign land of Babylon, Daniel the prophet suddenly realized that the time of captivity was over (cf. Dan. 9:2). In the days of Elijah, as in the days of Jeremiah, only 7,000 did not fall into apostasy (cf. Rom. 11:4-5). Even during the Arian heresy of the fourth to sixth centuries AD, many of the bishops of the Church sided with Arius, and only a few, like Athanasius, preserved the truth, yet is was an infallible truth which the infallible councils of Nicea, Constantinople and Chalcedon codified, and which the infallible Catholic Church has preserved to this day.

Patrick Madrid: I'm simply trying to force you to defend the WCF claim, but you seem unwilling to do so. You haven't explained how Scripture can be its own "infallible interpreter," where Scripture claims this, and when Scripture ever actually functioned as such. These elements must be proven if you're to vindicate the WCF version of *sola Scriptura*. I contend that you can't prove them since your position is epistemologically untenable. The "who decides?" dilemma pivots on the a priori question: "which 'church' is the Church?" Under the WCF rubric, you can't even determine that with certitude; just as you can't be completely certain the Anabaptist or any view (Rome's, for example) is incorrect. That certainty requires infallibility, otherwise, you're simply guessing.[6]

Douglas Jones: Actually, I've defended that WCF claim in each of my previous paragraphs; it's just another aspect of the teaching that Scripture is the "supreme judge" (I, X). If Scripture alone is ultimate and infallible, then it certainly doesn't contradict itself (I, IX). So, for our discussion, anything showing the infallibility of Scripture and the fallibility of the Church is an argument for *sola Scriptura*. I've supplied passages pointing to the Church's fallibility. I now argue by challenge that Rome's exegetical arguments for infallibility are simple non sequiturs. Moreover, your epistemological argument for infallibility starts an infinite regress: if we need infallibility to interpret Scripture, then we'll need it to interpret the Church, and so on. What help is that?[7]

---

6 Appropriately, Madrid keeps hammering away at the same points: (1) that Jones must prove *sola scriptura* from Scripture; (2) that without some form of infallibility, Jones cannot be certain of virtually anything he proposes, and (3) that Jones's previous appeal to a "genuinely authoritative" church is meaningless because Jones can't establish which church is the true church.

7 It is becoming obvious, despite Madrid's repeated requests, that Jones is not going to support *sola scriptura* by direct evidence from Scripture. Rather, he relies on the infallibility of Scripture (via the *Westminster Confession of Faith*), and on his opinion that the Church is fallible. Again, Jones believes he can win the debate by default. He then attacks the issue from a different angle by claiming that even if the Church provided infallible judgments, those judgments are subject to the fallible interpretation of the members of the Church. We can answer this in two ways: (1) attempting to deny the Church's infallibility by focusing on the possibility of fallible interpretations of the Church's infallible

Patrick Madrid: Please furnish even one example of Scripture interpreting itself. I reject your interpretation of the verses you cited and your premise that "Scripture alone is . . . infallible." On the contrary, Christ's Church is infallible (cf. Matt. 10:40, 16:18, 18:18, 28:20; Luke 10:16; John 14:25-26,16:13; 1 Thess. 2:13; 1 Tim. 3:15). Your argument entails the conclusion that the dogmas promulgated by Nicea I, Ephesus, and Chalcedon were merely fallible, as was the Church's determination of the NT canon. (If this is true, we're all in big trouble!) Your syllogism is flawed, and it's no non sequitur to claim that Scripture requires an infallible Church (cf. 1 Pet. 1:20-21; 3:15-16). And this debate is your perfect opportunity to prove otherwise: Please demonstrate how Scripture can "infallibly interpret itself" so as to solve this particular standoff.[8]

Douglas Jones: Your ongoing concern about self-interpretation is really not particularly relevant to *sola Scriptura*. "Interpreting itself" is just another way of saying that clearer passages shed light upon the less clear. Every ultimate norm, including yours, does that (Jn 10:35). More to the point are your proofs for Church infallibility. First, regarding councils, you again assume that fallibility entails falsehood. Must parents and courts always judge falsely? Second, the passages cited prove too much or too little. Those speak-

---

[7 cont.] judgments is a double-edge sword which also neutralizes Jones's position, since, by the same token, if the members are going to incorrectly interpret infallible Scripture (as the differing Protestant interpretations of Scripture have proven will continually occur) then Jones should conclude that *Scripture's* infallibility is of no practical use either. The "infinite regress" argument cuts both ways. (2) No matter how much infallibility an entity claims, there is always the "human" factor to confront. God has the same problem with humans. However, with its multitudinous voices of authority, Protestantism certainly has much more of the "human" factor to face than Catholicism does. Catholicism, despite the dissension among some of its members, has not changed one dogma in its two thousand years of history. As dissension surfaces, the Church refines and confines its dogma more and more so as to keep the "human" element to a minimum. Protestantism has no such controls. The more it refines and confines, the more denominations they create.

[8] Relentless in his pursuit, Madrid insists that Jones show *from Scripture* the very points he is trying to prove.

ing of leading the Church into "all truth" clearly go beyond Rome's very narrow subset of infallible truths. Why preclude science and economics? Others cited speak of preserving the Church, but something can be preserved without being infallible. Infallibility simply doesn't follow.[9]

Patrick Madrid: Actually, the claim that "the only infallible rule of interpretation of Scripture is the Scripture itself" lies at the very heart of this disputation. Can Scripture "decide" which passages are clear and which are unclear? (Matthew 16:18-19 seems quite clear to me.) Of course not, but the Church can, and before the

9 Jones attempts to neutralize Madrid's argument by saying that "interpreting itself" simply means that one must use clearer propositions to interpret unclear propositions, and that Catholicism itself uses this method. What Jones fails to see is that without a foundation of certainty he cannot be sure which passages are clear and which are unclear. For example, John 3:5 states that a man cannot enter the kingdom of heaven unless he is born of water and the Spirit. Catholics, Lutherans, Anglicans, Methodists, et al., look at this verse and conclude that it is very "clear," namely, that a person must be baptized with actual water — water that provides the means of grace — in order to enter heaven. Presbyterians, Baptists, and many other denominations look at this verse and also conclude that it is very "clear," except that they deny both that it teaches baptismal water is the means of grace and that the water is necessary for salvation. Now, who has the right interpretation of this supposedly "clear" passage? Appealing to other texts in the New Testament concerning baptism will not help, since all of them are just as "clear," (or should we say "just as ambiguous") as John 3:5. The point is that there is no way you can tell from the raw text whether John meant that the water's effects are literal or symbolic. The only way you can know is to ask the apostle John. The Catholic Church asserts that she indeed possesses that precise information from John, for it is information that she preserves in her living Tradition and which the ongoing Ecumenical Councils for two thousand years have infallibly confirmed. On another issue, Jones asks: "Second, the passages cited prove too much or too little. Those speaking of leading the Church into 'all truth' clearly go beyond Rome's very narrow subset of infallible truths. Why preclude science and economics?" Here Jones distorts the passage in John 16:13 concerning the Spirit guiding the Church into "all truth." The Church does not teach infallibly on "science and economics" simply because those subjects are not part of the "all truth" that the Spirit gave the Church. Not surprisingly, no early

Reformation the Church consistently taught the Catholic model of authority, not *sola Scriptura*. Since you've admitted the Church has real authority, why don't you adhere to its historic teaching? Or is this authority merely a convenient prop? Finally, fallibility entails the possibility not the necessity of error. Under your "fallible Church" rubric, you can never be certain which scriptural interpretations are erroneous and which aren't.[10]

Douglas Jones: Careful. Your challenge "can Scripture 'decide'?" again works only against *solo* not *sola Scriptura*. We both agree, along with classical Protestants and the WCF, that the Church alone should decide authoritatively. She weighs passages for clarity, allowing one passage to clarify another. This model is far more historic than Rome's late novelties, and I gladly adhere to it. And if an infallible Church provides the certainty you demand, why is Rome still debating the meaning of Trent? Subjectivism can't just stop with Scripture. You have yet to show how my arguments against

---

9 cont. Father or Church Council ever claimed the Church had infallible truth on such topics. All the truth that the Spirit wanted to give the Church he gave to her. It was the truth God wanted her to know. In fact, even the Spirit himself is limited in what He gives the Church, for according to the rest of John 16:13 he "will not speak on his own; he will speak only what he hears..." Thus the content of "all truth" depends on what the Father has given to the Spirit to say, and apparently it does not include "science and economics." Jones claims that "infallibility simply doesn't follow" from the Scriptures Madrid presented to him, yet it is precisely the Spirit's intrinsic *integrity* as the *Truth-giver* that proves the case for an infallible Church, for if the Spirit is going to lead the Church into the truth He hears from the Father, would not the Spirit's truth be infallible? If not, Jones must concede to the absurd proposition that the Spirit gives *fallible* information. If, as Catholicism asserts, the truth it receives is infallible, does it not follow that the Spirit would want that truth preserved for the life of the Church, especially since Jesus tells the faithful in John 14:16 that the Spirit will be with them "till the end of the age"?

10 Madrid continues to show the total subjectivity of Jones's position. Every time Jones attempts to take his argument back one step, he invariably exposes another subjective proposition that is supported by an equally subjective proof.

Roman infallibility fail. But can we at least agree that if the Church is fallible, then only Scripture can be ultimate and infallible?[11]

Patrick Madrid: We agree that the Church weighs passages, but notice that it has always done considerably more than that. The aforementioned councils show that since apostolic times the magisterium saw itself as teaching infallibly, imposing its interpretation of Scripture as dogmatic (Acts 15:28, 1 Thess. 2:13). St. Athanasius explained in De Decretis that First Nicea's definition of Christ as homoousios with the Father was not a merely fallible interpretation. This is hardly a "Roman novelty," as you allege. (The nascent Catholic model is visible in Acts 15:15-35, 16:4.) And remember, Orthodoxy also rejects *sola Scriptura*. Like the Catholic Church, they have preserved the ancient Christian teach-

[11] By creating a distinction between the more extreme *solo scriptura* and more moderate *sola scriptura*, Jones attempts to show that he respects Church authority and history, at least with more respect than the radical wings of the Reformation such as the Anabaptists. From this stance, Jones tries to create a consensus with Madrid by agreeing that "the Church alone should decide authoritatively." But as Madrid posed earlier to Jones, who does Jones think "the Church" is? The best Jones can do is to preface his concept of the Church with designations such as "classical Protestants and the WCF." But just who are "classical Protestants," and which denominations do the propositions of the WCF exclude as not being part of "the Church who decides authoritatively," and which of the various revisions of the Westminster Confession is Jones referring to? Although he asserts that "Rome is still debating the meaning of Trent," at least there is ***only one*** version of Trent that Catholics need consider. As for "classical Protestants," does this include Heinrich Zwingli, who Martin Luther said was under the influence of the devil because he didn't believe in the real presence of Christ in the Eucharist? Does it include Philip Melanchthon, who eventually repudiated the predestinarian views of Luther? Does it include John Calvin who denied Luther's view that baptism was a means of grace and salvation? In short, we can write a whole book listing the major doctrinal differences among the so-called "classical Protestants." Is this "the Church [which] should alone decide authoritatively" and the one with which Jones expects to form a consensus with Madrid?

ing that the Church, at least in its ecumenical councils, teaches infallibly. Historically, *sola Scriptura* is the novelty.[12]

Douglas Jones: There is simply no such thing as the historic view on these matters. Several competing views always existed side by side (though not the *solo* view). Even by the late medieval period, the Church still struggled to clarify notions of tradition and Scripture. And Athanasius's De Decretis is a particularly weak buttress for Rome, since Athanasius appeals to countless Scriptures to justify Nicea's language. Why not just cite the council and cease all disputing, as Rome's notion entails? And Eastern Orthodoxy openly rejects Rome's sweeping claims about definitive conciliar infallibility. But quite apart from these concerns, you still haven't provided any rebuttal to the arguments against Roman infallibility. If that fails, then *sola Scriptura* follows easily.[13]

---

12 Madrid has finally turned the tables on Jones. He rightly points out that it is precisely *sola scriptura* which is the "novelty" in this discussion. Moreover, Madrid will not allow Jones to hide behind the weak facade of the "Church alone should decide authoritatively," forcing him instead to address the Scriptures that speak of a strong, decisive, unwavering and infallible authority residing in the Church exemplified by such passages as Acts 15:15-35; 16:4; 1 Tim. 3:15; Matt. 16:18-19; 18:15-18; et al. The reader will notice, however, that Jones does not attempt to address these passages in the remainder of the debate.

13 Jones attempts to create the impression that as long as there is any controversy about doctrine, then the infallibility of the Church is invalid and impotent. This is far from the case. In fact, it is precisely the controversy about doctrine that leads the Church to formulate its infallible decisions, and subsequently conform its members more and more to that truth. As for the Church "struggling to clarify notions of tradition and Scripture [up until] the late medieval period," it was precisely the dissensions of Wycliffe and Luther in the late medieval period that forced the Church at the Council of Trent to finally and formally dogmatize its beliefs on Tradition and Scripture. This does not mean, however, that there was no consensus on Tradition and Scripture prior to Trent. Further, Jones's reference to Athanasius's "appeals to countless Scriptures to justify Nicea's language" does not support Jones's position as much as it does the Catholic position, for Catholicism holds that Scripture, Tradition and the Magisterium work in conjunction with one another, which is exactly what Athanasius is illustrating in the aforementioned citation. Anyone who doubts this should consult Athanasius's works, which Chapters 5, 8 and Appendix 1 of this book detail exhaustively.

Patrick Madrid: Your dismissal of De Decretis as "weak" evidence boggles the mind. Athanasius composed it precisely to refute the Arian claim that the Church teaches fallibly and erroneously. He did appeal "just to the council" to quell the dispute (as Orthodoxy does): "The Confession arrived at Nicea was, we should say, more sufficient and enough by itself for the subversion of all religious heresies and for the security and furtherance of the doctrine of the Church" (Ad Afros). Earlier, you mentioned "Rome's very narrow subset of infallible truths." Now you decry "Rome's sweeping claims about ... infallibility." You're dodging here. Ultimately, to vindicate *sola Scriptura*, you must explain how Scripture infallibly interprets itself. So far you haven't.[14]

Douglas Jones: You'll find the explanation of self-interpretation in my fourth through sixth paragraphs. My "Sweeping" and "narrow" describe different features. Interestingly, you don't cite De Decretis itself. There's nothing in it or Ad Afros contrary to a classical Protestant view. Sufficiency is far from Roman infallibility. I suspect you're still pursuing Anabaptist ghosts. Elsewhere Athanasius actually understates conciliar authority more than I would, claiming, "Vainly do they run about with the pretext that they have demanded councils for the faith's sake; for divine Scripture is sufficient above all things" (C. of Arm. & Sel.). I'm sincerely curious why you haven't rebutted my criticism that your case proves too much and too little. Without a response, doesn't my syllogism stand uncontested?[15]

---

[14] Persistently, Madrid keeps pushing his argument, i.e., that Jones must prove the tenets of *sola scriptura* from Scripture. So far, Jones has not offered one Scripture to support his view. Rather, Jones insists on having Madrid prove Church infallibility. All Jones has offered is theory, but he hasn't shown how either Scripture or the divisive history of Protestantism supports the theory. "Theory" may differ greatly from what actually works in practical life.

[15] Again, we refer the reader to chapters 5, 8 and Appendix 1 of this book for a most thorough cataloging and examination of the writings of the patristic witnesses. The reader will clearly see that Athanasius is not what Jones portrays him to be.

Patrick Madrid: Remember, fallibility entails the possibility, not the inevitability, of teaching error. This possibility creates your dilemma. Under *sola Scriptura*, you can't know with certitude if Scripture is being interpreted correctly. Agreeing with an interpretation is vastly different from knowing it's true. This is why your criticisms and syllogism fail. The passages cited here cannot, in 115 words, be adequately analyzed, but I have indeed rebutted your understanding of them repeatedly, showing that epistemologically, historically, and practically, *sola Scriptura* is a paper tiger. It's not taught in Scripture (you've provided no direct evidence), it's alien to historic Christian teaching and praxis, and it simply doesn't work. If it did, why doesn't Scripture infallibly resolve this standoff?

Douglas Jones: Why doesn't Roman infallibility resolve this standoff? In the end, all your epistemological and practical objections apply equally against your own position. Similarly, if fallibility always precluded "certitude," then unless we had infallible civil courts, we could never have justice with certitude. But that's absurd (Ezek. 45:9). Throughout, my argument has been: (P1) Either Scripture or the Church alone is infallible and ultimate; (P2) It's not the case that the Church alone is infallible and ultimate (my paragraphs three and five); (C) Scripture alone is infallible and ultimate. With this, the Church is a genuinely authoritative, sufficient (as with Athanasius), anti-individualistic, and reformable Court. Both Rome and modern evangelicalism join arms in rejecting these ancient truths.[16]

Well, Patrick, we have to stop somewhere. We both have more to say. I've wanted to have this little chat for some time. And you have been, as always, a gentleman and an honorable opponent. I wish we could be on the same side. You have my sincere thanks.

---

[16] Magisterial infallibility in the Catholic Church may perhaps be no more equipped to solve the "standoff" between Catholics and Protestants than was Jesus, who though infallible could not solve the standoff between himself and the Pharisees, the Scribes, the Teachers of the Law, and many other would-be interpreters of Scripture in his day.

The Second Debate[17]

Madrid's Question: The Westminster Confession of Faith asserted that "The only infallible rule of interpretation of Scripture is the Scripture itself." I contend that this proposition is unworkable. Given the substantive doctrinal divisions among Protestant denominations that adhere to *sola Scriptura* can you explain how Scripture infallibly interprets itself and show post-Reformation examples of this?

Jones's Response to Madrid's Question:

We should always find ourselves with some sorrow when entering into these sorts of discussions. Many things beautiful in medieval Christendom have been lost, and both Rome and Protestantism share the blame. But the issues surrounding the authority of Scripture and the Church are not light or dismissible, for they are stained with martyrs' blood and marked out by ancient covenantal threats. Most of the differences between classical Protestantism on one side and Rome and Constantinople on the other stem from a background clash between Hebraism and Hellenism. The Reformation was one of the fruits of the late medieval period's attempt to throw off the shackles of Hellenism and revive Hebraic, covenantal thinking. When classical Protestants, especially those of us in the Reformed tradition, gaze at the issues which separate these groups (redemption, authority, worship), many of us cannot help but see that Rome and the East have not yet extricated themselves from the dark labyrinths of Plato and Aristotle. Thematically, Protestants carried forth Athanasius's praise of the demise of Greek philosophy — "not only does the wisdom of the Greeks no longer make any progress, but that which used to be is disappearing." But the battle has been longer than he expected.

My friend Patrick Madrid, whom I greatly respect, asks a question above about *sola Scriptura* which shows some of this Hellenistic/Hebraic conflict. One of the biggest contemporary confusions about the Protestant doctrine is that between sola and what can be called *solo* Scriptura. These two notions are really worlds

[17] We offer the second debate without editorial comment.

apart. The former (sola) is the classical Protestant view with deep medieval and patristic roots, namely the teaching that Scripture is the only infallible and supreme criterion of truth. Whereas the latter view (*solo*) is the more anabaptistic, individualistic, evangelical view that Scripture is the only location of truth and authority. The difference between the two views is akin to the difference between a constitution as the highest law of the land over an authoritative court, on one side, and a constitution as the only law of the land without any courts. Tragically, the anabaptistic view has clearly taken the field in modern evangelicalism.

Richard Muller has noted that the Reformation arguments "against the idea of a co-equal authority of Scripture, tradition, and church, typically summarized by the phrase *sola Scriptura*, must never be taken as a condemnation of tradition or a denigration of the authority of the church... The Reformation took as its point of departure the late medieval debate over the relation of Scripture to tradition and assumed that tradition stood as a subordinate norm under the authority of Scripture and derived its authority from Scripture."

Patrick's question misses the heart of the debate, since all sides invoke self-interpretation. All "self-interpretation" means is that there is no higher epistemological appeal; the highest norm must be consistent with itself. I suspect Patrick is personifying "self-interpretation" and reading it as making the constitution also the court itself, but that is the anabaptistic position. Elsewhere the WCF teaches that the Church holds the power of interpretation. Chrysostom expresses self-interpretation well: "Sacred Scripture whenever it wants to teach us something like this, gives its own interpretation, and doesn't let the reader go astray... So, I beg you, block your ears against all distractions of that kind, and let us follow the norm of Sacred Scripture." Historical examples of this can be found at just about every ecclesiastical council, pre- and post-Reformation.

Since we share a commitment to the infallibility of Scripture, the heart of the debate with Rome over *sola Scriptura* really turns on the question of the Church's infallibility. If Rome can't justify that claim, then *sola Scriptura* prevails rather easily. *Sola Scriptura* maintains that the Church has genuine interpretive authority like a supreme court, but Rome's novelty is to insist that this authority must be infallible. That, however, runs contrary to Scriptural descriptions of an authoritative Church which in abnormal times may teach falsehood (Jer. 6:13; Is. 29:10; Ez. 22:25; 2 Pet. 2:2; Acts 20:29; I Tim. 4:1). Moreover, Rome's positive exegetical arguments for infallibility are simple non sequiturs. None of the appeals to the Church's perseverance or "leading into all truth" entail infallibility. And the stated need for an infallible Church creates a vicious infinite regress: if we need infallibility to interpret Scripture with "certitude," then we'll need it to interpret the Church with "certitude," and so on. What help is that?

Now when critics deny that the early Church held to *sola Scriptura*, they have to have the anabaptistic notion in mind. You certainly won't find the anabaptistic notion in the early Church or Scripture, but that's no great victory since you won't find the *solo* doctrine among the classical Protestants either. Among the fathers, though, we can often hear early forms of the sola notion, as in Basil's Moralia: "the hearers who are instructed in the Scripture should examine what is said by the teachers, receiving what is in conformity with Scripture and rejecting what is opposed to them." Now this is a bit too individualistic for classical Protestants, but it's a start. Yet the common reply to this claim is to take us immediately to Basil's famous statements about unwritten traditions. But notice how that reply misfires. It works only against the anabaptistic notion concerned with location of truth; unwritten tradition doesn't count at all against Scripture as the ultimate criterion of truth. If we aren't confusing *solo* for sola, then we can easily find the classical Protestant teaching throughout the fathers.

But then the howls start, since admittedly and shamefully, modern evangelicalism's fragmentation bears little resemblance to the unity of the Church in the fathers' time. One answer to that is that modern evangelicalism has abandoned sola for *solo* Scriptura. In addition, "Protestant fragmentation" is only an objection against *sola Scriptura* if we have a very unHebraic view of the Church. From Abraham's time on, the Church has faced both institutional unity and fragmentation, yet the Church persevered even during apostasy and exile. The Jewish sanhedrin in the first century had much more institutional unity than the early Christians, but it was apostate. In the Hebraic mindset, institutional unity is no guarantee of covenantal faithfulness. The Apostle Paul raised covenantal threats similar to those of Moses: "if God did not spare the natural branches, He may not spare you either" (Rom. 11:21).

Many of the fathers had a far more Hebraic understanding of the Church than does Rome. Jerome tells us that "The church does not consist in walls, but in the truth of her doctrines. The church is there, where true faith is. But fifteen or twenty years ago heretics possessed all walls here, for twenty years ago heretics possessed all the churches here; the church however was where true faith was." Similarly, Hilary teaches us, "I warn you of one thing: beware of Antichrist, for the love of walls has taken you badly; you venerate the church of God badly in houses and buildings. . . . Is it doubtful that Antichrist will have his seat in these?" Unity is sometimes a veneer for apostasy and fragmentation the scar of faithfulness.

Contemporary Protestant fragmentation won't stay with us forever. The Enlightenment joke is growing more stale by the minute. By the Spirit's work in fulfillment of divine promises, the Protestant Church will one day be both faithful and institutionally united. Until then, we have to imitate Elijah's patience. But we ought not reject the ancient doctrine of *sola Scriptura* for dangerous Roman novelties.

Patrick Madrid's Response:

Which "Church" do you mean? The Orthodox Church? The Catholic Church? What about the Lutherans, Anglicans, Orthodox Presbyterians, Church of Christ, Calvary Chapel, or the Reformed Baptists? Is it the Presbyterian Church in America, or the independent, "Bible-believing" fellowship down the street? The twin fallacies of ambiguity and of begging the question lurk at the heart of your question. Before you can deny the infallibility of the "Church," you must first define which Church you mean.

You accord "real authority" to the Church, but what does this mean? Where exactly is this authority located? Who exercises it? When and how is it used? What are its limits? The Catholic Church has concrete answers to these questions and can furnish 16 centuries of pre-Reformation evidence that its model of authority (Scriptura, Tradition, and Magisterium) worked. For *sola Scriptura* to be more than a mere slogan, it must be demonstrable in practice. Can you show us where *sola Scriptura* has actually worked?

This debate is not about the Church, but about the nature of the Scriptures the Church recognizes as canonical. *Sola Scriptura* entails formal sufficiency — that all revelation necessary for the Church to possess is presented formally in Scripture. Catholics and Orthodox reject this. Vatican II said, "Tradition, Sacred Scripture and the teaching authority of the Church ... are so linked and joined together that one cannot stand without the others" (Dei Verbum 10). St. Athanasius wrote: "The very tradition, teaching, and faith of the Catholic Church from the beginning was preached by the apostles and preserved by the Fathers. On this the Church was founded; and if anyone departs from this, he neither is nor any longer ought to be called a Christian" (*Ad Serapion* 1:28).

A major disproof of *sola Scriptura* is the New Testament canon. There's no "inspired table of contents" in Scripture listing the canonical books. This divinely revealed information comes to us from outside Scripture, through the Church. If Christ's Church is not infallible, then you can have no certainty that the books in your Bible belong there.

But Christ's Church indeed teaches with His infallible authority: "He who listens to you, listens to Me; and he who rejects you rejects me" (Luke 10:16; cf. Matt. 10:40, 16:18, 18:18, 28:20; John 14:25-26,16:13; 1 Thess. 2:13; Tim. 3:15). Christian orthodoxy has always been measured by adherence to the Church's doctrinal interpretations of Scripture.

In contrast, the WCF declared that "The only infallible rule of interpretation of Scripture is the Scripture itself." But where does Scripture teach this? The Westminster Catechism says: "The whole counsel of God, concerning all things necessary for his own glory, man's salvation, faith, and life, is either expressly set down in Scripture, or by good and necessary consequence may be deduced from Scripture" (6). For this to be true, *sola Scriptura* itself must be "expressly set down in Scripture, or ... deduced from Scripture."

But where does Scripture teach *sola Scriptura*? It doesn't. What pre-Reformation creed or council taught it? If *sola Scriptura* were part of "the faith once for all handed on to the saints" (Jude 3), we'd expect to find it everywhere in the early Church. But we don't. The patristic testimony alone leaves *sola Scriptura* squashed flat.

For example, the early Church taught the doctrine of baptismal regeneration, a doctrine you reject. Conversely, it did not teach *sola Scriptura*, a doctrine you embrace. So if we can at least agree that "The Church" equates with the Church Saints Athanasius and Augustine wrote about, isn't it safe to say that you are doctrinally at odds with that Church, at least on baptismal regeneration? And if so, why do you claim the Church has "real authority," if you are not bound by it? Or is this authority merely just a convenient prop?

St. Cyril of Jerusalem wrote that the Church "is called Catholic, then, because it extends over the whole world, from end to end of the earth, and because it teaches universally and infallibly each and every doctrine which must come to the knowledge of men, concerning things visible and invisible, heavenly and earthly, and because it brings every race of men into subjection to godliness (Catechetical Lectures 18:23 [A.D. 350]). The Catechetical Lectures are packed with Catholic doctrines: the Mass, the efficacy of prayers for the dead, the Real Presence of Christ in the Eucharist, the intercession of the saints, holy orders, baptismal regeneration, and many other doctrines Protestants reject as "unscriptural."

The First Council of Constantinople proclaimed the Church's belief in "baptism for the remission of sins" and warned it would "anathematize every heresy which is not of the same mind and the holy, Catholic, and apostolic Church of God" (Canon 7 [A.D. 381]). As a Reformed Christian, you don't believe in baptism for the remission of sins, basing your position on Scripture. *Sola Scriptura* has put you at odds with the Church you admit has authority over you.

St. Augustine defined orthodoxy as the assent to all the doctrines taught by the Church: "It is a fact that the Church is called 'Catholic' because it truly embraces the whole of that truth, some particles of which may be found even in various heresies" (Letter 93 7:23 [A.D. 408]). This "whole truth" didn't include *sola Scriptura*, nor was it transmitted according to the *sola Scriptura* model. St. Basil of Caesarea expressly denied *sola Scriptura*: "Of the beliefs and practices whether generally accepted or enjoined which are preserved in the Church, some we possess derived from written teaching; others we have delivered to us in a mystery by the apostles by the tradition of the apostles; and both of these in relation to true religion have the same force" (*On the Holy Spirit* 27);

St. Vincent of Lerins said: "I have often then inquired earnestly and attentively of very many men eminent for sanctify and learning, how and by what sure and so to speak universal rule I may be able to distinguish the truth of Catholic Faith from the falsehood of heretical depravity; and I have always, and in almost every instance, received an answer to this effect: that whether I or anyone else should wish to detect the frauds and avoid the snares of heretics as they rise, and to continue sound and complete in the Catholic Faith, we must, the Lord helping, fortify our own belief in two ways: first, by the authority of the Divine Law [Scripture], and then by the Tradition of the Catholic Church. But here some one perhaps will ask, 'Since the canon of Scripture is complete, and sufficient of itself for everything, and more than sufficient, what need is there to join with it the authority of the Church's interpretation?' For this reason: Because, owing to the depth of Holy Scripture, all do not accept it in one and the same sense, but one understands its words in one way, another in another, so that it seems to be capable of as many interpretations as there are men... Therefore, it is very necessary, on account of so great intricacies of such various error, that the rule for the right understanding of the prophets and apostles should be framed in accordance with the standard of ecclesiastical and Catholic interpretation' (*Commonotoria* 2:1-2 [A.D. 434]). That standard never included *sola Scriptura*.

Sola Scriptura is a paper tiger. It's not taught in Scripture, it's alien to historic Christian teaching and praxis, and it simply doesn't work.

Douglas Jones's Second Response:

I sincerely wish my always-honorable friend Patrick and I could be on the same side of these issues, but alas, we'll just have to keep talking and hoping for now. The sum of Patrick's answer to my initial question is that without an infallible church, Christians can have no certainty. He didn't elaborate on this, but as it stands it's rather problematic. Consider how this conflicts with our views of other authorities, such as civil courts and parents. Both of these are intimately involved in applying standards of justice, and yet both are fallible authorities. But on Patrick's view, we could never be sure about any questions of justice. In fact, we could never know what justice is.

Even more problematic is the infinite regress produced by Patrick's infallibility claim. If an infallible Scripture is so cursed by subjectivity that we need an infallible interpreter, then we can't stop there. We will also need an unending row of infallible interpreters at each subsequent stage. We end up in an almost postmodern subjectivism.

As to Patrick's scriptural proofs, notice that they prove too much or too little. They prove too much because they are so general as to include everything the church would say, but Rome severely narrows what it will count as infallible. They prove too little because they are wonderful exhortations to faithfulness and perseverance, but neither of these entails infallibility. And remember that the rub about the claim to church infallibility is that if it's false, then *sola Scriptura* follows rather quickly, since Scripture would be the only infallible authority left.

Patrick's other criticisms apply only against the *solo* location view. Note that even that favorite "major disproof" regarding the canon assumes the *solo* view — that is, no table of contents "in Scripture." And even if that criticism could be transformed to apply against the classical Protestant view, it would also prove that the Old Covenant Church never had authoritative revelation.

Patrick's other challenges about the definition of the church, patristic testimony, and pre-Reformation councils were already discussed in my opening essay. And as much as all sides of this issue long for the wonderful truths expressed by Vincent of Lerins, none of us can legitimately hold is up while the East and West remain divided. In the end, the most interesting part of this discussion for me is that continuing background conflict between Hellenistic and Hebraic assumptions.

Patrick Madrid's Second Response:

The Catholic position doesn't entail non sequiturs or an infinite regress. Scripture is infallible, yes, it cannot box our ears, rap our knuckles, or cry out, "Hold on! You've misunderstood!" But the Church can. The infallibility of the Church derives from the fact that She is a living organism, the bride of Christ, teaching and sanctifying with His authority and guidance (cf. Luke 10:16). She explains, clarifies, and answers questions in her councils, for example. When an Arius or a Pelagius pops up with heterodox interpretations of Scripture, the Church can point out where they went wrong. Scripture can't. There is no regress of infallible interpreters.

It's understandable that Doug would wish to shift the focus away from the nature of Scripture to the nature of the Church, doing so will avoid having to deal with thorny issues like the canon and defining what exactly he means by the "Church." His response didn't really answer the question "how does Scripture infallibly interpret itself?" We were told it "missed the heart of the debate." Not so. The WCF's expression of *sola Scriptura* (certainly a "classical" Protestant statement) pivots on this assertion. I don't see where Doug has made a case for this.

His appeal to the Fathers actually worsens matters for him. The quote he cited from Chrysostom, for example, makes my point a fortiori regarding the serious doctrinal divisions among Protestants who adhere to *sola Scriptura*. Chrysostom's writings brim with doctrines such as baptismal regeneration, the Real Presence of Christ in the Eucharist, and the sacrificial character of the Catholic priesthood — doctrines Doug vehemently disagree with. Was Chrysostom a bad exegete? Or is it possible that Doug's understanding of Scripture is incorrect on these matters? And if it is, what good does *sola Scriptura* do him?

And then there was the claim that the infallibility of the Church is a "dangerous Roman novelty." How does he account for Cyril of Jerusalem's (among others) teaching in A.D. 350 that the Catholic Church "teaches universally and infallibly"?

Doug Jones is a man of good will, and I admire the vigor with which he presents his position. But in spite of his considerable talent, the position he defends (*sola Scriptura*) remains untenable, as all errors are. Patristic testimony, logic, and, ironically, Scripture itself, demonstrate this. I invite our readers to study the evidence carefully, prayerfully, and without prejudice.

Selected Bibliography

Amidon, Philip, R., S.J., ed. and trans, *The Panarion of St. Epiphanius, Bishop of Salamis: Selected Passages*, (New York: Oxford, 1990).

Anderson, Floyd (ed.). *Council Daybook* (Vatican II; Session 3/ September 14-November 21, 1964). Washington: National Catholic Welfare Conference, 1965.

Armstrong, John, ed. *Roman Catholicism: Evangelical Protestants Analyze What Divides and Unites Us* (Chicago: Moody Press, 1994).

Armstrong, John. *A View of Rome: A Guide to Understanding the Beliefs and Practices of Roman Catholics* (Chicago: Moody Press, 1995).

Armstrong, Maurice. et al., eds., *The Presbyterian Enterprise: Sources of American Presbyterian History* (Philadelphia: Westminster, 1956).

Bainton, Roland H. *Here I Stand* (New York: New American Library, 1978).

Balthasar, Hans Urs von. "God Is His Own Exegete," *Communio*, 13 (1986) 280-287.

Barret, David B. *Oxford World Christian Encyclopedia* (NY: Oxford University Press, 1982).

Bauer, Walter. *A Greek-English Lexicon of the New Testament and Other Early Christian Literature*, 2nd ed. Revised by Gingrich, F. W. & Danker, F. W. (Chicago and London: The University of Chicago Press, 1979).

Beegle, Dewey M. *Scripture, Tradition and Infallibility* (Grand Rapids, Michigan: Eerdmans, 1973).

Berington, Jos. Rev. and Rev. John Kirk. *The Faith of Catholics*, 3 vols. (London: Dolman, 1846).

Bettenson, Henry. *Documents of the Christian Church*, 2nd ed., (London: Oxford University Press, 1963).

Berkhof, Louis. *Principles of Biblical Interpretation* (Grand Rapids, Michigan: Baker Book House, 1962).

Berman, Harold. *Law and Revolution: The Formation of the Western Legal Tradition* (Cambridge: Harvard, 1983).

Bird, Phyllis A. *The Bible as the Church's Book* (Philadelphia: Westminster Press, 1982).

Bloesch, Donald G. *Holy Scripture: Revelation, Inspiration and Interpretation* (Downers Grove: Intervarsity Press, 1994).

Blomberg, Carl. *New Oxford Review*, letter to the editor (Sept. 1991).

Boice, James Montgomery. *Foundations of the Christian Faith* (Illinois: Intervarsity Press, 1986).

Bossuet, Jacques Bénigne. *Histoire des variations des églises protestantes, Oeuvres completes de Bossuet*, Vol. XIV, F. Lachat, ed., (Paris, 1863).

Bousset & Baljon, *Die Schriften des New Testament*, 3rd ed. 1917.

Bottom, J. "Roman Roads: The Catholic Alternative to Nihilism," *Regeneration Quarterly* (Summer 1996).

Bouyer, Louis. *The Spirit and Forms of Protestantism*. Trans. A.V. Littledale (London: Harvill Press, 1956).

idem, *The Meaning of Sacred Scripture* (London: Darton, Longmann and Todd, 1960).

Bowman, Robert. *Orthodoxy and Heresy* (Grand Rapids: Baker Books, 1995).

Bromiley, Geoffrey W. "The Church Fathers and Holy Scripture," in *Scripture and Truth*, eds., D. A. Carson and John Woodbridge (Grand Rapids: Baker Books, 1992).

idem, *Zwingli and Bullinger* (Philadelphia: The Westminster Press, 1953).

Brown, Colin., ed., *Dictionary of New Testament Theology* (Grand Rapids: Zondervan, 1979).

Brown, Raymond and Joseph A. Fitzmeyer and Roland E. Murphy and O. Carm, eds., *The Jerome Biblical Commentary* (Englewood Cliffs: Prentice-Hall, 1968).

Bruce, F. F. and E. G. Rupp, eds., *Holy Book and Holy Tradition* (Manchester, England, 1968).

Bruce, F. F. *The Canon of Scripture* (Downers Grove: Intervarsity Press, 1988).

Burrows, Mark S. and Paul Rorem. *Biblical Hermeneutics in Historical Perspective* (Grand Rapids, Michigan: Eerdmans, 1991).

Butler, Scott and Norman Dahlgren and David Hess. *Jesus, Peter and the Keys* (Queenship Publishing, 1997).

Callahan, Daniel., Heiko A. Oberman, Daniel J. Ohanlon, eds., "Scripture, Tradition and the Church: An Ecumenical Problem." *Christianity Divided: Protestant and Roman Catholic Theological Issues* (New York: Sheed and Ward, 1964).

Calvin, John. *Institutes of the Christian Religion*, trans., Henry Beveridge (London: James Clarke and Co. 1957).

Calvin's New Testament Commentaries, trans., T. A. Smail (Grand Rapids, MI: Eerdmans Publishing).

Card, Michael and John Michael Talbot. *Brother to Brother* (Dallas: Word, 1996).

Carroll, J. M. *The Trail of Blood* (Lexington, Kentucky: Ashland Avenue Baptist Church, 1974).

Carson, D. A. and John D. Woodbridge. *Scripture and Truth* (Grand Rapids: Baker Books, 1992).

idem, *Hermeneutics, Authority and Canon* (Grand Rapids: Zondervan, 1986).

Carson, D. A., *Exegetical Fallacies.* (Grand Rapids: Baker Books, 1984).

Castellio, Sébastien. *De L'Art de douter et de croire, d'lgnorer et de savoir*, trans., C. Baudouin (Geneva: Éditions Jeheber, 1953).

Catechism of the Catholic Church (New York: Catholic Book Publishing Co. 1994).

Chapman, John (Abbot). *Studies on the Early Papacy* (New York: Benzinger, 1928).

Chemnitz, Martin. *Examination of the Council of Trent*, trans., Fred Kramer (St. Louis: Concordia, 1971).

Colson, Charles and Richard J. Neuhaus, *Evangelicals and Catholics Together: Toward a Common Mission* (Dallas: Word, 1996).

Congar, Yves. *Tradition and Traditions: An Historical and Theological Essay* (New York: Macmillian, 1967).

idem, *The Meaning of Tradition*, trans., A. N. Woodrow (New York: Hawthorne, 1964).

Currie, David. *Born Fundamentalist, Born Again Catholic* (San Francisco, Ignatius, 1996).

Denzinger, Henry. *The Sources of Catholic Dogma*, trans., Roy J. Deferrari (St. Louis: Herder, 1957).

De Sales, Francis. *The Catholic Controversy*, trans., Henry B Mackey (1886, rpt. Rockford, IL: Tan, 1989).

Dickens, A. G. *The Counter Reformation* (London: Harcourt, Brace and World, 1969).

Dillenberger, John, ed., *Martin Luther: Selections from His Writings* (Garden City, NY: Doubleday Anchor, 1961).

Dillenberger, John and Claude Welch. *Protestant Christianity* (NY: Charles Scribner's Sons, 1954).

Dix, Gregory and Henry Chadwick, eds., *The Treatise of the Apostolic Tradition of St. Hippolytus of Rome* (London: Alban, 1992).

Dobson, James. *Preparing for Adolescence* (Wheaton: Tyndale House, 1971).

Dodd, C.H. *The Authority of the Bible* (New York: Harper, 1958).

Douglas, J. D. ed., *New Bible Dictionary* (Wheaton: Tyndale House, 1984).

Dunn, James D. G. *The Justice of God: A Fresh Look at the Old Doctrine of Justification by Faith* (Grand Rapids, MI: Eerdmans, 1994).

Dupré, Louis. *Passage to Modernity: An Essay in the Hermeneutics of Nature and Culture* (New Haven: Yale University Press, 1993).

Eno, Robert, B., *Teaching Authority in the Early Church*, (Wilmington: Michael Glazier, 1984).

Farrar, Frederic W. *History of Interpretation* (Grand Rapids, Michigan: Baker Book House, 1961).

Fichtner, J. A. "Tradition" in *New Catholic Encyclopedia* (Washington, DC: Catholic University, 1967)

Fitzmeyer, Joseph A. *Romans* (New York: Doubleday, 1993).

Flannery, Austin. *Vatican Council II: The Conciliar and Post-Conciliar Documents* (Northport, New York: Costello Publishing Co. 1980).

Fosdick, Harry Emerson. ed., *Great Voices of the Reformation: An Anthology* (New York: Random House, 1952).

Frame, John. *The Doctrine of the Knowledge of God* (Phillipsburg, NJ: Presbyterian and Reformed, 1987).

Froehlich, Karlfried, ed. and trans., *Biblical Interpretation in the Early Church*. Philadelphia: Fortress Press, 1984.

Gamble, Harry Y. "Canon: New Testament" in *The Anchor Bible Dictionary*, vol. 1, eds., David Noel Freedman, et al., (New York: Doubleday, 1992).

Gasque, W. W. and W. S. LaSor, eds., *Scripture, Tradition and Interpretation* (Grand Rapids: Eerdmans, 1978).

Geiselmann, Josef R. "Scripture and Tradition in Catholic Theology" *Theology Digest* 6 (1958).

Geisler, Norman L. and Ralph E. MacKenzie. *Roman Catholics and Evangelicals: Agreements and Differences* (Grand Rapids: Baker, 1995).

Geisler, Norman. ed., *Innerancy* (Grand Rapids: Zondervan, 1980).

Giles, E. *Documents Illustrating Papal Authority* A. D. 96-454 (London: SPCK, 1952).

Godfrey, W. Robert. "Biblical Authority in the Sixteenth and Seventeenth Centuries: A Question of Transition," in *Scripture and Truth*, eds., D. A. Carson and John Woodbridge, (Grand Rapids: Baker Book House, 1992).

Gnuse, Robert. *The Authority of the Bible: Theories of Inspiration, Revelation and the Canon of Scripture* (New York: Paulist Press, 1985).

Goertz, Jurgen. ed., *Profiles of Radical Reformers* (Scottsdale, PA: Herald Press, 1982).

Gonzales, Justo. *A History of Christian Thought*, Vol III from *The Protestant Reformation to the Twentieth Century* (Nashville: Abingdon, 1975).

Graham, Henry G. *Where We Got the Bible: Our Debt to the Catholic Church* (Illinois: Tan, 1923).

Grant, Robert M. *A Short History of the Interpretation of the Bible* (New York: Macmillian, 1963).

Gruden, Wayne A. "Scripture's Self Attestation and the Problem of Formulating a Doctrine of Scripture" in *Scripture and Truth* (Grand Rapids: Baker Books, 1992).

Hagen, Kenneth, et al. *The Bible in the Churches: How Different Christians Interpret the Scriptures* (New York: Paulist Press, 1985).

Hanson, Richard C. *Tradition in the Early Church* (Philadelphia: Westminster, 1963).

Henry, Carl. "Biblical Authority and Social Crisis" in *Authority and Interpretation: A Baptist Perspective*.

Hill, David. "The Gospel of Matthew" in the *New Century Bible Commentary*, ed., Matthew Black (Grand Rapids: Eerdmans, 1972).

Hodge, Charles. *Systematic Theology* (1872, rpt. Grand Rapids: Eerdmans, 1952).

Hodges, Zane. *Absolutely Free! A Biblical Reply to Lordship Salvation* (Dallas: Redencion Viva, 1989).

Holmes, J. Derek and Robert Murray, *On the Inspiration of Scripture* (Washington: Corpus Books, 1967).

Howard, W. F. *Expositor's Times*, xxxiii, (July 1922).

Hughes, Philip. *The Church in Crisis: The History of the General Councils* 325-870 (Garden City, NY: Hanover House, 1961).

Hulse, Errol. "By What Authority?" in *Reformation Today*, No. 145, May/June 1995.

Jones, Douglas. "Scripture Teaches That The Word of God is the Supreme Norm" in *Antithesis* 1, no. 5 (September/October).

Jordan, Mark, ed., *A Catechism for Adults: The Church's Confession of Faith* (San Francisco: Ignatius Press, 1987).

Jurgens, William A. *The Faith of the Early Fathers* (Collegeville, MN: Liturgical Press, 1979).

Keating, Karl. *Fundamentalism and Catholicism: The Attack on "Romanism" by "Bible Christians"* (San Francisco, CA: Ignatius Press, 1988).

Kelly, J. N. D. *Early Christian Doctrines* (San Francisco: Harper and Row, 1978).

idem, *Early Christian Creeds* (London: Longman, 1972).

Kerr, Hugh T. Jr. ed., *A Compend of Luther's Theology* (Philadelphia: The Westminster Press, 1943).

Kilpatrick, G. D. *The Origins of the Gospel According to St. Matthew* (Oxford: 1946).

Kirn, P. and G Franz, eds., *Thomas Muntzer, Scriften und Briefe. Kritische Gesamtausgabe* (Guetesrslow, 1968).

Kistler, Don (ed.). *Sola Scriptura! The Protestant Position on the Bible* (Morgan, Pennsylvania: Soli Deo Gloria Publications, 1995).

idem, ed., *Justification by Faith Alone* (Morgan, PA: Soli Deo Gloria, 1995).

Kittel, Gerhard. *Theological Dictionary of the New Testament,* trans. Geoffrey W. Bromiley, (Grand Rapids: Eerdmans Publishing, 1964)

Kreeft, Peter. *Ecumenical Jihad: Ecumenism and the Culture War* (San Francisco: Ignatius Press, 1996).

idem, *Fundamentals of the Faith: Essays in Christian Apologetics* (San Francisco: Ignatius Press, 1988).

idem, *A Summa of the SUMMA* (San Francisco, Ignatius, 1990).

idem, "Gender and the Will of God" in *Crisis* (Sept., 1993).

Krehbiel, Greg. *A Defense of Roman Catholic Doctrine Against Reformed Protestantism* (Laurel, MD, 1992; privately circulated unpublished manuscript).

Kugel, James L. and Rowan A. Greer. *Early Biblical Interpretation.* Philadelphia: Westminster, 1986.

Küng, Hans. "Toward a New Consensus in Catholic Theology" in *Consensus in Theology? A Dialogue with Hans Küng and Edward Schillebeeckx*, L. Swindler, ed., (Philadelphia, 1980).

Lane, William., ed., *Praying with the Saints* (Doublin: Veritas, 1987).

Leonard, William and Dom. Bernard Orchard. "The Place of the Bible in the Church," in *A Catholic Commentary on Holy Scripture* (London: Thomas Nelson and Sons, 1953).

Liddell and Scott. *Greek-English Lexicon* (Oxford University Press, 1977).

Lienhard, Joseph T. *The Bible, the Church and Authority: The Canon of the Christian Bible in History and Theology* (Collegeville, Minnesota: Liturgical Press, 1995).

Lohse, Bernhard. *Martin Luther: An Introduction to His Life and Work*, trans., Robert C. Schultz (Philadelphia: Fortress Press, 1986).

L'Osservatore Romano, Vatican City. Weekly Edition in English (July 23, 1997).

Lull, Timothy F. *Martin Luther's Basic Theological Writings* (Minneapolis: Fortress Press, 1989).

Luther, Martin. *D. Martin Luthers Werke: Kritische Gesamtausgabe*. 103 vols. ed., J. C. F. Knaake, et al. Weimar edition: Herman Bohlaus, 1883f).

idem, Briefwechsel edition, 1930ff.

idem, Teschreden edition, 1912ff.

idem, *Lectures on Romans*, ed. W. Pauck (Philadelphia: Westminster Press, 1961).

idem, *Luther's Works*, ed. and trans. Jaroslav Pelikan, et al. (St. Louis: Concordia Publishing House (vols. 1-30); Philadelphia: Fortress Press (vols. 31-55), 1955-1979).

MacArthur, John. *Reckless Faith: When the Church Loses Its Will To Discern* (Illinois: Crossway, 1994).

MacIntyre, Alasdair. *Whose Justice? Which Rationality?* (Notre dame: University of Notre Dame, 1988).

Madrid, Patrick. *Surprised By Truth* (San Diego, CA; Basilica Press, 1994).

idem, "Sola Scriptura: A Blueprint for Anarchy," *Catholic Dossier* (March/April, 1996).

McCarthy, James G. *The Gospel According to Rome: Comparing Catholic Tradition and the Word of God* (Oregon: Harvest House, 1995).

McDonald, William J. ed., *The New Catholic Encyclopedia* (New York: McGraw-Hill Book Co. 1967).

McGrath, Alister. *The Intellectual Origins of the European Reformation* (Oxford: Blackwell, 1987).

idem, "Do We Still Need a Reformation?" in *Christianity Today*, Dec. 12, 1994.

idem, ed., *The Christian Theology Reader* (Oxford, UK: Blackwell Publishers, Ltd. 1995).

Megivern James J. ed., *Bible Interpretation* (Consortium Books: Wilmington, NC, 1978).

Melton, J. Mordon. ed., *The Encyclopedia of American Religions: Religious Creeds* (Detroit: Gate Research Company, 1988).

Mergal, Angel and George Williams, eds., *Spiritual and Anabaptist Writers* (Philadelphia: The Westminster Press, 1957).

Mickelson, A Berkeley. *Interpreting the Bible* (Grand Rapids: Eerdmans, 1974).

Migne, J.P., ed., *Patrologia Graeca Cursus Completus*, 161 vols. (Paris: Vives, 1857-1866).

Migne, J.P., ed., *Patrologia Latina Cursus Completus*, 221 vols. (Paris: Vives, 1844-1855).

Moffatt, James B. *The New Testament: A New Translation* (Harper and Brothers Publishers, 1935).

Moran, Gabriel. *Scripture and Tradition: A Survey of the Controversy* (New York: Herder and Herder, 1963).

Morgan, Richard Lyon. "Let's Be Honest About The Canon: A Plea to Reconsider a Question the Reformers Failed To Answer," *Christian Century* 84 (1967).

Most, William G. *Catholic Apologetics Today: Answers to Modern Critics* (Illinois: Tan, 1986).

idem, *Free From All Error* (Libertyville: Prow Books, 1985).

Moule, C. F. D. *An Idiom Book of the New Testament*, 2nd ed. (London: Cambridge University Press, 1959).

Moulton, James H and George Milligan. *The Vocabulary of the Greek New Testament Illustrated From the Papyri and Other Non-literary Sources* (London: Hodder and Stoughton, 1930).

Murray, Daniel A. *The Living Word in the Living Church* (New York: Thomas Nelson Publishers, 1986).

Murray, John. "Tradition: Romish and Protestant" in *Collected Writings of John Murray* (Carlisle: Banner of Truth, 1982).

Nestle, Eberhard and Kurt Aland, eds., *Novum Testamentum Graece*, 26th ed., (Deutsche Bibelstiftung, Stuttgart, 1979).

Nestle, Eberhard, ed., *Novum Testamentum Latine* (Wurttembergische Bibelanstalt, Stuttgart, 1906).

Neuner, J and J. Dupuis. *The Christian Faith in the Doctrinal Documents of the Catholic Church* (New York: Alba House, 1981).

Newman, John Henry Cardinal. *An Essay on the Development of Christian Doctrine* (Edinburgh: T & T Clark, 1988).

idem, *Apologia Pro Vita Sua*, ed. David J DeLaura (1864; rpt. New York: Norton, 1968).

idem, *The Development of Christian Doctrine* (Notre Dame: University of Notre Dame, 1989).

idem, *Lectures on the Prophetical Office*, 1837.

Nineham, D. E. "The Gospel of St. Mark" in *The Pelican New Testament Commentaries* (Harmondsworth, Middlesex, England: Penguin Books Ltd. 1963).

Noll, Mark. *The Scandal of the Evangelical Mind* (Grand Rapids: Eerdmans, 1994).

Oberman, A. "Quo Vadis? Tradition from Irenaeus to Humani Generis," in *Scottish Journal of Theology*, 16, 1963.

Oberman, Heiko. *The Harvest of Medieval Theology: Gabriel Biel and Late Medieval Nominalism* (Grand Rapids, MI: Eerdmans, 1967).

O'Hare, Patrick F. *The Facts About Luther* (Rockford, IL: Tan Books, 1987).

Olin, John C. *A Reformation Debate: Saldoleto's Letter to the Genevans and Calvin's Reply* (Grand Rapids: Baker Books, 1976).

O'Neil, Dan. *The New Catholics: Contemporary Converts Tell Their Stories* (New York: Crossroad, 1989).

Ott, Ludwig. *Fundamentals of Catholic Dogma*, trans. Patrick Lynch (Illinois: Tan, 1974).

Packer, J. I. *Fundamentalism and the Word of God: Some Evangelical Principles* (Grand Rapids: Eerdmans, 1958).

idem, *The Adequacy of Human Language*

idem, "Sola Scriptura in History and Today," in *God's Inerrant Word*, John Warwick Montgomery, ed., (Minneapolis: Bethany Fellowship, 1975).

Pache, Rene. *The Inspiration and Authority of the Bible* (Chicago: Moody Press, 1971).

Palm, David. "Oral Tradition in the New Testament" in *This Rock*, May 1995.

Payton, James R. Jr. "The New International Version and the De-Catholicizing of Scripture," *Perspectives* (formally *Reformed Journal*) (Nov. 1993).

Pelikan, Jaroslav. *Luther's Works: Companion Volume: Luther, the Expositor* (St. Louis: Concordia Publishing House, 1959).

idem, *The Christian Tradition: A History of the Development of Doctrine* (Chicago: University of Chicago Press, 1971).

Pesch, Christian. *De Inspiratione Sacrae Scripturae* (Frieburgi: Herder, 1906).

Pinnock, Clark H. *The Scripture Principle: A Systematic Defense of the Full Authority of the Bible* (London: Hodder and Stoughton, 1985).

Pontifical Biblical Commission. *The Interpretation of the Bible in the Church* (Vatican City State: Libreria Editrice Vaticana, 1993).

Popkin, Richard H. *The History of Scepticism from Erasmus to Spinoza* (Berkeley: University of California Press, 1979).

Preus, Robert D. "The View of the Bible Held by the Church" in *Inerrancy*, ed., Norman Geisler (Grand Rapids: Zondervan, 1980).

Provan, Charles D. *The Bible and Birth Control* (Monongahela, PA: Zimmer, 1989).

Quasten, Johannes. *Patrology* (Westminster, MD: Christian Classics, 1950-1986).

Quasten, J. and J. C. Plumpe, eds., *Ancient Christian Writers* (New York: Paulist, 1946ff).

Rahner, Karl. "Scripture and Tradition" in *Theological Investigation* 6 (London, 1969).

Ramm, Bernard. *Protestant Biblical Interpretation* (Grand Rapids: Baker, 1970).

Ray, Steven. "Did the Noble-Minded Bereans Believe in the Bible Alone?" *This Rock*, 1997.

Reid, J. K. S. *The Authority of Scripture: A Study of the Reformation and Post-Reformation Understanding of the Bible* (New York: Harper, n.d.).

Reventlow, H. G. *The Authority of the Bible and the Rise of the Modern World*, trans., John Bowden (Philadelphia: Fortress Press, 1985).

Richardson, Cyril C. *Early Christian Fathers* (New York: Collier, 1970).

Rix, Herbert David. *Martin Luther: The Man and the Image* (New York: Irvington Publishers, 1983).

Roberts, Alexander and James Donaldson and A.Cleveland Cox and A. Menzies, eds., *The Ante-Nicene Fathers: The Writings of the Fathers down to A.D. 325*, 10 volumes (Grand Rapids: Eerdmans, 1951-56).

Rogers, Jack and Donald McKim. *Authority and Interpretation of the Bible* (New York: Harper and Row, 1979).

Rorty, Richard. *Philosophy and the Mirror of Nature* (Princeton: Princeton University Press, 1979).

Rumble, Leslie. "The Bible Only Theory" in *This Rock*, Dec. 1992, Jan. 1993.

Runes, Dagobert D. *Dictionary of Philosophy* (Totowa, NJ: Littlefield, Adams & Co., 1962).

Samples, Kenneth R. "Does the Bible Teach 'Sola Scriptura'" in *Christian Research Journal*, Fall 1989.

Schaff, Philip. *History of the Christian Church* (Grand Rapids: Eerdmans, 1910).

Schaff, Philip. *Nicene and Post-Nicene Fathers* (Peabody, MA: Hendrickson, 1994).

Schaff, Philip and Wace, Henry, eds., *A Select Library of Nicene and Post-Nicene Fathers of the Church*, 28 volumes, 2 Series, (Grand Rapids: Eerdmans, 1952-56)

Schreck, Alan. *Catholic and Christian: An Explanation of Commonly Misunderstood Catholic Beliefs* (Ann Arbor: Servant, 1984).

Schweizer, Eduard. *The Good News According to Mark*, trans., Donald H. Madvig (Atlanta: John Knox, 1970).

Shapland, C. R. B. ed. and trans., *The Letters of St. Athanasius: Concerning the Holy Spirit* (New York: Philosophical Library, 1951).

Shea, Mark. *By What Authority? An Evangelical Discovers Catholic Tradition* (Huntington, IN: Our Sunday Visitor, 1996).

idem, "When Evangelicals Treat Catholic Tradition Like Revelation," *New Oxford Review* (Sept. 1996).

Shotwell, James T. and L. R. Loomis. *The See of Peter* (New York: Columbia, 1927).

Shroeder, H. J. *Canons and Decrees of the Council of Trent* (London: B. Herder Book Co. 1941).

Silva, Moisés. *Has The Church Misread the Bible*? (Grand Rapids: Zondervan, 1987).

idem, *Biblical Words and Their Meaning* (Grand Rapids: Zondervan, 1983).

Smith, Preserved. *The Life and Letters of Martin Luther* (Boston: Houghton Mifflin, 1911).

Sproul, R. C., and John Gerstner and Arthur Lindsley. *Classical Apologetics* (Grand Rapids: Zondervan, 1984).

Sproul, R. C. *Faith Alone* (Grand Rapids: Baker, 1995).

Stravinskas, Peter M. J. *The Catholic Church and the Bible* (San Francisco: Ignatius Press, 1996).

idem, ed., *The Catholic Encyclopedia* (Huntington, IN: Our Sunday Visitor, 1991).

idem, *The Catholic Response* (Huntington, Indiana: Our Sunday Visitor Press, 1985).

Stein, Robert H. *Gospel and Tradition: Studies on the Redaction Criticism of the Synoptic Gospels* (Grand Rapids: Baker Books, 1991).

Stevenson, James, ed., *Creeds, Councils and Controversies: Documents Illustrating the History of the Church AD 337-461,* (London: SPCK, 1989).

idem, *A New Eusebius: Documents Illustrating the History of the Church to AD 337* (London: SPCK, 1987).

Sturz, Harry A. *The Byzantine Text Type and New Testament Textual Criticism*, doctoral dissertation, 1979.

Sunberg, Albert C. "The Protestant Old Testament Canon: Should It Be Reexamined?" A Symposium on the Canon of Scripture," CBQ 28 (1966).

Sungenis, Robert A. *Not By Faith Alone: The Biblical Evidence for the Catholic Doctrine of Justification* (Santa Barbara, CA: Queenship Publishing, 1997).

idem, *Shockwave 2000* (Greenforest, AR: New Leaf Press, 1994).

Svendsen, Eric. *Protestant Answers* (Colorado, 1995, privately circulated unpublished manuscript). Will be published under the new title *Evangelical Answers.*

Swete, H. B. *Introduction to the Old Testament* (Cambridge University Press, 1914; rpt. Peabody, MA: Hendrickson, 1989).

Tate, Marvin. "Old Testament Apocalyptic and the Old Testament Canon" in *Review and Expositor*, 65 (1968).

Tavard, George. *Holy Writ or Holy Church: The Crisis of the Protestant Reformation* (New York: Harper, 1959).

Teske, Roland, trans., John E. Rotelle, ed., *Arianism and Other Heresies* (Hyde Park: New City Press, 1995).

Tillman, Mary Katherine, ed., *Newman and the Thoughtful Believer* (Florence, KY: Brenzel, 1993).

Todd, John M. (ed.). *Problems of Authority* (Baltimore: Helicon, 1962).

Vanauken, Sheldon. *Under the Mercy* (Nashville: Thomas Nelson, 1985, reprinted in San Francisco, Ignatius Press, 1988).

Volz, Carl A. *Faith and Practice in the Early Church* (Minneapolis: Augsburg, 1983).

Vorgrimler, Herbert (ed.). *Commentary on the Documents of Vatican II* (New York: Herder and Herder, 1969).

Vos, Arvin. *Aquinas, Calvin and Contemporary Protestant Thought: A Critique of Protestant Views on the Thought of Thomas Aquinas* (Grand Rapids: Eerdmans, 1985).

Warfield, Benjamin B. *The Inspiration and Authority of the Bible* (Philadelphia: Presbyterian and Reformed, 1948).

idem, *Revelation and Inspiration* (Grand Rapids: Baker Books, 1927).

Whelan, William J. *Separated Brethren* (Huntington, IN: Our Sunday Visitor, 1979).

White, James R. *Answers to Catholic Claims: A Discussion of Biblical Authority* (Southbridge, MA: Crowne Publications, 1990).

idem, *The Roman Catholic Controversy: Catholic and Protestants—Do the Differences Still Matter?* (Minneapolis: Bethany House, 1996).

idem, *The Fatal Flaw* (Southbridge, MA: Crowne, 1990).

Wiles, Maurice. *The Making of Christian Doctrine: A Study in the Principles of Early Doctrinal Development* (London: Cambridge, 1967).

Williams, Frank, ed. and trans., *The Panarion of Epiphanius of Salamis* (New York: E. J. Brill, 1987).

Williams, George H. *The Radical Reformation* (Philadelphia: The Westminster Press, 1962).

Williams, George H. ed., *Spiritual and Anabaptist Writers* (Philadelphia: Westminster, 1957).

Winter Ernst, trans. and ed., *Erasmus-Luther: Discourse on Free Will* (New York: Fredrick Ungar, 1961).

Woodbridge, John D. *Biblical Authority: A Critique of the Rogers/McKim Proposal* (Grand Rapids, Michigan: Zondervan, 1982).

Ziegler, Donald J. ed., *Great Debates of the Reformation* (NY: Random House, 1969).

Index of Scripture

The Old Testament

The New Testament

Romans

Index of Authors and Significant Persons

Index of Church Fathers, Councils, and their Opponents

Final Prayers

St. Augustine, blessed of God regarding the truth of the gospel, pray for us that God will grant to your earthly brethren in these turbulent times the same knowledge and wisdom he gave to you. Look down on us in pity and pray that we may be strengthened to bring forth truth in the face of all the opposition of the Devil.

St. Gregory the Great, noble and courageous successor of St. Peter, please obtain for us the graces necessary to adequately proclaim and defend God's revealed truth.

St. Thomas Aquinas, pray for us that we may be as diligent in our study of Scripture as once you were. Help us to answer all inquiries regarding the faith in the most effective and complete manner.

St. Francis de Sales, valiant defender of the faith, we beseech your intercession on behalf of our writing and teaching. May it always be faithful to Sacred Tradition, charitable, and efficacious in bringing souls closer to Christ and His Church.

St. Michael the Archangel, defend us in battle, be our protection against the wickedness and snares of the devil. May God rebuke him, we humbly pray; and do thou, Oh Prince of the heavenly host, by the power of God, thrust into hell Satan and all evil spirits who wander through the world for the ruin of souls.

Mary, Mother of God, we pray that you will beseech your Son, who alone provides grace and wisdom, to help us in our efforts to further the cause of the Church. May your holiness and faithfulness be brought to God on our behalf, so that he may have mercy and patience with us as we endeavor to honor his name.

Glorious Lord Jesus, we pray that your great prayer to God the Father for unity among all Christian brethren be realized before your return.

"We could say more but could never say enough; let the final word be: 'He is the all.'" (Ecclesiasticus 43:27).

Amen